Inuit Modern

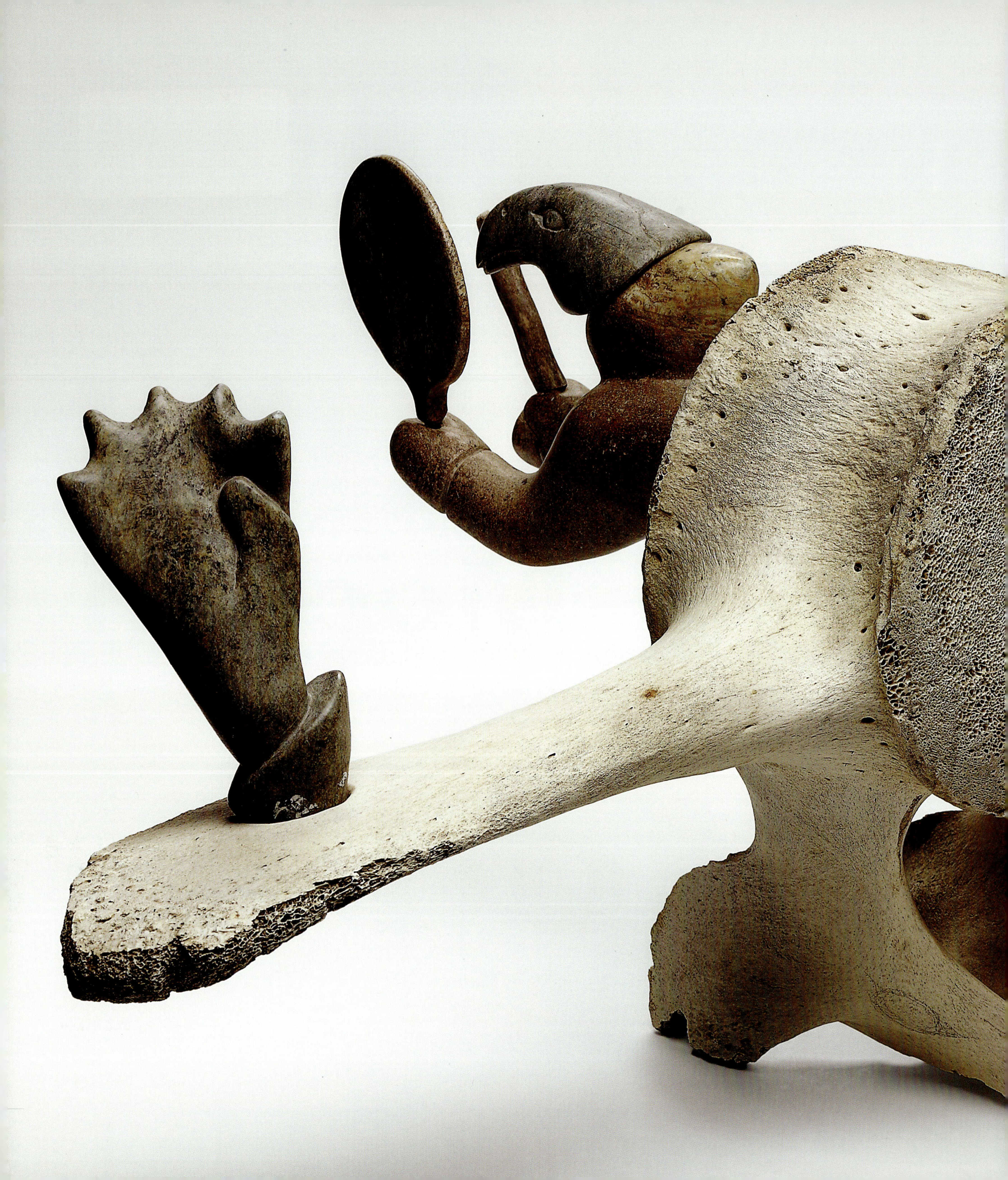

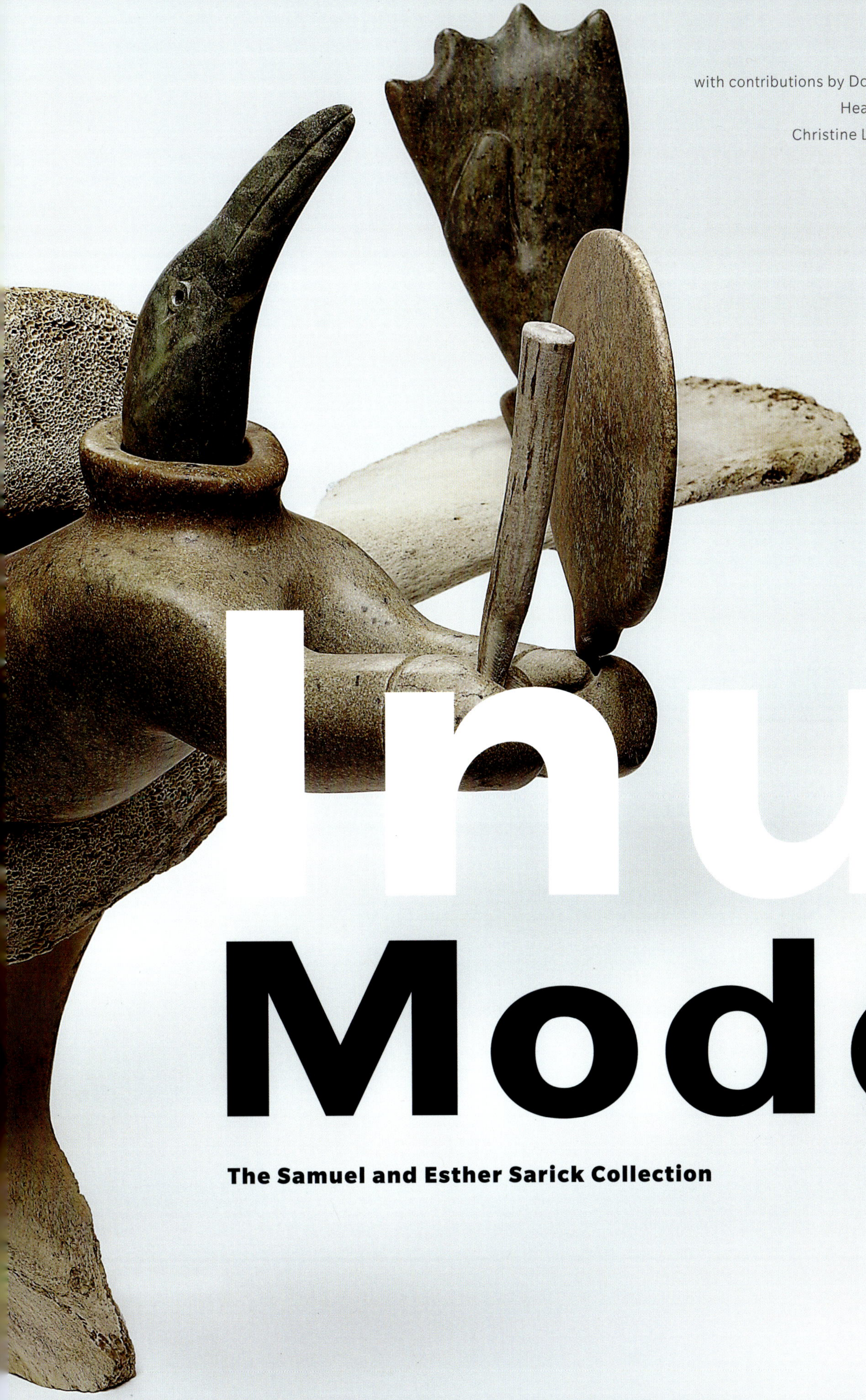

Gerald McMaster, editor and curator
Ingo Hessel, co-curator

with contributions by Dorothy Harley Eber, Bernadette Driscoll Engelstad, Heather Igloliorte, Alootook Ipellie, Zacharias Kunuk, Christine Lalonde, Robert McGhee, David Ruben Piqtoukun

Afterword by John Ralston Saul

Inuit Modern

The Samuel and Esther Sarick Collection

Art Gallery of Ontario
Toronto

Douglas & McIntyre
D&M Publishers Inc.
Vancouver/Toronto/Berkeley

First U.S. edition 2011
10 11 12 13 14 5 4 3 2 1

The *Inuit Modern* exhibition is organized by the Art Gallery of Ontario
April 2–August 21, 2011

Art Gallery of Ontario
317 Dundas Street West
Toronto ON Canada M5T 1G4
www.ago.net

Douglas & McIntyre
An imprint of D&M Publishers Inc.
2323 Quebec Street, Suite 201
Vancouver BC Canada V5T 4S7
www.douglas-mcintyre.com

Cataloguing data available from Library and Archives Canada
ISBN 978-1-55365-778-1

Editing by Meg Taylor
Cover and text design by Counterpunch Inc. / Linda Gustafson
Front cover: Eli Sallualu Qinuajua, *Fantastic Figure*, 1969
Back cover: Itee Pootoogook, *Qilalukat*, 2009
Cover photographs by Ian Lefebvre
Photos by Ian Lefebvre
Photo of Samuel & Esther Sarick by Craig Boyko
Maps by Eric Leinberger
Printed and bound in Canada by Friesens
Text printed on acid-free paper
Distributed in the U.S. by Publishers Group West

The Art Gallery of Ontario thanks the artists and the Inuit Art Foundation, Dorset Fine Arts and Canadian Arctic Producers for their generous participation in this project.

The Art Gallery of Ontario is partially funded by the Ontario Ministry of Culture. Additional operating support is received from the Volunteers of the Art Gallery of Ontario, City of Toronto, the Department of Canadian Heritage and the Canada Council for the Arts.

Supported by Canada Council for the Arts / Conseil des Arts du Canada

D&M Publishers Inc. gratefully acknowledges the financial support of the Canada Council for the Arts, the British Columbia Arts Council, the Province of British Columbia through the Book Publishing Tax Credit and the Government of Canada through the Canada Book Fund for its publishing activities.

Title page: Abraham Anghik Ruben, *Journey to the Spirit World*, c. 1995, Brazilian soapstone, whale bone, 43.5 x 118.0 x 68.5 cm. See page 207.
Page x: photo by Dr. Michael Tymianski
Pages xi, 39, 50, 51: poems copyright © 2010 Estate of Alootook Ipellie
Pages xiv–xv: Nungusuituq Qaqyuraqyuk, *Sea Goddess*, 1988, stone, ivory, plastic, 15.1 x 36.0 x 19.1 cm. See also page 98.
Pages 10–11: Inuksugalait, southwest Baffin Island; page 52: The doorway that the shaman passed through; pages 224–25: Barnes Ice Cap, central Baffin Island. Norman Hallendy Collection, Gift of Norman E. Hallendy, McMichael Canadian Art Collection Archives
Pages 48–49: Luke Iksiktaaryuk, *Family*, c. 1967, antler, 30.2 x 57.6 x 31.2 cm. See also page 133.
Page 219: photo by Oana Spinu, copyright Igloolik Isuma Productions
Page 220: photos copyright Igloolik Isuma Productions / courtesy of Vtape
Pages 221, 223: photos by Katherine Keum Ryun Lee Ruben
The credit information for the quotes from Inuit artists that appear throughout the book and on the back cover can be found on page 257.

The List of Works in the Exhibition on pages 247–57 constitutes a continuation of this copyright page. Every attempt has been made to trace ownership of copyright material in this book and to secure permissions. The publisher would appreciate receiving information on any inaccuracies in the credits for correction in subsequent editions.

Dimensions of artwork are given as height x width x depth

A Note on Inuit Names
Canadian Inuit traditionally had only one given name. If Inuit were baptized, they were given a Christian first name; also, to simplify things for government bureaucracy, all members of a family were expected to use the same surname, namely, the "last" name the father was called by, be it singular or a surname. In this book, the Inuit name commonly used by an artist and his or her family is used; sometimes this is the so-called first name, sometimes it is the second. For example, in discussing the life or work of Oviloo Tunnillie, we refer to her simply as Oviloo.

Contents

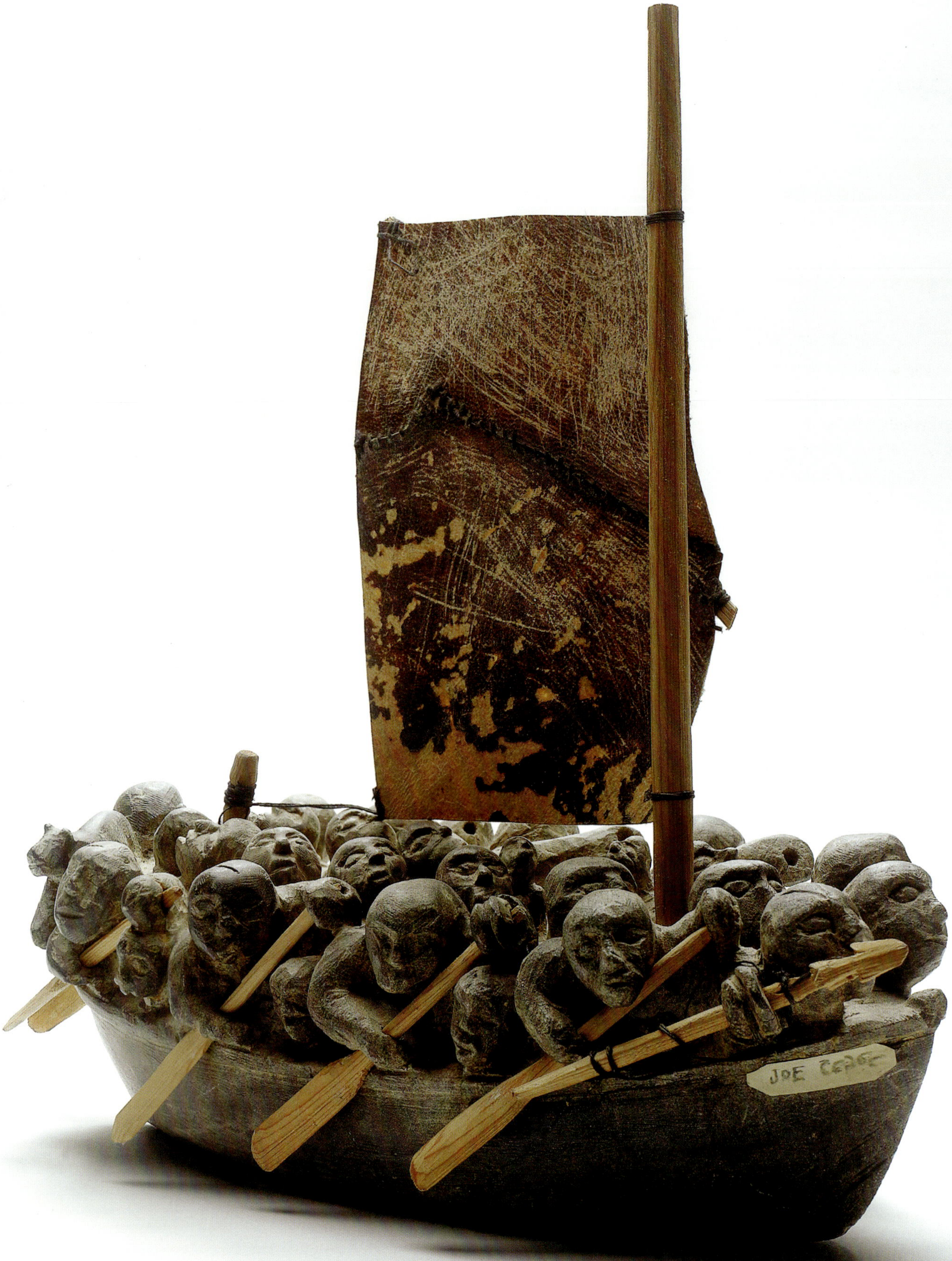

Joe Talirunili, *Migration*, c. 1974, stone, hide, wood, string, 33.7 x 39.5 x 19.5 cm

Director's Foreword

Since 1990 Inuit art has been clearly positioned at the Art Gallery of Ontario as an integral part of the story of Canadian art. In the reinstallation of our Canadian galleries in 2008, Inuit art was situated throughout the building to create dialogue with art from other times and places. Acknowledging the specific and dynamic storytelling attributes of Inuit art—both modern and historical—we sought to integrate the Inuit voice into the overarching history of art and demonstrate its relevance to audiences today.

As the writers in this volume attest, Inuit art is grounded in storytelling, creating markers in a narrative of communities confronting change. It is a dynamic tradition, as communities connect with and personalize belief systems, community values and image traditions from elsewhere. Styles and languages emerge, alternately resisting and integrating various attributes with personal vision. No longer does Inuit art merely reflect the remembered past; now it vibrantly engages with the conflicted present. And it is that tension between the old and the new—and the reality that experiences are never the result of following a single path—that lies at the centre of this publication and the exhibition it celebrates.

The genesis of this project lies in the dedication of Sam and Esther Sarick, who chose, more than forty years ago, to make a lifelong commitment to documenting and collecting contemporary Inuit art. More than twenty years ago, they ensured a broader and more profound recognition for Inuit art through the gift of their collection to the Art Gallery of Ontario. With the Sarick Collection, still active in its formation and marked by sustained advocacy and generosity, the AGO now boasts the most significant collection of Inuit sculpture in the world, with all major artists, communities and periods represented in depth. As the most important collectors of Inuit art of their generation, the Saricks have acquired sculpture, drawings, prints and textiles that reflect a range of creative ideas and life experiences. Their gift has ensured the integration of Inuit art fully into our national narrative, reflective of their fundamental belief that the North expresses Canada's evident uniqueness. It is collection building certainly, but it is nation building too, as all expressions of national value and varied experience are.

Gerald McMaster, editor and curator, and Ingo Hessel, co-curator of this exhibition, have found remarkable balance in their approach—celebrating the pioneering spirit of the Saricks, while expressing the complexity of belief systems in the work itself. They have looked to the past and the future at the same time, acknowledging the embrace of both tradition and the new in the trajectory of Inuit art history.

I would like to thank Scott McIntyre of Douglas & McIntyre, our co-publishing partner, for producing a remarkably cogent book on a subject that will appeal to many audiences. Finally, I would like to express my admiration to all the Inuit artists past and present, many of whom are in this book, for creating a distinctly characteristic expression that has won audiences around the world.

Matthew Teitelbaum
MICHAEL AND SONJA KOERNER DIRECTOR, AND CEO
ART GALLERY OF ONTARIO

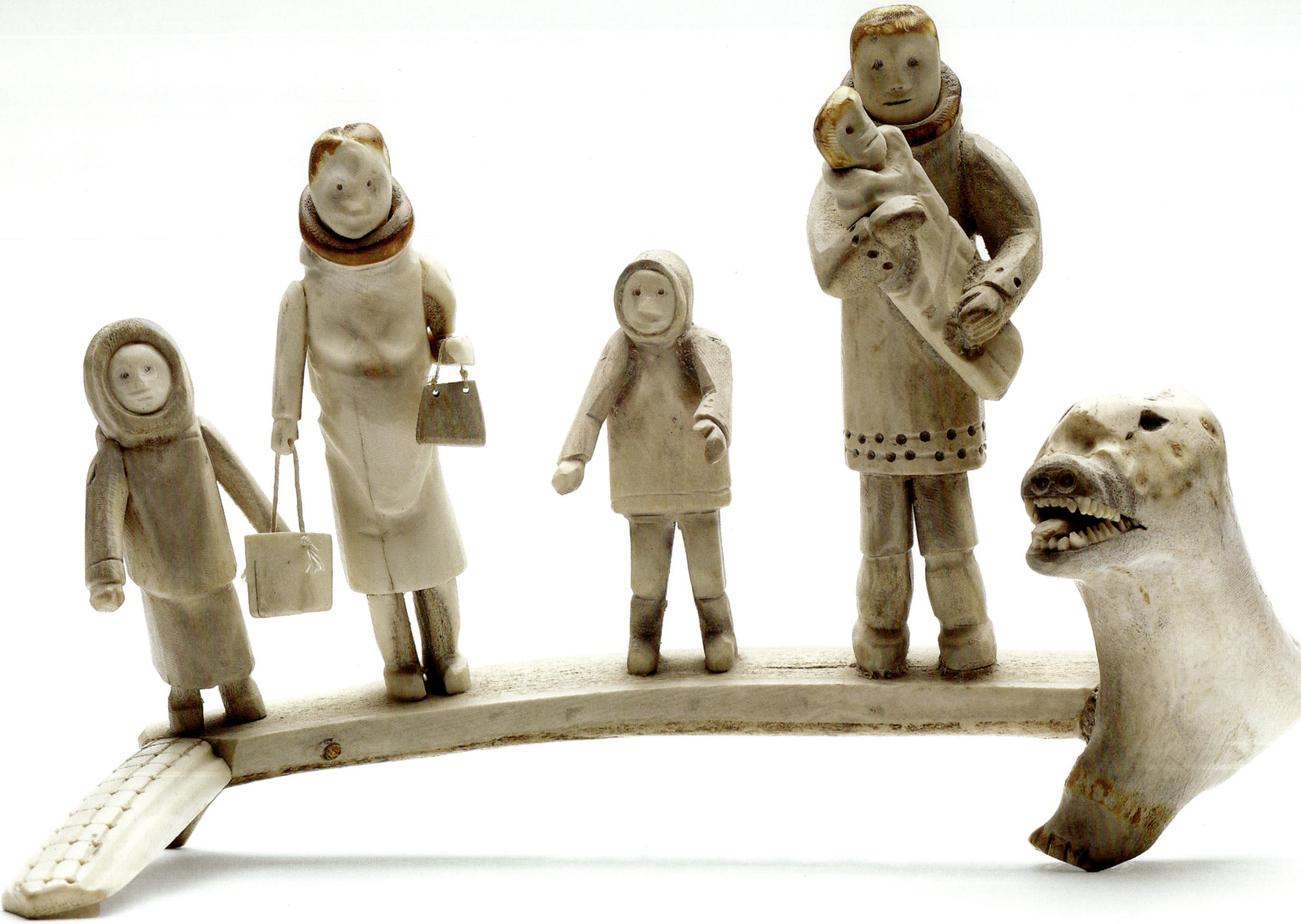

Romeo Eekerkik, *Family*, c. 1972, antler, bone, sinew, string, colouring, 20.6 x 31.3 x 18.3 cm

From the Collectors

Samuel and Esther Sarick

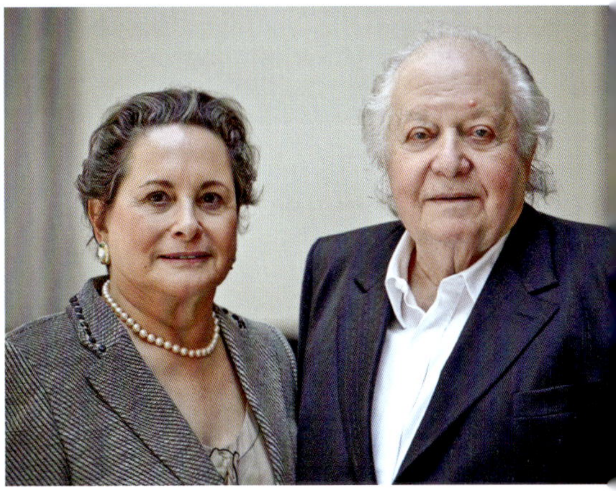

We are often asked how we became collectors. It's a simple question, but there's not always a straightforward answer. I don't think I became a collector—I was born a collector. If collecting is in your blood, it doesn't matter what you collect as long as you accumulate: baseball cards, Rembrandt etchings, Inuit art, Judaica, African art, Moorcroft pottery. You start with one piece, and by the time you acquire three or four thousand more, it is a collection.

I recall our first Inuit piece. It was acquired from Av Isaacs, when his gallery was on Yonge Street. It was a small bone carving of the head of a man and a woman. Inuit art was exciting, original and relatively affordable. The sculptures and prints were diverse, coming from numerous communities and created in a wide variety of materials. And perhaps most intriguing, the art portrayed a way of life that was rapidly disappearing. We were hooked.

As the passion for Inuit art took hold, we felt we had to see where this wonderful stuff was coming from and meet the artists who were creating it. This was before scheduled commercial flights to the Arctic, so I hitched a ride on government planes or with whoever was heading north. On a trip from Rankin Inlet to Repulse Bay, I was carrying a supply of fermented whale meat for some Inuit when Ches Russell, an old-time Hudson's Bay Company factor, came running up to the plane with a parcel for me containing a sleeping bag, a knife and a few other necessities and advised me that I had to be prepared.

On another trip north on which Esther accompanied me, we met Bud Orange, who had a Twin Otter and was electioneering in the North. We agreed to hand out election pamphlets in exchange for a ride with him. (I don't think he won.)

After very irregular commercial flights had begun, on one trip I was weathered in at Baker Lake with our good friends Boris and Liz Kotelewetz, when an Air Force Hercules radioed that they wished to land for refuelling. Boris was on the radio at the time, and he bartered two Arctic char and a lake trout for them to take me to their base in Edmonton. Esther joked after this that my true worth was just a couple of fish.

On landing in a community up north, we would head straight for the co-op and meet the artists themselves to add to our knowledge and to our growing collection. In every community we were continually amazed that so small a population could produce so many hugely talented artists.

After each trip many pieces usually followed on what was called "back haul." Since planes usually went north with produce and supplies and returned almost empty, there was usually room for some carvings and prints. We also left funds with co-op directors like Bob Billyard in Rankin Inlet and Boris Kotelewetz in Baker Lake to purchase pieces for us in our absence and provide the artists with ready cash as soon as their carvings came in.

After one such back haul shipment we were confronted with an ultimatum from our three children: "Either the stones go or we go." There wasn't room for both. The stones had taken over the entire house; they were on shelves in the basement, under the beds, on the piano bench and everywhere else. I really had no choice, so the next task was deciding where the stones were to go. We discussed this with friends,

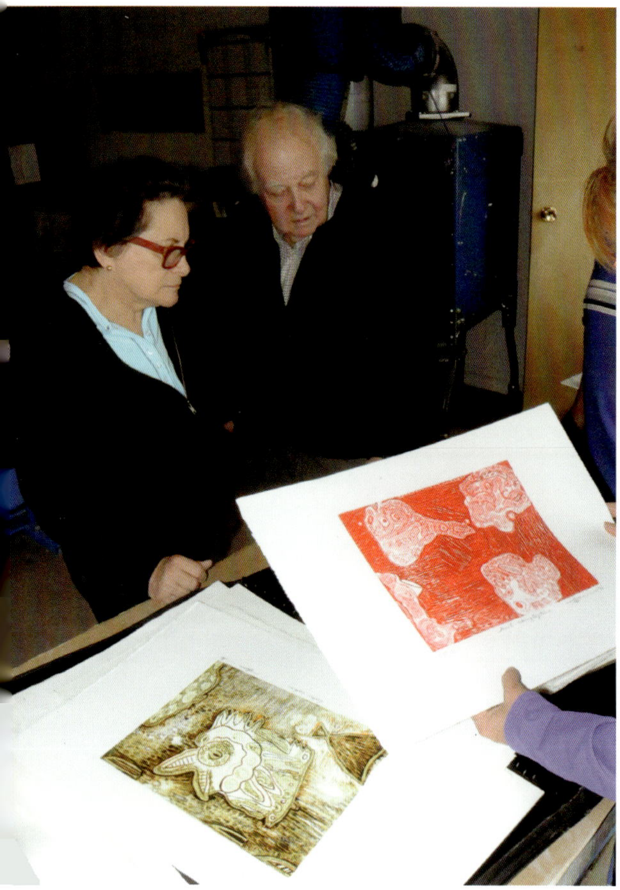

Esther and Sam Sarick at the Jessie Oonark Centre in Baker Lake, 2009

Bill Taylor, then director of the National Museum of Man (now the Canadian Museum of Civilization), Bill Withrow at the Art Gallery of Ontario, and others. Withrow and the AGO won. After all, Toronto is our hometown and we had grown up with the Art Gallery of Toronto (now the AGO).

The monumental task began. Soon after moving the "stuff" from our basement to the AGO's basement, the director of the Cultural Property Export Review Board intervened over the evaluation of the collection. Glenn Lowry, then CEO of the AGO, became incensed at the board's patronizing attitude to Inuit art and took them to court, where the CPERB was reprimanded and required to revisit the process. Glenn, the AGO and the Sarick Collection became instant case history.

We had many mentors, friends and advisers along the way: Bill Swinton and Jerry Twomey in Winnipeg; Budd Feheley in Toronto; Jim Houston and Alma Houston; Terry Ryan; Boris Kotelewetz; Brother Jacques Volant, who had started the Eskimo Museum in Churchill, Manitoba, and who often collected pieces for us to help offset his museum purchases; and many others. The dealers were also very helpful, among them Av Isaacs in Toronto, Theo Waddington in Toronto and Montreal, the staff at the Canadian Handicrafts Guild, Fay Settler in Winnipeg, Arnold and Helene Mazelow, Leon Lippel, John and Mary Robertson in Ottawa and, for more contemporary artists, Harold Seidelman and Pat Feheley here in Toronto. Waddington's auction house was helpful and yielded up some great treasures.

Harold Seidelman arranged for our acquisition of the Handel Collection, put together by his friend Jim Houston in the 1950s, and he introduced us to more contemporary artists who were not necessarily living in northern communities, like Abraham Anghik, his brother David Ruben Piqtoukun, Manasie Akpaliapik and Bill Nasogaluak.

We wish to thank them all for their friendship, advice and help.

Collections have a life of their own, but then ultimately they need a museum or a gallery to validate their existence. Collectors are only custodians for a little while, but the collections rightly belong to the public for posterity. We hope we have looked after your interest and helped to whet your taste for Inuit art at the AGO and for this exhibition curated by Gerald McMaster and his associate, Ingo Hessel.

We have certainly enjoyed our own quest over the years.

Let It Be Known

I would sit down here and see
The changes take place in the Inuit ways.
The life that stood still years ago
Now goes forward in many ways.

I see them go beyond their ways
With hopes of finding a place
Where they will pass their time
In such a way to help their race.

I do not foresee how their
Future will be, a while away
But I can see that it is brightly lit
If they will work their way.

Together into the future I hope
They land in success on their own
So they'll be happy to do what
They please and not be shown.

How I hope they will be given
A fair chance to meet the challenge
So they'll run their lives on
Their own to be on the balance.

I say these to you my friends
Of different races of many places.
I speak as one and speak for many
Who are Inuit of many faces.

For I am one – an Inuk, living
my dreams with high hopes of success.
I am no different than any,
I change with the changing
Arctic world.

Alootook Ipellie
(1951–2007)

Preface

Gerald McMaster

In 1978 the Art Gallery of Ontario accepted the Klamer Family Collection of Inuit Art, which included 602 sculptures, drawings and prints that were presented to the public in 1983 in an exhibition curated by Jean Blodgett called *Grasp Tight the Old Ways*. Five years later the AGO added the Samuel and Esther Sarick Collection of Inuit Art, which over the succeeding years totalled more than 1,800 sculptures and 1,300 prints and drawings. The Sarick Collection is surely one of the largest concentrations of Inuit contemporary art, assembled over several decades and representing more than four hundred artists from thirty-three communities across the Arctic. Together, the Sarick and Klamer collections constitute a comprehensive collection of Inuit art, now ranking among the top two or three in the world. The breadth and depth of the Sarick collection is virtually unrivalled. For many years a book and exhibition have been imagined; we are overjoyed that *Inuit Modern* has come to fruition.

From the beginning the focus of *Inuit Modern* has been on how artists and theorists represent and reflect the Inuit public sphere. Robert McGhee, for example, looks at the ancient archaeological period in which Inuit lived off the land; Dorothy Harley Eber presents the history of relations between Inuit and Europeans; Bernadette Driscoll Engelstad, Christine Lalonde and Heather Igloliorte redirect our attention from the nineteenth century to the second half of the twentieth century—that is, the time when processes of transition from traditional to modern reached their zenith. Ingo Hessel creates the all-important thread through his series of essays, providing a context for the artwork. In their interviews, Zacharias Kunuk and David Ruben Piqtoukun offer the perspective of Inuit artists in the twenty-first century. Finally, the distinguished philosopher John Ralston Saul presents his view of the new and changing North.

When asked by Sam Sarick whom I'd like to work with on the book as my co-curator, I immediately thought of Ingo Hessel, author of some of the most critically important texts on Inuit art. He had just finished curating *Arctic Spirit,* a major exhibition at the Heard Museum in Phoenix, Arizona. Over the past few years, while I was working on the placement of Inuit art within the reinstallation following the AGO expansion, Ingo and I travelled back and forth between Ottawa and Toronto to work out the concept. We also met with the Saricks to view their recent acquisitions and discuss what to include in the exhibit. Ingo was particularly astute at judging how the content of the book should be shaped. We conferred on the book's contributors. More importantly, we agreed that the Inuit voice would have a prominent place, since so many previous texts lacked their voice altogether.

In September 2009 I had the good fortune to board the cruise ship *Adventure Canada* in Kangerlussuaq, Greenland. We sailed to Sisimiut and Ilulissat before heading to Baffin Island and Arctic Quebec; along the way we stopped at Pangnirtung, Kimmirut, Cape Dorset, Kangiqsujuaq and Kuujjuaq. The trip radically changed the way I viewed the North—its land, its people and its art—and prepared me psychologically for work on this exhibition. Along the way my perspectives were gradually adjusted by Inuit, including two people who were on board the ship: Kananginak Pootoogook and Aaju Peter. I also understood why John Houston, who was also on-board, took every opportunity to return to the land where he was raised.

I began to understand how the North is critically important to Inuit, to the animals that live there and to our entire planet.

My curatorial journey would not have been possible without the assistance and guidance of the following people: Sam and Esther Sarick were gracious at every turn by repeatedly welcoming me into their home to look at their collection; without their generosity and vision *Inuit Modern* would never have become a reality. In my conversation with them, they said, "We believe that it is the only truly Canadian art form. Heads of state from other countries are always presented with a piece of Inuit art. We must foster this legacy. It's an inheritance not to be wasted." Matthew Teitelbaum, our institutional visionary, offered his support and guidance when most needed. Sue Gustavison and Sarah Chate were wonderful to work with as my research assistants. Pat Feheley always gave me assistance when called upon. Barry Appleton, a great collector of Inuit and Canadian art, offered me sage advice. Scott McIntyre continues to be a truly great publisher to work with. His team of Meg Taylor, editor, and Linda Gustafson, book designer, has given the world a great read and a handsome book. Photographing the artwork, especially the sculptures, was exceptionally difficult given the various media involved, but in the end, each work stands on its own for its depth of beauty and significance, thanks to photographers Ian Lefebvre and Craig Boyko. Other immensely talented people include Norman Cohn, Syvalya Elchen, Iain Hoadley, Heather Igloliorte, Lisa Landreth, Gillian McIntyre, Mara Meikle, Daniel Naccarato, Wanda Nanabush, Sherry Phillips, Katherine Ruben Piqtoukun, Jim Shedden, Sandy Sparks and Joan Weir. Selecting 175 works from a total of over three thousand from the Sarick Collection was an enormous task. Without my co-curator, Ingo Hessel, who deserves my enormous respect, it could not have been done.

Megwitch!

Inuit History, Inuit Art

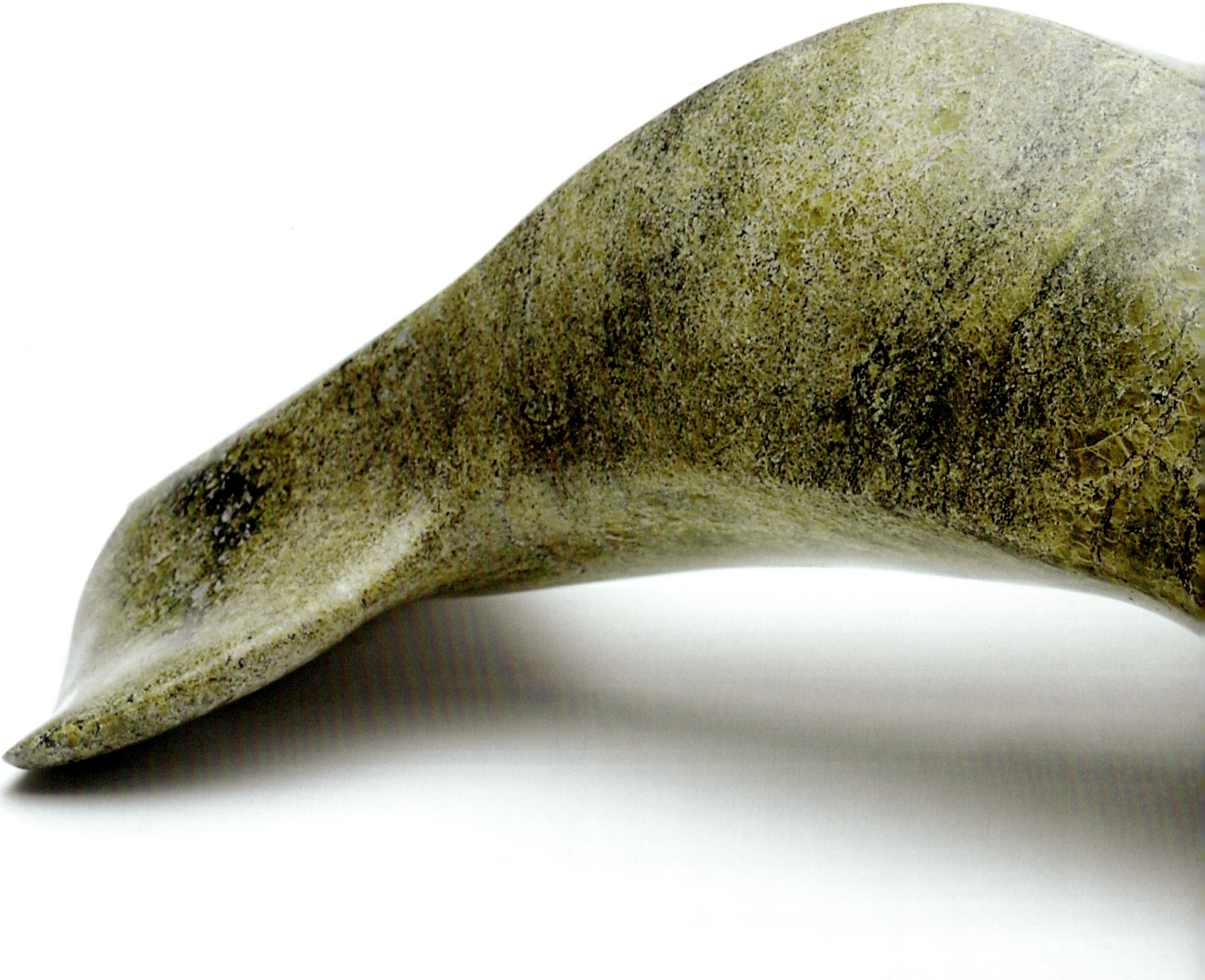

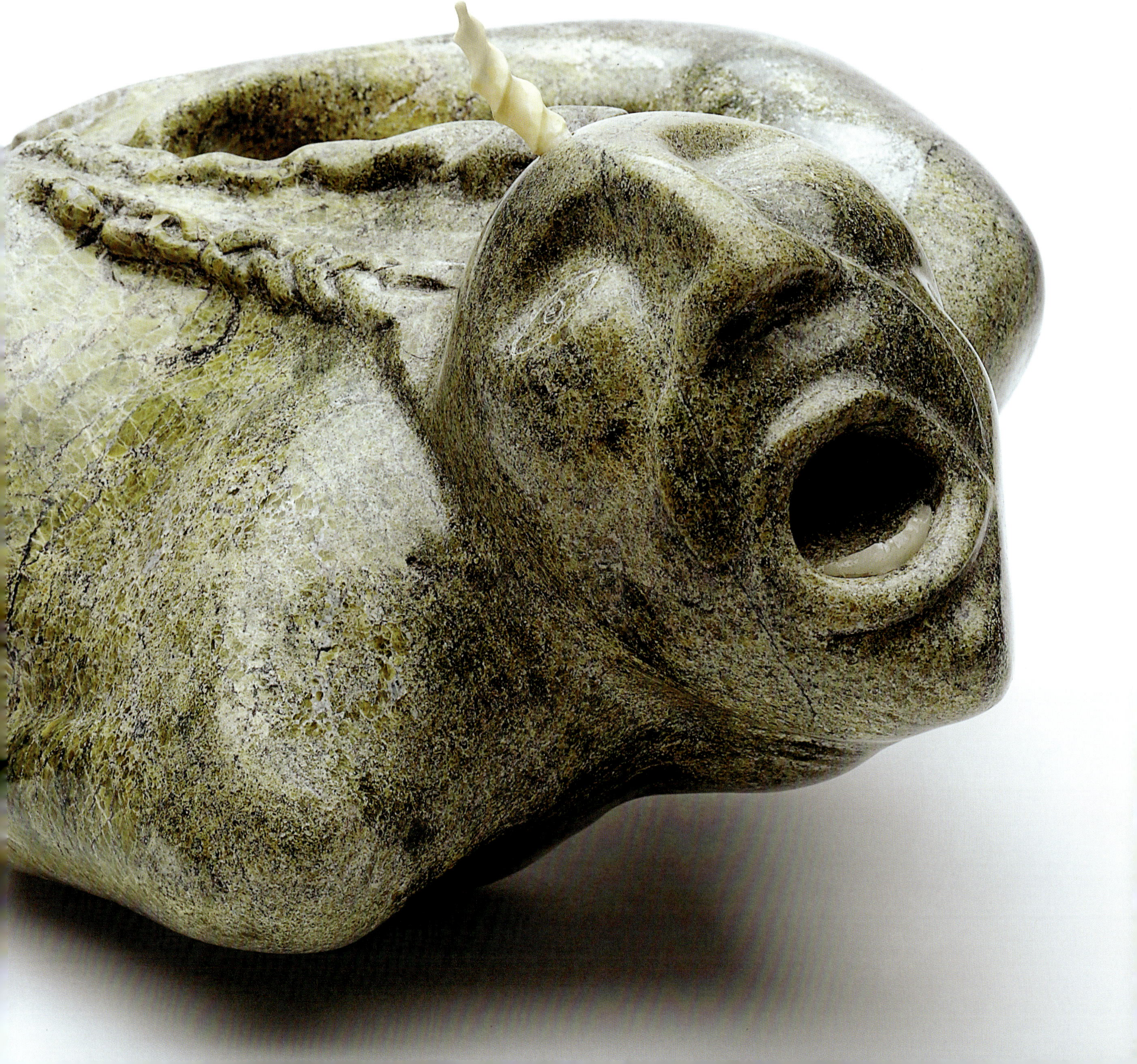

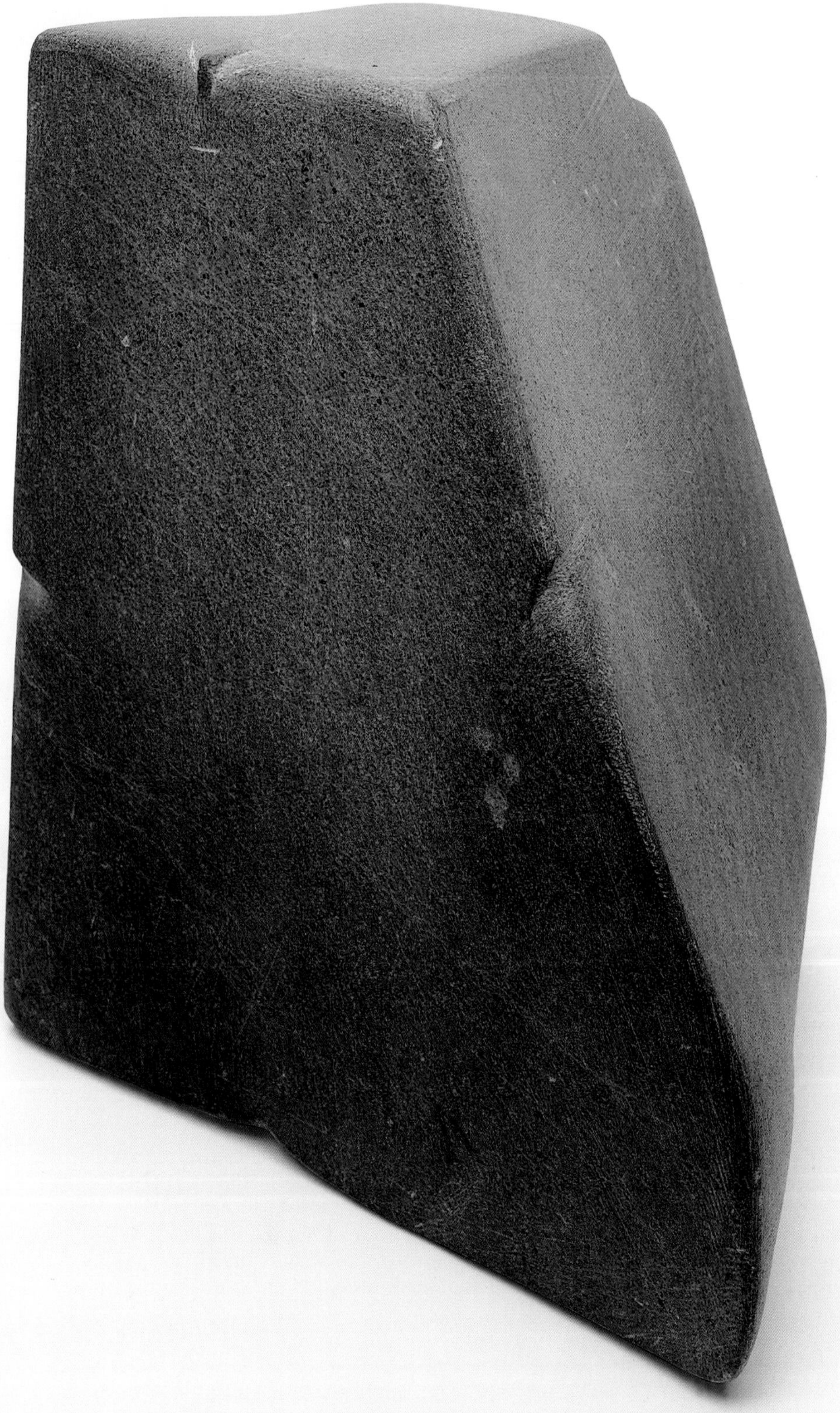

John Pangnark, *Figure*, 1974, stone, 21.5 x 22.3 x 18.3 cm

Inuit Modern: An Introduction

Gerald McMaster

Contemporary Eskimo art has indeed become a new art form. It is the art of the new Eskimo ... Still, although they have changed, the Eskimo and his art are intrinsically and uniquely Eskimoan. —George Swinton, 1972[1]

Can the word "Eskimo" legitimately be applied to this modern stone art? I think not. Its roots are Western; so is its audience. —Edmund Carpenter, 1973[2]

These two pioneers in Inuit art studies, the Inuit art scholar George Swinton and the anthropologist Edmund Carpenter, strongly disagreed on the phenomenon of the new artistic practice coming out of the Far North. Swinton was deeply involved in studying, collecting and promoting Inuit art throughout his life; Carpenter, in contrast, spent his early career studying the Inuit at a time when modern Inuit art was just emerging. They agreed that it was a new trend; however, they held opposing views on its authenticity as an art form. Typically, such issues characterize non-Western art studies, but for all the hand-wringing about its true nature, Inuit art has been embraced by Canadians as part of our national, multicultural, artistic identity.

In 1948 James Houston, who would become a prominent artist, writer and Inuit art specialist, travelled to a small Inuit community in Northern Quebec to paint the Arctic landscape. He quickly realized that the Inuit handicrafts he saw at Port Harrison (now Inukjuak) could be turned into marketable goods. The Inuit traditional way of life was changing; the Canadian government was interested in encouraging a money economy in the North. Inuit, as Dorothy Eber explicates in her chapter, had long been trading with southerners, especially in furs and meats. Trade in craft items was confined to smaller ivory pieces. It was not until the 1950s, with the shift from nomadic to settled communities, that the production of Inuit sculptures and drawings as commodities began in earnest.

What is it that characterizes Inuit art? Filmmaker John Houston said: "Their art must fulfill a need... in us. It is our own Western culture that has embraced Inuit art by curating travelling exhibitions, writing about it, and dedicating galleries around North America and Europe to it."[3]

The Inuit of our imagination continue into the present. At the Vancouver 2010 Winter Olympics the logo was the inukshuk—a human figure made of stones, traditionally used in the barren lands of the Arctic to frighten caribou into an ambush and to mark the landscape for travellers. The inukshuk has entered the popular imagination in Canada and is now created wherever and whenever a pile of stones is available.[4] When the logo was unveiled, the former premier of the territory of Nunavut, Paul Okalik, said: "We don't have any maple leafs where I come from. This is very special. It shows strength. Our inukshuk has been around a very long time. To be shown off to the rest of the world is very special for us."[5]

Until relatively recently, most of the world knew the North through images created by filmmakers such as Robert Flaherty, whose *Nanook of the North* (1922; filmed in 1920) made a "photoplay" about life in the Hudson Bay region of the Canadian Arctic. It was not until the release of Zacharias Kunuk's *Atanarjuat: The Fast Runner* (2001)[6] that Inuit and the North were imagined in new and authentic ways.

168, 169) and Simon Tookoome (pp. 180, 181), whose drawings must be viewed from multiple perspectives because horizon lines are non-existent; in other words, they are best viewed from above as the viewer walks around the work on the ground. It is in this regard that I agree with Carpenter as to how the hegemony of Renaissance perspective is non-existent. These artists have more in common with Australian Aboriginal desert artists, the dot painters of Papunya Tula, or the bark painters of Arnhem Land in the Northern Territory. All these artists paint while sitting on the ground; as well, they probably never heard of Jackson Pollock.

Another traditional observation on Inuit art is that so much of the work recalls a more-than-human world in which spirit forces abound. We see humans and animals living in the same space, often transforming into each other. Whether or not this is in response to southern demand, there is no doubt that it has become a popular theme, much to the chagrin of Christian missionaries bound on converting Inuit. Jean Blodgett, an Inuit art scholar, says that spirits were ubiquitous in the North; it was the shamans who more than likely were the main point of communication. Shamans, Blodgett says, "were capable of a number of spectacular feats which they employed to aid them in their duties."[18] Her work on Karoo Ashevak should be noted for presenting his unique exploration of the private world of dreams. Inuit shamanism is prominent in his mixed-media sculptures (pp. 93, 118, 119). His playful, experimental approach encompasses a large visual métier—animation and humour—vital elements in his carvings of spirits, shamans, Arctic wildlife and human figures.

We are seeing a new type of artist in the North—one who no longer draws on traditional themes and who sees life changing before their eyes. When we think of social realism, we think of depictions of social and racial injustice and economic hardship through unvarnished pictures of life's struggles. Although the artistic style of social realism varies from nation to nation, it almost always follows a form of descriptive or critical realism. This I would argue is the new kind of work coming out of Cape Dorset, led by Annie Pootoogook (pp. 198, 199). Pootoogook began drawing as recently as 1997. In her drawings, she represents the everyday life of contemporary Inuit in the North—the only world she knows. Unlike the older generations who depicted hunting, daily activities and a world imbued with spirits, Pootoogook knows a different world, a world where traditional and contemporary practices come together. Pootoogook's austere, often humorous pencil-crayon drawings are relentless in capturing the changing conditions of life in the North. Tradition often comes up against modernity, largely influenced, of course, by the inundation of the North in terms of southern goods, education, technology and media.

It is this inundation that is part of the neo-colonial process of globalization, which some would argue is cultural imperialism brought about by the consumption of cultural and material products. Nowhere else is this more evident than in the North, where the way of life is no longer as heavily invested in the land but depends more on products and services emanating from the South. This we can see in the works of Annie Pootoogook, Itee Pootoogook, Kananginak Pootoogook, Pudlo Pudlat and Shuvinai Ashoona. Although stopping short of suggesting that the men should be outside hunting, Annie Pootoogook's work (p. 198) shows three men playing cards in the comfort of their home, which is like any southern home; indeed, there are very few indications of northern identity. Perhaps this is the true intent of Pootoogook: to convey the almost complete overlay of the South on the North. The power imbalance between the North and the South, with winners and losers, reminds us of the dynamics of historical colonialism evolving into a new pattern of neo-colonialism.

Inuit Modern: An Introduction

Gerald McMaster

Contemporary Eskimo art has indeed become a new art form. It is the art of the new Eskimo ... Still, although they have changed, the Eskimo and his art are intrinsically and uniquely Eskimoan. —George Swinton, 1972[1]

Can the word "Eskimo" legitimately be applied to this modern stone art? I think not. Its roots are Western; so is its audience. —Edmund Carpenter, 1973[2]

These two pioneers in Inuit art studies, the Inuit art scholar George Swinton and the anthropologist Edmund Carpenter, strongly disagreed on the phenomenon of the new artistic practice coming out of the Far North. Swinton was deeply involved in studying, collecting and promoting Inuit art throughout his life; Carpenter, in contrast, spent his early career studying the Inuit at a time when modern Inuit art was just emerging. They agreed that it was a new trend; however, they held opposing views on its authenticity as an art form. Typically, such issues characterize non-Western art studies, but for all the hand-wringing about its true nature, Inuit art has been embraced by Canadians as part of our national, multicultural, artistic identity.

In 1948 James Houston, who would become a prominent artist, writer and Inuit art specialist, travelled to a small Inuit community in Northern Quebec to paint the Arctic landscape. He quickly realized that the Inuit handicrafts he saw at Port Harrison (now Inukjuak) could be turned into marketable goods. The Inuit traditional way of life was changing; the Canadian government was interested in encouraging a money economy in the North. Inuit, as Dorothy Eber explicates in her chapter, had long been trading with southerners, especially in furs and meats. Trade in craft items was confined to smaller ivory pieces. It was not until the 1950s, with the shift from nomadic to settled communities, that the production of Inuit sculptures and drawings as commodities began in earnest.

What is it that characterizes Inuit art? Filmmaker John Houston said: "Their art must fulfill a need... in us. It is our own Western culture that has embraced Inuit art by curating travelling exhibitions, writing about it, and dedicating galleries around North America and Europe to it."[3]

The Inuit of our imagination continue into the present. At the Vancouver 2010 Winter Olympics the logo was the inukshuk—a human figure made of stones, traditionally used in the barren lands of the Arctic to frighten caribou into an ambush and to mark the landscape for travellers. The inukshuk has entered the popular imagination in Canada and is now created wherever and whenever a pile of stones is available.[4] When the logo was unveiled, the former premier of the territory of Nunavut, Paul Okalik, said: "We don't have any maple leafs where I come from. This is very special. It shows strength. Our inukshuk has been around a very long time. To be shown off to the rest of the world is very special for us."[5]

Until relatively recently, most of the world knew the North through images created by filmmakers such as Robert Flaherty, whose *Nanook of the North* (1922; filmed in 1920) made a "photoplay" about life in the Hudson Bay region of the Canadian Arctic. It was not until the release of Zacharias Kunuk's *Atanarjuat: The Fast Runner* (2001)[6] that Inuit and the North were imagined in new and authentic ways.

Zacharias Kunuk, whose interview appears in this book, is now recognized around the world for his films and documentaries, which explore the changing portrayal of Inuit on the big screen over the past century. By using Inuit actors and a screenplay based on a traditional story, Kunuk assumed a voice of authority for his people.

In response to new thinking about the North, *Inuit Modern* situates its major themes within the context of a rapidly changing Arctic. It considers how Inuit have dealt with the swift transition from a traditional lifestyle to the current disturbing complexities of globalization and climate change. It describes how Inuit art reflects the reciprocal stimulus of contact with Euro-Canadians and concurrently analyzes the birth and evolution of a modernist Inuit aesthetic that springs from an ancient cultural context and, through acculturation, creates an exciting new hybridized art form.

"Some people say that it's bad to see the traditional things disappear, but for me, I say it's better because it makes life easier. I don't live a traditional life today."

Oviloo Tunnillie

The exhibition's message of artistic, social, political and cultural transformation will be seen through the two dynamic lenses of colonial influence and agency, which resonate across all regions of the North once thought of as geographically remote and intellectually inaccessible. Colonial influence is generally viewed negatively from a social/political perspective, but creative thinkers make independent choices. It is artists who adjust quickly by appropriating images and ideas from new sources, examples of which can be seen throughout this exhibition. In the 1950s Inuit quickly adjusted to the stereotypic view of them by outsiders, a moment we identified in this book as "Eskimo" art; but starting in the 1960s, they wrestled back their voice. Indeed, the Inuit voice became a critical component of *Inuit Modern,* complementing the scholarly essays.

Power relations proliferate in the modern world. The renewed calls for self-determination of indigenous peoples in various parts of the world, including the First Nations and Inuit in Canada, are based on implicit and explicit mandates of international law. Such calls have emphasized the legitimacy of indigenous culture as the principal force of authority in shaping such self-determination. Indeed, with the creation of the federal territory of Nunavut in 1999, Inuit have seen the dream of autonomy come to life. They can now experiment with how such autonomy can coexist with other systems. One such system is bringing together traditional values in a modern way.

With these critical issues in mind, the following questions are addressed in various ways throughout the book, and some I will address in this essay. What do we consider to be the signs of modernity in the North? How has modernity complicated everyday life in Canada's Far North? How has Inuit art changed the way that Canada and Inuit are viewed? How do we conceptualize colonialism, globalization and modernity in the context of the new North? How have Inuit taken control of notions of modernity?

The Myth of Primitivism

Although it appears that the glory days of Inuit art are gone, when artists such as Kenojuak Ashevak, Jessie Oonark, Karoo Ashevak and Kiugak Ashoona were receiving international praise for their distinctive artistic visions of the North, it was by sheer good fortune that they took an aesthetic form that was almost purely personal and cast it into a public sphere, thereby changing our view of an art that was once considered "primitive."

Through a great deal of art history, the artistic output of non-Western artists has been cast into marginal discursive categories of either "not art," or, if it was grudgingly deemed to be art, it was labelled "primitive art," "non-Western art," "ethnic art," "tribal art" or "craft." Art historian Colin Rhodes contends that it is "the distorting lens of Western constructions"[7] generated in the latter part of the nineteenth and early twentieth centuries that positions all artistic production outside the West in belittling terms. "The primitive," he points out, "was regarded, on the whole, as always more instinctive, less bound by artistic convention and history, and as somehow closer to fundamental aspects of human existence."[8] The debate has been further debased by the introduction of the false dichotomy of traditional versus contemporary: on the one hand, authenticity is said to exist in certain time-bound work, such as weaving, beading and pottery, in that they are more real because they draw on ancient forms; on the other hand, the so-called contemporary expressions are quite the opposite. The underlying hegemony of the colonialist agenda led to the creation of this false dichotomy. Numerous historical examples from the nineteenth century demonstrate that Aboriginal artists were freely drawing on new ideas and materials from the European newcomer. In this context, issues of authenticity were non-existent, since all artists were secure in their own cultural sphere. These artists were not slavishly bound by convention; in fact, they clearly welcomed new opportunities for artistic expression.

The productions of meanings are fairly distinct. Western definition of non-Western art is highly questionable; yet, without these definitions postwar Aboriginal art would not have the urgency to position itself. We are more apt to find Aboriginal contemporary artists, critics and curators articulating new definitions for their practice—arguing that such work must be viewed in the present tense as "contemporary," not as an anachronistic or essentialist phenomenon of a past that belonged to their ancestors. For example, there are many conceptual and discursive differences that distinguish the Inuit contemporary artists' works from the historical works we see most often in ethnographic[9] museums. The earlier artists produced works that were more closely related to, and constituted within, tribal cultures and language; today's artists by and large create works for any and all publics. In the case of Inuit historic art, the dialogue was internal; in Inuit contemporary art, the dialogue moves outward, with related dialogues that are aesthetic, political, moral and didactic.

Modernity and Inuit

How have Inuit experienced modernity in twentieth-century Canada? First, they experienced radical change from living on the land to living in communities, a shift that can be seen as either progress or transition. Inuit, of course, had long been in contact with white southerners, trading and mixing in some form or another over the past millennia.[10] McGhee begins with the Norse contacts; Eber presents the stories Inuit tell of contact with Europeans through the eighteenth and nineteenth centuries. Engelstad and Lalonde bring us into the present tense of these modernist influences, and Igloliorte articulates the resilient Inuit voice.

Inuit have experienced modernity amid a proliferation of choices. Whereas traditional cultural practices in the present are finite, modernity opens up a vast field of options, which can be a source of great anxiety. Traditionalists usually argue for certain restrictions, since they have experienced the turmoil of radical shifts through each generation. In all likelihood it is not so much the choices that create concern; rather, it is their uncontrollability. The schools are teaching less Inuktitut and more English; children spend more time in school than on the land learning how to hunt and fish; radio, television and the Internet replace storytellers and traditional music—the list of choices is enormous.

Describing modernity is not a particularly difficult or controversial task; indeed, there is a great deal of commonality among the features various writers have listed: a market economy, widespread literacy, the rise of government bureaucracy, the growth of science and industry. Shifts in personal philosophy include the conception of a person as free and autonomous, a reliance on reason and experience, and opposition or at least resistance to traditional forms of thought and life.

Different cultures have experienced modernization at different times. The conditions of modernity may vary, but essentially Europeans are regarded as the originators. Differential access to modernity and how modernity is introduced to non-Western cultures are hotly debated issues. It is often assumed that modernity in a Western sense is a conscious break from tradition; yet among the colonized peoples of the Americas, modernity was enforced, which is why it can be a controversial topic. Western forms of modernity have had tremendous influence into the present, to the extent that they have become inherently colonial, imposing many of the features listed above. Modernity is inherently globalizing and colonizing.

Modernity further suggests a process of social and cultural change, and a discontinuity with the past. In the case of Inuit culture, there is a strong argument to suggest that for traditionalists, modernity signified a decline; for progressives, it was an improvement. Certainly contemporary Inuit life in settled communities is fundamentally different from life on the land; yet, tradition, which is simply the idea that the present is continuous with the past, can actually benefit from some aspects of modernity. Mark Kalluak of Arviat says:

> The Arctic has gone through a very swift transition. Many of our leaders have examined the impact and made adjustments in support of language and cultural preservation. Modern technology has become a useful tool in fulfilling many of our aspirations in relation to preservation of culture and language. Compared to 40 or 50 years ago when the only reading material in Inuktitut for many of the Canadian Inuit were worn-out prayer books and biblical texts, we not only have a wider selection but are involved in publication of more materials.[11]

Like Heather Igloliorte in this volume, art historian George Swinton argues that Inuit were resilient in the face of modernity:

> It is mostly in regard to motivation that Eskimo culture purists get particularly upset. They decry the Eskimo's changing way of life and everything that goes with it. They are unwilling to appreciate the Eskimo's unbelievably matter-of-fact powers of adjustment to the incredibly fast pace of cultural evolution from the Stone Age to a money economy, mechanization, and rapid transportation, all within a single generation. They are equally unwilling to recognize the Eskimo's need for changing attitudes and motivations in his life and art during the process of acculturation... No doubt, these changes are destroying the Eskimo's indigenous culture, but they are also improving the tragic conditions of his life and are preferable to the purist's romantic illusions.[12]

Similarly, James Houston observes the old change to new:

> In 1948 Eskimo carvers in remote camps still lived lives little changed from the time when Rasmussen had travelled among them [in the 1920s], for even in his time they knew traders and missionaries. In the 1950s with the building of the DEW line, the intrusion of more outsiders, and the development of villages with school requirements for children, the Eskimos' lifestyle began to change at a more rapid pace, a pace that is accelerating today... with the development of oil and mineral deposits, air travel, and the introduction of industry in the Arctic.[13]

Critics such as Edmund Carpenter have suggested that modernity has had undue influence on the Inuit, and in a sense modernity is a *problem*. He, like many others, would argue that the traditional ways of life have been replaced with uncontrollable change and unmanageable alternatives; yet, when we consider the creation of the territory of Nunavut, we have to reconsider the argument in the present tense. At one time the Inuit in transition were not seen as having a clear future but rather were simply changing in response to forces outside their control—an interpretation that must now be cast in a new light.

Viewed from the present tense, the American Indian critic and writer Gerald Vizenor has suggested a new term—"survivance"—that would suggest Aboriginal peoples and cultures are dynamic, inventive and enduring rather than being passive victims of colonialist trappings such as absence, tragedy and powerlessness. Vizenor argues that survivance is an active sense of presence over social, cultural, political and historical erasure. (The nature of survivance, he argues, is unmistakable in Native stories, active traditions, customs and narrative resistance and is clearly observable in personal attributes such as humour, spirit, cast of mind and moral courage in literature.) Vizenor says, "Survivance is a practice, not an ideology, dissimulation, or a theory."[14] If we consider the work over the last fifty to sixty years by Inuit artists, surely it can be understood as a form of survivance within the framework of colonization.

For Inuit, modernity is the world experienced as fragmented, no longer an integrated world where social groups are based on real, biological kinship ties, and where social relations are stable and permanent. Modernity is changing this as communities are gradually getting larger and social relations are shifting rapidly. But is this a completely negative situation, or must we look at change differently? For the art and the artists in this exhibition change has been positive to a large extent.

First Nations cultures in the South have endured devastating changes to their way of life; yet they have managed to work with the changes, as Vizenor would attest. They have seen traditions take a beating, yet behaviour patterns, relations with indigenous peoples worldwide and rituals and ceremonies are new and innovative, such that the past is rarely repeated. The experience of modernity is to live in traditional ways and to repeat tradition in unrecognizable forms. Modern Inuit culture still performs traditional rituals, despite the influence of Christianity. Artists continue to create works that suggest and reference spirituality and shamanic practices. Since the Inuit of today are only a few generations removed from those who lived off the land, their culture is largely based on traditional ways of thinking. Modernity, often viewed as the present being discontinuous with the past, should now be viewed as an illusion. Inuit, like First Nations to the south, will continually adapt to their changing circumstances.

Modernization programs in the North started in the early 1950s and had far-reaching consequences for Inuit. On the way to modernity Inuit have been subjected to some instances of rapid relocation by the federal government, such as the creation of Grise Fiord, a community on Ellesmere Island and one of the coldest inhabited places in the world. In the process of moving off the land, Inuit moved into the more than two dozen communities that were built around trading posts. Unlike southerners, many of whom move to cities in search of opportunity and individual happiness, Inuit are more likely to seek a sense of fulfillment with their families. Yet for modern Inuit, community life has led to some sacrifice of nature for culture on a small scale; it may be through art that culture offers some of the exaltations of nature. New forms of wealth arrived from the South; commerce such as selling art and work with local community infrastructures or the tourism industry became new resources to be controlled and shared by Inuit. New systems of work and mobility have contributed to the reconfiguration of society. The displacement of traditional homes, of creating sedentary lives, has had a significant impact on Inuit life. Even modernist architecture and planning can be viewed as a colonial impact on the North; standardized housing appears in the works of Pudlo Pudlat (p. 171, *Modern Settlement—Traditional Camp*, 1978–79), Itee Pootoogook (p. 204, *Abandoned House*, 2009) and Annie Pootoogook (p. 198, *In the Kitchen*, 2002–03).

The transition to modernity is an ongoing process, and both traditional and modern ways coexist in the North. The new and emerging social groups are continually adjusting to the changing environment, making use of traditional practices that benefit them. For example, the underlying principle guiding relationships within small groups of people in pre-community life was—and still continues to be—reciprocity, in the form of exchange between people with different levels of status and wealth.

Alienation

A common ill in Western society is alienation, an individual's estrangement from traditional community and others in general. In Inuit society this has only recently become an issue. Artists rarely addressed alienation in the past, whereas we are now seeing social issues coming to light in some of the more contemporary works of Oviloo Tunnillie (p. 208, *Untitled*, 2001/341), Annie Pootoogook (*Guitar Player*, Sarick Private Collection) and Bill Nasogaluak (p. 216, *Sedna on Cross*, Sarick Private Collection). In each of their works the confrontation with modernity is something that was rarely expressed in the works of the older generation of artists. In the more recent generation, they have seen the changes wrought by modernity. David Ruben Piqtoukun and his brother Abraham Anghik Ruben attended residential schools and experienced forced removal from their families and Inuit society by the federal government. In many Inuit communities the influx of southern drugs and alcohol has created enormous societal tension, leading to suicides and unexplained deaths. Domestic violence is sometimes the focus of Annie Pootoogook's work; if we examine works by her mother, we find that Napachie was already depicting darker social issues. Inuit art was moving to another level of reality not previously seen.

"If I go back [home] for a few days, I'll be thrilled, then I'll get bored because it's not like the South. After a few months, I'll get used to it but it takes time. When I come down, I'm happy for a few days, then I get depressed. For me I feel I'm caught in the middle. I don't really have a place here, or don't really have a place up there. Somewhere in the middle would be comfortable I guess... I'm stuck in between."

Manasie Akpaliapik

Piliriqatigiinniq is the concept of developing a collaborative relationship or working together for a common purpose. This is the essential Inuit belief that stresses the importance of the group over the individual. Yet, the North has changed significantly over the last sixty years. Not only have Inuit shifted from living off the land to living in communities, but many of these communities have grown larger and more complex. Southern-style administration has greatly influenced how Inuit live today. One outcome of a modern community lifestyle is the relation between the individual and the community. In the case of the artists in this exhibition, we have created a section called "I Am an Artist" to suggest that Inuit art in the South has created a sophisticated discourse around the individual, in which the named artist is critical.

How are artists who are known to the outside world understood within the community? The academy and the art world have long loved individuals and individualism as a way of looking at the artwork—the genius effect, the artist, troubled or otherwise. The individual artist was viewed as an outsider, living on the margins of society. Artworks are analyzed by looking at the social, cultural, political views of the individual, in an attempt to see the world the way the artist sees it and represents it. No doubt in contemporary Inuit society individualism is both praised and condemned, making it a tricky situation, especially in small communities. Traditionalists are usually the first to criticize individualism as a way of protecting group cohesiveness; southerners, however, have valued Inuit artists as individuals through art collecting.

Western civilization has long believed in the dignity and worth of the individual. Coupled with this view is the idea that individuals are separated from each other and from the natural world, an idea that would be countered by Inuit. For Inuit individualism is largely practised in relation to outside society; artists leave to go south, not as a withdrawal from the community but to attend exhibitions or participate in public events.

Edmund Carpenter's view of Inuit individuality is fairly negative. In 1973 he wrote:

> I am aware that there are modern Eskimo who use art as a means of lonely self-identity. I have known such men. But I believe they are new on the Arctic scene, products of Western influence. Their art should not be confused with aboriginal Eskimo art, which is of an entirely different order. Some of this new art is genuine enough: as people change, so their art changes, and the Eskimo are changing rapidly. Among them there are growing notions of individualism, new attitudes

> toward controlling the external, and, hence, a way of perceiving that separates time and space... The new stone carvings, each with its base and its favored point of view, reflect all this and are therefore much easier for the Western art connoisseur to appreciate.[15]

In a campaign to control the Inuit, the federal government allotted discrete numbers to individuals. These "disc numbers" appear on the bottom of some of the older sculptures. With some investigative work we now know the identity of many individuals identified only by their numbers until recently. In Ruth Annaqtuusi Tulurialik's *On the Land*, 1990 (p. 179), for example, the woman in the centre carrying her child also carries her disc number "E62" as she would an amulet.

Another method of individualizing artists advocated by southerners was by having them sign their work. Christian missionaries had developed a written script for what had traditionally been a purely oral culture. The Bible was translated into a syllabic form that could be understood by people in local communities across the North. Inuit quickly picked up this syllabic system, to the point that artists began signing their work using the new written language; as well, southern institutions mounted exhibitions and books on Inuit art in French, English and Inuktitut.

In Inuit communities today, the values of community and individuality, far from being in opposition, are mutually supporting and mutually sustaining. We see this in the work of many of these artists. This may change in the future; in the meantime they struggle through modernity in their own ways. They would see it as pointless to attempt to restore the small-scale community of the past.

Inuit Art and Aesthetics

The disciplines of aesthetics and aesthetic theory are inseparably bound up with modernist art practices. Modernism's abiding interest and influence are generally in formal experimentation and experience. It has been the formalist aesthetic values where Inuit art has attracted attention, aside from its exotic otherness. Formalism is often described as looking at art outside of its historical and/or social context, privileging the work's design principles. Its effect on the appreciation of Inuit art occurred about the same time that George Swinton, a European-trained art historian, came onto the scene. Without pulling punches, he describes the criteria used to evaluate Inuit art as one based on Western values. "Even more significant for the development of contemporary Eskimo art," he says, "is the fact that it is mainly because of our Western criteria and aesthetic values that we have become interested in the new carvings. Thus it would be hypocritical to deny that the appreciation of Eskimo art is based on Western values and aesthetic considerations. It is important, therefore, to clarify these criteria and values."[16] In contrast, Swinton's critic Edmund Carpenter argues for the return of the art before the modern period: "Most of [the modern] carvings," he pronounces, "are massive, heavy, and fragile, designed to be set in place and viewed by strangers. The traditional role of art is gone: object has replaced act. Traditional perspective is gone: stability and single perspective have replaced mobility and multiple perspectives. Traditional notions of discovering and revealing are gone."[17] Inuit were never part of the Western discourse of form versus content; rather it was the critics and collectors who made these arguments.

If works by artists such as John Tiktak, Lucy Tasseor Tutsweetok, Paniluk Qamanirq, John Pangnark or Andy Miki are viewed primarily from a formalist perspective, then so be it; there is a timeless quality to their approach that has so attracted critics and collectors. For Inuit artists, one does not overpower the other: form is always a significant aspect of content; it is only the modern function that has overtaken traditional use.

Some artists recall the traditional aesthetic perspective, as in the works of Luke Anguhadluq (pp. 103,

168, 169) and Simon Tookoome (pp. 180, 181), whose drawings must be viewed from multiple perspectives because horizon lines are non-existent; in other words, they are best viewed from above as the viewer walks around the work on the ground. It is in this regard that I agree with Carpenter as to how the hegemony of Renaissance perspective is non-existent. These artists have more in common with Australian Aboriginal desert artists, the dot painters of Papunya Tula, or the bark painters of Arnhem Land in the Northern Territory. All these artists paint while sitting on the ground; as well, they probably never heard of Jackson Pollock.

Another traditional observation on Inuit art is that so much of the work recalls a more-than-human world in which spirit forces abound. We see humans and animals living in the same space, often transforming into each other. Whether or not this is in response to southern demand, there is no doubt that it has become a popular theme, much to the chagrin of Christian missionaries bound on converting Inuit. Jean Blodgett, an Inuit art scholar, says that spirits were ubiquitous in the North; it was the shamans who more than likely were the main point of communication. Shamans, Blodgett says, "were capable of a number of spectacular feats which they employed to aid them in their duties."[18] Her work on Karoo Ashevak should be noted for presenting his unique exploration of the private world of dreams. Inuit shamanism is prominent in his mixed-media sculptures (pp. 93, 118, 119). His playful, experimental approach encompasses a large visual métier—animation and humour—vital elements in his carvings of spirits, shamans, Arctic wildlife and human figures.

We are seeing a new type of artist in the North—one who no longer draws on traditional themes and who sees life changing before their eyes. When we think of social realism, we think of depictions of social and racial injustice and economic hardship through unvarnished pictures of life's struggles. Although the artistic style of social realism varies from nation to nation, it almost always follows a form of descriptive or critical realism. This I would argue is the new kind of work coming out of Cape Dorset, led by Annie Pootoogook (pp. 198, 199). Pootoogook began drawing as recently as 1997. In her drawings, she represents the everyday life of contemporary Inuit in the North—the only world she knows. Unlike the older generations who depicted hunting, daily activities and a world imbued with spirits, Pootoogook knows a different world, a world where traditional and contemporary practices come together. Pootoogook's austere, often humorous pencil-crayon drawings are relentless in capturing the changing conditions of life in the North. Tradition often comes up against modernity, largely influenced, of course, by the inundation of the North in terms of southern goods, education, technology and media.

It is this inundation that is part of the neo-colonial process of globalization, which some would argue is cultural imperialism brought about by the consumption of cultural and material products. Nowhere else is this more evident than in the North, where the way of life is no longer as heavily invested in the land but depends more on products and services emanating from the South. This we can see in the works of Annie Pootoogook, Itee Pootoogook, Kananginak Pootoogook, Pudlo Pudlat and Shuvinai Ashoona. Although stopping short of suggesting that the men should be outside hunting, Annie Pootoogook's work (p. 198) shows three men playing cards in the comfort of their home, which is like any southern home; indeed, there are very few indications of northern identity. Perhaps this is the true intent of Pootoogook: to convey the almost complete overlay of the South on the North. The power imbalance between the North and the South, with winners and losers, reminds us of the dynamics of historical colonialism evolving into a new pattern of neo-colonialism.

The Future

Film has become an effective medium to express narrative to a wider audience. Zacharias Kunuk's *Atanarjuat* is an epic piece of storytelling. It was also the first Inuit film to receive a theatrical release. The film was shot in Igloolik, using local cast and crew. "Inuit have learned through the millennia that people cannot overpower reality. Our objective was not to impose southern filmmaking conventions on our unique story, but to let the story shape the filmmaking process in an Inuit way."[19] Beside Kunuk's Isuma Productions, Arnait Video Productions incorporated in 1999 as the first women's collective independent production company in the Arctic. These companies now bolster local control to present and promote an alternative to Western-style film and television and to conserve Inuit knowledge and broadcast it beyond the North.

> *"My art has been a way for me to see the world."*
>
> Pudlo Pudlat

In the past several decades we have begun to understand that there are many modernisms; for Inuit, they are experiencing and participating in the newest version. Curator and essayist Marie Bouchard wrote a remarkable essay on the AGO's Sarick Collection that was presented in the Inuit community of Baker Lake in 2000. In it she writes about the new changes in the North that have had some effect on how institutions are now regarding Inuit art:

> The establishment of Nunavut... has significantly changed the relationship between Inuit and the rest of Canada and will continue to do so... Inuit are no longer relegated to a neo-colonial status of exotic "other" in this country. In postcolonial Nunavut, Inuit traditions, knowledge and opinions are openly acknowledged to have equal if not greater value to that of the white dominant culture that has surreptitiously infiltrated every aspect of Northern life.[20]

Curiously she refers to post-colonial Nunavut. Post-colonialism is usually understood as a period marker of what came after colonialism. Although some would argue that First Nations and Inuit will always be in a colonial condition, we can take from it that the practice of post-colonial theory is a way of imagining, a style of thinking and a set of reading strategies. Post-colonial theorists seek to focus on problematic issues of representation, the interconnections between knowledge and power.

Industrialization, urbanization, the focus on the individual, secularism, rationality, the impact of science and technology, and colonialism are closely associated with modernism. The effect of climate change on the North is an additional pressure on the culture. To the extent that Inuit are won over by modernity, they struggle to adapt while remaining resilient.

Nevertheless, instead of Inuit losing their sense of place in the face of ever-increasing global influences, globalization has highlighted the importance of local Inuit culture in negotiating the process of a kind of cultural hybridization. The push back—the resistance and resilience that characterize Inuit culture—has always been reflected in the creation and production of art. Many of the artists featured in *Inuit Modern* have merely found a new medium to control the process. Oviloo Tunnillie's telling work (p. 208) shows a woman covering her eyes with her hands, suggesting the unknown future. We live in the creative present looking back. In such an unsympathetic yet rapidly changing climate, I believe Inuit have always lived the right way: they have stayed put and let the South come to them; in so doing, it is we who change when we go North.

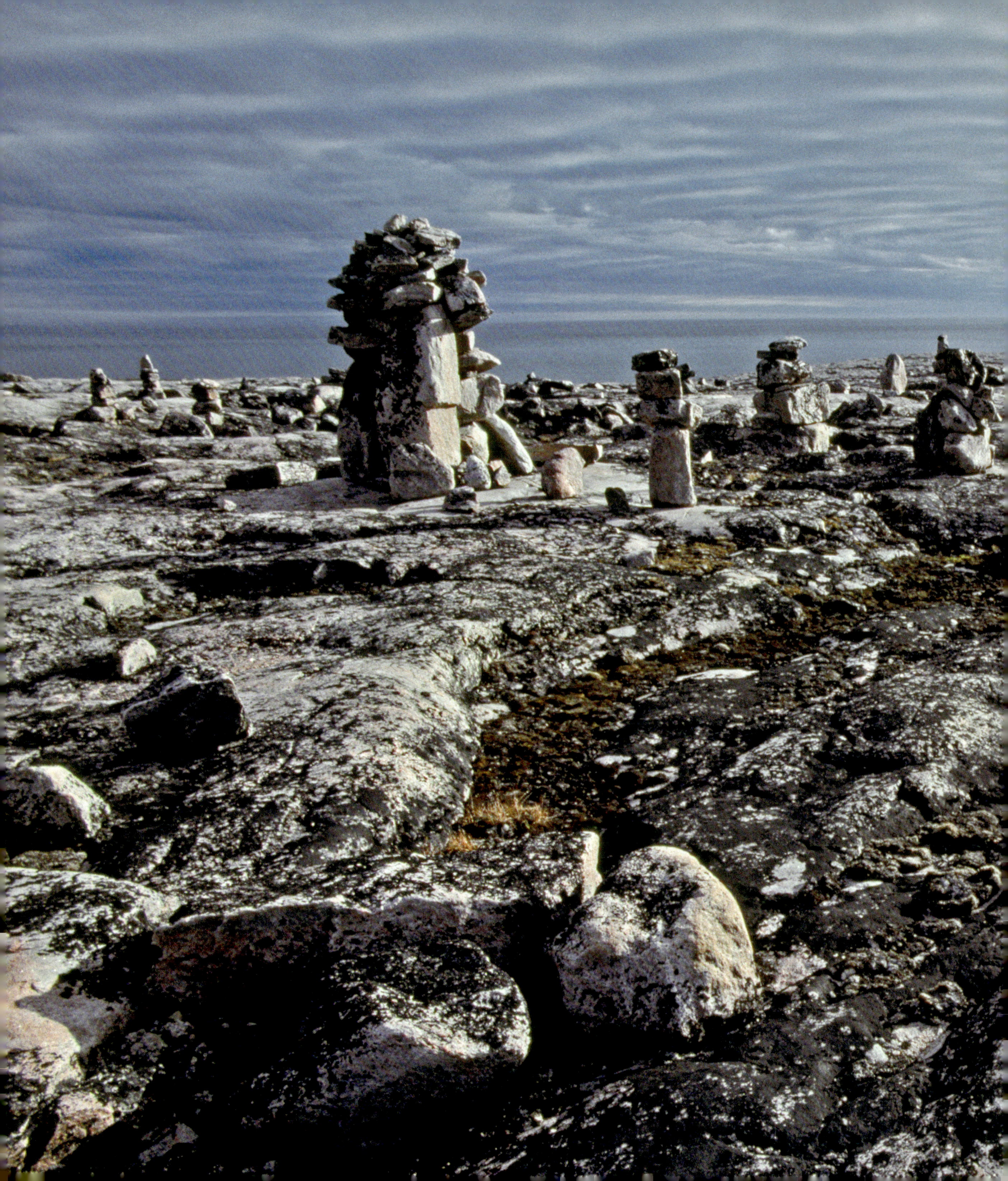

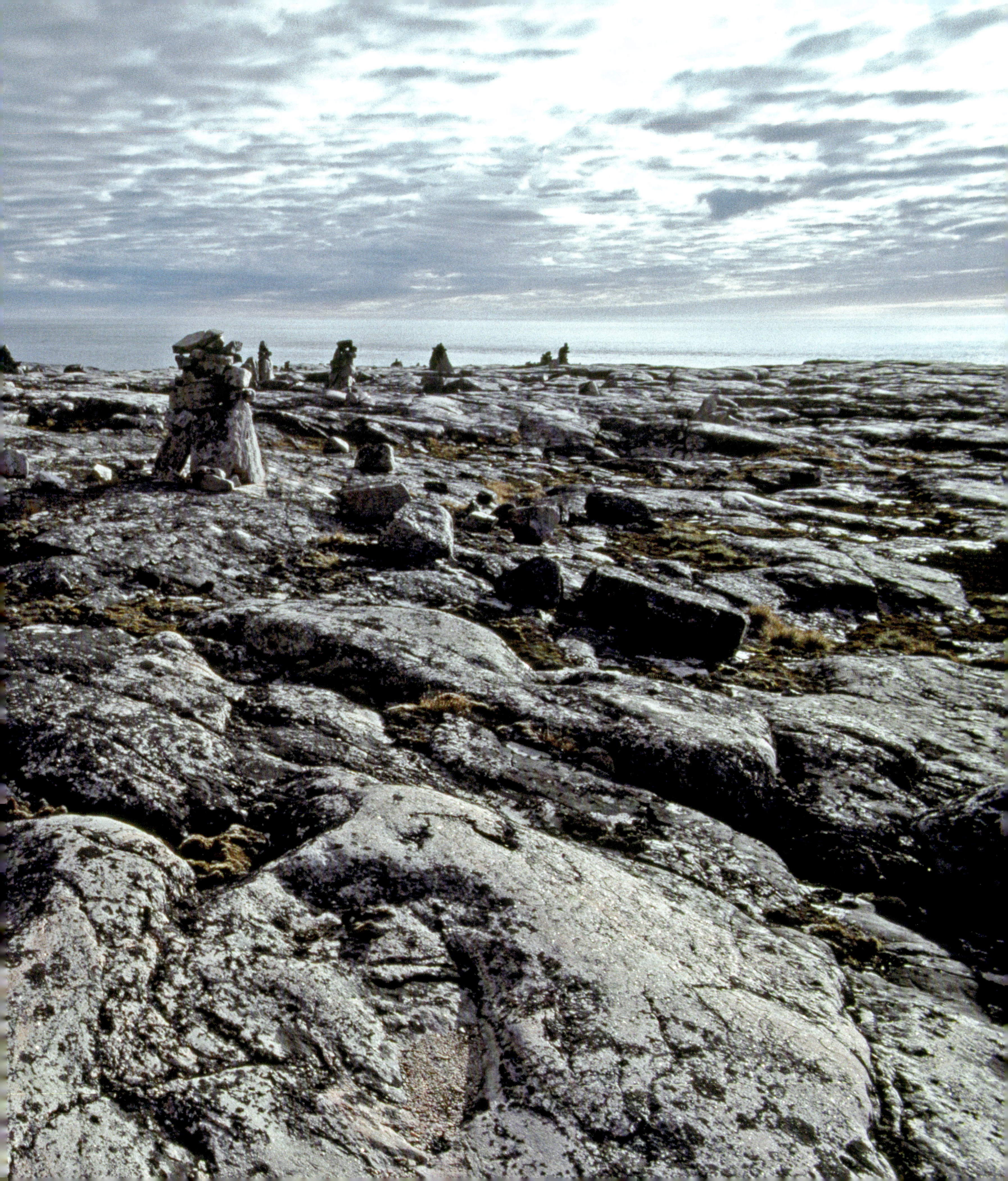

Inuit History, Inuit Art

Robert McGhee

The coasts and islands of Arctic North America lie far beyond the urban world of the mid-latitudes. The distance is not only geographical but also environmental and experiential. Accustomed to the reassuring presence of forest and farmland, southerners find Arctic landscapes of rock and ice so alien that they could well be on another planet. Even the sky is unfamiliar, in summer glowing with perpetual daylight, whereas in winter the flickering aurora and the circling moon illuminate a night that lasts for weeks or months. The darkness and cold of an Arctic winter are beyond the experience, and even the imagination, of most southerners.

This is the Arctic that we have come to know through the literature of Arctic exploration—a barren land of unrelenting cold and danger as described by the men who, facing its worst ordeals, set out to find the Northwest Passage. But there is another Arctic world, one that we can perceive through the eyes of people to whom the Arctic is a homeland. This world is a place of beauty, security and comfort, a place that has provided a livelihood for them and for their ancestors over countless generations. The ancestors of northern peoples long ago realized an essential fact: that the wealth of the Arctic is in its animals. Although Arctic environments support few species of animals, most of these species boast large numbers, and as in any commercial harvesting endeavour, this situation allows very efficient use of resources. Moreover, the extreme range of seasonal variation in Arctic environments promotes dense aggregations of these animals at certain times of the year: heavy runs of salmon and char in summer rivers, vast herds of migrating caribou, islands covered with nesting seabirds, massive clumps of sea mammals concentrated by sea ice. For hunters who have learned when and where to expect such concentrations of animals in their local environment, and how to schedule their yearly round of activities to best use these seasonal aggregations, the Arctic is a rich and rewarding land.

None of this complex adaptation was apparent to the European explorers who began to penetrate the channels of Arctic North America over the past four centuries. To their eyes the Inuit whom they encountered were small and wandering bands of "primitives" who barely managed to survive in a land of appalling hostility and who had probably been driven to this most marginal of regions by more powerful southern neighbours. Others saw them as the last remnants of the Paleolithic peoples who had occupied European caves during the time of the last Ice Age and whose descendants had retreated northward as mid-latitude climates warmed to present conditions. The picture of the Inuit as an antique people preserving an ancient way of life in the isolation of the Arctic captured the imaginations of southerners and influenced the world's view of Inuit life. This widespread impression of the Inuit has also been influential in the perception and marketing of the arts that developed in northern communities over the past half-century, a florescence that has been attributed to the tensions that arise when an ancient way of life is suddenly juxtaposed with the modern world.

Attractive as this view of Inuit history may be, it has long been questioned by the science of archaeology, which finds no evidence of an ancient and unchanging way of life extending from the historic Inuit into the ancient past. The history of the Inuit seems to be much more complex than had once been assumed, and only in recent years have archaeologists begun to form a plausible picture of Inuit history from the stray pieces of evidence preserved over several millennia and across a vast landscape.

We can trace this history back to the end of the last ice age. Approximately ten thousand years ago the ice caps that had lain over Eurasia and northern North America were melting rapidly. As meltwater flooded off the land, sea levels rose in the Bering Sea separating Asia from America. For centuries before this, the seasonally dry bed of the Bering Sea had been used by the ancestors of most Native Americans to reach the American continents. Nomadic hunters began following herds of caribou migrating northward into the summer pastures of the Arctic mainland, but it would be several millennia before there was evidence of humans living throughout the year in the Arctic tundra. When such evidence began to appear, at some time around five thousand years ago, it was apparent that these first Arctic explorers were a Siberian people who brought with them two Old World inventions that made Arctic life possible: the bow and arrow, and finely tailored skin clothing. These people were soon displaced from present-day Alaska but survived across Arctic Canada and in Greenland until early in the past millennium. According to their oral history, when ancestral Inuit arrived in Arctic Canada, they found it occupied by a people they called Tuniit, a race of large and strong people who had very simple technology and who were easily killed or chased from their homelands. This accords exactly with the archaeological evidence, which points to the disappearance of the Tuniit (known as the people of the Dorset culture), together with their very distinctive technology, at the same time that ancestral Inuit moved into and across Arctic North America.

During the millennia that the Tuniit were perfecting their Arctic adaptation and carrying it across the Arctic world, ancestral Eskimos (of whom the Inuit are a distinctive component with their own language) appear to have been living on the Pacific coast of Alaska, adjacent to their linguistic relatives the Aleuts, whose descendants still occupy the volcanic Aleutian chain of islands that separates the Pacific from the Bering Sea. By about ten thousand years ago a series of maritime hunting cultures was beginning to evolve around the northern rim of the Pacific, from Japan in the west to California in the east. Their descendants include the socially complex and artistically renowned cultures of Canada's west coast, similar societies on the coasts of Kamchatka and Sakhalin, and the rich Jomon culture in Japan. The marine resources of the North Pacific are exceptionally abundant, and it is not surprising that the area saw the early development of rich and complex hunting cultures that shared many aspects of their maritime hunting and travelling technology as well as other elements of their ways of life. The early Eskimos and Aleuts are easily pictured as the most northerly peoples of this cultural continuum, and the Pacific coast of southwestern Alaska is still home to large communities of their descendants.

The next major step in the development of Eskimo culture involved a movement by some communities away from the relatively warm waters of the North Pacific and the adaptation of their maritime hunting technology to the cold and seasonally frozen Bering Sea. This venture gave them access to massive populations of northern sea mammals: walrus and several species of seals that lived in and on the ice, as well as whales that summered in Arctic seas to feed on the small creatures that flourished in icy waters bathed by a never-setting sun. The nature and timing of this northern venture is very unclear. A bewildering variety of archaeological finds dating to the first millennium BC are found near the coasts of Alaska and Chukotka, suggesting the occasional presence of various peoples whose technologies hint at connections to either northeastern Siberia, the North Pacific or the Alaskan interior. However, by the end of this period—perhaps as early as 200 BC—ancestral Eskimos had established a major occupation along both coasts of the Bering Strait and on the islands of the Bering Sea. These peoples lived in villages of substantial log houses, heavily banked with turf to provide insulation from winter cold, with heat and light supplied by lamps burning sea-mammal oil. They were hunters of seals, walrus and small whales, capturing these animals with harpoons thrust from boats or from the sea ice. Most elements of the complex technology used by historic Eskimos can be traced to this period, including well-designed clothing, multi-component harpoons with attached floats, kayaks, and large open skin-covered boats capable of transporting an entire camp.

Archaeologists know this phase of Eskimo development as the Old Bering Sea (OBS) culture, and some form of this way of life continued for most of the first millennium AD. The art of the Old Bering Sea people is justly celebrated, if not entirely understood. The permafrost soils of Chukotka and Alaska have conserved in pristine condition large numbers of ivory sculptures that were placed in burials or lost beneath the collapsed houses of ancient villages. OBS art is based on the portrayal of animals, humans and what seem to be creatures of mythology or dreams. The sculptures are of

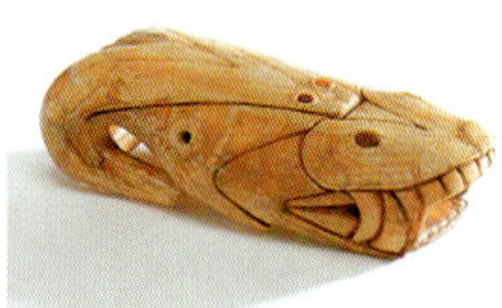

Old Bering Sea carving of an imaginary or mythical beast. Photo: Bryan Alexander, RC 0255-09

a size that can easily be held in the hand and turned to appreciate the transformation of forms as viewed from different angles. Animals and animal-like creatures merge into one another to form compositions that suggest cryptograms or perhaps an artistic grammar that has long been lost. Patterns of finely engraved lines swirl around the creatures, and points of particular interest are marked by graceful ovals or small conical swellings. The most finely decorated pieces are hunting weapons: harpoon heads, sockets for harpoon shafts, butterfly-shaped counterweights mounted on harpoon shafts, and various toggles and handles for harpoon-float equipment. This has suggested a magical function for much of OBS art, which was perhaps believed to increase the efficacy of weapons by harnessing the power of the creatures incorporated in their ornamentation. Less frequently the OBS artists decorated other tools: handles of men's knives and adzes, knives and skin scrapers used by women, and the bone or ivory cases in which seamstresses stored their needles, thimbles and other tools. Occasional stylized representations of humans may be portraits of individuals or of mythological characters, whereas the function of a variety of small non-representational sculptures is totally unknown.

On the basis of his very detailed study of OBS art, Russian archaeologist Mikhail Bronstein suggests that it may have also had a social function. Several distinct styles of ornamentation can be identified, associated with particular villages or regions, though occasionally objects with different styles of decoration are found in the same village or even accompanying the same burial. Bronstein thinks that these styles served as identity markers, helping to validate the owner's membership in a particular community, or perhaps in a particular clan or lineage. On this assumption, the styles of objects can be used to trace a series of complex social relationships among the inhabitants of northeastern Siberia, western Alaska and the Bering Sea islands. What must have been an important development can be deduced from the carving and engraving of these objects: the work is so fine, detailed and complicated that it could only have been accomplished with metal tools.

Although all earlier Arctic peoples had based their technology on cutting and piercing tools made from chipped stone, the Old Bering Sea culture marks the exit of Eskimo technology from the Stone Age. The beginning of the OBS period coincides with the massive development of iron technology by Han dynasty metallurgists in China. Iron first appeared around the second century BC in Japan, Korea and Mongolia, and it had obviously reached as far north as Bering Strait. Metal and other southern goods probably reached the region through trade routes extending along the Pacific coast of Asia, in return for the furs, ivory and other luxury goods that the Arctic has traditionally supplied for luxury markets far to the south. When Russian merchants penetrated the area during the eighteenth and nineteenth centuries, they found a flourishing and jealously guarded trade across Bering Strait, and it seems likely that this pattern extended two thousand years into the past.

The centuries around AD 1000 saw a series of changes and additions to the OBS way of life. Hunters were now able to successfully hunt, retrieve and butcher bowhead whales, the largest animals in Arctic seas. Harpooned from an umiak powered by a skilled team of paddlers, a bowhead provided many tons of meat and blubber for use as food and winter fuel, which in turn concentrated wealth and economic power in the hands of a few boat owners and captains of their select crews. Bowhead hunting also expanded the range of Eskimo settlement, with large communities now established along Alaska's northern coast, where whales could be efficiently hunted as they migrated along narrow leads in the ice. Another important element of technology appeared in the form of the compound bow based on a Mongol design, powered by a thick cable of twisted sinew and much more dangerous than earlier weapons known in the area. It is clear that this was not solely a hunting weapon, as its appearance was accompanied by that of body armour based on the Asiatic slat-armour design, with slats made from ivory or whale bone. Low-level but continuous warfare was endemic among the large and rich trading communities of the Bering Strait area during the eighteenth and nineteenth centuries, and this seems to be another pattern that can be traced for at least a millennium into the past.

Although artistic production continued during the centuries around AD 1000, the graceful and complex sculptures of the OBS period gave way to simpler and less skilfully executed pieces. Straight lines replaced elegant curves, and engraved ovals were replaced by mechanically drilled dot-and-circle motifs. Harpoon components took on more utilitarian forms, with ornamentation either lacking or greatly reduced. A decrease in the energy and creativity applied to art or the adornment of everyday life is often thought to be associated with poverty and economic insecurity, when neither time nor energy is available to be expended on artistic endeavours. However, the apparent decline in the ornamentation of Eskimo weapons and tools is not associated with any apparent decline in the economic security or wealth of Bering Sea communities during these centuries. One might even argue that increased efficiency in the attainment of food and fuel could have decreased the perceived need for the magical assistance sought in the ornamentation of weapons with designs alluding to spiritual power. Or perhaps the function of art as validation of community identity lost its importance in an era of rapid social change.

During this period the relative long-term stability and distinctiveness of the Old Bering Sea way of life was replaced by a mix of OBS elements with those brought by new peoples from both the southern Bering Sea (Punuk culture) and the northern coasts of Chukotka and Alaska (Birnirk culture). By the twelfth or thirteenth centuries, this mélange had fused into a new way of life, known to archaeology as the Thule culture. In Alaska to the north of Bering Strait this culture can be identified with speakers of the Inuktitut language, the people who have become known as Inuit. These were the people who would take the next major step in the expansion of the Eskimo community—a step that took them eastward across Arctic North America as far as Greenland and the coasts of the northwestern Atlantic.

The Inuit expansion across more than four thousand kilometres of Arctic terrain—more than one-quarter of the distance around the circumpolar world—was one of the most extraordinary episodes in human history. This event used to be thought of as a gradual expansion, beginning about AD 1000 and ending with the sixteenth-century Inuit settlement of Greenland and Labrador, of a hunting people into new territory opened up by the warming climate of the Medieval Warm Period. However, information attained over the past few years has shown that this interpretation cannot be correct. We now know that the warming climate recorded in late medieval Europe was largely a local event, and evidence from Arctic regions shows that warmer conditions occurred only sporadically and at different times in various areas. More importantly, recent advances in radiocarbon dating techniques have indicated that the eastward movement did not begin until the twelfth or more likely the thirteenth century—rather than in the warmer tenth or eleventh century—and that Thule settlements in the central Arctic are not significantly earlier than those in the east. The earliest dated Thule villages now known are found in northwestern Greenland and adjacent regions of Arctic Canada, consistent with the 1260s Norse account of first contact with peoples far to the north of the farming settlements that had been established in southwestern Greenland more than two centuries earlier by Erik the Red and his followers. Pottery recovered from one of these early Thule villages was made from Alaskan clay, and the frame of an umiak abandoned during the thirteenth century on the northern coast of Greenland was made from Alaskan spruce—aside from a small replacement part made from oak that had probably been obtained from the Norse.

Current interpretations of the Inuit expansion suggest an extremely rapid initial movement by a relatively small number of people—perhaps one or more groups of a few related families. Rather than the subsistence motive that we usually ascribe to indigenous people—"searching for a better hunting ground"—only a commercial motive makes sense of this episode. This theory is supported by the fact that the styles of artifacts found at these sites resemble most closely those used by the Alaskan Inuit of northwestern Alaska, those who were likely to have been most intimately involved with the iron trade across Bering Strait. Recent discoveries show that the Tuniit people of the eastern Arctic had significant contact with the Norse and also that at some time between AD 500 and 1000 they had discovered the large iron meteorites that had fallen near Cape York in northwestern Greenland. Small chunks of iron were widely traded through Tuniit communities, and news of new metal sources to the east might have filtered along these trade routes, eventually reaching the Inuit of northwestern Alaska. Whatever the actual sequence of events, the earliest-known Inuit

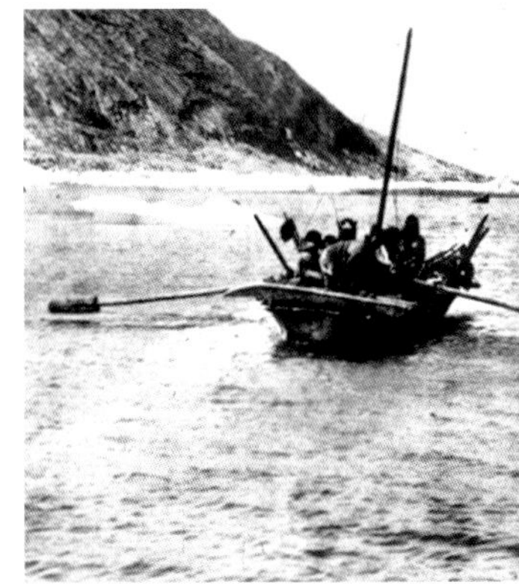

Family travelling by umiak on Hudson Strait, early 1900s. © Canadian Museum of Civilization. Photo: Albert Peter Low, 1897, 2239

settlements in Arctic Canada are located in the far northeast, in the vicinity of the Cape York meteorites and of the Norse hunting grounds. The sites of these early winter houses have produced large numbers of objects that had obviously been obtained from the Norse, and the nature of this material—woolen cloth, pieces of kegs and boxes, rivets from ship planks, chunks of chain-mail armour—has suggested to Peter Schledermann, an archaeologist who excavated this material, that it came from a Norse shipwreck or an abandoned Norse camp in the Far North. Inuit piracy of a small Norse hunting ship would seem more likely and would be consistent with the records of Inuit encounters with Martin Frobisher, John Davis, Henry Hudson and other explorers who reached the eastern Arctic a couple of centuries later.

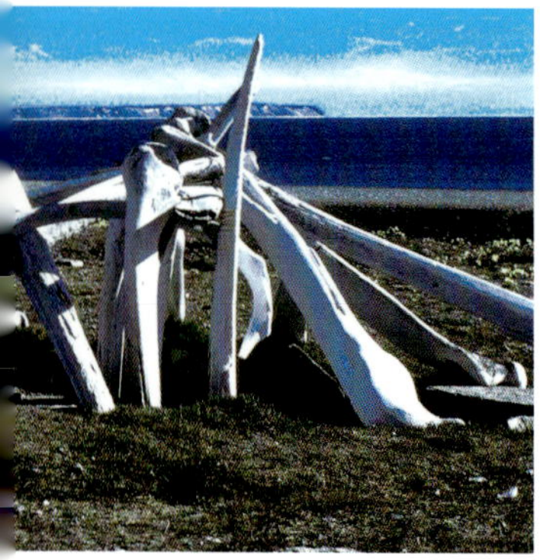

Reconstructed Thule house near Resolute Bay, Nunavut. © Canadian Museum of Civilization. Photo: Robert McGhee, IMG2010-0179-0002

The descriptions of Inuit met by these sixteenth- and seventeenth-century explorers indicate that they had quickly adapted their Alaskan technologies to the environments of the eastern Arctic and were living a way of life very similar to that of their Alaskan cousins. Summers were spent in sea hunting from kayaks and umiaks, bow hunting for caribou, and spearfishing in rivers during runs of char and salmon. Winters were passed in communities of permanent houses, built on the Alaskan pattern except that frames and rafters were whale bones rather than logs; they survived on food and fuel stored during the summer. In the travelling season of late winter and spring, dogsleds pulled by large teams fuelled on abundant supplies of sea-mammal meat and fat linked the Thule world into a widespread network of trade and communication. Archaeological excavation of Thule settlements shows that some houses were significantly larger than average and contained more objects that can be construed as evidence of wealth—finely decorated tools and rare materials obtained through distant trade—which in turn suggests that the stratified social structures of the Alaskan Eskimos were maintained in the east. The Inuit whom Martin Frobisher met on Baffin Island in the 1570s were eager to trade for metal and other European goods. They were very capable of defending themselves in skirmishes with the English, and they managed to hijack a ship's boat, which would have made its new owner a very wealthy and influential man. These sophisticated maritime hunters and traders were far from the ancient primitives that have been imagined as the ancestors of present-day Inuit.

The early Thule people brought from Alaska the artistic traditions of their Bering Sea ancestors, preserved primarily in the form of ornamented weapons and tools, though the occasional find of frozen clothing provides hints of a well-developed form of artistic expression practised by women. Women's combs and sewing tools, especially the carved ivory cases in which they kept their needles and thimbles, were among the most highly ornamented objects produced by early Inuit carvers. Women were also consistently represented in the few non-utilitarian sculptures in the Thule inventory. These took the forms of small images that may have been children's dolls, and flat-based ivory carvings of floating waterfowl that often bore human upper torsos and heads with the distinctive hairstyles of women. Thule craftsmen also maintained the traditions of ornamenting weapons designed for hunting sea mammals, though the shapes were far simpler and the engraved decoration less delicately executed than were the weapons of their Old Bering Sea ancestors. Occasionally artists engraved scenes of hunting or other activities on their artifacts, using a simple stick-figure style that provides casual insights into what may have been particular episodes in the lives of the artists and their companions. Whaling scenes were particular favourites, hinting at the importance of this activity both in providing food for the community and in enhancing the status of the individual hunter or boat crew.

The sixteenth century saw the abandonment of the central Canadian Arctic, as Inuit communities moved eastward to both the Greenland and Canadian coasts of Davis Strait, the Labrador Sea and the waters of Hudson Bay. There, they increasingly came into contact with European whalers, fishermen, traders and, from the eighteenth century onward, missionaries and representatives of the governments of Greenland, Newfoundland and Canada. The Inuit desire for metal tools and wooden boats, both of which made their lives easier and their work more productive, drove the need for contact with Europeans. In return the Inuit had furs, ivory, the skins of sea mammals, baleen from the mouths of the great whales and other valuable goods that attracted European merchants. When whalers moved

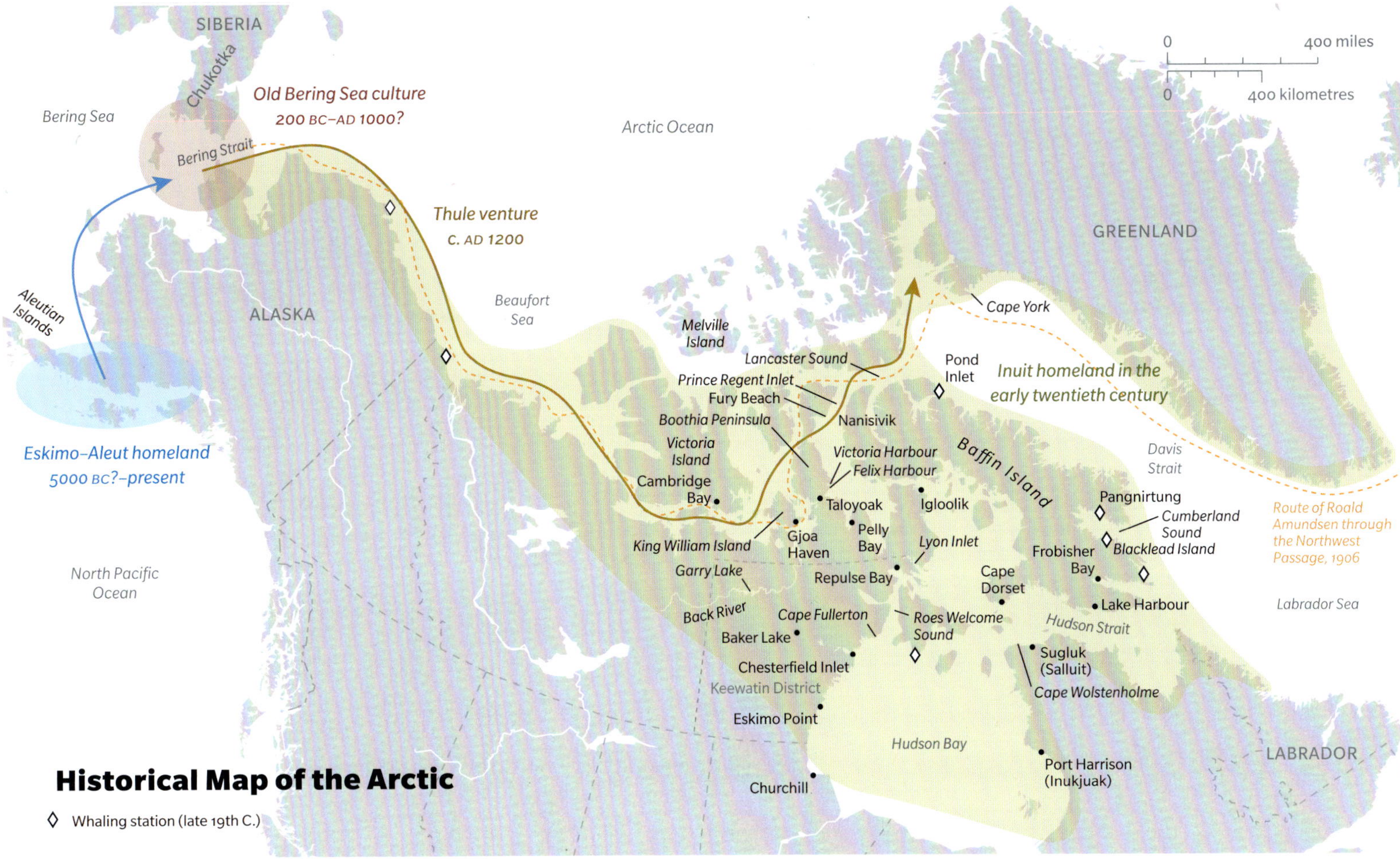

Historical Map of the Arctic

into Canadian waters during the nineteenth century, the Inuit also marketed their local knowledge and expertise by supplying transport and fresh game. In addition, the Inuit were often hired to supplement whaling crews. As the Canadian fur trade moved westward across the boreal forests, the Inuit reoccupied the central Arctic, quickly developing the nomadic way of life spent in summer tents and winter snow houses that was misinterpreted as the original primitive form of the Eskimo culture.

The Inuit's increasing involvement in commercial contacts, and the adoption of a growing range of European technologies, seems to have lessened their interest in the ornamentation of weapons and other tools that had once been the basis of their life. Clothing was an exception to this trend—probably because Inuit clothing has not yet been surpassed for Arctic winter use—and the addition of glass beadwork and needlepoint simply increased the range of ornamentation applied to skin and fur clothing over the past century or so. In contrast, aside from small ivory carvings produced for sale to visitors, and the occasional piece of scrimshaw in the style of the American whalers, the Inuit traditions of sculpture and engraving were in abeyance.

The florescence of Inuit art during the past half-century began with the introduction of stone sculpture, drawings and prints as craft products with commercial potential. Although none of these crafts had direct roots in Inuit artistic traditions, they provided an avenue through which Inuit intellect and skill could be applied. A significant number of Inuit surpassed the limitations of the original crafts and developed new and original forms of art. For communities whose ancestors had a history of accomplishing rapid change, undertaking great ventures and establishing beneficial relations with alien peoples, the development of twentieth-century Inuit art is surely not a surprising achievement.

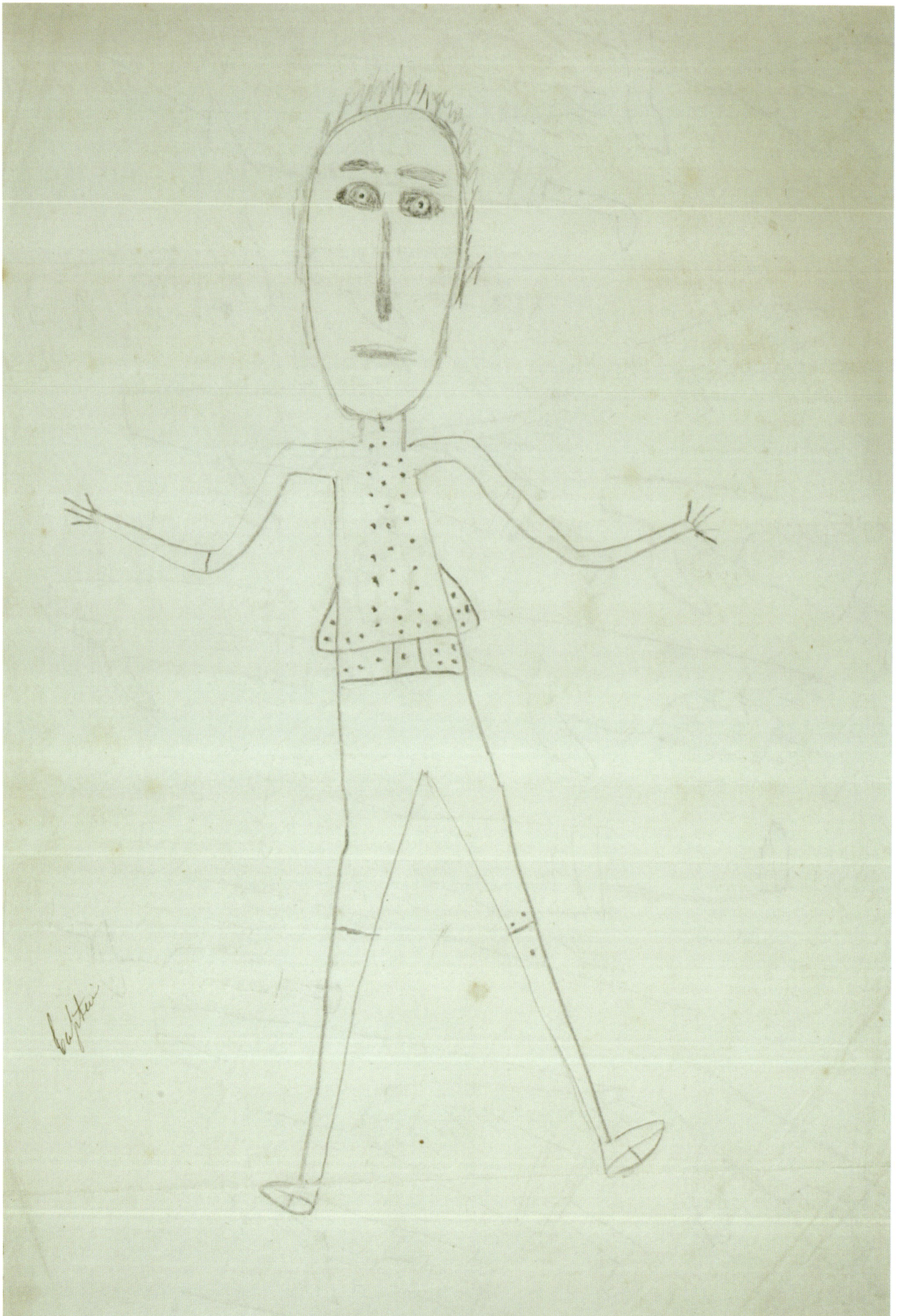

Inuit portrait of Edward Parry, drawn during his 1821–23 expedition. Courtesy of Scott Polar Institute, Cambridge, UK

The Start of Change

Dorothy Harley Eber

Inuit retain poignant and often wrenching memories of the last days of camp life. Pitaloosie Saila of Cape Dorset recalled the snow house built by the last family to leave their camp on the land for settlement living. They put up their igloo just outside Cape Dorset, living there until the new house being built for them was ready. "You could see the light shine out at night," remembers Pitaloosie.[1] The Inuit referred to the new southern-type government housing as "match boxes."

George Pitseolak of Kimmirut (formerly Lake Harbour) told writer Ann Meekitjuk Hanson, who later became the second commissioner of Nunavut, how it felt to be suddenly a settlement dweller. After hearing repeated government announcements over the shortwave radio that all campers were required to move into settlements so that their children could go to school, he said, "We delivered ourselves to a new life."[2]

The moves that would end Inuit camp life all across the North began in the 1957–58 winter of severe starvation in what was then the Keewatin District of the Northwest Territories (now Nunavut). Famine had always been a fact of life for people of the Keewatin. "When the migration changed and the caribou didn't come, sometimes a whole tribe died out," according to Mark Kalluak of Arviat, a former editor of the *Keewatin Echo* and *Isumasi* magazine. In that year of many deaths, survivors from camps in areas along the Back River were relocated with government assistance to Arviat (formerly Eskimo Point) and inland to the Hudson's Bay Company (HBC) post on Baker Lake. Simon Tookoome, whose family continued living on the land for a few years longer, recalls that dreadful year:

> We were affected, but we survived... Through prayer we got by, only by prayer. We'd catch caribou or fish. God gave us the food. We would run out of food but only for a short time. Fish would come. Caribou would come. We were around Garry Lake but we never stopped; we would go from place to place. The time I was most afraid was when my father said he didn't want to walk further distances just to starve to death. He wanted to camp and not move again, even if we starved. But we didn't do that; we survived.

Hard times on the land and the increasing southern presence brought about the end of Inuit camp life by the early 1970s, with most Inuit moving to the fur-trading posts of the HBC, which now became permanent settlements with schools and nursing stations.

Dramatic and harrowing though the changes of the last decades of the twentieth century have been, Inuit were never strangers to change and its demands. Students of Inuit life often count the Vikings as the first "outsiders." Inuit who grew up on the shores of Frobisher Bay and today live in Iqaluit, Nunavut's capital, retain stories, passed down through the generations, of Martin Frobisher and his crews, who arrived on three voyages, in 1576, 1577 and 1578. In his youth Inookie Adamie of Iqaluit heard the stories in camp:

> The Inuit were just in awe. The Qallunaat [white people] came with their huge ship. The Inuit themselves had only sealskin boats... They had never seen a ship... When the ship was spotted, the Inuit took their kayaks and went to meet the ship. They had never seen such a big ship and the people were strange, just different. Right away there were some grudges.

Giant vessels belonging to British explorers and British and American whalers, and much bigger than Frobisher's, dominate Inuit history in the nineteenth century. James Houston's underappreciated novel *The White Dawn* (a fictional account of an incident involving Cape Dorset photographer and historian Peter Pitseolak's ancestors[3]) and the fine film *Before Tomorrow,*[4] with an all-Inuit cast, both paint evocative pictures of the start of change. The English, Scots and American whalers, in pursuit of the massive bowhead, stayed for one hundred years and left the population of the eastern Arctic forever transformed.

In 1817 the first ships to arrive out of British ports were the *Elizabeth* and the *Larkins,* appearing in whale-rich waters in Lancaster Sound, off north Baffin Island; they were harbingers of great fleets to come. The British vessels had previously whaled off the Greenland coast, but they had not before crossed the Davis Strait over to Baffin Island. Europeans are known to have been whaling off the east Baffin coast in the eighteenth century; in an appendix to Charles Francis Hall's *Life with the Esquimaux* (published in 1864), a 1754 newspaper article reports Danish ships familiar with the coast and conditions above Hudson Strait for more than twenty-five years.[5] Joe Curley of Arviat grew up on a whaler in Hudson Bay and in 1983, a few months before his death, recalled,

> The first whalers spoke German [probably Danish or Dutch]. They came in by a different route than the later whalers. They used to go through the Northern Quebec Strait before they came up... Around the area of Pond Inlet when there wasn't too much ice, these ships would come in by a different route [from that used later by British whalers who crossed Baffin Bay]. I've heard some of these people came even from Germany [probably Denmark or Holland].

With the advent of the Scots and English whalers, Arctic whaling began in earnest. At times during the 1820s and 1830s, seventy to one hundred vessels would be fishing for the great bowhead off north Baffin Island. Soon they "rock-nosed" south, down the Baffin coast. In 1840 the whalers entered Cumberland Sound, and it quickly became the principal eastern Arctic whaling theatre. In 1851 the Americans, at the time the world's pre-eminent whalers, joined the chase and introduced the practice of "wintering." They froze-in their ships amid icebergs and craggy cliffs. In 1857 the British created the first land station and within a year or two the Americans did the same. "How tiny the houses were; they looked as if there was not enough wood to build them any bigger," said Leah Nutaraq, a survivor of the whaling days, who in the 1980s was living in Iqaluit.

Well into the twentieth century these small stations were the centre of life in Cumberland Sound. Inuit left their camps to gather at the shore stations. A new hierarchy developed: the whalers appointed Inuit "bosses," or mates, and in turn, Inuit provided the whalers with their knowledge of the land, their seamanship and their labour in the whaleboats. The men supplied country food (caribou, seal and fish), and women made the whalers handsome fur clothing. In return, Inuit benefited from southern goods that were suddenly available. "We used to call the whalers the Arctic postmen," recalled one elderly Inuk, "because they brought so many things." The presence of the whalers meant new equipment, new concepts, new attitudes and new delights. This was the era when Inuit of the eastern Arctic acquired rifles, ammunition and wooden boats, displacing bows and arrows and skin boats with sails of intestine. Inuit also discovered teakettles, ship's biscuits, glass beads, cloth and accordions. According to Peter Pitseolak, the first Inuit photographer and Cape Dorset's own historian, Inuit had had from ancient times their own stringed instrument—perhaps like the one depicted in the 1959 Cape Dorset print *Woman with Musical Instrument* by his brother Josephie Pootoogook and printed by Lukta Qiatsuq. "It was true Inuit," he said. Now the decks of whaling ships resounded to the squeezebox, sometimes with Inuit songs sung to new music; American tunes such as "Oh! Susanna" were popular. Contact with the whalers was close and intimate. An interpreter, after translating the words of her elders, was heard to remark, "It would certainly be a surprise to people down south to know they have so many relatives up here."

Whalers traditionally left fished-out waters behind them. After wintering skills proved their worth in Cumberland Sound, the search for new whaling waters led the whalers onward around south Baffin Island, through Hudson Strait and into the great whaling theatre of Roes Welcome Sound. The whalers built no land-based stations here but instead froze-in their vessels in the winter. And as they did on the east coast of Baffin Island, they formed strong partnerships with the Inuit.

Inuit elders recalled the whaling days as happy ones. In 1983 Joe Curley recalled,

> I can't really remember any disagreements between the Inuit and the Qallunaat. Sometimes the whalers would have the [Inuit] mate do something he didn't want to do, but there were never feelings of inferiority or superiority between whalers and Inuit. They would help each other out as best they could... They were pretty good among the Inuit people.

Leah Arnaujaq of Repulse Bay, a great storyteller and another of the last generation to have first-hand memories of the whalers, echoed Joe Curley's sentiments:

> When the whalers left and didn't come back, I was a bit too young to feel really sad, but I think there were people who did... We were kind of regretful because we remembered how good their food had tasted and we remembered everybody getting together like a big family. When the whalers left, that big family feeling was gone.

One of the most famous American whaling captains was George Comer; he appeared in Roes Welcome Sound in 1896 and whaled with the Aivilik Inuit. Like many of the whalers, he lived with an Inuit woman. According to Joe Curley, "The Captain's girlfriend was Nivisinaaq—her whaling name was Shoofly. She was a brilliant woman." Curley recalled the name given to Captain Comer:

> The Inuit called Comer the white shaman, giving him the name Angakkuq – shaman – because he was able to take photographs. They would appear just like that, out of a piece of paper... An Inuk knows a shaman as a person who is able to make things appear or happen, in a way no ordinary person can. If he had not produced these magical things – so exciting and so fascinating – they would not have called him Angakkuq.

Comer collected material for the American Museum of Natural History in New York, and after his last voyage in 1919 he left comments on record about interactions between Inuit and whalers:

> We got attached to the natives... they have worked among the whalers since Civil War times, and coming in contact with them has changed the natives... While whalers perhaps have not always been what they should be, still I have found them just as good as any other people I ever met.[6]

The heydays for whaling were in the nineteenth century. During the first two decades of the twentieth century, the last of the whalers were traders as much as whalers; either the Hudson's Bay Company or the Inuit themselves were the last to take whales. As a little boy, Osoochiak Pudlat of Cape Dorset recalled watching Inuit conduct a successful hunt for the HBC:

> Those animals were so big, as high as the ceiling. The whale I saw caught that day they said was only a young one, but to me it looked like a giant whale. I know there were whales caught so huge that if you put the kayak upright it would reach to the top of the flipper. That's how they used to measure a big whale.

Other outsiders also made their mark on Inuit life during the nineteenth century. In the aftermath of the Napoleonic Wars, the British Admiralty decided to pursue a program of Arctic exploration: men and ships needed employment. Thus, in 1819, two years after British whalers first appeared off Baffin Island, twenty-eight-year-old William Edward Parry (later Sir Edward) sailed into Lancaster Sound at the head of the first Royal Navy expedition to enter the Arctic Archipelago. With two vessels under his command, Parry sailed far west to winter at Melville Island, which he named after the first lord of the Admiralty. (For thirty years, no one would sail farther west.) He returned to England to tell the Admiralty that a Northwest Passage must exist. In 1821 Parry set out again, hoping to find a Northwest Passage closer to the continental mainland. He wintered twice, the second time at Igloolik, where his presence became the stuff of legend (stories passed down have been recorded by Igloolik elders with the help of young bilingual interpreters for the archives of the Inullariit Elders Society at the Igloolik Research Centre). Inuit were helpful to the explorers, and the Qallunaat were generous in return; however, near the end of Parry's sojourn, sensitivities developed. When the explorers left, it is said "they were cursed by a shaman not to return." No foreign vessels would reach Igloolik for one hundred years.

In pursuit of the Northwest Passage, Parry made a third and final effort in 1824, but this voyage was a failure. He had to give up and left one of his vessels, the *Fury,* at Fury Beach in Prince Regent Inlet. The abandoned ship saved the lives of the next explorers in the region: Royal Navy Captain John Ross (later Sir John) and his crew on a privately financed search for the passage in 1829.

Ross was an early proponent of steam vessels for naval use. He had proposed to the Admiralty an attempt on the Northwest Passage by steam, but the Admiralty turned him down. Instead, gin manufacturer Felix Booth came to his aid with £10,000, and with £3,000 of his own he acquired the paddle steamer *Victory,* which had previously delivered mail. He equipped the steamer with newly patented paddles and boilers, and other new machinery. His friend Parry visited the ship, and Parry later wrote to his brother that the expedition was bold and public spirited, "but there is, in the whole thing, rather too much that is new and untried."[7] Ross took the *Victory* into Lancaster Sound and then south into Prince Regent Inlet; he passed the spot where Parry, in 1825, had had to abandon the *Fury* along with her supplies. Ross continued down the coast, naming various points of the landscape after his sponsor. He anchored his vessel at Felix Harbour, off the Boothia Peninsula. There he discarded his engine; from the journey's start he said it was "a heavy grievance."[8]

On January 9, 1830, the *Victory* received her first visitors. Contemporary Inuit all like to tell stories of the moment when the Netsilik Inuit—the last uncontacted Inuit—met the Qallunaat for the first time. This one is told by Lena Kingmeatook, Taloyoak's master storyteller:

> Abiluktuk—"Long Strides"—was seal hunting in the wintertime. There were quite a number of people, and it was a very snowy day. Abiluktuk had a dog that was very well trained for smelling out seal holes. Every time the dog smells something he goes toward the smell. The dog began running and Abiluktuk was running with it, and soon he starts smelling something strange that he had never smelled before. And then he saw something that looked like mountain, not quite a mountain but so big he compared it to a mountain, on the ice where he had never seen anything before. Abiluktuk gets closer and sees smoke coming out of the mountain and also people. This man was so scared that he started running with all his might, running away from this strange thing he had just witnessed. He was running so hard and so fast that the tail of his parka was straight out. (At that time the men's parkas had a long tail.) When Abiluktuk—"Long Strides"—got home, everyone was scared, not knowing what was in their hunting territory.

Jose Angutingunirk of Pelly Bay, whose great-great-grandmother was a baby packed on the back of one of his other ancestors who visited the ship, recounts what happened next:

> Abiluktuk told the Inuit hunters, "I saw some masts and people walking around them. I didn't go to them because I was afraid of those masts and what they might do to me... the other hunters got together and started to go to the masts, but then they began to think that the white people might think they were spirits, not people. What if they think we are not Inuit, not men? So they went back home and began their shaman practices. Through his spirit a shaman spoke to a white man. They spoke in English. Then the shaman told the Inuit that the Qallunaat were not dangerous and that the masts would do no harm to anyone. The next day, they went to the ship."

Relations between Qallunaat and Inuit were cordial. Soon Inuit made regular visits to the *Victory* and gave the sailors new warm clothing, provided them with seals, fish and fresh meat and helped them on sledging expeditions. "They were kind," John Ross observed in his book, *Narrative of a Second Voyage in Search of a North-West Passage*, "and the cause of kindness in those around them."[9]

Ross had reason to be grateful for the help the Inuit provided because his stay in their territory was prolonged. He was forced to spend three winters in the area when severe conditions locked his ship into the ice. After the third winter, which he spent in Victoria Harbour, just a few miles from his first harbour, he abandoned his ship. Inuit found the wreckage and the supplies, which lasted them for years. Bibian Neeveeovak of Taloyoak, in the 1990s the most senior elder on the coast, said, "I am grateful the Qallunaat made it up here because their wreck let the Inuit people survive."

Ross eventually marched his men up the coast to the point where Parry had left the *Fury,* and they lived on the abandoned supplies from the ship. The following spring, after four winters in the ice, he and his men rowed out into Lancaster Sound, where they were rescued by passing whalers.

Although Parry's sojourn at Igloolik and Ross's stay with the Netsilik had an impact on the Inuit and created a rich oral history, the presence of the explorers did not bring the great changes to the central Arctic that the whalers had brought to the eastern Arctic. Their time among the Inuit had been of short duration; farther west, the white man remained a ghostly entity—and often occasioned fear.

In 1845 the British Admiralty dispatched the *Erebus* and the *Terror* under command of Sir John Franklin on a superbly equipped expedition that many in naval circles confidentially believed would complete the passage. After recent expeditions there was not, some thought, much territory left to be discovered. The Franklin expedition entered Lancaster Sound and was never seen again by Western eyes. The Admiralty launched massive searches, said to have involved some forty vessels, but only in 1859, on a final search organized by Jane Franklin, Sir John's widow, did Leopold McClintock (later Sir Leopold) and his second-in-command, Lieutenant William Hobson, recover the only official communication from the expedition ever found. The ships had been abandoned on April 22, 1848, after having been locked in the ice northwest of King William Island for two winters. Sir John had died on June 11, 1847, and nine officers and fifteen men were also dead. Captain Francis Crozier, who had taken over after Franklin died, was heading for the mainland and the Great Fish River (the Back River) with 105 souls. McClintock thought the position of the lifeboats found, together with other impressions he formed, suggested that one or both of the vessels might have been remanned; most subsequent investigators have subscribed to this belief. The wrecks of Franklin's ships have never been found, and the tragedy and the mysteries associated with the Franklin disaster still rivet attention, to the extent that in 2008 Parks Canada committed itself to a three-year search for the missing vessels.

Recently the elders of Cambridge Bay have revealed that a story survives in their oral history of an exploring ship that wintered in the Royal Geographical Society Islands, on the south shore of the most northern island.[10] Inuit visited the ship, perhaps because "they were the first to try to come through." Oil slicks from their cooking fires—"Inuit would never use oil like that"—can still be seen in midsummer. There were quite a few white men, and all were thought to have left with the ship in the spring. "Whether they made it or not we do not know," said Frank Analok, who was able to point out on a map the position where the ship is reported to have wintered.

Cambridge Bay elders also tell of Inuit sinking a white man's ship. Earlier investigators, including Charles Francis Hall, and William H. Gilder, the newspaper reporter who accompanied the Schwatka expedition in search of Franklin records, heard stories from Inuit of how they had boarded a vessel and inadvertently sunk her by making an entrance hole in the side; when the ice broke up, it caused the ship to take on water and sink. The stories of the Cambridge elders, however, are rather more specific. This one is from Moses Koihok:

> In the 1800s they were pushing toward the east. But they couldn't succeed—because of the ice. When one of the first ships came up here, I've heard that the Inuit didn't want to have anything to do with the people. In those years the Inuit were well off from the land and they were leery, cautious to accept them. They weren't given reason to fear them, they were not given cause; they really didn't have any problem with them. But they were intruding on the Inuit land, and I've heard the Inuit sank the ship. The Inuit had no idea why the first explorers were coming onto their land and they were afraid. Perhaps they decided the best thing was to sink their ship. The shamans may have played a role. They were protectors in the old days.

Frank Analok added to this account:

> Yes, I've heard the stories about Inuit sinking ships. My stepfather told of a premeditated incident. Because Inuit were afraid of the unknown they may have sunk the ship. The shamans may have played a role. Because they were shamans, they were able to do this. The Inuit were afraid of the white men—of the way they approached, of the language the Inuit didn't understand—and because of this, they looked to the shamans to deal with these strangers.

Despite Parry's and Ross's sojourns, the great ships of the British in the central Arctic were intrusive and frightening. In 1999, the elder Alice Anguttitauruq of Gjoa

Haven recalled how, in her childhood, her parents used to talk about strangers in strange clothing "all black, no fur" (apparently Franklin crews), who sometimes appeared on the southwest side of King William Island; this was about seventy-five years before her birth. "Not many people saw them, but people passed on the stories. When Inuit saw them, they thought they were spirits. They would never go close; they were always afraid. They thought they were spirits because the people of that time had never really heard of the white man."

Shamans and spirits were ever-present in the old Inuit world. Such strong spiritual belief and cosmology was still in place all over the Arctic. Long after the missionaries came in 1771 on the Labrador coast, and as late as the 1950s in parts of the central Arctic, shamanism and Christianity coexisted. Indeed, in 1999 Bibian Neeveeovak reported, "We still have people who practise—toward Gjoa Haven and Pelly Bay—but a lot of them are dying out."

The Anglican missionaries established their first Baffin Island mission on Blacklead Island in Cumberland Sound in 1894. Among the mission's gifts was literacy, in the form of a syllabic system of writing. Its use spread like wildfire, and by the early twentieth century most south Baffin people were literate in their own language. Reading and writing came later in the central Arctic. Bibian Neeveeovak remembered how, perhaps in the late 1920s or early 1930s, she went by dog team to Gjoa Haven, where Qallunaat were spending the winter in a boat with an Inuit crew. "We had heard that there you could learn." She recalled how people used to chant the syllabic table to memorize it. "Reading and writing helped with everything," she said. "It was new knowledge."

The centuries-long search for the Northwest Passage—it would turn out that there were several routes—reached its conclusion in the early twentieth century when the Norwegian Roald Amundsen successfully reached the Pacific with his tiny fishing smack, the *Gjoa*. En route he spent two winters with the Inuit in what is now Gjoa Haven on King William Island. Inuit there still speak of him fondly. But when asked if they missed him when he and his crew left Gjoa Haven in 1905 to complete the historic passage, Jimmy Qirqut replied, "We were nomadic in those days, so we were not dependent upon them."

The last period of life on the land for Inuit began in 1909 with the establishment of the first Hudson's Bay Company Arctic post at Cape Wolstenholme in Arctic Quebec. The HBC post was located there primarily for the white fox fur trade with Inuit. In 1911 the HBC crossed the Hudson Strait and established its first Baffin Island post at Kimmirut. In the central Arctic the first HBC post went up in 1912 at Chesterfield Inlet on the west coast of Hudson Bay. Soon there were HBC posts throughout the Arctic, and Inuit became fully involved as trappers in the fox fur trade. The camp leader or boss now became "first trade man" for the company. James Houston, who lived in Cape Dorset and was the first to help the Inuit market their art, referred to the Inuit camp bosses in a 1981 telephone interview: "They were powerful in the sense of the old kings of England." Their word was law. The trade relationship with the HBC altered the Inuit way of life; the nomadic days were over. Today, Inuit make a distinction between what they call "the old, old way" and "the old way"—the last period of life on the land when "the Bay" and the vagaries of the fox fur trade were controlling forces.

Since the relocation of the Inuit to settlements, which began in the late 1950s, many HBC posts have grown into small towns. In their art, the Inuit have made a magnificent response to the dislocation and difficulties brought about by the new lifestyle. Their sculpture, prints, drawings and wall hangings have captured international attention, and leading artists from tiny northern communities have became household names: Kenojuak Ashevak, Pitseolak Ashoona, Kananginak Pootoogook, Oviloo Tunnillie and Peter Pitseolak of Cape Dorset; Karoo Ashevak of Taloyoak; Jessie Oonark, Simon Tookoome, Luke Anguhadluq and Nancy Kangeryuaq Sevoga of Baker Lake; Judas Ullulaq of Gjoa Haven, and many more. Like the artists of Pangnirtung who brought memories of the whales to life in their prints, the first artists recreated the world they knew: the snow houses and traditional stories, the animals and birds, the spirits and shamans. Today, talented younger artists do the same, depicting their contemporary world with its problems and pleasures.

Today Nunavut is a work in progress. The Inuit homeland has its own democratic government but is

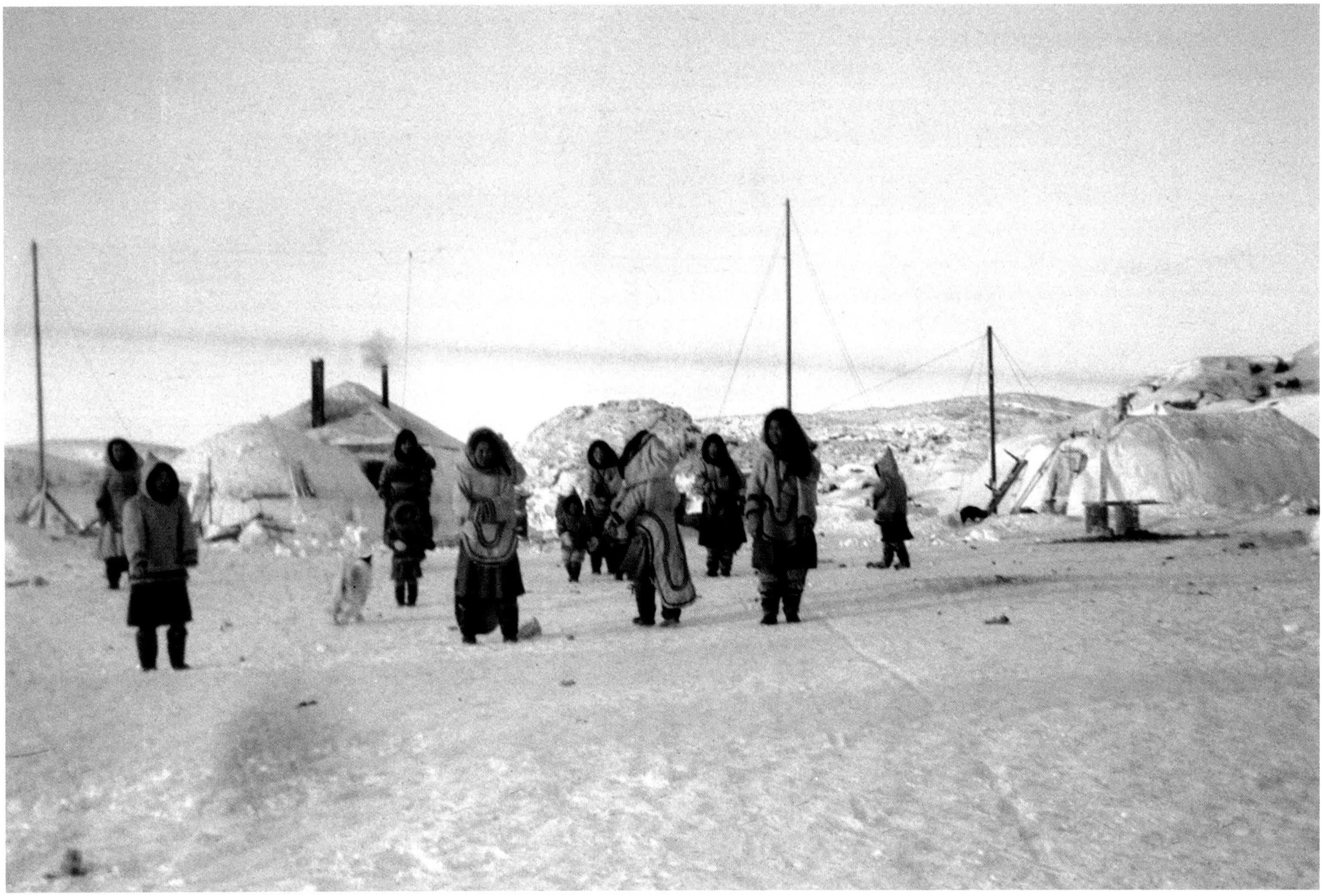

"Last Days of Camp Life," Keatuk camp, c. 1940s. © Canadian Museum of Civilization. Photo: Peter Pitseolak, 2000-199

troubled by many social problems, high unemployment being the most serious, but also including drugs and high suicide rates. In 2008, Madam Justice Beverley Browne, then senior justice for Nunavut, told an interviewer she preferred not to discuss statistics. "There are lots of hopeful signs in Nunavut," she said. "The courthouse is a microcosm. We have mostly young Inuit people working in the courthouse. They are awesome. They get compliments from every judge that comes from away and from local judges as well. These talented, with-it young people are the future of Nunavut." Indeed, Nunavut now has some ten new Inuit lawyers, graduates of a special four-year law course organized in Iqaluit under the aegis of the University of Victoria, British Columbia. These graduates follow in the footsteps of Paul Okalik, a graduate in law from Carleton University in Ottawa, who returned to article in Iqaluit. One week after he was called to the bar he became first premier of Nunavut.

Amid their involvement with the present, like their artists, Inuit draw strength from the heroic past and are likely to continue to do so. Although cameras are not rare in Cape Dorset today, people continue to take pride in the work of Peter Pitseolak, who obtained a camera in the early 1940s and photographed the last days of Inuit camp life. After his death in 1973 schoolchildren told his widow, Aggeok, that they saw from the pictures "how it really was." Peter Pitseolak himself was well aware of the challenges those schoolchildren faced. "Not all of our young people will learn the new ways," he said in the last words of his life story. "But the better ones, the ones who care about themselves, will learn the new ways with happiness." Then he added, "For myself, I am sad that the Inuit way has gone."[11]

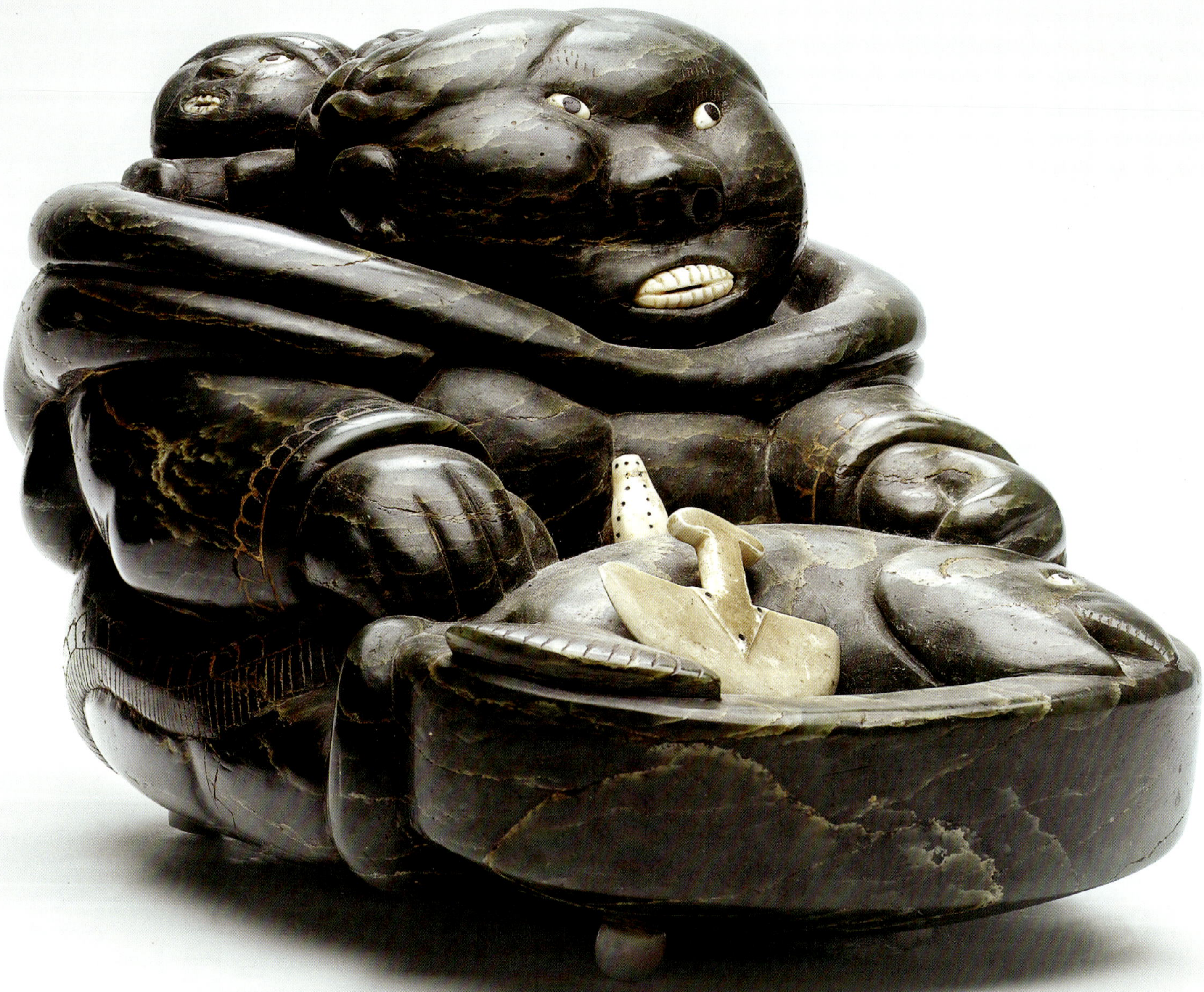

Colonialism Changes Everything

Christine Lalonde

As the late Iqaluit writer Alootook Ipellie describes in his 1992 essay "The Colonization of the Arctic," cultural exchange, change and adaptation have long been a part of Inuit history. Contact between Inuit and the rest of the world occurred over centuries, in waves. Yet as he observes, "Inuit were unconcerned about their initial encounters with outsiders since they came and went like the wind. Even when these transients began setting up their gear in convenient places on the land, the Inuit found them acceptable since they went about their business in a friendly manner, providing goods and needed assistance in times of hardship."[1]

Although these encounters brought both opportunity and crisis, deleterious effects in the earlier centuries did not compare with the widespread cultural and social upheaval that took place in the 1940s and 1950s. With the collapse of the fur trade, Inuit lost their income from trapping. In the same period, caribou migration patterns changed and animal populations declined in several parts of the Arctic, which led to a desperate shortage of "country food" normally available through subsistence hunting. In these postwar years, when Canada was building a new identity as a social welfare state, the Canadian government responded to the famine in the North by moving many of the Inuit from their seasonal camps into settlements to receive services, which were administered from afar without the input of Inuit themselves. The government's new-found sense of responsibility for Inuit as citizens also served other nationalistic agendas.[2] A growing awareness of the richness of natural resources in the North coincided with a need to assert sovereignty over Arctic lands. All these factors combined to turn the government's attention northward.

Out of this morass, incredibly, was born a modern art movement in the Arctic. What had been a sideline—making objects for trade—became a mainstay in this period of transition. Most accounts trace the development from ivory to stone carving through the catalyst of Toronto artist James Houston and his work for Montreal's Canadian Handicrafts Guild. The Guild had on previous occasions attempted to support the fabrication of Inuit traditional objects, yet only with the willingness of Houston to travel to the Arctic did the organization, in partnership with the Hudson's Bay Company, find the means to incorporate Inuit creations in their shows and sales.[3] Although the Inuit had for decades been using ivory to make small-scale replicas (commonly called miniatures) of everyday objects and animals for occasional trade, the figurative stone sculpture encouraged first by Houston and the Guild was something else—and this is the starting point of the debate about authenticity and continuity raised by Edmund Carpenter and George Swinton, among others. Ivory pieces depicted life as it was then experienced, camp scenes as they existed and even elements of cross-cultural exchange, such as rifles, kerosene lamps, cribbage boards and boats (see pp. 58–60). When working in stone, however, Inuit focused on a traditional way of life with little reference to the outside world. The somewhat idealized depictions of the past became the iconic images associated with Inuit culture (pp. 66–69). Their immediate popularity set audience expectations, which in turn had an influence on succeeding generations of artists who, in repeating the same themes and often the same compositions, ironically reinforced stereotypes of Inuit life, as if untouched by the modern world.

The origins of Inuit art production for markets in the South and the simultaneous bureaucratic assimilation of Inuit into modern Canadian society have been extensively commented upon. More recently Inuit themselves have begun to make known their experiences of this period through oral and written narratives, providing much-needed perspective on the struggles endured and hardships overcome.[4] Not fully considered in accounts of this transitional period is another side effect of colonization, which was a radical change in the

Johnny Inukpuk, *Mother and Child with Fish*, before 1959, stone, ivory, inlay, 18.0 x 21.0 x 29.0 cm.
Gift of Samuel and Esther Sarick, Toronto, 2001

concepts of representation by Inuit. Inuit art history, for example, logically focuses on carving activities of the Historic Period because it is a predecessor to modern stone sculpture, even though the importance of ivory miniatures in Inuit life and society was limited. Traditional modes of expression that held a more prominent place in Inuit culture, by contrast, have not received equal attention largely because the story of Inuit art has focused on sculpture and graphics.[5] Before the introduction of these art forms, the Inuit created objects with skill and artistry, as expressions of collective and individual identity, affording both visual and tactile pleasure. That these objects were often viewed as utilitarian did not mean they were without a clearly articulated aesthetic.

Clothing is an excellent case in point. Essential to survival, and requiring a highly developed level of knowledge and technical skill to create, articles of clothing were culturally significant markers of affiliation and kinship with distinguishable regional and familial designs. Moreover, in creating articles of clothing, the makers could exercise their aesthetic preferences and even flaunt their virtuoso talents. As the artist Paulosie Kasudluak once wrote, "We do not reveal ourselves only in stone. The work of the women shows the type of clothing which we as people had. That, too, contributes to the truth."[6]

Within certain parameters—for example, those relating to region and gender—clothing design was among the most flexible of customs informed by individual interpretation. This only increased with access to glass beads, new materials and other external influences (such as playing cards for decorative motifs or imported styles, as in the full-length "Mother Hubbard" parka in the western Arctic) that resulted in evolving styles. Clothing was not, however, viewed as collectable. It was considered functional and therefore outside Western concepts of artistic expression. Likewise, since it was tied closely to traditional life, articles of clothing were categorized as ethnographic artifacts rather than art. Yet the importance of clothing fabrication and design in Inuit culture continues to be underscored by its frequent appearance as subject matter in the newer forms of sculpture and graphic arts; rarely, however, have articles of clothing been included in publications and exhibitions of modern Inuit art.

As Inuit moved into settlements and took up artmaking as a profession, a division occurred between objects made to stay within the local communities and those made for sale to an outside market. This division represents the nuanced difference between the more holistic view of cultural expression held by Inuit and modernist notions of fine art prevalent at the time. It is often stated that Inuit have no word for "art" (yet seemingly infinite words for snow).[7] Most of us recognize this as a problematic cliché that suggests a conceptual void and lack of vocabulary in Inuktitut for aesthetic expression. The stereotype is also harmful in that it perpetuates the romanticized notion of the Inuit artist as one whose creativity flows effortlessly from some primordial wellspring, when in fact most have dedicated long hours to perfecting their talent and vision.

Several authors on Inuit art have attempted to understand and articulate artmaking from an Inuit, rather than Western, viewpoint. George Swinton, drawing on conversations with artists, popularized the term *sananguaq* for sculpture, meaning "carved in the likeness of (replica)."[8] In his exploration of the differing aesthetic criteria of Inuit and non-Inuit, anthropologist Nelson Graburn recorded several terms—among them, *sulijuk*: "it is true or real"—as core qualities that artists value and therefore aim to achieve.[9] Norman Hallendy has written about how Osuitok Ipeelee described "a state of mind beyond dreaming" that offers a view on the creative state *siilatujuk*, which the artist said,

> allows me to see a different world, which is my very own place... It is a very strange place because you know that it can never be, yet when you leave it and come back to the world we know, you discover that you have created a beautiful thing that you have brought back with you. I am a carver, so I bring forth carvings – but there are songs, stories and magical things that have been brought back by others from their own worlds.[10]

Marie Bouchard, curator for *An Inuit Perspective: Baker Lake Sculpture*, worked closely with the artists to select sculpture "based on their assessment of what constitutes a successful carving within their own aesthetic system," as well as to rethink the way it was presented in the exhibition context. The outcome of their discussions provides insights into concepts such as the reiterated idea of *sanaguaq* and naturalistic representation as a highly valued quality, the status of the artist, the place of artmaking in relation to other occupations and, significantly, the restatement, as articulated by Bouchard, that "the Inuit aesthetic exists as part of an integrated whole and is not segregated into a separate category as in Western forms of classification."[11]

These efforts to understand artmaking from an Inuit viewpoint create a foundation for acknowledging Inuit aesthetic perspectives. Yet, once again the focus is on modern forms of artmaking; we have only a partial glimpse of Inuit perspectives, since they were being overshadowed by Western notions of art at the time. That a well-developed Inuit aesthetic existed long before the mid-twentieth century is generally acknowledged, but—by questioning Inuit artists exclusively about the visual arts rather than older forms of cultural expression—this aesthetic has not been the one that art historians and others have tried to understand and record. As has been noted, to understand Inuit concepts requires exploration of a more holistic view of artistic expression, one that is connected to other aspects of culture and includes the diversity of objects made by Inuit, both past and present.

In fact, in the earliest exhibitions, sculpture and graphic arts were presented within the context of a variety of traditional and experimental forms. Curator Darlene Wight documents that James Houston was given an itemized list of things to purchase on his first trip for the Guild. The broad range of these objects fell squarely within the Guild's mandate "to encourage, retain, revise and develop Canadian handicrafts and art industries… [with the goal] to prevent their loss, extinction, and deterioration."[12] In the summer of 1949, Houston acquired the following: seven pairs of kumiks (boots), three dozen sealskin slippers, one dozen sealskin bags, two dozen wall hangings, four dozen goose-wing brushes, one eider duck wall mat, three caribou parkas, six carved ivory tusks, twelve match holders, twelve paperweights, six paper knives (letter openers), three ivory harpoons, one model kayak, one dozen stone sculptures, twelve dozen baskets, one dozen caribou gloves and one sealskin kayak.[13] The stone sculptures sold out within three days of the Guild's sale of these items in November 1949. The success of this first show is well known within the Inuit art community, yet rarely mentioned are the many other types of objects in the same show.

It was a similar situation ten years later in 1959 with the landmark show organized by the Department of Northern Affairs and National Resources in Stratford, Ontario, to coincide with the influx of visitors for the new Shakespeare Festival. The Canadian Handicrafts Guild sale in Montreal ten years earlier had caught the attention of the department, and its success established the potential that art and crafts could offer an economic opportunity for Inuit.[14] The department was then open to a wide variety of initiatives—some rooted in Inuit culture, others more experimental, such as the canning of seal meat.[15] In a 1956 letter outlining the new crafts program in Cape Dorset, Deputy Minister R.G. Robertson wrote:

> We have every reason to feel optimistic about the venture, because conversations which Mr. Houston has had with [Inuit] of the Baffin Island area satisfy us that they themselves are eager to participate in a further development of their handicrafts… It is interesting to note that the [Inuit] themselves feel that, in addition to those… who have marked ability in stone carving, there are others who should also be given a craft outlet. For example, there are many who have been unable to produce stone carvings of the highest quality, but who nevertheless in their daily life have evidenced by the manufacture of harpoon heads and other tools their ability to fabricate objects which we feel would find a ready market in southern Canada.[16]

On display in the 1959 exhibition, but not for sale yet, were objects from eighteen communities across the Arctic, from Tuktoyaktuk to Kuujjuaq.[17] Organized into sections with headings (in English and Inuktitut) such as "The Eskimo Hunter," "The Craftswoman" and "Stonecut prints (New Art from Old)," were displays that included parkas in muskrat, caribou, sealskin, eiderdown and duffel, sealskin and caribou slippers, woven belts, dolls made of caribou, sealskin and cloth, willow baskets and mats, uluit, skin softeners, a drying frame, a kayak, fish spears, jiggers and gaffs, harpoons, a sealskin float, bird spears, a dog whip, boots, snow goggles, even a bow and arrow set; as well as models of some hunting implements, ivory and stone carvings and, for the first time, stonecut and stencil prints.[18]

In his opening speech on July 2, 1959, Abraham Okpik said,

> The Exhibition you are about to see will show you the skills of an ancient Canadian people who for centuries have endured the cold of the barren lands and have developed a way to survive. This simply because being human, with human needs and feelings, they had a great determination to live. When I think of the difficulties and discomforts and the few hard-gained materials they had to work with I am proud to be an [Inuk]... You will see in this Exhibition what my people have achieved with very little.[19]

Although the scope of the handmade items was clearly meant to educate the public about Inuit culture, the other intended aim was to test the marketability of the objects. As the introduction to the accompanying catalogue states, "This display officially heralds the beginning of the Department of Northern Affairs and National Resources market research programme... Production of crafts is being organized in the north and will be geared according to public interest in specific articles."[20]

The 1949 and 1959 shows came closest to representing the holistic view held by Inuit at the time. And they mark a turning point. The greater response by the public to sculpture and graphic arts meant that henceforth the department did not give equal support to other forms of expression.[21] Several handicraft initiatives did continue, particularly sewing centres, but with different policies and less promotion than sculpture and prints; eventually the sewing centres were taken over at the local level. Although traditional objects continued to be made, Inuit artists by and large focused instead on the visual art forms introduced by the department's arts advisers. These became the main mode of expression known the world over.

It deserves mention here that Inuit artists, particularly those in the first generation to focus on sculpture and graphics, were able to negotiate and navigate between their individual inclinations and the aesthetic preferences of their audience. Just as Inuit society at large demonstrated itself to be highly adaptable to change in other areas of life, so in artmaking Inuit were able to work with introduced media but retain elements of the ingrained concepts linked to communal camp society, a semi-nomadic way of life and close relationship with the environment. Art historian Marion Jackson demonstrated this in her dissertation on the ideological and stylistic approaches of two generations of artists, for example, by pointing out how the use of multiple perspectives replicates the spatial and temporal concepts developed from the experience of travelling great distances across the land.[22]

The shift in artistic expression, based on how the new Inuit art was received by outside audiences, was at the centre of the debate between George Swinton and Edmund Carpenter. Swinton saw it as a "new Eskimo" art, whereas Carpenter thought of it as a Western-influenced development. One can understand Carpenter's point in exposing the discrepancy between pre-existing forms that Inuit made for themselves and the newer ones tailored to a southern audience, but I believe he was reacting to the promotional claims that overemphasized a cultural continuity meant to authenticate the newer forms of sculpture and prints.[23] Ironically Carpenter, in his consideration of "art," included not only ivory carvings and incised two-dimensional representation but everything from snow goggles, clothing and tattooing to songs and poetry. What he excluded from this holistic view were the stone carvings and newer graphics, because "the traditional role of art is gone; object has replaced act."[24] He did not believe that Inuit themselves would accept these new forms and was especially scathing in the notion that they did not invest themselves in their work since they were "directly trained by Houston; others followed the government manual."[25] He could not foresee the role that art would have for Inuit in the face of colonialism. Swinton, in this regard, was more forward thinking in his argument that Inuit art, made by Inuit artists, is just as valid and meaningful a reflection of Inuit culture, despite its focus on the outside market. Lastly, to suggest, as Carpenter does, that all artists were passively influenced to the same degree by market demands is a grave generalization that denies the individual artist's ability and the right to express, interpret, invent and reinvent cultural heritage as it evolves and changes.

If Inuit art does not reflect pre-existing concepts, then is it without meaning for the artists and other Inuit? I would suggest that meaning itself is evolving and mutable, formed and reformed over time and circumstances. With the new modes of expression came new meanings and new roles. Certainly, it has been well recorded in interviews with artists that artmaking has had an immediate importance as a source of income, for the artists and their communities, since the 1950s. Making art has given many Inuit an economic foothold in the modern world. Their success has allowed them to continue a way of life that maintains hunting and fishing. Kananginak Pootoogook and other Inuit of his generation have spoken about the mutual relationship between carving and hunting, in terms of the income it allows for necessities such as ammunition and the flexibility of time to be out on the land. As expressed succinctly by Johnny Maiko, "Carving is my hunting weapon."[26]

Although perhaps this was not a conscious aim of all artists, the first appearance of sculpture in exhibitions countered the depictions of impoverished Inuit being reported in newspapers, magazines, popular literature and film. The suggestions of a culture in decline were set against images of a rich cultural heritage created by Inuit themselves. Sculpture had a strong visual presence at a time when Inuit voices were yet to be heard, and it reminded the world that they were still alive and well and capable of creating works of unexpected eloquence and power. Art thus acted as a means of communication for Inuit that transcended language and geography. In this sense, Inuit art can be viewed as a form of "survivance"—a term coined by Gerald Vizenor that combines "survival" and "endurance"—to counter the dialectic of victimization and domination and to reflect how an empowered presence acts as a means of active resistance against oppression and acculturation.[27]

The earliest work of the 1940s and 1950s is now recognized to contain the wealth of *Inuit Qaujimajatuqangit*, which is to say a traditional cultural knowledge that embodies not only technical details but also the values and principles that guide Inuit society. The same hands that made the *qamutiq* (sled), the *amauti* (woman's parka)—the same knowledge was seamlessly transferred from one form to the other. Inuit artists perceive that their works are made for an outside market, but many have said they are keenly aware that in the face of a radically changing way of life, artmaking is their legacy for future generations of Inuit and to all Canadians.

Finally, it must be noted that the holistic, cosmological view still exists. In contrast to the Western canon, the understanding of Inuit art today in the Arctic is expansive enough to encompass sculpture, graphics and even newer media that southern audiences have yet to fully accept. This viewpoint was reflected in the exhibition *Our Land: Contemporary Art from the Arctic*, held at the Peabody Essex Museum, in Salem, Massachusetts, in 2004. *Our Land* was the first major exhibition of the Government of Nunavut's collection and was organized by the Department of Culture, Language, Elders and Youth. The introduction to the catalogue states: "Inuit art is nourished by its ancient cultural roots. In the past, these roots sustained stories, song, dance, carving, and exquisitely designed functional objects. Now, in addition, they give life to printmaking, photography, video, and popular music, among other art forms."[28] For this exhibition, objects were paired and juxtaposed according to themes, rather than categorized separately as fine art or handicraft; additionally, the inclusion of film brings in storytelling and performance as a recognized means of expression. It is a presentation that I imagine would have pleased both Carpenter and Swinton. Not only has Inuit art taken its place as a significant form of cultural expression, but we are finally learning to appreciate those items designated as handicraft for their unique aesthetics and are rethinking the definitions of art itself.

At a time when Inuit contemporary artists are pushing boundaries that may have limited them in the past, it makes sense to avoid situating them exclusively in Inuit culture when their works, although rooted in northern realities today, speak to world issues. For Inuit art from the early years after the shift to sculpture and graphics for the southern market, however, we can hope to truly understand and appreciate it only by revisiting and reconsidering the context in which it arose. In the end, Inuit artists have accomplished a synthesis of familiar content and foreign materials, of a way of viewing the world with introduced concepts—a hybrid art form that has risen beyond the debates and above all expectations.

"An Eskimo woman had only time to sew... It is very cold and the clothes always need mending. The men did not make art either, their only art was making weapons."

Jessie Oonark

"Carving is my hunting weapon."

Johnny Maiko

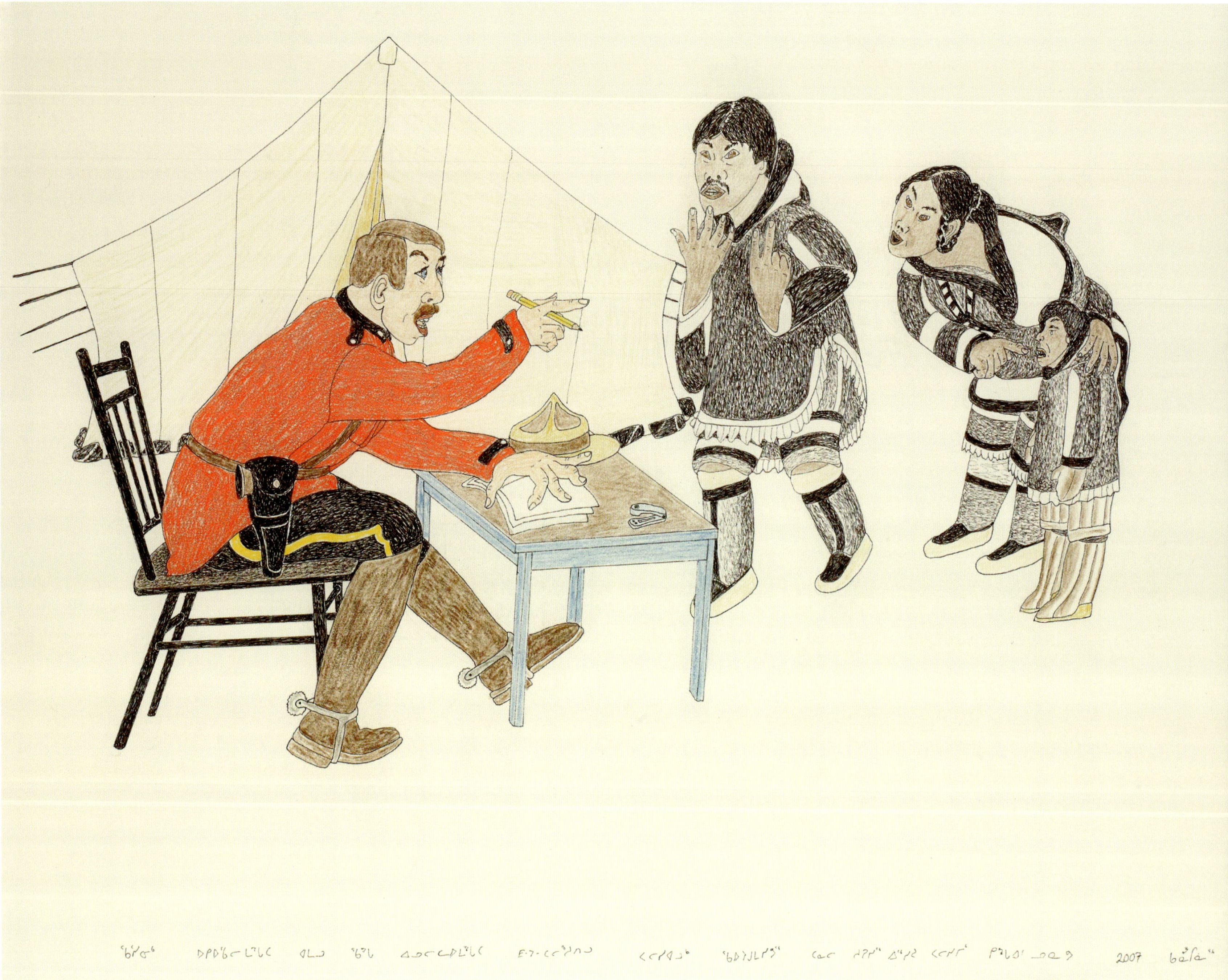

Kananginak Pootoogook, *RCMP and Inuit Family*, 2007,
coloured pencil and ink on paper, 57.0 x 76.0 cm

Inuit Art and the Creation of Nunavut

Bernadette Driscoll Engelstad

The federal territory of Nunavut encompasses much of the extensive homeland of Inuit in the Canadian Arctic.[1] Nunavut was created on April 1, 1999, the year that also marked the fiftieth anniversary of contemporary Inuit art production in Canada, dating from the first exhibition of carvings acquired by "wandering artist" James Houston. Sponsored by the Canadian Handicrafts Guild in Montreal in 1949, this exhibition introduced Inuit art to the Canadian public. Inspired by the exhibition's commercial success, the federal government recruited Houston to direct an ambitious arts program, encouraging Inuit to create stone and ivory sculpture for a southern market. The strength of the carving effort in Povungnituk prompted Father André Steinmann, an Oblate missionary, to organize the Société des sculpteurs de Povungnituk—a forerunner of Arctic art co-operatives—in 1958. At Houston's suggestion, artists at Cape Dorset formed the West Baffin Eskimo Co-operative in 1959, with Kananginak Pootoogook serving as the first president.[2] From these initial efforts, the model of art-producing co-operatives spread, creating vital economic centres in Inuit settlements across the Arctic.

In addition to providing a necessary economic resource to artists, their families and communities, Inuit art production served as a critical means of strengthening Inuit cultural identity, preserving memory and relaying cultural ideas and ideals across generations. During this period of radical social change in the North, art provided a creative and intellectual focus—a centring device and a mindful means of reflecting on, and reacting to, the turbulent change confronting Inuit society. Closely aligned with art production in the North, the co-operative movement has played a central role in building economic strength and political acuity among Inuit in the rapidly expanding settlements of the Arctic.[3]

From the vantage point of history, it is evident that the creative work of Inuit artists, in conjunction with the co-operative movement, has played an essential role in forging the path to Nunavut. Through sculptures, prints, drawings, textile art and video, artists provided critical insights into northern life, introducing generations of Canadians to Inuit social and cultural traditions and laying the groundwork for cross-cultural understanding. Building a solid foundation of public interest and awareness, Inuit artists fostered respect for Inuit culture, facilitating the later negotiations between Inuit political leaders and the federal government of Canada, eventually culminating in the creation of Nunavut. Today, governed by an elected Legislative Assembly, Nunavut has become a full political partner in the nation-state of Canada.

Since its political formation in 1999, the Nunavut government has stressed the ancestral values that reflect its identity as an Aboriginal homeland, striving to preserve these values in the institutional framework of Nunavut.[4] As philosophical concepts directing Inuit life through the generations, these principles, articulated in *Inuit Qaujimajatuqangit* (Inuit traditional knowledge), have inspired and motivated Inuit artists, shaping the co-operative movement and community-based approach to Inuit art production for more than fifty years. By applying these principles to their cultural practice, Inuit artists transformed a historical period marred by poverty, ill health, family separation and displacement into an era that celebrates the strength, courage, wisdom and resilient nature of Inuit society, past and present. Modelling the cultural principles of *tunnganarniq* (fostering good spirit by being open, welcoming and inclusive), *qanuqtuurniq* (being innovative and resourceful in solving problems), *pilimmaksarniq* (acquiring knowledge and skill), *pijitsirniq* (providing for family and community), *piliriqatigiinniq* (working together for a common cause) and *aajiiqatigiinniq* (decision making through discussion and consensus), as well as *inuqatigiitsiarniq* (respecting others, sustaining relationships and caring for people) and

ᖃᓄᖅᑑᕐᓂᖅ ***qanuqtuurniq***
being innovative and resourceful in solving problems

ᐱᔨᑦᓯᕐᓂᖅ ***pijitsirniq***
serving and providing for family and community

ᓴᓇᑦᑎᐊᖅᓯᒪᔪᑦ ***sanattiaqsimajut***
these things that are finely made

ᐱᓕᒻᒪᒃᓴᕐᓂᖅ ***pilimmaksarniq***
acquiring knowledge and skill through practice, effort and action

ᐊᕙᑎᑦᑎᓐᓂᒃ ᑲᒪᑦᓯᐊᕐᓂᖅ
avatittinnik kamatsiarniq
respect and care for the land, animals and the environment

ᐃᓅᖃᑎᒌᑦᓯᐊᕐᓂᖅ ***inuqatigiitsiarniq***
respecting others, nurturing relationships and caring for people

ᑐᙵᓇᕐᓂᖅ ***tunnganarniq***
fostering good spirit by being open, welcoming and inclusive

ᐱᓕᕆᖃᑎᒌᓐᓂᖅ ***piliriqatigiinniq***
working together for a common cause

ᐃᓄᐃᑦ ᖃᐅᔨᒪᔭᑐᖃᖏᑦ
Inuit Qaujimajatuqangit
traditional knowledge

ᐋᔩᖃᑎᒌᓐᓂᖅ ***aajiiqatigiinniq***
decision making through discussion and consensus

avatittinnik kamatsiarniq (respect and care for the land, animals and the environment), artists' efforts helped to sustain the cultural, political and economic vitality of Inuit society while simultaneously earning the attention and respect of the outside world. This interplay of social tenacity and public respect seeded the vision of Nunavut, nurturing its concept within Inuit society and beyond—a vision that has become a reality, promising a more secure future for generations of Nunavummiut.

Contemporary Inuit Art: An Economic Invention?

The art historical canon describing the development of contemporary Inuit art consistently—and persistently—overlooks a basic fact: that art has always been fundamental to Inuit culture. Design sensibility, aesthetic appreciation and skill in craftsmanship are richly evident in the archaeological and historical record, informing the utilitarian function of objects and enhancing the efficacy of hunting tools, clothing and other forms of cultural production.[5] As stated by Charlotte St. John, a seamstress and clothing designer from Arviat, "In my family, it was important that things be made well."[6] This integration of function, aesthetic form and skilful production was elemental in ensuring Inuit success in inhabiting the Arctic. The architectural design of the igloo, sheltering families in an extreme climate; the efficient movement and elegant lines of the kayak; the protective nature and striking appearance of caribou and sealskin clothing; the efficacy and graceful form of composite bows, arrows, crescent-shaped ulus, and ivory needle cases are evidence of the complementary nature of superior function, aesthetic design and skill that characterize Inuit production.

Despite the dominant Western tendency to separate function from art, Inuit material culture reflects their intimate connection, one implicit in the other. Although it is often repeated that there is no word for art in the Inuktitut language, this should not suggest that there is no concept of art, in the manner of aesthetically pleasing objects. Quite the opposite: the term *sananguaq*, usually offered as the closest Inuktitut counterpart, means "the making of something." A recent publication, however, introduces the more precise term, *sanattiaqsimajut*, "these things that are finely made."[7] Intimately tied to the observation of nature and the design principles of natural forms, the Inuit aesthetic is so closely bound to the concept of making something that there is no need to make aesthetic concerns explicit—they are fully implicit in the design and fabrication of Inuit material culture.

Art and *Inuit Qaujimajatuqangit*

Throughout the historical period of European and American exploration, whaling and trading, Inuit were widely respected for their skill as carvers and seamstresses. Cribbage boards, incised ivory tusks, clothing made of fur, gut and birdskin, as well as carvings of human and animal forms, dolls and models of everyday implements were exchanged, bartered or presented as gifts to outsiders. Miniature ensembles of camp scenes and families journeying with heavily laden sleds pulled by dog teams were delicately carved in ivory, particularly by Inuit along the Labrador coast, and are found in several early museum collections. Beyond the narrow purpose of trade, however, these objects also reflect the cultural principle of *tunnganarniq:* fostering good spirit by being open, welcoming and inclusive. Indeed, the gift of a small carving presented by Nayoumealook to Houston during his first visit north in 1948 was undoubtedly inspired by this principle—a spontaneous and fortuitous act that initiated this era of contemporary Inuit art production.[8]

The economic activities introduced by whalers and traders during the nineteenth and early twentieth centuries provided the opportunity and necessity for Inuit to demonstrate *qanuqtuurniq:* being innovative and resourceful in adapting to new situations. Recruited to join whaling crews and to trap fox for the lucrative fur trade, Inuit families began to abandon subsistence hunting and camping patterns. Newly imported trade goods often supplanted traditional materials, transforming cultural practice. Rifles, telescopes and wooden whaleboats improved hunting success, and steel needles, imported cloth and sewing machines eased women's labour in sewing clothing. In addition, women became highly inventive in adapting glass beads and metal objects for clothing decoration. Geometric motifs used in women's traditional tattooing emerged as patterns in beadwork, along with skilfully designed images and narrative scenes from the whaling and trading era. Judging from their presence in museum collections, beaded parkas became a valued trade item. More importantly, however, beaded parkas reveal women's skill in graphic design, which in combination with men's drawing skill in incising ivory tusks, serve as significant historical precedents for drawing and printmaking in the modern period.

As a pedagogical tradition, Inuit families emphasize a non-didactic teaching method, learning by observation rather than direct instruction. Raised to be thoughtful, observant witnesses of nature, children also observe the work of skilled artisans, learning the combination of discipline and skill necessary for success in hunting, sewing and art production. Observation features as an important attribute in the principle of *pilimmaksarniq:* acquiring knowledge and skill through practice, effort and action. The acquisition of traditional skills depended on the presence of gifted family members in their small nomadic hunting camps. Having left her family's camp to marry at a young age, the renowned Baker Lake artist Jessie Oonark once lamented her own sewing skills, stating, "I never had anyone to teach me."[9] Respect for exceptional craftsmanship is evident in the words of artist Marion Tuu'luq, also of Baker Lake. Turning over a wall hanging, Tuu'luq noted the stitches visible on the underside of the duffle and asked in an incredulous voice, "Don't people have eyes?" intimating not only the artist's failure to hide her stitches but also a serious lack of discernment on the part of the viewer.[10]

The move from hunting camps to settlements around the Hudson's Bay Company (HBC) trading posts increased the exposure to skilled artisans in the community. As carvers presented their work for sale at HBC posts, and later at community co-operatives, these settings became informal venues for observing the accomplished work of others. When the quality of sculpture being produced in Inukjuak was falling off in the late 1970s, sociologist Marybelle Myers wrote that the art "was suffering because the last vein of the beautiful green stone they loved to work had been used up."[11] Although a new vein was eventually made available to the carvers, the Purchaser of Carvings, Pauloosie Weetaltuk, also advised that a more prominent section in the new community co-op be set aside to purchase carvings, stating, "Until you get a good place for people to bring their soapstone, you will not get good sculpture."[12]

The commitment of Inuit to art production in the newly settled communities demonstrates two key cultural principles: *qanuqtuurniq* (being innovative and resourceful in solving problems) and *pijitsirniq* (serving and providing for family and community). In the postwar era, a period marked by extreme poverty, cash payments for artwork assisted families in purchasing imported food, fabric for clothing, rifles, ammunition, gas, canvas tents and basic camping supplies. As artists' reputations grew, so did their income. Realizing its economic benefit, many artists, such as Pitseolak Ashoona of Kinngait (Cape Dorset), encouraged family members to develop their artistic skills. Pitseolak's daughter, Napachie Pootoogook, and granddaughter, Annie Pootoogook, have since gained international reputations in their own right. Jessie Oonark was also the matriarchal head of a large family of artists, including Janet Kigusiuq, Josiah Nuilaalik, Victoria Mamnguqsualuk, Miriam Nanurluk Qiyuk, Mary Yuusipik, Nancy Pukingrnak and William Noah.

Although some critics still characterize Inuit art production as a largely commercial endeavour, this narrow perspective demonstrates a limited understanding of the relevance of art production within Inuit society. Providing cash at a time when there were few alternative sources allowed an artist (or spouse) to continue to hunt, thereby providing for the needs of the family *(pijitsirniq)*, as well as demonstrating *avatittinnik kamatsiarniq* (respect and care for the land, animals and the environment). Cash income also helped artists to fulfill social obligations following the principle of *inuqatigiitsiarniq:* respecting others, nurturing relationships and caring for people. The personal and social value of carving may be found in the words of one of the earliest sculptors, Johnny Inukpuk—"Carving gave us independence that we never had before"[13]—as well as in the statement of Arviat artist Lucy Tasseor Tutsweetok: "I do not want anyone else to copy my style of carving except my daughter. I have taught her to carve so that when I die she can keep on carving."[14]

Despite its origins as an economic endeavour, artmaking fuelled the creative spirit on a personal and collective level. Shaping the emerging form of a sculpture before the watchful eyes of a grandchild, or transforming a pencil drawing through the process of printmaking, the Inuit artist gained a feeling of personal accomplishment and sensed the affirmation of others. Most importantly, art allowed sculptors, graphic artists and printmakers to experience the personal autonomy so highly valued in Inuit social and intellectual culture. As members of an art co-operative, artists also participated in a communal institution—an alternative to the hierarchical system imposed by Qallunaat institutions in which educational, legal and medical decisions affecting the well-being of individuals, families and the community at large were being made by outsiders in positions of authority. In contrast, the economic and social structure of the co-operative provided a more egalitarian setting, reflecting the values of collaborative effort *(piliriqatigiinniq)* and decision making through discussion and consensus *(aajiiqatigiinniq)*.

With the formation of community co-operatives, Inuit art production thrived in smaller, more remote communities with few wage-earning alternatives. Indeed, Arctic communities such as Kinngait (Cape Dorset), Qamanittuaq (Baker Lake), Ulukhaktok (Holman Island), Pangnirtung and Clyde River enjoy national and international recognition based primarily on the reputation of their art programs. Judging by the fact that the larger administrative centres, notably Iqaluit and Cambridge Bay, failed to build an art base reflecting their community size, one wonders if the strength of these more remote artmaking programs also reflects the less intrusive presence of outsiders.[15] In recalling the early settlement days of Inukjuak, Marybelle Myers cites Peter Murdoch, a former HBC factor and later general manager of La Fédération des coopératives du Nouveau-Québec:

> It is his conviction that the "Inoucdjouamiut" went through a long period of insecurity in their relations with the Kablunak [*sic*: Qallunaat]... They didn't really feel at home in the village but exhibited guarded, slightly defensive, behaviour. It was as if they were merely visiting in this strange land and their *real* [Mitchell's emphasis] place was somewhere else—back in the ruins of what had once been a camp.[16]

The institutional nature of the co-operative helped Inuit to move away from this "spirit of deference" by encouraging collaborative work, strengthening social and cultural identity and nurturing a spirit of self-awareness and self-reliance. Co-operatives also offered a safe place to express individual autonomy and develop a personal artistic style. In an essay entitled "That I am old is the trouble," Terry Ryan sketches a touching portrait of the elderly artist Parr and his playful exchange with fellow printmakers in the Kinngait print shop, accepting their banter while maintaining his confidence in his own work as a graphic artist.[17]

By virtue of their mission and internal organization, printmaking shops formed an especially collaborative environment. The separate but interdependent roles of graphic artist and printmaker freed the artist's hand, leaving printing decisions to a trained, often gifted technician. The extraordinary success of so many Inuit prints is due to the close collaboration of artist and printmaker, each bringing skill, creativity and artisanship to the successful completion of the work.

Skilled art advisers—some of legendary note such as Terry Ryan, Jack and Sheila Butler and Wallace Brannen—mentored and challenged individual artists, lending stability to the printmaking program and serving as administrative directors and liaisons between the print shop and the outside world. The preparation of the annual print collections relied on the communal effort of the printmakers as they worked to meet deadlines. As recalled by Av Isaacs, the Toronto art dealer, the release of the annual portfolios generated considerable excitement among collectors across North America, with lines gathering at galleries in anticipation of the new Cape Dorset or Baker Lake collection.[18] News of such events made their way back to the print shop, building a sense of communal pride. Fully illustrated print catalogues documenting the annual edition, now regarded as an essential archival resource, were also an important source of affirmation.

The multiplicity of print-images and their public exhibition have allowed graphic artists to become identified with personal styles, raising the profile of individual artists and of Inuit society as a whole. Exploring ideas in a comprehensive, almost serial manner, Inuit artists have created a remarkable compendium of graphic images recording their own cultural history. Luke Anguhadluq's drawings describe hunting techniques and implements of the central Arctic; Pitseolak Ashoona's work preserves the memory of communal camp life; Jessie Oonark has left behind a remarkable portrayal of womanhood—one that stands on par with that of any Western artist, from Botticelli to De Kooning. An adept illustrator of nature, chronicler of Inuit artisanship and observer of social change, Kananginak Pootoogook remains an insightful contributor to the Kinngait print shop.

Growing increasingly aware of the cultural value of their own work, many artists have developed thematic collections of images. Victoria Mamnguqsualuk conveys a detailed knowledge of Inuit mythology, and in a light-hearted yet keenly reflective manner, Pudlo Pudlat describes the urbanization of northern communities, often with airplanes flying overhead and power lines stretching across the landscape. Particularly in her drawings, Napachie Pootoogook has drawn attention to social and domestic issues in the North. William Noah, Pitaloosie Saila and Annie Pootoogook, among others, have offered incisive visual commentaries on Qallunaat personhood and institutional roles.

Although drawings provide a wider and deeper understanding of an artist's oeuvre, the multiplicity of print-images allows public museums to acquire substantial graphic collections, increasing the exhibit quotient of prints. Individual images remain more consistently in the public eye, allowing singular images, such as Kenojuak's *The Enchanted Owl* (see above and p. 174), to become almost iconic representations of Inuit art. Print shops and the production of prints, however, depend on large-scale funding, and over the years undulating waves of financial support have severely challenged print-producing communities. It stands as a singular tribute to graphic artists, printmakers and art advisers that this form of Inuit art production has attained the quality and strength it has, despite the challenges that have faced the printmaking programs over time.

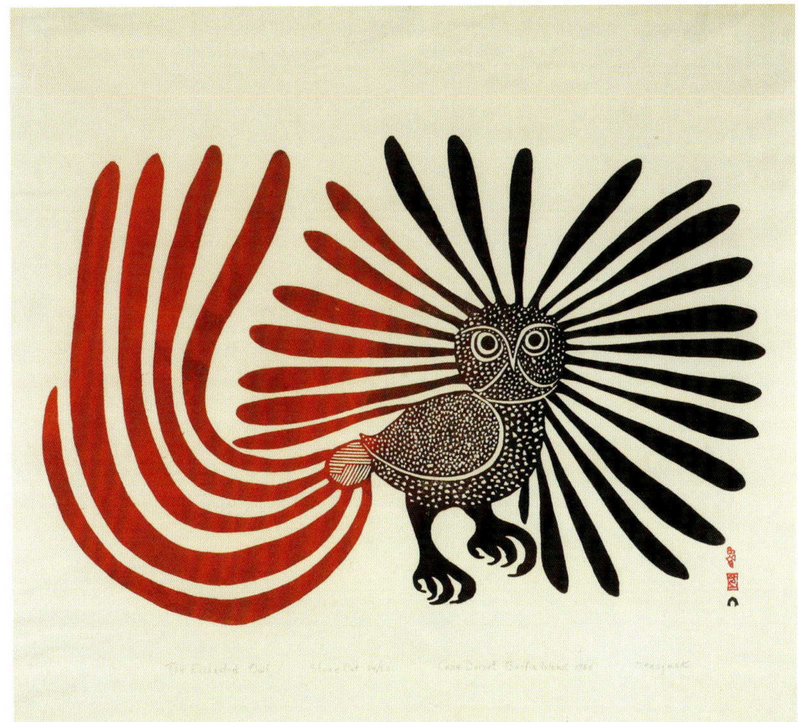

Kenojuak Ashevak, *The Enchanted Owl*, 1960, stonecut on paper, 59.7 x 65.0 cm. © Dorset Fine Arts

"I have seen so many changes in my life and I like to express my thoughts. In the past, families would drift away on ice floes and never be seen again, but now a helicopter goes out to rescue them and there is great rejoicing. Airplanes and helicopters make me happy because they are able to rescue hunters."

Pudlo Pudlat

Conclusion: Nunavut and Inuit Art

For more than fifty years, contemporary Inuit art has served as a remarkable means of cross-cultural communication. Displayed in public museums and commercial galleries across Canada and around the world, art has carved out a space for Inuit culture in the public mind, playing a prominent role in the public arena from state visits to major sporting events. Even "airport art" has served a purpose, keeping the Inuit presence in the mind of travelling Canadians and international visitors. In the course of Canadian modern history, Inuit sculpture and graphic art has become synonymous with Canadian culture, universally recognized as a national symbol—a point emphasized in the choice of the inukshuk as the emblem for the 2010 Winter Olympics in Vancouver, British Columbia.

Undoubtedly, this public acknowledgement, gained through respect for the visual quality of Inuit art as well as the cultural insight provided by Inuit artists, helped to pave the road to Nunavut. From the postwar period to the present, art has stood in the place of Inuit, serving to represent Inuit throughout southern Canada and around the world, even in their absence. Throughout this period a strong commitment to Inuit art has existed at the highest level of the Canadian federal government. The number of Inuit artists and southern art scholars, advisers and supporters of Inuit art honoured as recipients of the Order of Canada speaks to the formal recognition of Inuit art and its contribution to the nation.[19] Thus, when Inuit leaders began negotiating with the federal government to divide the geographically and politically cumbersome Northwest Territories, establishing Nunavut as a political entity within the nation of Canada, they were able to build upon a foundation of understanding, respect and familiarity with Inuit culture, established through the work of generations of Inuit artists.

In communities across Nunavut, Inuit are taking the lead in developing and preserving the cultural traditions that nurture the creation of art. New voices and experiences are emerging. In 2005 Bernadette Miqqusaaq Dean and Zacharias Kunuk brought together a group of elders to visit museum collections in Toronto, Ottawa, New York, Philadelphia and Washington, D.C., for their documentary film, *Inuit Piqutingit: What Belongs to Inuit.* As the film concludes, the elders meet with Inuit youth at a school in Ottawa. One cannot help but be moved by the comments of Rhoda Karetak, an elder who speaks with deep emotion about how this journey awakened in her such strong feelings of pride for her culture and respect for the strength and fortitude of her ancestors.[20]

Just as the ancestral legacy held in ethnographic collections remains virtually unknown to Inuit, contemporary Inuit art—created for, and marketed to, a non-Inuit audience—is largely unknown to Inuit as well. This point was brought home to me in preparing the exhibition *Inuit Myths, Legends and Songs*. Visiting the community of Qamanittuaq (formerly Baker Lake), I interviewed artists whose works were featured in the exhibition. I cannot forget the words of Janet Kigusiuq as she reviewed slides of her drawings in southern collections. In a voice that was almost a whisper, she said, "I never knew that I had created such beautiful things."

In years to come, as Inuit become more fully aware of their own art history—of the sculptures, prints, drawings and textile art stored in museums around the world, published in exhibit catalogues, illustrated in books of Inuit art and held in private collections—their pride in the creative work of their fellow artists will certainly grow, evoking the same respect and awe voiced by elder Rhoda Karetak. Inuit artists have created—and continue to create—a cultural legacy that enriches the vision of Canada and offers a fuller understanding of the indigenous social and cultural history of the Americas.

Thirty-six

So this is how life is supposed to be lived
Oops...
I had no idea...

I feel like a damn fool
For having tried to learn how to be a great Eskimo hunter
Like Papa wanted me to become that fateful day
When I was unceremoniously thrust into this world
How embarrassing for my beautiful parents
They had no idea this was going to be happening to little O me

These crafty Qallunaat
These social experimenters
These arbiters of the old Brit empire-building
These greatest of all caretakers
These psychological warfare instigators
These Eskimo traditionalist haters
These God-like humankind make-up artists
These clothing design experts
These greatest of all chefs
These incredible inventors of snow machines
These Jack-of-all-trades humankind
These ESP people
These aliens
They have arrived...

Does it mean we are better Eskimos for it?

Alootook Ipellie

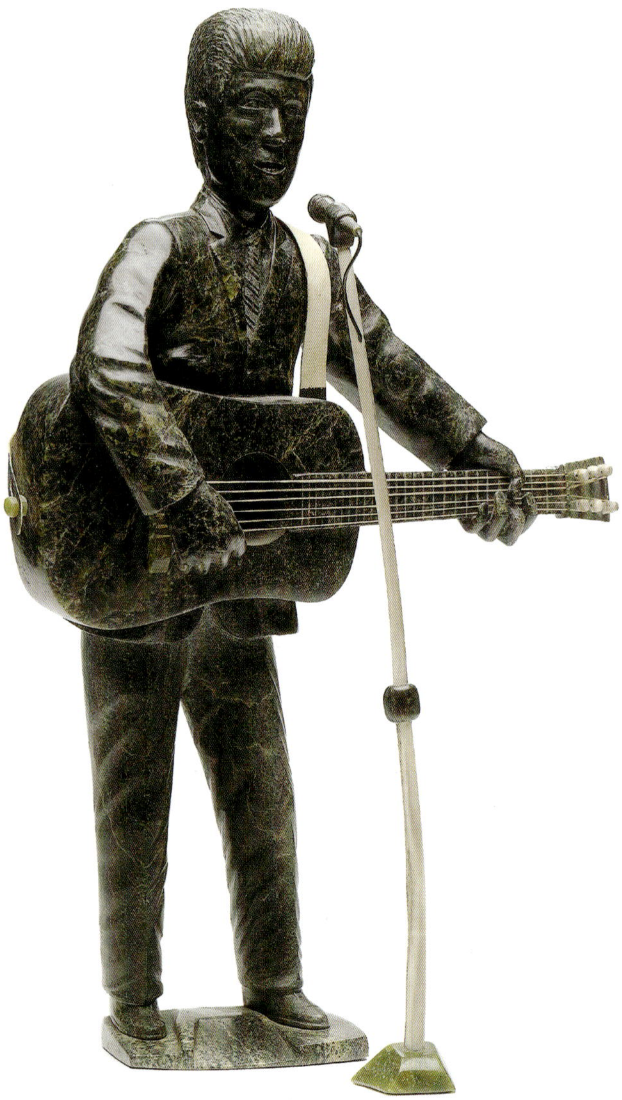

Paulassie Pootoogook, *Tommy Hunter with Guitar at Microphone*, 1992, stone, antler, leather, sinew, plastic coated wire, 44.0 x 33.0 x 12.5 cm. Collection of Samuel and Esther Sarick, Toronto. © Dorset Fine Arts

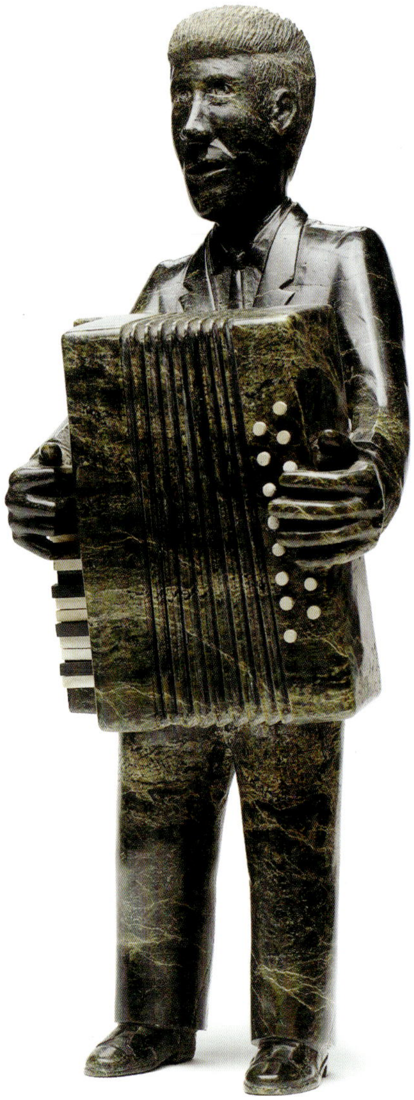

Paulassie Pootoogook, *Tommy Hunter with Accordion*, 1992, stone, ivory, painted wood, 50.0 x 17.5 x 18.5 cm. Collection of Samuel and Esther Sarick, Toronto. © Dorset Fine Arts

The Inuit of Our Imagination

Heather Igloliorte

In recent decades, the North has undergone a remarkable social, political and cultural transformation. With the formation of Nunavut in 1999 and the ratification of land claims in other Arctic and Subarctic territories, Inuit are regaining some of the autonomy that had been lost to them since Qallunaat (non-Inuit) culture first encroached upon the Arctic. The Inuit have begun to take control of their global representation by speaking out against the legacies of colonization in the North and by asserting their rights to sovereignty, self-determination and custodianship over the land and its natural resources. Although the right to maintain stewardship over our ancestral territories has been in jeopardy ever since the first arrival of Europeans, it has never been more urgent than now, as environmental pollutants and climate change threaten to irrevocably alter both the landscape and the health and well-being of the inhabitants. The rapidly melting sea ice also enlivens old international disputes over state control of the Far North and its waterways; as the ice recedes, new resources reveal themselves for development and exploitation, and the fabled Northwest Passage becomes a viable transnational shipping route, risking further contamination to Arctic waters and promising a dramatic increase in foreign traffic and trade. The Inuit are responding to these escalating complexities of globalization and climate change with tremendous strength, grace and resilience, demanding to be heard, and with a voice much greater than a people of our population (approximately 55,000 in Canada) would be expected to command.

Parallel to the strides toward Inuit sovereignty and self-governance made since the 1990s in politics, the economy and social health and well-being, the Inuit art world has been experiencing a similar slow-to-build yet monumental shift in its artistic production. In the 1950s, during a period of dramatic and devastating cultural and economic upheaval for the Inuit, art production was introduced as a means for Inuit to regain a foothold in the economy and some measure of autonomy. The new art form was enthusiastically accepted as both "primitive" and modern, and Inuit artists were celebrated for their community and personal styles. This recognition of individual style afforded Inuit artists a unique position within the field of global indigenous arts, where at this time most "primitive" artworks were considered the anonymous products of a collective people rather than of individual artists. Since the 1970s we have seen the rise of the new Inuit artist: fiercely individualistic and strongly committed to personal expression, with a growing tendency toward socially conscious art and subversively critical commentary. These new hybridized works, uncommon and contemplative, mirror the rising societal and cultural awareness of the Inuit as they take their place in the new North, while reflecting the culmination of decades of prolonged contact and reciprocal influence between Inuit and Qallunaat in the Arctic.

Colonization and Sovereignty in the Arctic

To understand the important role that these contemporary Inuit artists play in fostering and maintaining Inuit autonomy and cultural identity, it is necessary to put the issues of colonization and sovereignty, and the interrelation of these issues to the Arctic environment, into historical context. While First Nations communities in southern Canada had undergone several centuries of colonization and missionary involvement, Inuit communities remained relatively unaffected by European culture until the early twentieth century and had maintained a mutually beneficial relationship with those Qallunaat living in the North.[1] In the 1910s and 1920s semi-nomadic camp life began to change as many Inuit moved into settlements around trading posts, which resulted in the over-hunting of land and sea animals in the immediate area and an increase in dependence upon preserved food and packaged goods imported from southern Canada; it also led to the rapid spread of devastating diseases such as smallpox and tuberculosis.[2] Parallel to this settlement into communities, Inuit were rapidly converted to Christianity, often through the missions that were set up near the trading posts, effectively ending the observation of Inuit spiritual customs and cultural traditions because missionaries and the clergy proclaimed these to be heathen and savage practices.[3]

Before the Second World War, the federal government's policy for dealing with the Inuit had been one of non-interference and limited economic support, but in the period after the war and at the beginning of the Cold War, growing concerns about Canada's sovereignty over the Arctic brought national media and public attention to Inuit living within Canada's northern border.[4] This new and sudden involvement in the Arctic of the dominant, southern population had a rapid, deleterious and lasting impact on the Inuit.

By 1955 the federal government instituted the northern Federal Day School system, the residential school system for the Inuit, where children were forbidden to speak their own language or practise any aspect of their culture in the schools, dormitories, hostels and other residences, and where many suffered terrible abuses.[5] The harmful long-term effects this cultural turmoil had on the health and well-being of survivors and their families is still evident today in Arctic communities. Alootook Ipellie's pivotal essay "The Colonization of the Arctic" allows us to penetrate with profundity this nearly incomprehensible part of our history and to see how this project fits within the "civilizing" mission of the pervasive European epistemology of evolutionism in the late nineteenth and early twentieth centuries, which judged all cultures by a Eurocentric standard. The Qallunaat carried out this paternalistic mission in the belief that they had the power and cultural superiority to dictate how Inuit should live. In Ipellie's words,

> In all of the Inuit communities across the Arctic, the story was the same. The government did what it wanted to do and when it wanted to do it. There was absolutely no opposition from the Inuit to any of the projects the government brought in. All Inuit people in the Arctic were treated like infants by the paternalistic government.[6]

Despite all this, one of the greatest violations of Inuit human rights occurred in the 1950s in Nunavik (Arctic Quebec), where several Inuit communities were entirely relocated to the unfamiliar terrain of the High Arctic, and in the same period in Nunatsiavut (Labrador), where the long-settled communities of Hebron and Okak were dismantled and the families split up into more southern coastal communities, with devastating consequences to both of the relocated populations.[7] In Nunavik, the relocation was part of the Canadian government strategy to assert sovereignty in the High Arctic;[8] in Nunatsiavut, the government deceived the families into leaving so that they could close the only trading post in the area, which was expensive to stock and maintain.[9] The relocated Inuit families of both Nunavik and Nunatsiavut faced numerous hardships in the unfamiliar areas, and many continued to suffer the after-effects of this ill-treatment for decades to follow. The Nunavik Inuit, who had been treated like pawns by the federal government, faced the further indignity of the government's vehement denial of any wrongdoing.[10]

Underlying all these events is the vastly imbalanced historical power relationship between the Qallunaat and the Inuit. As Rosemary Kuptana, the former president of Inuit Tapirisat of Canada (now Inuit Tapiriit Kanatami), has observed,

> They took their authority for granted and presented a greater air of superiority since the Inuit were obviously so appreciative, so eager to please and becoming increasingly dependent. The prejudices and ideologies of the day asserted that the Inuit were indeed inferior, and that the Qallunaat knew what was best for Inuit.[11]

In the face of such overwhelmingly skewed control, Inuit acted in their own best interests by submitting to the dominant power as a matter of survival, and the Canadian government acted in its own self-interest to maintain sovereignty over the Arctic lands and sea ice. In her essay "The Inuit and Issues of Arctic Sovereignty" Violet Ford, executive council member of the Inuit Circumpolar Council, protested that Inuit are too infrequently included in discussions of Canadian Arctic sovereignty and stated that Inuit can and should play a determining and protective role in their ancestral and contemporary territories. As

Ford points out, "Inuit are, and expect to remain, the permanent majority population of the Arctic. Inuit are centrally placed in the region. They are the key players, and they are the most affected by the Arctic sovereignty processes and by the outcomes and solutions Canada proposes."[12] Furthermore, Inuit sovereignty in the Arctic, as Canadian peoples, would serve to strengthen Canada's claim to Arctic territory. Sheila Watt-Cloutier of Kuujjuaq, northern Quebec, former president of Inuit Tapiriit Kanatami and Nobel Prize nominee in 2007, suggested,

> Our government could go a long way toward defending our Arctic sovereignty by providing the tools for Arctic communities to succeed and thrive. This would include making a dedicated effort to ensure the highest standards of culturally appropriate education; investing in community infrastructure, not just the military; and undertaking respectful stewardship of the land through natural resource co-management bodies. We must insist that Canada's investments for sovereignty be directed first to peoples and communities.[13]

She further points out that the main factor protecting Canadian Arctic sovereignty today is the frozen sea ice, which naturally prevents foreign interlopers from accessing our vast coastal resources.[14] It would be wiser, she insists, to protect the environment and slow the breakup of land-fast ice[15] in order to protect Canada's northern interests, rather than mobilize the military in the rapidly melting sea. As current Inuit Tapiriit Kanatami president Mary Simon affirmed in "Climate Change, Sovereignty and Partnership with the Inuit," today's situation is very different from that of the 1960s and 1970s, when the government viewed the Arctic as a "frozen treasure chest"; rather, the establishment of Nunavut and the implementation of land claims agreements in other self-governing Inuit bodies ensure that Canada will fulfill its commitments to Inuit people, who have a right to play a deciding role in what happens in the Arctic and in their own lives. Simon argues that only Inuit sovereignty—with the full support and cooperation of the federal government and driven by a thriving economy, healthy people and a renewed, fortified and dynamic living culture—will truly protect Canadian Arctic sovereignty. The sooner that Canada realizes that it should collaborate with, and not work against, its greatest allies in the North, the better, wealthier and more secure the whole country will be.[16]

Perhaps the most urgent need for Inuit Arctic sovereignty is driven by the rapidly changing Arctic climate. While the world debates the existence of global warming and what to do about climate change, Inuit living in the Arctic experience the changes to their fragile ecosystem daily: the rapidly melting sea ice and proliferation of environmental toxins present numerous threats to northern species and biodiversity. The melting ice may open doors to resources and development previously unheard of, but rapid global warming leaves Inuit in an extremely vulnerable position as Arctic waters open up into vast shipping lanes, drawing international traffic as well as escalating interest in the untapped oil, gas and mineral resources that become available as the ice recedes.[17] Watt-Cloutier has urged the world, "In this age of globalization and ever-increasing connectivity, we must strive to answer these questions while recognizing how the global affects the local and the local affects the global."[18]

To maintain a harmonious relationship with the land and to pass on environmentally based traditional knowledge—in our case *Inuit Qaujimajatuqangit*[19]—we must maintain a safe and healthy environment that retains its defining characteristics, biodiversity and ecological soundness.[20] Laura Westra, professor emerita at the University of Windsor and environmental justice advocate, argues in *Environmental Justice and the Rights of Indigenous Peoples* that neither self-governance nor cultural integrity can exist if Aboriginal peoples do not have the authority or ability to control and manage their lands and resources. Although today most Canadian Inuit live in self-governing territories, their agency over the land is limited by forces beyond their control or by environmental impacts that occurred before self-governance. Northerners are becoming increasingly concerned about rapidly shifting climate disruptions, the level of environmental contaminants in country foods (local fish and game),[21] and foreign hostility to Inuit traditions in the form of international trade bans and anti-sealing campaigns by groups like PETA or the International Fund for Animal Welfare, which garner financial and popular support through their opposition to the seal hunt.[22] The knowledge

"Lying in bed at night, I start to remember the time we lived out on the land and I long to go back. I remember vividly how Inuit used to live as I experienced it myself and can express this way of life easily in my carvings. We lived a hard life. We were always hungry. It was a happy time when somebody would catch a fish like this woman has... There is a special meaning in my carvings; the stories they tell are meant for my grandchildren."

Mathew Aqigaaq

base of Inuit, our very way of life, is threatened by international forces. As a young Inuk, I share in the concern that *Inuit Qaujimajatuqangit*—put simply, Inuit traditional knowledge and collective social memory—is being rapidly and irrevocably forgotten. Also of concern is that English is replacing Inuktitut as the dominant language of Inuit, even in the North, and that, although many young Inuit do not have the traditional skills necessary for survival on the land, education and job opportunities are severely limited. We continue to struggle against the legacy of nearly a century of intense colonial influence to maintain our cultural practices and to wrest back our stewardship over the land and its natural resources.

These challenges are not unique to Inuit, of course; historically, indigenous peoples all over the world have had to struggle to maintain their sense of place and their rightful custodianship over ancestral territories in the face of geographical and cultural imperialism. In an increasingly cosmopolitan world, ideas of land, place and ownership become tricky to traverse and maintain. In Canada, Inuit territories function as neo-colonial states, with no expectation of total independence. Yet it might be possible to achieve a form of internal sovereignty if we work toward self-determination over our lives, lands and natural resources by demanding a mutual respect on a government-to-government level alongside the many other sovereign nations that exist within Canada's boundaries. The establishment of Nunavut and the settling of Inuit land claims are important first steps toward asserting Arctic sovereignty and power-sharing with the federal government. Action must also be taken to maintain our culturally distinct practices and artistic traditions and to draw on these practices as sources of strength and cultural resilience. Steven Loft, an Iroquois curator, has recently theorized the important role of arts and cultural practices in asserting indigenous sovereignty. He says,

> When members of a community assert control over their own lives and culture, politically, socially, and artistically, they go beyond oppression. Thus, control of "our" image becomes not only an act of subversion, but of resistance, and ultimately, liberation... What is at stake here is not how the image is presented (aesthetics aside) but who controls it. This is the fundamental challenge to Aboriginal artists and cultural producers.[23]

Loft is writing about Alanis Obomsawin, an Abenaki filmmaker, but his essay resonates with the work of contemporary Inuit cultural producers, who have assumed the responsibility of providing the wellspring of our collective cultural identity and of shifting the perception of Inuit by non-Inuit away from their historical representation in the popular media and art world alike as "modern primitives" and toward a more balanced and accurate portrayal of the present-day Inuk in a modern landscape. Our ancestors—shamans, hunters, storytellers—were the keepers of collective social memory; now our artists share that responsibility for preserving *Inuit Qaujimajatuqangit* in their works, by asserting themselves as the true authorities on Inuit culture and confronting the legacies of colonial influence and the more recent mediation of Inuit identity by both the media and the art markets.

Artmaking, Resilience and *Inuit Qaujimajatuqangit*

Many of the new artists of the Inuit avant-garde have begun this practice of frank self-representation by making art that responds to, and provides commentary on, the many entangled impacts of almost a century of colonial influence in the Arctic. Whereas other scholars following recent indigenous art theory may identify these works as sites of resistance, I would argue instead that these new artworks should be viewed as expressions of cultural *resilience*. The distinction is significant: resistance implies a violent opposition, a struggle against an oppressor. Although it is certainly true that these new works respond to colonial legacies as equally and consistently as they challenge the Inuit art market, I believe that viewing these artworks as acts of resilience—fortifying the culture from within, rather than reacting to outside opposition—is more in line with the Inuit world view as communal and based on the well-being of the collective.

Resilience, as defined by Aboriginal health specialists Madeleine Dion Stout and Gregory Kipling, is the capacity of communities, families and individuals to spring back from adversity more fortified and resourceful despite decades of cultural stressors. Resilience is cultivated through the adoption of "mature defenses"—such as humour and altruism—which can help individuals overcome a lifetime of adversity. On the societal level cultural resilience can strengthen the collective capacity to withstand negative forces from within and without. As Stout and Kipling observe, "the resurgence of Aboriginal beliefs and practices, accompanied by traditional resilience promotion strategies, has given rise to promising interventions."[24] It is my conviction that the production of contemporary art in the Arctic is one of the "interventions" that has fostered and safeguarded Inuit culture in the face of numerous affronts to our sovereignty. Despite the remarkable individual talents of this Inuit avant-garde and the incredible distinctiveness and particularity of each artist's personal style, I believe that collectively these artists are expressing the strength and resilience of Inuit culture from an emic, or internal, perspective, showing the world that Inuit are a sovereign people who can reflect on and adapt to the world around them in a manner that reinforces our centuries-old beliefs and practices while allowing the culture to flourish. Inuit art that expresses cultural resilience takes part in the consolidation and rejuvenation of indigenous culture and the assertion of autonomy while providing a valuable and nuanced critique of the complex interactions of nearly a century of colonialism and the aggressive evangelization of the Arctic, demonstrating that even a society with a limited population can exercise agency over its own future.

Although rare in the first decades of the contemporary period of Inuit art, increasingly, Inuit artists today are creating artworks that examine the influence of the Qallunaat incursion into Inuit territory. In a recent article for *Inuit Art Quarterly* I tested my theory of resilience and found much evidence in support of this idea.[25] The beginnings of Inuit cultural resilience occurred in the mid-twentieth century, during the period described above, a period marked by the general erosion of traditional life in the North. Concurrent with the devastating changes sweeping the Arctic, Inuit contemporary art debuted on the global art scene to critical acclaim, supported by the Canadian public, the modern art market and the government.[26] Somewhat ironically, while Inuit culture was being debased, devalued, exploited and eroded in the North by the dominant colonial presence that sought to wholly assimilate Inuit culture into the mainstream, in the mainstream culture these same Inuit values were being celebrated through the enthusiastic purchase of Inuit art in the national and even international art market. Significantly, Inuit had the opportunity to create works that reflected their otherwise forbidden cultural practices, through, for example, depicting the teaching and practices of shamanism, as well as Inuit origin stories and oral histories passed down through countless generations. In the wake of the many devastating converging impacts of colonization and evangelization in the North, artmaking provided a significant opportunity for us to foster and maintain our cultural resilience and to know, through affirmations from the world outside the Arctic, that our culture, knowledge and expressions are of value.

The roots of this art of cultural resilience were forged in the earliest years of the contemporary art period by artists such as Cape Dorset's Pudlo Pudlat, who depicted in his drawings and prints what life was like before colonization and during the early contact period. Although Pudlat's work frequently presented whimsical impressions of Qallunaat culture, he, along with others, also looked critically at spiritual matters, specifically the conflict between Christianity and Inuit belief systems. Other important artistic precursors include Napachie Pootoogook and Kananginak Pootoogook, both of Cape Dorset, who created great bodies of autobiographical and historical works that chronicled community life during a critical period of transition. Today artists exhibit an even greater awareness of southern influences and often evidence a new, hybridized identity that reflects their contemporary reality. Cape Dorset artists Shuvinai Ashoona and Jutai Toonoo, for example, are among the many artists who have critically examined religion in their artwork.[27] Shuvinai's cousin Annie Pootoogook, in contrast, is famous for her daring and sensitive critiques of the colonial legacy in her works on alcohol and substance abuse and for revealing the influence of pop culture in the North in the form of video games, trashy television and sensationalized news coverage. Siblings David Ruben Piqtoukun and Abraham Anghik Ruben of Paulatuk, Northwest Territories, have revealed through their sculptural practice the complexities and nuances of the history and lingering impacts of residential schools with great solemnity, whereas the more lighthearted mixed-media sculptures of Labrador's Michael Massie and Floyd Kuptana of Cape Parry, NWT, demonstrate how Inuit maintain cultural integrity while creating imaginative, bold, hybridized works of art.

"I hope to tell Inuit people that when they adopted Christianity and gave up the old beliefs, they gave up a lot... They have forgotten that the shamans taught... respect for the animal world, for human life, for a spouse and for children, and the principal idea of sharing that has been lost to a lot of communities."

Abraham Anghik Ruben

These artists provide inspiration and demonstrate, through the depiction of Inuit cultural knowledge or in the act of carving itself, how artmaking can be creatively used to preserve and fortify threatened cultural knowledge and practices. These emergent, socially conscious works are indicative of the renewed ability of Inuit to reflect upon and respond to the multiple pressures of modern life. This new approach to Inuit art, which reflects the Inuit experience of the contemporary world, is just beginning to gain recognition and acceptance in the artistic community and global art market, and it is exciting to imagine the future manifestations of this practice and the influence these strong cultural expressions might inspire.

New Directions for Inuit Art and Scholarship

Although I am encouraged by the positive direction of these new Inuit artworks and believe they reflect a growing self-confidence within Inuit society, there are still serious challenges to asserting Inuit cultural sovereignty. It is easy for me to be optimistic about our near future when I observe the tremendous strides made by the inspiring new artists of the Inuit avant-garde, and this optimism is probably heightened by my separation from the daily reality of many communities; I am an urban Inuk, who has lived in the nation's capital for several years and has fully acclimated to life in the South. I know that there are many Inuit who are still, to paraphrase the post-colonial theorist and filmmaker Trinh T. Minh-ha, the Third World living within the First World. Our suicide rate is the highest on the planet; our northern educational and employment opportunities are few. As for the field of Inuit art, I am currently the sole active Inuit member of the Aboriginal Curatorial Collective, an organization of indigenous Canadian and international academics, museum professionals and curators that has over one hundred members.

Although much has been written, we are still just at the beginning of our art history, and there are still so many challenges to be overcome. The problem was identified years ago by Inuit art scholar Jean Blodgett in an essay in *On Aboriginal Representation in the Gallery*: "Compared with First Nations art, the power relationships in Inuit art still leave much of the decision making in the hands of outsiders... While there are many Inuit artists, there are few Inuit curators and researchers working with their own artistic culture. This has been changing, but until recently, only at a slow rate."[28] There are no Inuit working in our national arts institutions; at present, I don't know of any other Inuit studying our art history and visual culture at the doctoral level, but I have hope that I will not be so alone for much longer—there is so much work to be done by Inuit in the arts and so many leadership roles to be filled. In an essay in *Vision, Space, Desire: Global Perspectives and Cultural Hybridity,* Gerald McMaster offered a hopeful direction for the new critical discourse on post-colonialism in curatorial and museological practice: he suggested that, "on an increasingly complex and connected globe, the art world is expanding far beyond the Western trajectory. The old patterns of exclusion have reversed, bringing new voices into the mainstream."[29] Most of the Inuit population in Canada is my age or younger—I was born in 1979—and our generation is becoming increasingly better educated. Our leaders have gained a higher political profile, garnering national media attention, and even a Nobel Prize nomination.[30] Our territories have made huge strides in just a few short decades. Although the real success of the Inuit is yet to come, I believe it will not be long before many more new voices enter the discourse of Inuit studies.

Modern Map of the Arctic

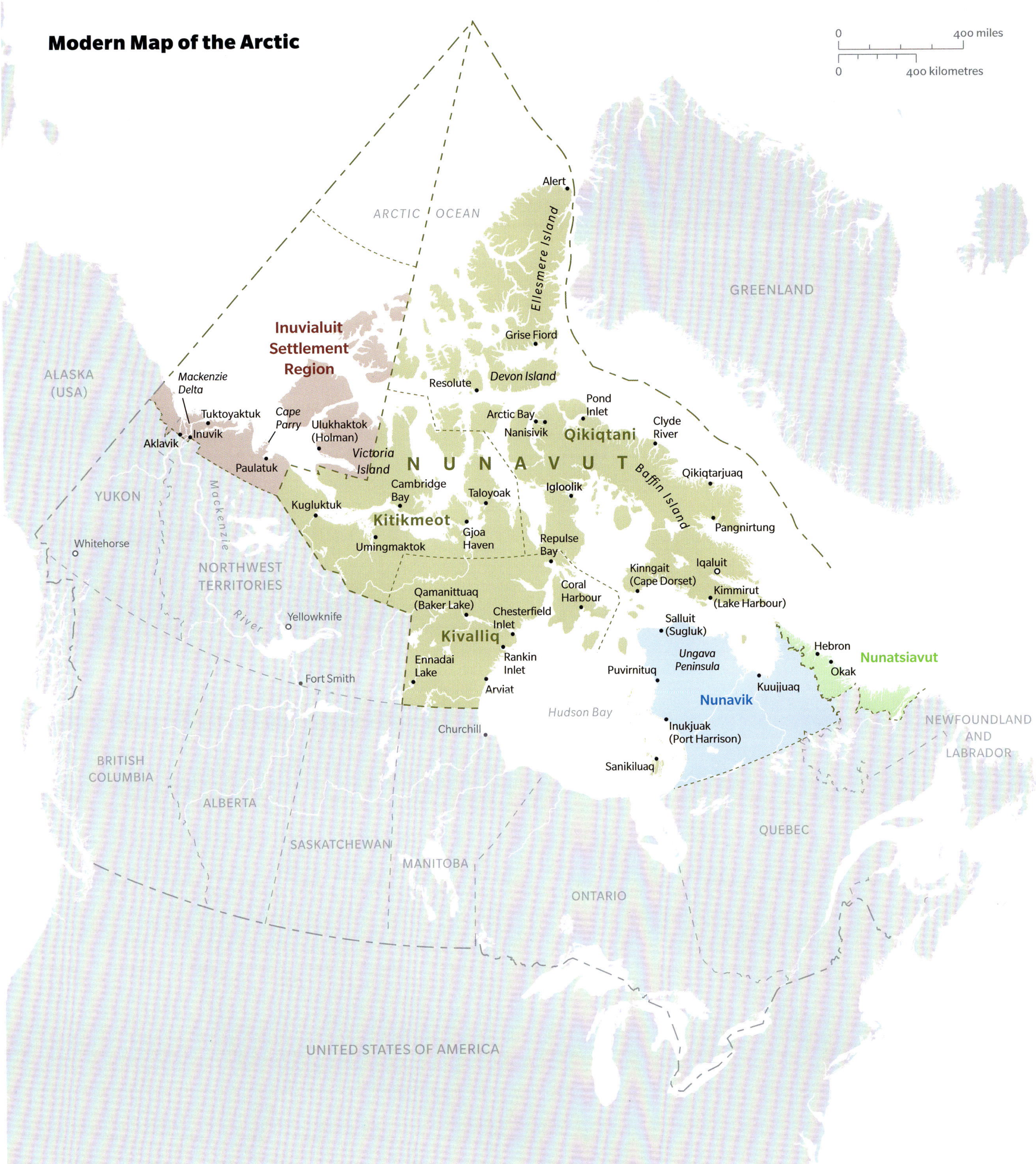

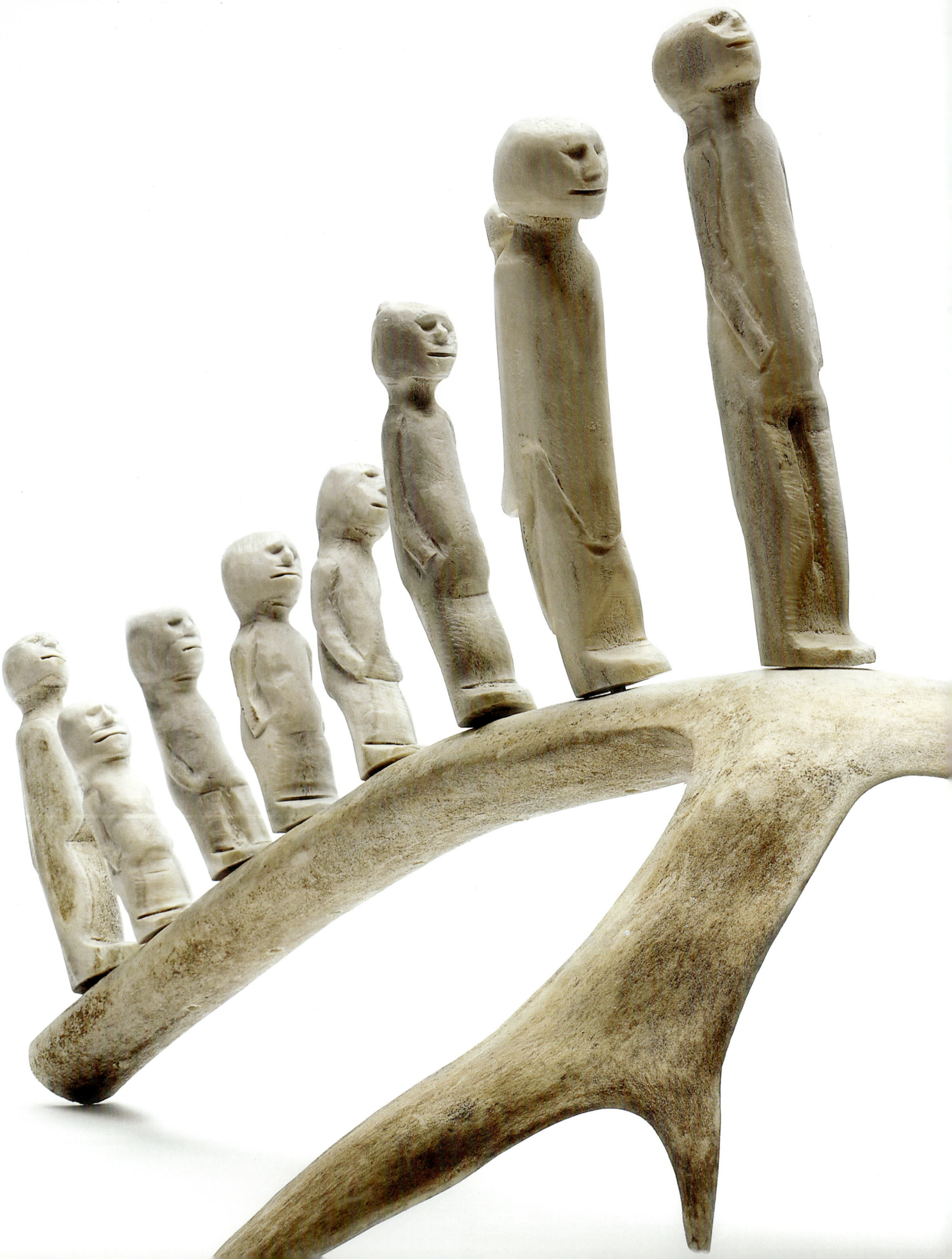

Inuit Modern

The Samuel and Esther Sarick Collection

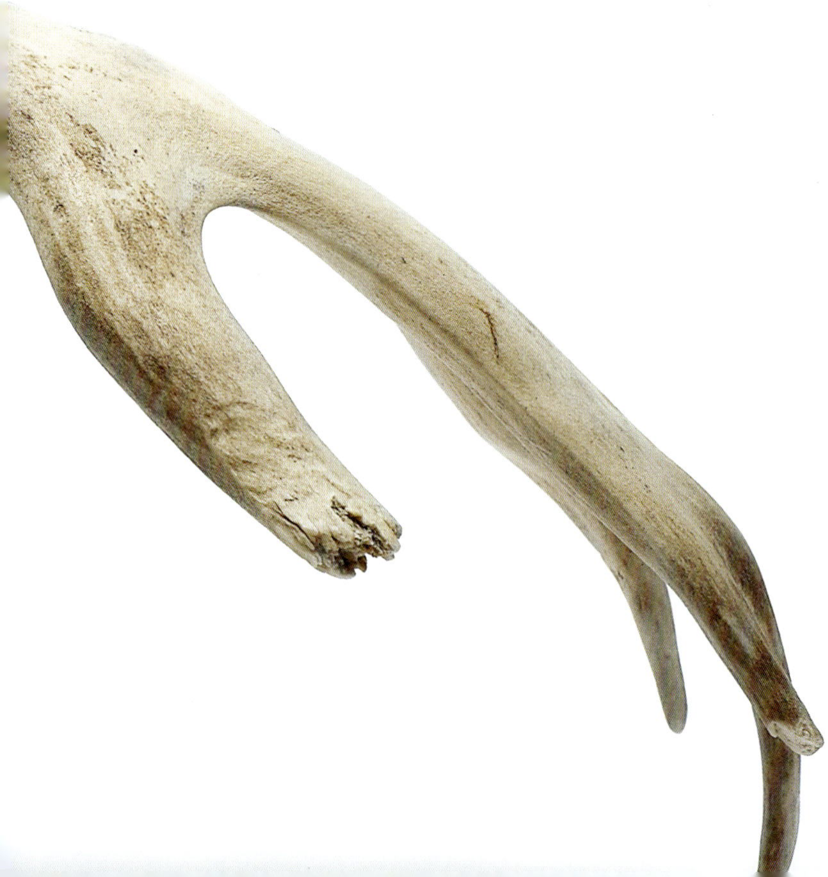

Poems

Alootook Ipellie

Walking Both Sides of an Invisible Border

It is never easy
Walking with an invisible border
Separating my left and right foot

I feel like an illegitimate child
Forsaken by my parents
At least I can claim innocence
Since I did not ask to come
Into this world

Walking on both sides of this
Invisible border
Each and every day
And for the rest of my life
Is like having been
Sentenced to a torture chamber
Without having committed a crime

Understanding the history of humanity
I am not the least surprised
This is happening to me
A non-entity
During this population explosion
In a minuscule world

I did not ask to be born an Inuk
Nor did I ask to be forced
To learn an alien culture
With an alien language
But I lucked out on fate
Which I am unable to undo

I have resorted to fancy dancing
In order to survive each day
No wonder I have earned
The dubious reputation of being
The world's premier choreographer
Of distinctive dance steps
That allow me to avoid
Potential personal paranoia
On both sides of this invisible border

Sometimes this border becomes so wide
That I am unable to take another step
My feet being too far apart
When my crotch begins to tear apart
I am forced to invent
A brand new dance step
The premier choreographer
Saving the day once more

Destiny acted itself out
Deciding for me where I would come from
And what I would become

So I am left to fend for myself
Walking in two different worlds
Trying my best to make sense
Of two opposing cultures
Which are unable to integrate
Lest they swallow one another whole

Each and every day
Is a fighting day
A war of raw nerves
And to show for my efforts
I have a fair share of wins and losses

When will all this end
This senseless battle
Between my left and right foot

When will the invisible border
Cease to be

The Great and Mysterious Northern Lights

I once heard my grandmother say:

If you ever see the northern lights at night,
Do not whistle once, or even twice, or more.
For if you do, they will come after you.

When you are passing through the porch
Of your home, they will, without a care
In the world, cut off your head and
Play ball with it in the dark, quiet night.

If you have ever seen them dancing up there,
They are restless and ready, if by chance
One night they will hear a whistle...
And then, with happy hearts, they will
Go after the person who had carelessly
Called them to get the ball.

Perhaps you have also seen the beautiful
Different colours they often show for you to see.
Those are conflicting colours of anger.

So, if you ever see the northern lights at night,
Never whistle once, or even twice, or more.
For if you do...

Laughing sounds echo throughout the igloo.
A sure sign of happiness among the throng.
With joyous hearts they devour the caribou.
The noise is sounding like a song.

Then...
The clock struck the midnight hour!
Heads rose from chests with virgin power!
Rushing legs swiftly run into the pitch darkness!
Not a single soul says a word of thankfulness!

Still...
The wind was soft, smooth and warm...

Thirty-four

It seemed easy to take advantage of the Eskimo savages
A desperate people stuck in the middle of nowhere
Always on the edge of certain starvation
Perhaps on the brink of extinction as a distinct people
At their most vulnerable
They were easy pickings for a colonial empire

Those Brits...
Having "discovered" and swallowed up as many new lands
As they could find in their global path

Then one day
They found themselves in an awkward situation:
Suddenly...
There were no more lands or peoples to conquer in the known world
What to do
But turn to the impoverished hunters and gatherers of the barren lands
Where they could get down to the level of the savages
And gradually penetrate the armourless Eskimo savages
And like the sleight of hand of the greatest magician of the world
Gingerly stripped the once proud savages

Not just their traditional garb
But also their psychological makeup

Was there no greater humiliation an individual could experience

The silent cultural holocaust made its way from camp to camp
Slowly brainwashing each individual savage Eskimo
Slowly changing his garb
Slowly changing his diet
Slowly changing his view of the greater world
Beyond the confines of the hunting camp

This is how we do things in this world
Pray like we do to the Almighty Goddess
Learn what we learn in our schools
This is how we view the world
This is our philosophy about life on Earth
Watch...
Do as we do
You will be a much better people for it

No...
No need to thank us...

Welcome to our roundabout world...

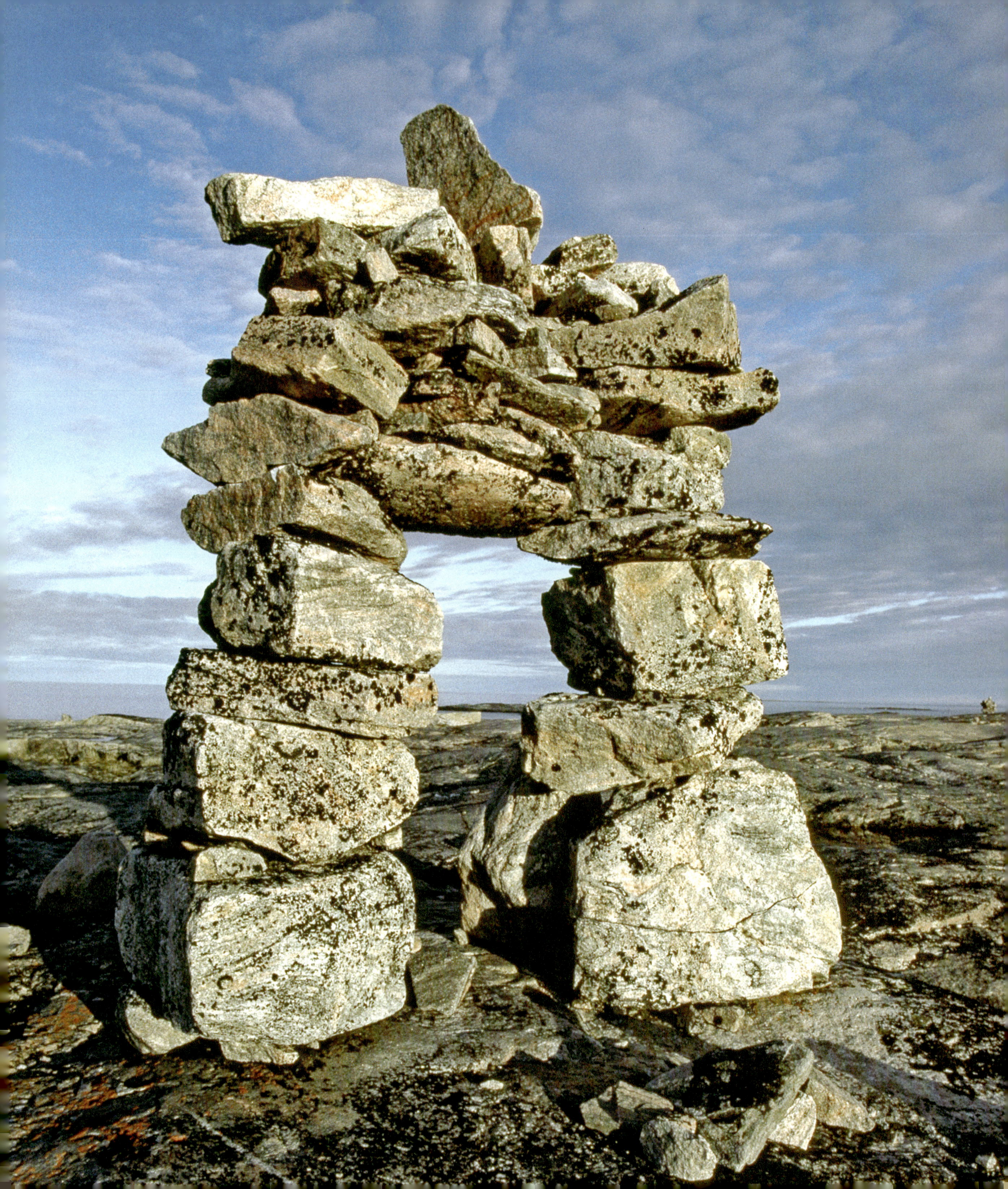

Art of the Historic Period
The Spirit of the Thule

Ingo Hessel

Recent writings by the Arctic archaeologist and historian Robert McGhee concerning ancestral and early Inuit history encourage us to adjust our ideas about the origins and development of Inuit and their art. Briefly, McGhee's premise is this: from their homeland in northern Alaska, the Thule ancestors of the Inuit quickly swept across Arctic Canada and reached northern Greenland by AD 1260; in the process they overran the Dorset/Tuniit people and probably plundered and/or traded with the Norse. The Thule/Inuit pursued commercial contacts with Europeans with increasing frequency from the sixteenth to the early twentieth centuries, always adjusting to newly acquired technologies.

In his essay "Inuit History, Inuit Art," McGhee not only posits a more recent arrival (c. mid-thirteenth century, as opposed to c. 1000, as has long been thought) and hence a more compact time frame for the Thule culture in the Canadian Arctic, but he also suggests a highly adaptive, trade-oriented, even entrepreneurial mindset for the Thule culture. McGhee's image of eighteenth- and nineteenth-century Inuit not as the remnants of Thule culture but rather as their highly mobile and adaptive descendants who, by their nature, enthusiastically—and on occasion even aggressively—sought out contact and commerce with outsiders, forces a re-evaluation of many of our dearly held notions about Inuit history, culture and art. As if that were not enough, my recent telephone conversation with McGhee, during which I voiced my reaction to his latest work, evinced his opinion that Inuit have been and are "just like us"—which I take to mean "just like any other people." This opinion (which he, quite rightly, sees as somewhat radical) is contrary to many decades of pronouncements about Inuit.

McGhee's revised time frame for the Thule occupation of Canada and his ideas concerning the Thule mindset are supported in part by recent archaeology and by advances in radiocarbon dating techniques. His second claim—that Inuit are in many ways just like the rest of us—is more contentious but, to me, has the ring of truth about it. Both assumptions help to explain some of the controversies and contradictions that have complicated the study of Inuit art.

I will use these ideas as new lenses through which to view the story of Inuit art. Moreover, since the intellectual framework that Gerald McMaster and I have created for this exhibition is also novel, I will in fact be looking at Inuit art through a new set of bifocals: that is, I am looking at Inuit art through an intellectual framework and at the same time viewing it through the archeological breakthroughs as described by McGhee. My underlying questions will be these: How did Inuit art evolve from a virtually anonymous souvenir art into an important school of contemporary Canadian art? Were Inuit passive participants in the Inuit art "project," or did they take an active role in shaping events and creating their destiny as artists? What are the attitudes—southern and Inuit—that, conscious or not, helped to define Inuit art over the past six decades? My answers will not be definitive or categorical—it is much easier to ask these questions than to answer them—but I think there is some value in re-evaluating our notions about the development of Inuit art and artists in the light of questions like these.

According to Renée Fossett,[1] the first century of written accounts of European exploration in the eastern

Arctic (from Martin Frobisher in the 1570s to about 1670) are replete with stories of Thule aggression against outsiders on the one hand and, on the other, an eagerness to trade for—or, alternatively, plunder—useful objects of European manufacture, particularly metal implements. She neatly describes the ambivalent attitude of the Thule (and then Inuit) toward Europeans, and toward their First Nations neighbours, as being rooted in the search for and protection of resources.

This pattern of behaviour persisted into the late eighteenth century and beyond. Naturally, Inuit in different regions of the Arctic had varying degrees of contact and trade with foreigners. For example, Labrador Inuit, feared by European settlers and fishermen because of their incessant raiding, were eventually colonized, in part influenced by permanent Moravian missions from the 1770s. Moravian missionaries and the later Grenfell missions[2] fostered arts and crafts production among Labrador Inuit.

Inuit across the Arctic had sporadic contact with explorers for much of the nineteenth century. Captain George Lyon's fascinating account of his Arctic voyage with Captain Parry (1821–23) contains this report of an encounter with the Inuit of northern Hudson Strait: "We soon had a large assemblage of canoes alongside our floe, and a most noisy but merry barter instantly took place: all of us anxious to purchase Eskimaux curiosities, as they were to procure iron and European toys."[3] And at Lyon Inlet in Hudson Bay: "In every family we found proof of some intercourse having existed with Europeans, although apparently through an intermediate channel; knives, tools, two large copper kettles, and beads having been met with..."[4] It should be noted that the Hudson's Bay Company (HBC) had established its first trading post at Churchill in 1685. In the nineteenth century, in addition to trade, abandoned exploration ships provided Inuit with rich sources of useful materials and goods.

Inuit contact with foreign whalers had an even more profound impact. Fossett describes early (mid-1820s) Inuit encounters with foreign whalers in Cumberland Sound (on eastern Baffin Island) as tense but goes on to state that by the 1830s, Inuit were attempting to lure whaling captains into Cumberland Sound by describing it as a rich whaling ground. She characterizes these actions as "a hedge against recurring hard times."[5] In the 1850s American and European whalers began wintering over and constructing land stations in the Canadian Arctic (see Dorothy Harley Eber's "The Start of Change," pp. 19–25). Up until the early decades of the twentieth century, commercial whaling provided extensive employment and trading opportunities to many Inuit groups.[6] Eber's essay describes the profound influence of whaling in some detail; her book *When the Whalers Were Up North: Inuit Memories from the Eastern Arctic* goes into even greater depth.[7] As whaling began to wane in the late nineteenth century, commercial fur trapping took its place as the primary economic activity in the Canadian Arctic.[8] The Hudson's Bay Company eventually swallowed up its competitors and exerted considerable control over the lives of the Inuit for the first half of the twentieth century.[9]

For more than a century and a half in the so-called Historic Period (the post-Thule but pre-modern period) of Inuit art (c. 1770s–1940s), explorers, whalers, missionaries and fur traders, and eventually also anthropologists and Canadian police and government administrators, bartered with Inuit for artifacts and artworks, mostly as souvenirs and curios but also sometimes for resale or for museum collections. At first these objects consisted of tools and weapons, clothing, toys, amulets, and so forth, made by Inuit for their own use. It is likely that very quickly, foreigners began commissioning objects (and showing off their own handiwork), and Inuit began creating new objects.[10] A new class of Inuit-made souvenir art object—primarily carved in ivory—emerged: model kayaks and sleds, sets of miniature animals, human and animal carvings (p. 56), camp scenes, cribbage boards (pp. 58–59), elaborately carved or engraved tusks, pipes and miniature implements and weapons (including replicas of European-style objects). Artworks in the Sarick Collection from this era that clearly reflect the deepening influence of outsiders and their technology on Inuit and their art include *Fox with Leg Trap* (p. 56), *Sailor* (p. 57) and *Whaling Ship* (p. 60).

It is interesting to note that some outsiders were interested in *any* art made by Inuit, even if it was a reflection of themselves rather than the typical ethnographic souvenir illustrating life in the Arctic.

One can only imagine the scene of "merry barter" repeated countless times during this period of post-contact Inuit history. The number of small carvings and more elaborate display objects made by Inuit specifically for trade with outsiders during the Historic Period—and now widely dispersed in collections in Europe, the United States and Canada—is no doubt in the many thousands. This might not be much smaller than the number of objects that would qualify as "traditional art objects" (amulets, toys, gaming pieces, shamanic implements) produced by Inuit for themselves (but often also traded away) in the same period. And since there were no specialist artists among Inuit (with the possible exception of shamans), many carvers were liable to have made both types of artworks. Consequently, the two types of art—"indigenous," personal, often stylized and sometimes magical, versus "prompted," commercial, increasingly naturalistic and almost always secular—probably influenced each other in style, function and format.[11]

It has been generally assumed that for the most part, the Qallunaat who collected these works viewed them as little more than trinkets and curios, quaint but primitive. And it has been likewise assumed that for their part, the ever-pragmatic Inuit makers probably viewed their creations as simply another trading commodity. The late Eric Anoee, a respected Anglican deacon, scholar, elder and sometime artist from Arviat, offered up this assessment in 1982: "Because figures of people and animal carvings were merely objects to look at, they were not as important to the Inuit as tools."[12] Nevertheless I would suggest that we formulate some new assumptions: that Historic Period carvings were made with skill and pride, in the spirit of entrepreneurship; and that they were collected with considerable appreciation and delight. It is quite likely that the sometimes condescending accounts of nineteenth-century Arctic travellers do not accurately reflect the real pleasure that a beautifully decorated cribbage board, or animal figurine, or miniature rifle would have afforded the average whaler, fur trader or other visitor.

In *The Labrador Eskimo,* the anthropologist E.W. Hawkes considered the form and finish of Labrador ivory carvings to "excel the other eastern tribes and more nearly approach the ambitious work of the Alaskan Eskimo."[13] He also noted that Labrador Inuit paralleled almost all of their ivory carving in wood. In his memoirs (which cover the years 1923–39), the HBC trader A. Dudley Copland ("Coplalook") recalls the work of Isaacie ("a master carver") and others from Port Harrison (Inukjuak). "I admired the early work I saw in ivory and soapstone, and purchased many carvings of polar bears and other arctic animals to send home to my family."[14] The tiny community of Lake Harbour (Kimmirut) on Baffin Island was renowned as an ivory-carving centre in the 1930s and 1940s;[15] the HBC factor in Sugluk (Salluit), Quebec, purchased 100 to 150 ivory carvings a year between 1939 and 1941.[16]

Obviously, Inuit were ready and able to make excellent work in the first half of the twentieth century and had no lack of appreciative buyers.[17] It was likely difficulties in material supply and distribution that stymied the efforts of the Canadian Handicrafts Guild and the Hudson's Bay Company to market Inuit carvings and other crafts in southern Canada in the 1920s, 1930s and 1940s.[18] Also during this period, some thoughtful federal government officials realized the potential for handicrafts production to alleviate poverty and suffering among Inuit.[19] Fur trading was definitely the top commercial priority in the Canadian Arctic during this period, but there was always some level of interest in arts production.[20] Roman Catholic and Anglican missionaries in Pelly Bay (Kugaaruk), Chesterfield Inlet, Repulse Bay, Pangnirtung and elsewhere actively encouraged carvers in the late Historic Period, as had their Moravian colleagues along the northern Labrador coast. The Diocese of Churchill–Hudson Bay had collected enough artworks and artifacts to establish a small museum in Churchill, Manitoba, in 1944 (now the Eskimo Museum, which houses one of the finest collections of Inuit art in the country).[21]

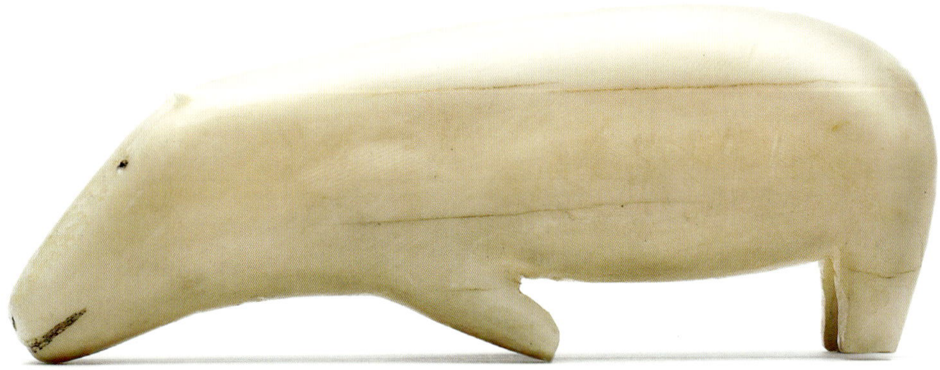

Unknown Artist, *Bear*, early 1900s, ivory, colouring, 2.9 x 2.1 x 8.1 cm

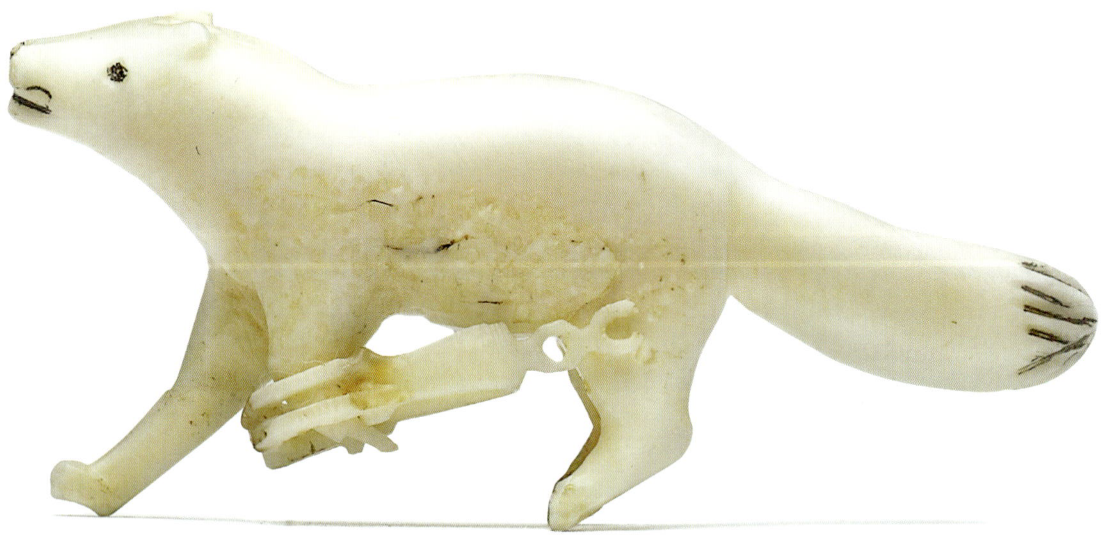

Unknown Artist, Eastern Arctic, *Fox with Leg Trap*, 1941–42, ivory, colouring, 2.5 x 1.1 x 6.4 cm

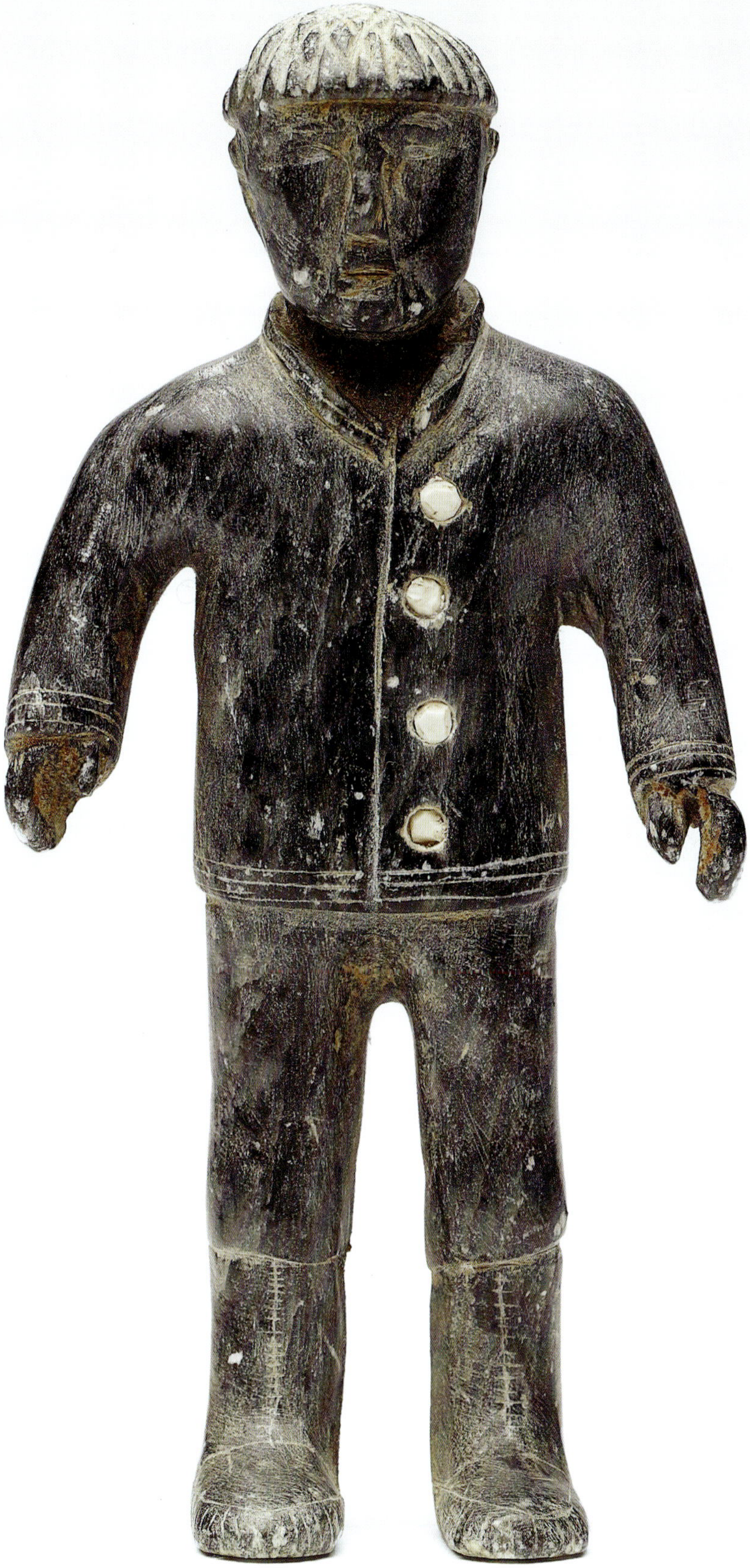

Unknown Artist, *Sailor*, 1900–1925, stone, ivory, 12.5 x 6.0 x 2.5 cm

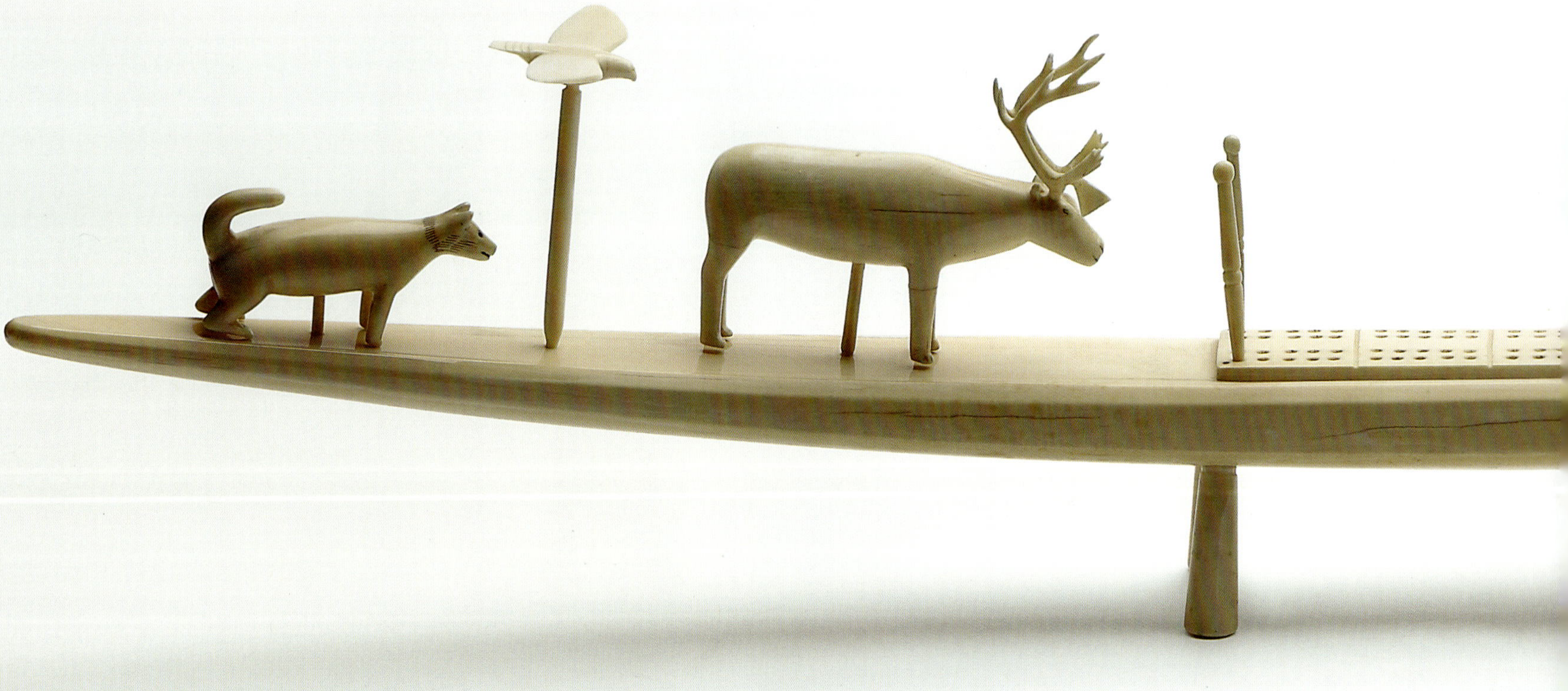

Koviak, *Cribbage Board*, 1942–45, ivory, stone inlay, 16.6 x 87.3 x 11.7 cm

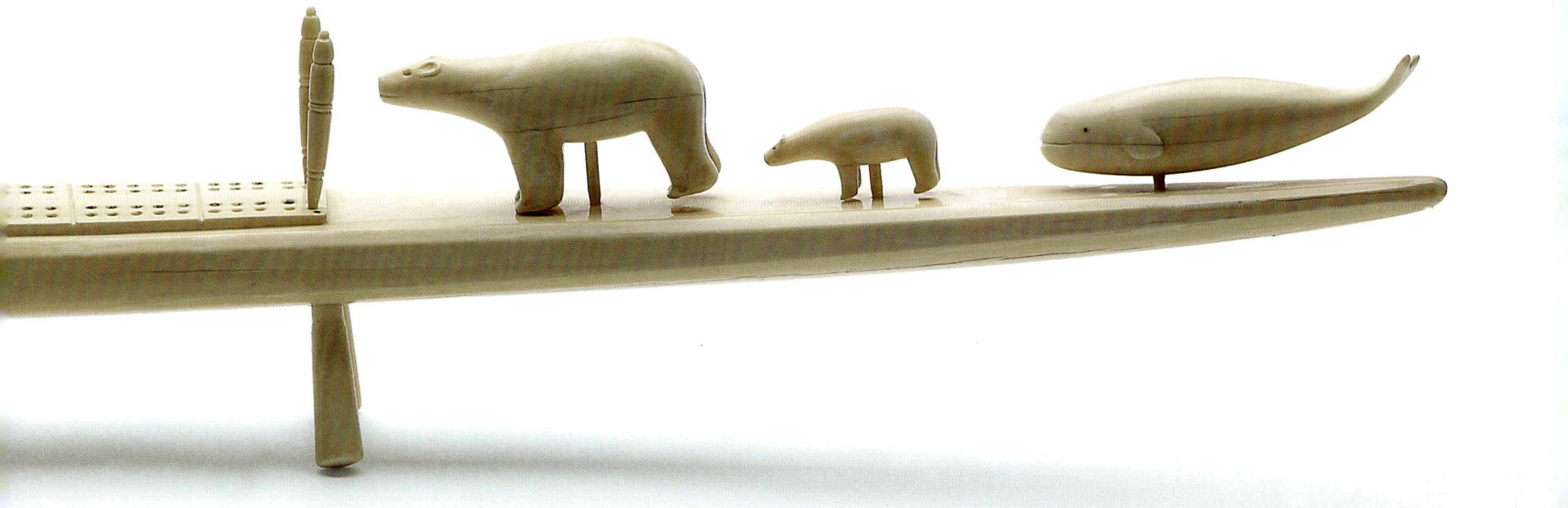

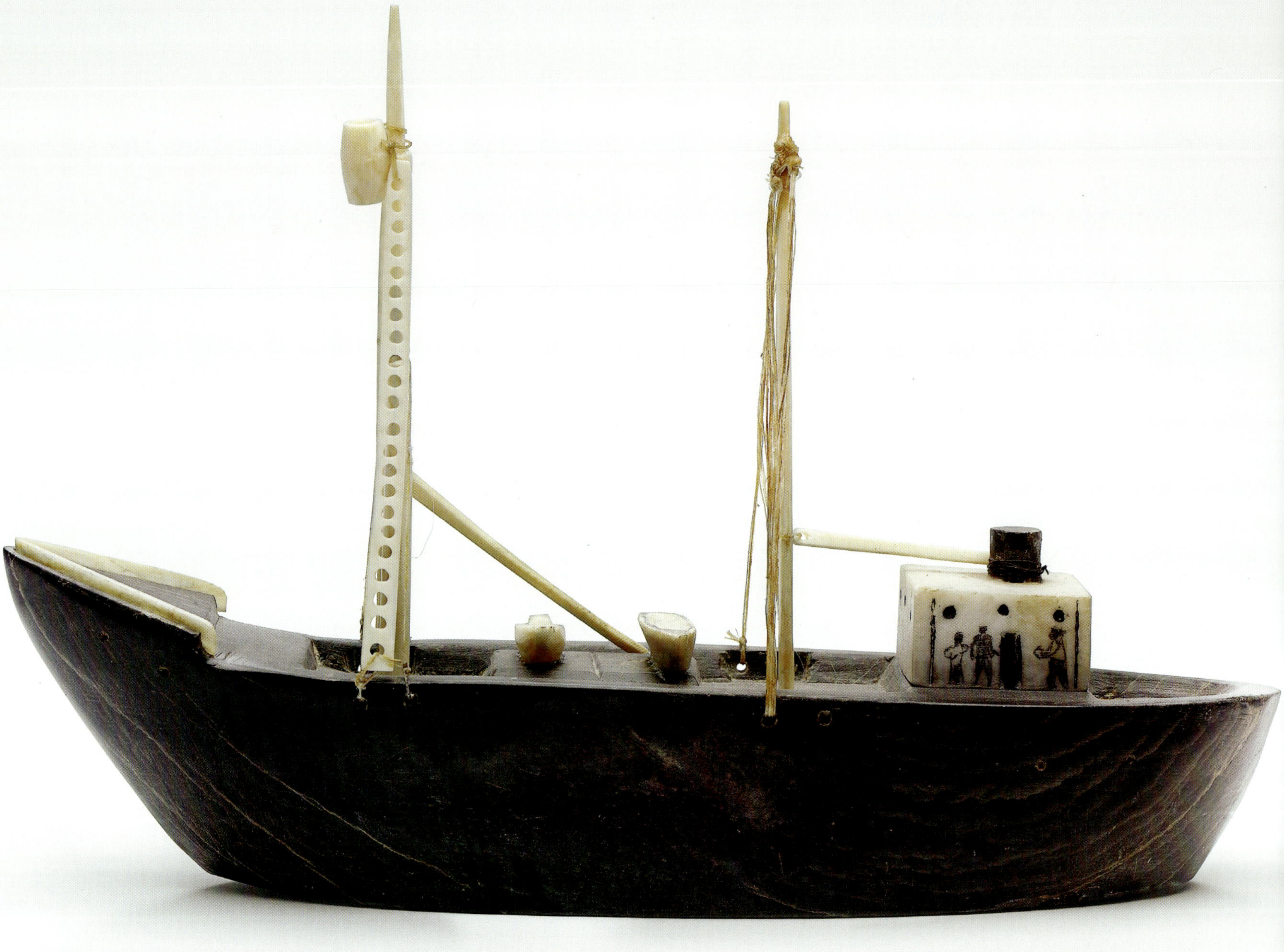

Josephee Angnako, *Whaling Ship*, c. 1950,
stone, ivory, sinew, thread, pigment, 17.5 x 25.7 x 5.8 cm

The World Rediscovers "Eskimos"
A New Art Is Born

Ingo Hessel

At the end of the Historic Period (1948)[1] the world still knew relatively little about "Eskimos" and certainly nothing of "Eskimo art." As the pioneer Inuit art collector Ian Lindsay wrote, "Eskimos were often thought of as being some sort of Indian (when they were thought of at all), who dwelt in igloos and travelled by dogsled in a cold, inhospitable, and remote land. And that was about the sum of it."[2] When the young artist James Houston "discovered" Eskimo carvings at Port Harrison (Inukjuak) in Arctic Quebec in the summer of 1948 and met excitedly with the Handicrafts Guild in Montreal later that year, he was completely unaware of the almost two-hundred-year history of souvenir-art production and "merry barter" in Canada's Arctic and of the efforts of the Guild and others to develop and market Eskimo crafts.

The far-reaching results of that meeting—namely the development of modern Inuit art; its promotion, beginning with the famous sale at the Canadian Handicrafts Guild in November 1949; and its evolution as a major Canadian art form—have been well documented. It is always useful, however, to recall some of the events of this early period, both in the light of the prevailing attitudes of the time concerning Inuit and their art and in the hindsight of history. Something worth emphasizing here is that it is somewhat of a miracle that the "Eskimo art project" ever got off the ground at all. The considerable skepticism with which many greeted the very idea of soliciting and marketing Eskimo arts and crafts might have stopped the venture in its tracks.[3] And perhaps (as might be inferred from early correspondence between federal officials and the Handicrafts Guild), the Guild just barely prevented "Eskimo art" from becoming a dull crafts industry that would have scarcely merited a footnote in the history of Canadian art.[4] After working closely with the Guild for years, the federal government stopped giving it grants in 1953. Houston was hired on as a civil servant; the government had ideas about incorporating arts and crafts development into a larger "industrial" strategy for the Arctic.[5] Houston himself had commented on the "industrial" potential of "Eskimo" handicrafts as early as 1951. Perhaps he was playing up that aspect of art production as a way of garnering support for it; also, he truly believed (or hoped) that it would "in no way disturb [the Eskimo's] present way of life."[6]

We have James Houston to thank for the earliest written impressions of early modern Inuit art. Houston was a born storyteller, as was later revealed in his more than twenty books for children and adults. Houston's early magazine articles and promotional booklets were based on first-hand knowledge working with and living among Inuit and as such, gave many readers their first glimpse of the Inuit way of life and Inuit creativity. However, they also reveal an unabashed enthusiasm that sometimes led to embellishment of the truth.[7] Houston wrote the influential article "In Search of Contemporary Eskimo Art" for *Canadian Art* in 1952; the article inspired the British art dealer Charles Gimpel to request an exhibition at his gallery in London.[8] In the article Houston flirted with romanticism by suggesting that the new carvings might still be made to "bring good fortune in hunting."[9] The 1954 promotional publication *Canadian Eskimo Art*[10] (which, inexplicably, was kept in print with no changes in text for more than two decades)[11] repeats this suggestion; in this booklet Houston also stated, "Even today, after more than a century of exposure to European culture, this primitive art persists, original, creative and virile." In the same booklet, he stated that because "the

Eskimos had few materials with which to create works of art... they turned to the stones of their land, from which they were compelled to fashion their tools, as a medium for artistic expression," when he himself was encouraging Inuit to carve in stone because there was no longer enough ivory to keep up with southern demand.[12]

The latter statement, although partly based in fact, helped to perpetuate the notion that Eskimos were a Stone Age people, when in fact the Alaskan Old Bering Sea culture had marked the end of that era some two thousand years earlier (see "Inuit History, Inuit Art" by Robert McGhee, pp. 12–17). The February 27, 1956, *Life* magazine article in its "Epic of Man" series was accompanied by photos of Ennadai Lake Caribou Inuit in skin clothing, under the title "A Mesolithic Age Today."[13] Featured in the photos are the future artists Luke Anowtalik and his wife, Mary Ayaq, and their infant son. Interestingly, the 1961 book *The Epic of Man* includes a similar photo spread, followed by a short article with a photo of one of the Inuit women (possibly Ayaq's mother, Elizabeth Nutaraaluk Aulatjut wearing a dress and jacket.[14] The staged presentation of "primitive Eskimos" in the articles is in the spirit of Robert Flaherty's classic 1922 silent documentary *Nanook of the North*.

What possibly spurred *Life* magazine's interest in the Ihalmiut (Caribou Inuit) was the publication of Farley Mowat's controversial 1952 bestseller *People of the Deer*. The front flap of the American edition states that Mowat describes how the intrusion of outsiders "has driven these primitive folk to the verge of extinction."[15] Mowat's books popularized a belief already held by many specialists; according to the distinguished Canadian anthropologist Diamond Jenness, much of Inuit culture had already been "completely shattered" before 1920.[16]

The stereotypical view of Inuit that evolved in the 1950s both coloured the perception of Inuit art and was in turn reinforced by it. The image of a happy, stoic, peaceful[17] race, barely emerged from the Stone Age, threatened by modern civilization, on our very northern doorstep, was immensely appealing to Canada's still-forming identity as a northern power and as a multicultural society with an exotic yet homegrown Aboriginal component.[18] The images of a hunter patiently waiting at a seal breathing-hole (p. 69) or stalking a polar bear; the mother with a child snug in her capacious hood (p. 66); the snarling bear (p. 71)—surely these had deep roots in time immemorial.

To many viewers these images seemed to spring from a collective unconscious. Even some anthropologists fell into the trap of forming a romantic impression of an anonymous, generic Inuit world view.[19] As late as 1973, Edmund Carpenter pronounced that Inuit had no sense of individualism.[20] Already in 1952, Houston had asserted the very opposite: "We are aware of the Eskimos' proud sense of individualism."[21] The Inuit art scholar George Swinton agreed with Houston: "The success of contemporary Eskimo art—with its largely individual (rather than collective) character—depends mostly on individual form and not on collective style."[22] But as early as 1957 Swinton had begun to develop his typically nuanced view of things, taking into account the complexity of the situation. Although he acknowledged earlier "collective" styles, he proposed that early modern Inuit art was actually at its most individualistic when it first started and suggested that the rapid development of regional styles in the 1950s was proof of increasingly repetitive work.[23]

The art historian Janet Berlo also refuted Carpenter's claim: "A blindness to individuality and creativity under conditions different to our own has been one of the fictions of western culture and western scholarship."[24] To be fair to Carpenter, the Inuit sense of individualism might have been considerably different from that of the Euro-American, which in recent times has been fairly pronounced; for him to declare that it was non-existent strikes me as far-fetched. As art historian Christine Lalonde put it, "given the small scale of Inuit society, it might be more reasonable to assume that individuals had a *greater* sense of self than those born into the anonymous Western masses."[25]

Swinton pointed out the dangers of viewing Inuit art through an anthropological or ethnological lens;[26] he clearly saw the danger in "primitivizing" the art and the people who made it, for failing to understand the culture properly and for overlooking the importance of acculturation as a force in Inuit society and art. Swinton viewed this acculturation not as "passive" but rather as "unquestionably dynamic."[27] The art historian Charlotte Townsend-Gault has called the prevailing idea that Inuit culture had never before changed "a convenient fiction."[28] Swinton was correct in assuming that the general public might easily fall into—or had to some extent already fallen into—this romantic primitivizing trap. Swinton himself, in 1957, still referred to the earliest modern Inuit works as "a genuinely primitive art form" that he saw as having quickly morphed into a "newer phase" characterized by the artists' increasing consciousness and premeditation.[29] Swinton had every reason to worry; in 1959, and reiterated in 1973, Carpenter was making comments like this one: "As the carver holds the unworked ivory lightly in his hand, turning it this way and that, he whispers, 'Who are you! Who hides there!' And then: 'Ah, Seal!'... Then he brings it out: Seal, hidden, emerges. It was always there: he did not create it, he released it; he helped it step forth."[30] This, coming from an anthropologist, rivals anything that James Houston might have dreamed up! In Houston's 1954 article "Contemporary Art of the Eskimo" in the British art magazine *The Studio,* he labelled Inuit art primitive, implied that Inuit artists carved for their own enjoyment (but admitted that they were now feeling the benefit of sales), stated that "the link between past and present in their art remains as yet unbroken" and pondered the questions, "What motivates this man? What inner spring of consciousness demands an art of him? Perhaps it is a clinging remnant of a forgotten civilization of the Asiatic continent where he almost certainly originated."[31] The anthropologist Charles Martijn aptly described this kind of thinking and writing about Inuit and Inuit art as "the sham facade of primitiveness."[32]

For their part, Inuit artists have rarely if ever taken part in the discussion of these issues. These are outsiders' quibbles and quandaries, not theirs. With great pragmatism, Inuit artists in the 1950s either carried on with materials, styles, formats and themes already developed in the Historic Period or happily experimented with new materials, tools and themes as they were suggested or offered. The controversial 1951 instructional booklet *Sanajaqsaq (Eskimo Handicrafts)*—already recommended by federal officials to the Guild in the fall of 1949—is a case in point.[33] Using 1940s Alaska Native Arts and Crafts booklets as models, James Houston wrote and illustrated a thirty-two-page booklet (translated into Inuktitut) giving explicit directions for making carvings and other "crafts" such as baskets, kamiks and mitts, games and tools. These included tips on the proper choice of materials and careful craftsmanship but sometimes went further, counselling Inuit to fashion or compose works in specific ways to make them more saleable. Widely circulated (mostly in Arctic Quebec) and rapidly withdrawn a few years later, the booklet spawned many quirky, imitative carvings and functional objects. What is seldom realized is the preponderance of illustrations of crafts and functional objects in this publication; they outnumbered those of carvings by two to one. This would suggest that the booklet had a far greater influence on crafts production than on carving. Perhaps its lasting impact, in the end, was in spurring arts and crafts production across the Arctic.[34] The charming pair of ivories, *Woman Holding Ulu* and *Man with Snow Knife* by an unidentified Inukjuak carver, dating from c. 1954 (p. 66), might or might not have been inspired by a drawing by Houston on page 3 of his booklet; the *Figure and Animal Totem* attributed to Amidlak (p. 65) shows the booklet's influence more obviously, since no Inuit artist would otherwise have been aware of Northwest Coast totem poles.

The 1951 booklet was superseded in 1953 by *Senangoat,* a smaller manual that contained eleven drawings of carvings only and which, while obviously suggesting a range of formats and themes, recommended that artists make original, high-quality works.[35] Houston's 1954 *Canadian Eskimo Art* (illustrated with almost forty photographs—mostly sculptures, and a few crafts) may have had an even greater impact in this regard;

Houston stated in his first memoir[36] that the booklet was distributed to every Inuit family in Canada. Both of these later publications were potentially more influential than the 1951 instructional manual.[37]

In the final analysis, though, the factor with the most influence, on subject matter and on quality, was direct communication between artists and advisers (Houston and eventually others) and local buyers. Sometimes this took the form of direct suggestion; at other times it was "not by direct suggestion, but by the more subtle and more effective method of paying most for the best work."[38] But Houston insisted in 1954 that "Eskimos regard originality to be of utmost importance."[39] In all likelihood, the better artists initially listened to advice and noted what sold well but eventually chose their own favourite media and themes and developed their own styles, whereas many lesser talents followed outside influence more closely and produced souvenir-style work; a good number of the latter group probably ceased production after a few experiments. As George Swinton put it, "One of the continuing miracles of the current art renaissance is that the inuit [*sic*] artists are flexible enough to reject as much as to accept what we have to offer."[40]

An interesting shift occurred in 1952 with a new emphasis on art as opposed to handicrafts production and marketing. This coincided with the switch from ivory to stone as the primary carving medium (p. 66).[41] Significantly, it also came on the heels of James and Alma Houston's trip to Cape Dorset in 1951; Houston was very impressed by the work of carvers such as Kiugak Ashoona and Osuitok Ipeelee (p. 67). Exhibitions of "Eskimo Art" in the early 1950s, including shows at the National Gallery of Canada in Ottawa (1952) and at Gimpel Fils in London (1953),[42] reinforced this shift in nomenclature, as did a flurry of articles by Houston in art magazines. Expanding the market to the United States (Eskimo Art, Inc. in Ann Arbor, Michigan) and Great Britain (Gimpel Fils) made up for the fact that supply was beginning to exceed demand in Canada. The Gimpel show received rave reviews in the British press.[43]

To give Houston his full due, he was not merely a promoter; his enthusiasm was grounded in his appreciation, as a fellow artist, of the quality and novelty of the artworks being produced—and these works of art were being created, to a large extent, as the result of his development efforts (augmented, of course, by the efforts of many others at the Guild, the Hudson's Bay Company and the Canadian government).[44] The shift from handicraft to art status would not have succeeded through clever promotion alone; obviously, the most talented Inuit artists were finding their personal voices and styles, gaining confidence and refining their skills.[45] Swinton said that the new art of the mid-1950s should be called "sculpture," not because of any presumed quality (and Swinton had strong views on this matter), but rather because of its larger scale and its new function as an art commodity and because of the new objectives of the artists themselves—namely the "individual's ability to transform experience into art," increasing technical perfection, and the idea of art as communication of ideas.[46] To illustrate this point, compare two works: the small carving *Mother and Child,* c. 1950, by an unknown artist from Inukjuak or Puvirnituq (p. 66), and Isa (Aqiattusuk) Smiler's 1953 impressive *Seated Mother with Child*, from Inukjuak (p. 84).

Houston noted: "There seem to be two schools of thought among the Eskimo artists: one man will carve with infinite care, his sculpture showing the finest details; the next man will create on a much wider plane, merely suggesting the details while concentrating on the form and movement."[47] Swinton wrote that only the weaker carvings resembled each other closely, whereas the best works demonstrated strong personal styles.[48] A few individual artists were being recognized in the mid-1950s—Akeeaktashuk and Johnny Inukpuk from Inukjuak, and Osuitok Ipeelee from Cape Dorset are three early examples. Akeeaktashuk's style and range of subject matter extended beyond his iconic (if rather static and stereotypical) "Eskimo hunters" (p. 69), but his career was cut short by an early death. Osuitok Ipeelee's illustrious career was to last five decades; his early stone sculptures profited from the finesse gained from his ivory carving. Even so, it would be some years before there was a widespread appreciation of individual Inuit artists.

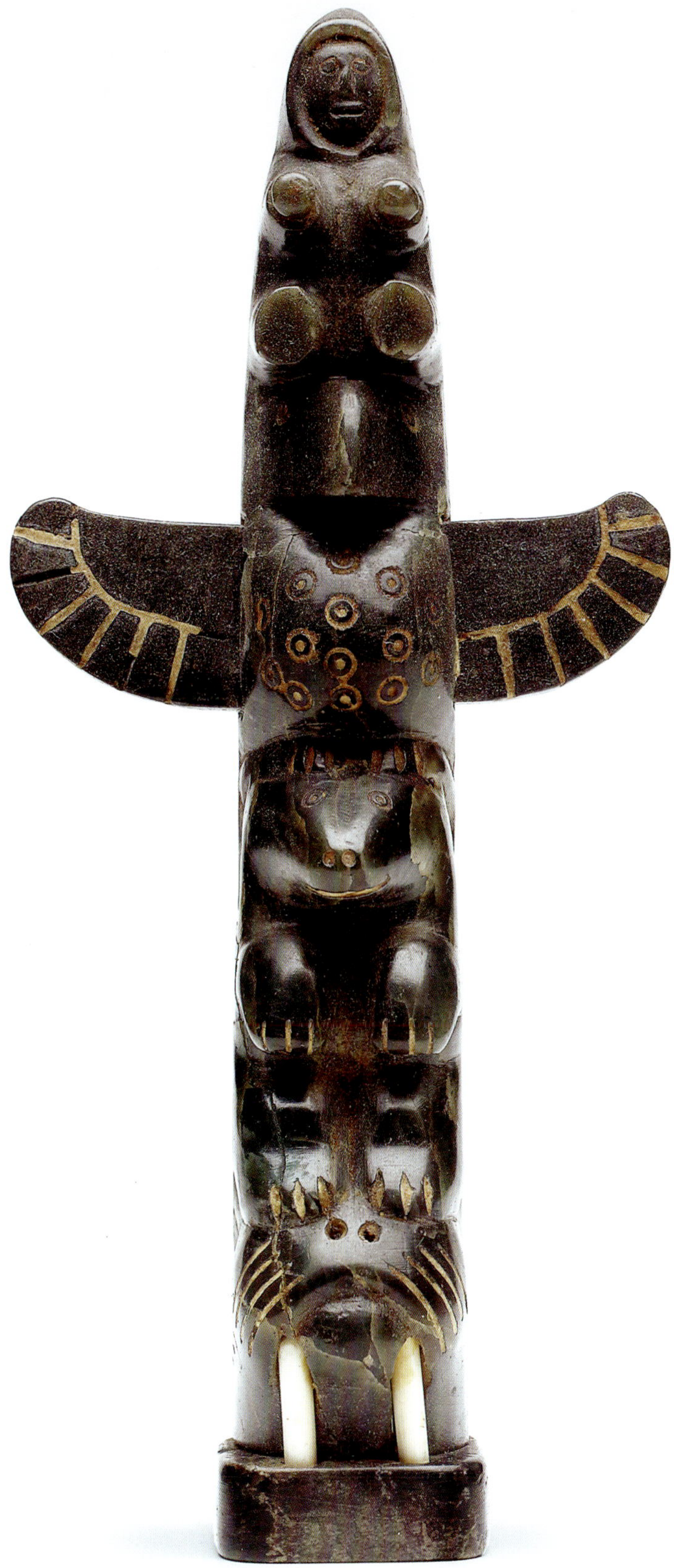

Amidlak, *Figure and Animal Totem*, 1951–55, stone, ivory, colouring, 21.4 x 9.4 x 4.4 cm

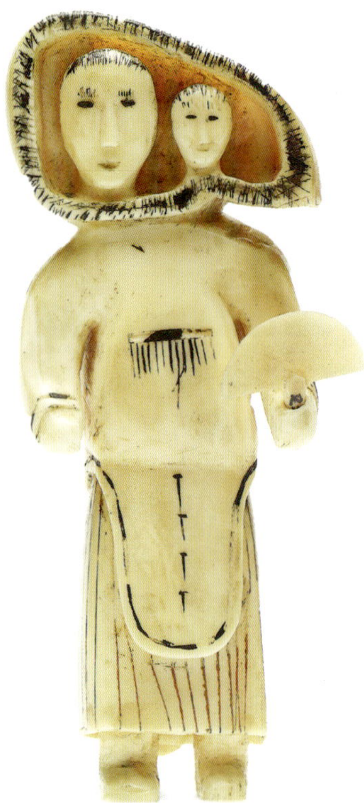

Unknown Artist, Inukjuak, *Woman Holding Ulu*, c. 1954, ivory, colouring, 11.0 x 4.0 x 3.0 cm

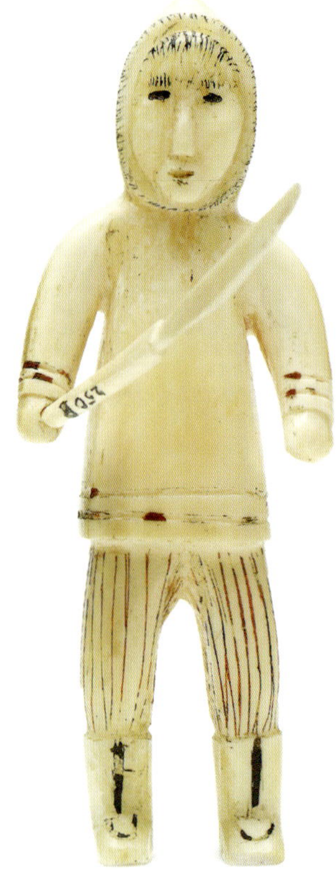

Unknown Artist , Inukjuak, *Man with Snow Knife*, c. 1954, ivory, colouring, 10.5 x 4.5 x 6.0 cm

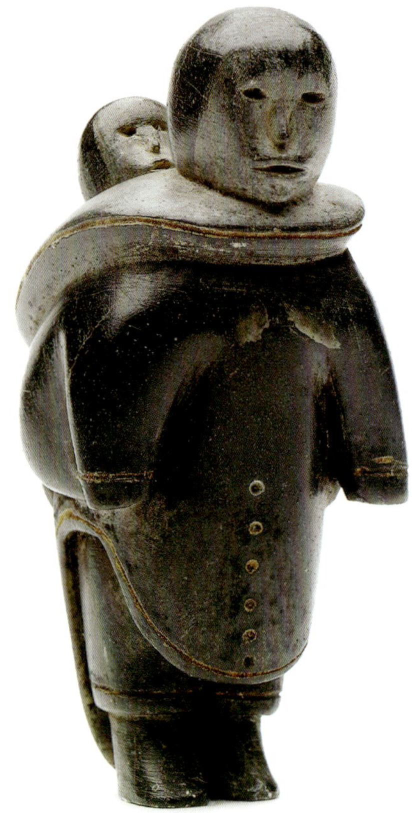

Unknown Artist , Inukjuak, *Mother and Child*, 1948–53, stone, colouring, 11.0 x 6.0 x 5.3 cm

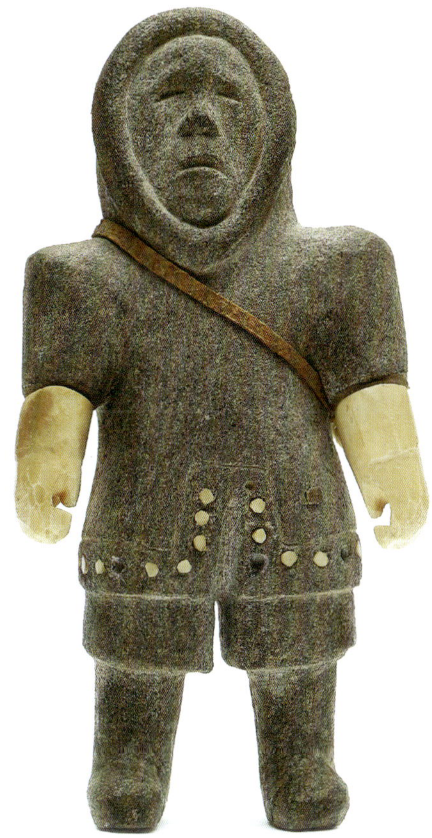

Toonoo, *Man*, before 1959, stone, ivory, hide, 15.4 x 8.6 x 8.0 cm

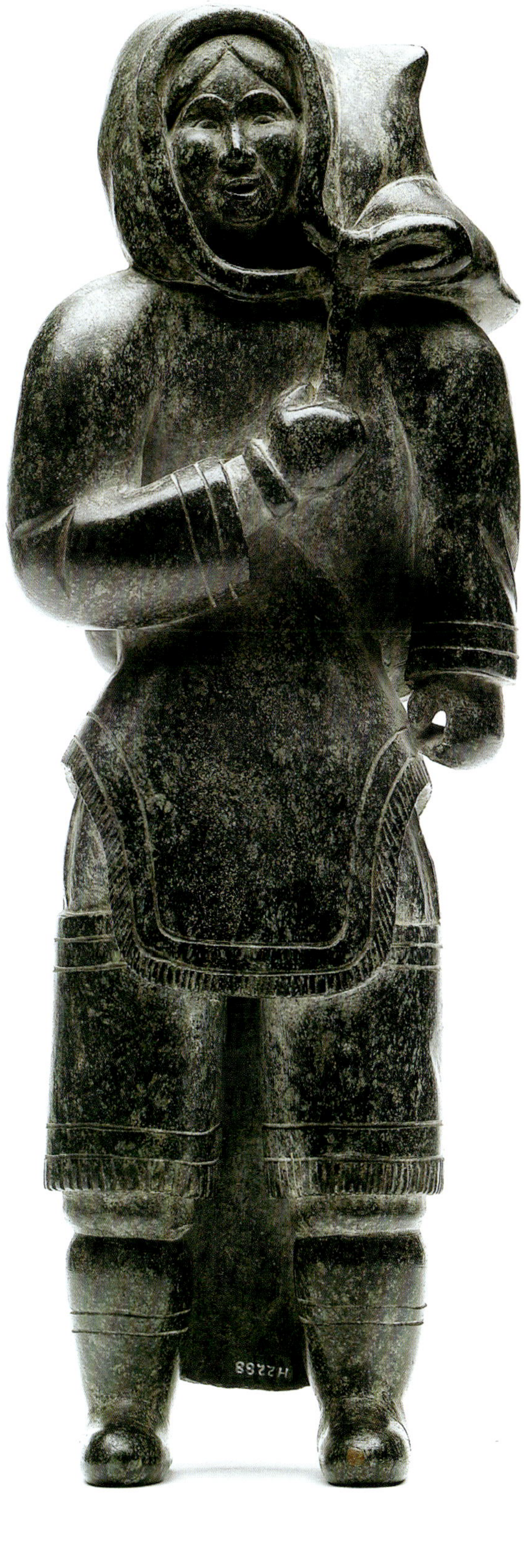

Osuitok Ipeelee, *Woman*, c. 1957, stone, 32.1 x 11.4 x 6.8 cm

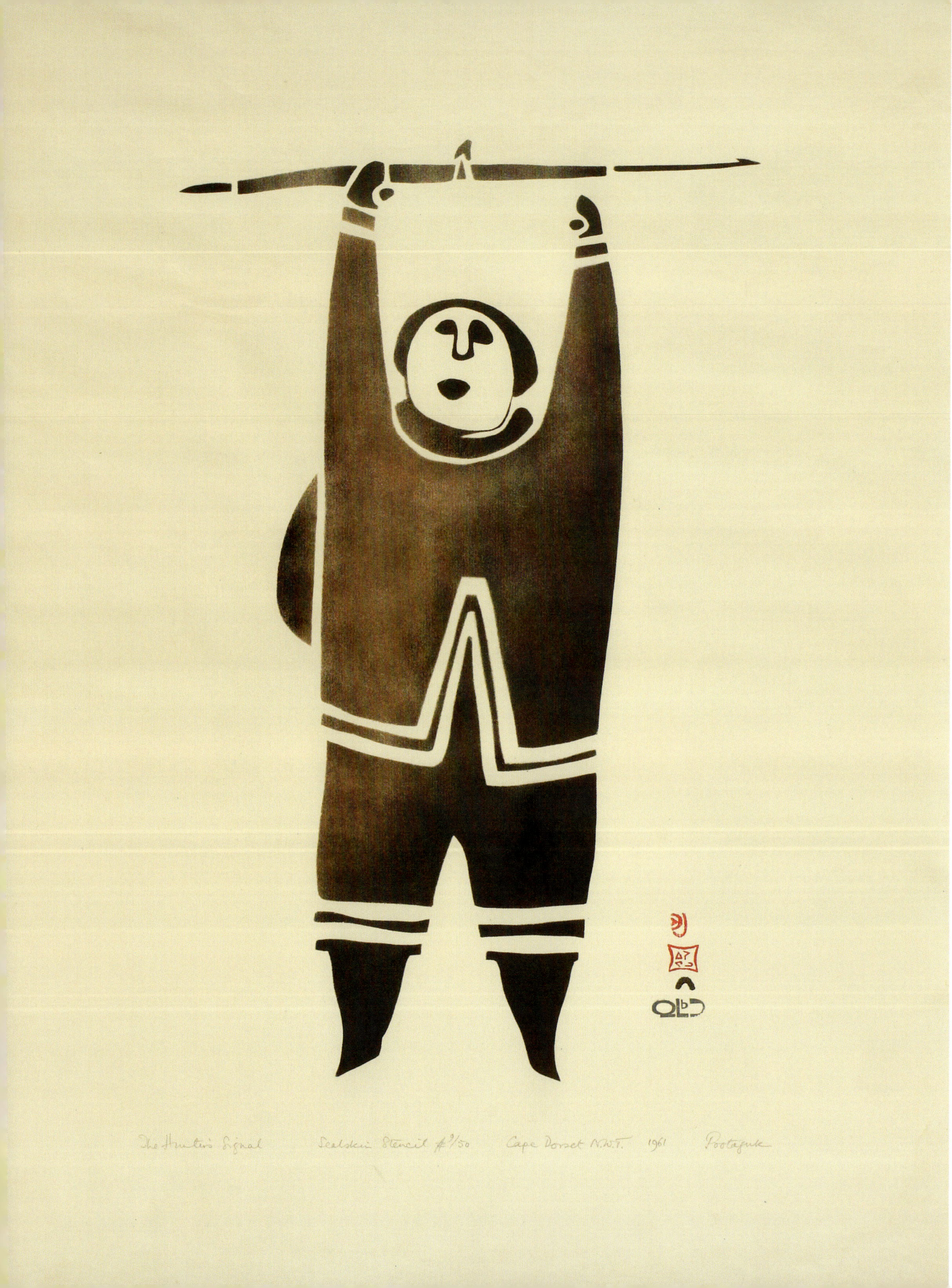
The Hunter's Signal
Sealskin Stencil # 9/50
Cape Dorset N.W.T.
1961
Pootagok

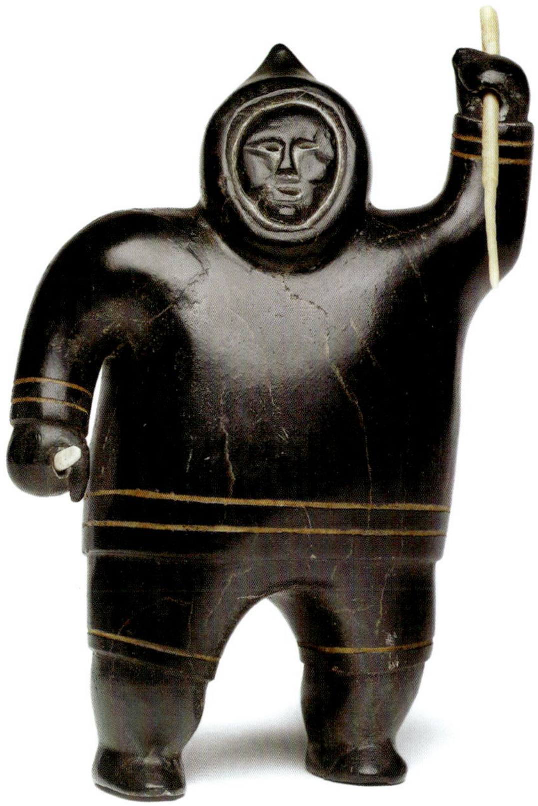

Akeeaktashuk, *Hunter*, before 1954,
stone, ivory, inlay, 17.5 x 13.0 x 8.0 cm (without harpoon)

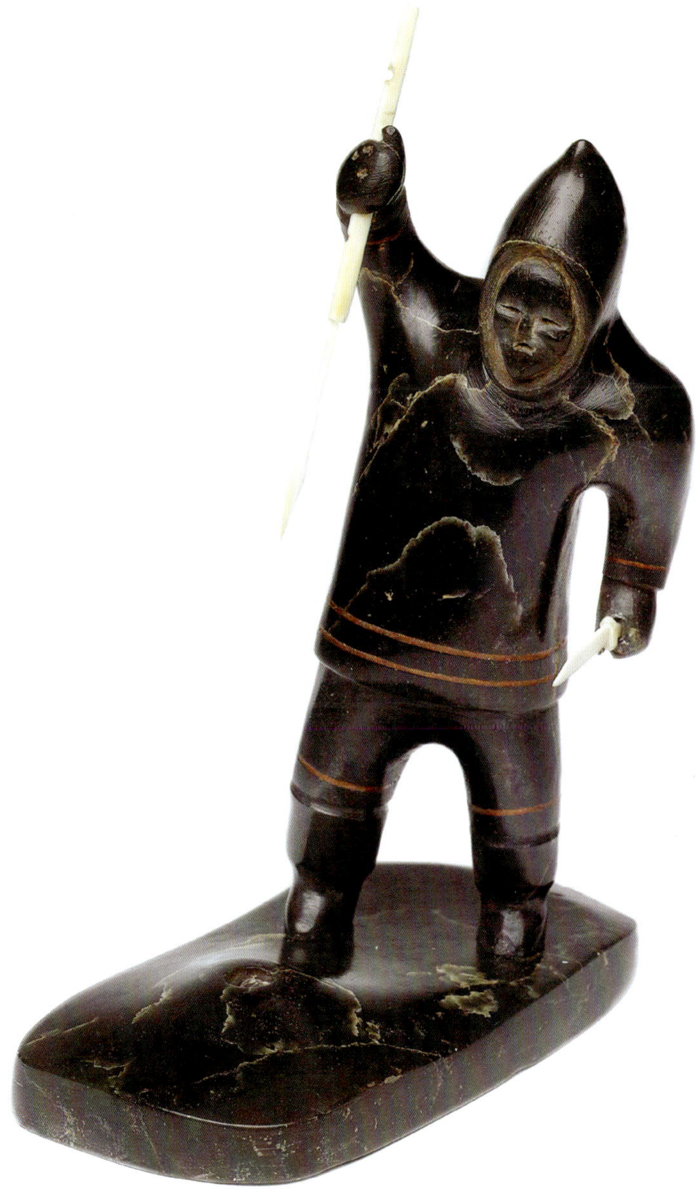

Akeeaktashuk, *Seal Hunter*, before 1954,
stone, bone, inlay, 23.5 x 10.6 x 16.4 cm

Left: **Josephie Pootoogook**, *The Hunter's Signal*, 1961,
stencil on paper (posthumous print) 63.7 x 48.4 cm

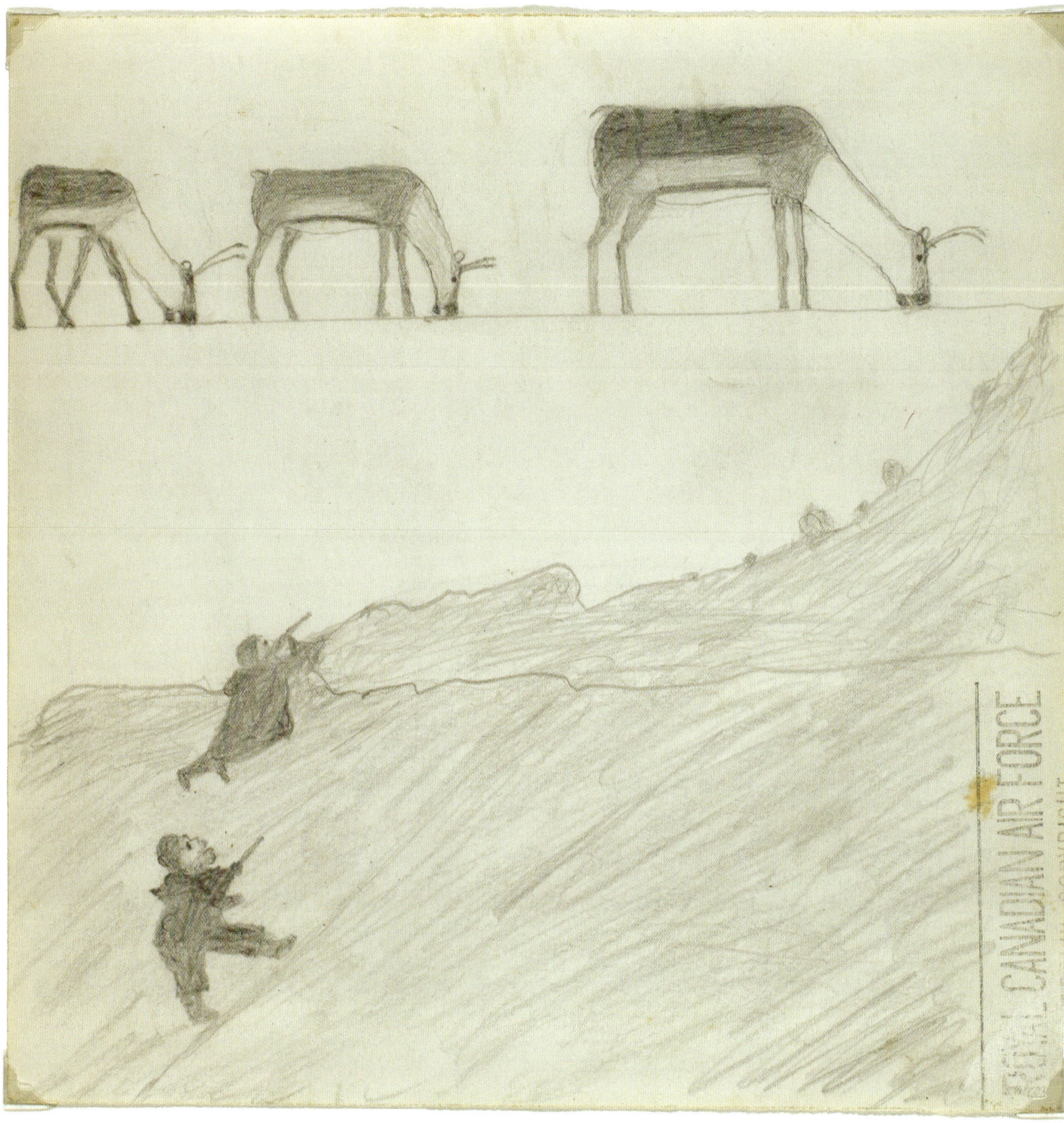

Josephie Pootoogook, *Grazing Caribou*, c. 1957, graphite on paperboard, 22.9 x 22.7 cm

Josephie Pootoogook, *Grazing Caribou*, 1957, stonecut and lino block, 15.0 x 24.0 cm

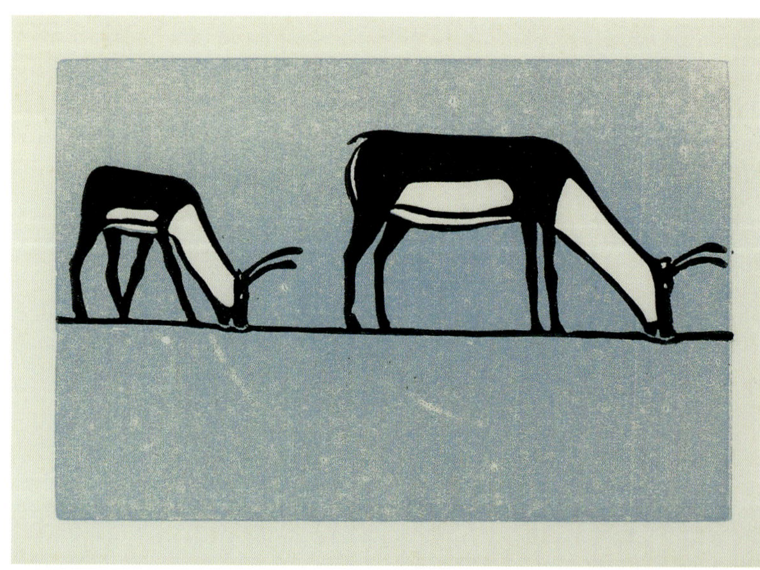

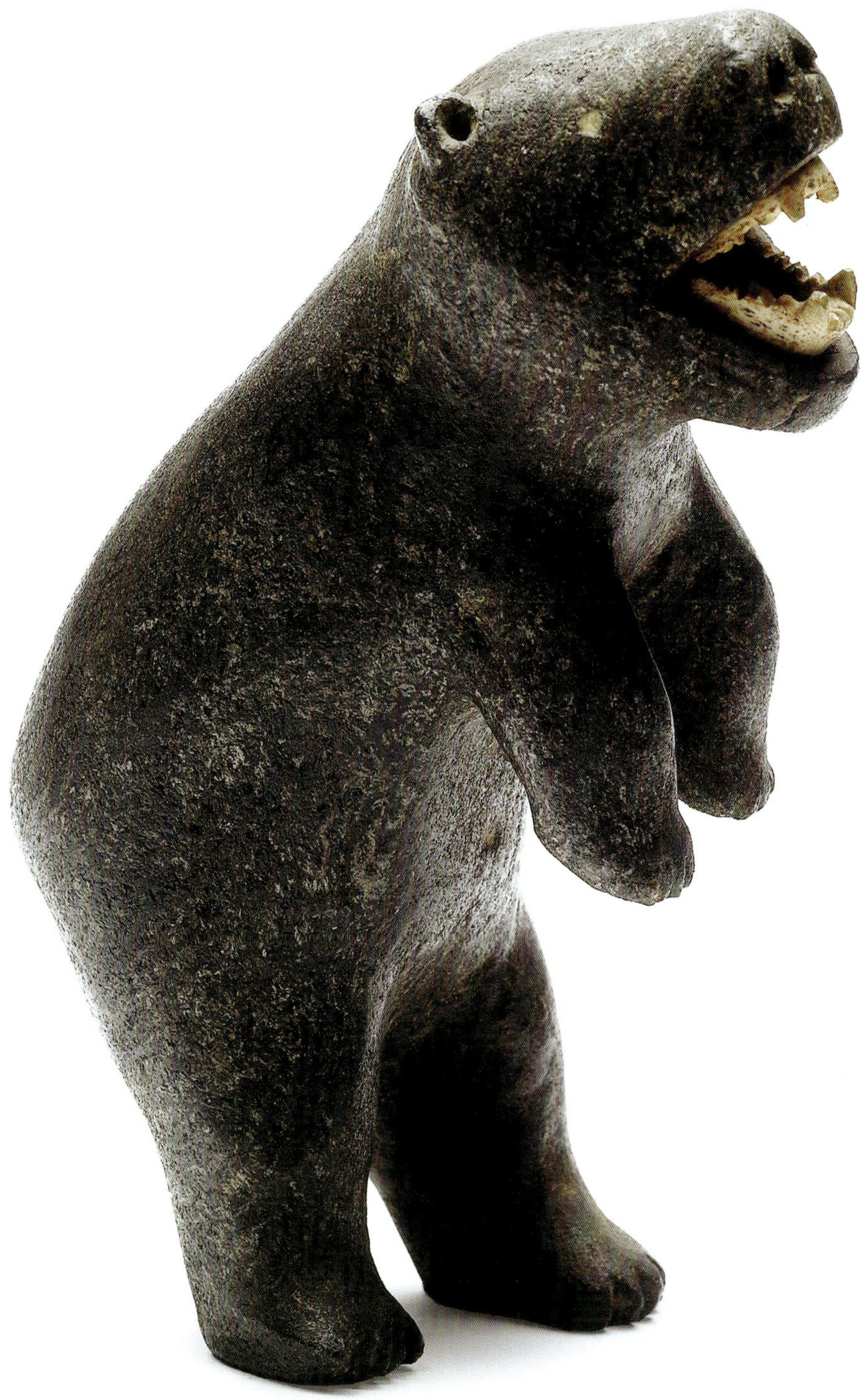

Tudlik, *Bear Standing on Hind Legs*, c. 1955, stone, antler, 18.6 x 13.5 x 7.8 cm

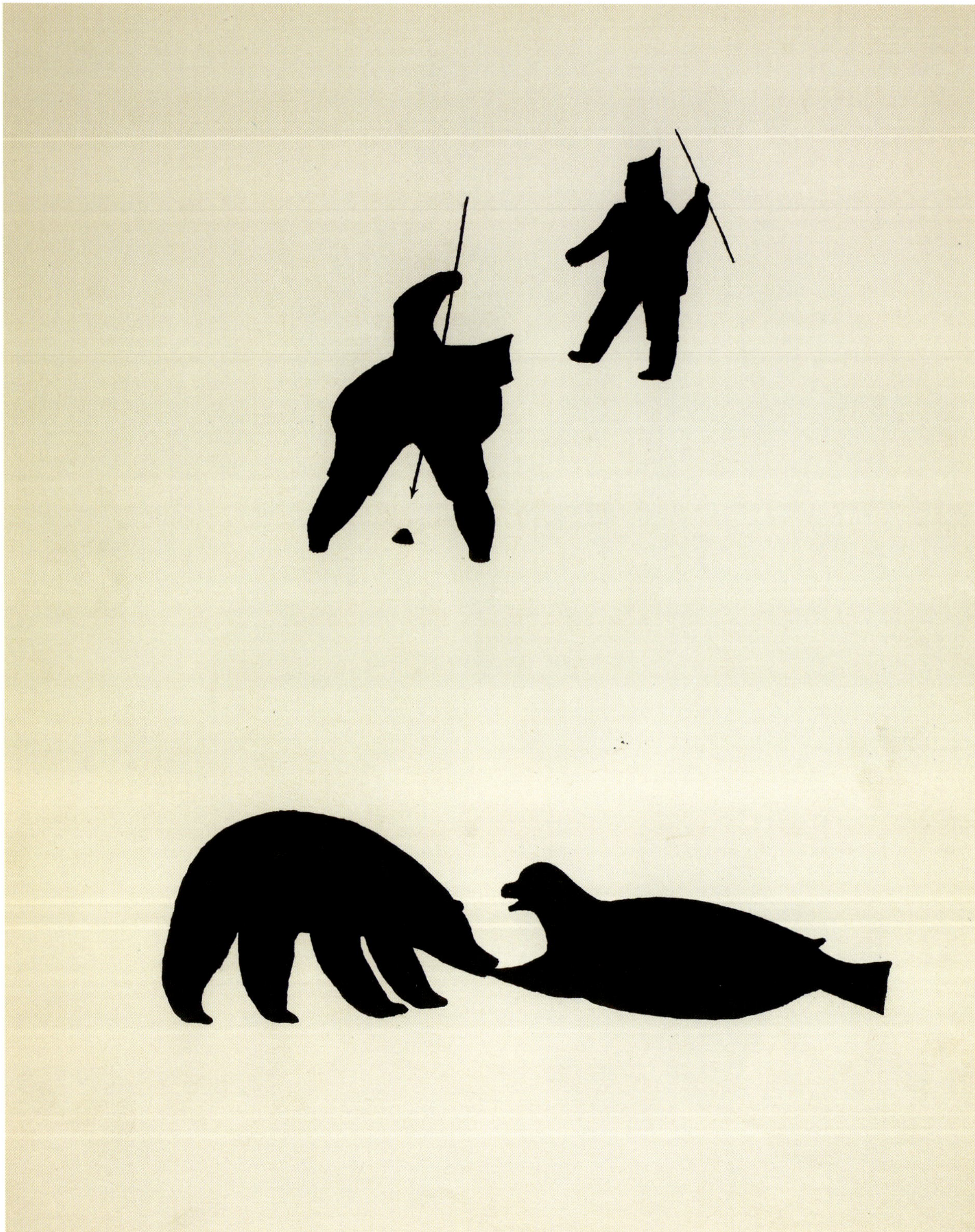

Niviaksiak, *Man Hunting at a Seal Hole in the Ice*, from *Niviaksiak Sketchbook*, 1950s, ink and graphite on paper, 43.0 x 35.5 cm

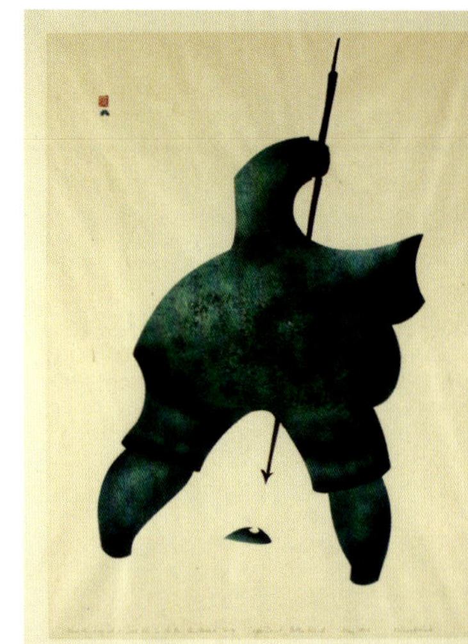

Niviaksiak, *Man Hunting at a Seal Hole in the Ice*, 1959, stencil on paper, 59.8 x 45.7 cm

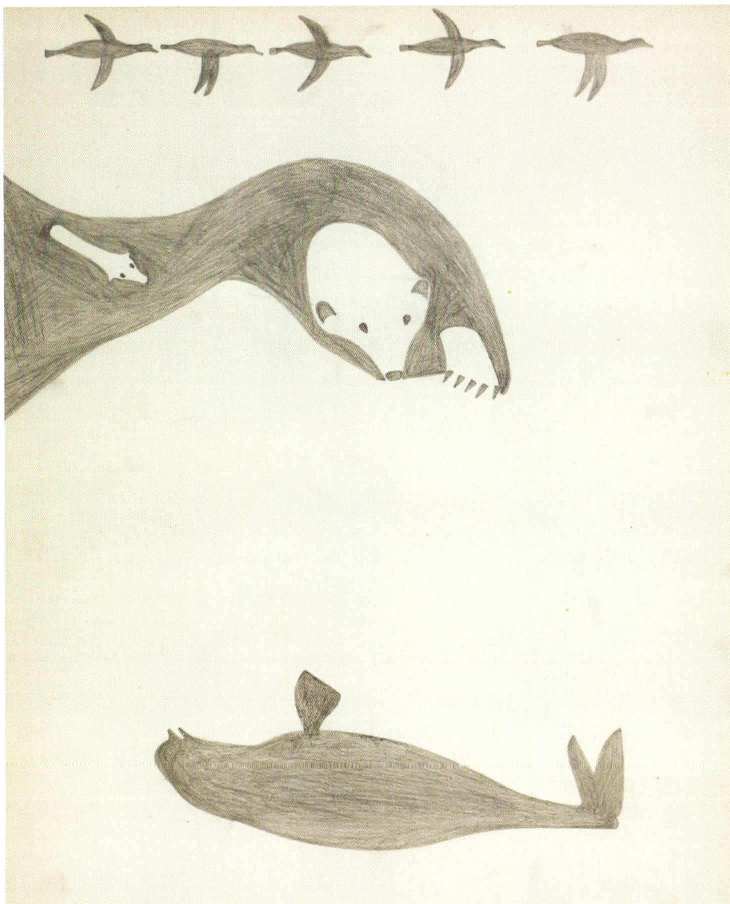

Niviaksiak, *Polar Bear and Cub in Ice*, from *Niviaksiak Sketchbook*, 1950s, ink and graphite on paper, 43.0 x 35.5 cm

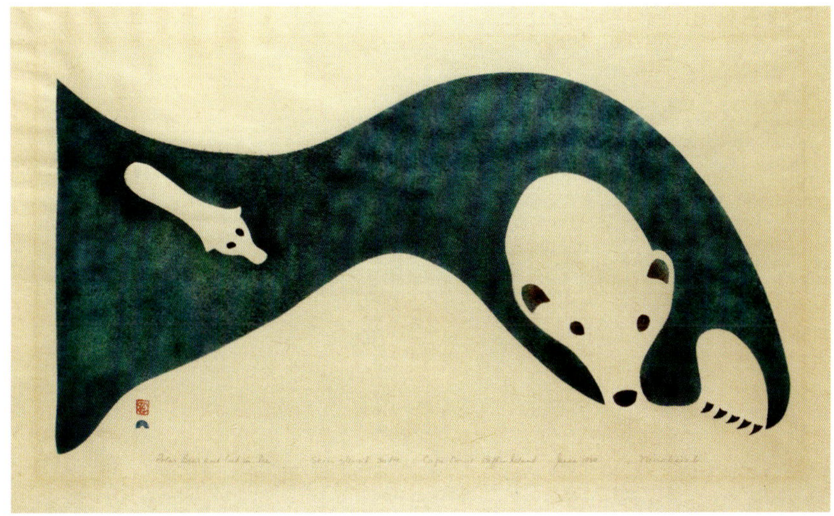

Niviaksiak, *Polar Bear and Cub in Ice*, 1959, stencil on paper, 34.1 x 65.8 cm

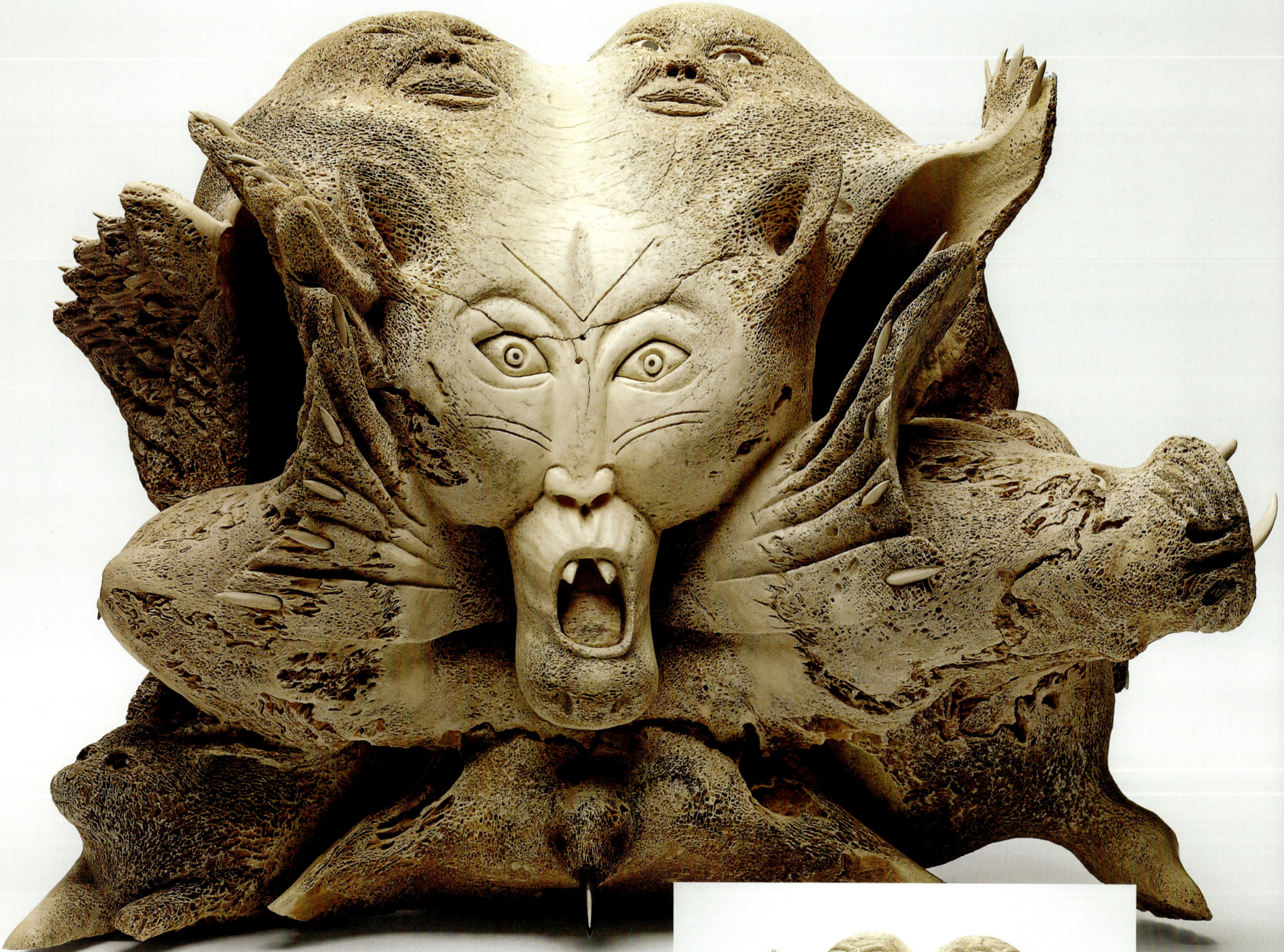

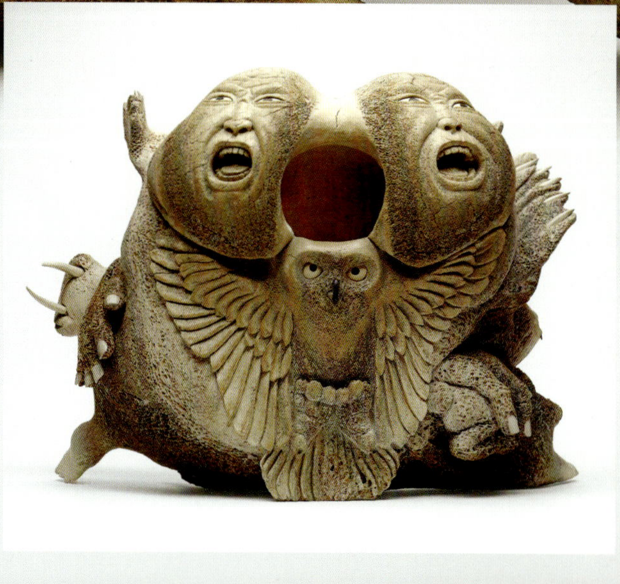

Manasie Akpaliapik, *Respecting the Circle*, 1989,
whale bone, ivory, stone, antler, baleen, horn, 52.0 x 71.4 x 40.0 cm.
Gift of Samuel and Esther Sarick, Toronto, 1996, 96/1294,

"We Are Inuit" Art and Identity

Ingo Hessel

The rapid transformation of Inuit life and artmaking brought about shifts in attitudes both in the North and outside the Arctic. These new attitudes were evident by the late 1950s and accelerated in the 1960s. For their part, Inuit were forced to rapidly formulate new ways of thinking about their own "Eskimo" identity; for many Inuit, this meant adapting themselves to new roles as makers of what was still known as "Eskimo art."

The shift in thinking outside the North was prompted in large part by a broader view of "Eskimo" culture as seen through the lens of "Eskimo art." Quite understandably, it lagged behind the new ideas of Inuit about themselves, but it was a subtle shift away from the stereotypical view of Eskimos as anonymous "primitives" and their art as quaint handicraft, to a subtly different idea of Eskimos (as they were still called) as northern Canadians with a distinct ethnic identity, and "Eskimo art" as an important marker of that identity, and even of Canadian identity.

Inuit culture and identity were, of course, in a state of turmoil. The collapse of the fur market[1]; the relocation of Inuit closer to, and eventually into, permanent settlements; schooling (in some cases residential); tuberculosis outbreaks and the forced evacuation of thousands of patients to southern hospitals; the welfare and cash economy—all of these factors, occurring simultaneously in the 1950s and early 1960s,[2] destabilized Inuit society and demoralized individual members of that society.[3] Seen against this backdrop, art and craft production seems like little more than occupational therapy with spending money. But perhaps under the circumstances—namely, being powerless against the onslaught of so much social disruption—occupational therapy, and some cash, were just what many Inuit desperately needed.[4] Art critic Thomas McEvilley in *Art and Otherness: Crisis in Cultural Identity* writes that "it is perhaps in the midst of catastrophic change, or in a time of anguished endings and beginnings, that artists have the greatest opportunity to offer something of crucial value to the culture around them, by seeking, through the image, ways to deal with the destruction of an old identity and to begin to shadow forth a new one."[5]

To me it seems to matter little if Inuit artists made their art of their own accord or through prompting; they did in the end manage to "shadow forth" a new identity—in other words, to reinvent themselves. The American anthropologist Nelson Graburn suggests that Fourth World peoples (minority ethnic groups who lack the ability to direct their collective lives) sometimes use their arts as a survival tactic—cultural retrenchment, assimilation or other "psychosocial" responses—in dealing with the dominant culture.[6] I think Charles Martijn put it best when he characterized early modern Inuit art as "a splendid new art of acculturation."[7]

Not just Inuit artists but Inuit as a people were "shadowing forth" a new identity. That this was a new, hybridized identity (or perhaps even a dual one) was ignored or denied by some and lamented or criticized by others. Writing in 1979, art historian Dorothy Jean Ray saw the similar state of affairs in Alaska this way: "Although the Eskimos have successfully amalgamated portions of both cultures, they have refused parts of the new life and retained so tenaciously parts of their own that they appear to be in possession of two separately identifiable cultures."[8]

In the 1950s Inuit began "shadowing forth" new ways of making art and new reasons for making it. Collectively and individually, they had to sort out economic and market forces, material and technical challenges and opportunities, subject matter and stylistic concerns, and personal and artistic motivation. As Swinton astutely observed in 1958, "No longer can the Eskimo express himself without inhibitions, for he has created for himself an artistic consciousness which hampers his flow of unpremeditated art. In order that it may be art, he must not only think as an Eskimo but also as an artist."[9]

Some would say that it is an exaggeration to say that Inuit "seized" the opportunity to experiment with producing art in the 1950s, but I suspect this was often the case. As Houston wrote in a 1951 report, "As soon as the [Eskimos trading into Cape Dorset] understood that we desired to purchase handicrafts of all types, they started to bring us many articles..."[10] This sounds much like Captain Lyon's description of "merry barter" from 1825. Osuitok Ipeelee of Cape Dorset had this to say about the situation: "Before the government came up here there was only one way of making money. People could make money from fox furs and the other things we used to bring in, but only a little money. Then it was learned that carvings here in the Arctic have a price and when there were no jobs available people quickly learned their value. That is why they have tried so hard at it. If people hadn't started carving we'd all be supported by the government."[11] Louis Tapardjuk, then president of Canadian Arctic Co-operative Federation Limited, had this perspective in 1980, looking back on a phenomenon that no one could have predicted: "Arts and crafts is our largest industry that does not require skill or knowledge that is developed by southern training or educational institutions."[12]

Osuitok (pp. 138–39) was one of many Cape Dorset–area Inuit who responded early and quickly to the opportunity. James and Alma Houston spent a few months in Cape Dorset in 1951 soliciting all manner of handicrafts. Having very little ivory and little soft stone at first, the local Inuit soon found a new quarry site. Osuitok brought in three carvings and was paid forty-two dollars, and as a result, according to Houston, "the Eskimos all learned of this in a short time, and all settled down to carving in earnest."[13]

Inuit certainly responded in large numbers—in some areas, up to 75 per cent of the population, including men, women, and even children. With encouragement and monetary incentive from the Qallunaat, and few other options, Inuit created a veritable flood of works. A *Time* magazine review of the May 1953 Gimpel Fils exhibition in London stated that thirty thousand Inuit artworks had already been shipped south.[14] The Inuit "psychosocial" response (which comprised the sum total of thousands of individual psychosocial responses to cultural and social stress) was neither cultural retrenchment nor assimilation; it was a rapid adaptation born of human resilience and the kind of economic opportunism with which Inuit had greeted foreign influences in the past.

Swift and decisive economic opportunism by Inuit has clearly been a major factor in the speedy expansion and development of their art, both in the beginning and in subsequent decades. A case in point is that William Larmour's efforts to further stimulate art production in Baker Lake in 1962 were stymied because the Inuit were "contemptuous of earning money through carving rather than hunting." When he paid thirty-five dollars for a carving, however, he was "inundated" with carvings.[15] Amazingly, in 1964, a scant two years after the "contemptuous" response of Baker Lake Inuit, the Winnipeg Art Gallery organized its first exhibition of their art; *Eskimo Carvers of Keewatin N.W.T.* included 118 works by Baker Lake men and women. Almost overnight, Baker Lake had become a major sculpture-producing centre, and in less than a decade the community became famous for its vibrant prints, drawings and wall hangings as well.

Graburn has discussed Inuit art extensively in his writings on Fourth World arts. According to his theory, "the study of Fourth World arts is, par excellence, the study of *changing* art—of emerging ethnicities, modifying identities, and commercial and colonial stimuli and repressive actions."[16] Despite their disadvantaged position, Inuit perhaps recognized the advantage of projecting their cultural identity clearly through their art. They no doubt understood the economic advantage of doing so fairly quickly, even if they might not yet, in the early years, have recognized the cultural importance of this project. Marybelle Mitchell quotes artist and Fédération des coopératives du Nouveau-Québec (FCNQ) president Paulosie Kasudluak as saying, "I became more and more aware that our sculpture was having a big effect on everything that was happening in the North and of the use of sculpture as a means of livelihood and also as a means of expressing ourselves as Inuit."[17]

Even if Inuit artists had not been encouraged to do so, they would have chosen subject matter that was familiar to them; and so the great classic themes of Inuit art established themselves in the 1950s: Arctic animals, hunting, camp life, mother and child, mythology, shamanism and the spirit world, the human figure. The Canadian art critic Peter Millard quite rightly pointed out that, unlike Northwest Coast First Nations artists, for example, Inuit visual artists "did not inherit a clearly established stock of images to work upon" and speculated that memories, and a store of legends and beliefs, might have been the inspiration.[18] Zebedee Nungak, writing in 2008, confirms this: he describes traditional Inuit culture as a "deep and natural well of inspiration" for Inuit visual artists. "Having never known anything else, Inuit artists tapped into what they were totally knowledgeable about: their *unikkaatuat* [legends], their *unikkaat* [historical accounts], their *inuusirminitait* [life experiences], and their *isumaminitait* [inspired imaginations]."[19]

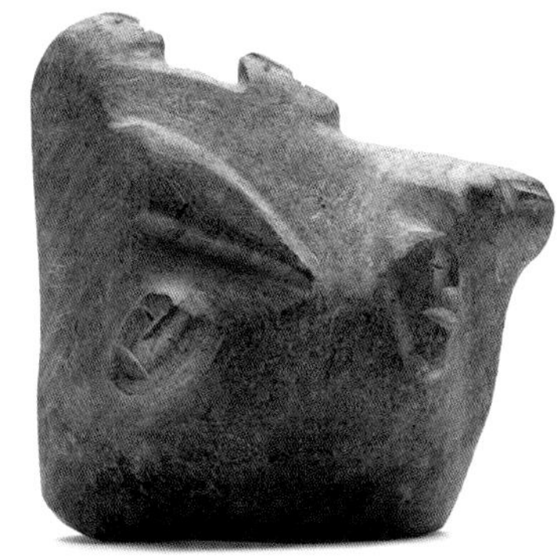

Lucy Tasseor Tutsweetok, *Family*, c. 1977, stone, 11.5 x 11.7 x 6.6 cm. Gift of Samuel and Esther Sarick, Toronto, 1996

Elsewhere I have described Inuit art as "an almost encyclopedic visual catalogue of traditional (and to a lesser extent transitional and modern) Inuit culture."[20] Here, I would like to emphasize my opinion that Inuit artists have depicted not simply what they knew about (and yes, sometimes what was suggested to them) but also what they passionately *cared* about. Beginning in the 1950s but well beyond that decade, generations of Inuit artists have described and illustrated the beauty, physical characteristics and habits of Arctic animals (pp. 56, 58–59, 70, 71, 97); the techniques, excitement and dangers of the hunt (pp. 69, 90); the occupations and pleasures of camp and community life (p. 83); the close physical and emotional bonds of family life (pp. 84–87); the stories and myths derived from the oral tradition (pp. 93, 94, 98, 99); the supernatural, including the spiritual intersection of the human and animal worlds (pp. 65, 74, 88, 89, 90) and the role of the shaman (pp. 88, 98, 104); and the portrayal of the human figure (pp. 67, 91).

In other words, artists explored themes that reflected the essence of Inuit identity. As Swinton put it, "Yes, the Eskimo were influenced by white men; but the true Eskimo artist created works that no white man could possibly have conceived."[21] The Inuit scholar and educator Mark Kalluak summed it up this way: "Each carving is a replica, shape or form of Inuit culture. It speaks of something from the past, an imitation of Inuit tradition created through the mind of an artist."[22] One could argue that the repetition of these traditional themes simply prolonged stereotypical imagery for decades. Elsewhere I have surmised that although Inuit artists were willingly complicit with marketers and collectors who desired "Eskimo" imagery for their own reasons, they also celebrated the past as a way to preserve it.[23] The Baker Lake artist William Noah, born on the land but raised in a community and schooled in the south, sees it this way: "In art you can remember your homeland and your tradition and your way of daily life…" But he realizes the limitations of this for him: "Artmaking is a really good start at getting your culture back, but it's still not the real thing."[24]

Janet Berlo came to a similar conclusion: "It often seems that to draw the old ways rather than to continue to enact them, is a way of maintaining identity"; and, "These arts are multivocal, simultaneously fulfilling the differing needs of Native artist and southern audience."[25] I would suggest, however, that the best Inuit art, when its styles and themes flow genuinely from the soul of a people, is not mere stereotype. It moves beyond it, into that ineffable realm of the symbolic, the archetypal and the iconic (pp. 86, 162–63,

166–67, 168–69, 174–75). It does that regardless of prompting, marketing and promotion, and regardless of scholarship and exhibition methodology or other forms of interpretation and appropriation by the dominant society.

The above assertion hinges on the idea of the "genuine." Attacks on the authenticity of Inuit art have dogged it almost from the beginning. At the risk of giving Carpenter's opinions more attention than they deserve, I will cite him a few more times. In 1959 he was willing to grant some legitimacy to post-1949 Inuit art: "The new art is genuine enough: as people change, so their art changes, and the Eskimo are changing rapidly." However, he cautioned against confusing it "with aboriginal Eskimo art, which is of an entirely different order."[26] His 1973 book, *Eskimo Realities,* rehashed many of his ideas from 1959. Although he still granted that post-1949 work was a "new, delightful art,"[27] he felt he could no longer grant it true authenticity: "Can the word 'Eskimo' legitimately be applied to this modern stone art? I think not. Its roots are Western; so is its audience."[28] Carpenter believed that anthropologists who accepted the new art as "Eskimo" were swallowing Canadian government "propaganda."[29] He dismissively described Inuit artists as, variously, following a government manual; working at craft centres or at TB sanatoria; being Hong Kong Chinese; producing Ookpik dolls, totem poles, pots and prints. "We let the Eskimo know what we like, then congratulate them on their successful imitations of us."[30] Carpenter's "purist" position both reflected and fuelled decades of prejudicial opinions by some academics, curators and art critics. The debate may never end, since, as art historian Deborah Root says, "'authenticity' is a floating category, able to migrate and legitimize or delegitimize certain kinds of images."[31]

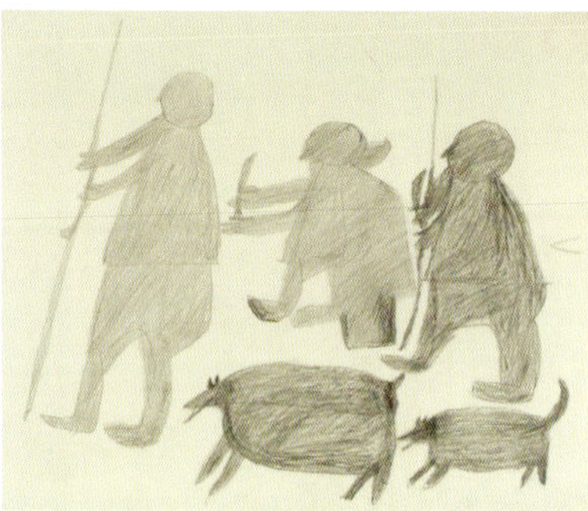

Parr, *Hunters with Dogs*, 1961–65, graphite on paper, 50.7 x 65.5 cm. Gift of Samuel and Esther Sarick, Toronto, 2002. © Dorset Fine Arts

As for Inuit identity, Carpenter suggests that the modern culture that Inuit art has shadowed forth is at best a shallow (and false) replacement for the real thing: "Having deprived him of his heritage, and even the memory of his heritage, we offer him a substitute which he eagerly accepts, for no other is permitted. And so he takes his place on stage, side-by-side with the American Indian whose headdress comes from a mail-order catalog, who learned his dances at Disneyland, and picked up his philosophy from Hippies. He knows no other identity..."[32]

Carpenter's comments are insulting on many levels, and yet there is a germ of truth in all of them. They are based on his observations of early (and sometimes faltering) steps at development and promotion, low-end souvenir production[33] and cheap (often foreign-made) imitations;[34] presumably these provided the best foil against which to promote his idea of "pristine" Inuit art, frozen in time. I can only assume that at some point (quite early on in the development of Inuit art) Carpenter and others like him simply stopped looking at the physical evidence—namely, the new art itself. For example, I can see no other reason for Carpenter's ignoring the fact that many Inuit prints and drawings from the 1960s and early 1970s look remarkably like some of the early Inuit drawings that Carpenter presented as authentic in his own books.[35]

Carpenter simply could not bring himself to accept that Inuit culture and art could adapt and change and still remain truly "Eskimo." McEvilley's assertion that artists can offer something vital to their culture "by seeking, through the image, ways to deal with the destruction of an old identity and to begin to shadow forth a new one" is not only more generous than Carpenter's, but it is also less romantic. My only quibble is that I see the old Inuit identity as having been damaged, not actually destroyed. And I believe that most Inuit would firmly agree with Nungak's view of Inuit culture as a "deep and natural well of inspiration." New cultural identities do not have to rise, phoenix-like, from the ashes of old ones; they can evolve, suffer rude shocks and absorb outside influences. And the arts can be the shapers of identity, not merely reflections of it. The Inukjuak sculptor Johnny Aculiak stated his opinion in a 1997 interview: "It seems to me that our culture will die off one day if we do not keep carving."[36] The way in which Inuit art has helped to shape Inuit identity could not have been programmed or predicted, either by Inuit or by outsiders; it takes hindsight to see how the process evolved. As Deborah Root states, "the constructed tradition became real, through the lived experiences and artistic practices of the artists."[37] Folklorist and curator Susan Fair, writing of Alaskan Native artists, had a similar view: "Tradition is not product, but process… Further, tradition is not simply of and about the past, it is the present and the future."[38]

Consciously or not, Inuit in some real sense "took control" of Inuit art and began using it as a vehicle for cultural identity. If we consider this to be one of the primary, if unintended, "functions" of Inuit art, what of its other functions? One of the most interesting and puzzling aspects of Inuit art is the question of its functions, and hence its importance to Inuit artists (and ultimately, to Inuit society). One could argue that the basic function or purpose of Inuit art is simply as a commercial souvenir and folk art, made for sale to outsiders. In this completely utilitarian view of Inuit artmaking, the artist is simply the producer of a commodity. (Strictly speaking of course, *all* art made for sale is simply a commodity, in the utilitarian sense.) The utilitarian view does not take into account those things that Inuit artists have in common with artists everywhere: pride of craftsmanship; pride in one's artistic vision, style and accomplishments; personal and/or shared community themes, subject matter and values; relationships with fellow artists and collectors/admirers—and in the larger sense, the artist's status as keeper and shaper of community traditions and history. The very process of making art, by thousands of Inuit, even if most works disappear into a southern market—constitutes hundreds of thousands of acts of creation, statements of self, affirmations of identity; it creates tradition in Susan Fair's sense of the word. This has become an important, though unintended, function of Inuit art. In 1967 Swinton was noting that Inuit art had become a focal point of "a decidedly ethnic consciousness or, almost, an Eskimo nationalism, with a corresponding ethnic self-affirmation."[39]

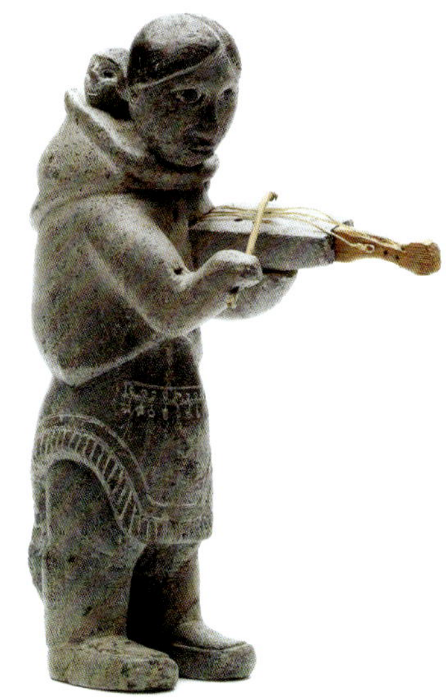

Joe Talirunili, *Woman Playing Fiddle*, c. 1965, stained stone, 27.0 x 17.0 x 8.9 cm. Gift of Samuel and Esther Sarick, Toronto, 1996

The other important function of Inuit art is communication—between artist and observer, and between cultures. The fact that much Inuit art can claim status as a folk art puts it in an unusual position on the Canadian art scene.[40] As a popular art with few artistic pretensions, it appeals to a broad range of ordinary people and sophisticated collectors alike (though not always, as we have seen, to academics and critics). Whether through the simpler, exotic appeal of materials and subject matter, or the more complex attractions of style or psychological, emotional or symbolic content, Inuit art's power to communicate has acted as a bridge between cultures.[41] In the final analysis it is primarily for this reason, and not because of government support or promotion, that Inuit art has matured and endured as a symbol of Canada's own hybrid national identity. As Nelson Graburn has conjectured, the message delivered by Canadian Inuit through their art has been this: "We exist; we are different; we can do something we are proud of; we have something that is uniquely ours."[42] The message, and the art, are genuine.

In the 1950s, artmaking was a part-time activity for all but a few Inuit. Graburn points out that HBC traders in the 1950s preferred to purchase carvings from successful trappers in order to ensure the continued supply of lucrative pelts; Graburn speculates that this temporarily impeded the participation of "women and disabled men."[43] Houston does not seem to have gone out of his way to encourage women once the primacy of stone carving was established in the early 1950s; in his 1954 promotional publication *Canadian Eskimo Art,* he stated that "few women have interested themselves in carving," suggesting that they preferred sewing and basketry.[44] For a time, the exception to this rule was Sugluk (Salluit) on the northern tip of the Ungava Peninsula in Arctic Quebec. In this village, where fully 75 of the 110 Inuit over the age of ten were carving in 1955,[45] many of the best works were created by women.[46]

The late 1950s and 1960s brought significant developments. The most important event—indeed a pivotal moment so far as this discussion is concerned—was the introduction of printmaking by James Houston to the Inuit of Cape Dorset in 1957. Houston's famous anecdote about his conversation with Osuitok, in which the carver, having seen Houston's demonstration using an engraved tusk, ink and toilet tissue, said, "We could do that," is part of Inuit art mythology.[47] We now know that this eureka moment was not the germ of the project. Houston had the idea earlier than that; he had solicited drawings from Caribou Inuit at Ennadai Lake in the Keewatin region in 1955 and published one of them in a short article he wrote in 1956.[48] But obviously, once Houston proposed the idea in Cape Dorset, the prominent carver Osuitok's enthusiasm for the idea and his cooperation, and the support of the respected elders Josephie Pootoogook (pp. 68, 70) and Kiakshuk (pp. 164–65), were crucial to the undertaking.[49] The Inuit of Cape Dorset could indeed do that, and still do. In her autobiography the graphic artist Kenojuak Ashevak (pp. 174–75) describes the atmosphere in the late 1950s: "It was a time of excitement, for we sensed that many things were happening."[50] After two years of experimentation, which began very modestly with Christmas cards and small editions of prints made using mostly old linoleum tiles, the first official collection of limited-edition prints was released in 1959.[51] The Kinngait Studios flourished under four decades of Terry Ryan's management beginning in 1960 and just celebrated its fiftieth anniversary in 2009.[52]

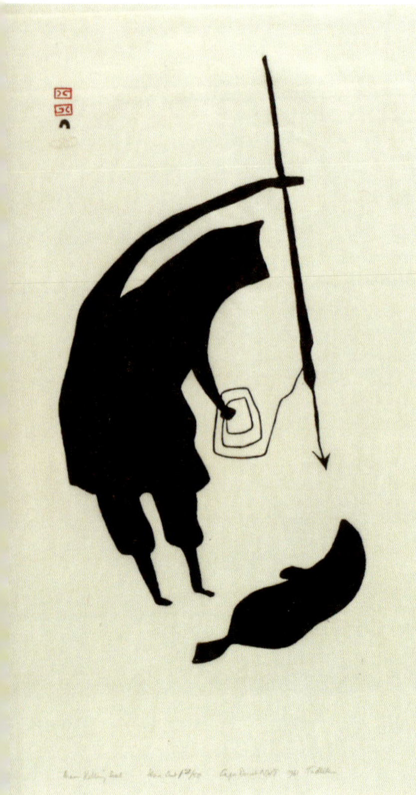

Tudlik, *Man Killing Seal*, 1961, stonecut on paper, 76.1 x 50.9 cm. Gift of Samuel and Esther Sarick, Toronto, 2002. © Dorset Fine Arts

The Cape Dorset prints were marketed differently from Inuit carvings almost from the very beginning. The federal Department of Northern Affairs and National Resources quickly took charge of marketing the work[53]; after an initial showing of the 1959 collection at the Stratford Shakespeare Festival to great acclaim, the collection was officially relaunched at the Montreal Museum of Fine Arts in February 1960. Soon major public galleries in Canada and the United States were snapping up Cape Dorset prints. Clearly the strategy was to aim directly at the fine arts market.

Doubts about the authenticity of Inuit prints, as an entirely "introduced" art form and thus even less grounded in tradition than Inuit sculpture, were countered by Houston's assertions in his 1960 article "Eskimo Graphic Art" in *Canadian Art,* that graphic imagery was based on appliqué clothing patterns and incised ivory work, and his descriptions of "sealskin stencils," brushes of "seal and polar-bear hair" and inks mixed from "commercial paint and seal oil."[54] We now know that these and other descriptions (which Christine Lalonde has termed attempts to "indigenize the processes"[55]) were clever inventions of the literary variety.[56] Using stone blocks to make relief prints (a homegrown adaptation of the well-known woodcut technique) was a brilliant move that used local materials, used existing carving skills and satisfied those with lingering doubts about the legitimacy of the art (pp. 81, 99). No mention was made of the early linocut relief printing experiments, which had preceded the stonecut method.

Compared with the flood of articles and booklets dealing with Inuit sculpture in the early to mid-1950s, there was little promotional material concerning prints written by Houston or anyone else. Interestingly, in his 1960 article Houston never used the word "primitive"; in fact, he stressed experimentation and innovation. The article seemed to speak more of the future and less of the past. Notably, he did not mention his own involvement or Osuitok's eureka moment.[57] The 1959 collection had been so well promoted and so well received that perhaps the illustrated annual catalogues were deemed to be enough for the time being. The introduction to the 1960 catalogue pointed out "international interest" and the fact that "prominent galleries and museums were quick to grasp the significance of this graphic art."[58] Significantly, the catalogue also included fourteen portrait photographs of Cape Dorset artists and printmakers.

In 1960 limited-edition Inuit prints were an easier "sell" in the art market than small stone carvings were in 1950, intermingled as they had been with handicrafts such as mittens and baskets. In addition, in 1961 the federal government established the Canadian Eskimo Art Committee (CEAC), an advisory body made up of influential art experts to oversee the development and promotion of the new art form. One of the CEAC's main functions was to jury, and thus approve for sale, the Inuit prints created each year.[59] There are other factors that came into play as well. Inuit prints appealed to a whole new segment of the art market because, for a variety of reasons, most people naturally gravitate toward pictures rather than sculptural objects. Also, unlike with carvings and sculptures, where virtually everything was put on the market to be sold—and judged[60]—the great majority of Inuit graphic images (almost all original drawings and experimental prints deemed "unsuccessful") were not made public.[61] Visual appeal, scarcity and presumed quality all played their part. In the end, though, because of the "originality and aesthetic merit of those images,"[62] the prints practically sold themselves; then "the huge reception from the south opened up creative floodgates,"[63] and the virtuous cycle continued. It not only continued for Cape Dorset prints; in my opinion, it also perceptibly altered the public's notion of what Inuit art was, and could be.

Printmaking spread to Puvirnituq in 1962 and Holman (Ulukhaktok) in 1965. The federal government hired crafts officers who worked to set up various arts programs in several communities in this period—most notably, a ceramics project in Rankin Inlet. This period saw the first serious book on Inuit art (George Swinton's 1965 *Eskimo Sculpture Esquimaude*), the formation of collections of Inuit art at the Winnipeg Art Gallery and at the National Museum of Man (now the Canadian Museum of Civilization, Gatineau, Quebec), as well as the Toronto-Dominion Bank collection of Inuit art and the promotion of Inuit art at Expo 67; all of these served to raise the status of the art form.

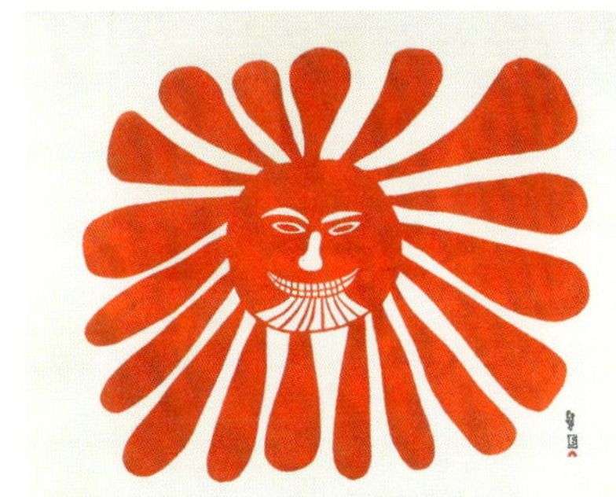

Johnniebo Ashevak, *The Woman Who Lives in the Sun*, 1960, stonecut on paper, 49.7 x 66.2 cm. Gift of Samuel and Esther Sarick, Toronto, 2002, 2002/9464. © Dorset Fine Arts

By the mid-1960s it was clear that Inuit art had been adopted—some would say appropriated—as a national symbol by the federal government, and through its promotional efforts, recognized as such by the Canadian and international publics as well. Nelson Graburn has theorized that the Canadian government was motivated to use Inuit art as a national icon by a need to establish a unique national identity after the Second World War, for political as well as cultural reasons; his claims have some validity but were debated in Inuit art circles.[64] Canada was continuing to promote itself as a northern nation, and one whose identity included Aboriginal as well as English and French foundations.[65] Graburn has noted many examples of nations that have "borrowed" the cultural features of "exotic" ethnic minorities as symbols of "national ethnicity."[66]

During this decade the co-operative movement, which was spawned in Arctic Quebec (at the suggestion of and with the full support of the federal government) in the late 1950s, quickly spread to other regions. Furthermore, in 1965 the government instigated the establishment of Canadian Arctic Producers (CAP), a southern co-op marketing agency for Inuit arts and crafts.[67] Co-ops gave Inuit greater control in the purchasing and distribution of their art and involved them in various other commercial enterprises.[68] The co-op movement also offered Inuit a new political voice.[69]

The idea of Inuit co-ops did not, therefore, as is often supposed, spring forth from the "collective spirit" of Inuit themselves but was actually introduced by federal government bureaucrats; it did, however, seem to strike an egalitarian chord among Inuit across the Canadian Arctic.[70]

The egalitarian nature of Inuit art is noteworthy. The fact that both men and women, the elderly, and even children, have been consistently allowed to experiment with making art, and are encouraged to market their art, is a comment on Inuit society but also speaks to the sensitivity of many of the Qallunaat (both men and women) who have worked with Inuit artists. That children are encouraged to carve,[71] and the elderly are encouraged to draw, has increased the Inuit talent pool considerably. In more general terms, egalitarianism means that potentially all can contribute to the livelihood and prestige of their family and community, and everyone is seen as a potential artist. Little wonder, then, that so many Inuit have achieved just that. Dorothy Jean Ray noted a similar artistic egalitarianism—though only among men—among Alaskan Eskimos and remarked how different this was from the "non-Eskimo world."[72]

Some Inuit art media are segregated by gender—for example, most sculptors and printmakers are male, and the great majority of textile artists and weavers are female—but there are many successful female sculptors.[73] The art of drawing was more evenly divided in the early years, but women are in the majority today.[74] According to the late Cape Dorset artist Joanasie Salomonie, prints by female artists influenced the work of many male carvers in his community.[75] This is interesting since, according to Terry Ryan, a number of Cape Dorset men had originally questioned the "manliness" of making prints derived from women's sealskin appliqué picture designs.[76] The prominent role that women play in modern Inuit art, if not unique in the history of art, is certainly unusual. Another art "movement" that comes to mind in this regard is modern Southwest Native art; the high status attained by Canadian Inuit women artists has few other equivalents anywhere in the world. How the relative gender equality among artists might have directly affected the "rise of the Inuit artist" and the importance of the art form as a whole is open to discussion; it most certainly has enriched Inuit art's overall character.

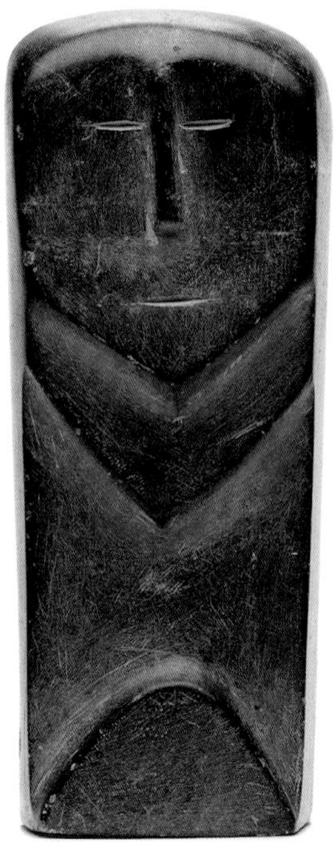

John Tiktak, *Figure*, 1961, darkened stone, 20.7 x 8.7 x 6.7 cm. Gift of Samuel and Esther Sarick, Toronto, 1996

By the 1960s Inuit artists had forged a distinctive new art form that drew from and represented a new collective ethnic identity. However, even if the themes they chose to explore could be considered somewhat nostalgic and stereotypical, the styles of Inuit art were anything but homogeneous. In fact, in the 1960s community styles were quite sharply differentiated from each other; in sculpture, the reasons included the relative isolation of the villages from one another, differing stone types and the varying tastes of local buyers and arts advisers—as well as an important new factor: the growing influence of talented and successful individual local artists (pp. 116–17, 125–26). By the mid-1960s many Inuit in communities on Baffin Island, in Arctic Quebec and in the Keewatin were producing art as their chief economic activity, supplemented by subsistence hunting and welfare payments. It was only logical that the best artists—the ones with distinctive, successful personal styles—would become full-time artists, but also that artists who chose to work full-time making art might develop distinctive personal styles (pp. 79, 83, 120–21, 152–53). George Swinton noted that a growing emphasis on individual artists was beginning to supersede the importance of "collective styles" in Inuit art.[77] Janet Berlo has noted that this was "in contrast to most ethnic art traditions that are marketed to the western world."[78]

Swinton was referring specifically to sculpture, but his observation is valid for graphic art as well. Graphic artists such as Kenojuak Ashevak (pp. 174–75), Parr (pp. 166–67), Kiakshuk (pp. 164–65), Pitseolak Ashoona (pp. 160–61) and Lucy Qinnuayuak from Cape Dorset; Joe Talirunili (pp. 111–13), Davidialuk Alasua Amittu (pp. 114–15), Juanisialu Irqumia and Annie Mikpiga from Puvirnituq; and Helen Kalvak and Victor Ekootak from Holman rose to prominence quickly in the 1960s. Significantly, many important graphic artists were "women and disabled men," who from the very start were given the opportunity to submit drawings to the print studios.[79] Kenojuak, in particular, became a "star"; the photogenic artist and her family were featured in an evocative 1963 National Film Board documentary, *Eskimo Artist: Kenojuak*.[80] The film, shot in late spring in 1962, includes charming footage of the family in their igloo—which, according to Kenojuak, had to be constructed out of Styrofoam because the snow was already too soft.[81] It is quite likely that the success of Inuit print collections—the Cape Dorset collections in particular—with their published catalogues (which clearly identified artist names and titles of works, and often featured artist photos and biographies), actually paved the way for the rise of the individual Inuit artist.[82]

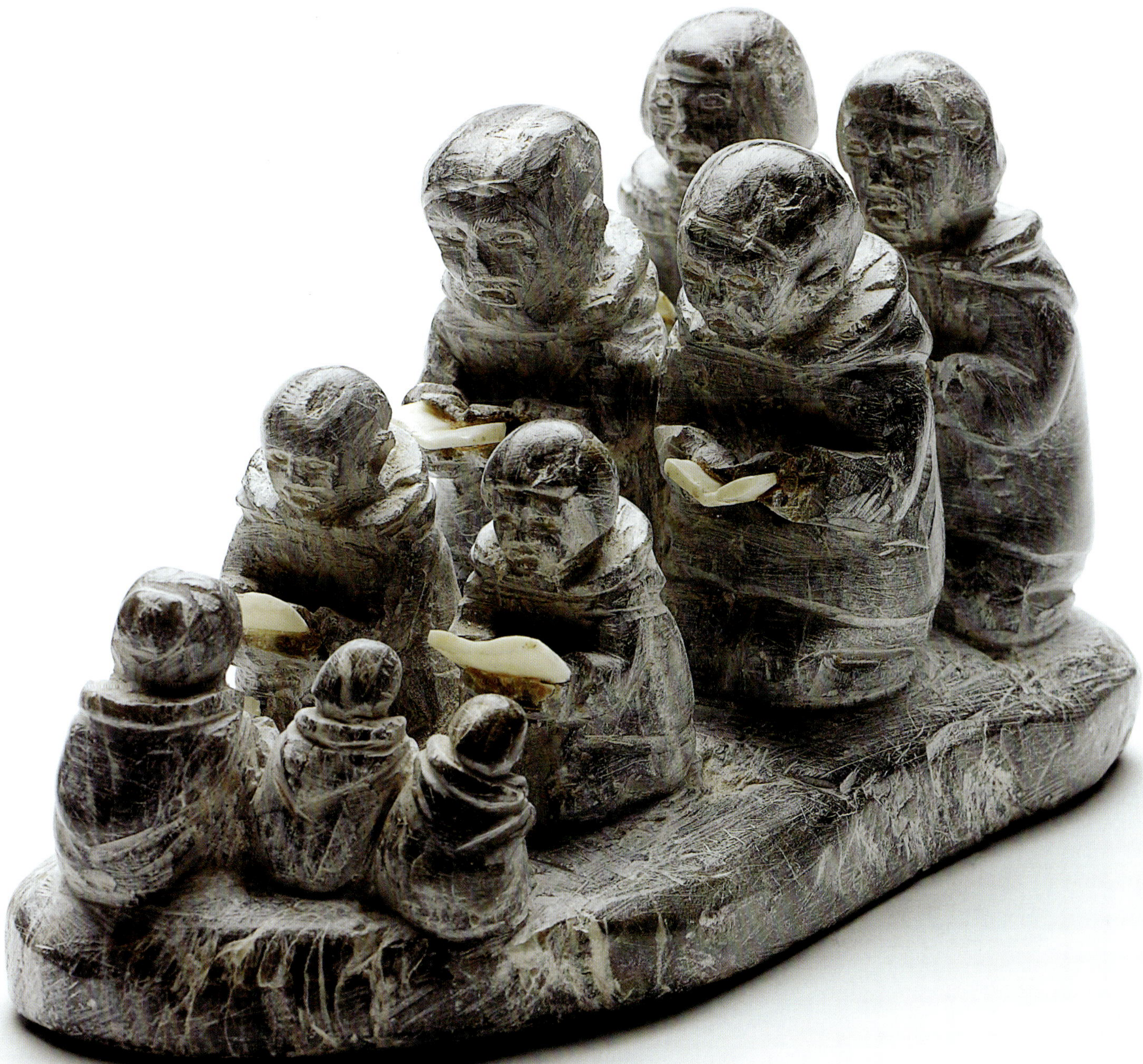

Ennutsiak, *Book Reading Scene*, c. 1959, stone, ivory, 9.0 x 7.2 x 17.3 cm

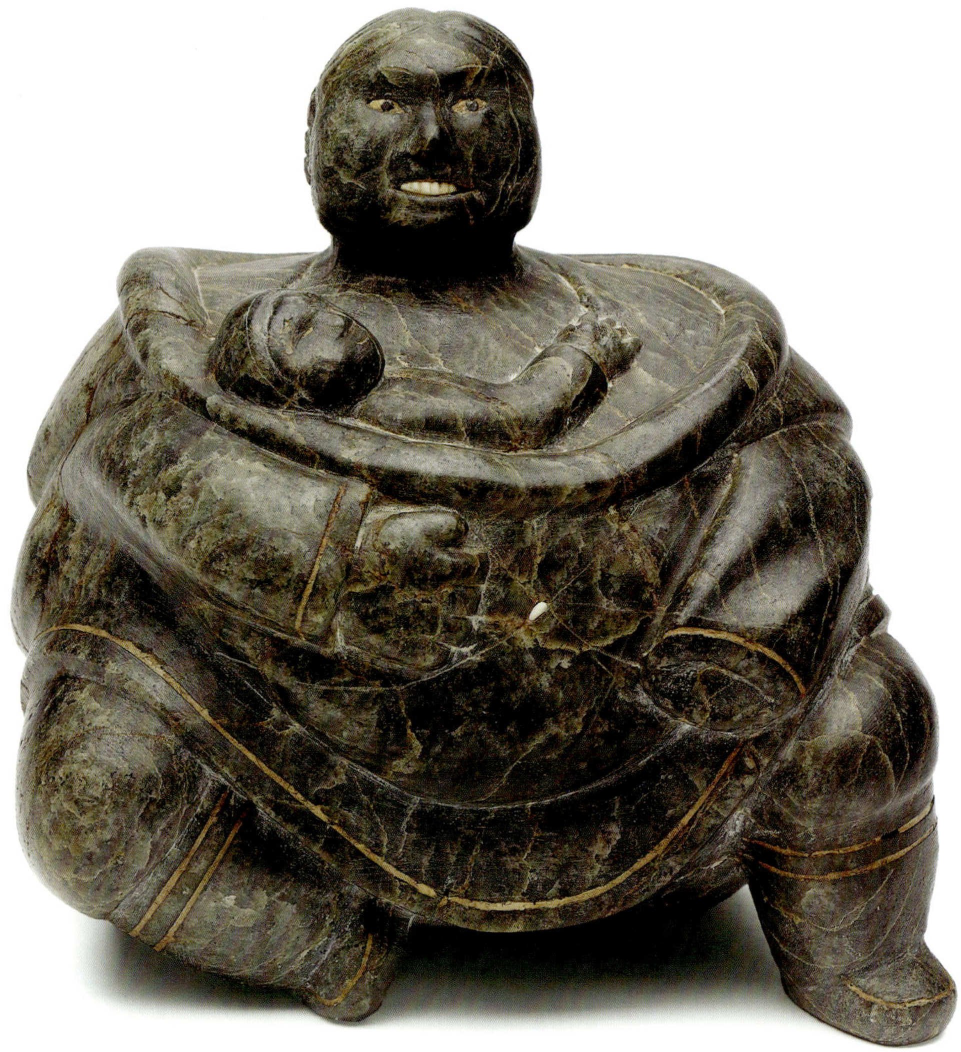

Isa Aqiattusuk Smiler, *Seated Mother with Child*, c. 1953,
stone, ivory inlay, 14.5 x 15.0 x 9.5 cm

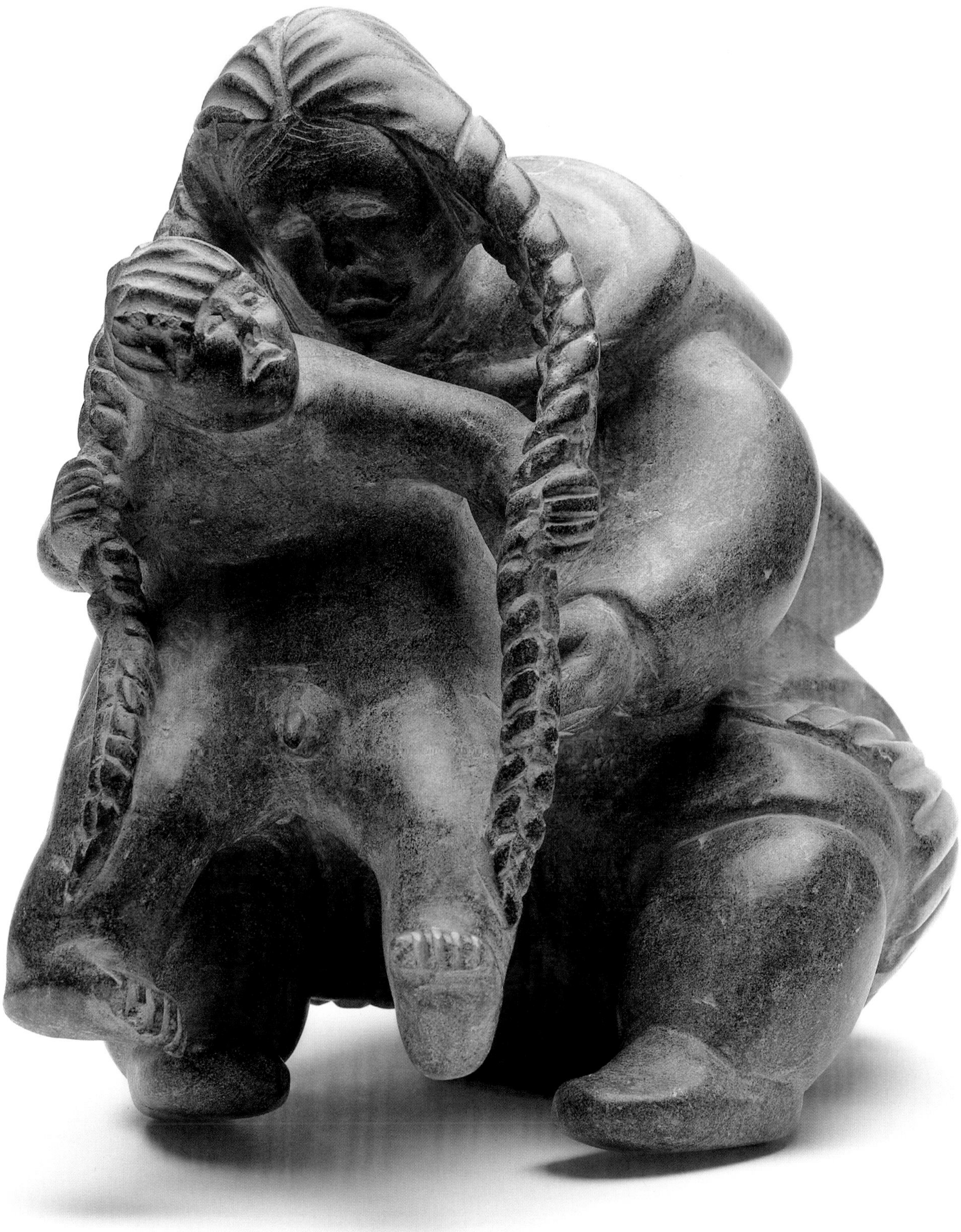

Paulusikotak Alaku, *Mother and Children*, c. 1959, stone, 26.9 x 32.0 x 22.4 cm

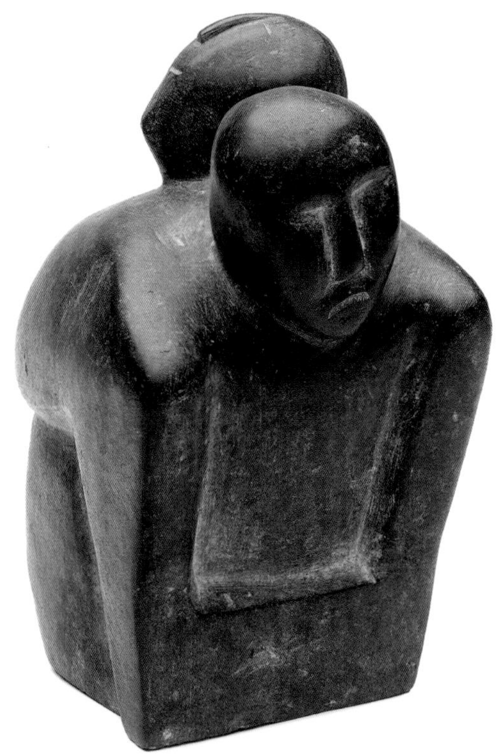

Mary Kahootsuak Miki, *Mother and Child*, before 1979, darkened stone, 22.6 x 16.4 x 13.8 cm

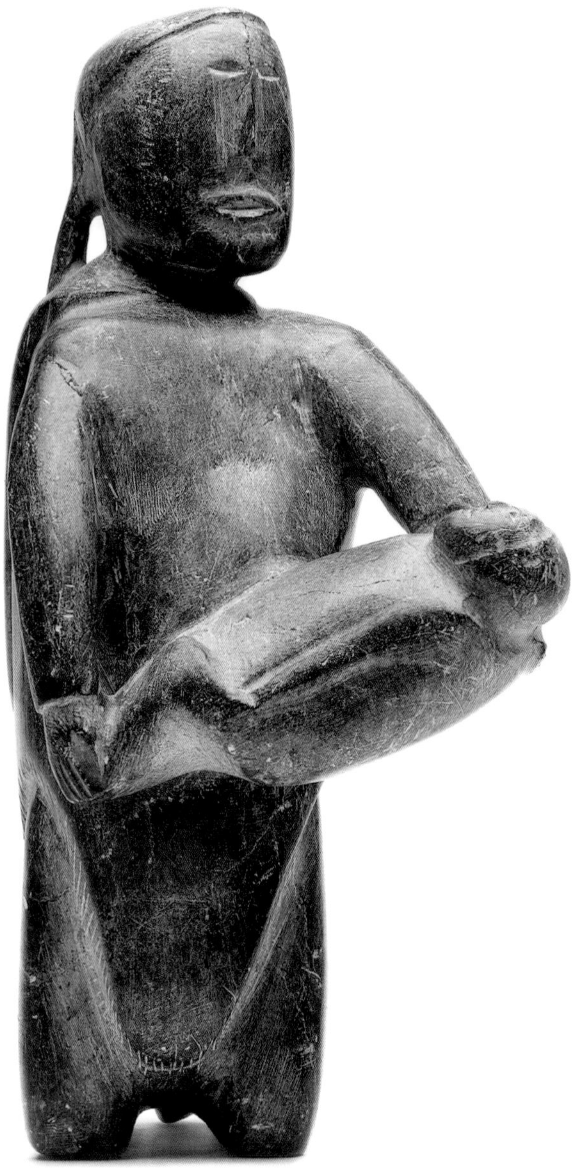

Margaret Uyauperq Aniksak, *Mother and Child*, c. 1964, darkened stone, 26.5 x 16.5 x 12.8 cm

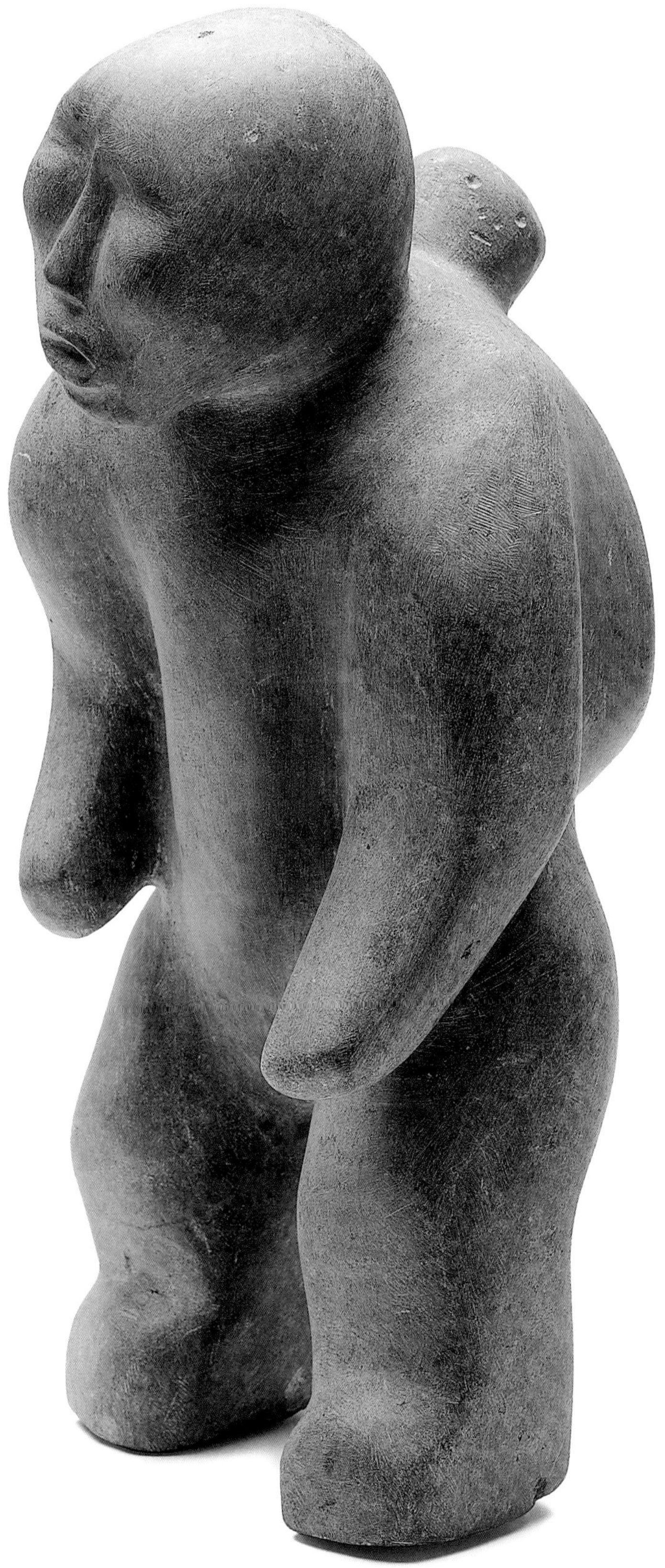

Marc Alikaswa, *Mother and Child*, 1980, stone, 40.5 x 20.0 x 19.5 cm

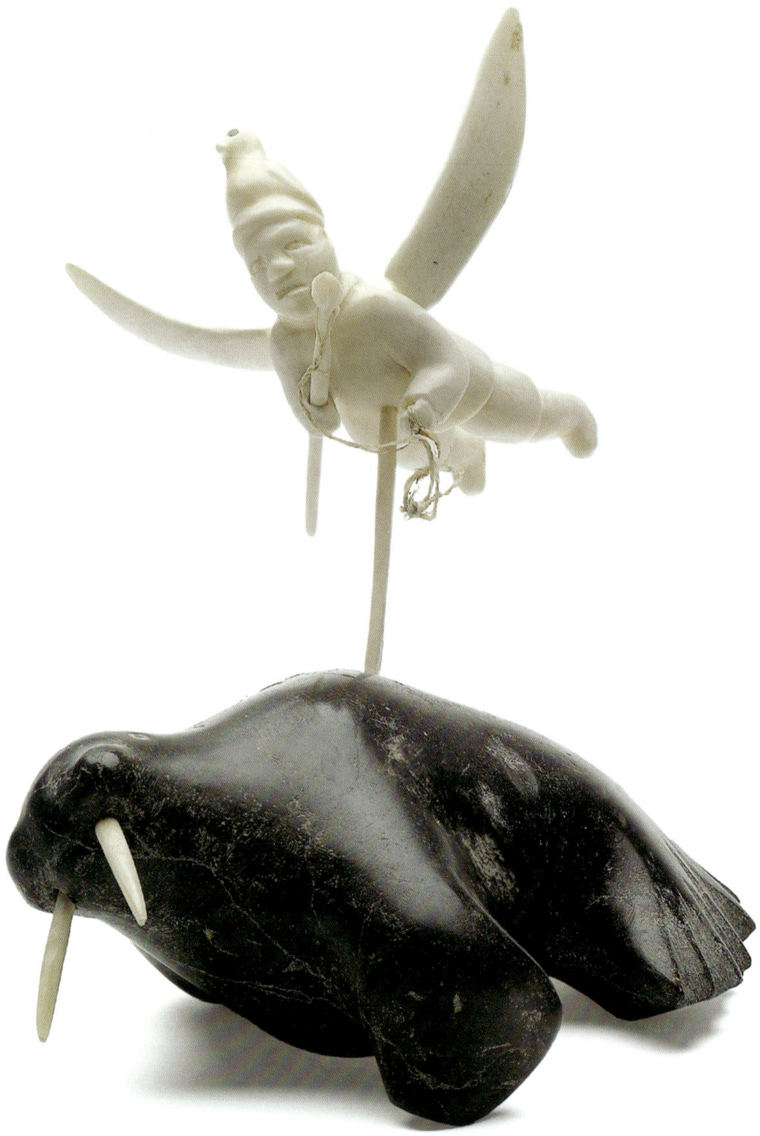

Bernadette Iguptark Tongelik, *Transformed Shaman and Walrus*, c. 1973, stone, ivory, sinew, inlay, 17.5 x 21.5 x 17.4 cm

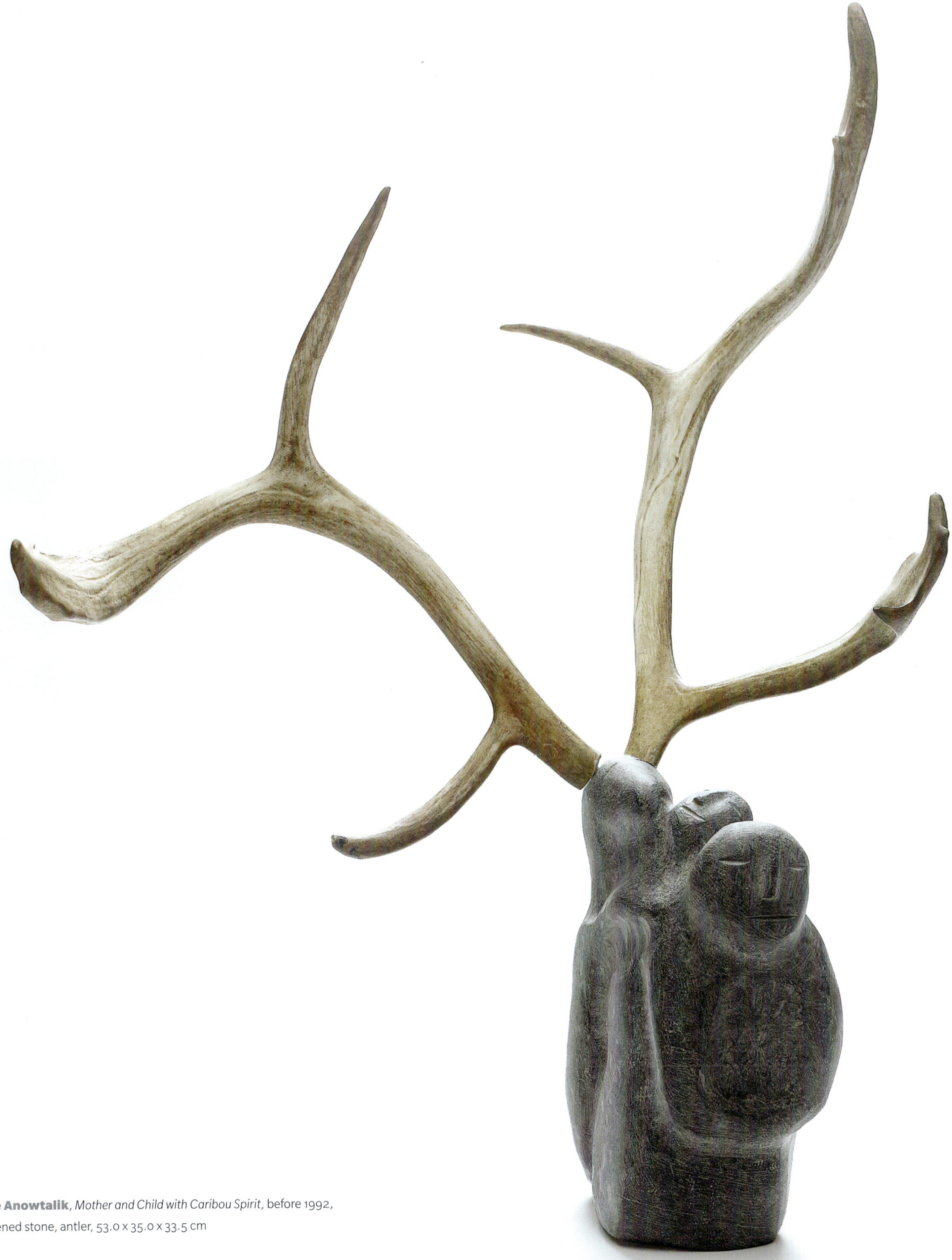

Luke Anowtalik, *Mother and Child with Caribou Spirit*, before 1992, darkened stone, antler, 53.0 x 35.0 x 33.5 cm

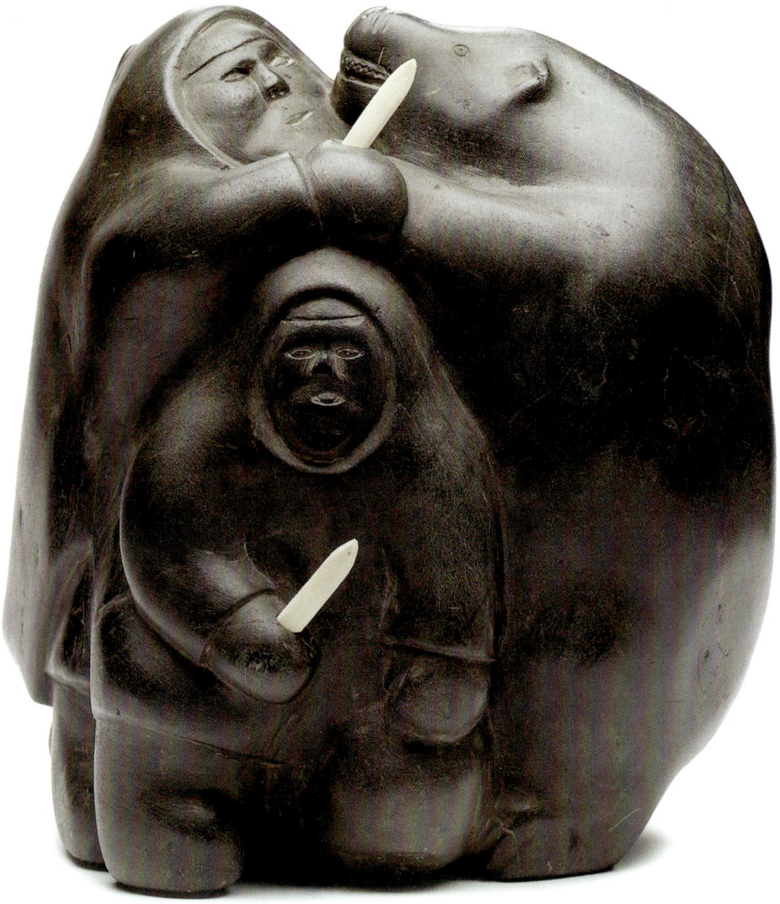

Mathew Aqigaaq, *Figures with Bear*, 1975–76, darkened stone, antler, 37.5 x 37.9 x 28.0 cm

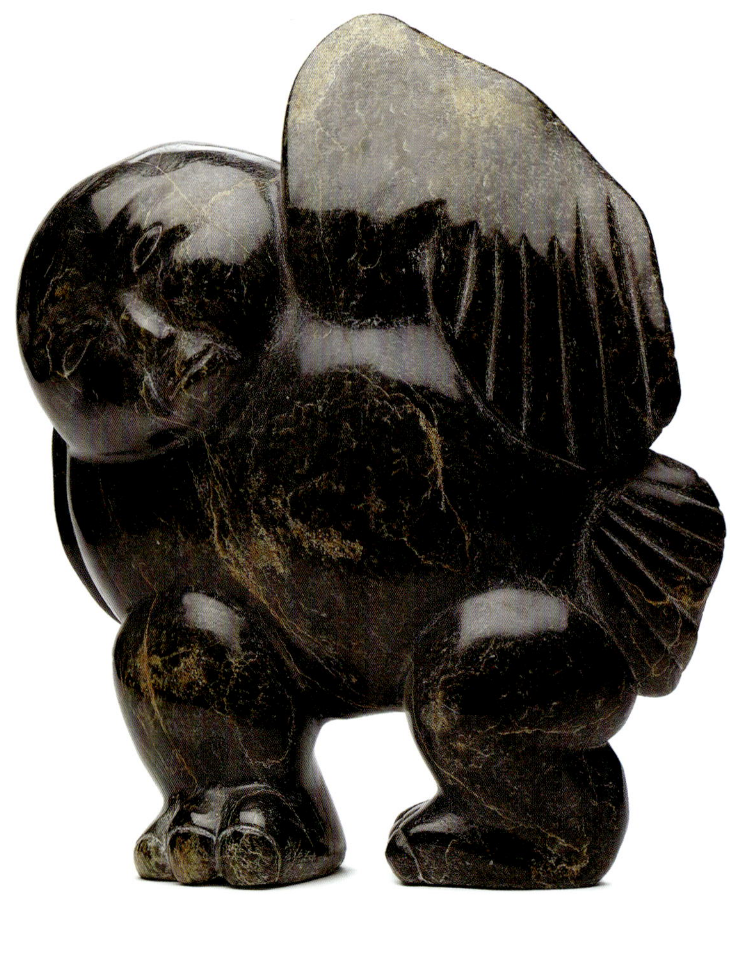

Qaqaq Ashoona, *Bird/Human Transformation*, 1986, stone, 42.2 x 36.4 x 13.4 cm

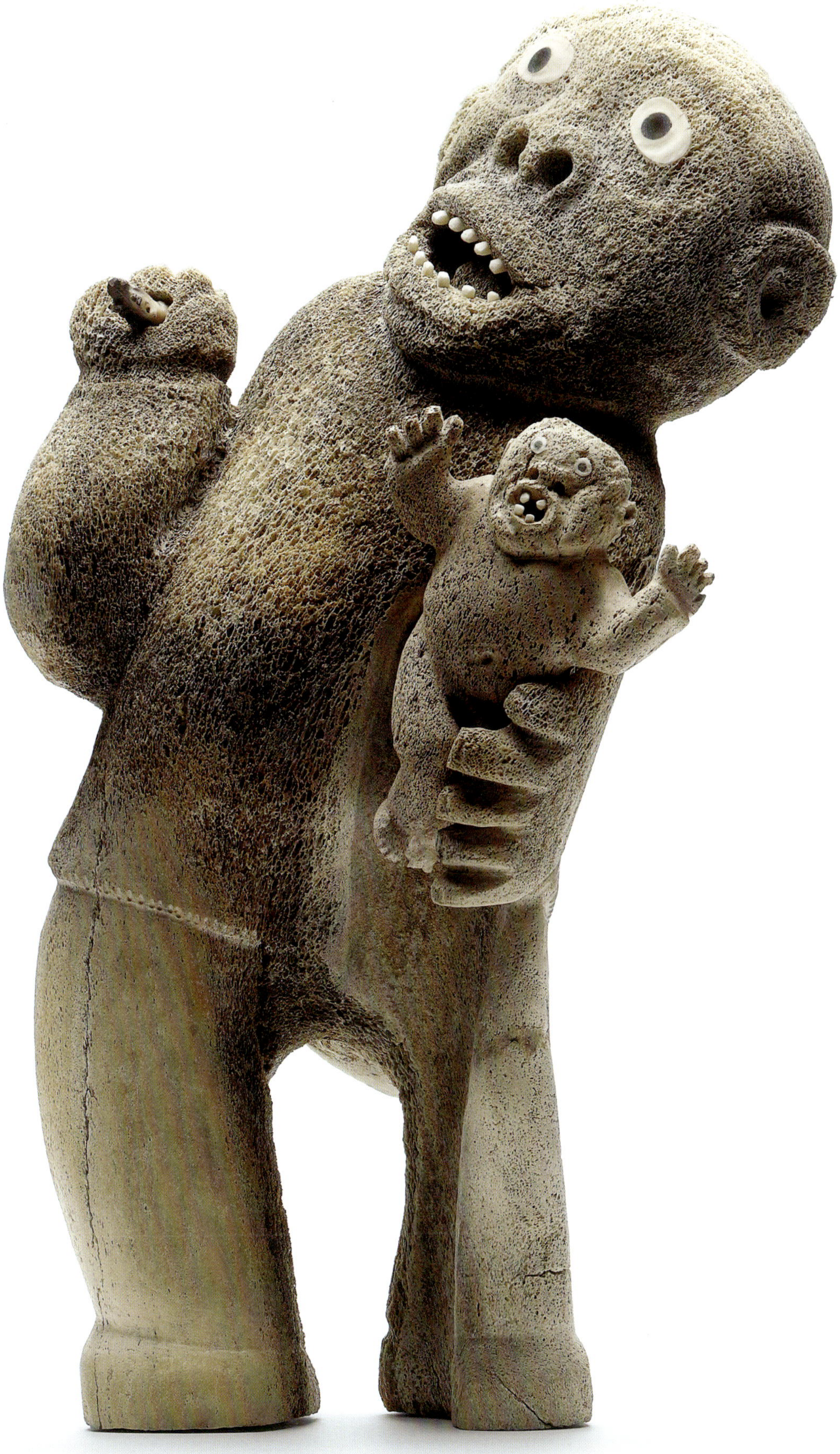

Nelson Takkiruq, *Mother Delousing Child*, 1992,
whale bone, ivory, stone, horn, 58.8 x 35.0 x 25.2 cm

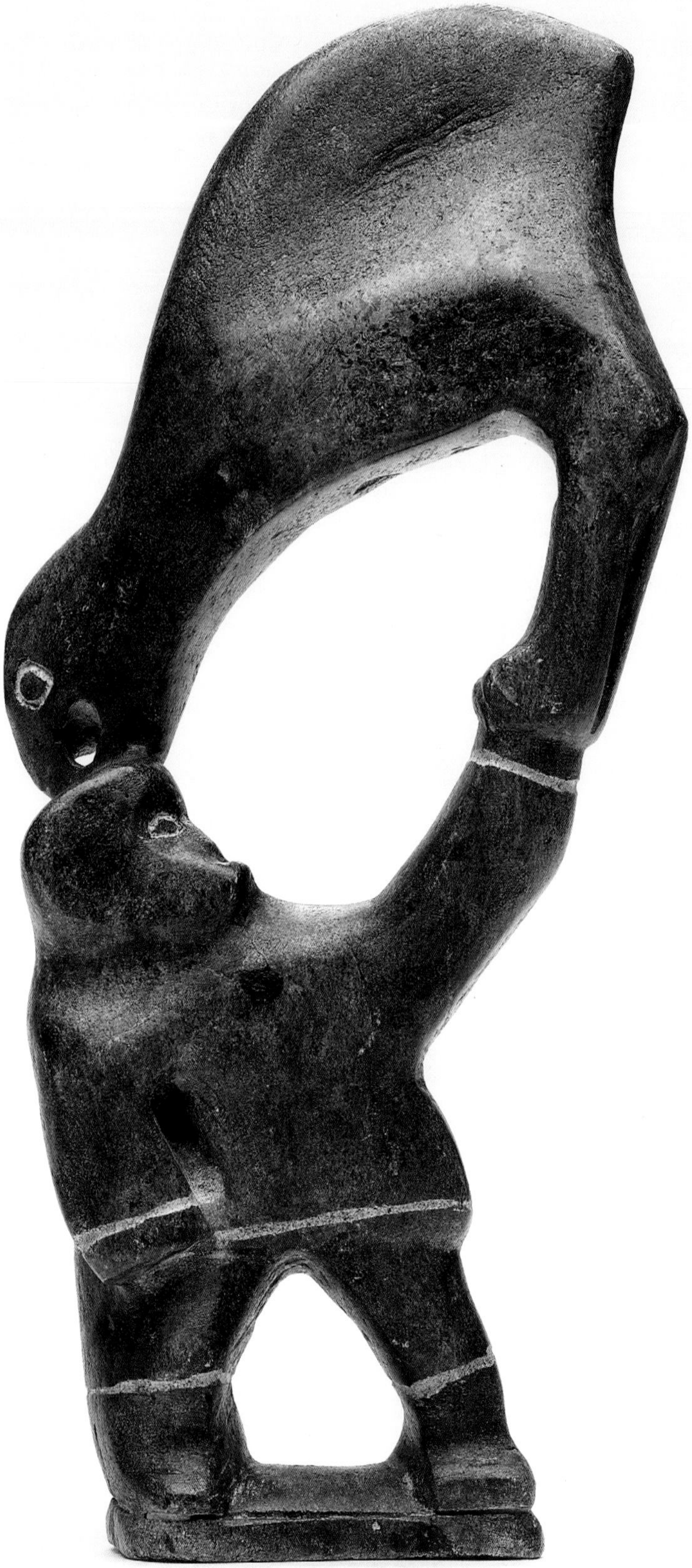

Thomassie Kudluk, *Stacked Up Together*, 1980, darkened stone, 29.8 x 13.8 x 4.4 cm

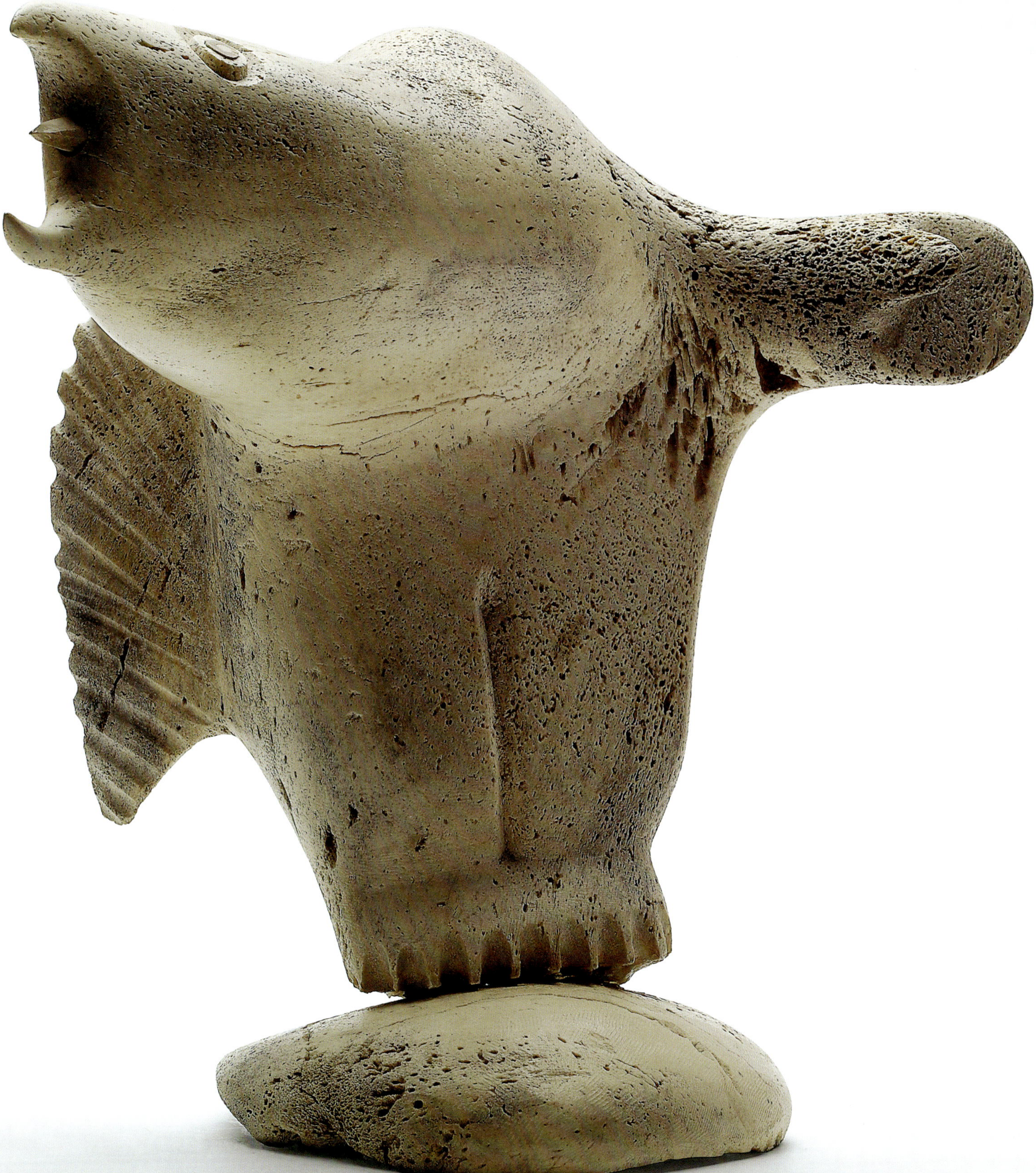

Karoo Ashevak, *Bird Spirit*, 1972,
whale bone, antler, ivory, 26.6 x 28.3 x 24.3 cm

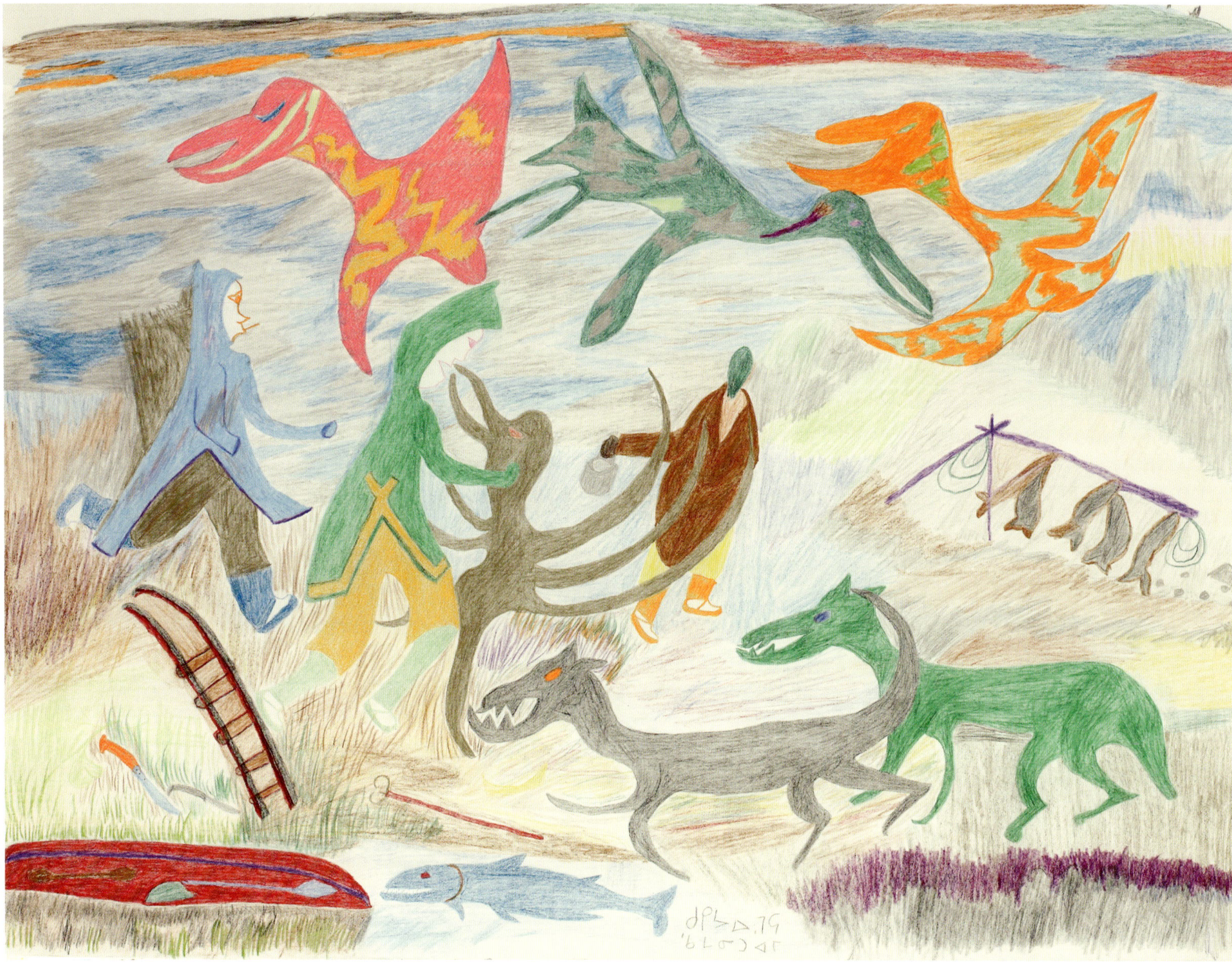

Myra Kukiiyaut, *Imaginary Scene*, c. 1980s, coloured pencil on paper, 57.8 x 76.2 cm

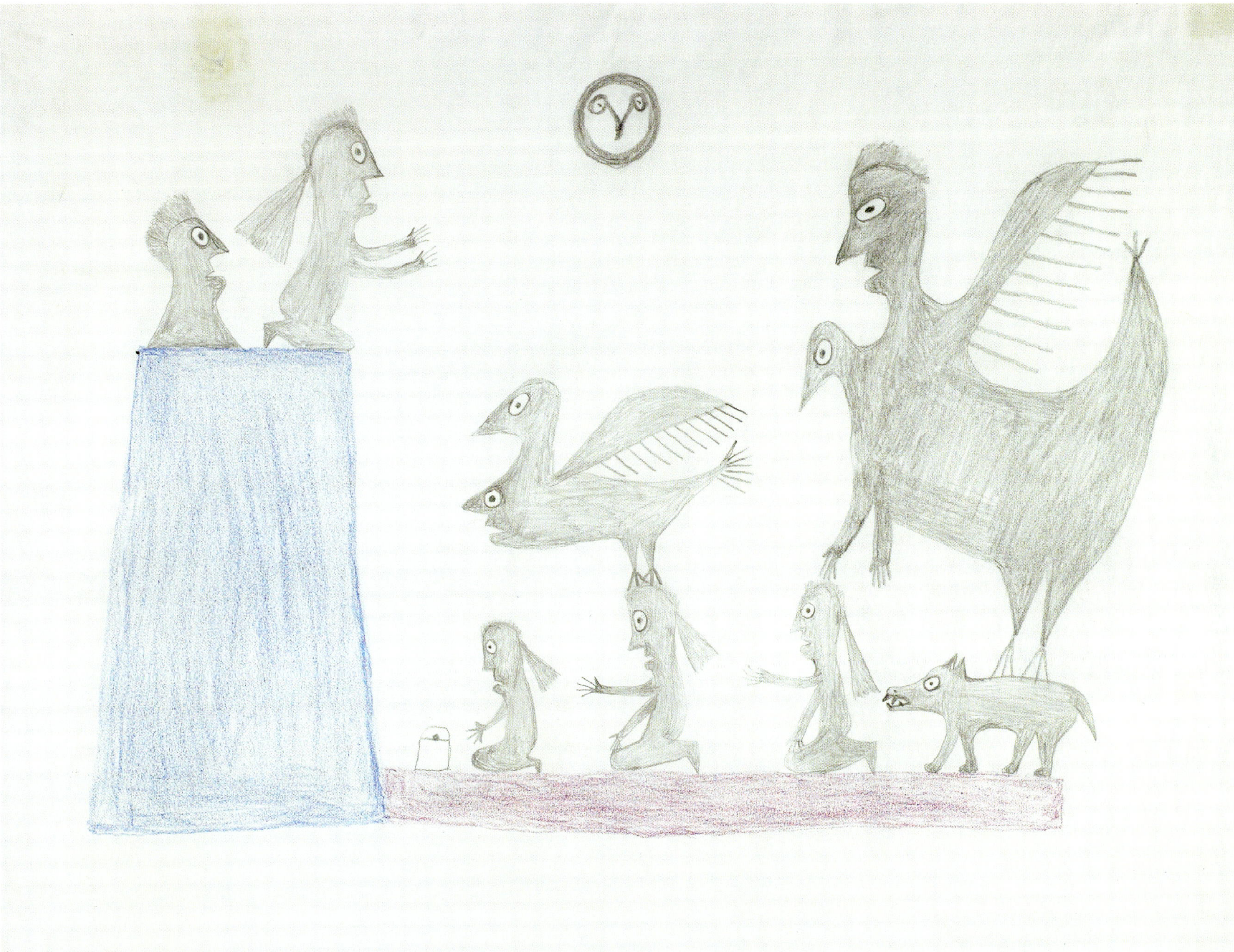

Anirnik Oshuitoq, *Drawing for the print "The Oracle,"* 1965,
graphite and coloured pencil on paper, 49.7 x 63.1 cm

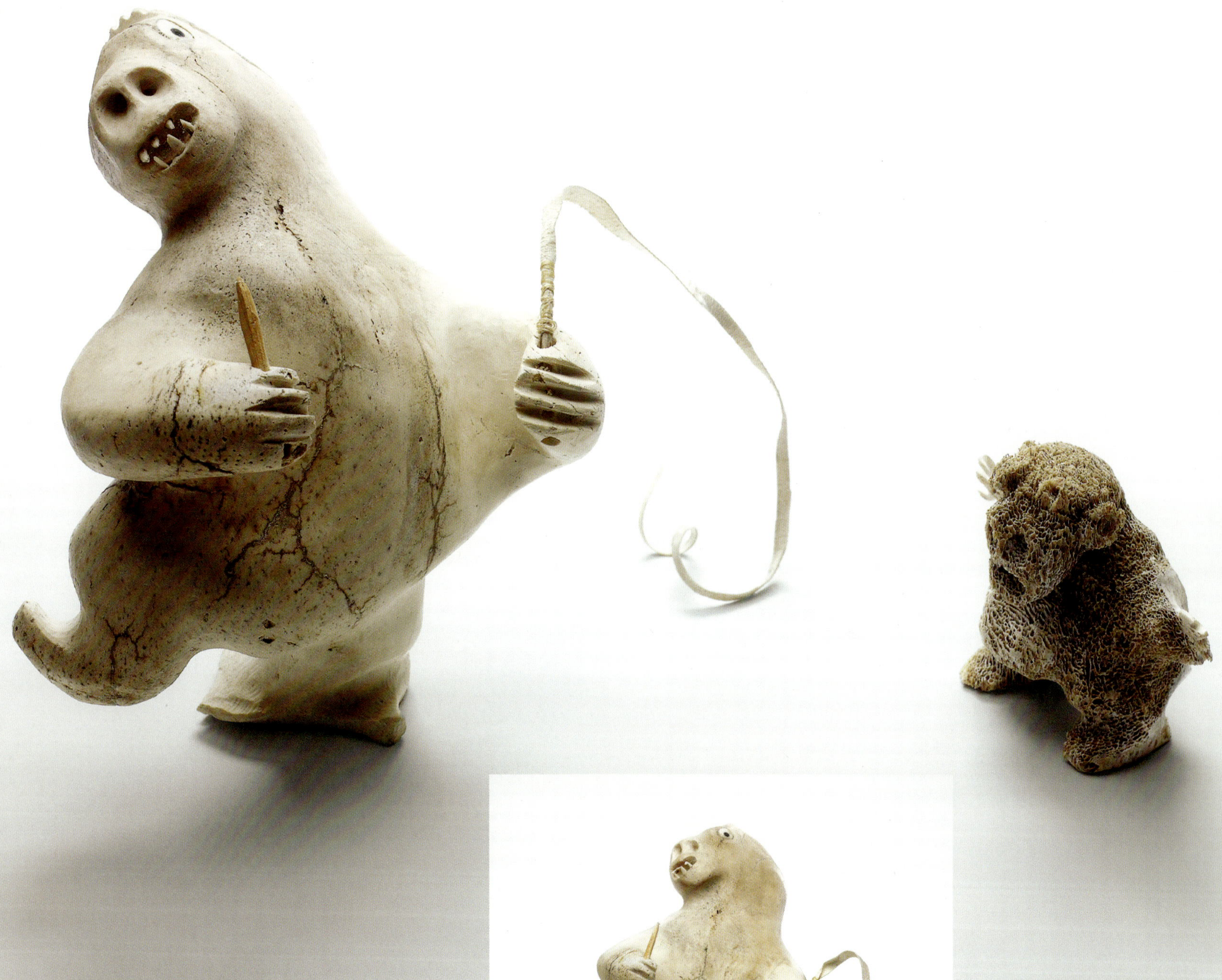

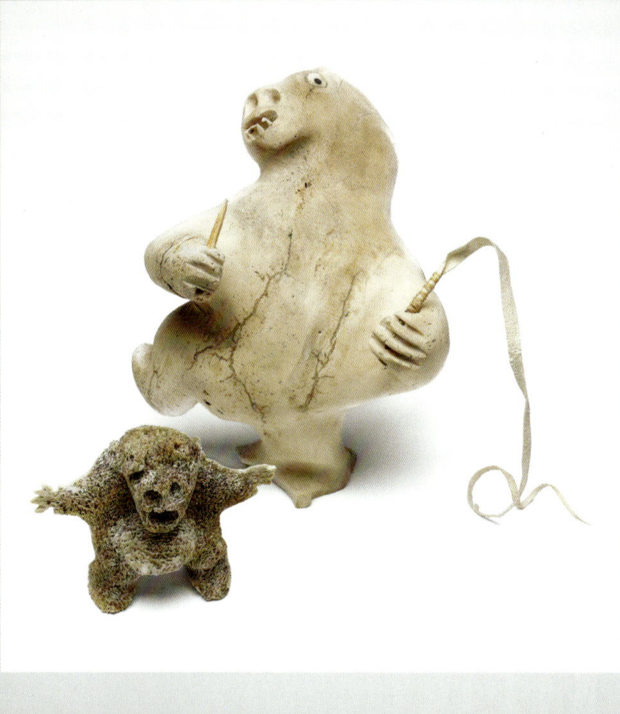

Judas Ullulaq, *Untitled*, c. 1990, whale bone, wood, sinew, hide, 22.1 x 19.8 x 18.2 cm (large figure), 10.0 x 13.2 x 7.0 cm (small figure)

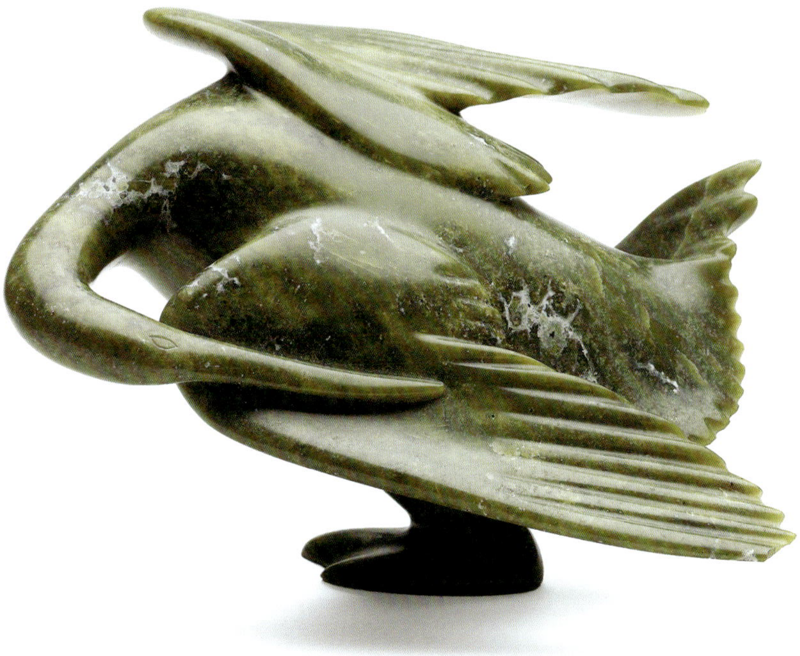

Lukta Qiatsuq, *Bird Preening*, 1983, stone, 20.9 x 28.2 x 22.5 cm

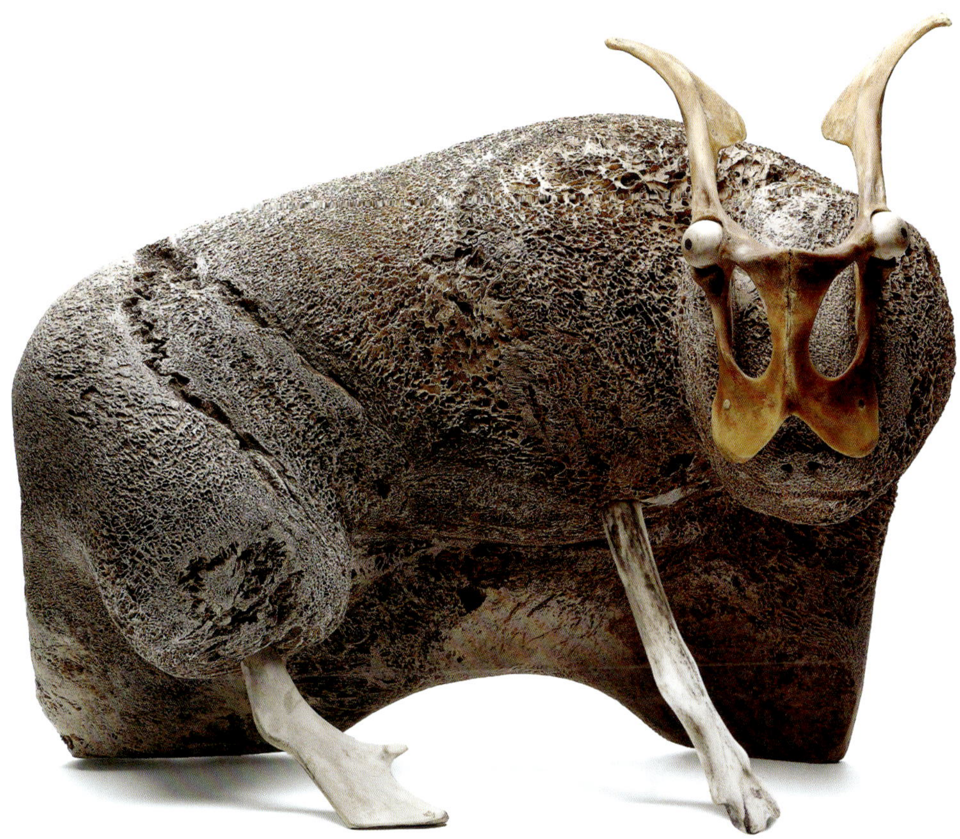

Augustin Anaittuq, *Muskox*, 1990,
whale bone, antler, bone, stone, 50.7 x 62.0 x 36.0 cm

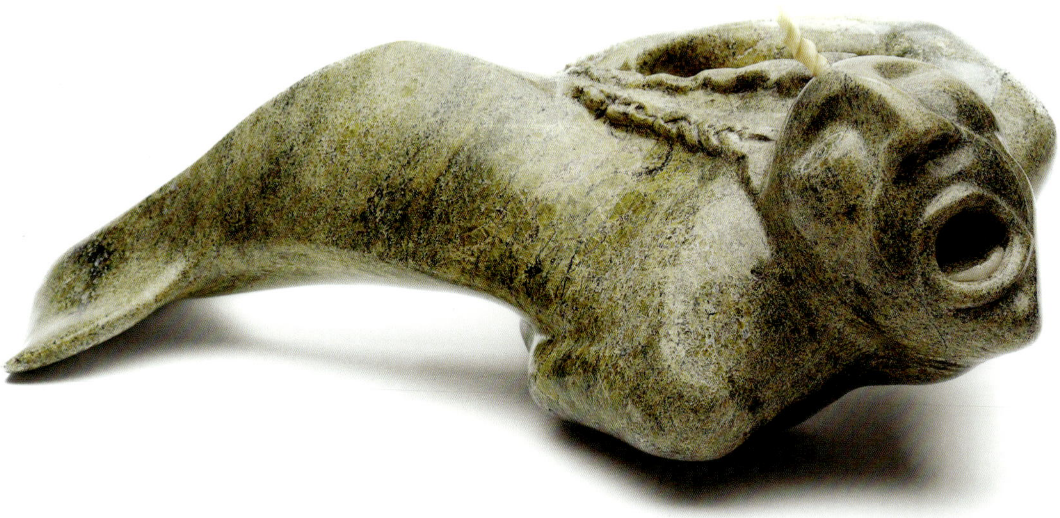

Nungusuituq Qaqyuraqyuk, *Sea Goddess*, 1988,
stone, ivory, plastic, 15.1 x 36.0 x 19.1 cm

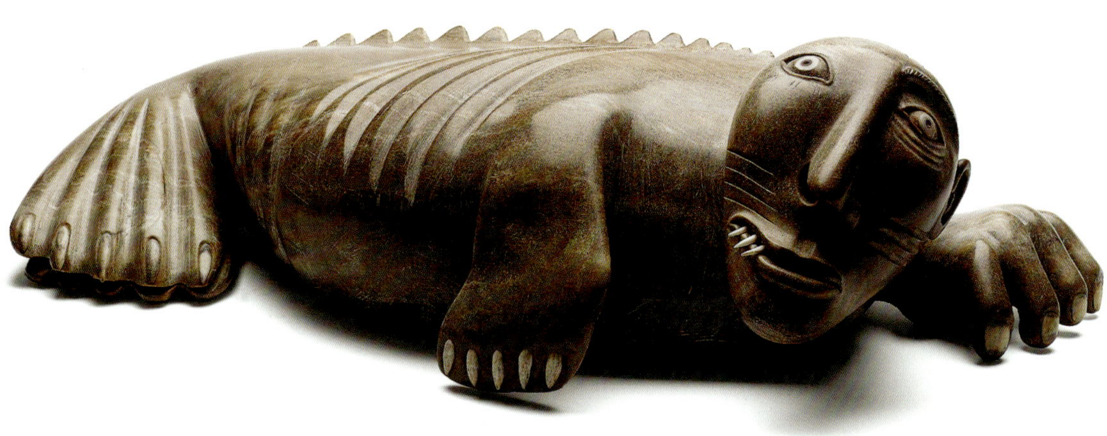

David Ruben Piqtoukun, *Shaman*, 1989,
Brazilian soapstone, antler, ivory, Arizona pipestone, stone inlay, 19.9 x 66.6 x 38.2 cm

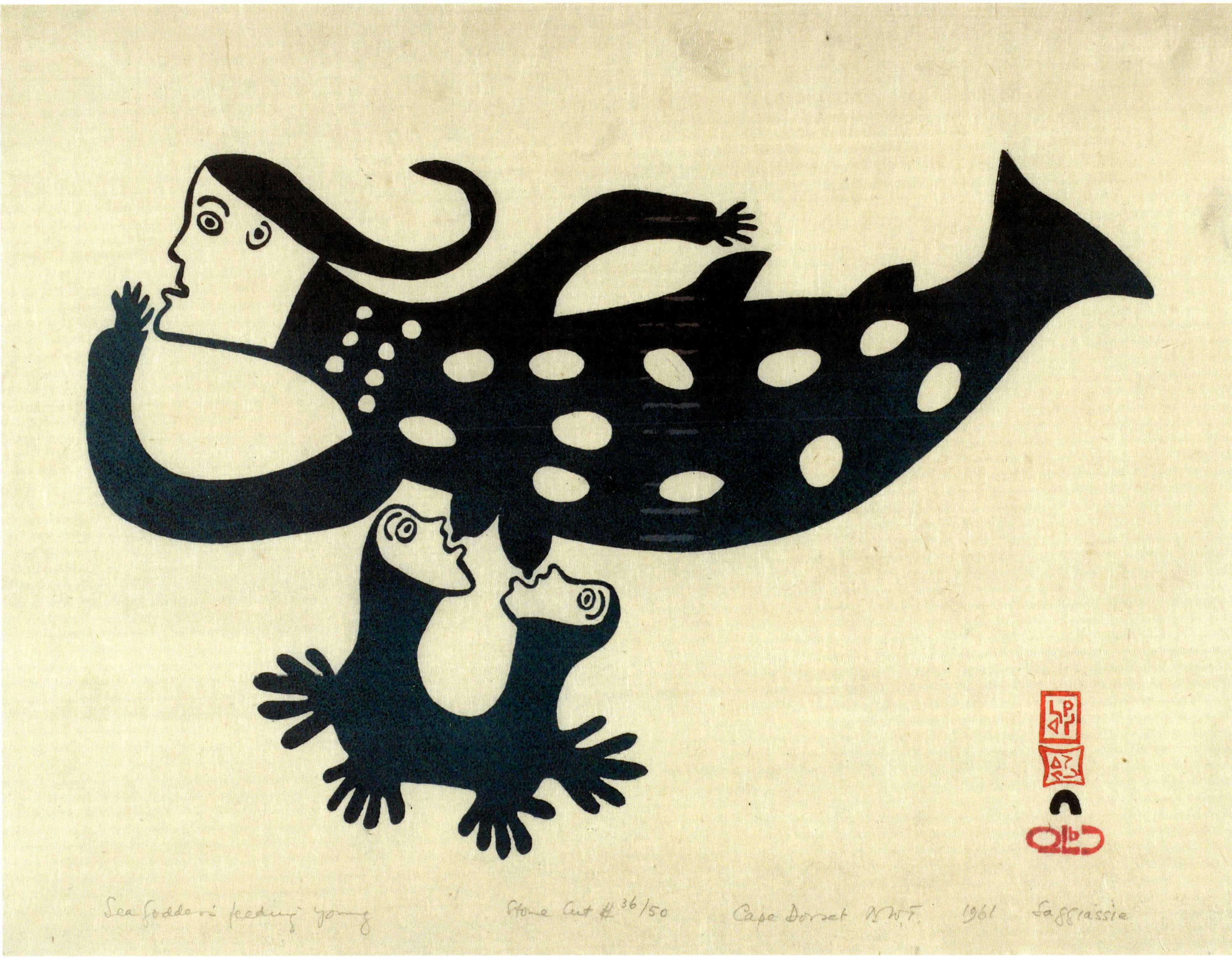

Sakiassie Ragee, *Sea Goddess Feeding Young*, 1961, stonecut on paper, 31.0 x 41.3 cm

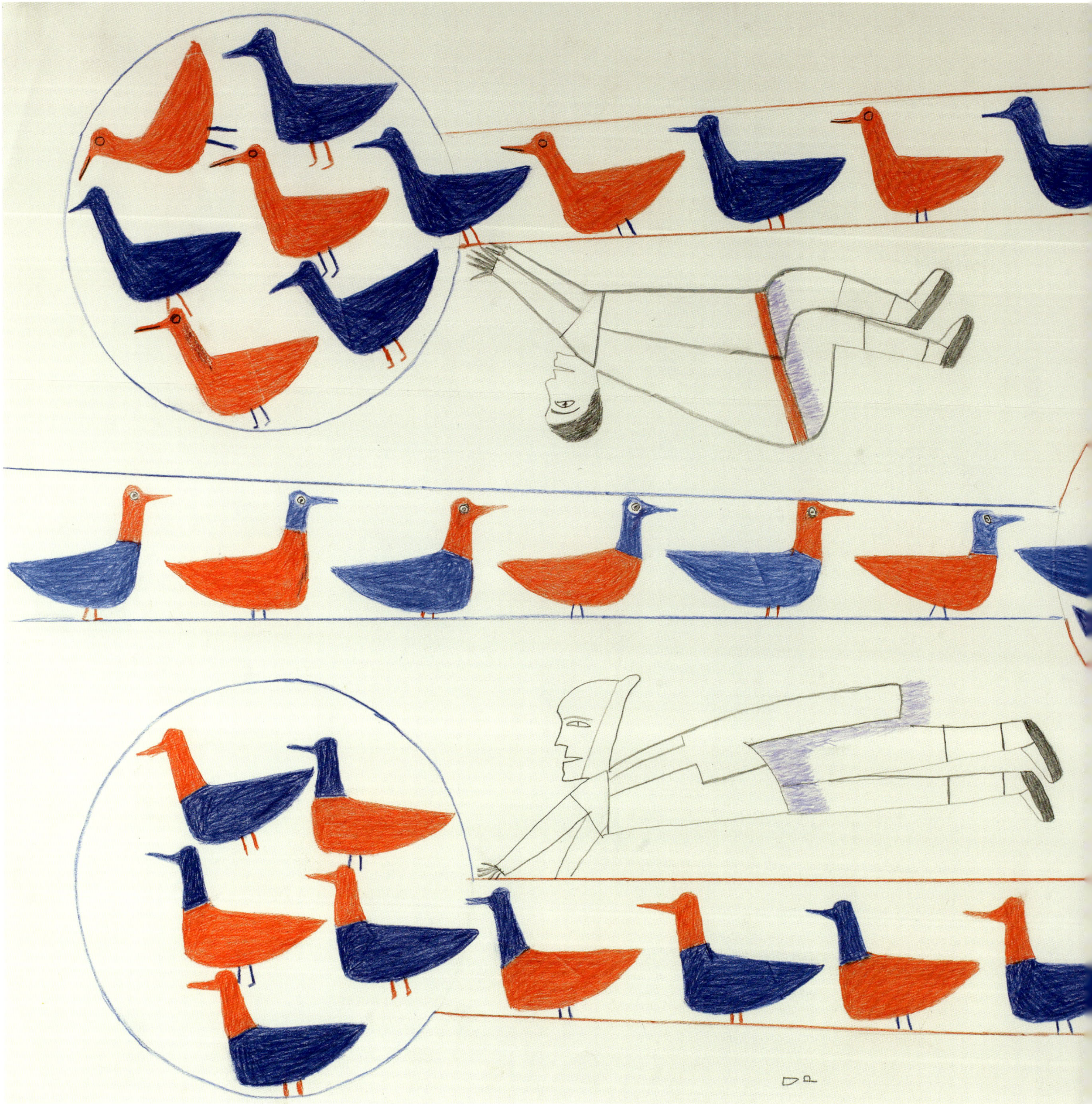

Jessie Oonark, *Capturing Geese*, early 1970s, coloured pencil and graphite on paper, 56.0 x 76.6 cm

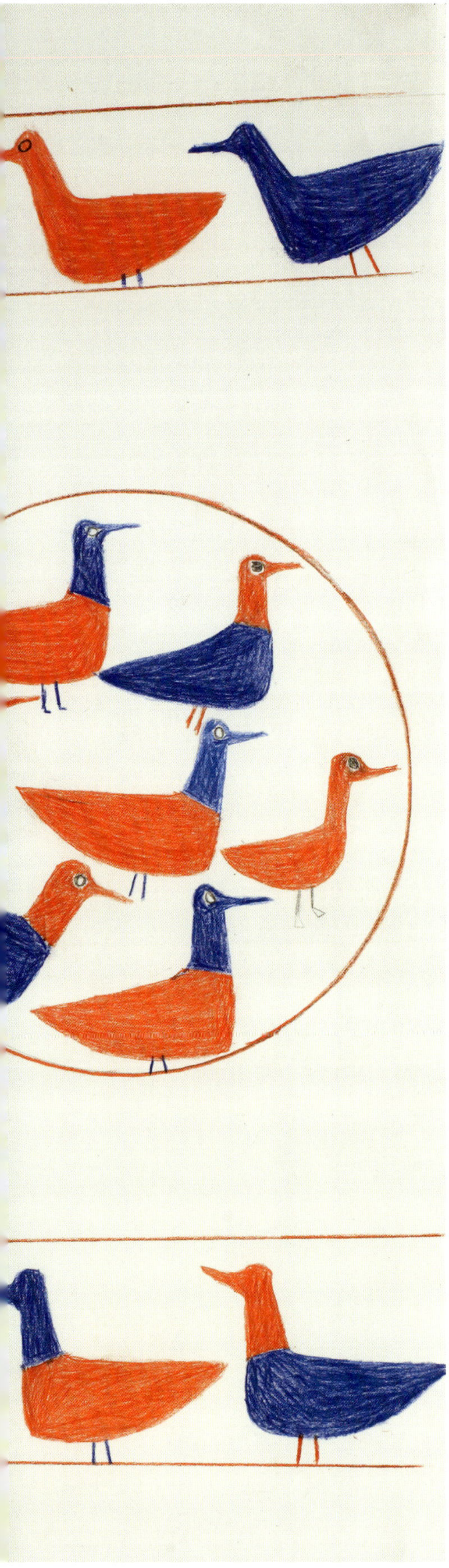

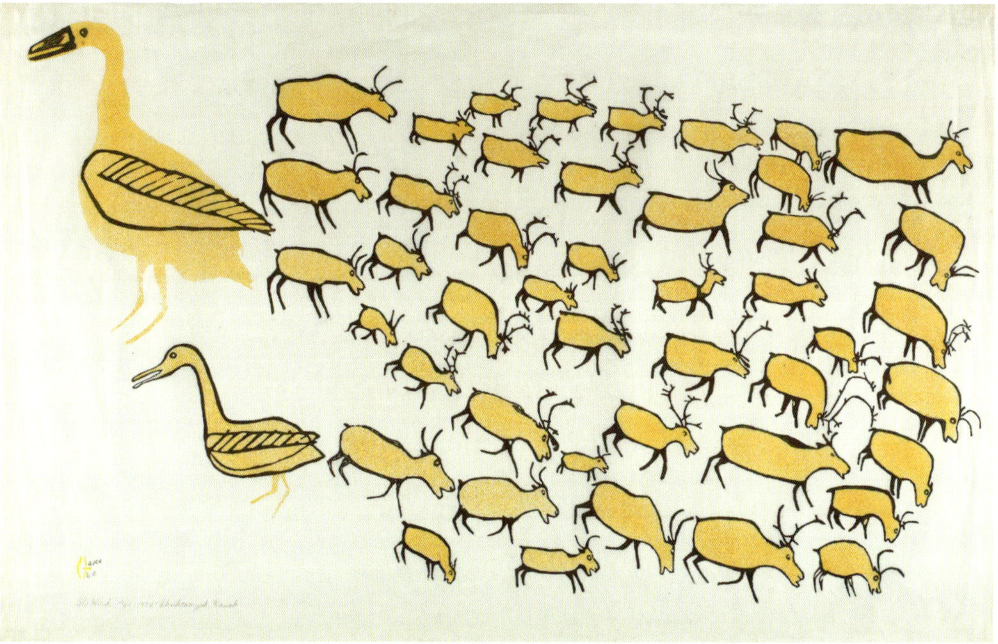

Luke Iksiktaaryuk, *The Herd*, 1972, stonecut and stencil on paper, 62.9 x 100.7 cm

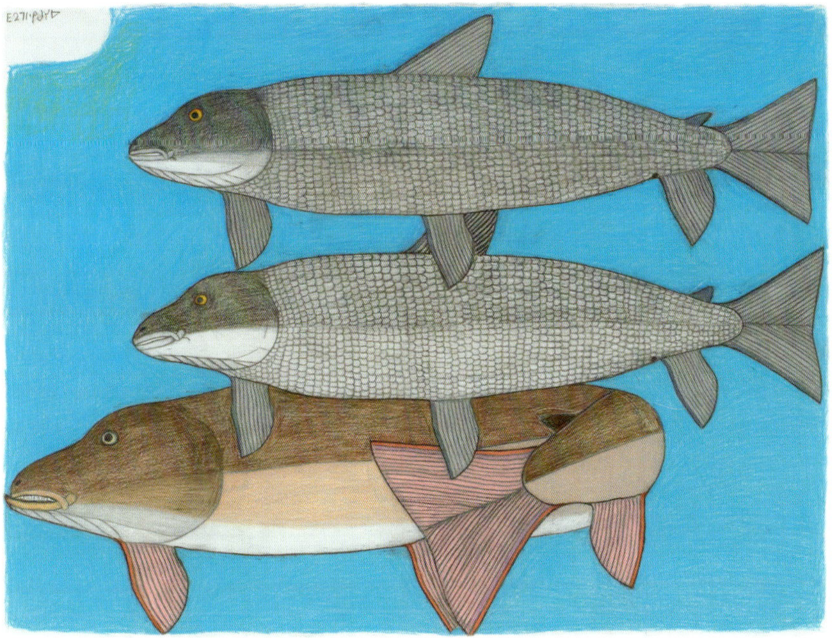

Janet Kigusiuq, *Three Large Fish*, 1984, coloured pencil and graphite on paper, 56.5 x 76.3 cm

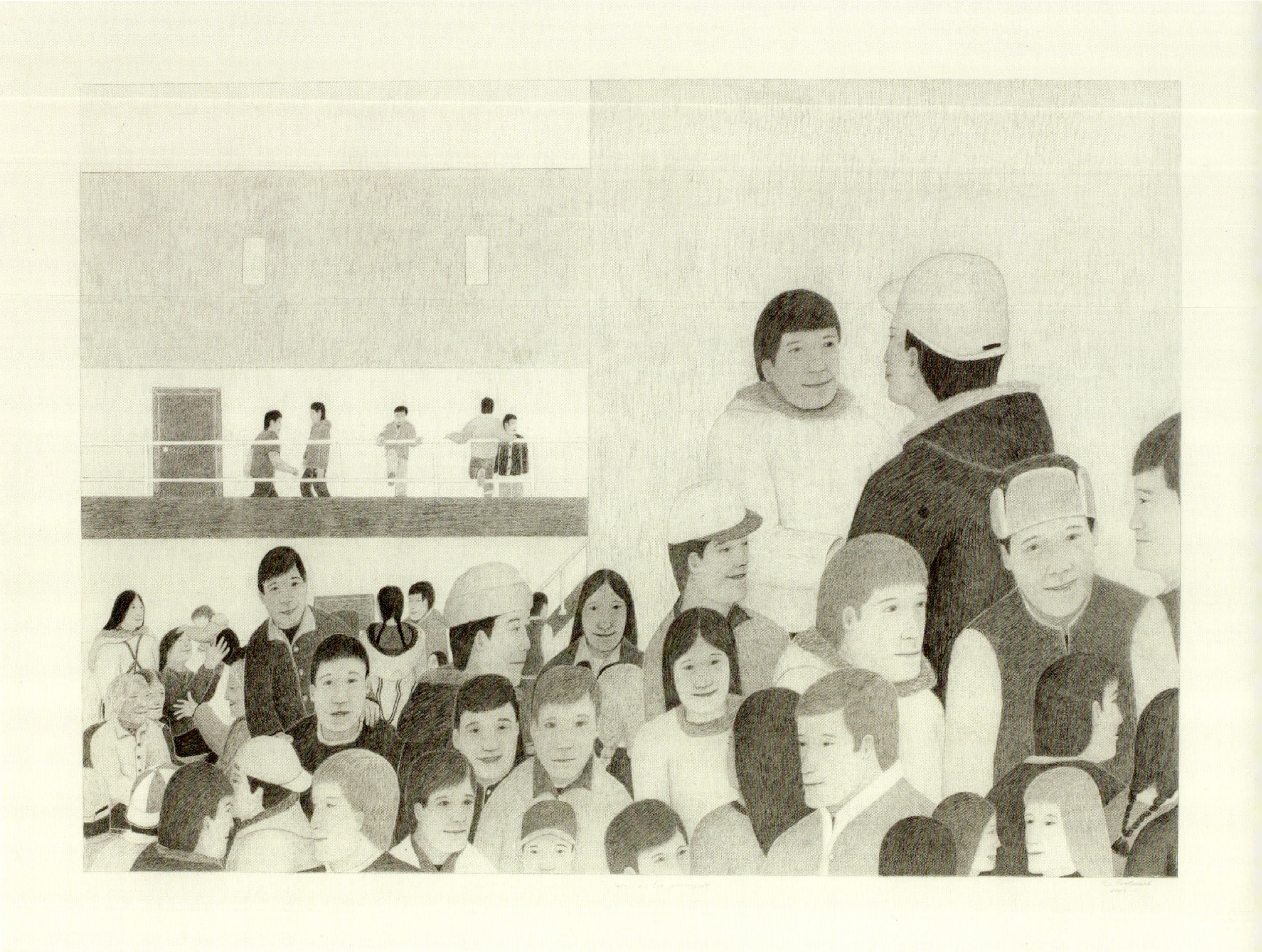

Itee Pootoogook, *Waiting for Penny Sale*, 2009, graphite on paper, 55.9 x 76.2 cm

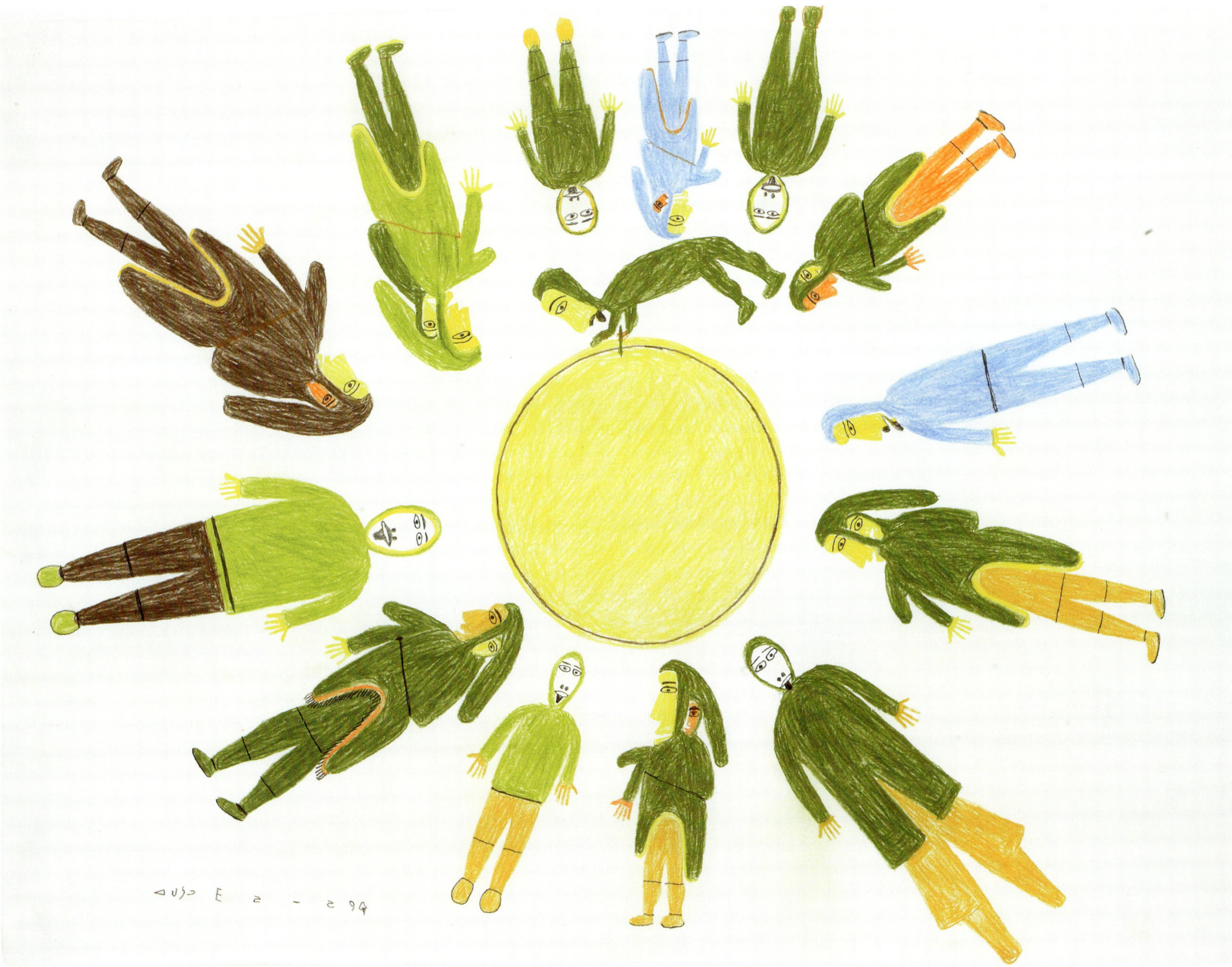

Luke Anguhadluq, *Drum Dance*, c. 1972, coloured pencil and graphite on paper, 58.3 x 79.9 cm

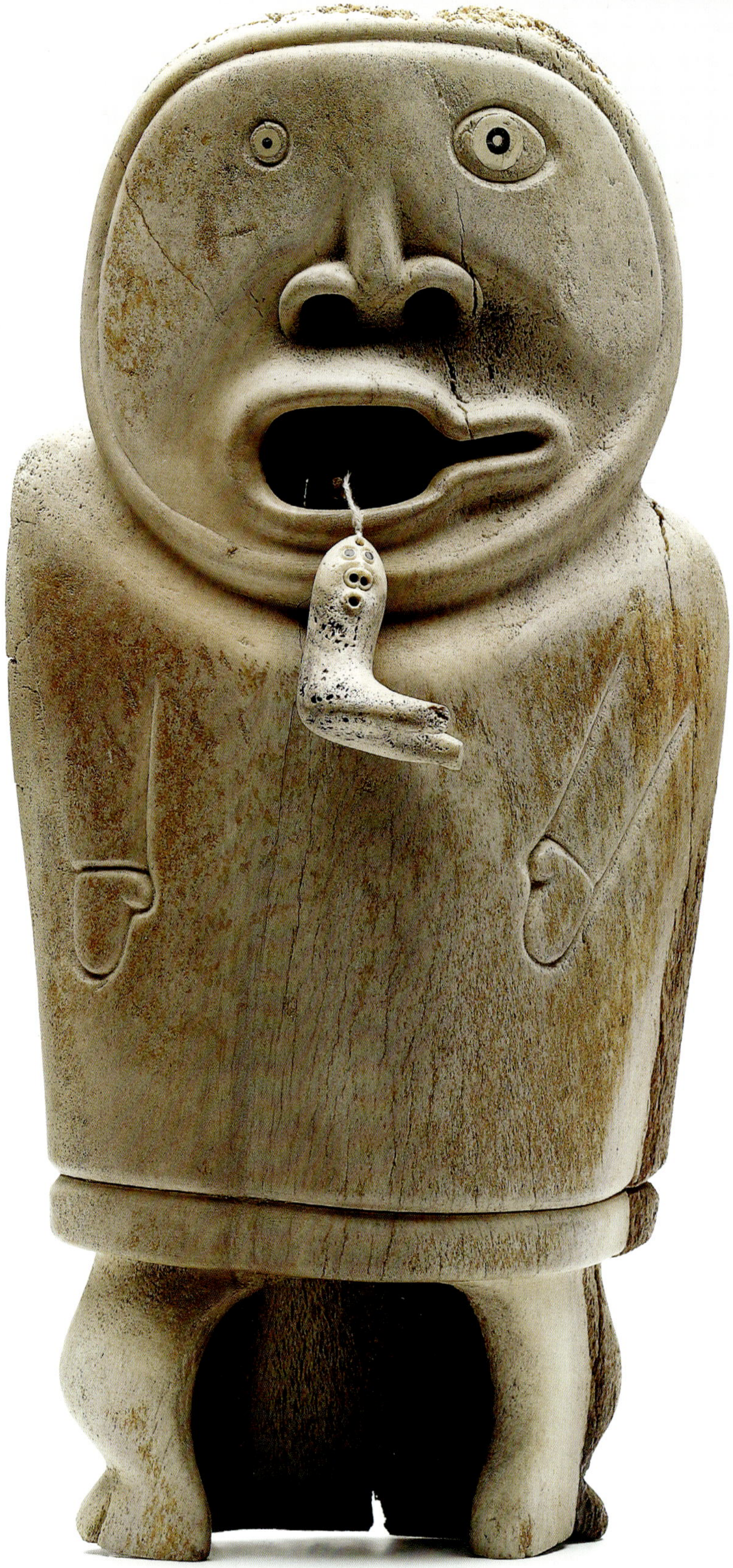

Karoo Ashevak, *Shaman with Spirit Helper*, 1972,
whale bone, ivory, stone, sinew, 47.7 x 23.6 x 16.6 cm

"I Am an Inuit Artist"
The Rise of the Individual Artist

Ingo Hessel

James Houston had begun identifying individual carvers in his articles and publications almost from the start.[1] His 1954 booklet *Canadian Eskimo Art* identified the artists for almost all illustrated works; interestingly, only a handful of these carvers became truly famous—and only in the 1960s, once their styles had matured. By the mid-1960s works by sculptors such as Johnny Inukpuk in Port Harrison (Inukjuak) (p. 26); Charlie Sivuarapik in Puvirnituq; Osuitok Ipeelee (pp. 138–39), Tudlik, Latcholassie Akesuk (pp. 136–37), Pauta Saila (pp. 116–17), Qaqaq Ashoona (p. 90) and his brother Kiugak (pp. 140–41) and others in Cape Dorset; Mathew Aqigaaq (p. 90) and George Tatanniq (pp. 130–31) in Baker Lake; John Tiktak (pp. 126–27) and Tuna Iquliq in Rankin Inlet were held in major public and private collections and illustrated in books. Note the switch from the term "carver" to "sculptor"; the term *sculptor* carries a bit more prestige and in the 1960s was beginning to replace the more modest *carver*.

One impediment to the early recognition of sculptors was the problem of signatures and titles of works. As a rule, sculptors did not title their works, and art dealers were content to assign generic titles to them. More importantly, many early sculptures were not signed at all; others were signed with RCMP-issued disc numbers or were signed in Inuktitut syllabics; these identifiers were not meaningful as signatures to dealers and collectors in the south.[2] Furthermore, names and spellings were inconsistent; consequently, many sculptures remain unattributed or misattributed to this day. The system of signature chops (and/or pencilled signatures) for graphic artists and printmakers was much more straightforward. Despite the fact that Inuit artists' names are difficult for many "southerners" to remember, spell and pronounce, a number of them became quite famous.

Needless to say, Edmund Carpenter had an opinion on publicizing the works and names of certain artists: he attacked it as "a new concept, out of keeping with the complete anonymity of aboriginal Eskimo art."[3] As usual, he was partly right; the concept was new, but his assertion that "aboriginal Eskimo art" was "completely anonymous" is false; presumably, the artists and their community would have known who had made which works.[4] Nelson Graburn quite rightly suggested that Inuit were probably encouraged to sign their works because, as the most highly valued artworks in Western culture are produced by identifiable artists, the art-collecting public would therefore naturally value art made by "name" artists from another culture.[5] These criticisms do not alter the fact that Houston enthusiastically promoted certain artists because he believed they merited it.

The real implication of the "rise of the artist" in Inuit art goes far beyond mere name recognition in the South. The true importance lies in the shift in self-image for some makers of Inuit art objects. This shift may result from some or all of the following realizations: that the artist possesses a well-defined personal style and unique vision; that her peers recognize her special ability; that Qallunaat buyers, advisers, dealers and collectors give him special attention; that she is paid premium prices; that his work appears in exhibitions and publications; that she may feel "compelled" to produce art (or a certain type of art, or art devoted to a particular theme) even in the absence of significant monetary incentive; that the artist feels he is leaving a cultural legacy to his children or his community; that her work is emulated by others; that he works in a spirit of friendly competition with other artists; and, importantly, that she loves creating art and finds it fulfilling. Modesty sometimes prevents Inuit artists from seeing themselves as "true artists"; interestingly, there seem to be relatively few Inuit who err in the opposite direction, thinking themselves to be artists when in fact they are not. Outsiders sometimes describe someone as an artist before the person in question really understands or accepts the label.[6] The sense of one's status as an artist is strongest in communities such as Cape Dorset and Baker Lake, where important elder artists such as Pitseolak Ashoona (pp. 160–61) and Jessie Oonark (pp. 162–63) have produced veritable dynasties of artistic children and grandchildren. As Kenojuak has said, "When I am dead, I am sure there will still be people discussing my art."[7]

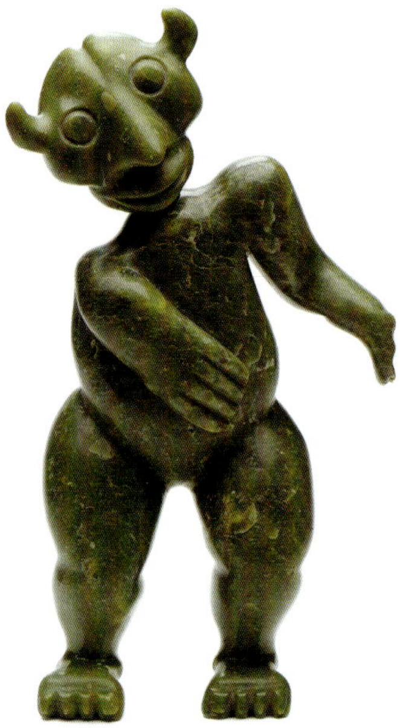

Kiugak Ashoona, *Spirit Figure*, c. 1961, stone, 37.0 x 21.6 x 13.6 cm. Gift of Samuel and Esther Sarick, 1989, © Dorset Fine Arts

In stark contrast, there was a deliberate attempt in the co-op system in Arctic Quebec, beginning in the late 1960s, to de-emphasize the importance of individual artistic talent, to foster egalitarianism and a more collective spirit of enterprise, to limit the influence of outsiders and to turn over sales quickly.[8] This might explain why highly original talents such as Joe Talirunili (pp. 111–13), Davidialuk Alasua Amittu (pp. 114–15) and Josie Papialuk were celebrated and promoted in the South with considerable reservations on the part of Arctic Quebec co-op management. One can only speculate on the tensions created by the differences between the egalitarian nature of Inuit society and the meritocratic nature of the art world. In any case, in this discussion I am more interested in the "sense of self" as a creator and less in the relative merits of particular artists.

The term "artist" has, of course, been used to describe any Inuk who has ever picked up a file, pencil or needle. There is a delightful *New Yorker* cartoon by Boris Drucker, depicting an Inuit couple: the husband carves a bear, the wife sews a kamik. The husband declares, "What you're doing is art, too—everything we do is art!"[9]

We are dealing once again with a relatively subtle shift in emphasis, not a revolution. The shift in emphasis, beginning in the early 1960s, and clearly evident in the 1970s and 1980s, is from "Inuit who make art" to "Inuit artists." The first category of artmaker is still with us and will always be in the majority. The second category comprises artists for whom, to *some* degree, formal or stylistic concerns, personal history, favourite themes and originality take precedence over adherence to community artistic concerns or styles. These artists work either within or outside the Inuit art mainstream; hence, their work might be either respected by other artists and imitated by lesser talents, or ignored or even gently derided by their peers. In Inuit villages, where a fairly egalitarian attitude is still the norm, talented or successful artists are respected as good role models and providers for their extended families, in much the same way that good hunters or good seamstresses might be admired. Furthermore, technical skill, originality of composition, and to a considerable extent, adherence to realism, are highly regarded by Inuit.[10] Inuit art historian Marie Routledge confirmed that in general, among Inuit sculptors at least, there was a growing sense of professionalism in the 1970s; furthermore, she sensed that artists such as the brothers Qaqaq and Kiugak Ashoona of Cape Dorset (p. 90 and pp. 140–41) "were acutely conscious of the manner in which they composed their pieces."[11]

The works of these artists do not necessarily transcend the styles or themes of Inuit art. Often, quite the opposite is true; the images actually epitomize classic Inuit themes or styles. Dancing bears by Pauta Saila of Cape Dorset (pp. 116–17)—an artist who obsessively carved images of ferocious or playful bears for decades—or the iconic drawings and prints of owls and other birds by Kenojuak Ashevak (pp. 174–75) are the quintessential Inuit images of polar bears and birds by which all others are judged. In the case of Karoo Ashevak (pp. 118–19) of Taloyoak (formerly Spence Bay), we see an artist whose radical new style spawned an entire school of sculpture in the Kitikmeot region. In contrast, the highly abstracted figures by John Pangnark of Arviat (pp. 120–21) and Paniluk Qamanirq from Arctic Bay (pp. 122–23) might be thought of as idiosyncratic, atypical Inuit sculpture, even in the context of the style of their respective communities. Modern Inuit art continues to be considered through the work of the sculptors and graphic artists who comprise the broad and varied category of true Inuit artists.

In the final analysis, it is the individuality and originality of the artist's style or view of the world that is of paramount importance. Some would argue that individuality in Inuit art is the result of outside influence. To some extent that is obviously true, but I believe that Robert McGhee's hunch is correct—Inuit are not really so different from the rest of us. In Inuit art, as in all art, there is room for work that springs naturally from a collective spirit and a shared aesthetic (and indeed helps to shape it), and room for work that stands somewhat apart.

Marion Jackson studied the evolution of artistic self-consciousness among Baker Lake graphic artists in 1985.[12] In the course of her research she formulated an interesting "two generation" theory; although this theory was intended to explain differences in Inuit drawing styles between older and younger Inuit graphic artists, Jackson mused that it might be applicable even beyond Inuit art.[13] Briefly, Jackson posited that older graphic artists "did not aspire toward innovation" and had "little consciousness of self-as-artist" and suggested that furthermore, in their drawings, "content and form merge." She concluded that younger artists were more self-conscious because they were aware of more choices and also that they were compelled to choose either information or aesthetic expression, rather than fusing the two.[14] Jackson's theory explains why the art of many elderly Inuit artists appears somewhat fixed in terms of style or theme and points to why the art of some younger Inuit artists tends either to be strongly descriptive or emphasize form and aesthetics. The theory is flexible enough to allow for some evolution in the style of older artists, some latitude in the boundaries between generations, and the successful fusing of content and form among gifted younger artists. And it is certainly applicable, as Jackson hoped, to Inuit art in general.

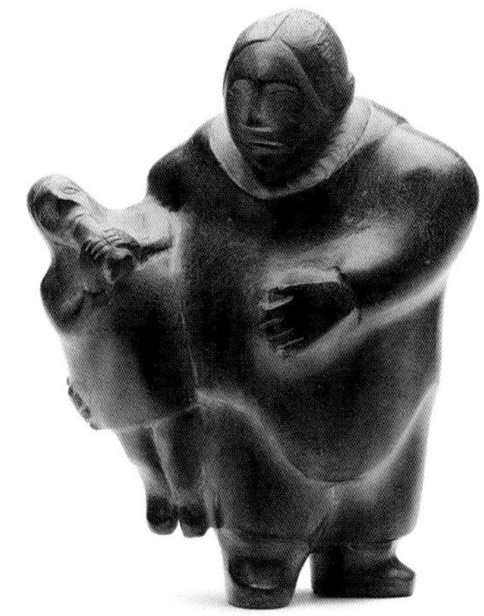

George Tatanniq, *Mother and Child*, 1976–77, darkened stone, 21.1 x 16.7 x 10.2 cm. Gift of Samuel and Esther Sarick, Toronto, 1996

Sorting sculptures or graphics by generation is relatively simple, but the next step—discovering the affinities between artists—is the gratifying (if somewhat subjective) part. There are no hard and fast categories, of course; furthermore, we are dealing with stylistic continuums and with artists who have developed distinct personal styles. Comparing sculptures and graphics can be a bit like comparing apples and oranges, so I will discuss those media separately. I believe that clear generational and stylistic affinities do exist across media, however; one way to discover these affinities is to focus on single figures in the more complex compositions.

The art of four first-generation sculptors from the Kivalliq (Keewatin) region—John Kavik and John Tiktak from Rankin Inlet, and George Tatanniq and Luke Iksiktaaryuk from Baker Lake—shares a rugged simplicity of form and a sobriety of mood. The hunters and other figures of Kavik, the oldest (born 1897), are both the crudest and the most energetic (pp. 124–25); they are sawn, rasped and drilled to form raw, elemental forms. Tiktak's faces and figures range from the subtly carved and coolly elegant to the starkly expressive (pp. 126–27). Tatanniq's humans, animals and transforming figures, with their stolid, gentle elegance, have an air of tentativeness (pp. 130–31). Iksiktaaryuk, working caribou antler exclusively, created otherworldly, ethereal shamans, seances and family groups (pp. 132–33).

Although the slightly younger John Pangnark and Andy Miki from Arviat are typically (and quite logically) discussed together with some or all of the four previously mentioned Kivalliq artists,[15] I have chosen to group them with their contemporaries Pauta and Latcholassie from Cape Dorset. These two pairs of artists spring from separate (some would even say disparate) community aesthetics, but I think they share a penchant for streamlined volumes and simplified shapes; their subjects sometimes fuse with the stone itself or become almost purely abstract shapes. Pauta's bears (pp. 116–17), with their powerful truncated forms, are infused with "bear-ness"; much copied over the decades, they are seldom equalled. Despite their lack of naturalism, their subject matter is anything but ambiguous. Latcholassie's chunky, quirky birds and bird-people (pp. 136–37) are more so; they are by turns comic and solemn. Miki's pristine animals (pp. 134–35) and Pangnark's radically pared down human forms (pp. 120–21) wander more obviously into abstract territory, as the indicators of species and sex are eliminated. Paniluk Qamanirq from Arctic Bay (pp. 122–23) has a clear artistic kinship to this group as well. Her work is completely atypical of her small north Baffin community, and she often found herself justifying her radically streamlined animal and human forms (or "ordinary pointed objects") to her neighbours.[16]

Pauta and Latcholassie are at the margins of the Cape Dorset mainstream, whereas Osuitok Ipeelee epitomizes it. Beginning with his elegant early ivory and stone works in the 1950s (p. 67), Osuitok helped to forge the dominant Cape Dorset style. A true virtuoso with stone, Osuitok effortlessly alternated between naturalism and stylization, imbuing his birds, caribou and other sculptures with elegance, poise, drama and sheer exuberant sculptural form (pp. 138–39); his work embodies the idea of personal style. Kiugak Ashoona's dramatic spirit sculptures from the early 1960s exemplify the fascination with transformation imagery in Cape Dorset at the time (p. 140); Kiugak pursued his interest in spirit and mythological subjects (p. 141) throughout his career. Aqjangajuk Shaa's robust, sometimes even contorted works (pp. 142–43) and Quvianatuliak Takpaungai's borderline erotic female figures (pp. 144–45) bring a more macho sensibility, while conforming to the Cape Dorset aesthetic of theatrical composition and carefully balanced form.

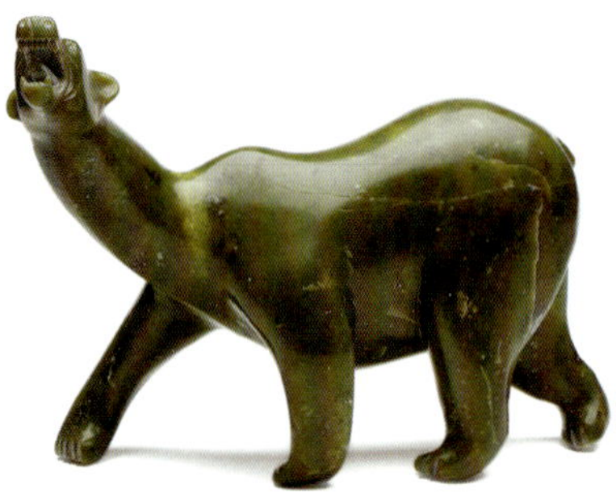

Osuitok Ipeelee, *Bear*, before 1982, stone, 23.7 x 16.8 x 32.6 cm. Gift of Samuel and Esther Sarick, Toronto, 2001. © Dorset Fine Arts

Influenced in the late 1960s by the work of the older artist Sakkiassee Anaija and by his own uncle Charlie Ugyuk, the Taloyoak artist Karoo Ashevak departed from the monolithic method of whale-bone carving early in his brief but brilliant career, inventing what curator Darlene Coward Wight has termed a "collage-like" approach, in which works are pieced together from several parts.[17] Karoo's style ideally suited his two favourite themes: shamans and spirits; according to his sister Eeteemunga Niviaqsiaq, Karoo exorcised his former fear of these through his art.[18] The influence of Karoo's humorous but angst-ridden works from the early 1970s can be felt across the Kitikmeot region—in the "surprised" faces of the hunters, fishers and shamans by his uncle Judas Ullulaq (pp. 146–47) of Gjoa Haven, and even more so in the morbidly amusing spirits and shamans constructed by Nick Sikkuark from Kugaaruk (pp. 148–49). Of the artists in this group, Maudie Okittuq, the only well-known female artist in the region, shows the least influence. Her stone sea goddesses, spirits and women simultaneously exude strength and vulnerability (pp. 150–51).

Davidialuk Alasua Amittu from Puvirnituq was an elder respected for his knowledge of local oral tradition, which included stories and memories of murder, cannibalism and suffering from his childhood, as well as graphic accounts of myths, legends and evil spirits.[19] Davidialuk began carving as early as the late 1940s; then, prompted in 1958–59,[20] and obsessively driven during about the last dozen years before his death in 1976, he recorded oral history and legend in drawings, prints and sculptures, and in interviews. In a rustic, folk art realist style all his own, he vividly portrayed myth and memory (pp. 114–15). Eli Sallualu Qinuajua, a generation younger than Davidialuk, was also prompted to push the limits of his artistic expression; he ended up winning a 1967 contest sponsored in Puvirnituq by Nelson Graburn.[21] As bizarre and monstrous as Sallualu's sculptures are (pp. 152–53), they have more than a passing resemblance to Davidialuk's works. Their compositions are similar but, even more importantly, as fantasy art they share not only a certain grotesqueness but also "repetitiousness and ambiguity, disorder and fragmentariness, [which] are all elements of a gradual arrival at a meaning."[22]

Peter Sevoga of Baker Lake and Lucy Tasseor Tutsweetok from Arviat are more likely to be compared to artists from their home communities. Sevoga, part of a second wave of Baker Lake sculptors who rose to prominence in the early 1970s, imparts to his massive yet elegantly poised family groups, with their broad volumes and sensuous curves, a sturdy delicacy (pp. 154–55). Tasseor's carvings from her "classic" early period are usually smaller, considerably more abstracted, less polished and more solidly rooted to the ground, yet no less graceful (pp. 158–59). Both artists symbolize the closeness of the family by merging the individual figures. Furthermore, the way in which the figures or faces gaze outward and upward lends a timeless, monumental quality to their works.

Three first-generation graphic artists, men all born in the nineteenth century, took up drawing in their sixties and seventies: Kiakshuk and Parr from Cape Dorset, and Luke Anguhadluq from Baker Lake. Parr had the most naive style of the three; his early drawings, especially, are reminiscent of the art of young children. Some are narrative, typically hunting scenes, whereas other drawings are simply arrangements of animals and people; the figures seem randomly chosen and arbitrarily sized, but they are deliberately positioned to fill the page (pp. 166–67). Kiakshuk, the oldest (born 1886), was the most accomplished draughtsman and an excellent sculptor as well. His subject matter ranged more broadly, from carefully crafted images of hunting and camping to the dreamlike images of spirits and transformation in vogue in Cape Dorset in the early 1960s (pp. 164–65). In this group Anguhadluq's drawings are distinguished by their vivid colour schemes, typical of Baker Lake graphic art, and by their unique system of multiple perspectives, which Anguhadluq invented to help him capture the world he depicted (pp. 168–69).

Pitseolak Ashoona from Cape Dorset (pp. 160–61), a woman slightly younger (born 1904) than the aforementioned artists, combined a love of colour (which was introduced to Cape Dorset at about the time of Kiakshuk's death in 1966) with an autobiographical impulse in her art (resulting in the 1971 book collaboration with Dorothy Eber, *Pitseolak: Pictures Out of My Life*).[23] Joe Talirunili from Puvirnituq (Davidialuk's cousin) shared this urge to chronicle the past, focusing particularly on a harrowing tale of shipwreck and survival from his youth. Talirunili's prints are documented and his sculptures highly prized, but his drawings depicting his early life and historical events are less well known (pp. 111–13).[24]

Jessie Oonark of Baker Lake is renowned not only for her drawings, prints and wall hangings but also for the fact that she founded an artistic dynasty. She brought to her art a sophisticated synthesis of symbolism and decoration, a stunning colour sense and a flair for composition based on symmetry and pattern (pp. 162–63). Her work manages to look simultaneously playful and regal. Thematically, Oonark was inspired mostly by the past, whereas Pudlo Pudlat from Cape Dorset enthusiastically welcomed the new iconographic possibilities brought about by contact with the South (pp. 170–71). Pudlo shared Oonark's love of pattern and composition; quirky decorative details appear already in his graphite drawings of the early 1960s; by the late 1970s whimsical symbols representing the influence of southern technology and culture—airplanes, houses, angels—commingled with more typical Inuit imagery, creating new metaphors of transformation. Ever willing to experiment, by the 1970s Pudlo had fully embraced colour, as well as new techniques such as lithography and acrylic wash. The early drawings of Oonark's eldest daughter Janet Kigusiuq are complex and narrative in nature, providing the viewer with myriad details of traditional life. By the 1980s, however, her compositions became simpler, bolder and more dominated by fields of vibrant colour (pp. 172–73). By the end of her life, colour and shape led to near-abstraction.[25] Over the decades, Kigusiuq showed herself to be the inheritor of that aspect of Oonark's artistic sensibility.

Kenojuak Ashevak from Cape Dorset is the reigning queen of the Inuit art world, and her 1960 print *The Enchanted Owl* (pp. 37, 174) is its most famous icon. Over the decades Kenojuak's style has evolved and her palette has brightened, but the artist frequently reworks the iconography she developed with her early graphite drawings, primarily stately owls and other birds, on their own or in combination with other compositional elements (pp. 174–75). The forms of the birds themselves, their naturalistic or decorative plumage, shapes reminiscent of seaweed or other flora, and other figures are all drawn with Kenojuak's sure, fluid hand. Simon Tookoome explores the typical Baker Lake themes of shamanism, transformation

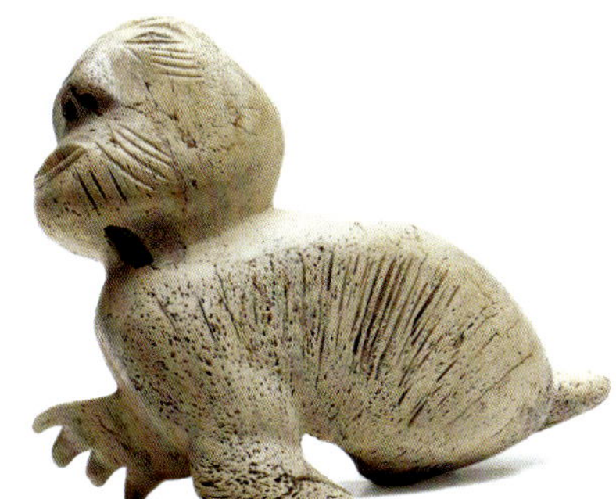

Maudie Rachel Okittuq, *Sea Goddess*, c. 1982, whale bone, 21.2 x 35.2 x 19.0 cm. Gift of Samuel and Esther Sarick, 1990

and the strong spiritual connection between humans and animals in his complex, exuberant drawings (pp. 180–81). Where Oonark might have used symbolism, and others might have chosen a narrative approach, Tookoome opts for an in-your-face multiplicity of exploding and radiating forms and colours. Like Kenojuak, Tookoome reworks separate elements into seemingly endless variations. In the work of both artists, aesthetic considerations outweigh others.

Victoria Mamnguqsualuk, another of Oonark's artist-children, has created great numbers of drawings and wall hangings that celebrate myth and legend, most famously the exploits of the Odysseus-like wandering shaman-hero Qiviuq. Fascinated by both the grand sweep and the small details of these narratives, Mamnguqsualuk chooses a pictorial approach in which several episodes of a story, or a sequence of events within one episode, are presented in a single drawing.[26] Mamnguqsualuk opts for clarity of expression rather than aesthetics; for her the narrative is of paramount importance (pp. 176–77). Her contemporary Ruth Annaqtuusi Tulurialik, also of Baker Lake, seamlessly blends personal narrative, history, myth and the supernatural in her exuberant drawings (pp. 178–79) that, according to Marion Jackson, "throb with strong organic rhythms."[27] Both artists illustrate multiple events, but whereas Mamnguqsualuk's are logically and temporally connected, Annaqtuusi's seem thrown onto the page with joyous, haphazard abandon.

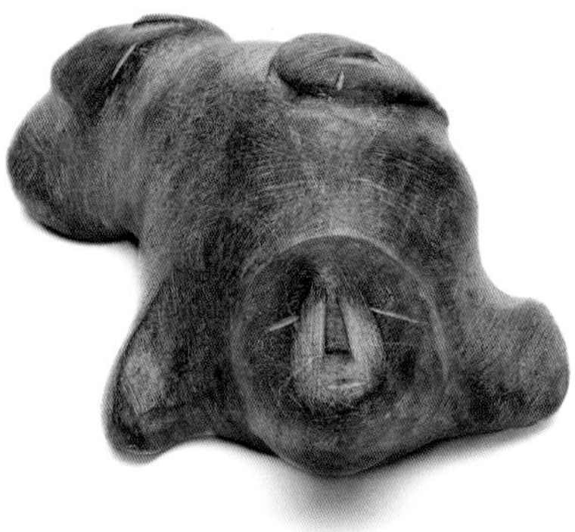

George Arluk, *Seal Form with Human Faces*, 1975, stone, 6.5 x 18.9 x 10.4 cm. Gift of Samuel and Esther Sarick, 1988

Kananginak Pootoogook, son of the artist Josephie Pootoogook (p. 70)—one of the original Cape Dorset printmakers and eventually an important artist in his own right—set himself apart almost from the beginning with his naturalistic style. At first interested primarily in animal subjects, he eventually also developed a "documentarian" approach by illustrating the changing life of south Baffin Inuit in the mid-twentieth century (pp. 182–83). He sees himself as someone whose life has successfully spanned the transitional period of modern Inuit history.[28] Napachie Pootoogook, Pitseolak Ashoona's daughter, began illustrating transitional life around the same time in the 1970s (pp. 184–85). Her artistic career culminated in a deeply personal series of three hundred drawings in the last five years of her life, works that presented a decidedly unromantic view of family and community life and history. Images that included scenes of violence, abuse, religious fervour and murder were accompanied by syllabic inscriptions; since 2002 artists such as Annie Pootoogook (Napachie's daughter) and others have continued this brand of art.

Marion Jackson recognized that there is a continuum of artistic self-consciousness among and between the first two generations of Inuit artists. At one end of this range we witness their seeming imperviousness to the outside world and the place of Inuit art in it, as seen in the memory-inspired drawings of Parr and Anguhadluq and the primal sculptures of Kavik. Pitseolak's famous statement, "I know I have had an unusual life, being born in a skin tent and living to hear on the radio that two men have landed on the moon,"[29] showed her awareness of being on the cusp of radical cultural change even if her art continued to look resolutely back for inspiration. Artists such as Kenojuak have cultivated strong personal styles and strong artistic personalities and are perfectly aware of their status as celebrities in the pantheons of Inuit and Canadian art. Pudlo's curiosity and the quirkiness of his depiction of cultural change, Karoo with his virtuosity and humour and angst, Kananginak's documentarian approach to the realities of life at the crossroads — these are just three examples of artists whose works have foreshadowed and paved the way for the qualities of experimentation, irony and idiosyncrasy that mark the work of the newest generation of Inuit artists.

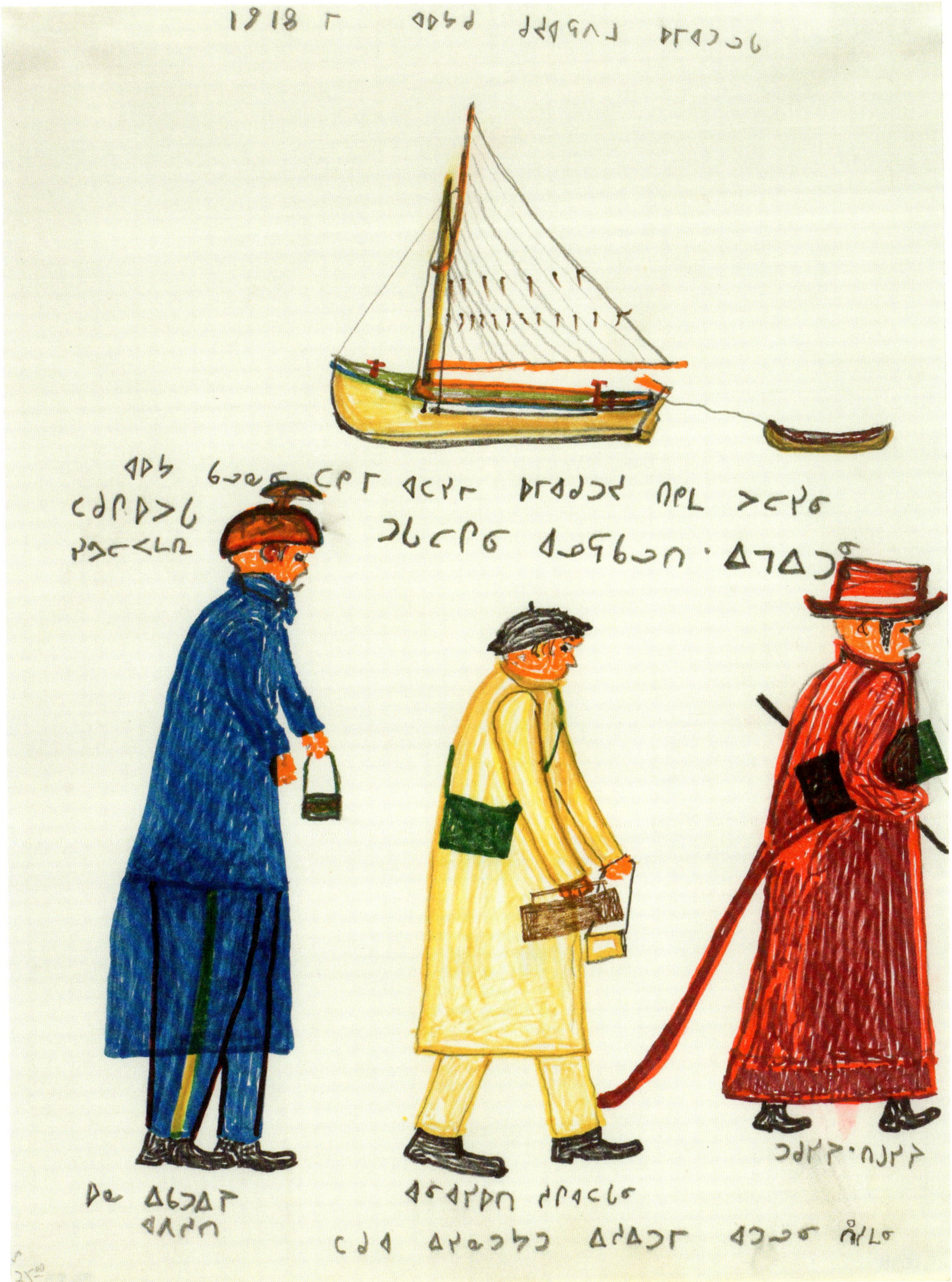

"In 1918 in the summer as I was going to Kuujjuaraapik by boat."

"That summer for one whole month the white people came with their very big boat and it was the first time I saw police. Their positions followed their clothing as depicted – those very first ones."

"This is the judge, the one who asks questions." (blue)

"A medical worker, a neutral person." (yellow)

"The one who can kill people and take them away." (red)

"Those seemed to be quite terrifying if you had done something inappropriate back then."

Joe Talirunili, *Three Large Figures*, 1971,
porous pointed pen and graphite on paper, 35.7 x 27.2 cm

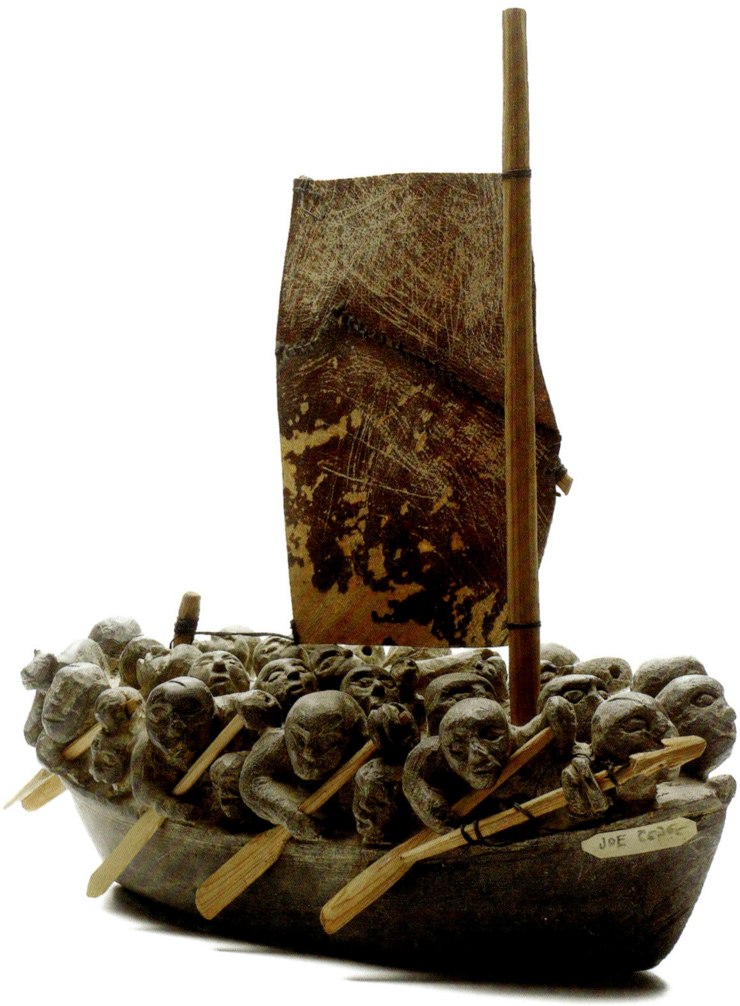

Joe Talirunili, *Migration*,
c. 1974, stone, hide, wood, string, 33.7 x 39.5 x 19.5 cm

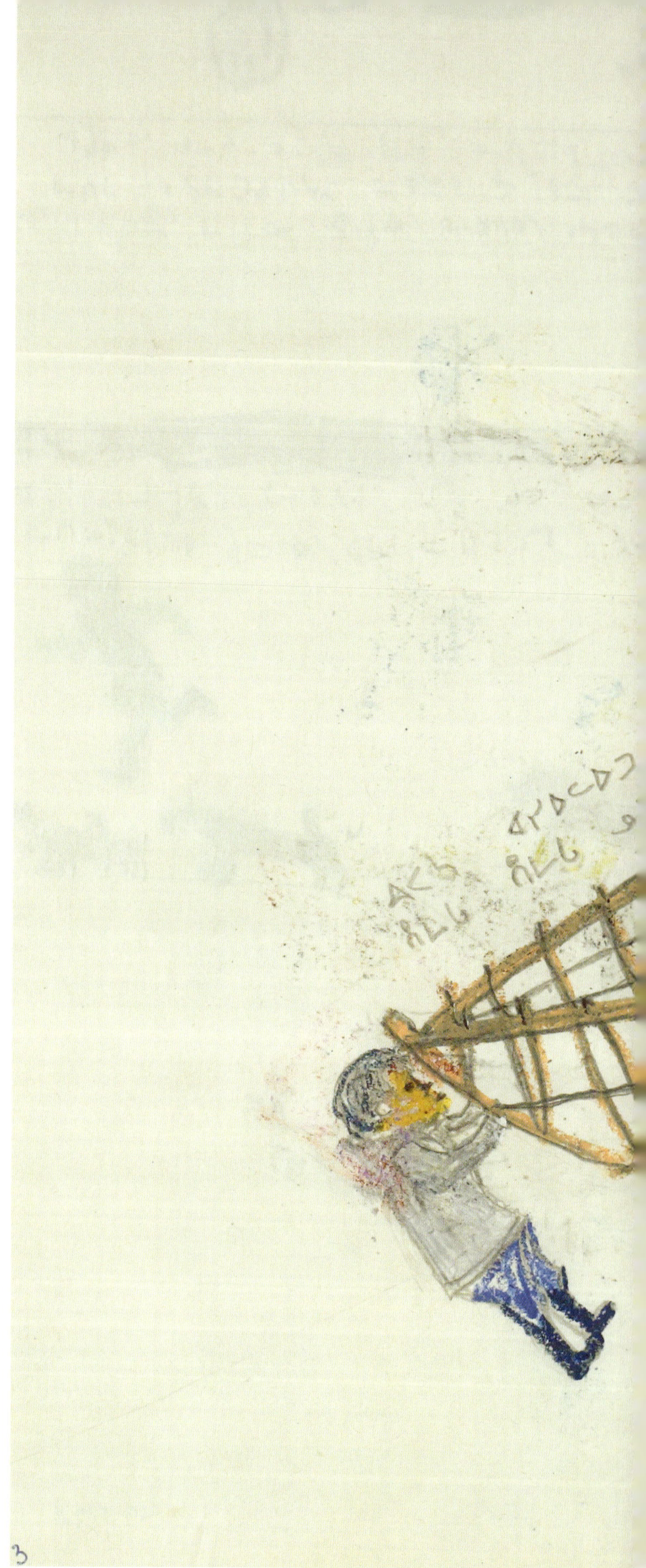

Joe Talirunili, *Building a Large Skin Boat*,
1970s, pencil and wax crayon on paper, 30.1 x 45.0 cm

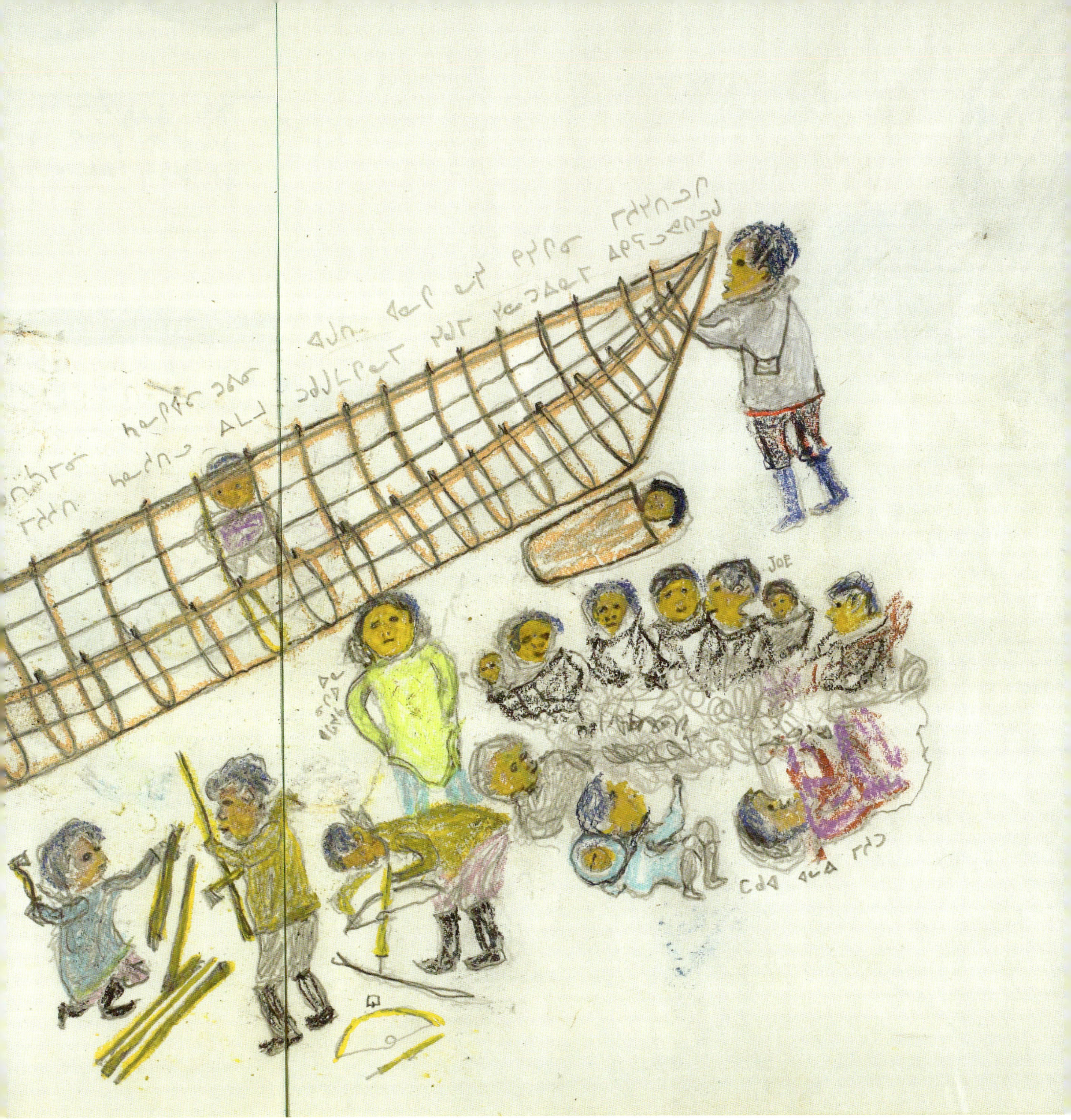

"Yesterday they lost the means to survive. So they began to make more again. The men's wives began to sew the sealskins. They sewed and sewed for a very long time without ever stopping, just working away. They did not want people to die in the water, near the ice, in the wild where there are large channels of water."

"This is the old lady, their leader."

"Those women are sewing."

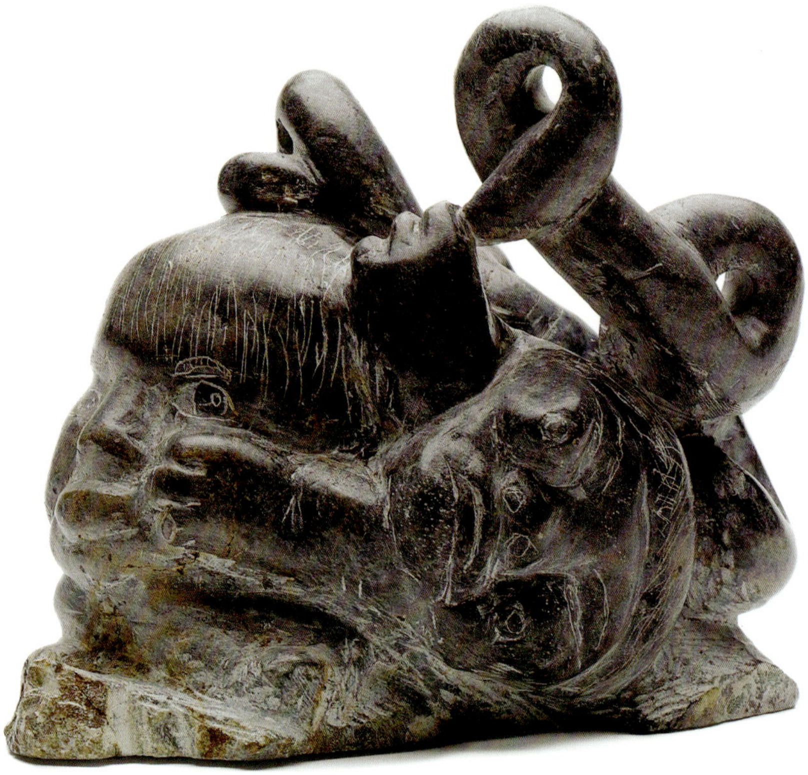

Davidialuk Alasua Amittu, *Kajjutajuk and Tunnituaqruk*, c. 1972, darkened stone, 19.2 x 24.0 x 14.0 cm

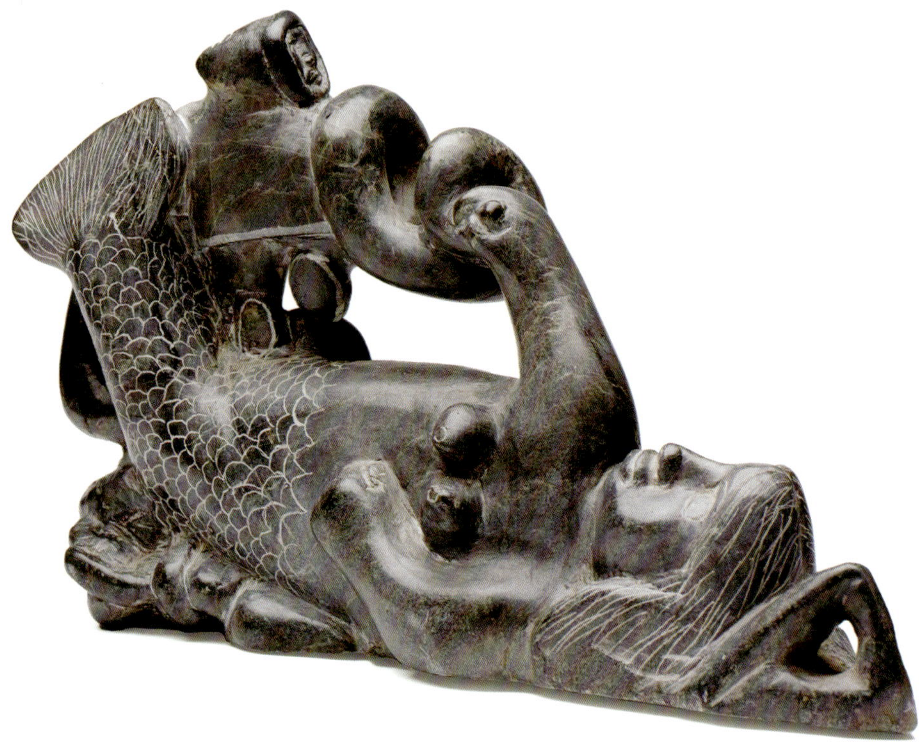

Davidialuk Alasua Amittu, *The Hunter Who Encountered the Iqalunappa*, 1972, stone, 24.1 x 41.9 x 8.9 cm

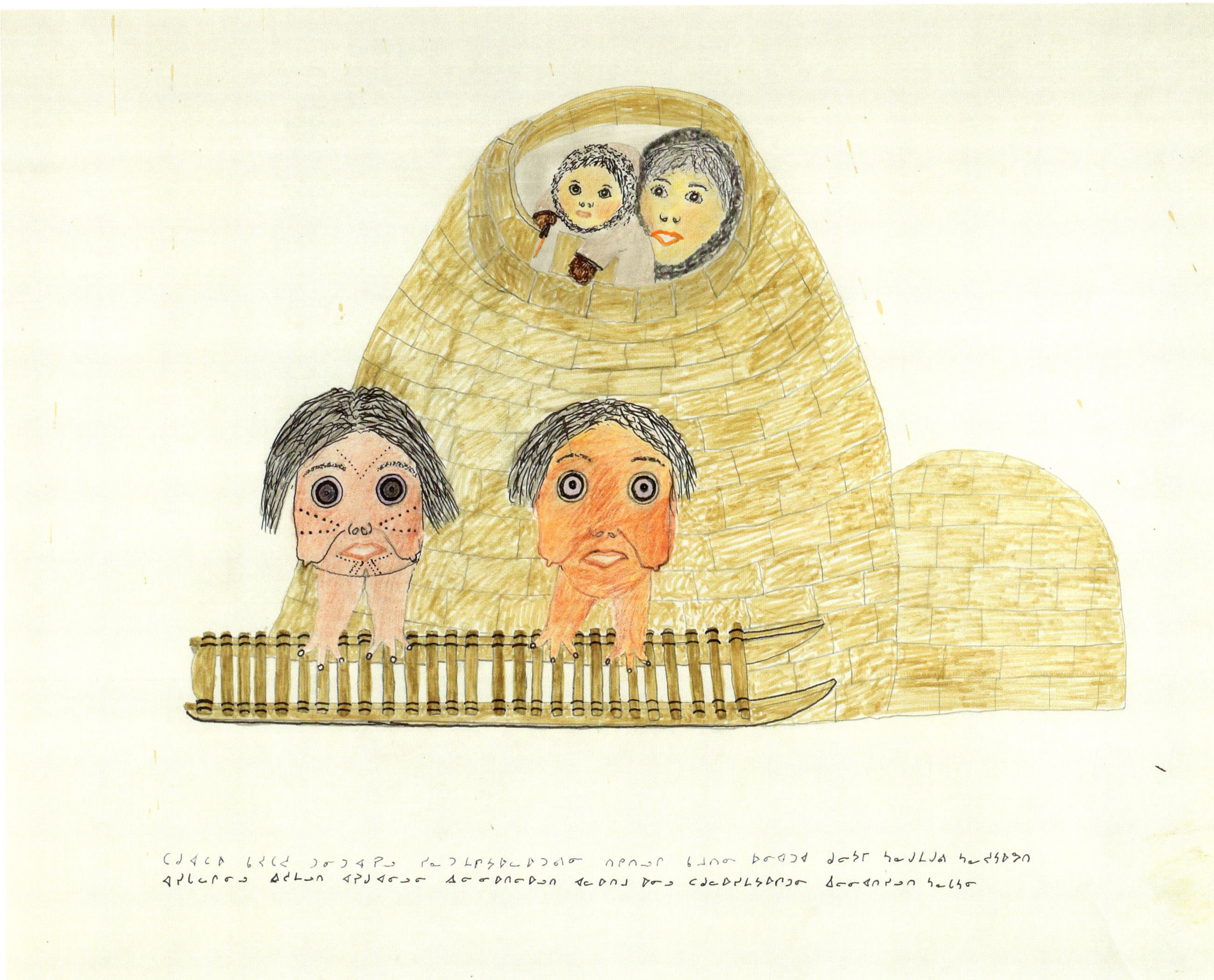

Davidialuk Alasua Amittu, *Two Kajjutajuit on a Sled*, c. 1970, porous pointed pen, coloured pencil and graphite on wove paper, 59.1 x 66.1 cm

"These beings were dreamt about a very long time ago. They came hauling a sled and said, 'If you want to make a stone lamp you just have to make one now.' And they implied that this included other items as well, including artwork. And the people were shown how to make different tools that had never been seen before by anyone. They were there teaching them how to make all different kinds of things."

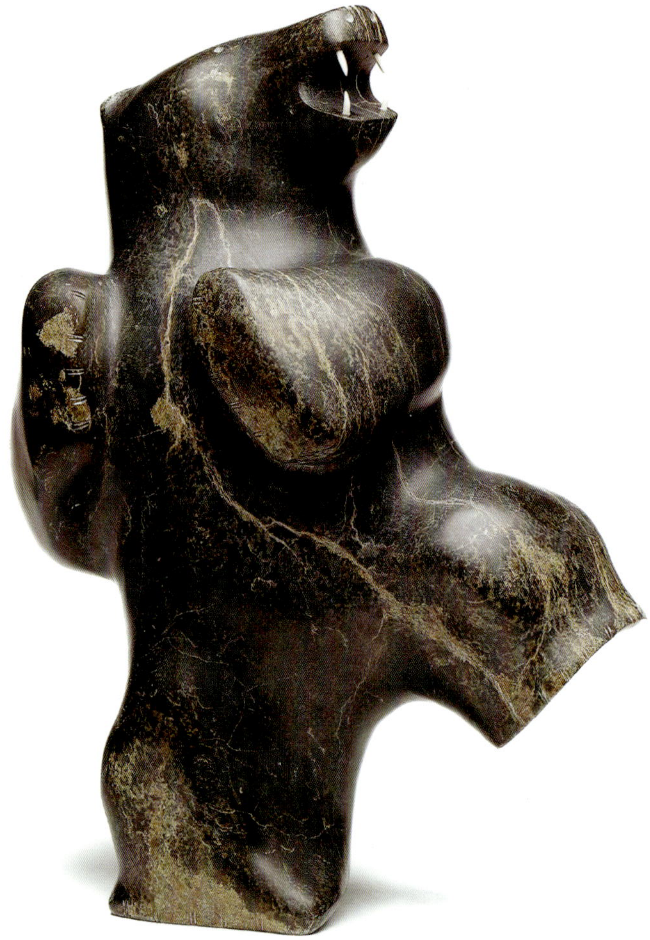

Pauta Saila, *Dancing Bear*, 1984, stone, ivory, 51.2 x 38.8 x 22.8 cm

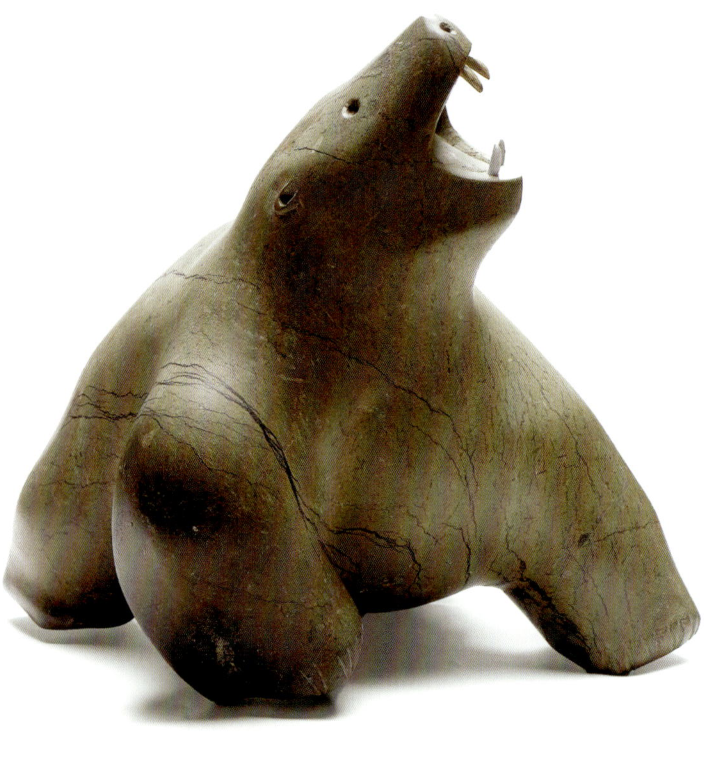

Pauta Saila, *Bear*, 1967, stone, 46.0 x 42.0 x 40.0 cm

Right: **Pauta Saila**, *Dancing Bear*, c. 1973, stone, 48.5 x 36.5 x 19.0 cm

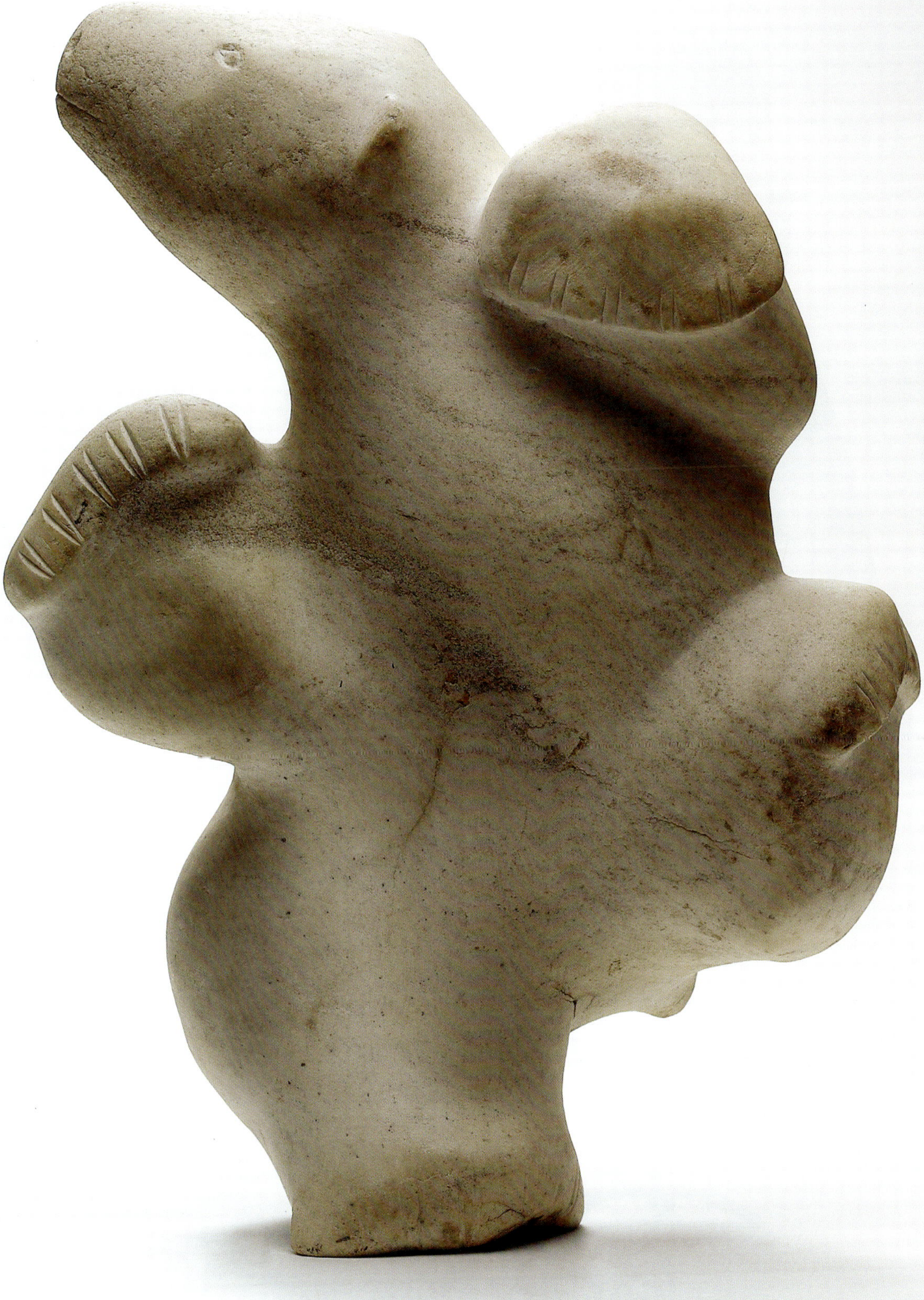

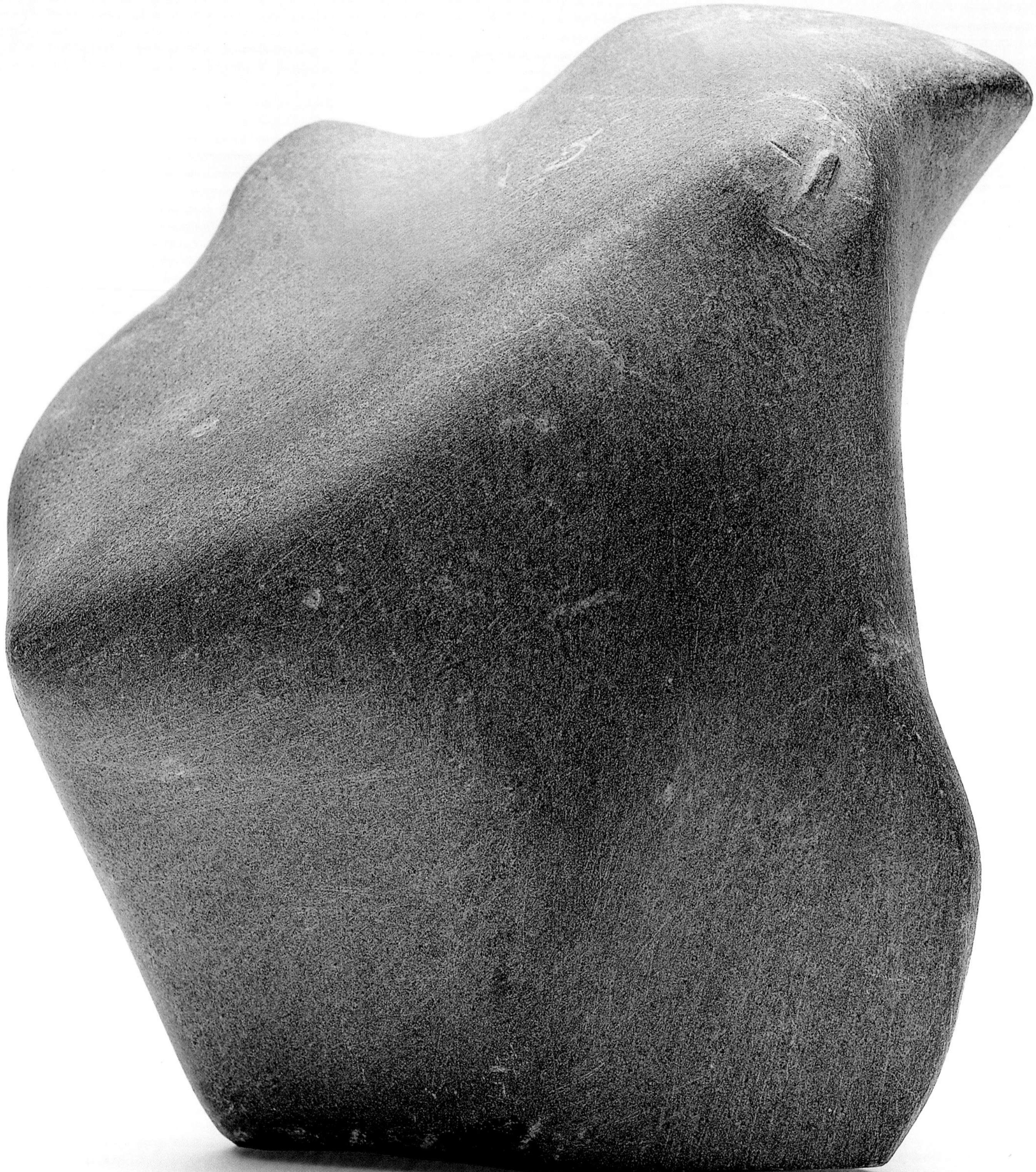

John Pangnark, *Figure*, 1970, stone, 13.3 x 13.1 x 9.2 cm

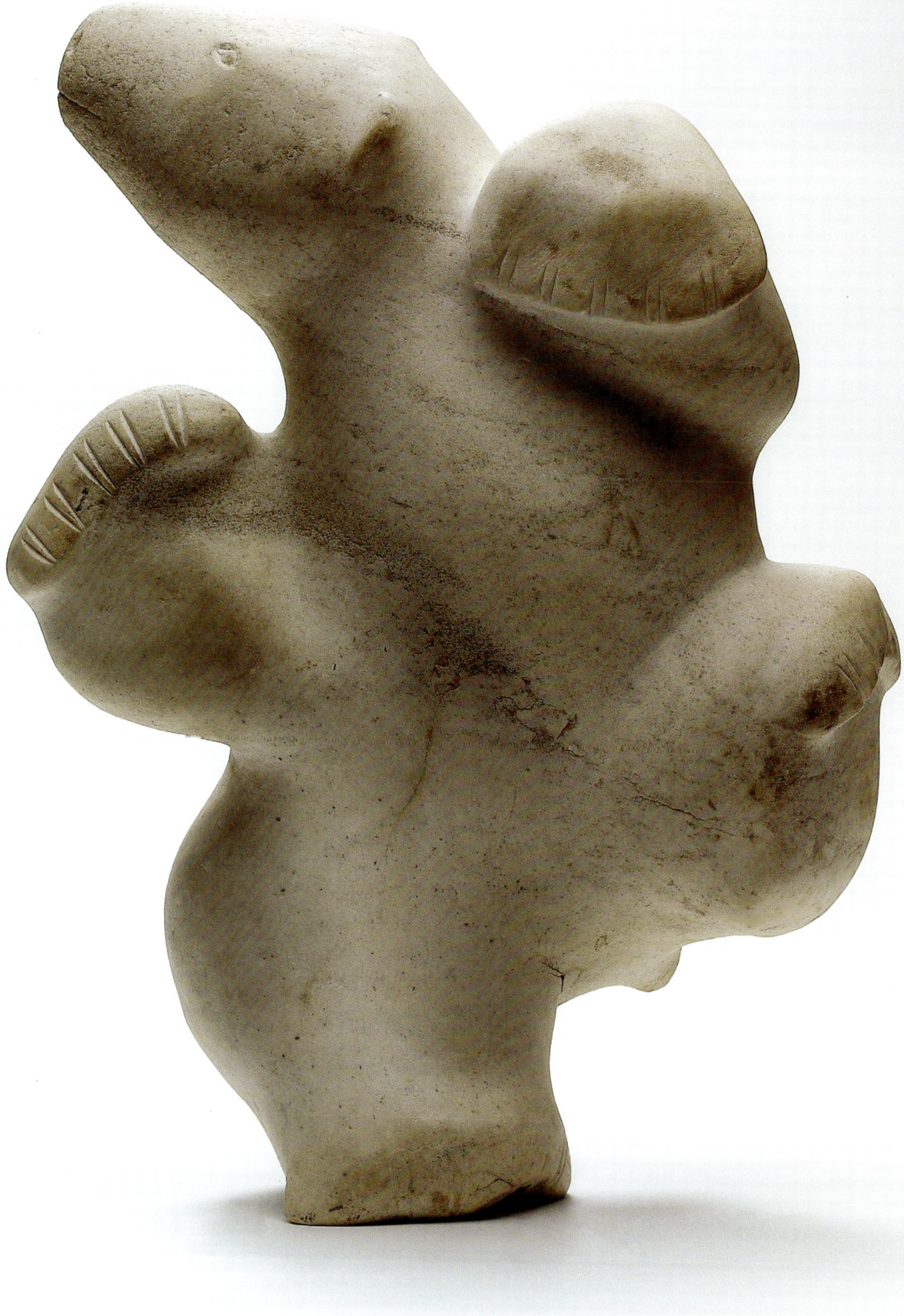

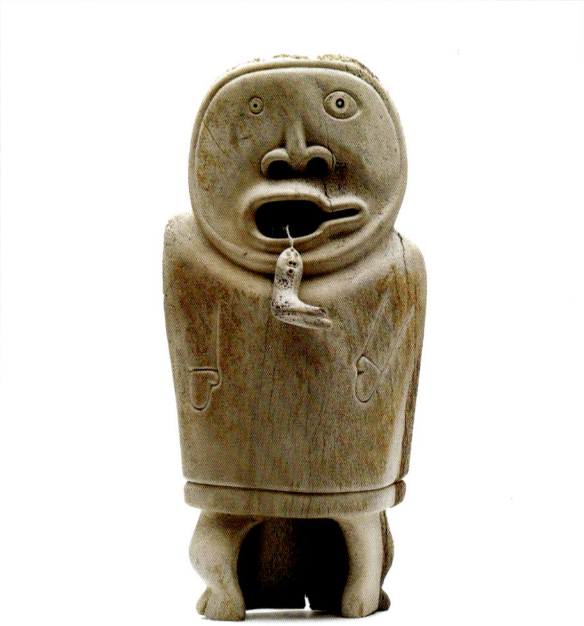

Karoo Ashevak, *Shaman with Spirit Helper*, 1972, whale bone, ivory, stone, sinew, 47.7 x 23.6 x 16.6 cm

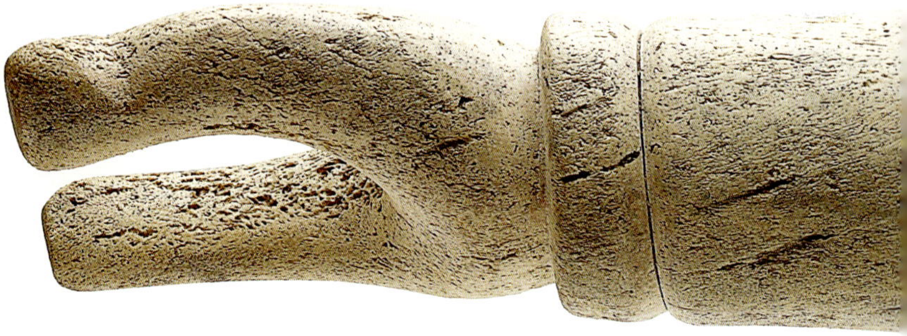

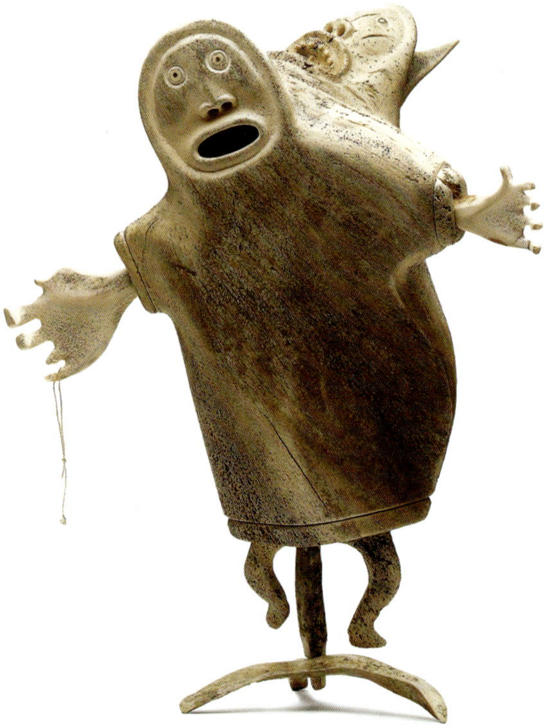

Karoo Ashevak, *Mother and Child with Pulled Tooth*, c. 1972, whale bone, antler, stone, ivory, sinew, 50.9 x 40.7 x 33.6 cm

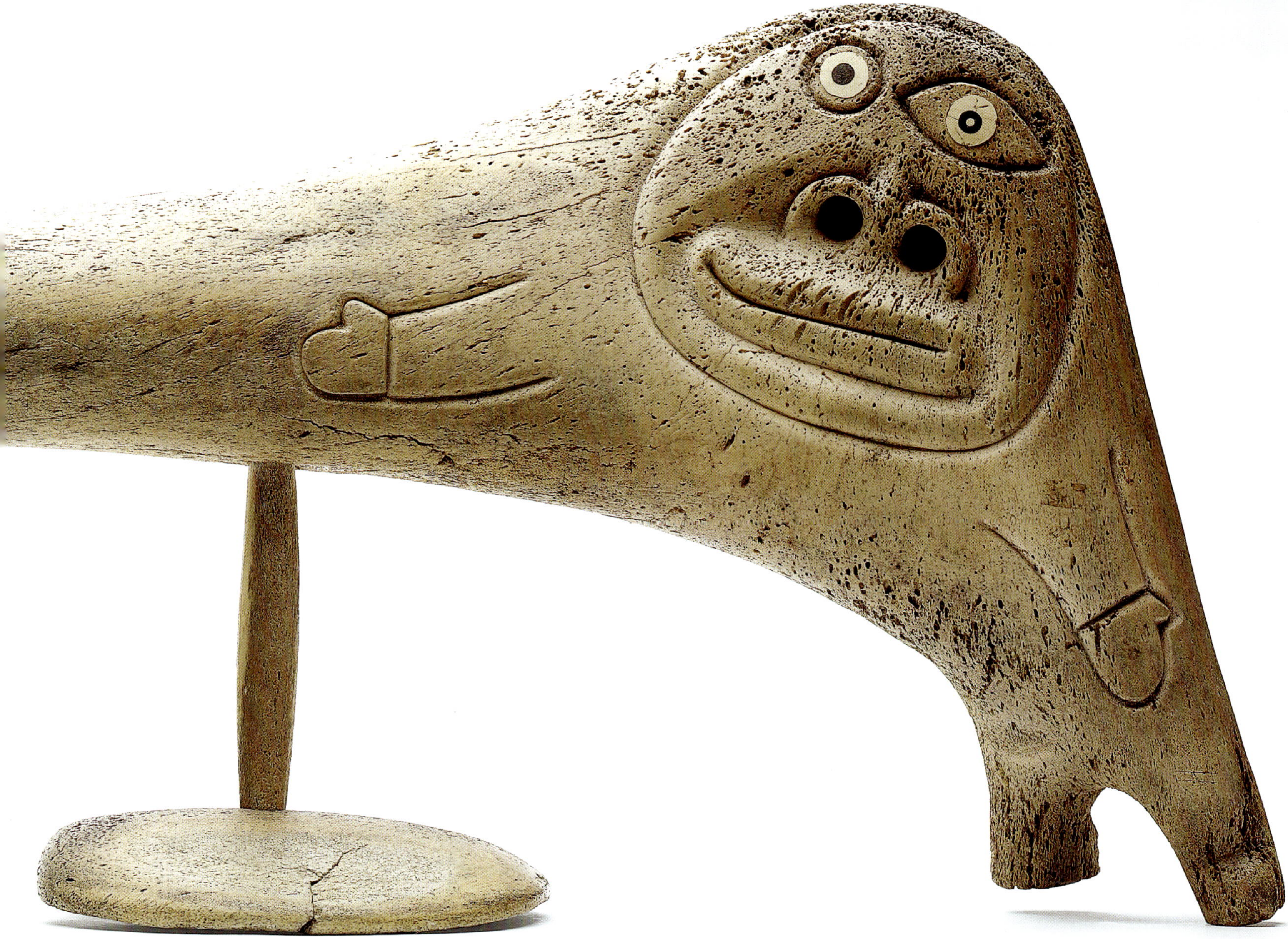

Karoo Ashevak, *Spirit Figure*, c. 1972, whale bone, antler, ivory, stone, 32.7 x 65.5 x 10.5 cm

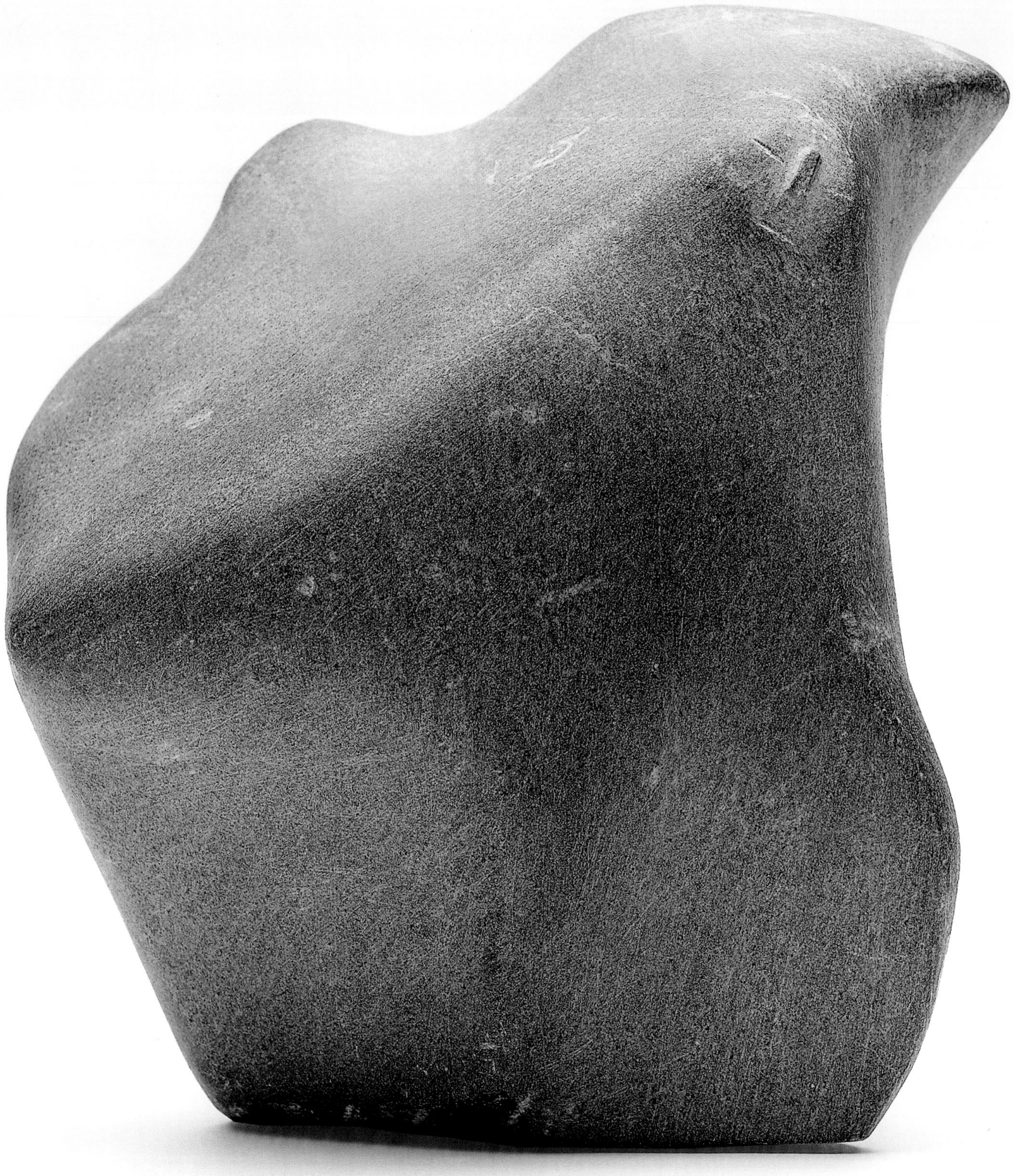

John Pangnark, *Figure*, 1970, stone, 13.3 x 13.1 x 9.2 cm

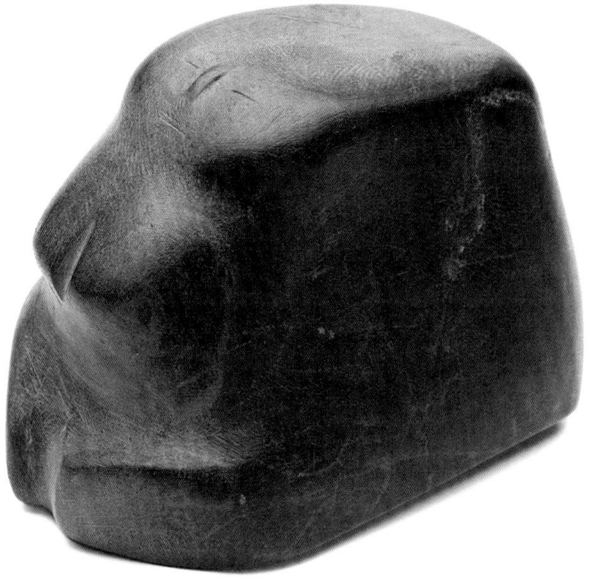

John Pangnark, *Figure*, 1969, darkened stone, 10.5 x 13.9 x 9.2 cm

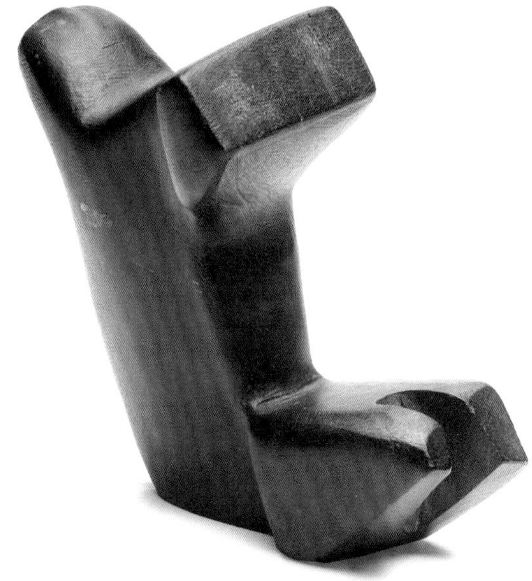

John Pangnark, *Figure*, 1968, stone, 9.8 x 10.4 x 4.9 cm

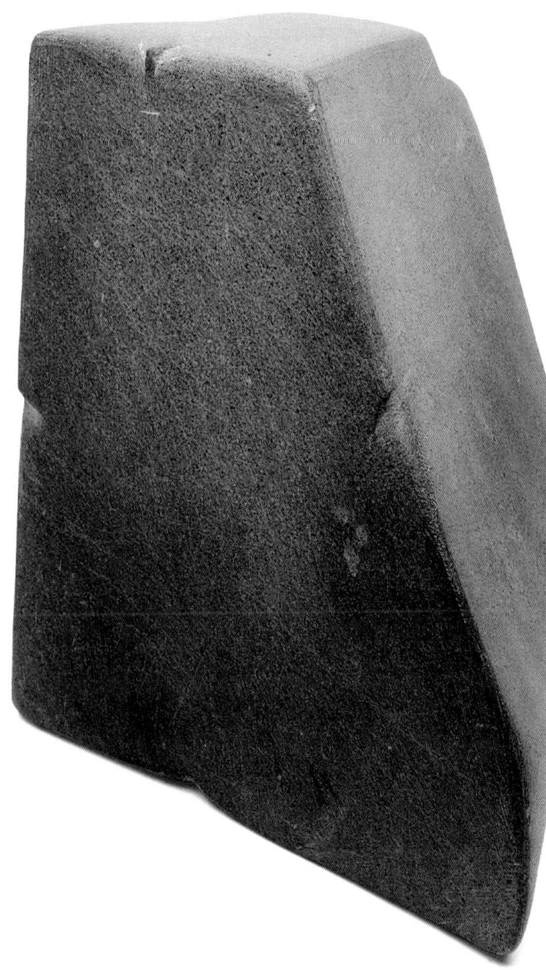

John Pangnark, *Figure*, 1974, stone, 21.5 x 22.3 x 18.3 cm

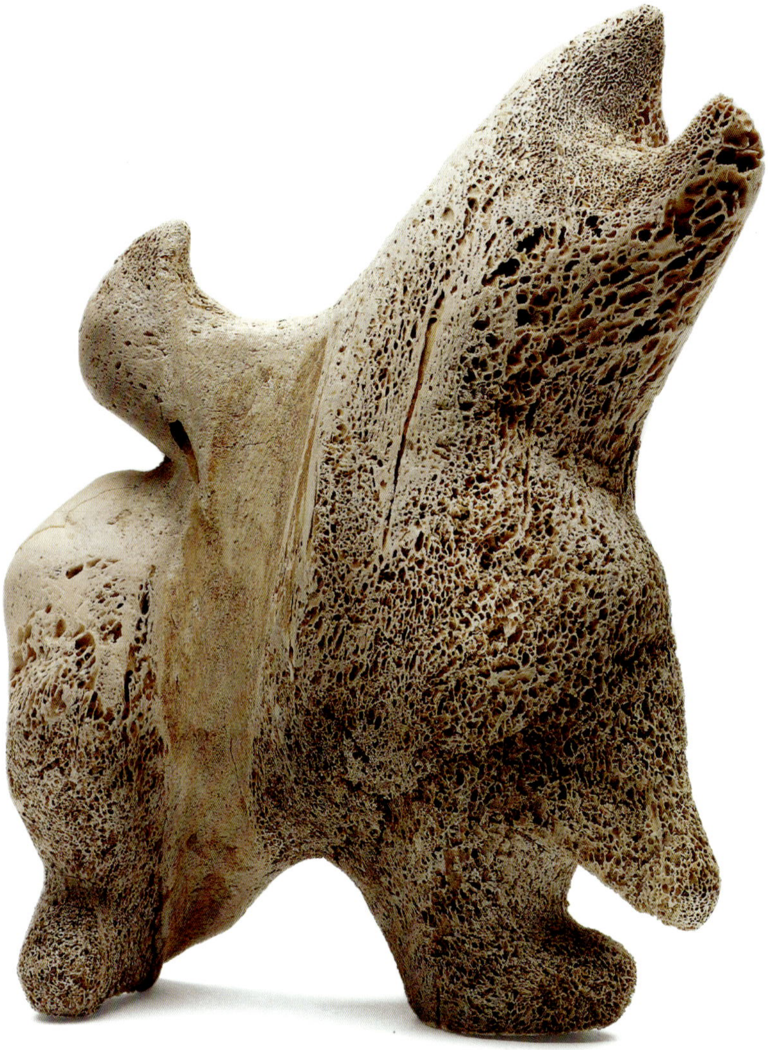

Paniluk Qamanirq, *Bird Transformation*, 1971, whale bone, 25.4 x 20.2 x 10.1 cm

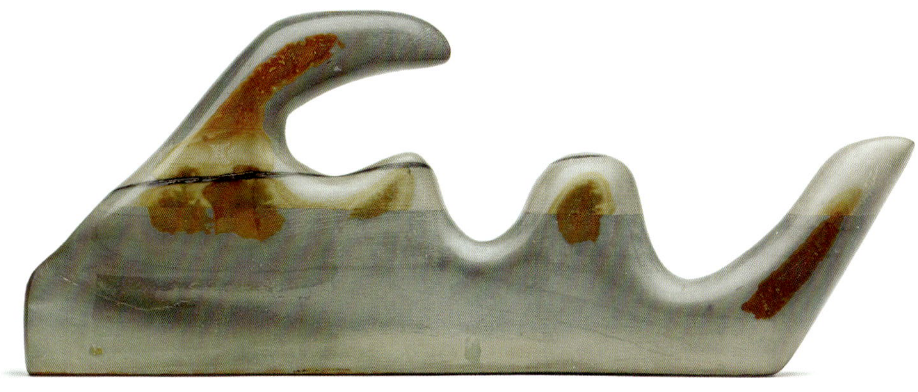

Paniluk Qamanirq, *Animal*, c. 1973, stone, 5.4 x 20.9 x 3.7 cm

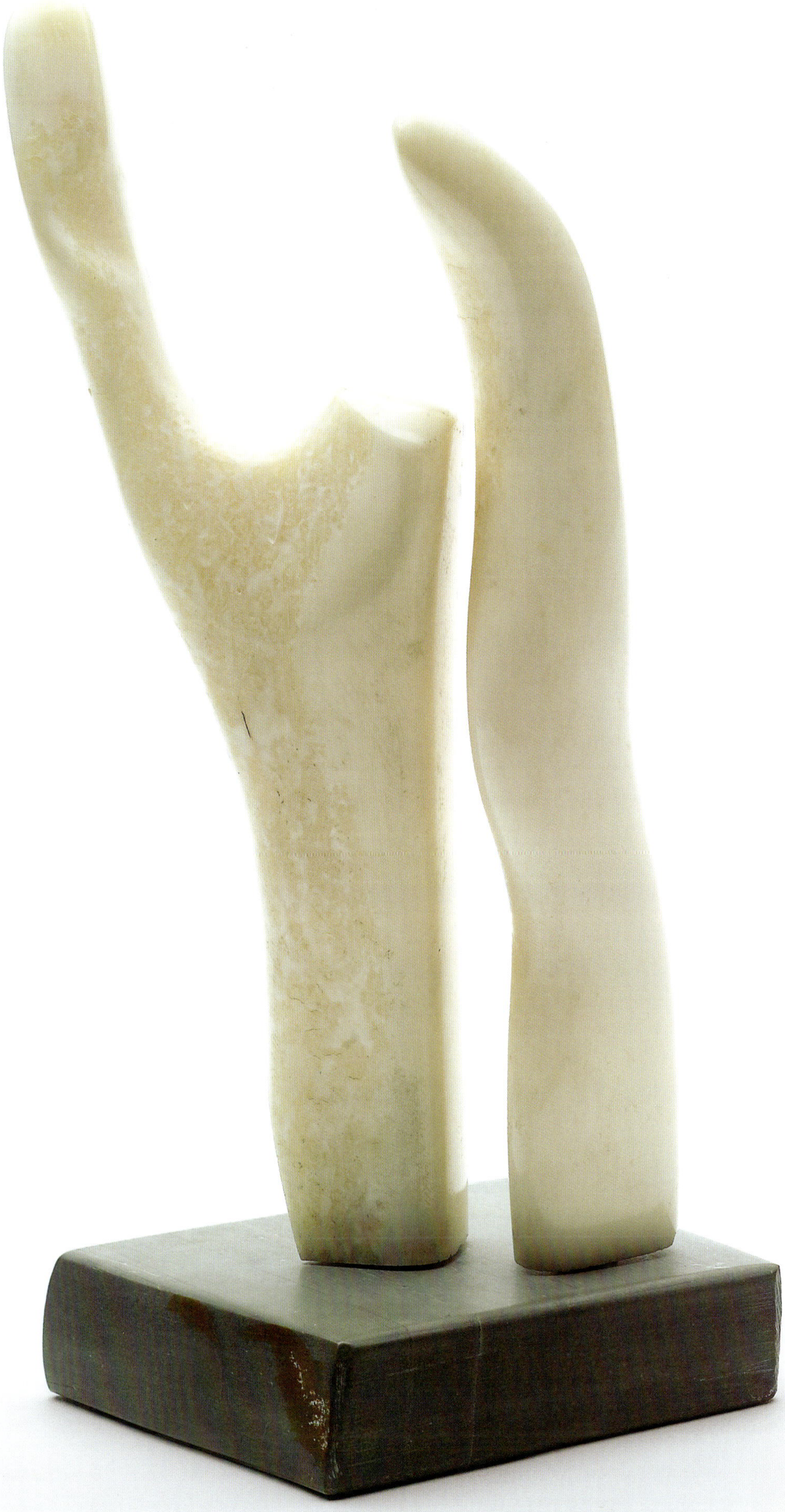

Paniluk Qamanirq, *Two Forms on Base*, c. 1971,
stone, ivory, 13.3 x 5.7 x 5.0 cm

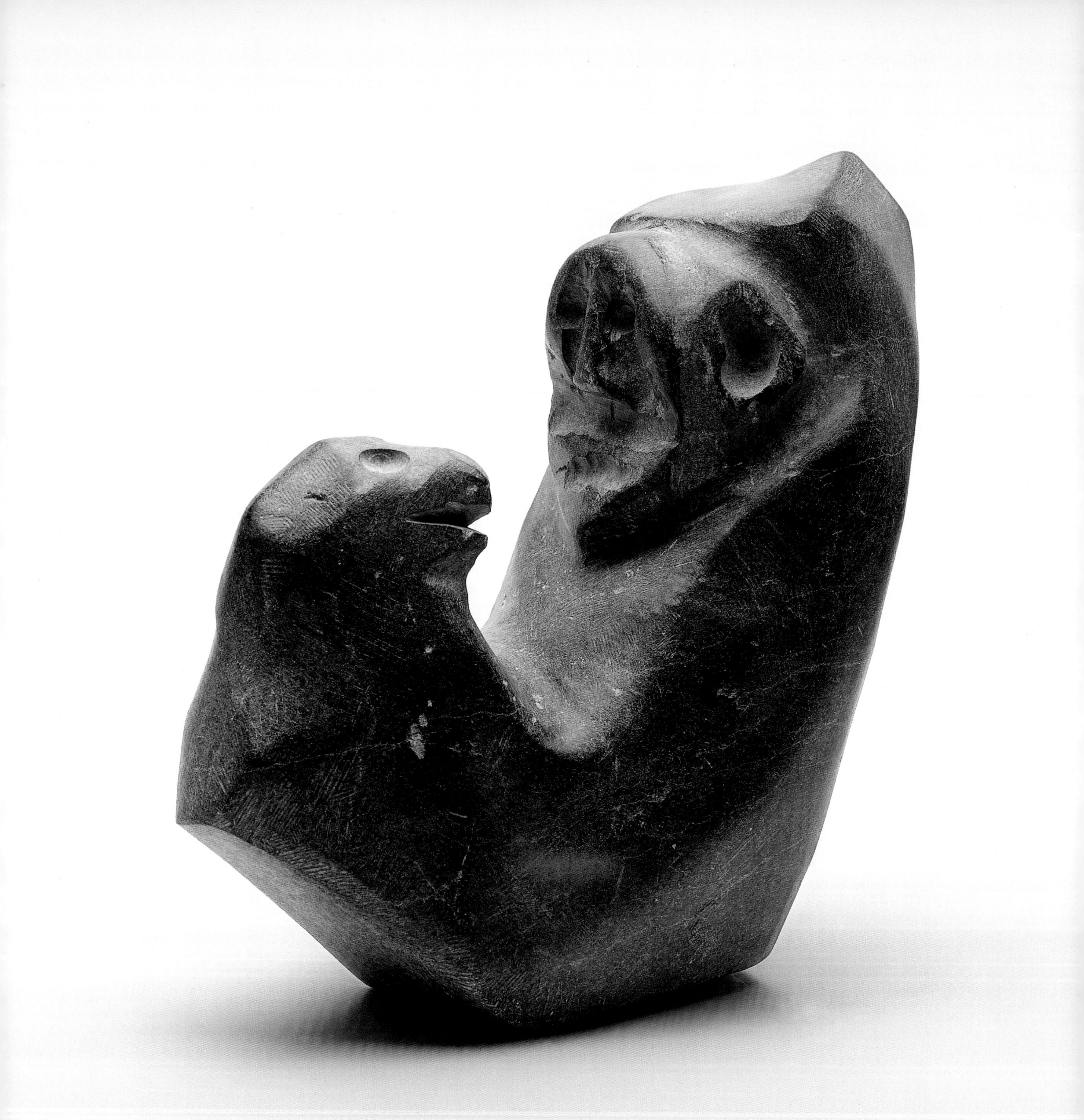

John Kavik, *Figure and Bird*, c. 1972, stone, 20.4 x 22.3 x 11.4 cm

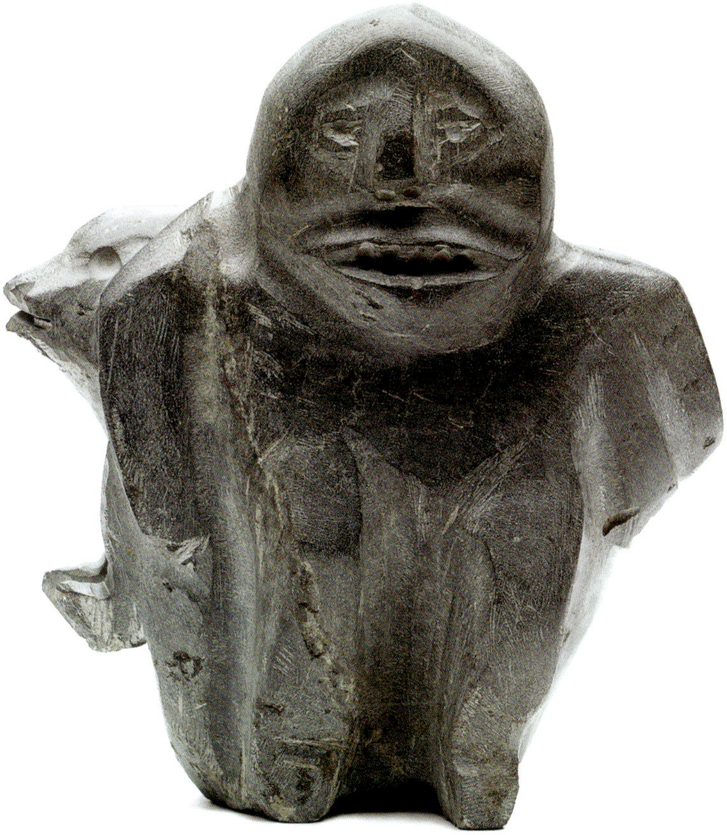

John Kavik, *Man Carrying Animal*, 1970–71, stone, 12.6 x 10.5 x 6.8 cm

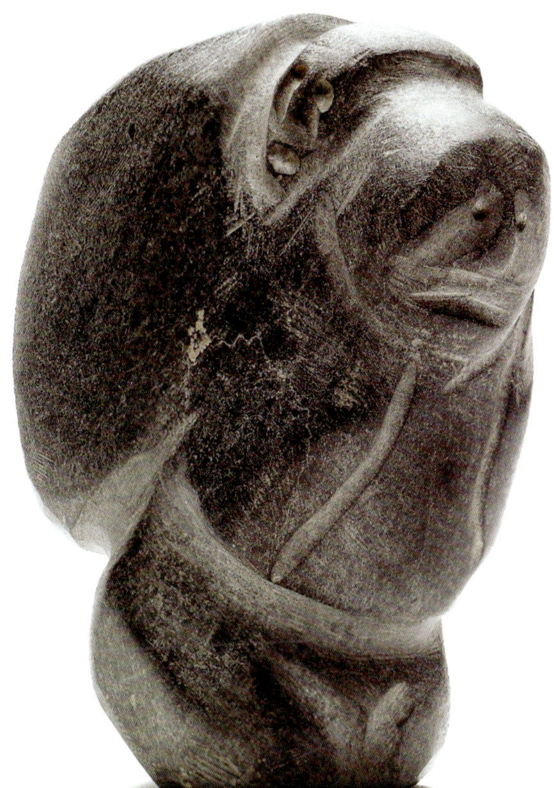

John Kavik, *Mother and Child*, c. 1974, stone, 14.2 x 13.2 x 7.0 cm

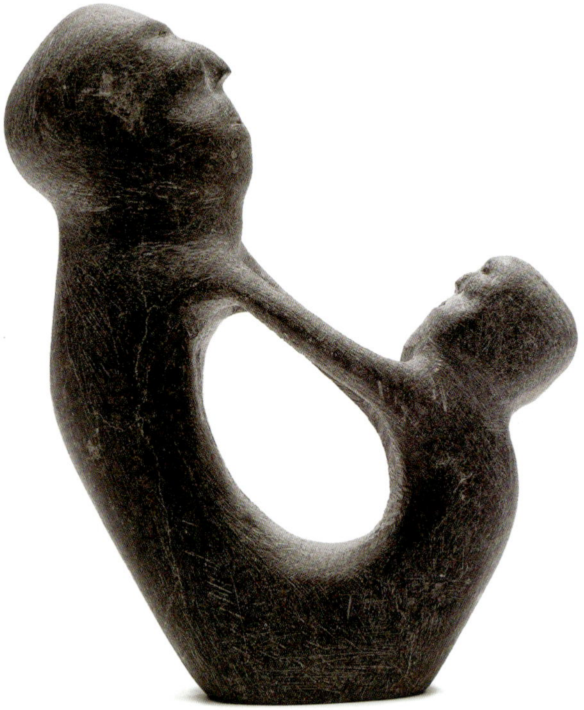

John Tiktak, *Mother and Child*, c. 1966, stone, 20.1 x 17.3 x 6.0 cm

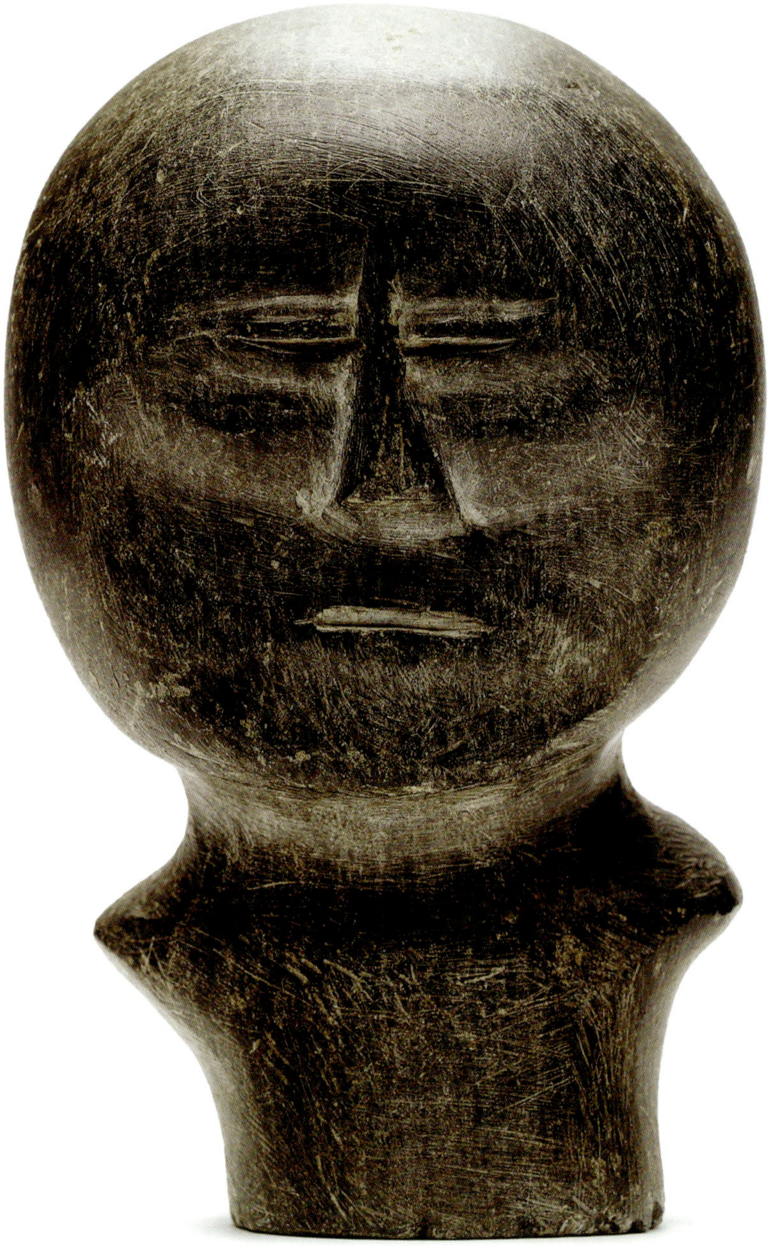

John Tiktak, *Head*, c. 1965, stone, 18.0 x 13.2 x 8.0 cm

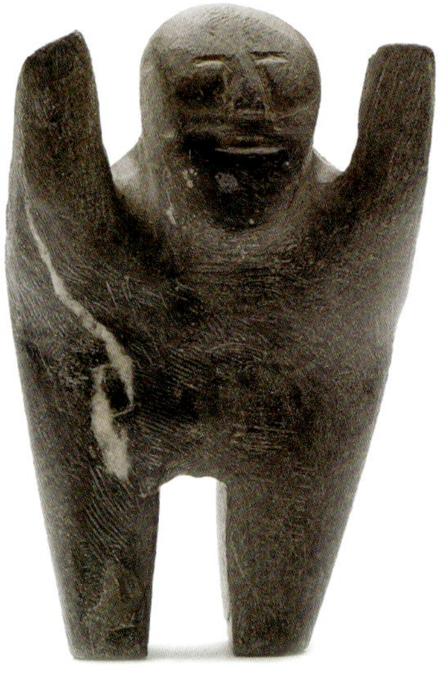

John Tiktak, *Man with Arms Raised*, 1969, stone, 15.0 x 10.2 x 7.9 cm

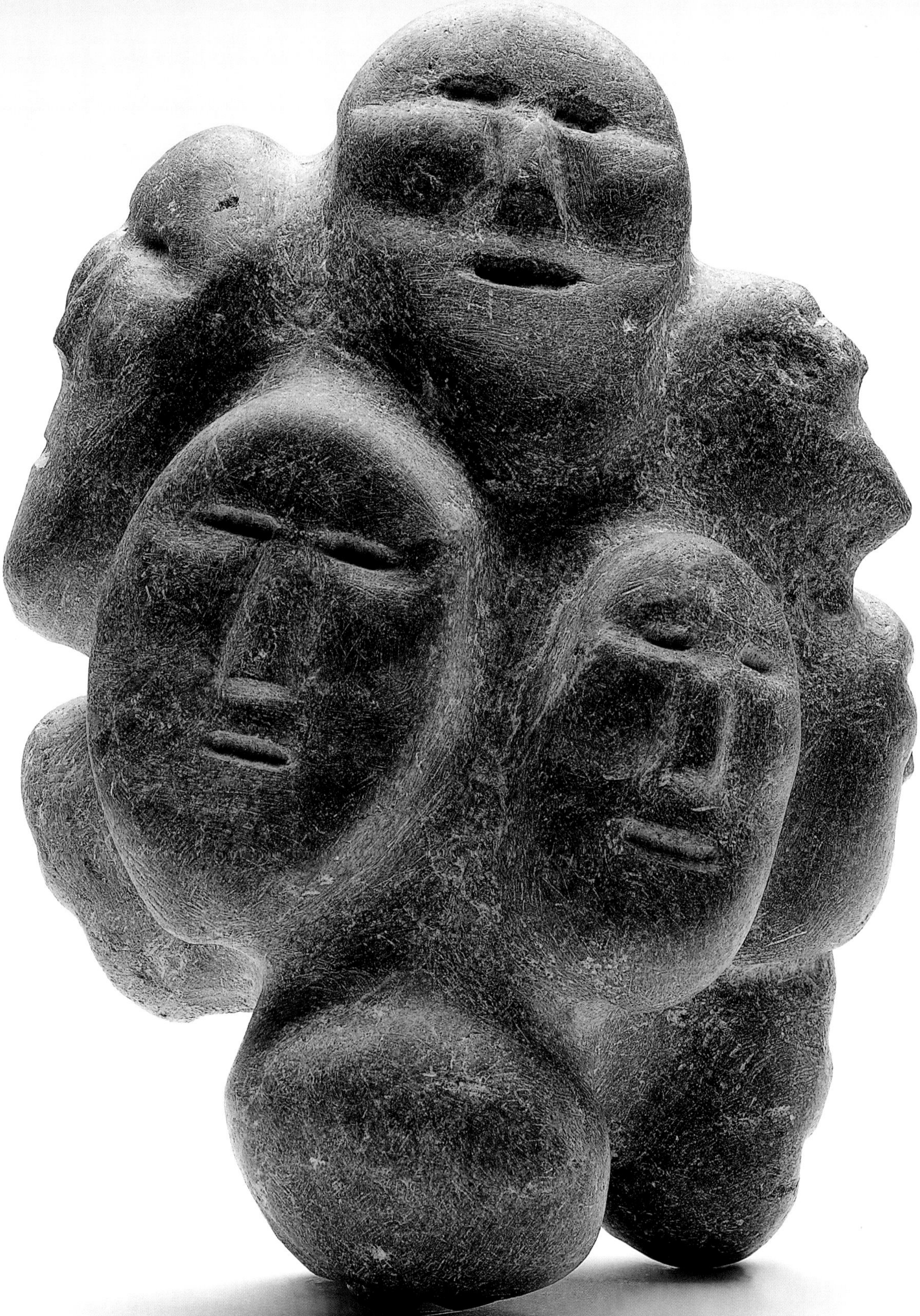

John Tiktak, *Faces*, c. 1971, stone, 13.8 x 25.3 x 20.3 cm

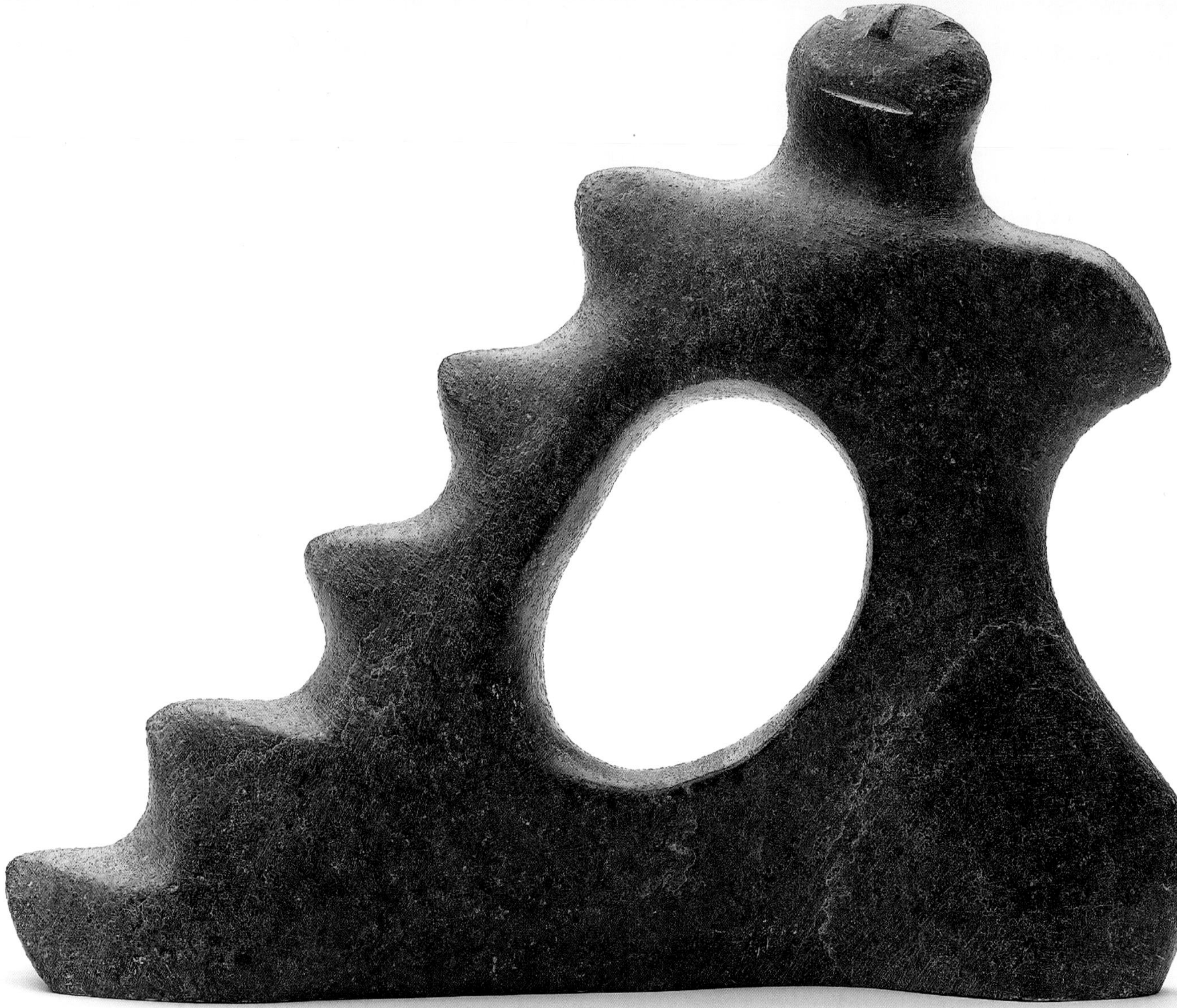

George Arluk, *Figure*, 1975, stone, 12.2 x 15.4 x 2.8 cm

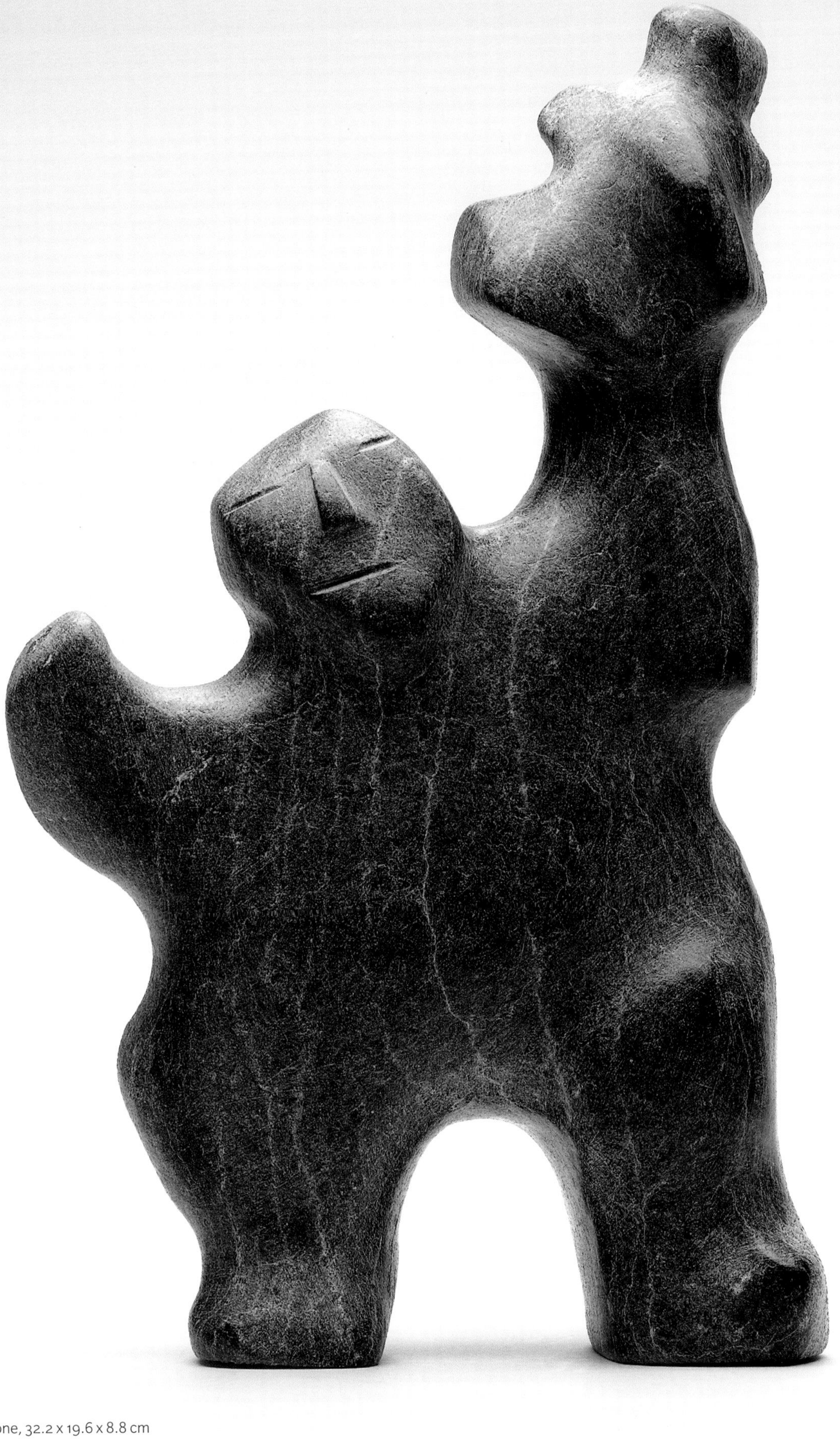

George Arluk, *Father and Child*, 1970–71, stone, 32.2 x 19.6 x 8.8 cm

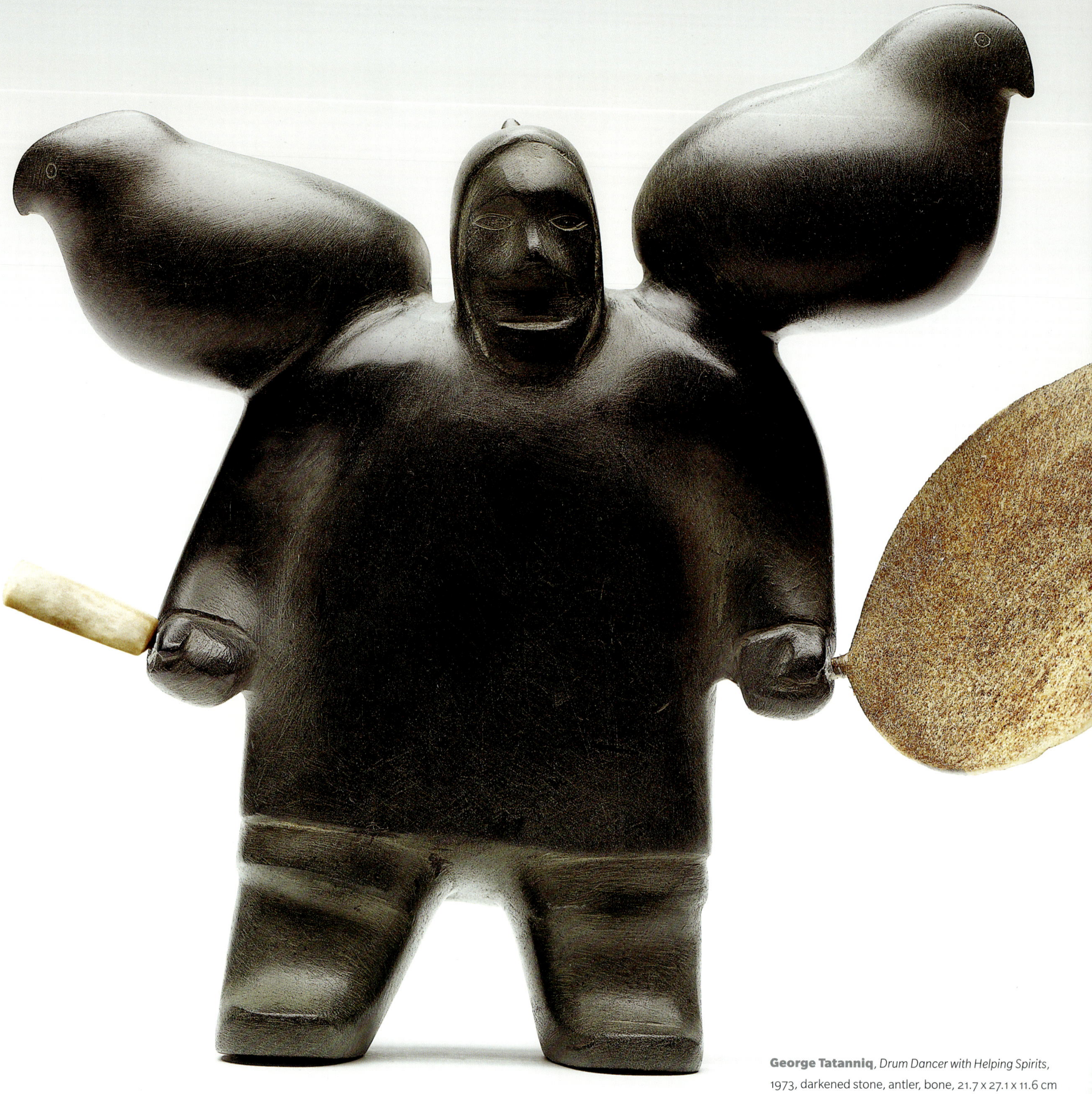

George Tatanniq, *Drum Dancer with Helping Spirits*, 1973, darkened stone, antler, bone, 21.7 x 27.1 x 11.6 cm

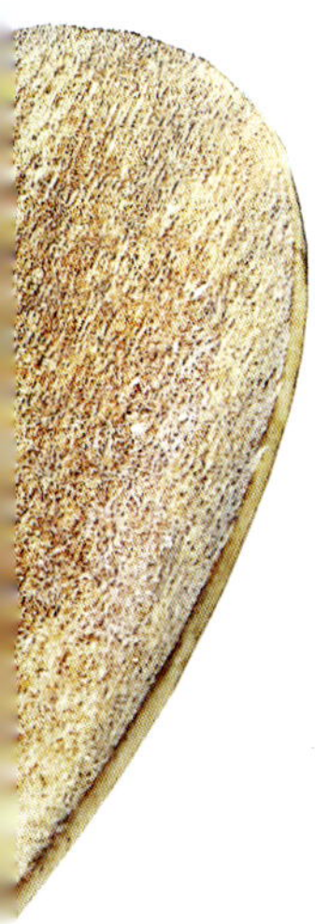

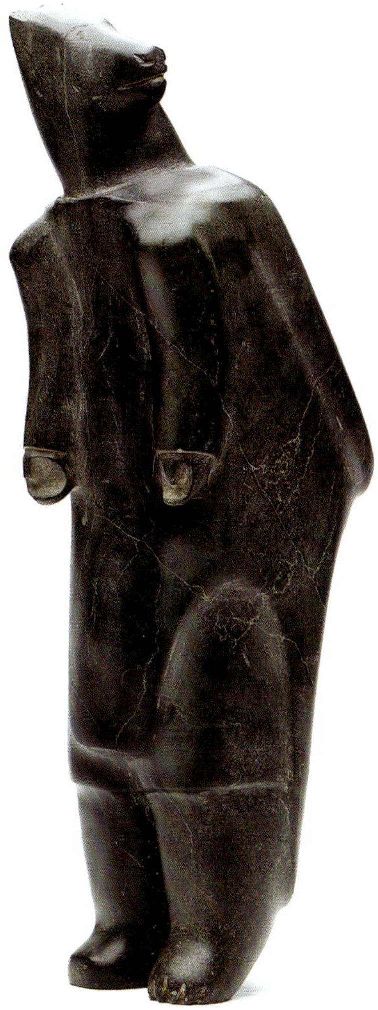

George Tatanniq, *Fox-Woman*, c. 1970, stone, 39.1 x 16.3 x 11.0 cm

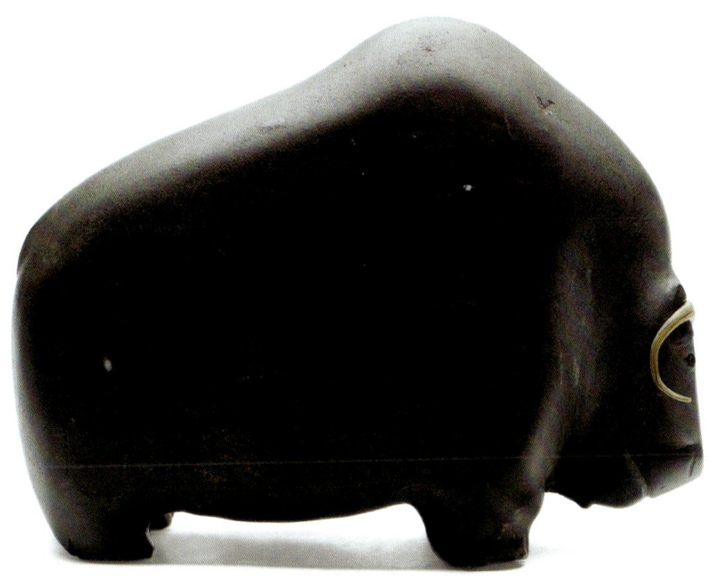

George Tatanniq, *Muskox*, c. 1971, stone, horn, 24.5 x 32.5 x 14.0 cm

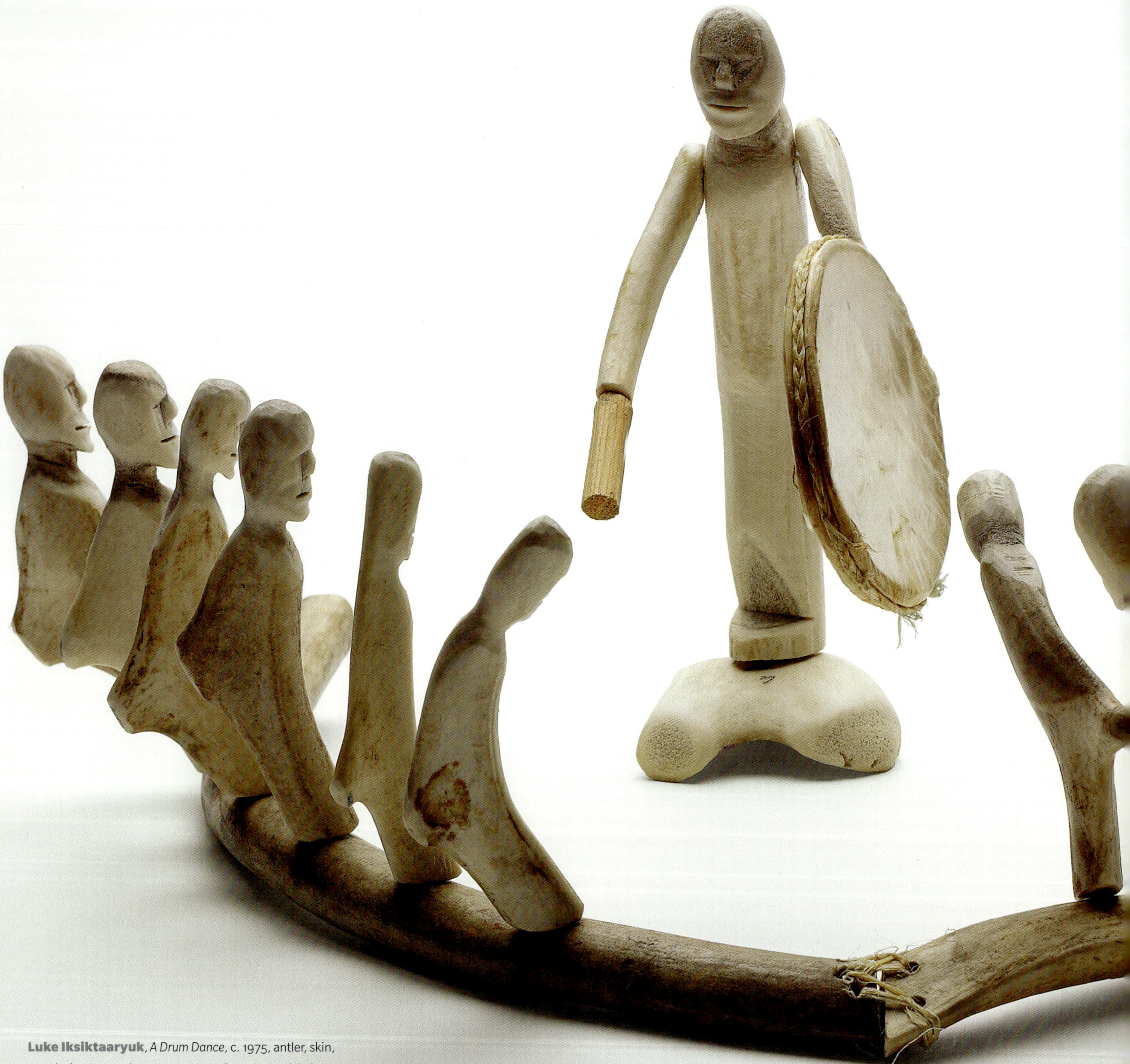

Luke Iksiktaaryuk, *A Drum Dance*, c. 1975, antler, skin, wood, sinew, metal, 21.0 x 40.5 x 33.8 cm (assembled)

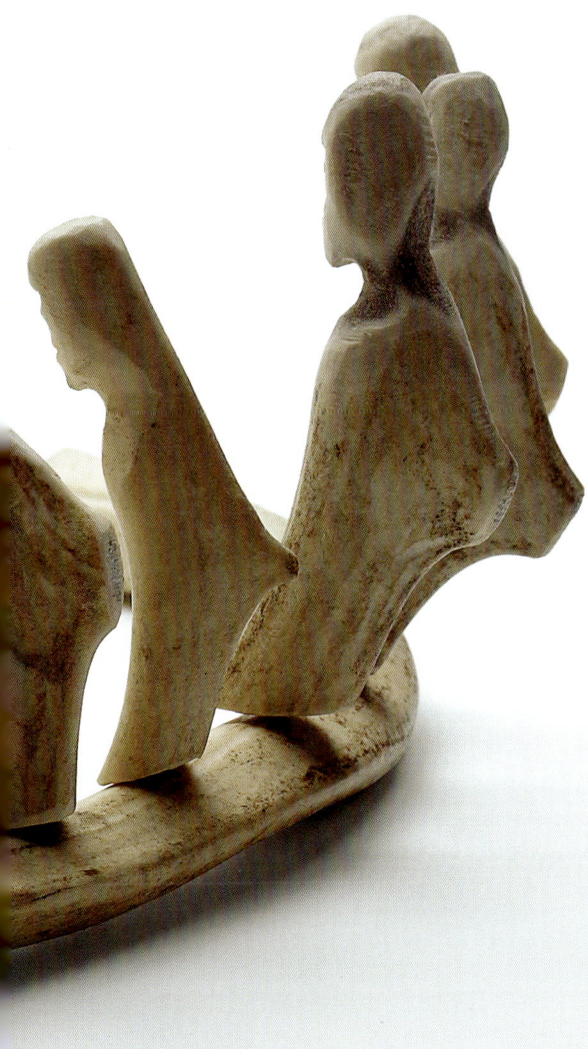

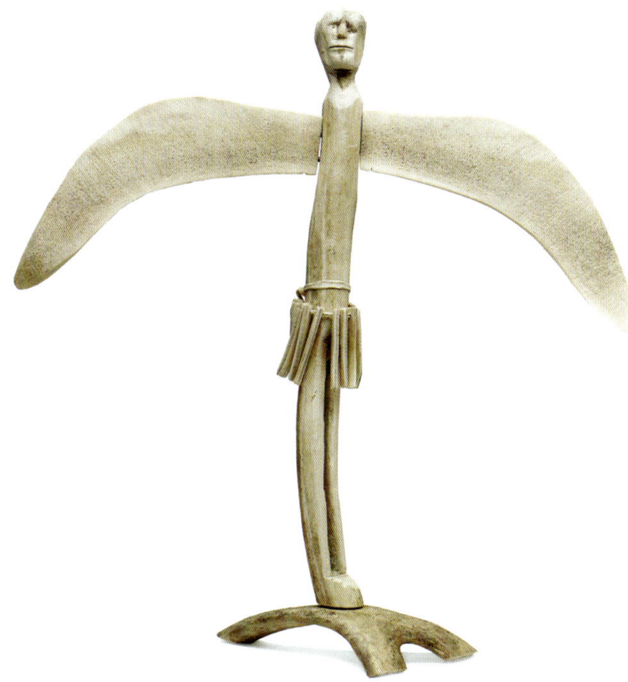

Luke Iksiktaaryuk, *Shaman in Flight*, c. 1975, antler, hide, 46.6 x 46.2 x 20.0 cm

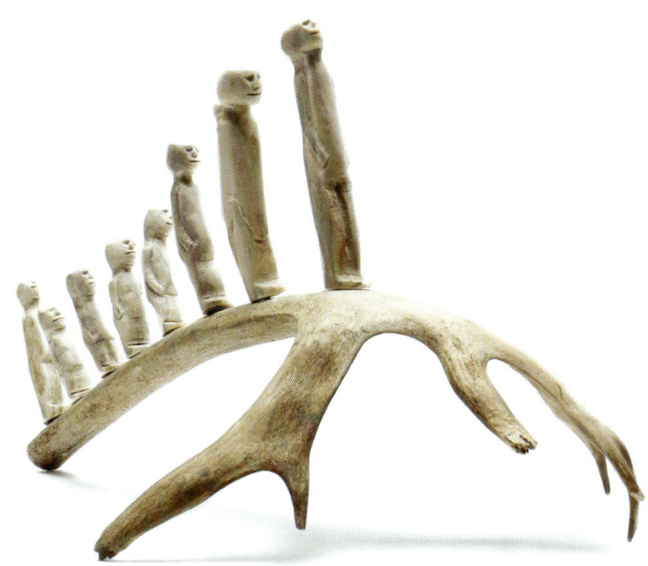

Luke Iksiktaaryuk, *Family*, c. 1967, antler, 30.2 x 57.6 x 31.2 cm

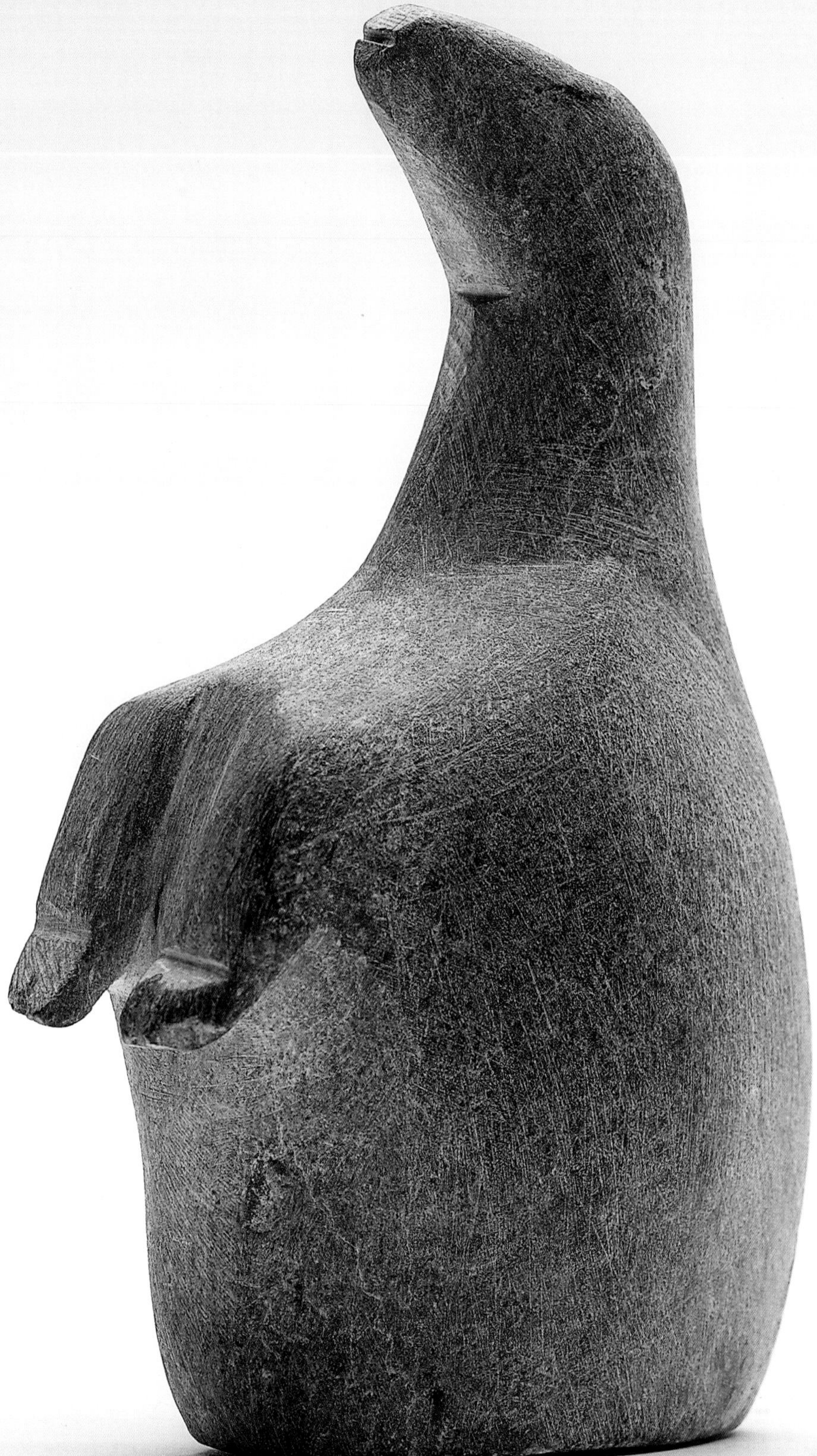

Andy Miki, *Animal*, c. 1967,
stone, 12.4 x 8.2 x 3.8 cm

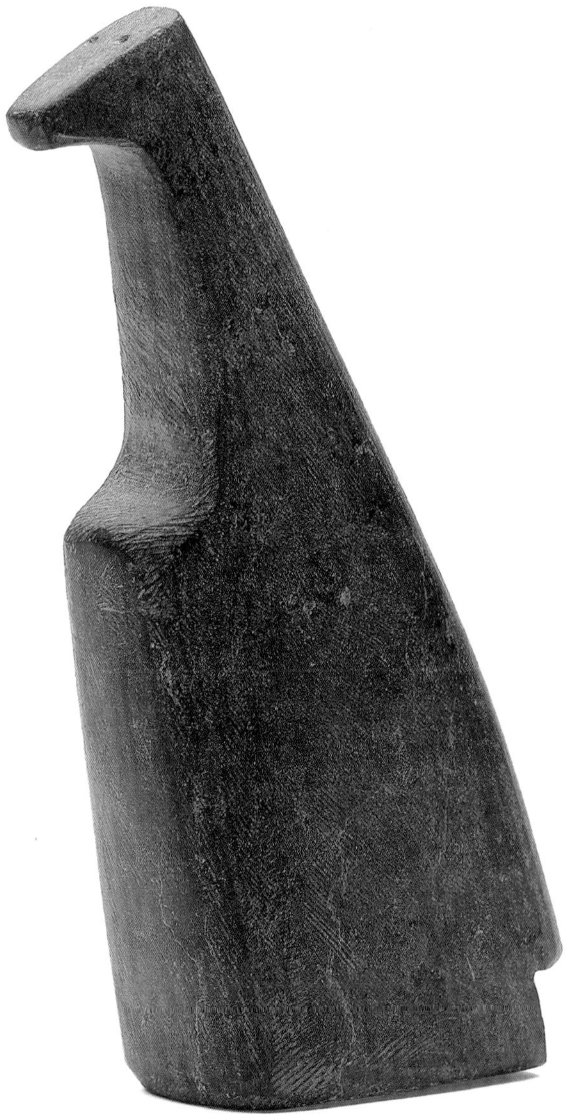

Andy Miki, *Bird*, 1972–73,
darkened stone, 14.2 x 3.7 x 8.2 cm

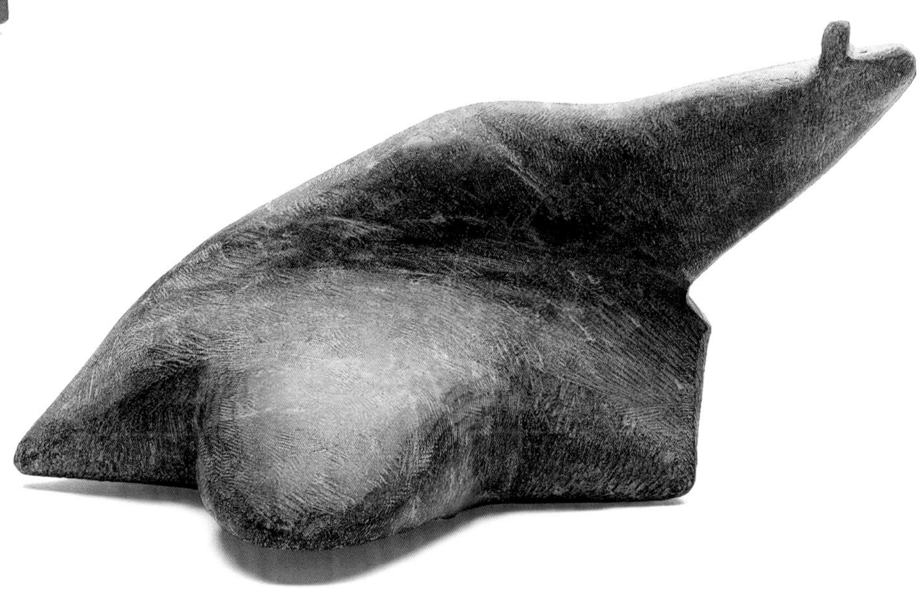

Andy Miki, *Animal*, c. 1970,
darkened stone, 10.9 x 22.0 x 15.7 cm

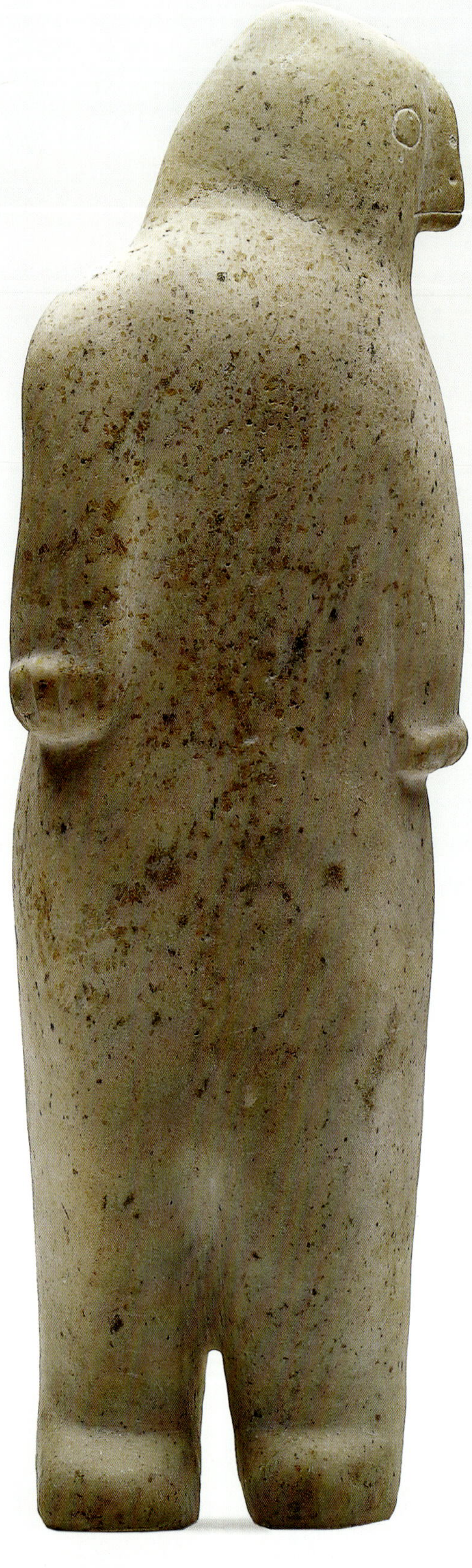

Latcholassie Akesuk, *Bird/Man Transformation*, c. 1973,
stone, 56.8 x 18.0 x 12.5 cm

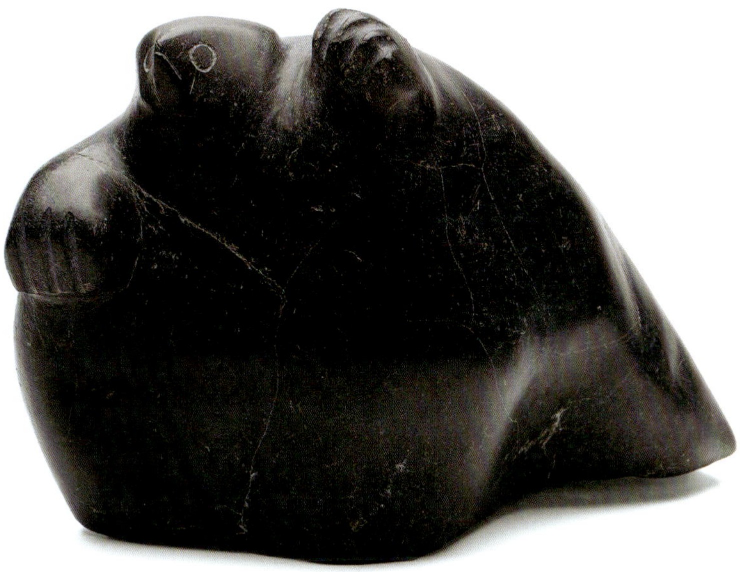

Latcholassie Akesuk, *Bird*, c. 1973, stone, 23.6 x 37.3 x 21.5 cm

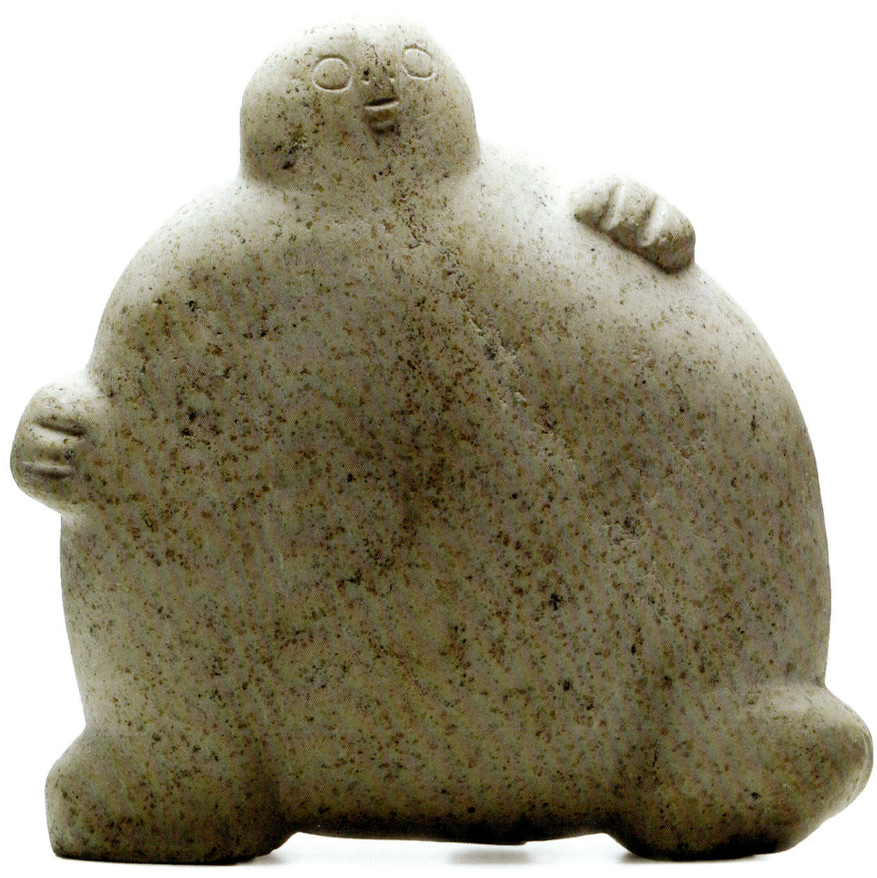

Latcholassie Akesuk, *Bird*, c. 1973, stone, 41.6 x 43.0 x 16.8 cm

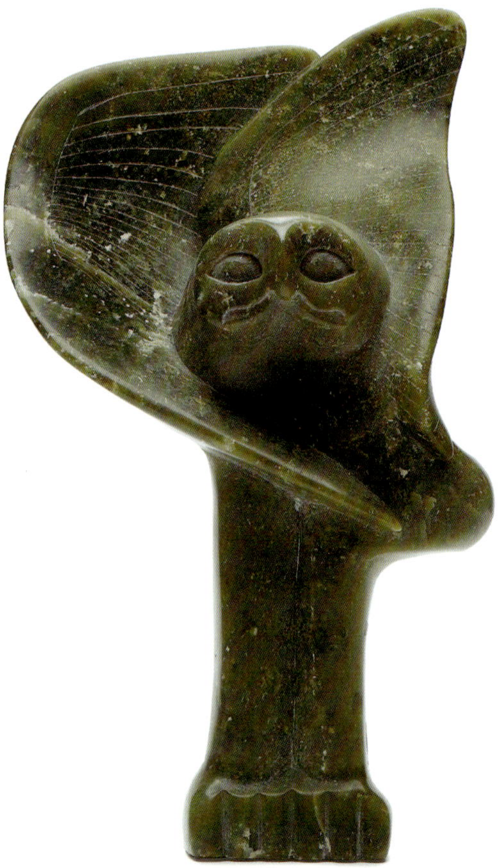

Osuitok Ipeelee, *Bird*, 1983, stone, 27.3 x 16.5 x 7.6 cm

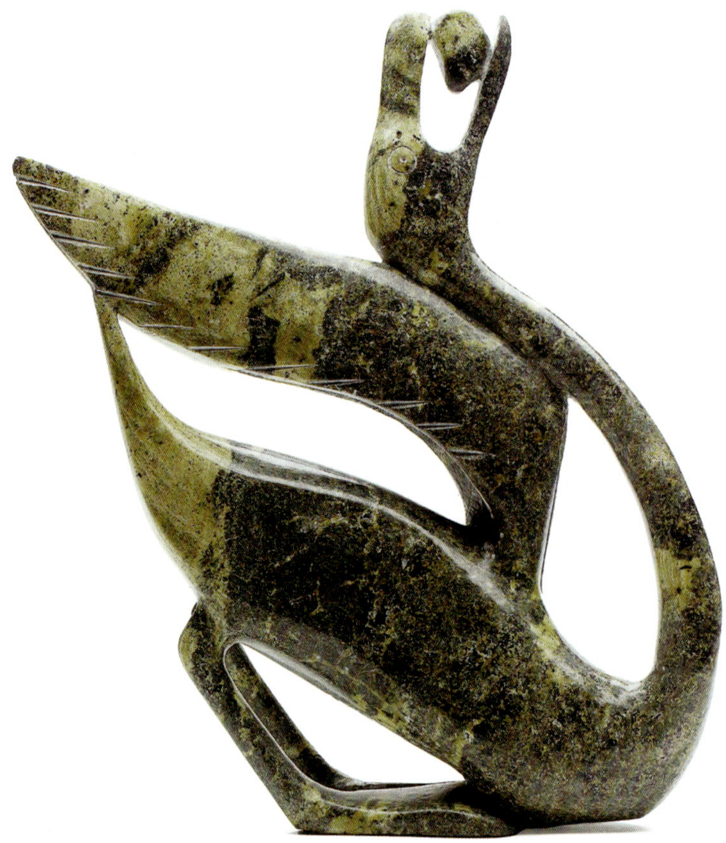

Osuitok Ipeelee, *Bird*, 1982, stone, 30.2 x 26.5 x 7.4 cm

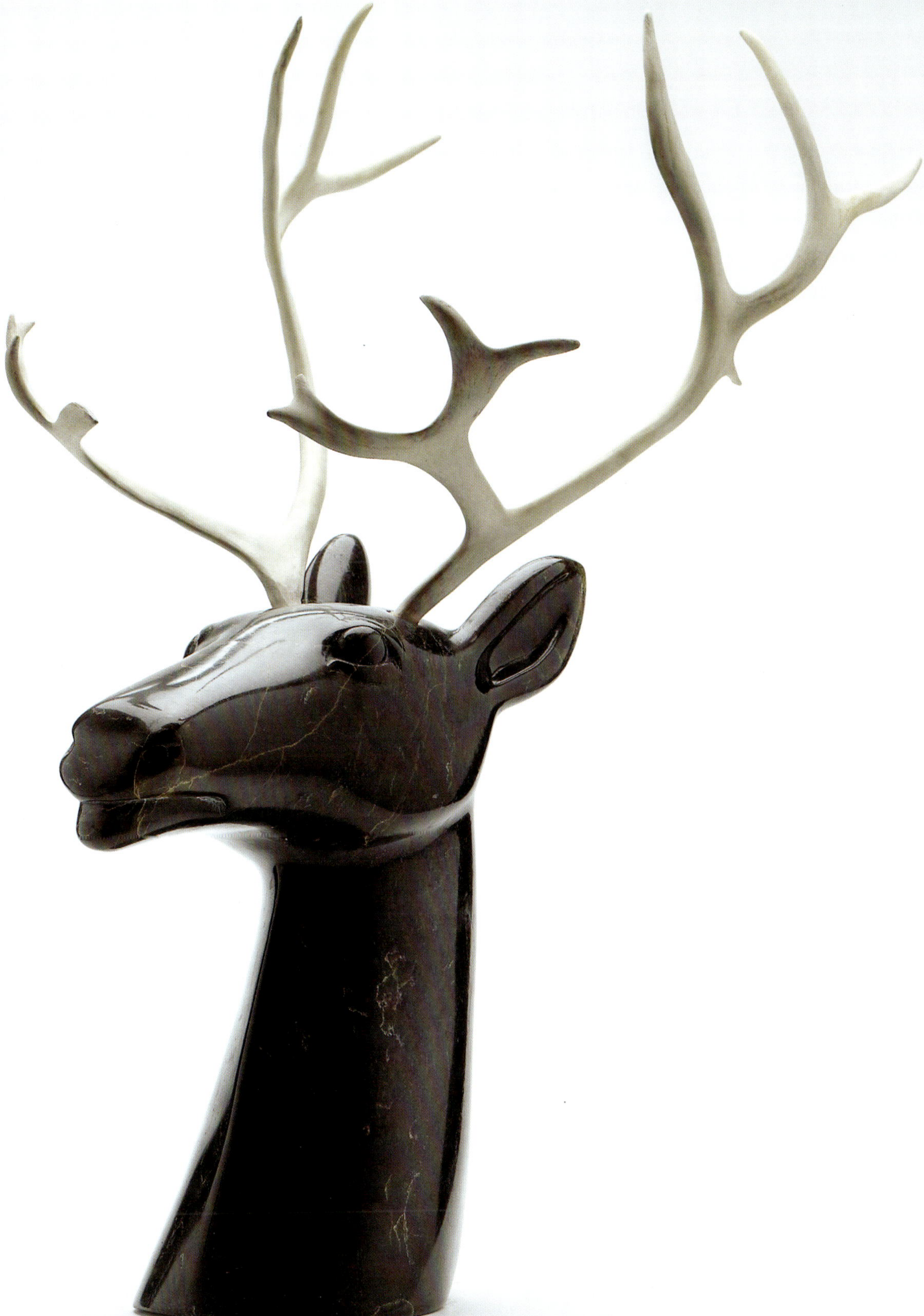

Osuitok Ipeelee, *Caribou Head*, before 1988, stone, antler, 63.7 x 54.0 x 31.3 cm

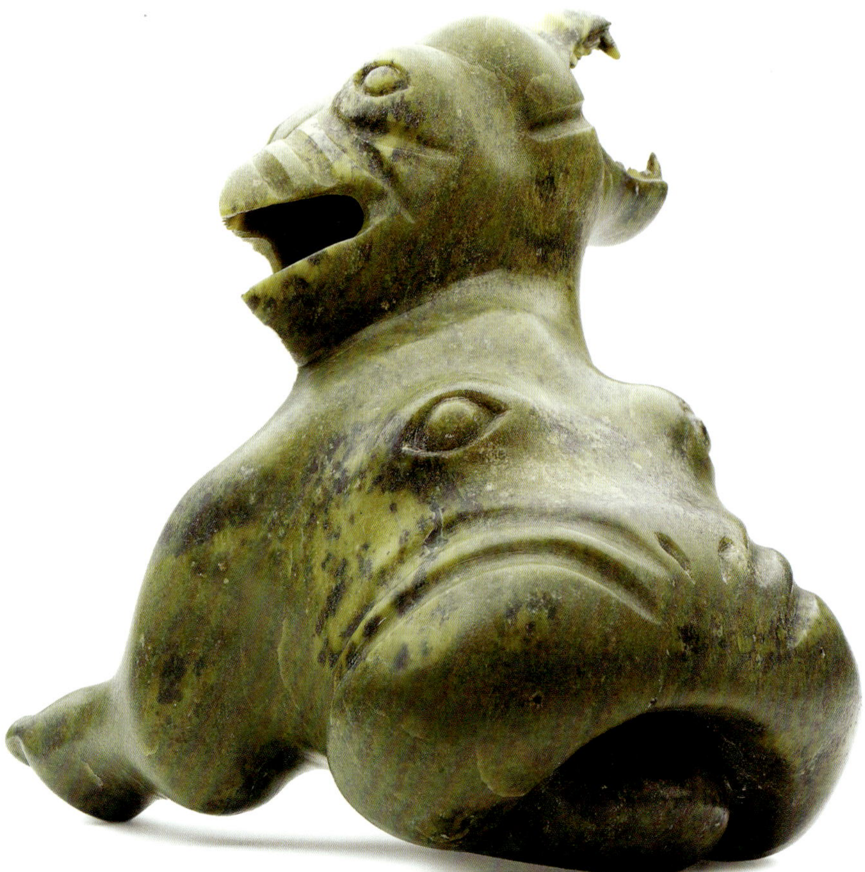

Kiugak Ashoona, *Bird and Animal Head Cluster*, early 1970s, stone, 16.3 x 17.1 x 12.3 cm

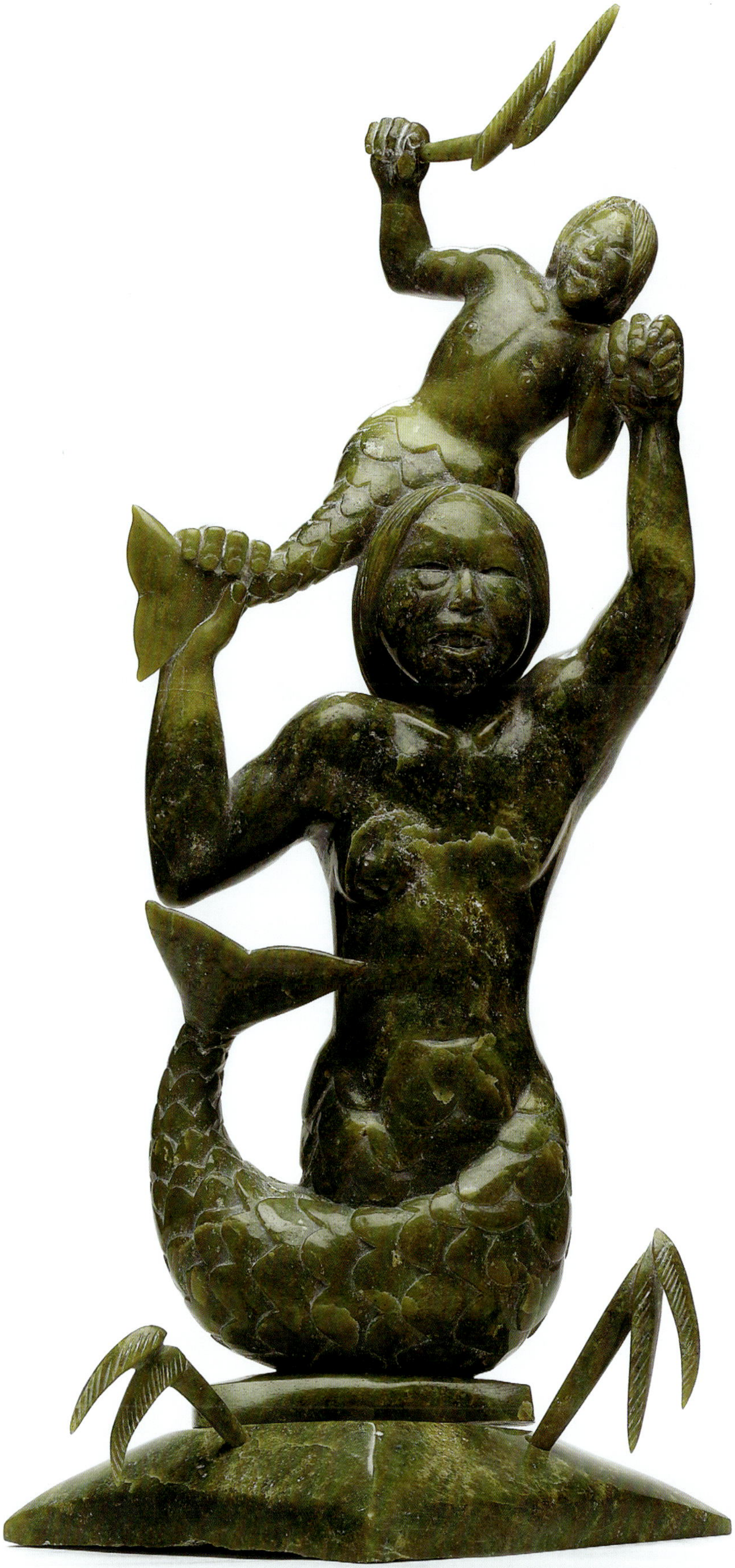

Kiugak Ashoona, *Sea Goddess and Young*, before 1986, stone, wood, 49.8 x 26.5 x 19.9 cm

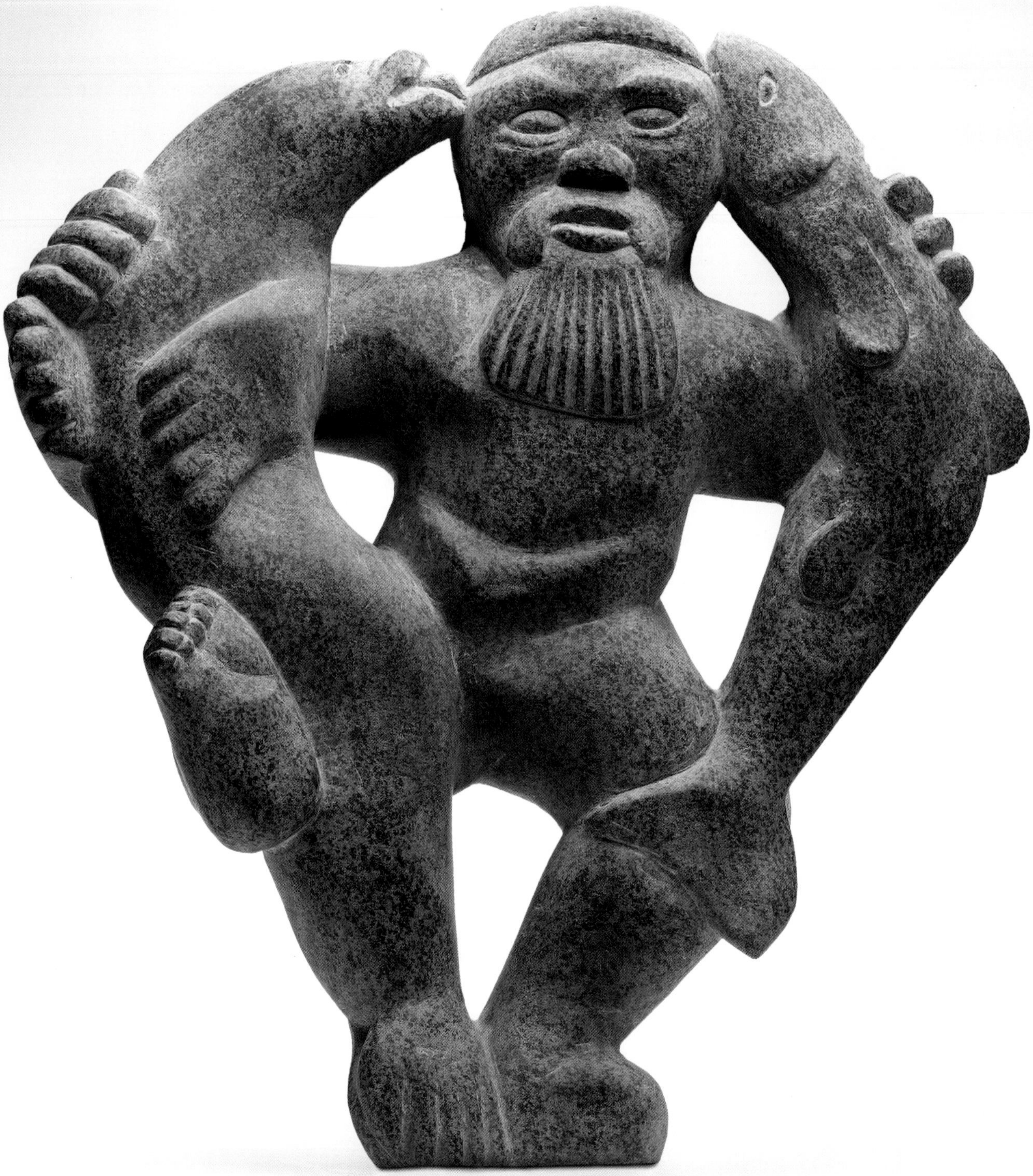

Aqjangajuk Shaa, *Man with Fish and Seal*, before 1974, stone, 54.4 x 51.5 x 22.0 cm

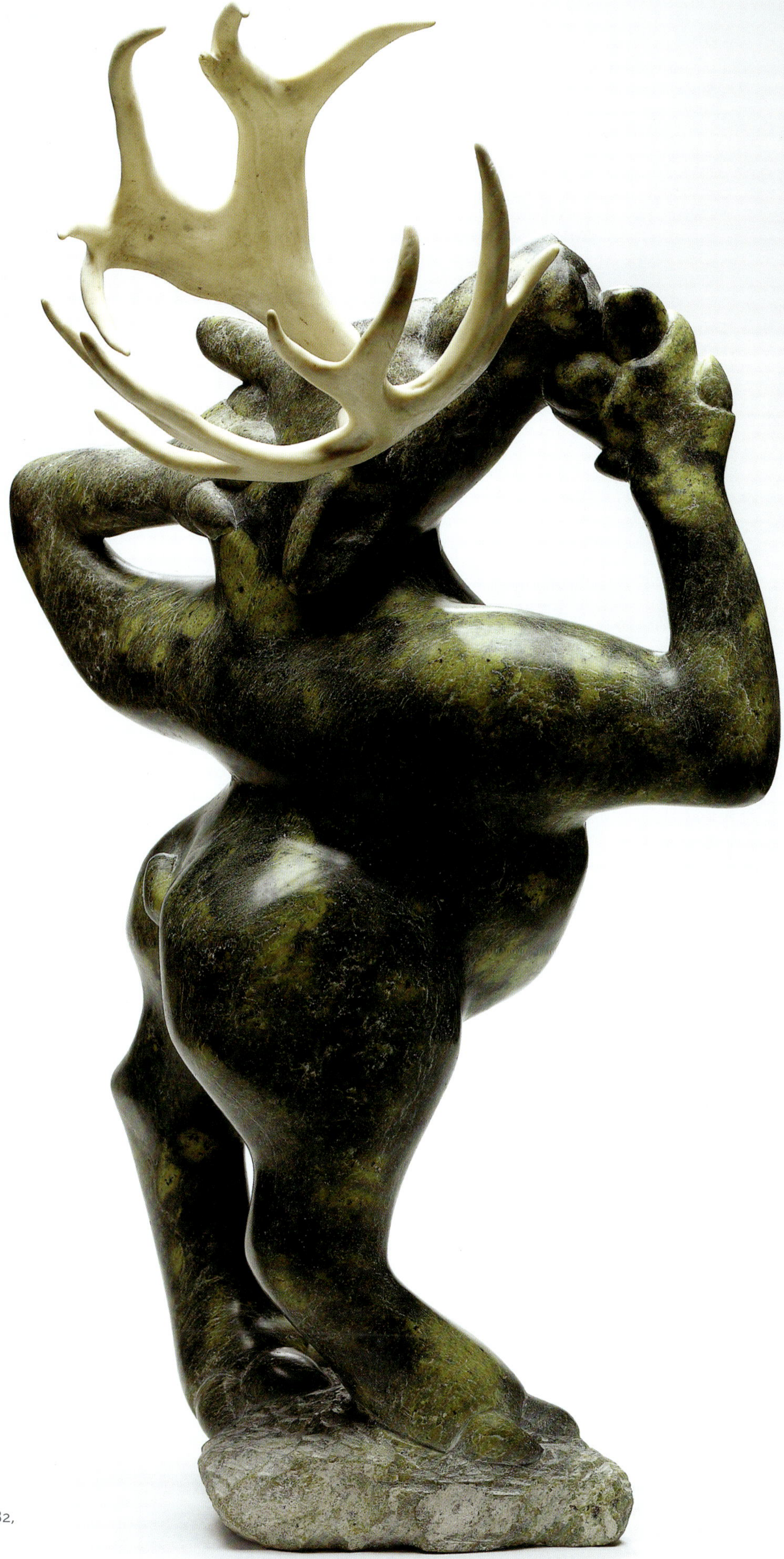

Aqjangajuk Shaa, *Caribou Standing on Hind Legs*, 1982, stone, antler, 64.0 x 37.8 x 36.0 cm

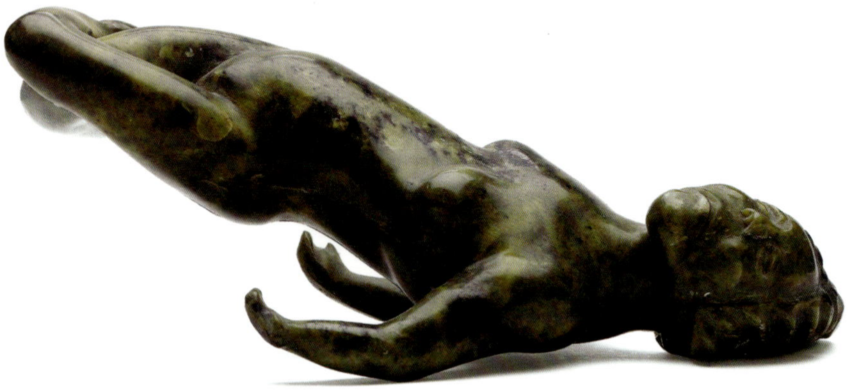

Quvianatuliak Takpaungai, *Female Nude*, before 1982, stone, 12.3 x 29.2 x 15.3 cm

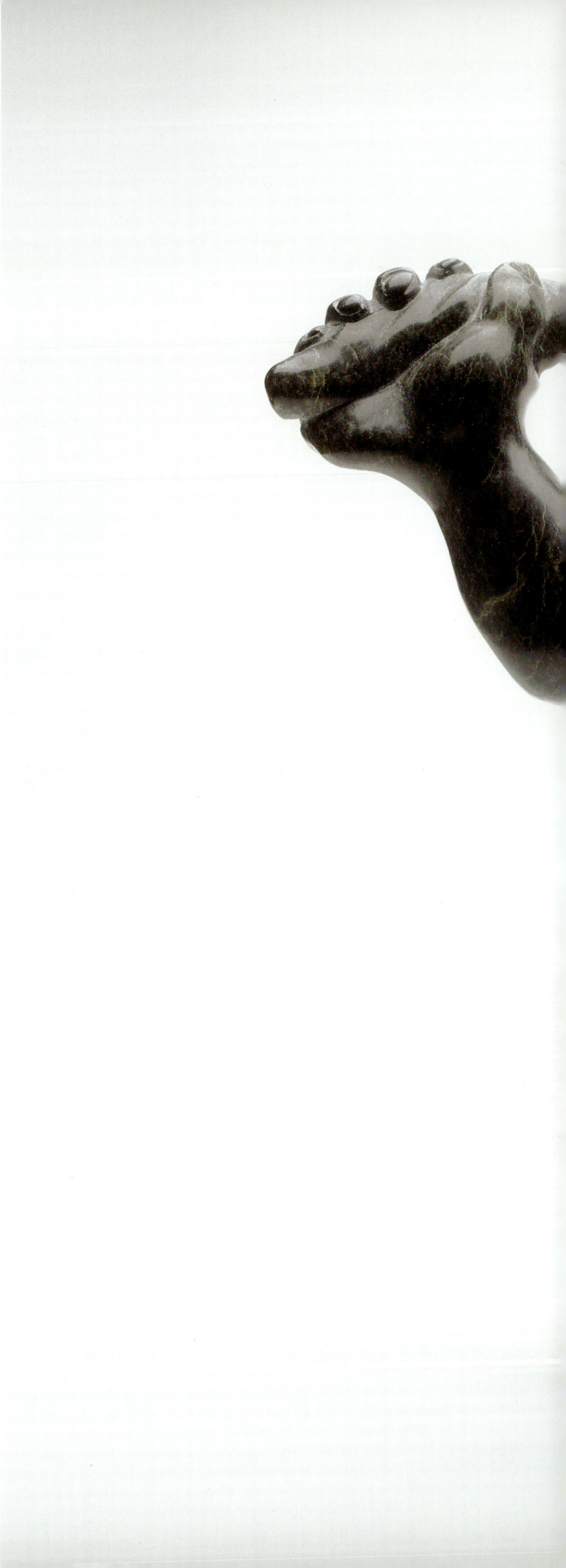

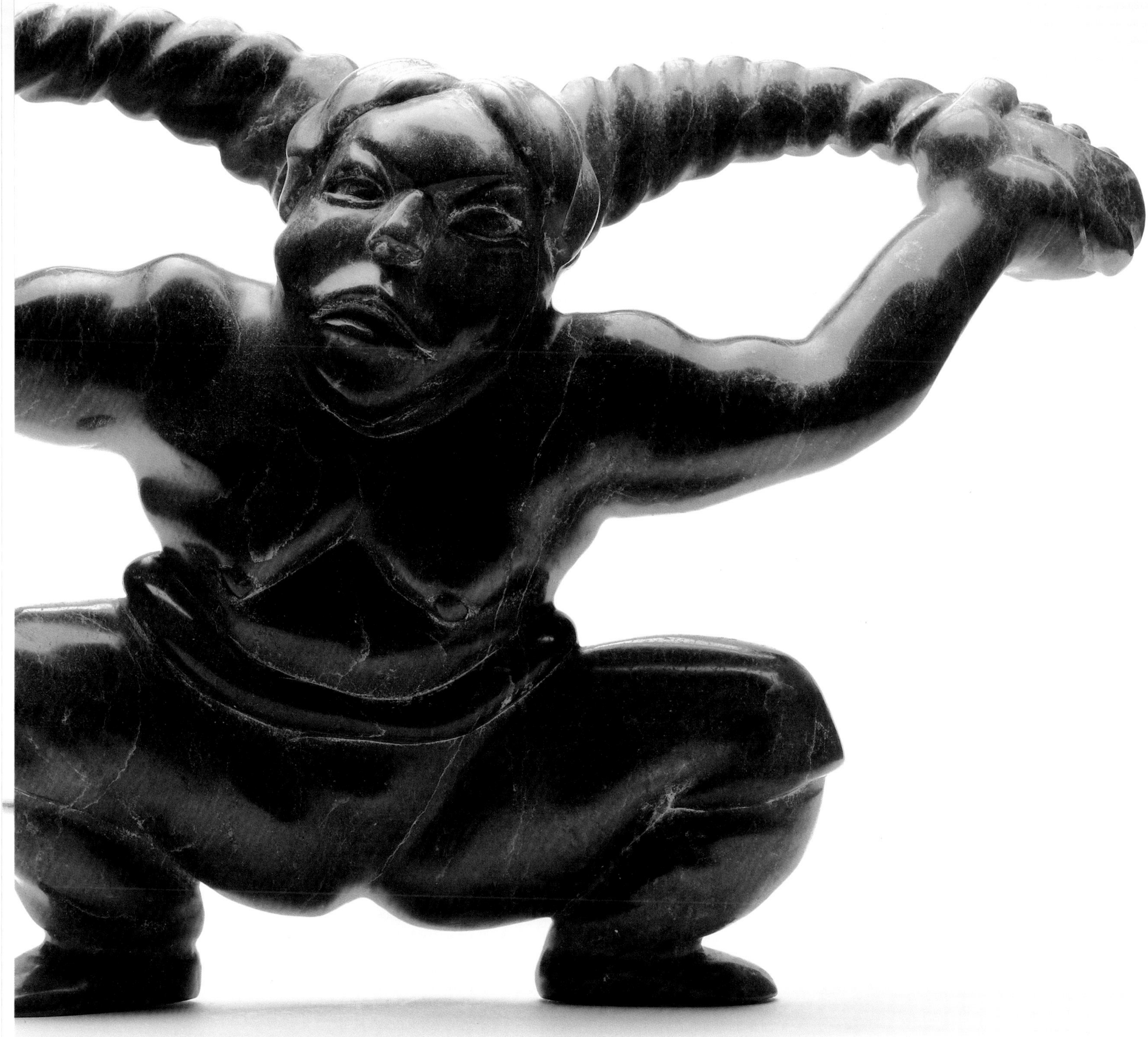

Quvianatuliak Takpaungai, *Woman Holding Braids*, before 1987, stone, 29.9 x 45.5 x 14.0 cm

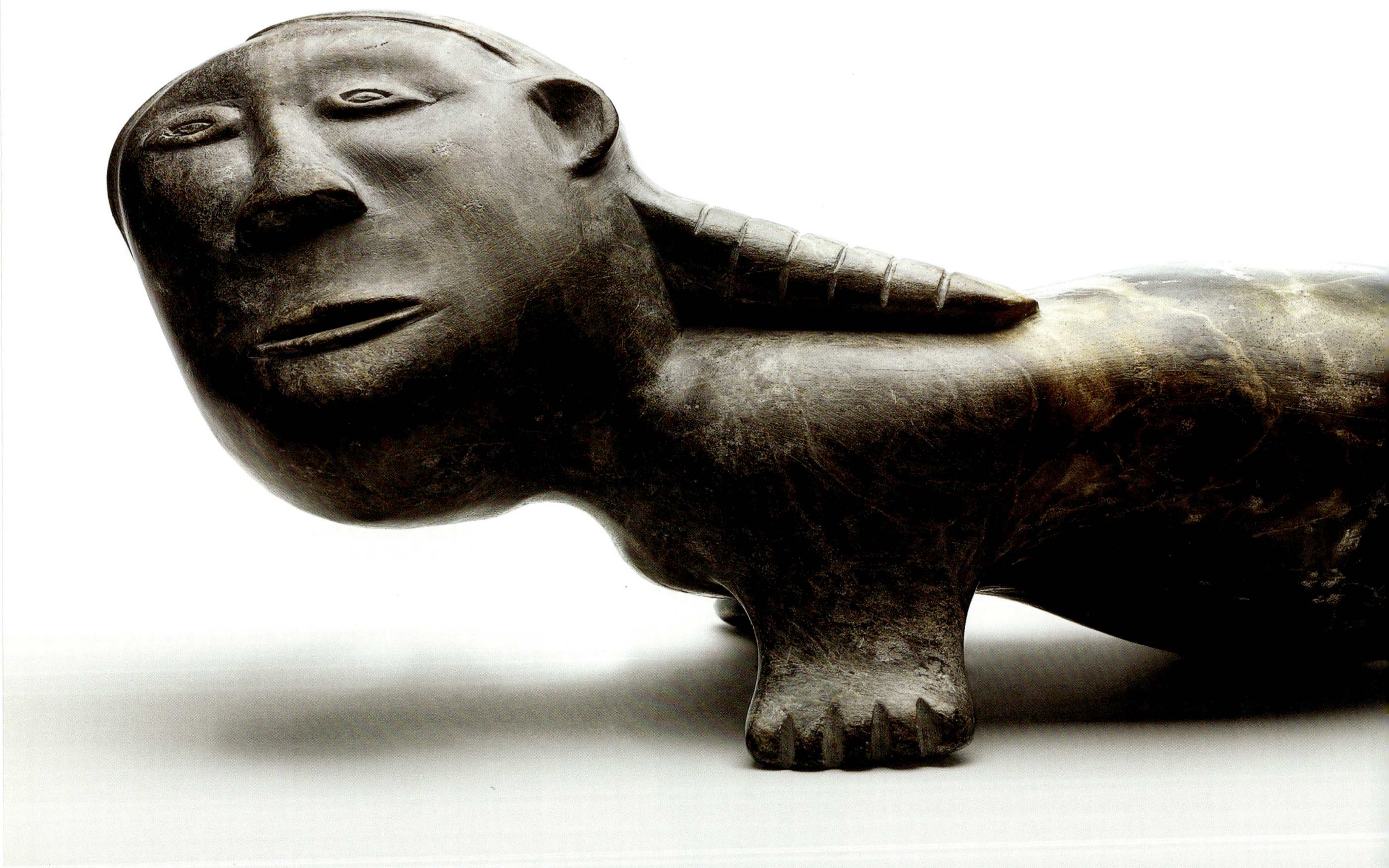

Maudie Rachel Okittuq, *Sea Goddess*, 1978, stone, 12.8 x 35.6 x 14.9 cm

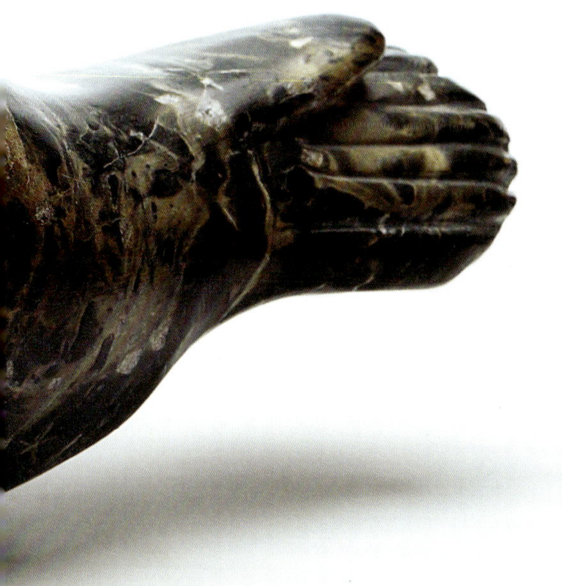

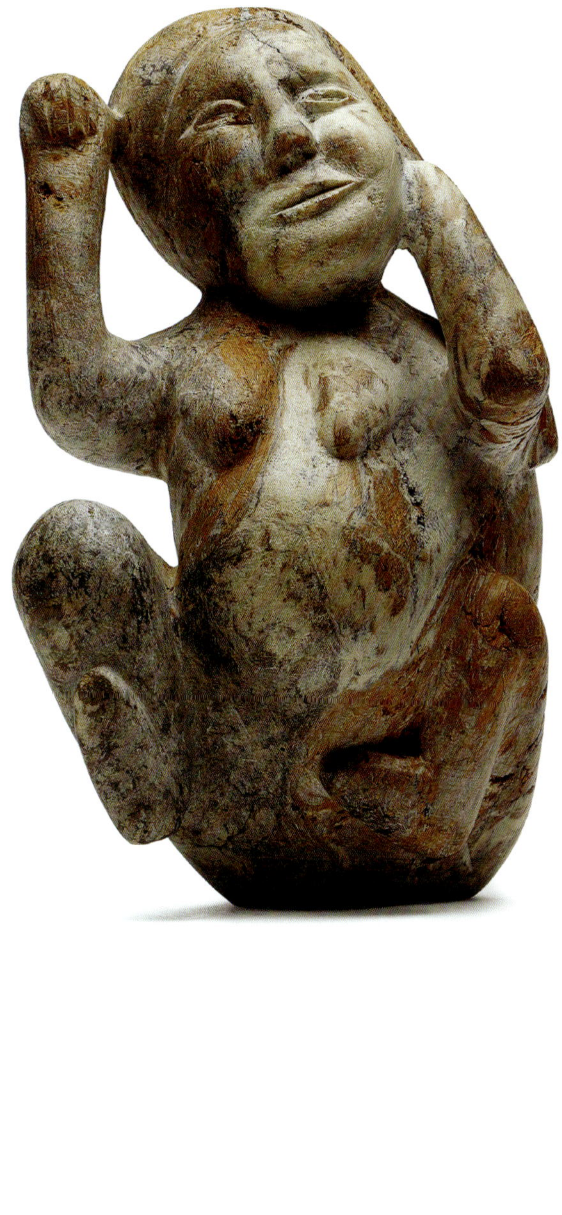

Maudie Rachel Okittuq, *Woman Giving Birth*, c. 1980, stone, 19.4 x 12.0 x 11.4 cm

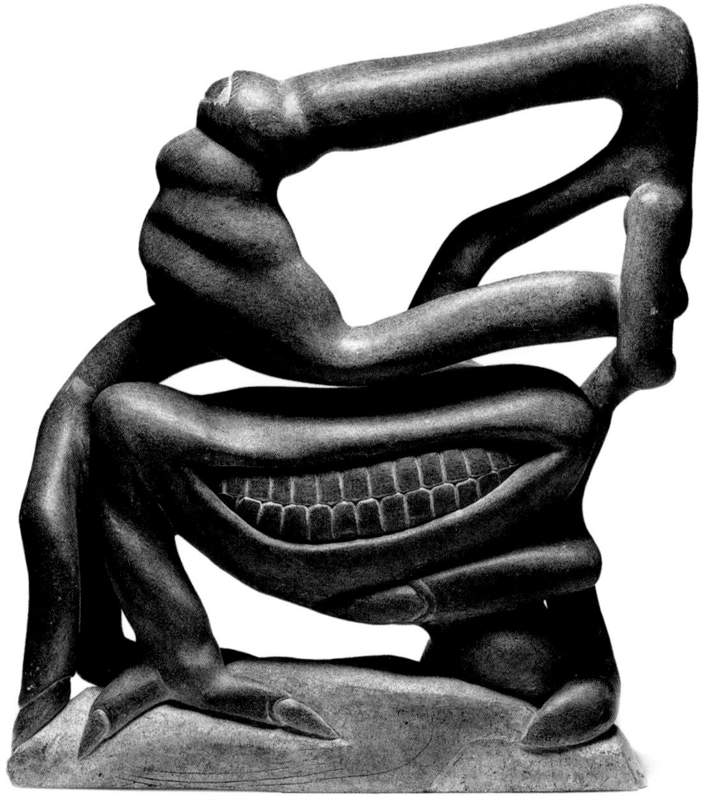

Eli Sallualu Qinuajua, *Fantastic Figure*, 1969, stone, 54.2 x 47.4 x 14.3 cm

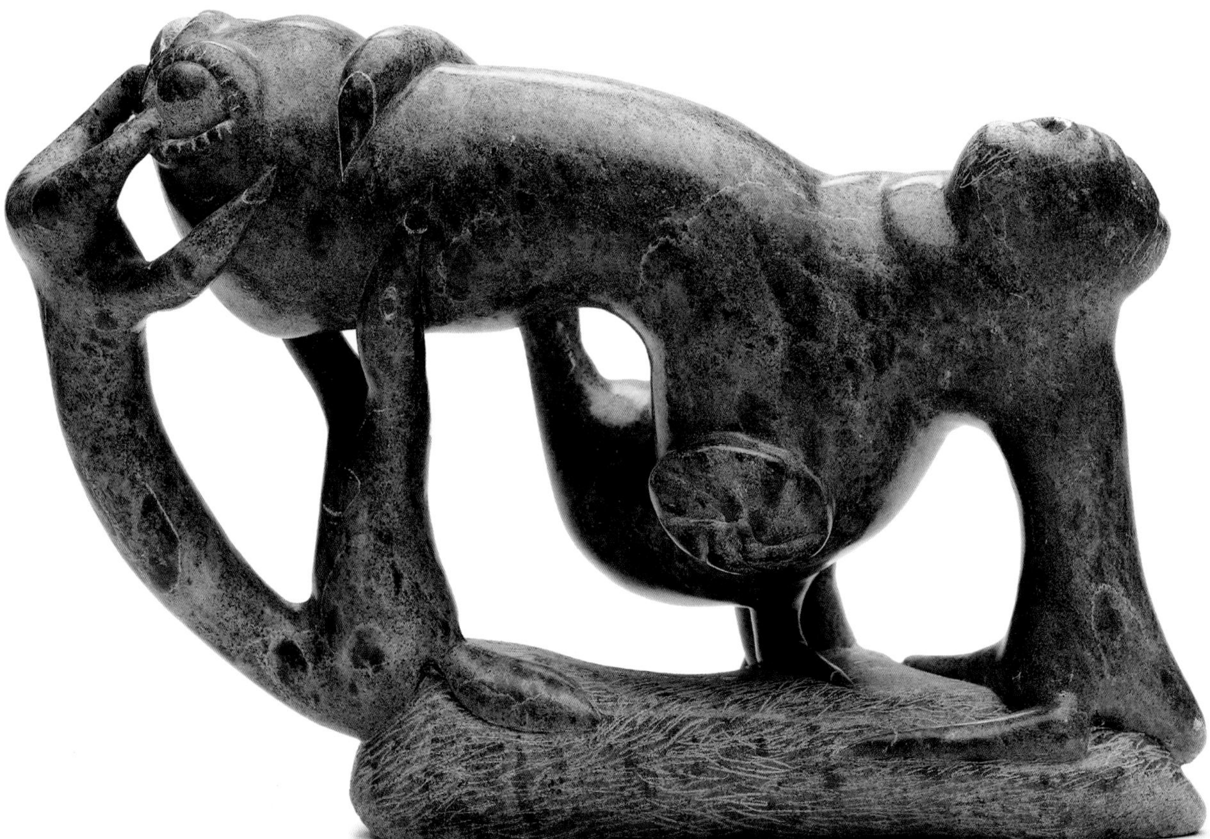

Eli Sallualu Qinuajua, *Fantastic Figure*, c. 1970, stone, 19.2 x 28.6 x 13.5 cm

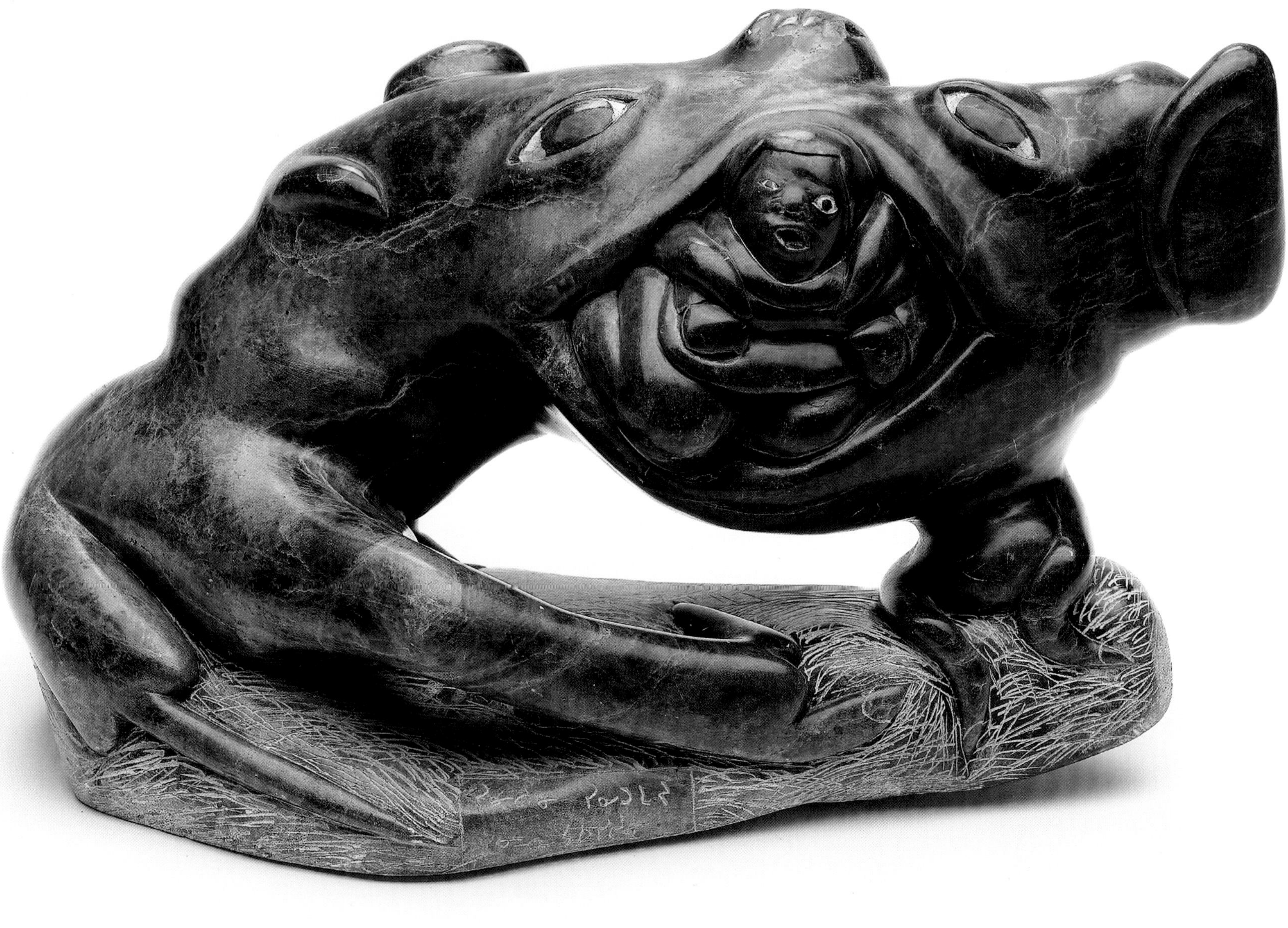

Eli Sallualu Qinuajua, *Fantastic Figure with Man in Mouth*, 1975, darkened stone, 16.3 x 29.6 x 14.7 cm

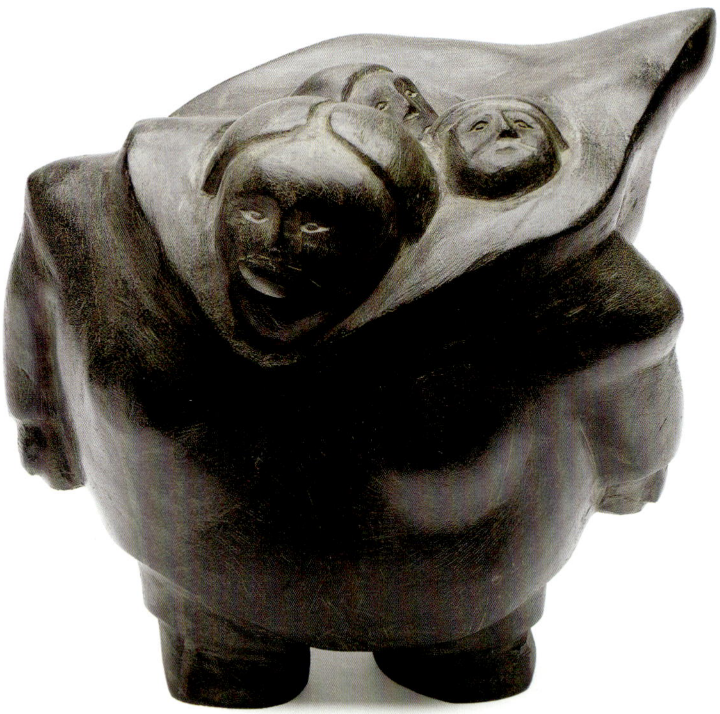

Peter Sevoga, *Mother and Children*, 1973,
darkened stone, 21.2 x 23.7 x 19.3 cm

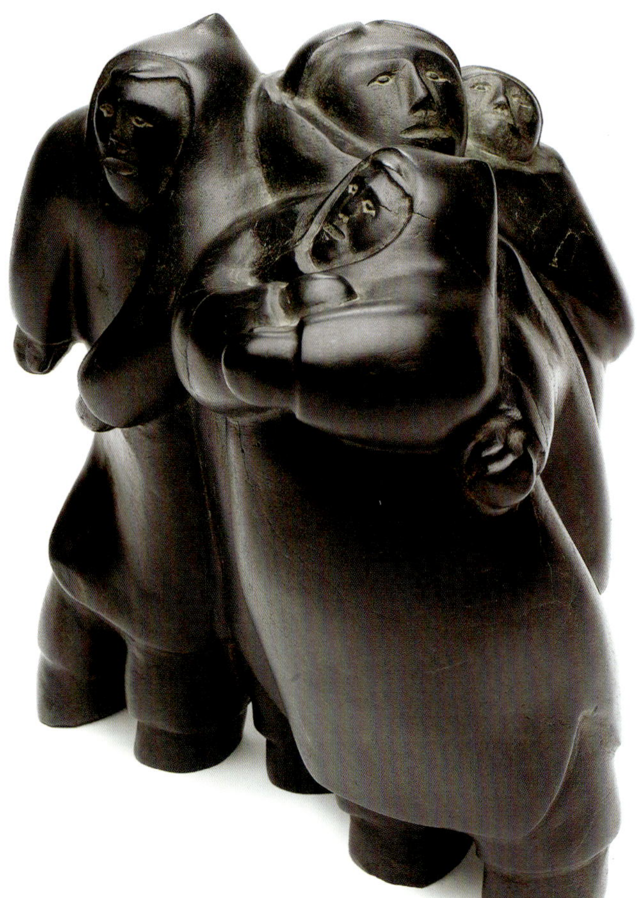

Peter Sevoga, *Family*, 1972,
stained stone, 25.2 x 22.7 x 22.5 cm

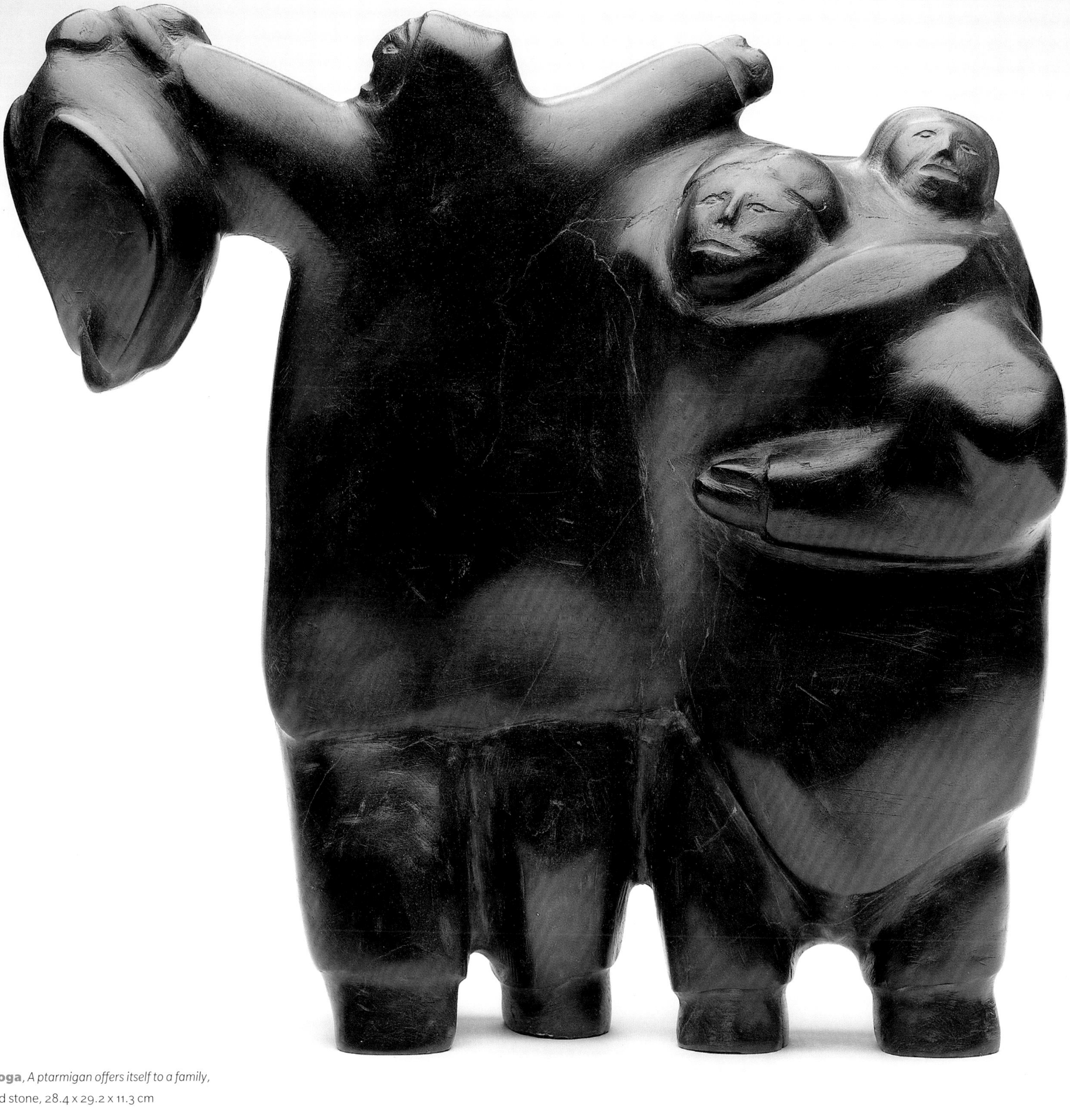

Peter Sevoga, *A ptarmigan offers itself to a family*, 1971, stained stone, 28.4 x 29.2 x 11.3 cm

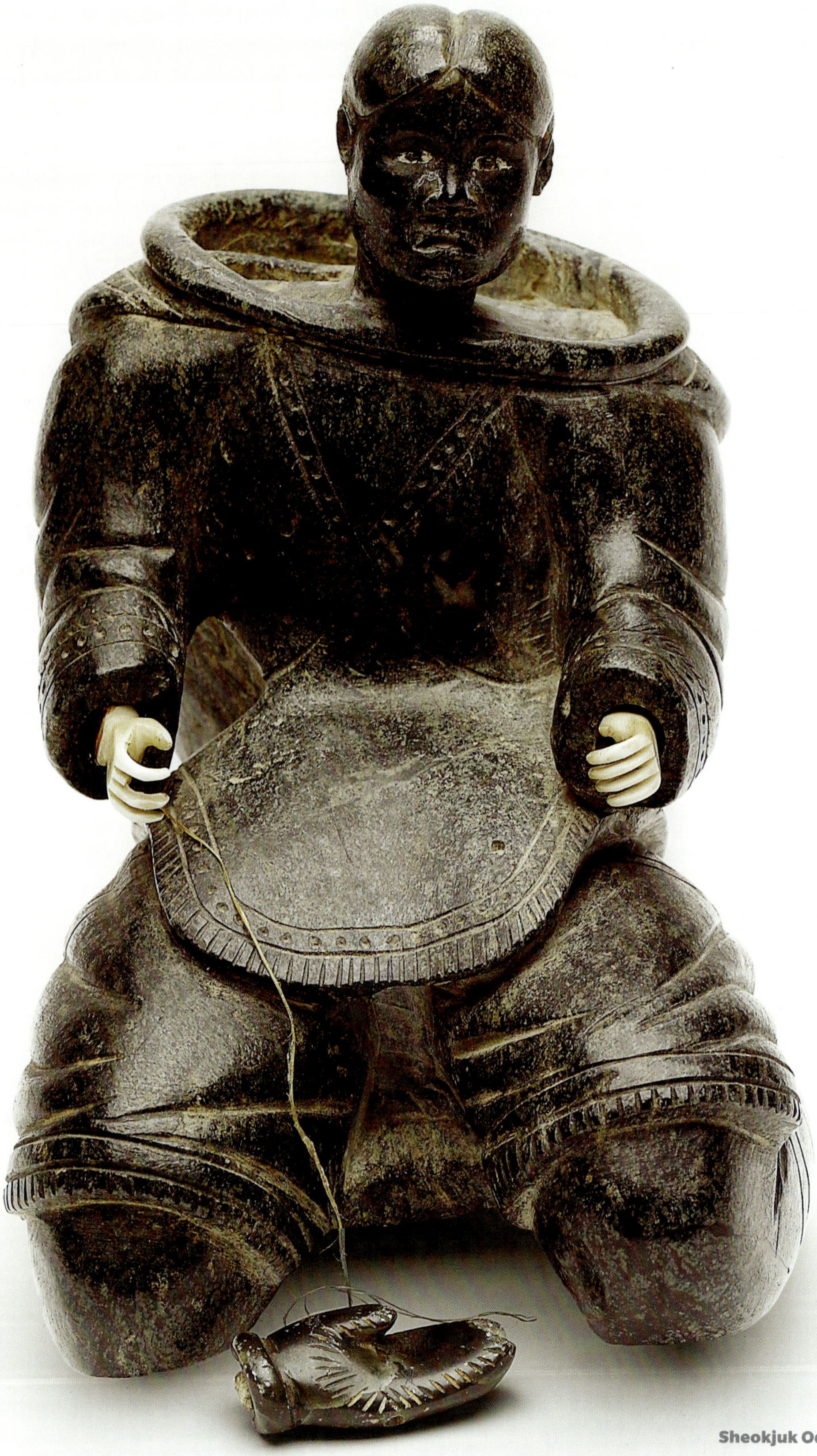

Sheokjuk Oqutaq, *Glove Maker*, c. 1955, stone, ivory, sinew, 15.4 x 10.5 x 14.0 cm

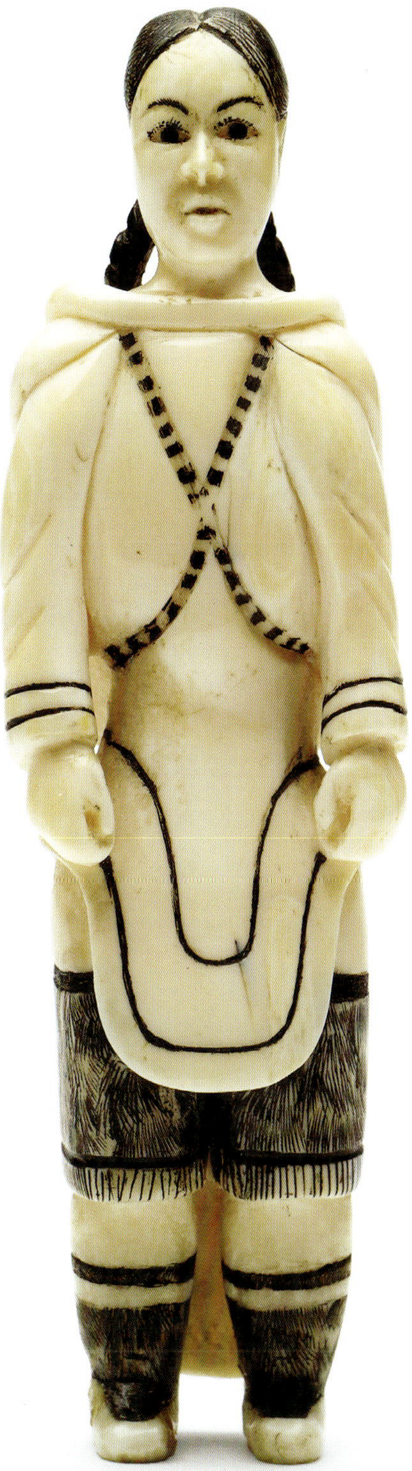

Sheokjuk Oqutaq, *Woman Standing*, c. 1955, ivory, colouring, 14.9 x 4.6 x 4.1 cm

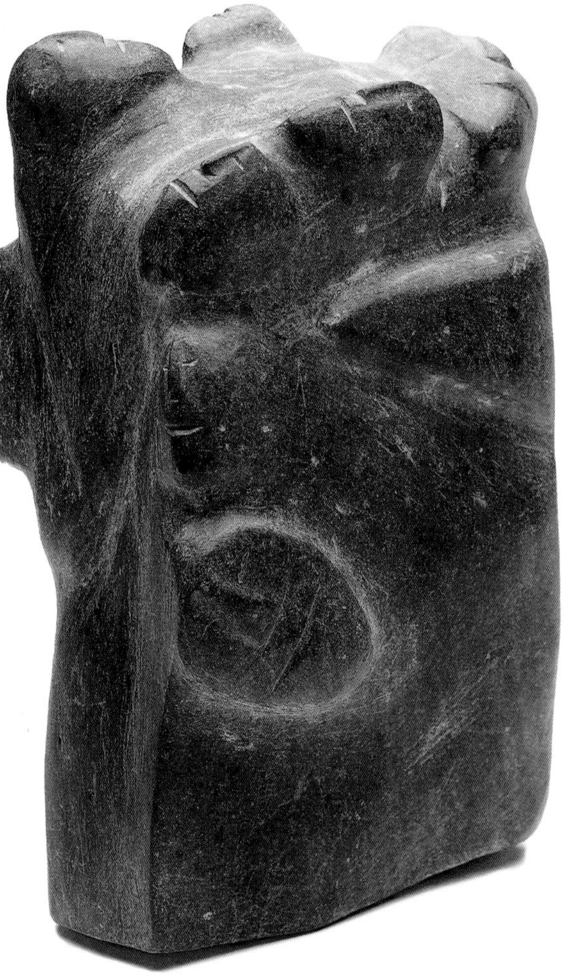

Lucy Tasseor Tutsweetok, *Face Cluster*, c. 1969, darkened stone, 25.5 x 20.4 x 11.0 cm

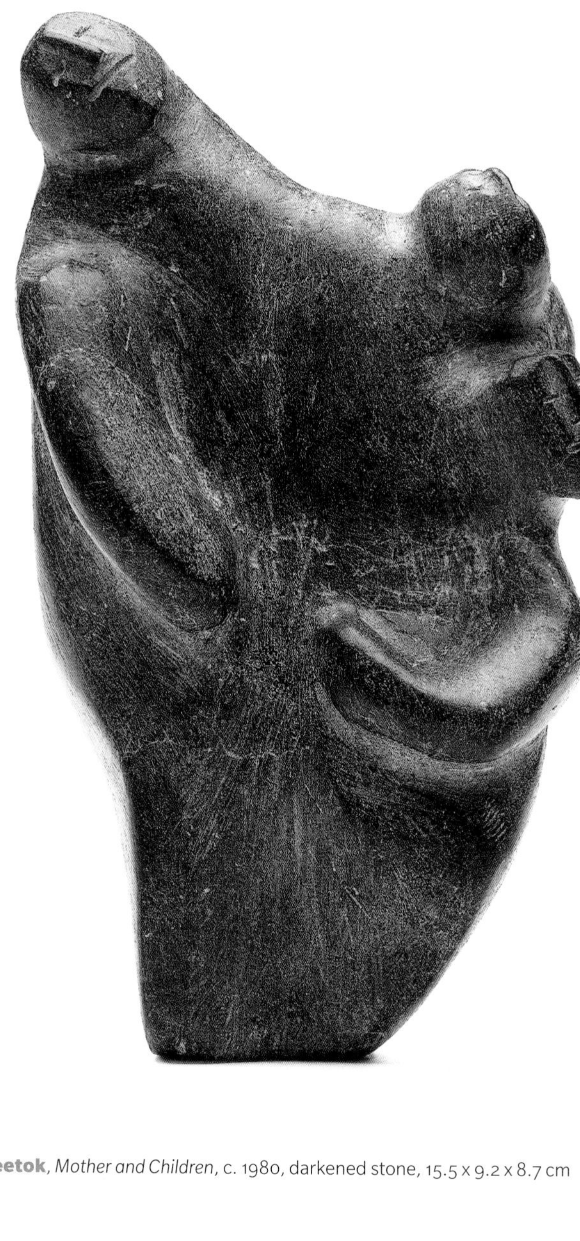

Lucy Tasseor Tutsweetok, *Mother and Children*, c. 1980, darkened stone, 15.5 x 9.2 x 8.7 cm

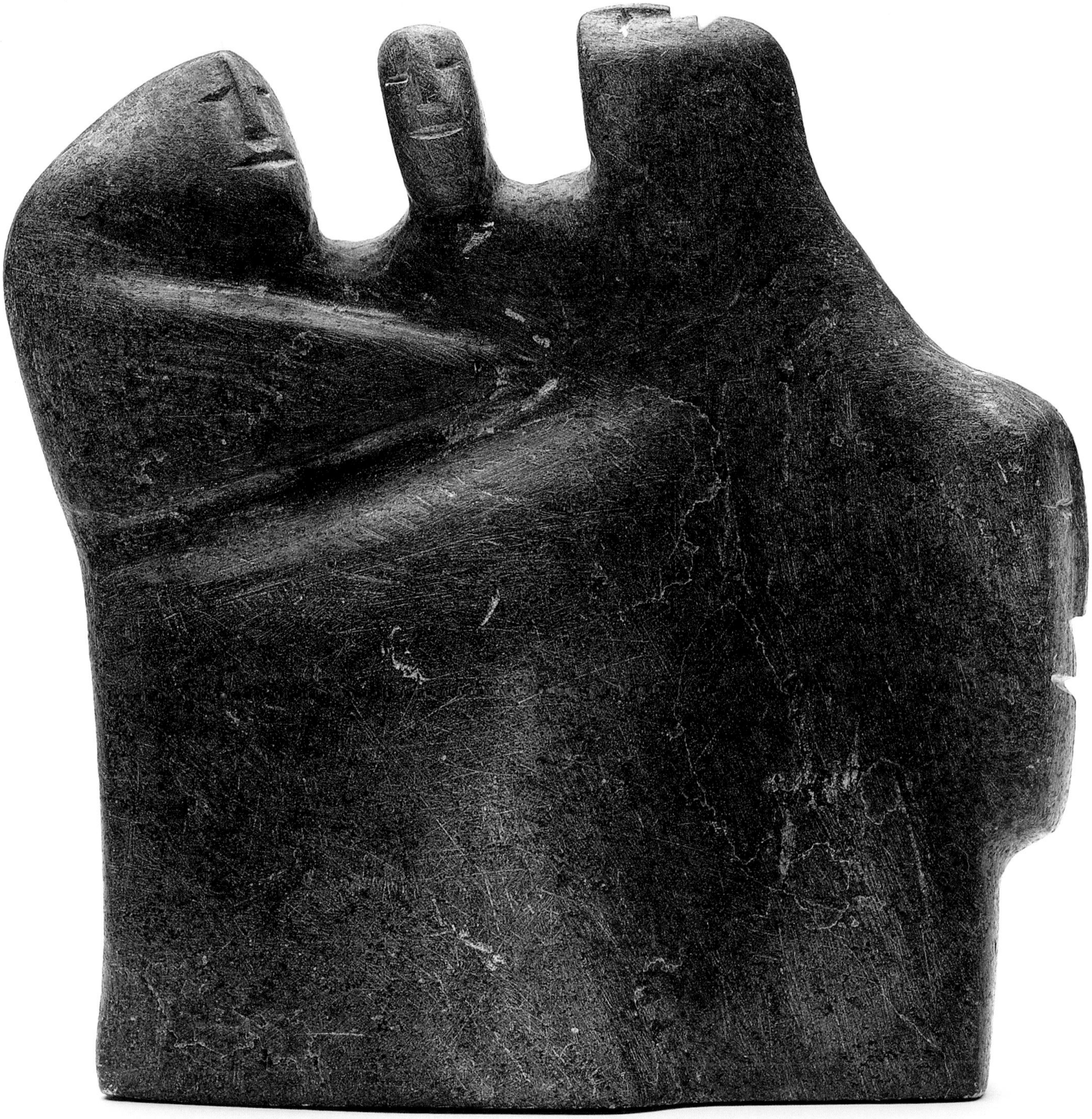

Lucy Tasseor Tutsweetok, *Family*, c. 1969, darkened stone, 16.4 x 17.0 x 4.6 cm

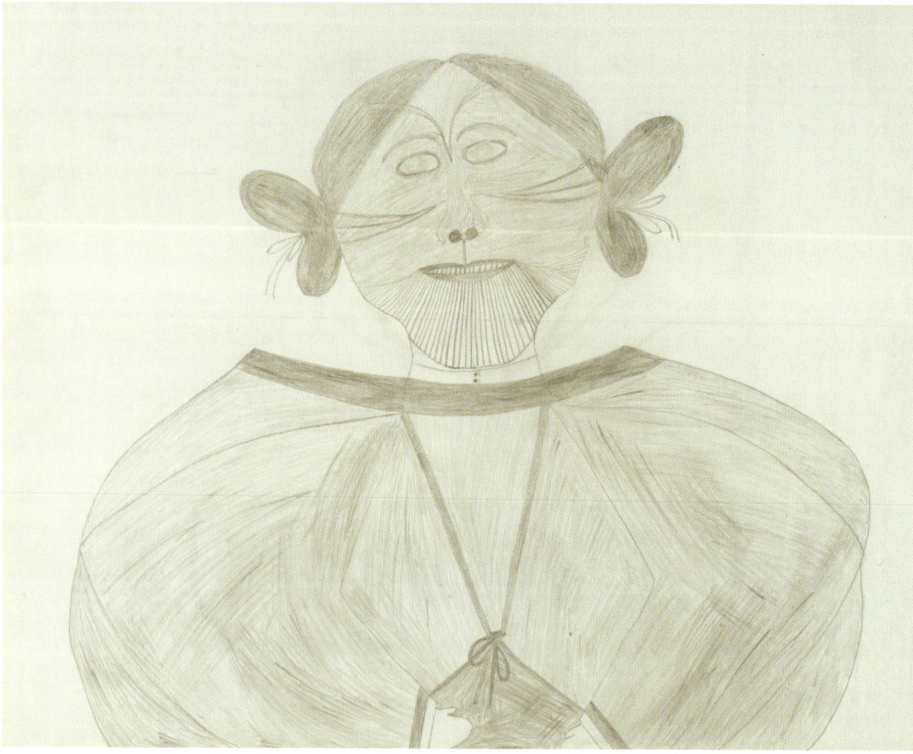

Pitseolak Ashoona, *Tattooed Woman*, 1960, graphite on paper, 41.9 x 53.4 cm

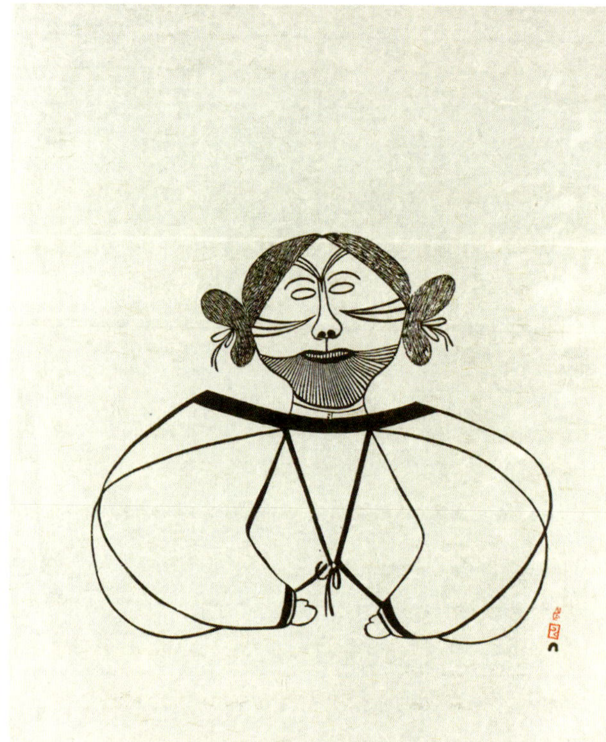

Pitseolak Ashoona, *Tattooed Woman*, 1963, stonecut on paper, 75.2 x 62.9 cm

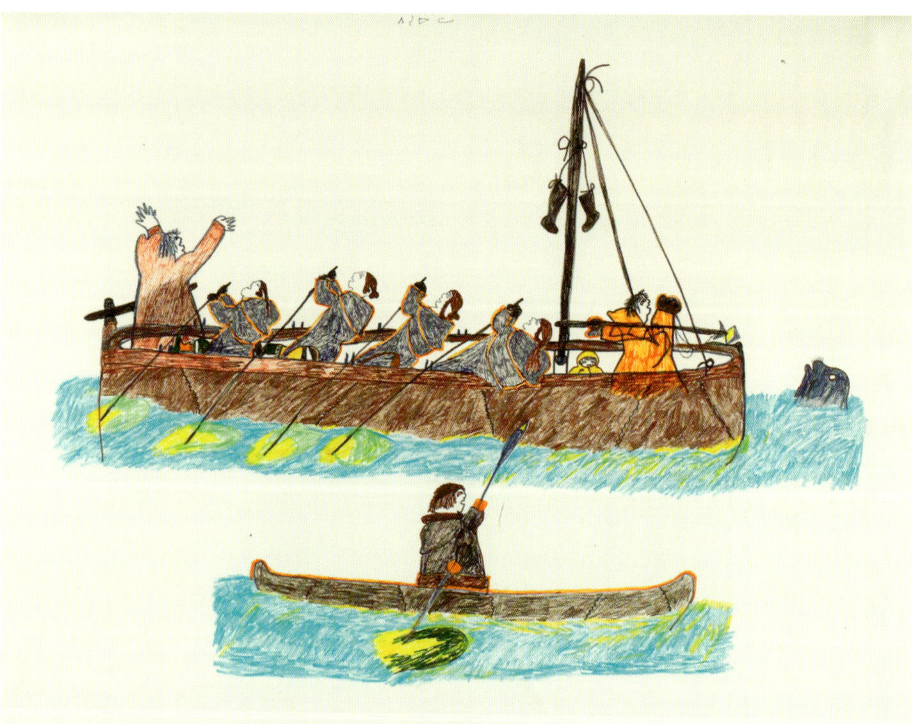

Pitseolak Ashoona, *Travelling by Umiak and Kayak*, 1966–76, coloured pencil and porous pointed pen on paper, 50.8 x 66.3 cm

Right: **Pitseolak Ashoona**, *In summer there were always big mosquitoes*, 1970, porous pointed pen on paper, 68.6 x 53.5 cm

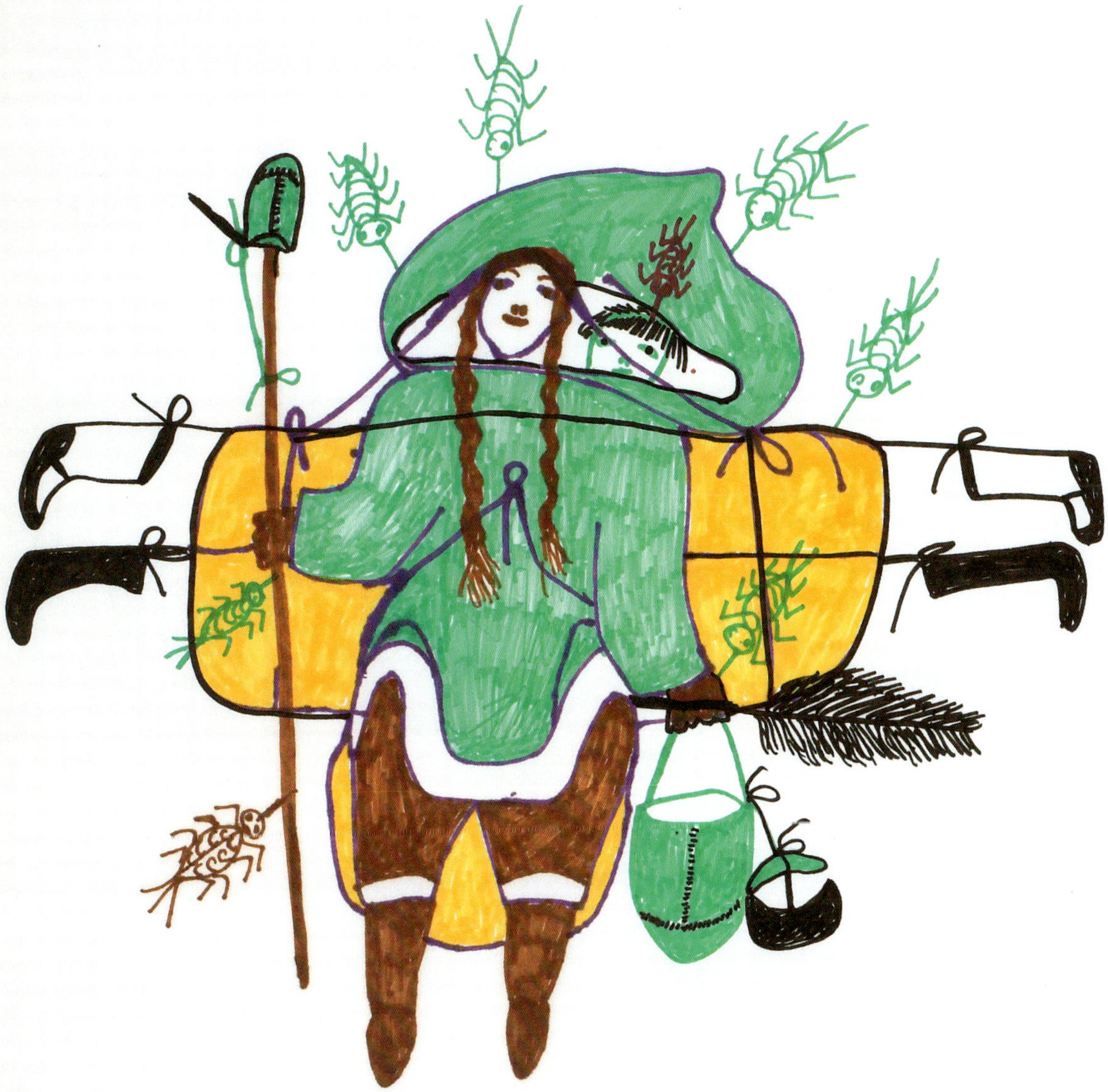
ᐱᓯᐅᓚ

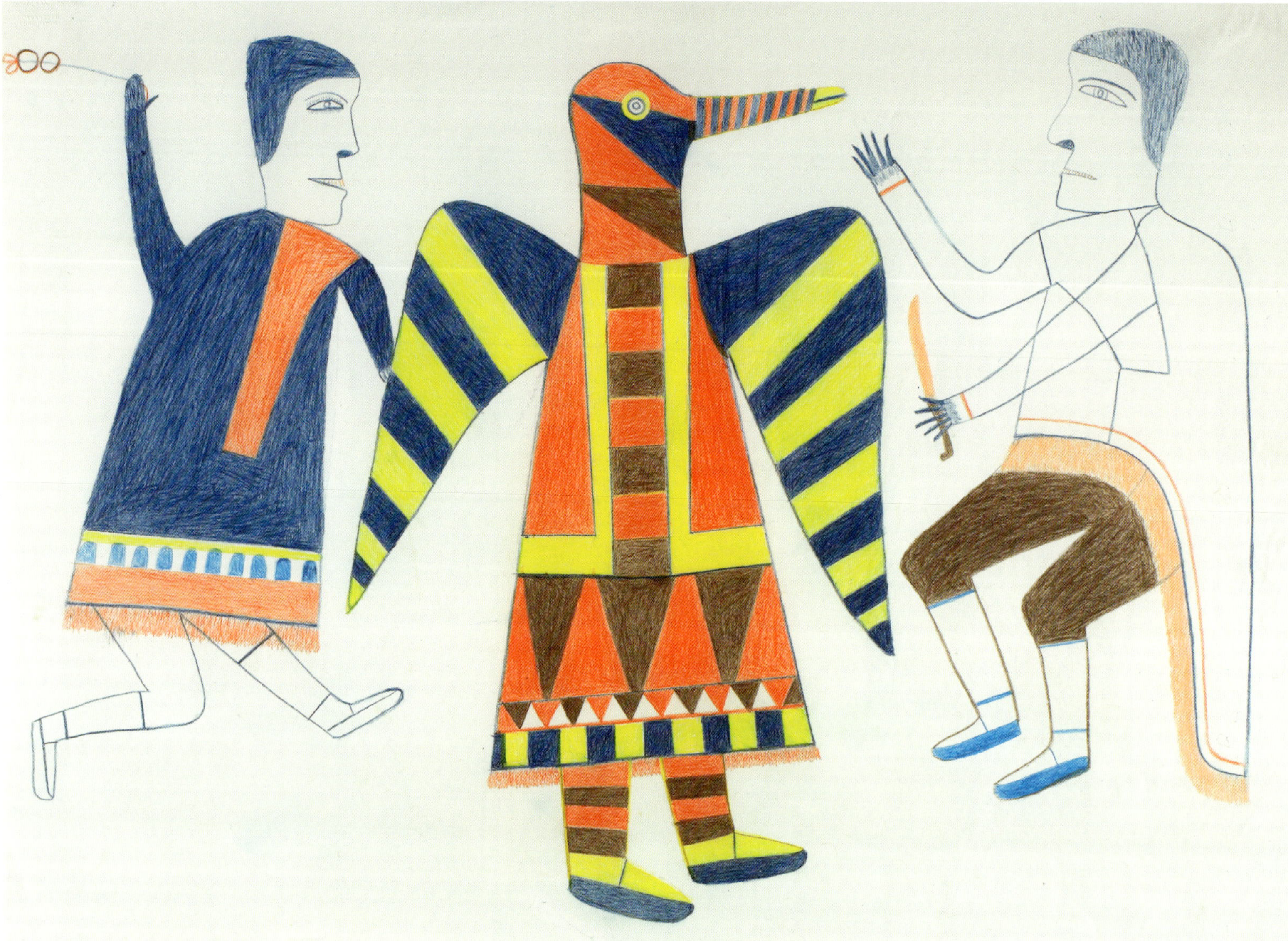

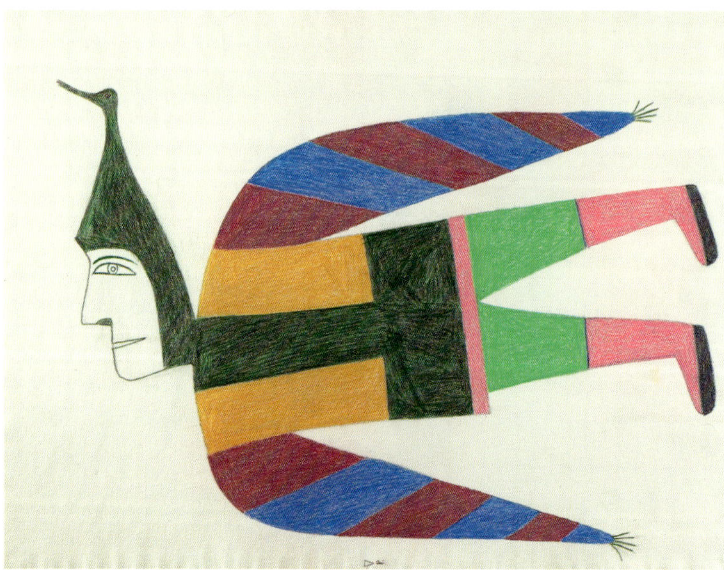

Above: **Jessie Oonark**, *Female Shaman with Spirit Helpers*, c. 1970, coloured pencil and graphite on paper, 51.0 x 66.1 cm

Left: **Jessie Oonark**, *Shaman's Flight*, c. 1970, coloured pencil, porous pointed pen and graphite on paper, 58.0 x 77.4 cm

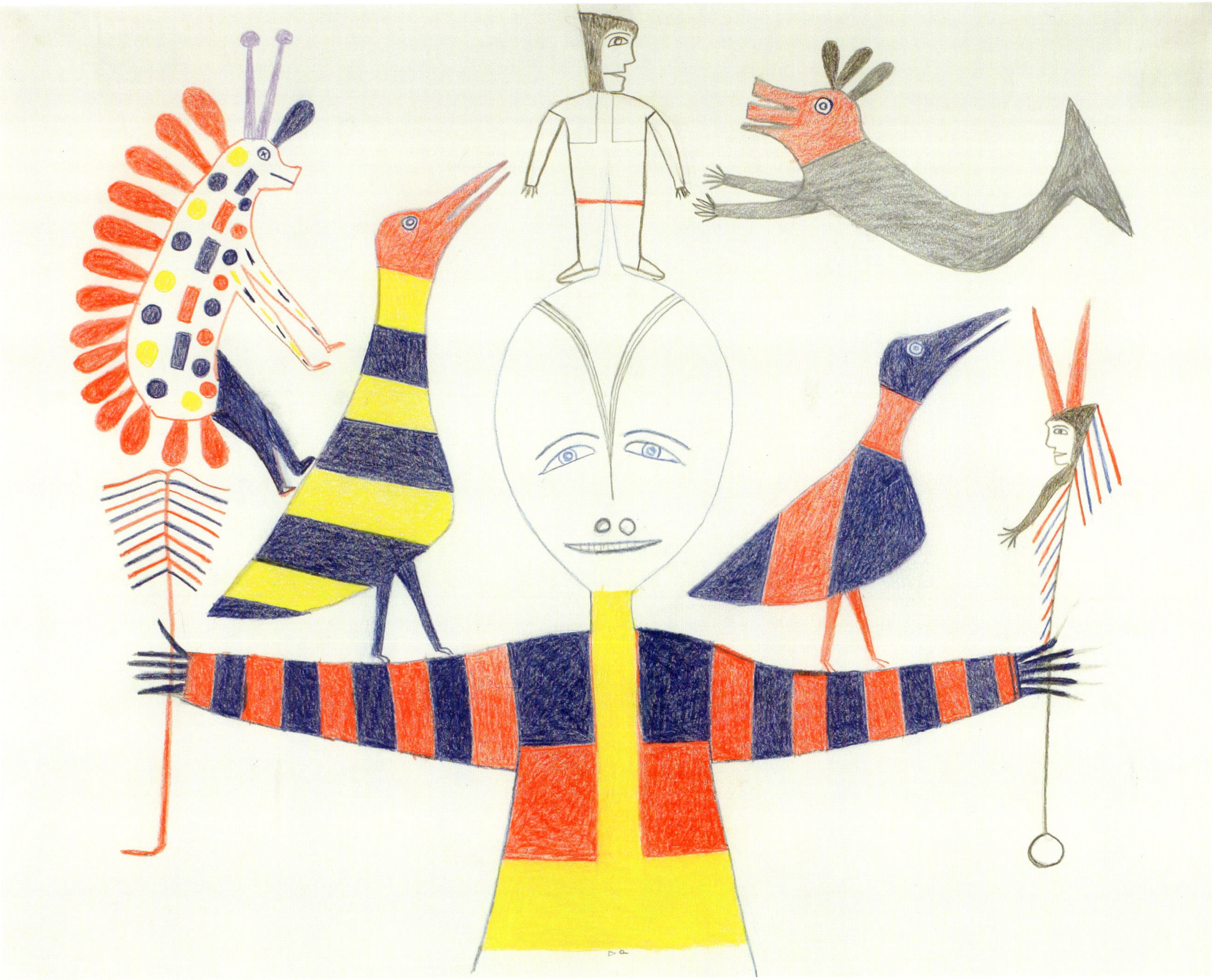

Jessie Oonark, *Hunters and Bird Spirit*, c. 1970, coloured pencil on paper, 58.0 x 79.8 cm

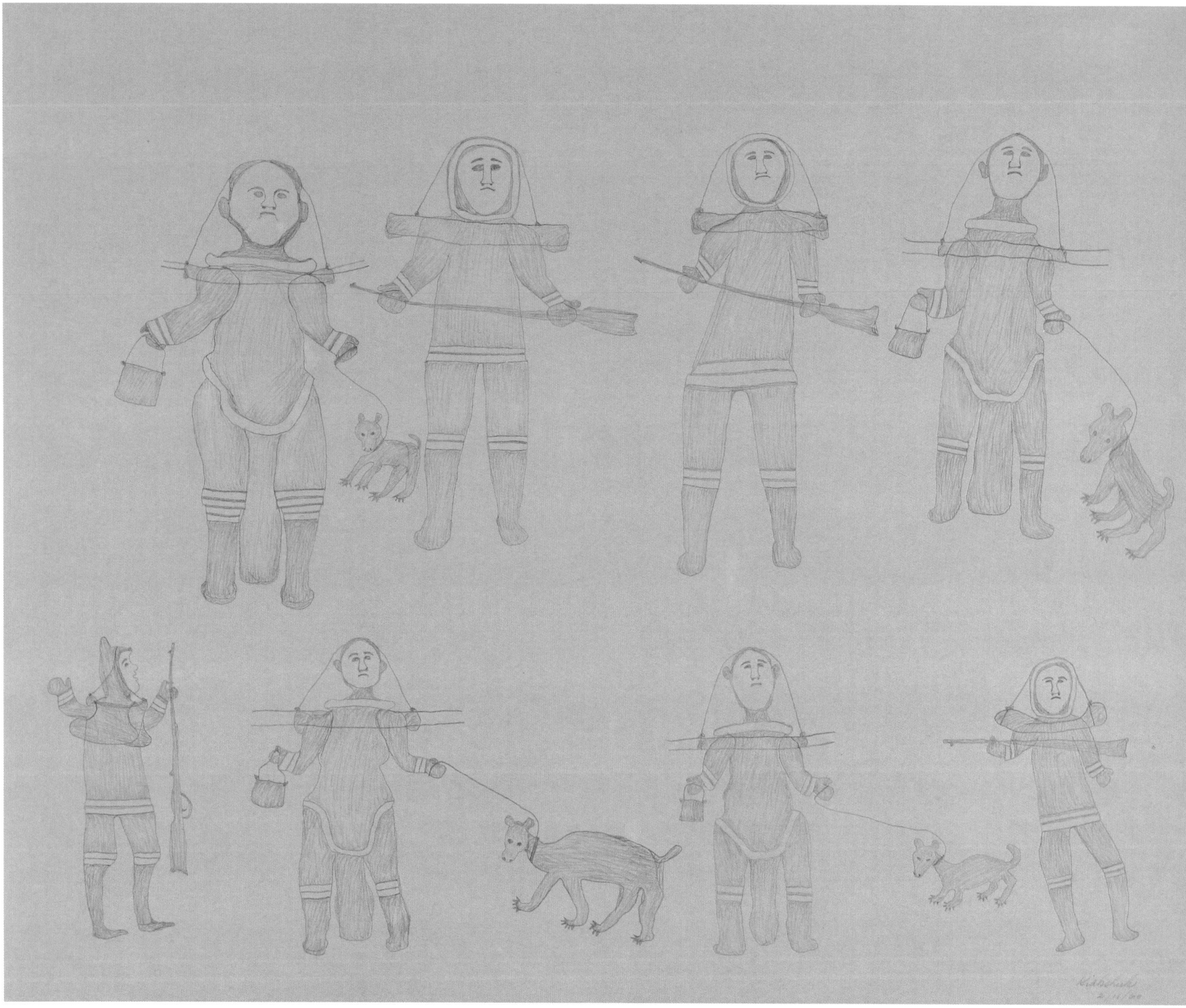

Kiakshuk, *Four Couples*, 1960, graphite on paper, 46.0 x 56.5 cm

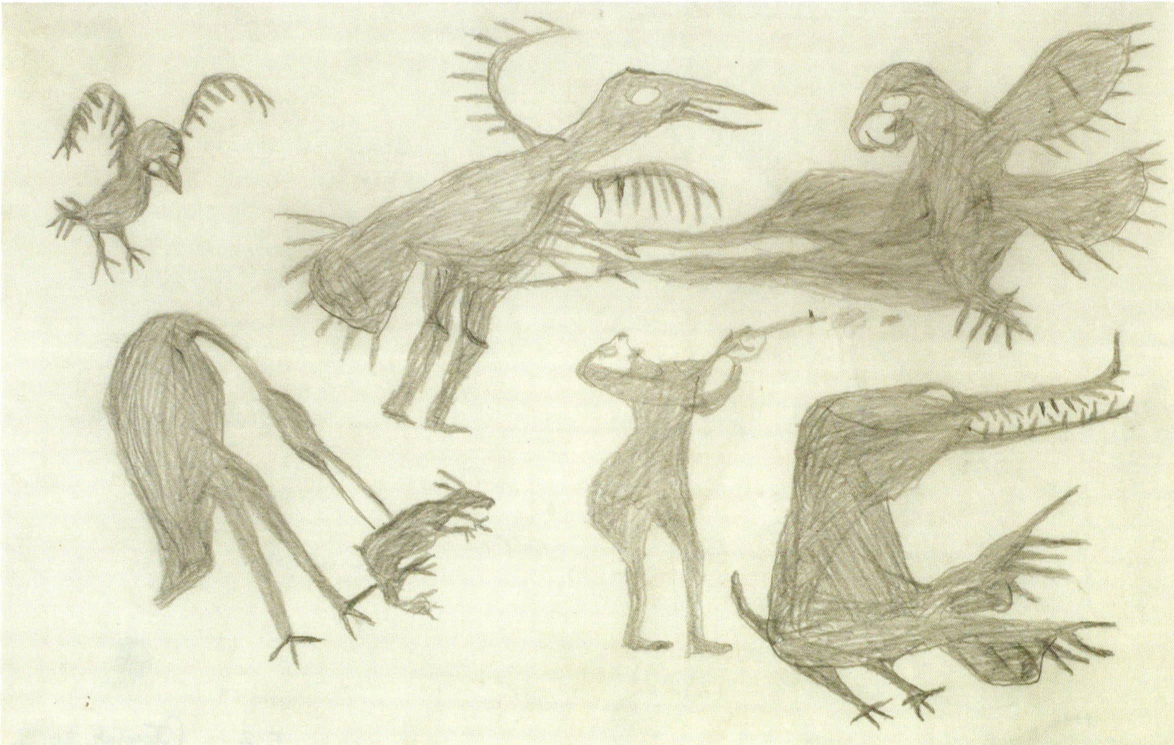

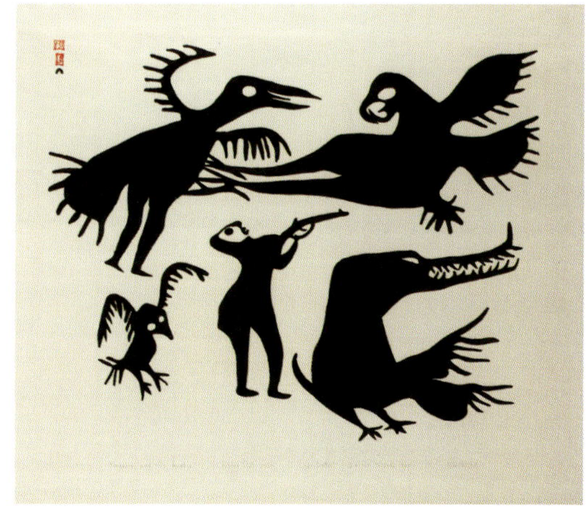

Kiakshuk, *Kikgavik and the Hunter,* 1960, stonecut on paper, 60.1 x 71.3 cm

Kiakshuk, *Kikgavik and the Hunter*, 1960, graphite on paper, 20.4 x 33.2 cm

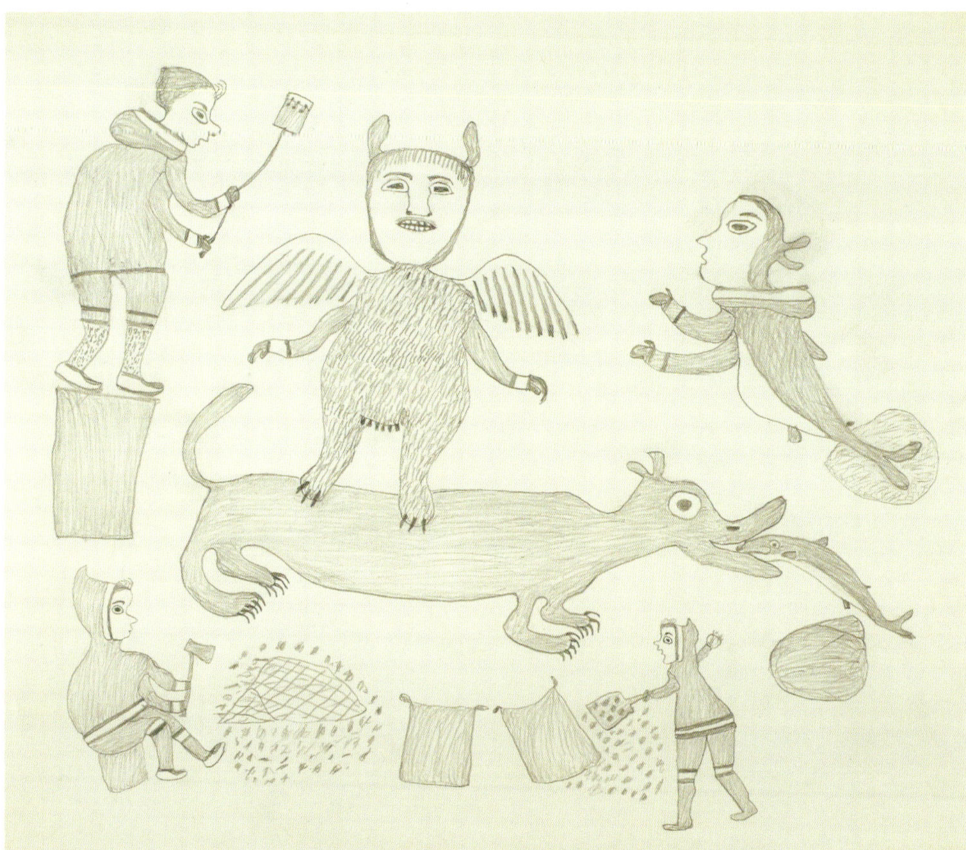

Kiakshuk, *Spirits and Men*, 1960–65, graphite on paper, 46.0 x 53.5 cm

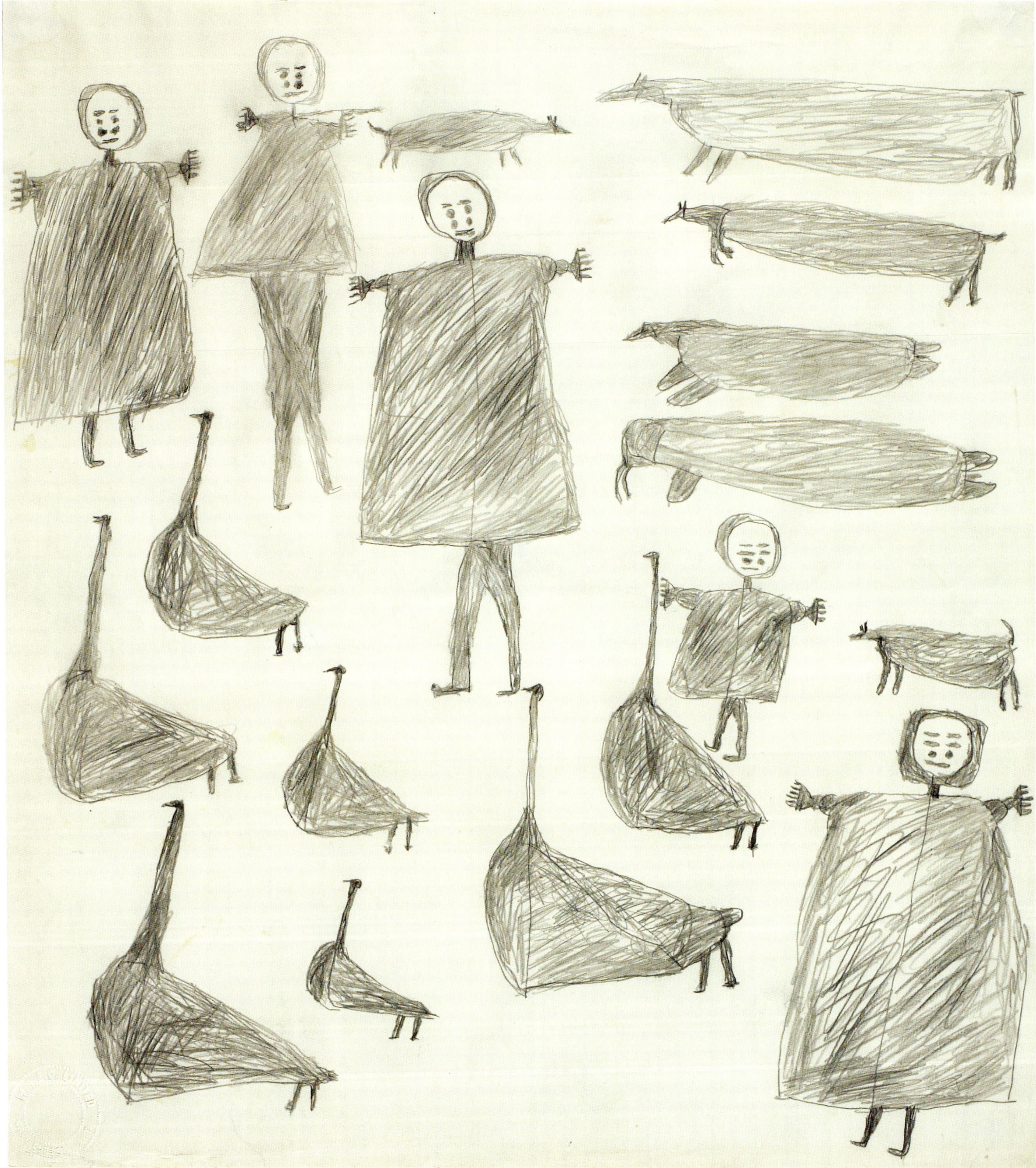

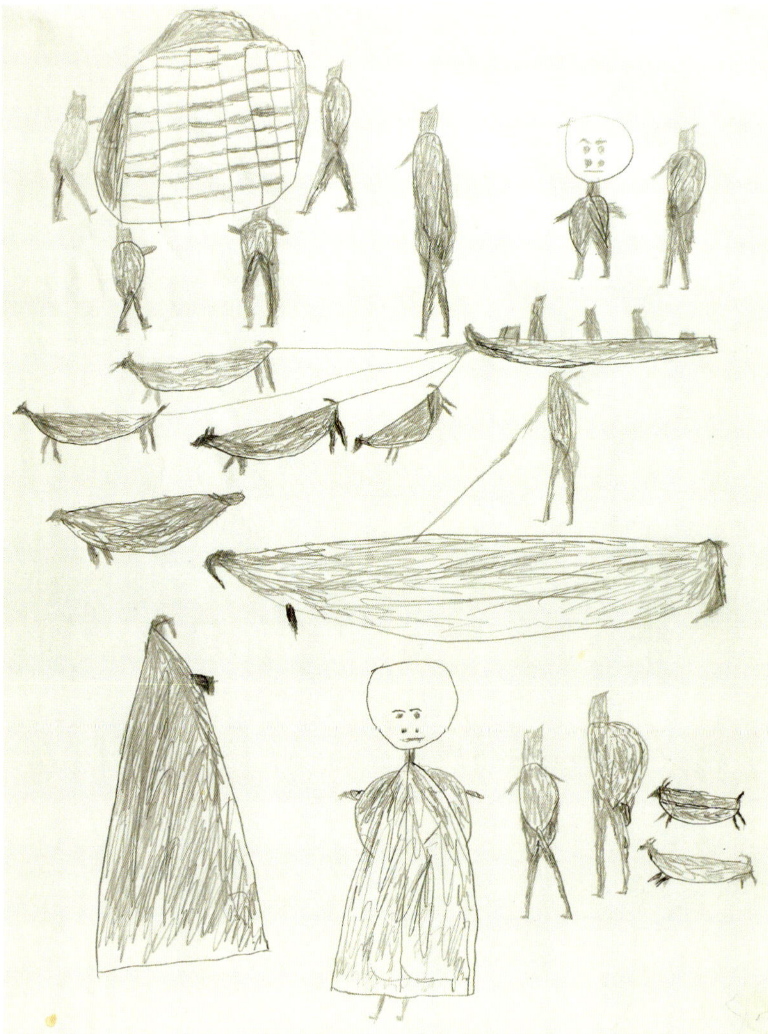

Parr, *Dog Team, Figures, Walrus and Igloo*, c. 1960, graphite on paper, 61.0 x 45.8 cm

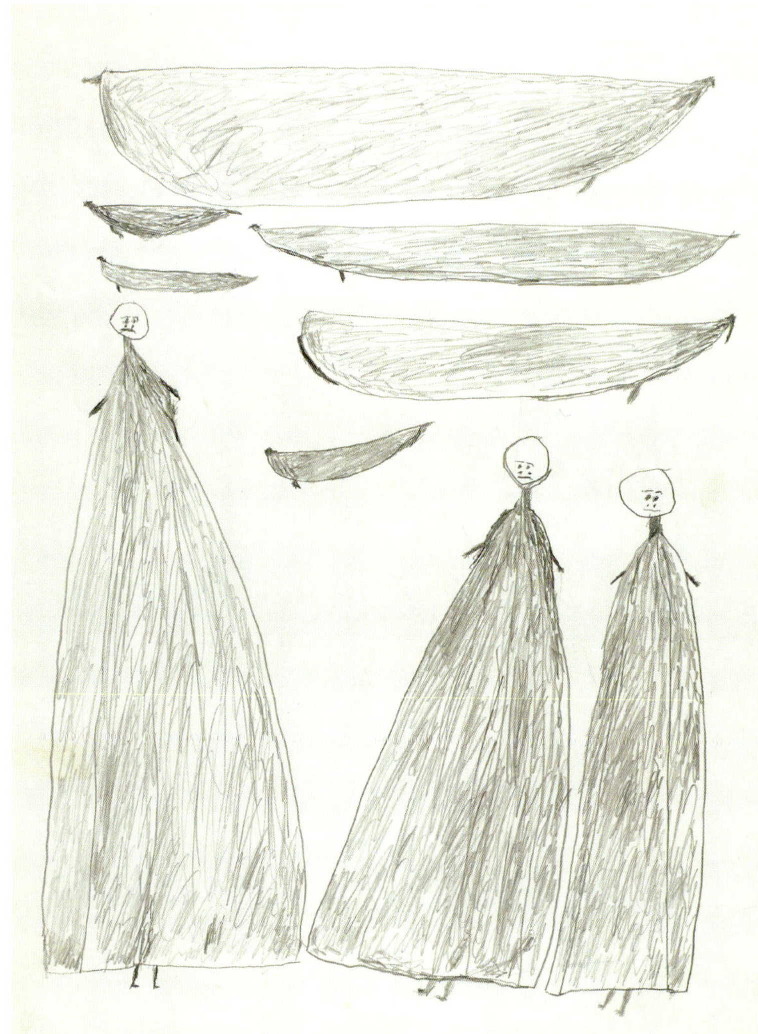

Parr, *Figures and Sea Mammals*, c. 1960, graphite on paper, 60.7 x 45.7 cm

Left: **Parr**, *Figures with Geese and Animals*, 1961, graphite on paper, 50.4 x 45.8 cm

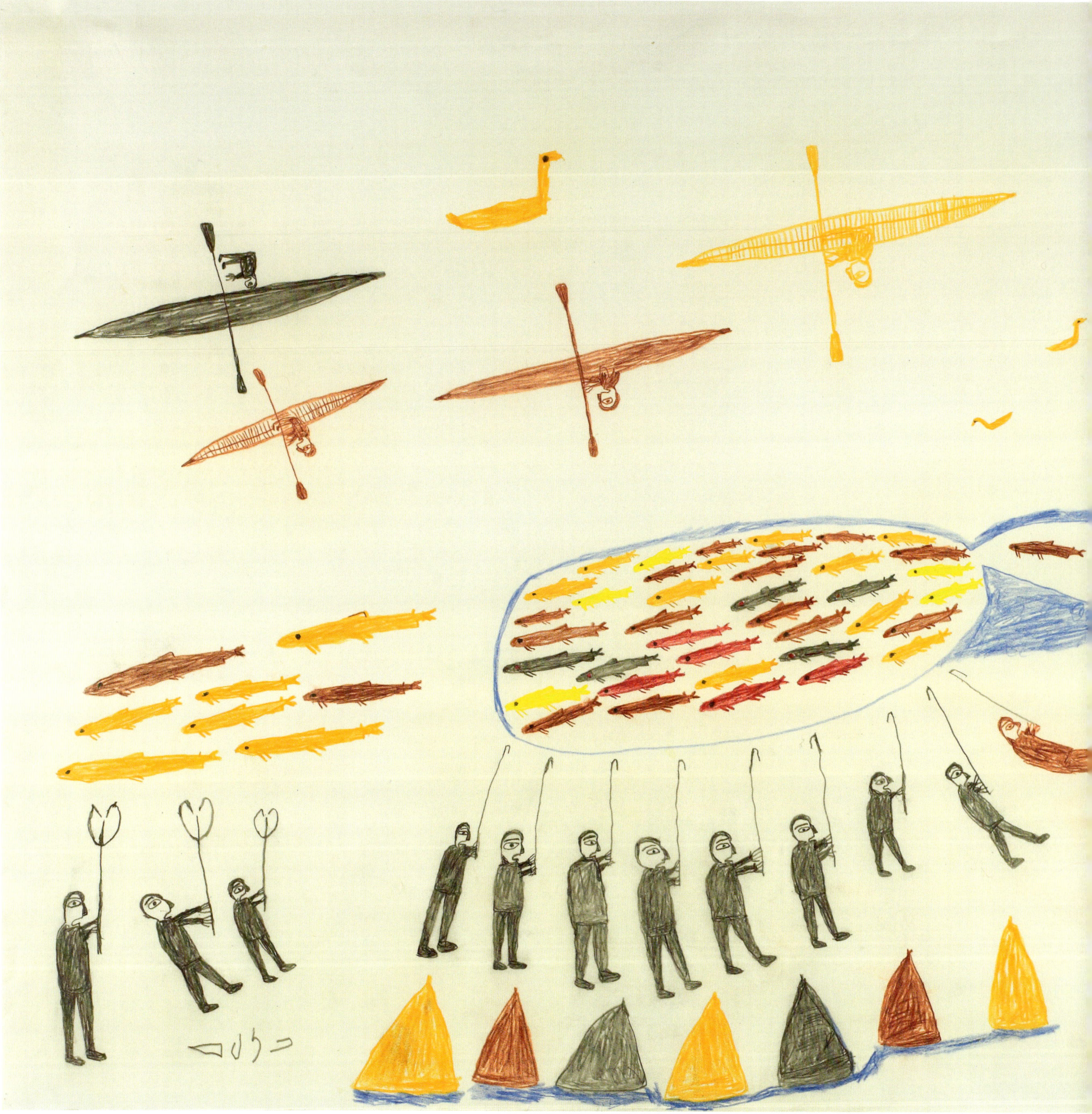

Luke Anguhadluq, *Fishing and Hunting Birds*, 1970, coloured pencil and graphite on paper, 56.1 x 76.1 cm

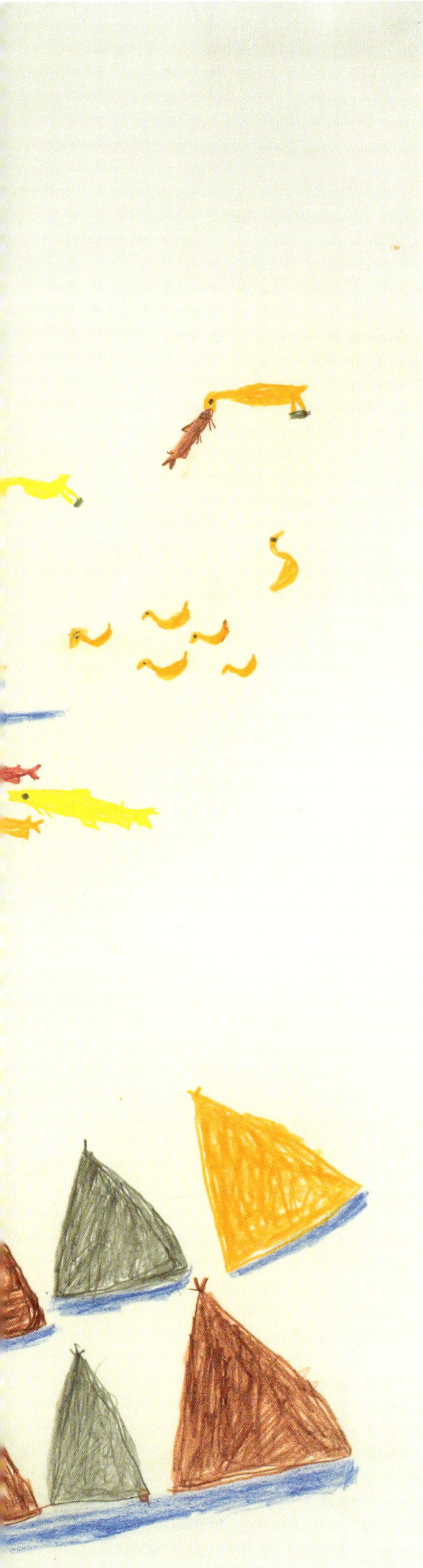

Luke Anguhadluq, *Caribou Hunting*, 1973, coloured pencil and graphite on paper, 58.4 x 79.8 cm

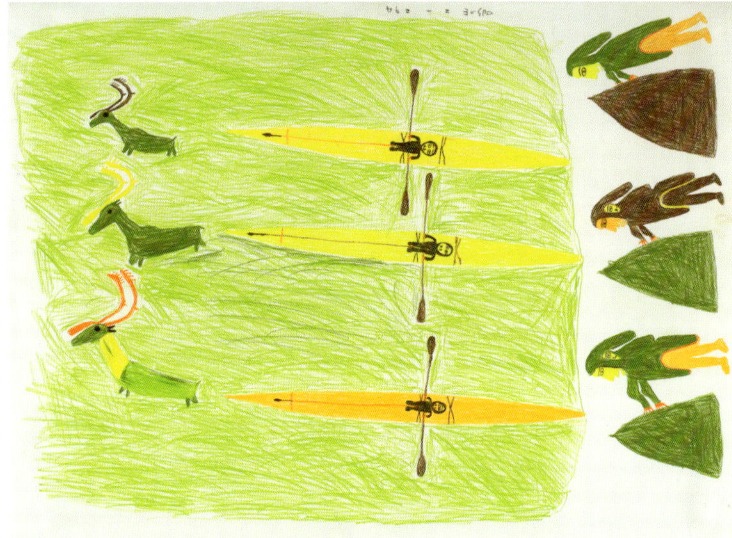

Luke Anguhadluq, *Muskox and Hunter*, c. 1973, coloured pencil and graphite on paper, 58.7 x 73.9 cm

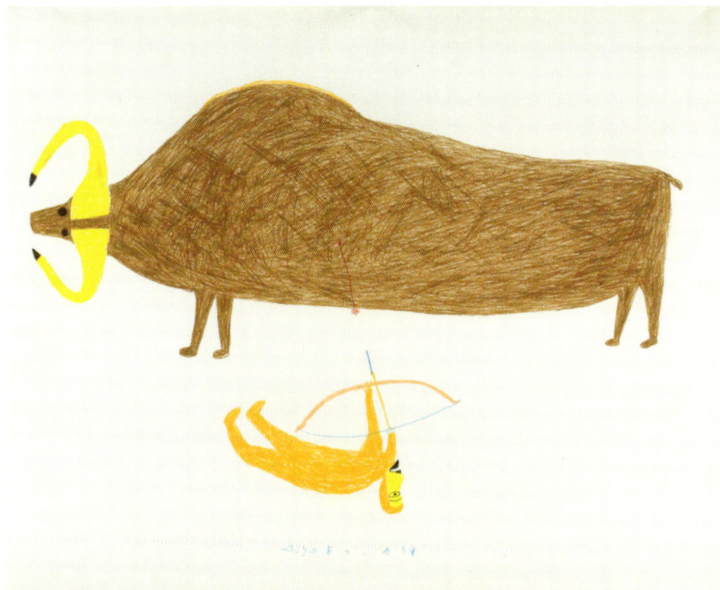

Luke Anguhadluq, *Hunting Bears*, c. 1975, coloured pencil and graphite on paper, 58.9 x 79.6 cm

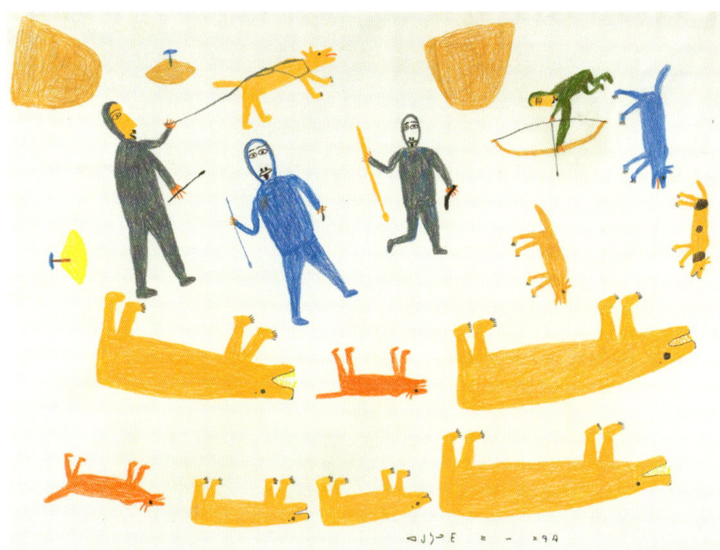

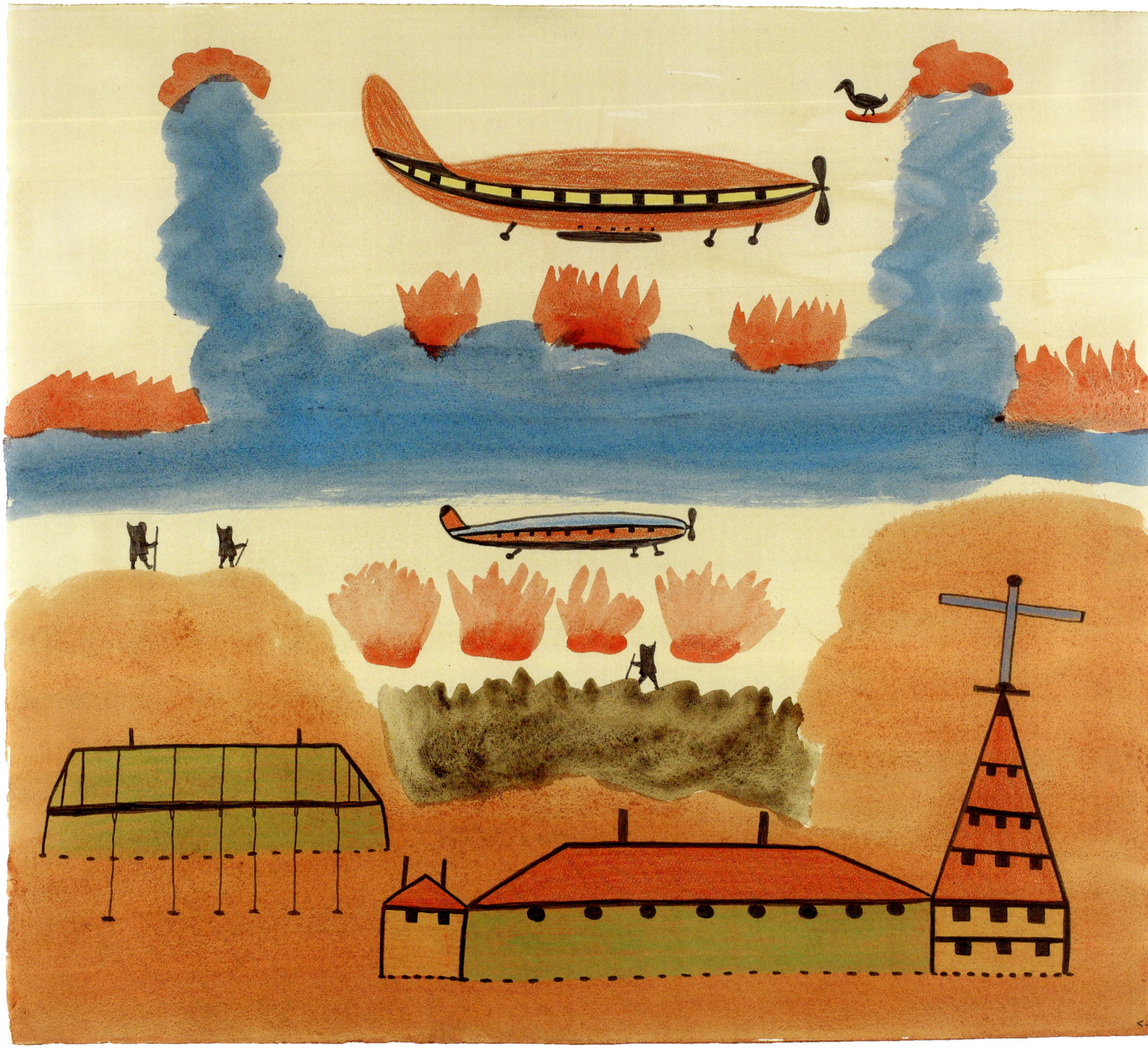

Pudlo Pudlat, *Scene with Two Airplanes and Church*, 1976,
acrylic, coloured pencil and porous pointed pen on paper, 49.1 x 56.2 cm

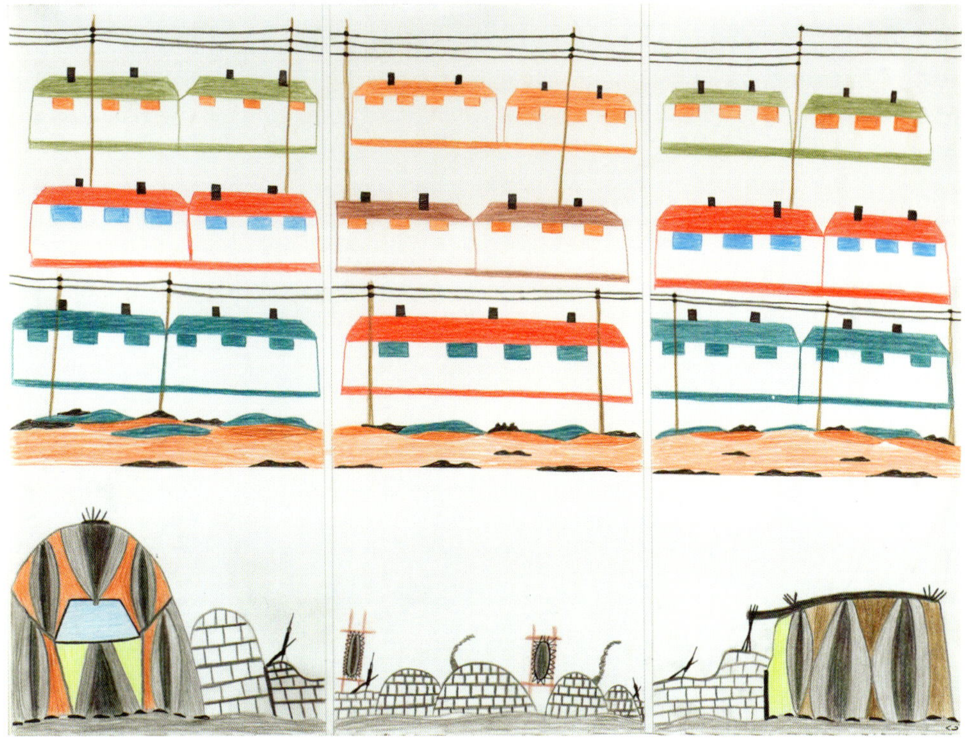

Pudlo Pudlat, *Drawing for the print "Modern Settlement — Traditional Camp,"* 1978–79, coloured pencil, graphite and porous pointed pen on paper, 56.9 x 76.2 cm

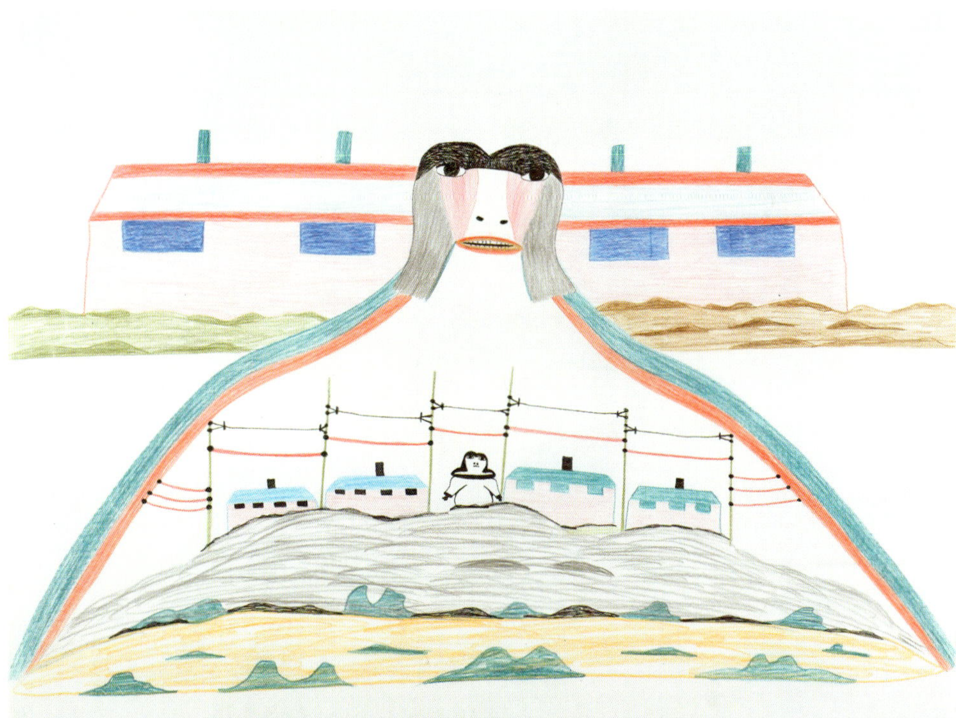

Pudlo Pudlat, *Drawing for the print "Spirit Embracing Settlement,"* 1978–79, coloured pencil and porous pointed pen on paper, 56.5 x 76.5 cm

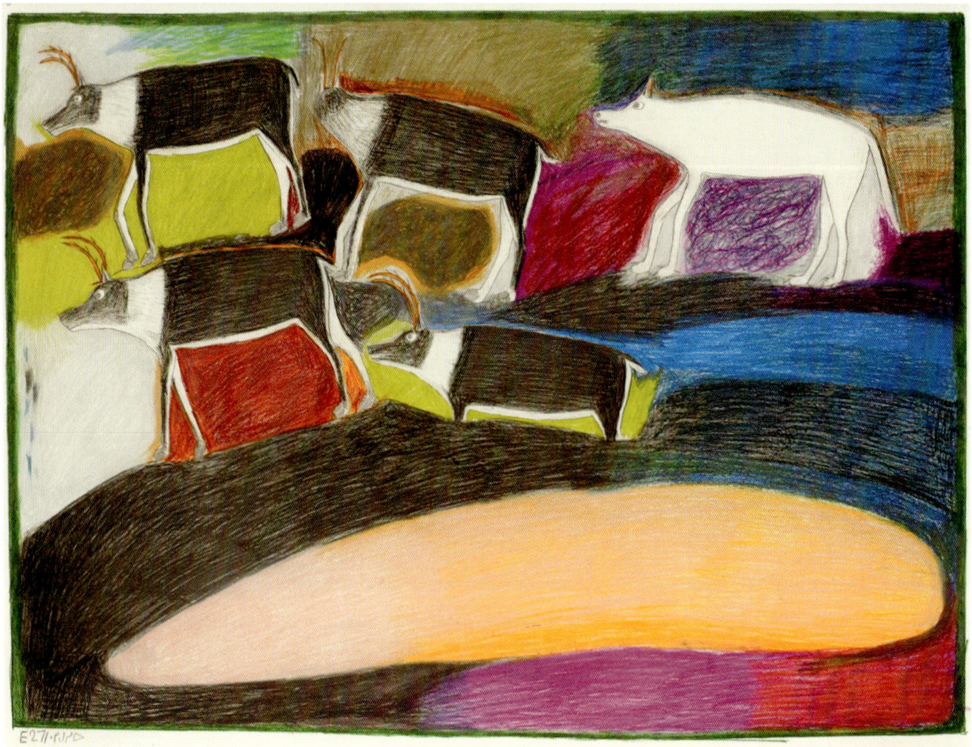

Janet Kigusiuq, *Caribou*, c. 1990s,
wax crayon and graphite on paper,
57.0 x 76.0 cm

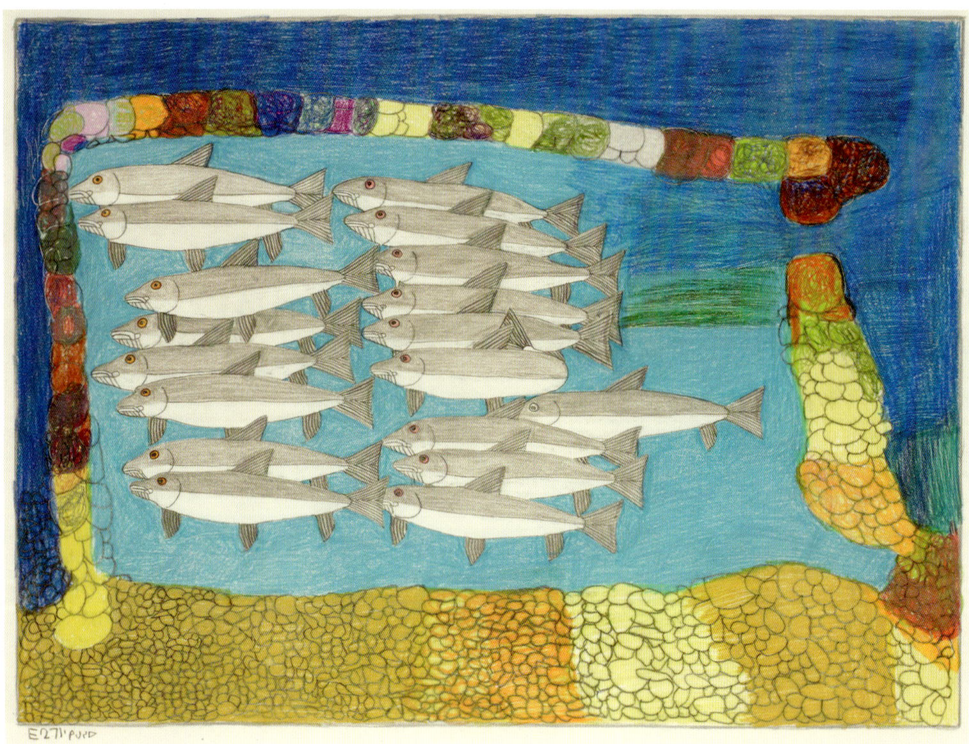

Janet Kigusiuq, *Fishing Weir*, c. 1970s,
wax crayon, coloured pencil and graphite on paper,
56.5 x 76.5 cm

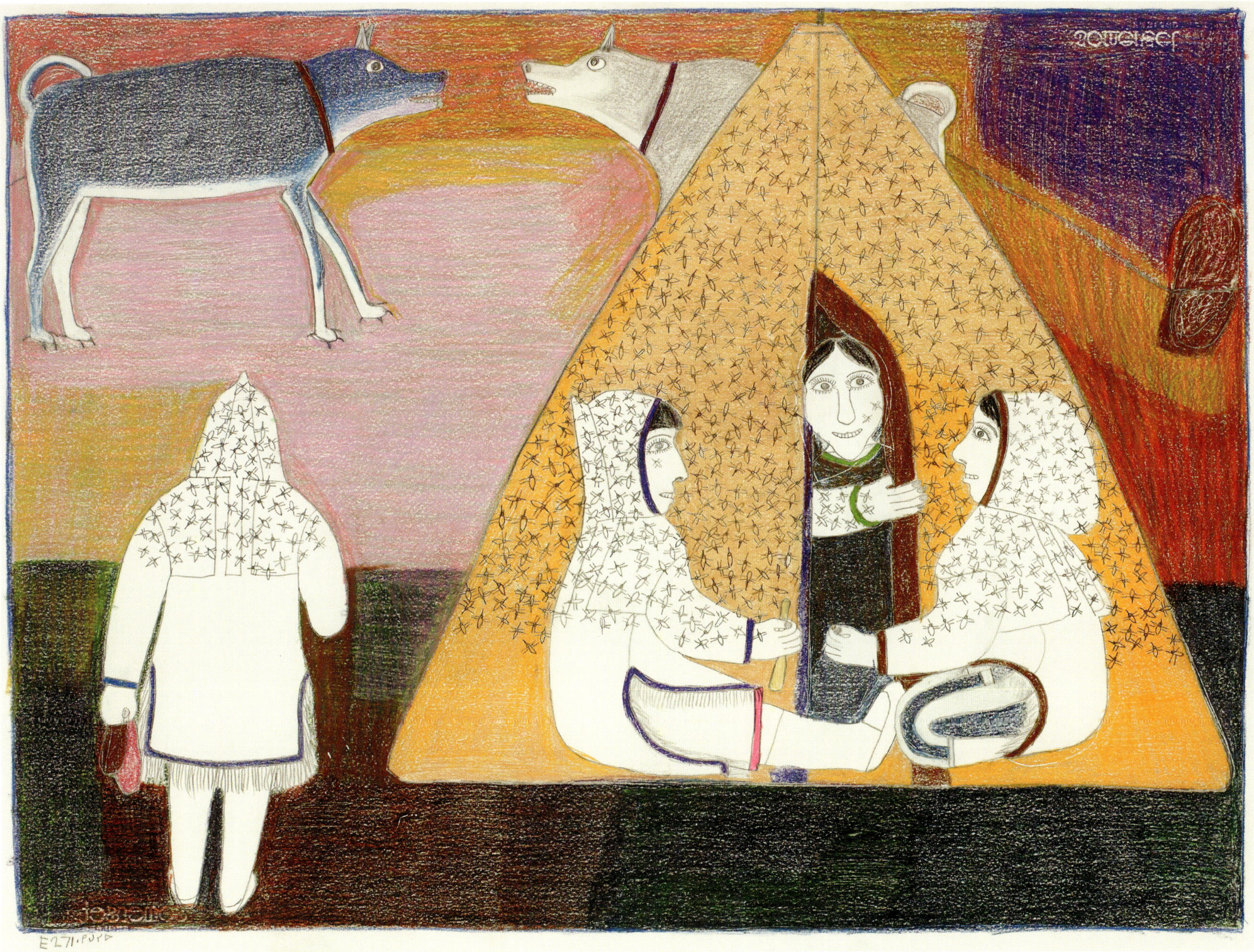

Janet Kigusiuq, *Camp Scene with Mosquitoes*, c. 1980s,
coloured pencil, wax crayon and graphite on paper, 56.5 x 76.5 cm

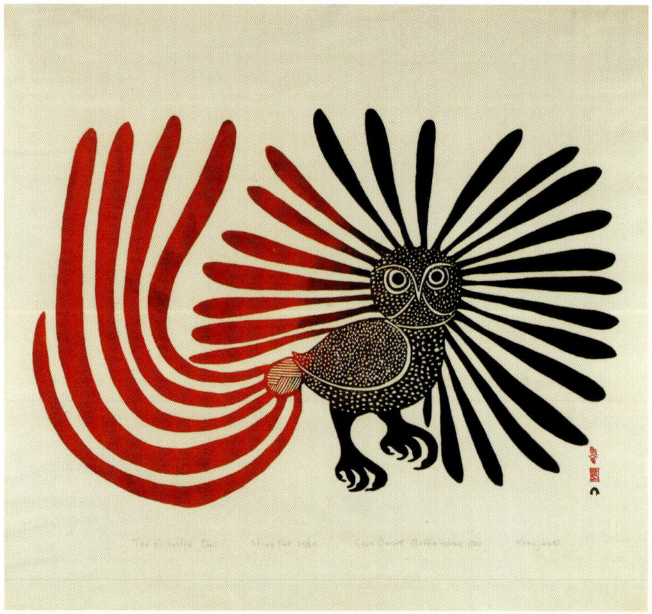

Kenojuak Ashevak,
The Enchanted Owl, 1960,
stonecut on paper,
59.7 x 65.0 cm

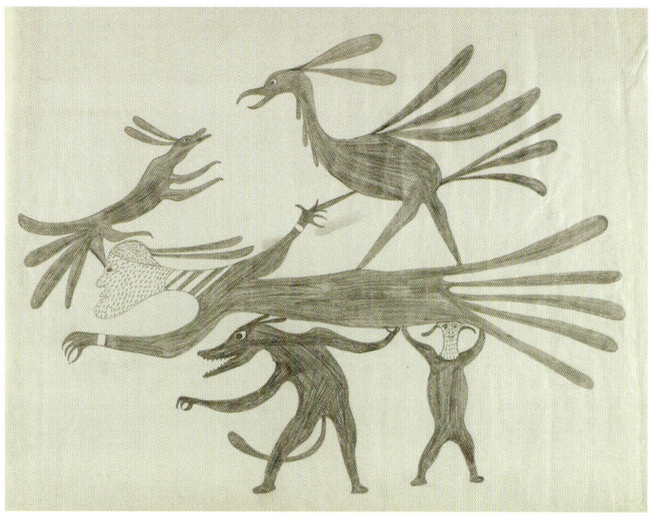

Kenojuak Ashevak,
Five Creatures, 1960–65,
graphite on paper,
46.0 x 60.5 cm

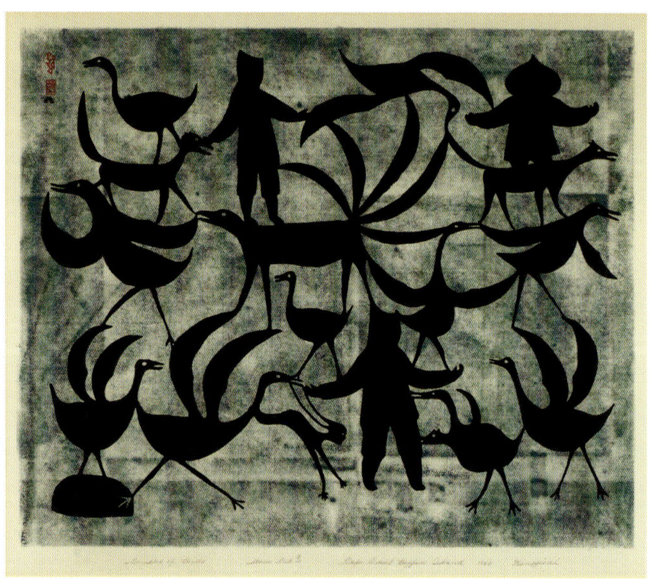

Kenojuak Ashevak,
Complex of Birds, 1960,
stonecut on paper,
61.1 x 66.1 cm

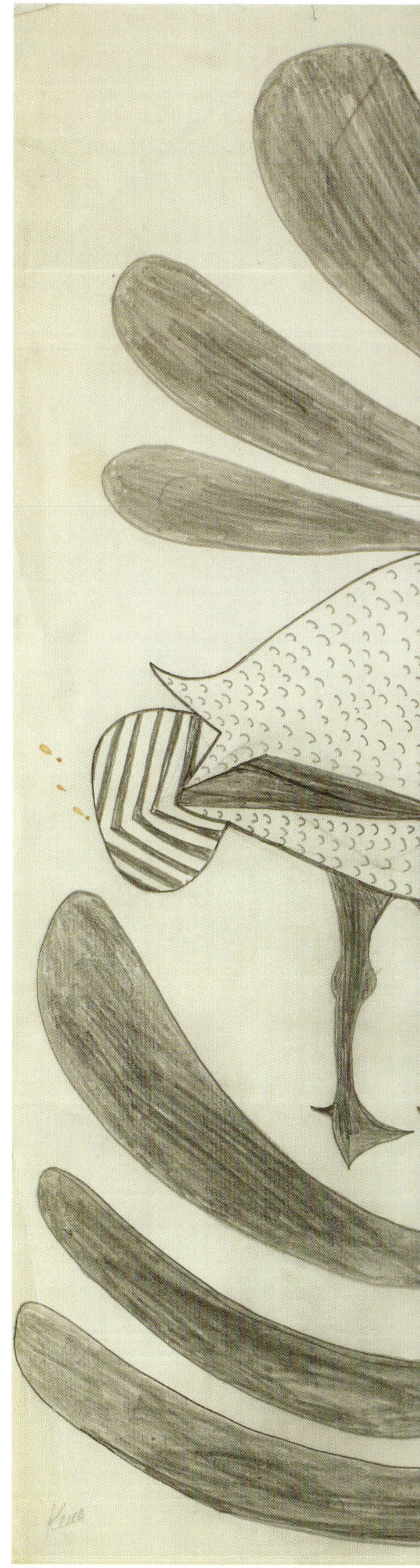

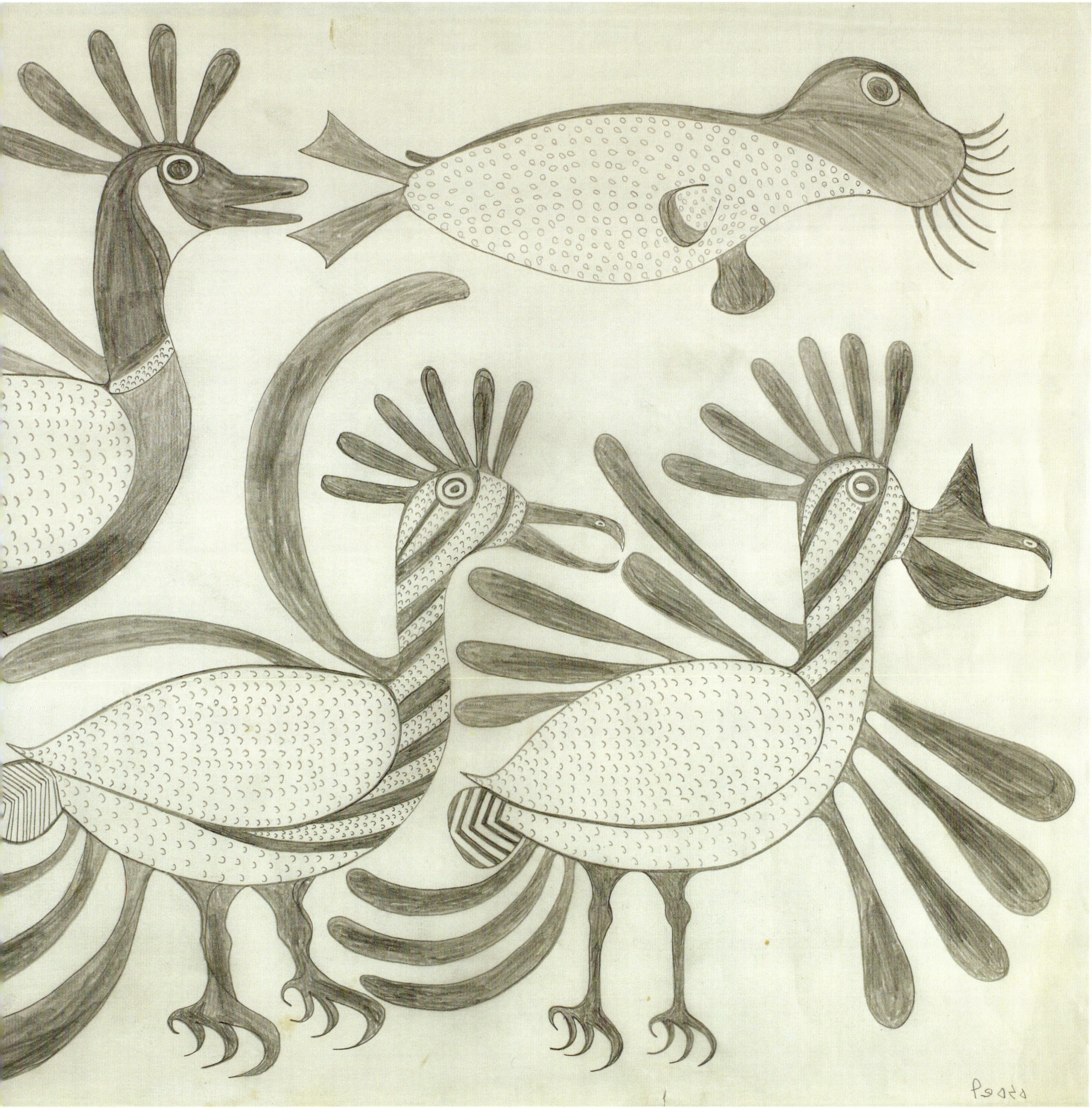

Kenojuak Ashevak, *Three Birds and Seal*, 1960–63, graphite on paper, 48.5 x 66.5 cm

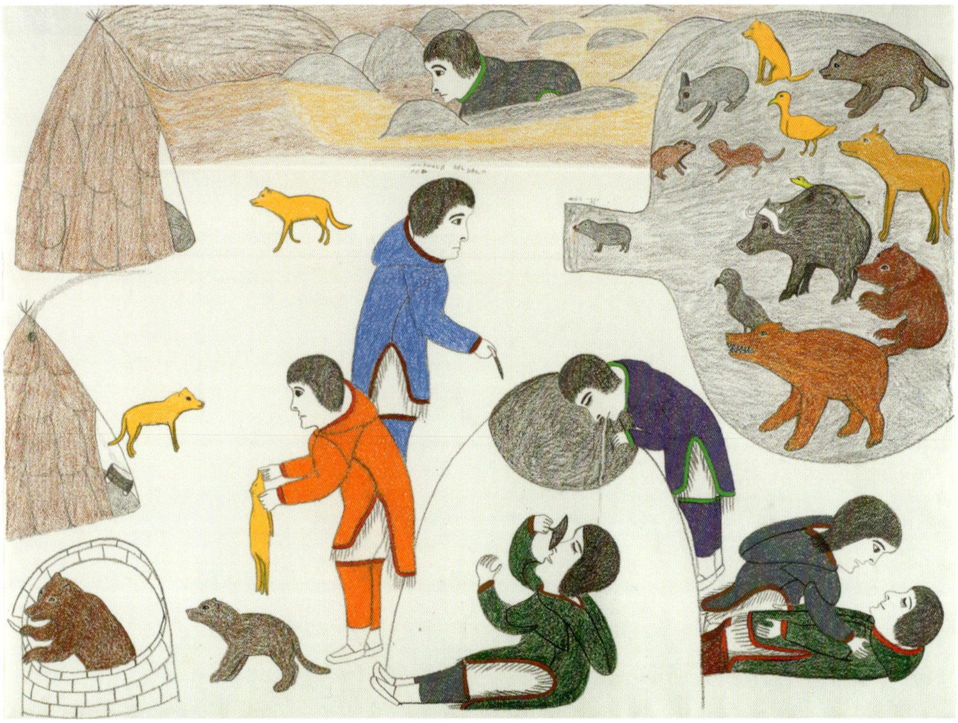

"Qiviuq: You are bleeding. You don't want this anymore."

"Lemming says, 'It is mine!'"

Victoria Mamnguqsualuk, *Tales of Qiviuq*, 1980s, coloured pencil and graphite on paper, 59.0 x 80.0 cm

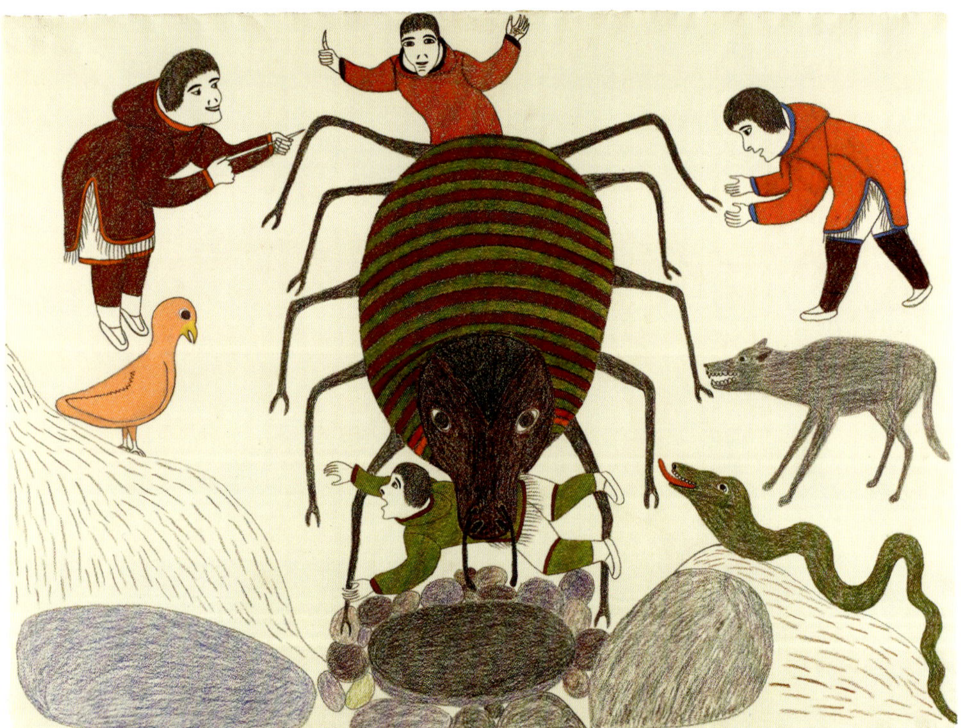

Victoria Mamnguqsualuk, *Giant Insect*, 1980s, coloured pencil and graphite on paper, 58.5 x 80.0 cm

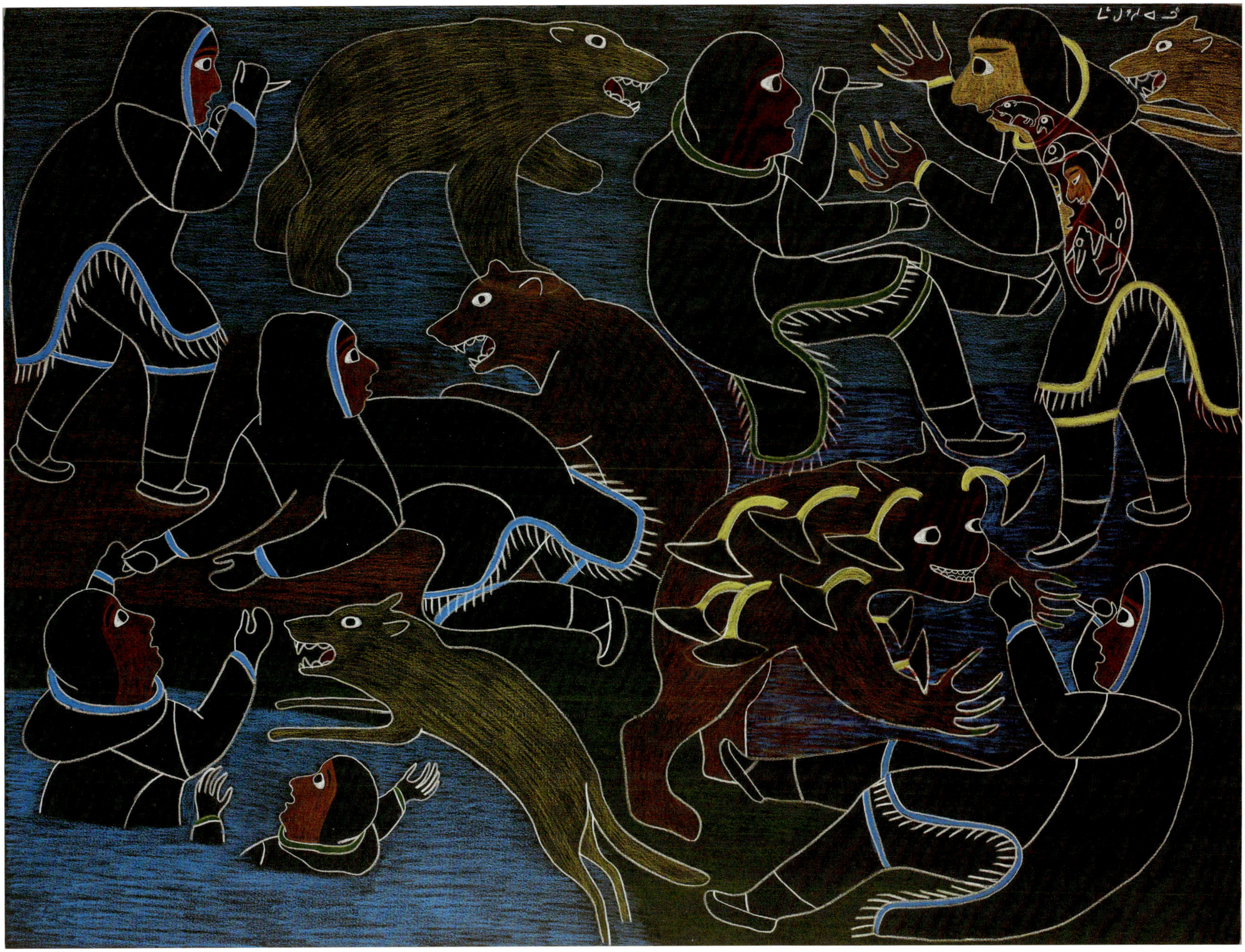

Victoria Mamnguqsualuk, *Imaginary Scene*, c. 1980s,
wax crayon on paper, 56.5 x 76.0 cm

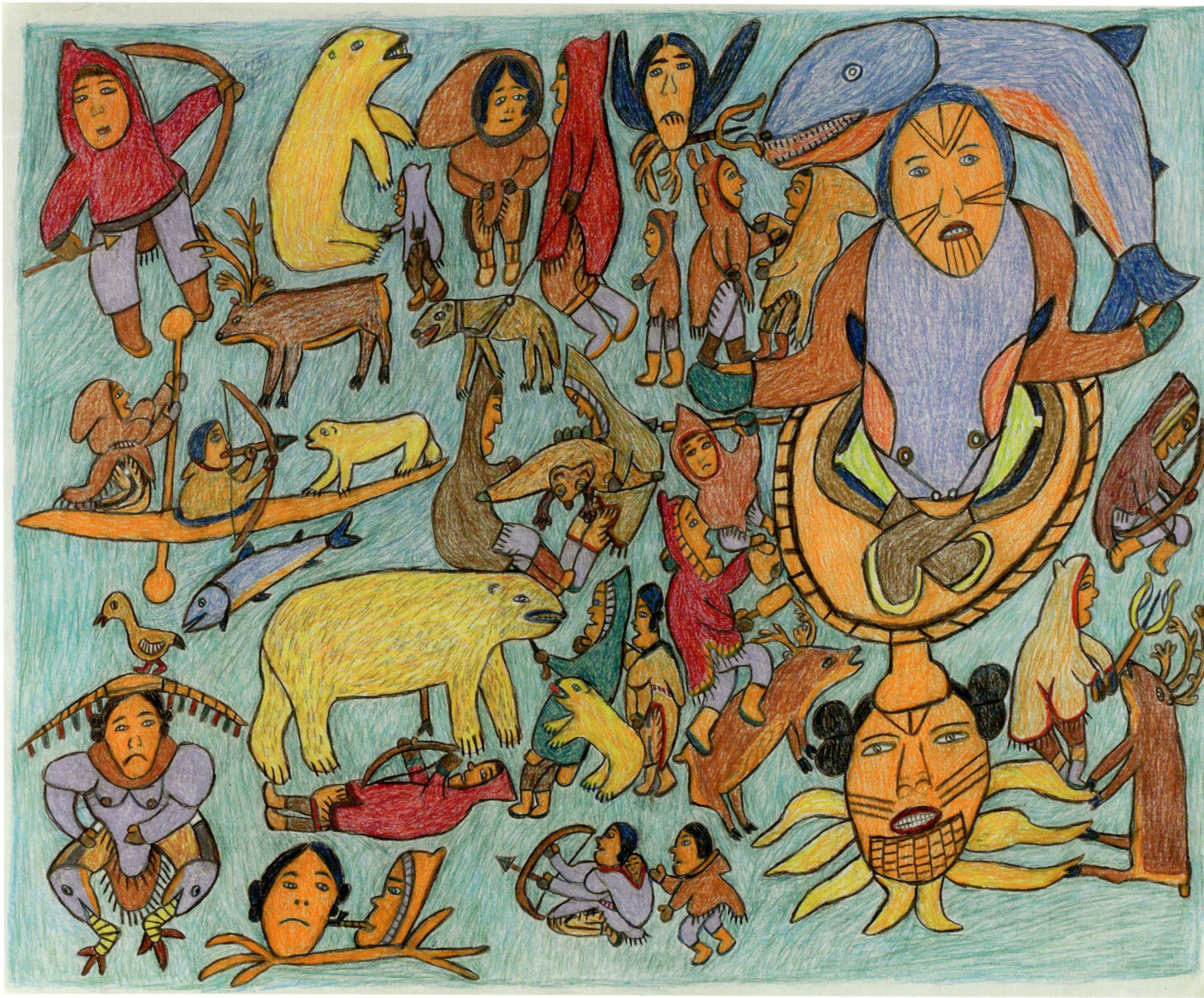

Ruth Annaqtuusi Tulurialik, *Camp Scene with Spirits*, 1980s, wax crayon, coloured pencil and graphite on paper, 59.0 x 74.0 cm

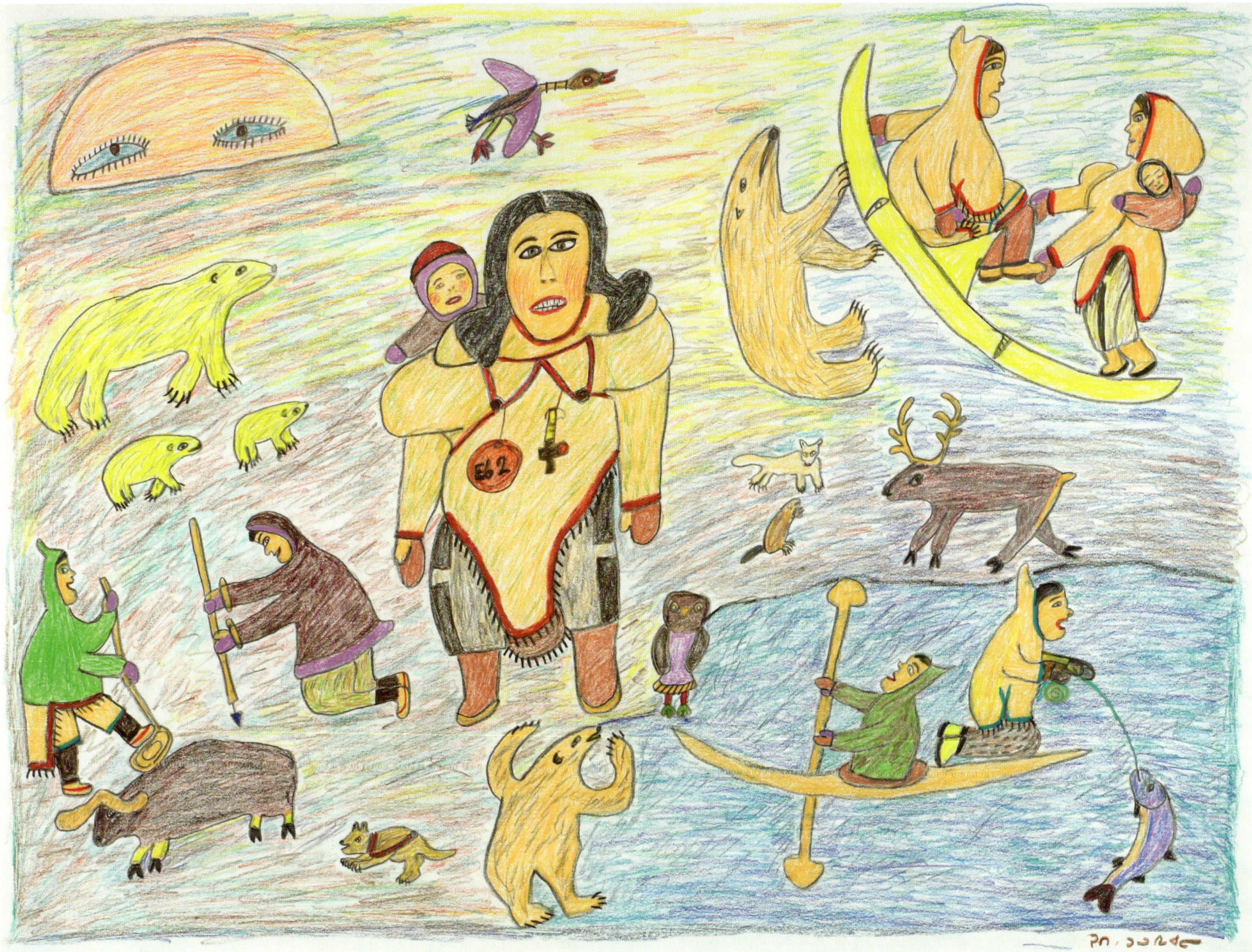

Ruth Annaqtuusi Tulurialik, *On the Land*, 1990, coloured pencil, graphite on paper, 56.1 x 76.2 cm

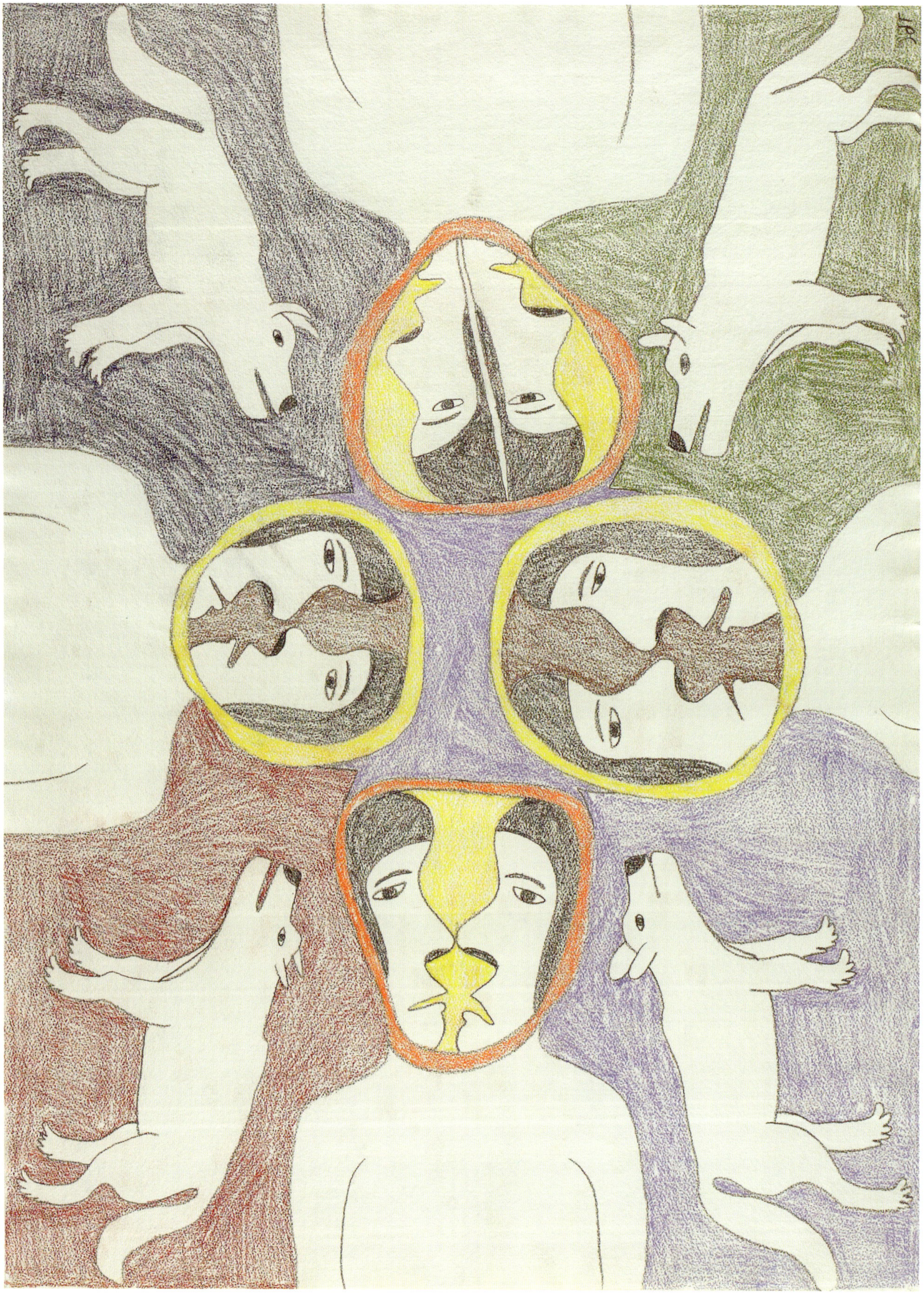

Simon Tookoome, *Four Dogs, Four Double-Faced Humans*, 1980s, coloured pencil on paper, 78.5 x 58.0 cm

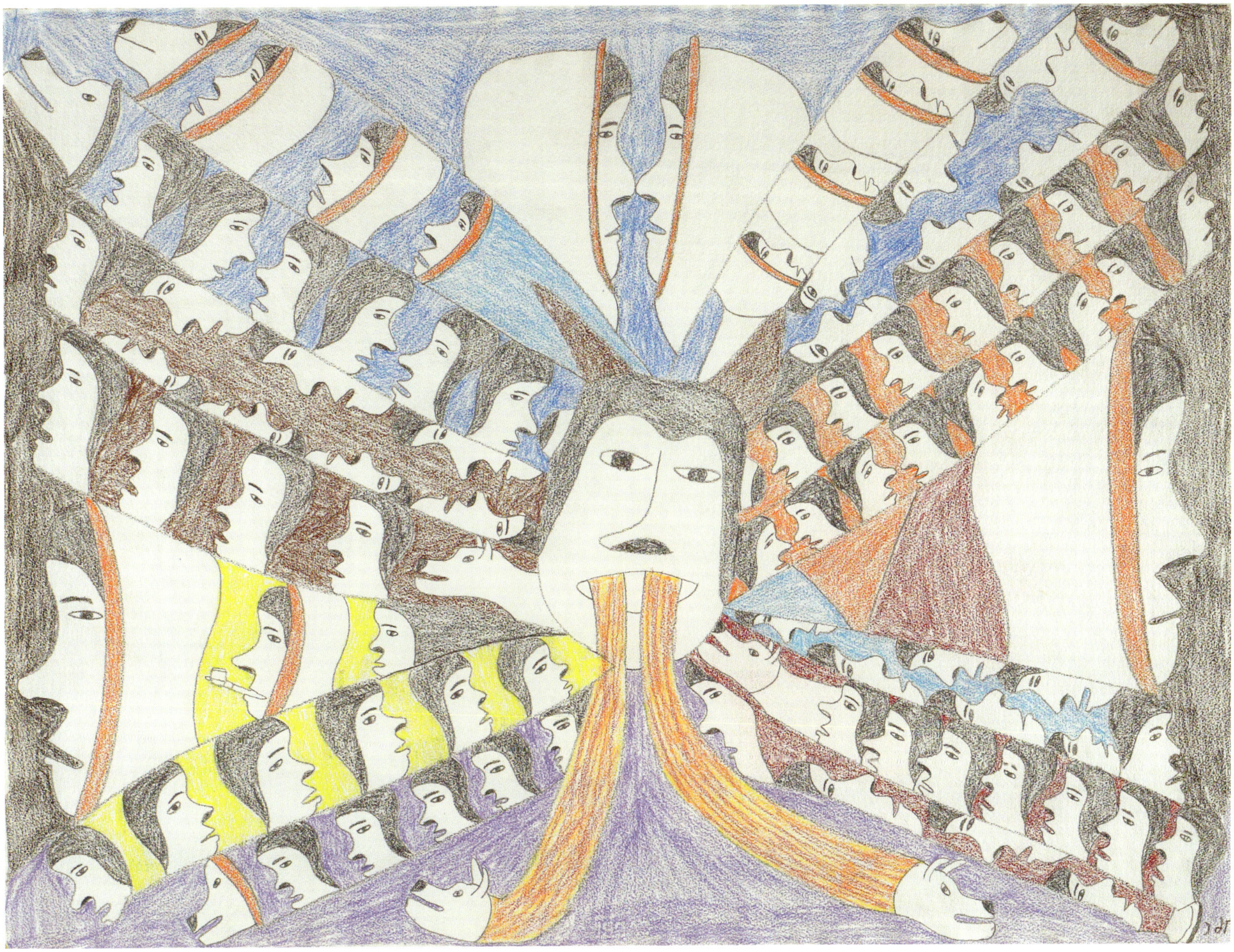

Simon Tookoome, *Wolf and Inuit*, 1980s, coloured pencil on paper, 58.5 x 78.0 cm

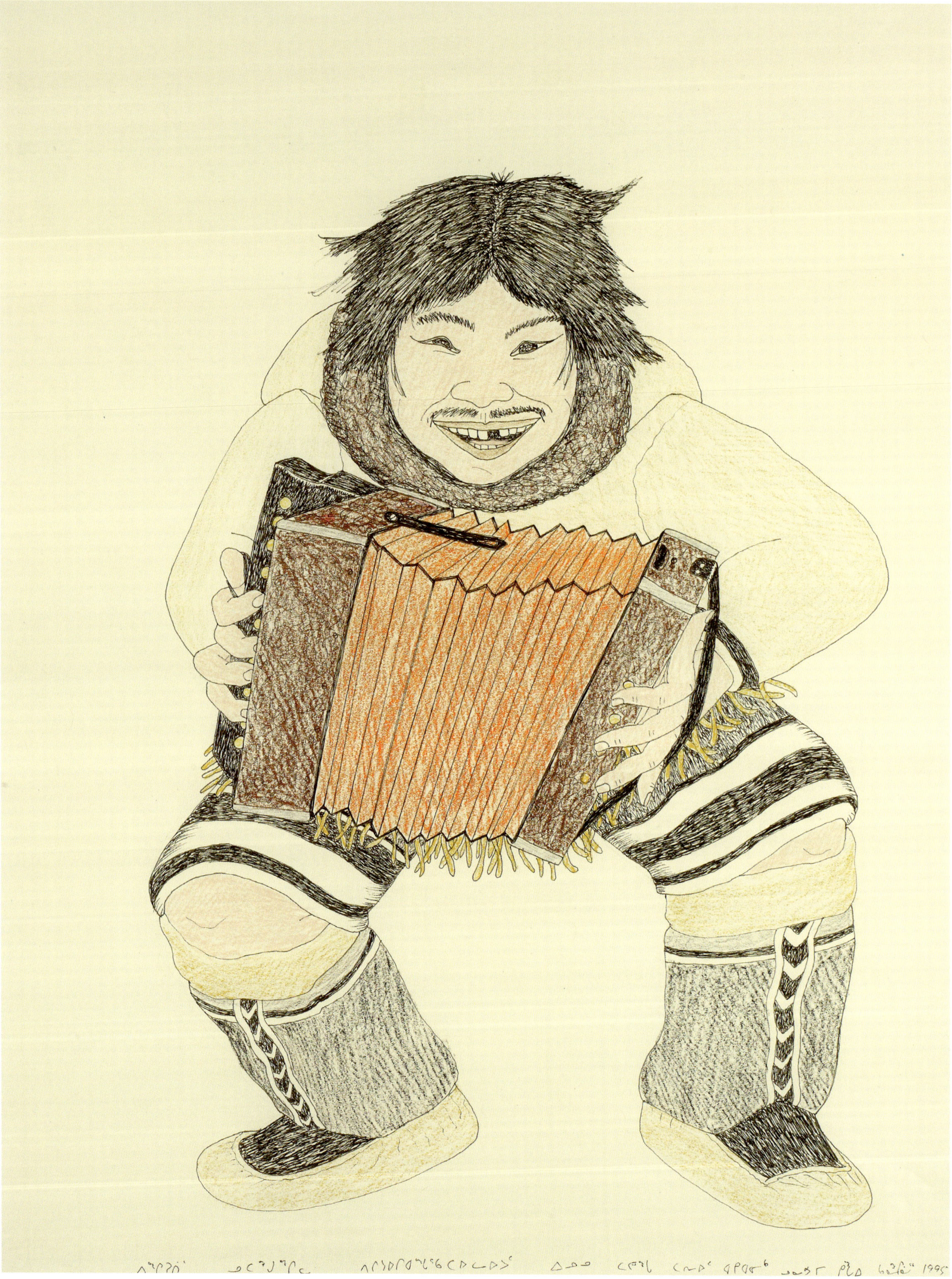

Kananginak Pootoogook, *Accordion Player*, 1995, coloured pencil and ink on paper, 66.0 x 50.8 cm

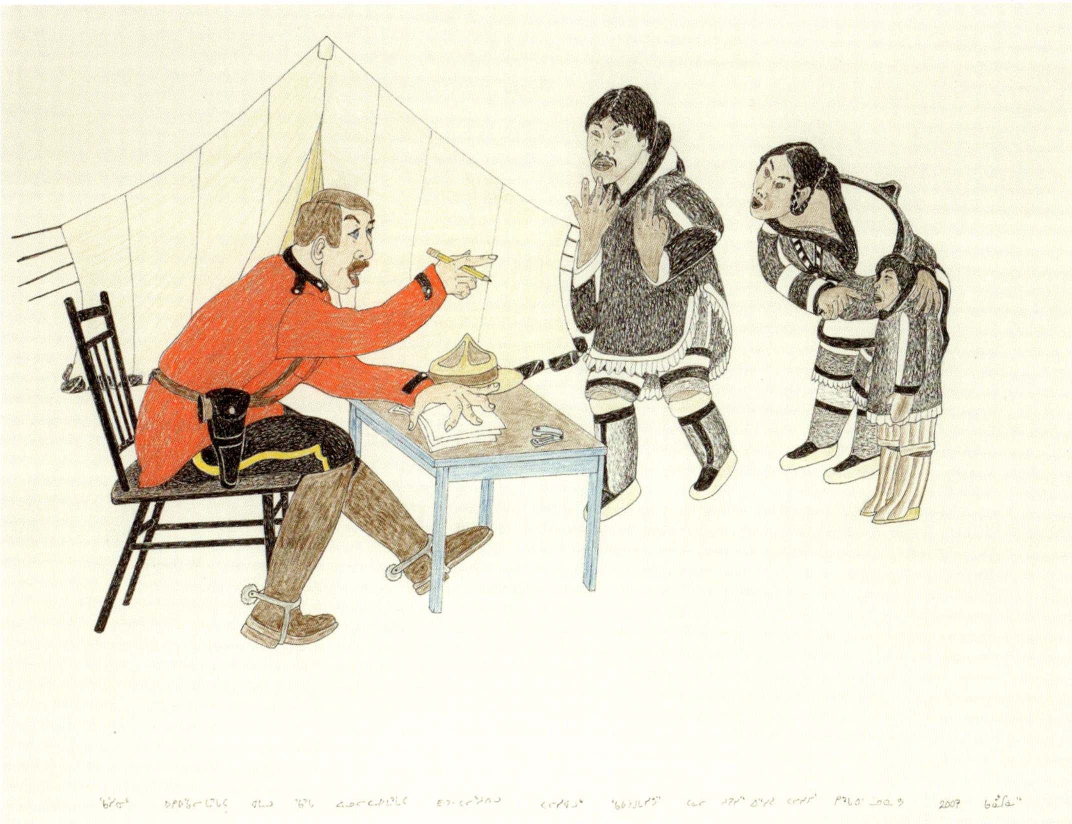

Kananginak Pootoogook, *RCMP and Inuit Family*, 2007, coloured pencil and ink on paper, 57.0 x 76.0 cm

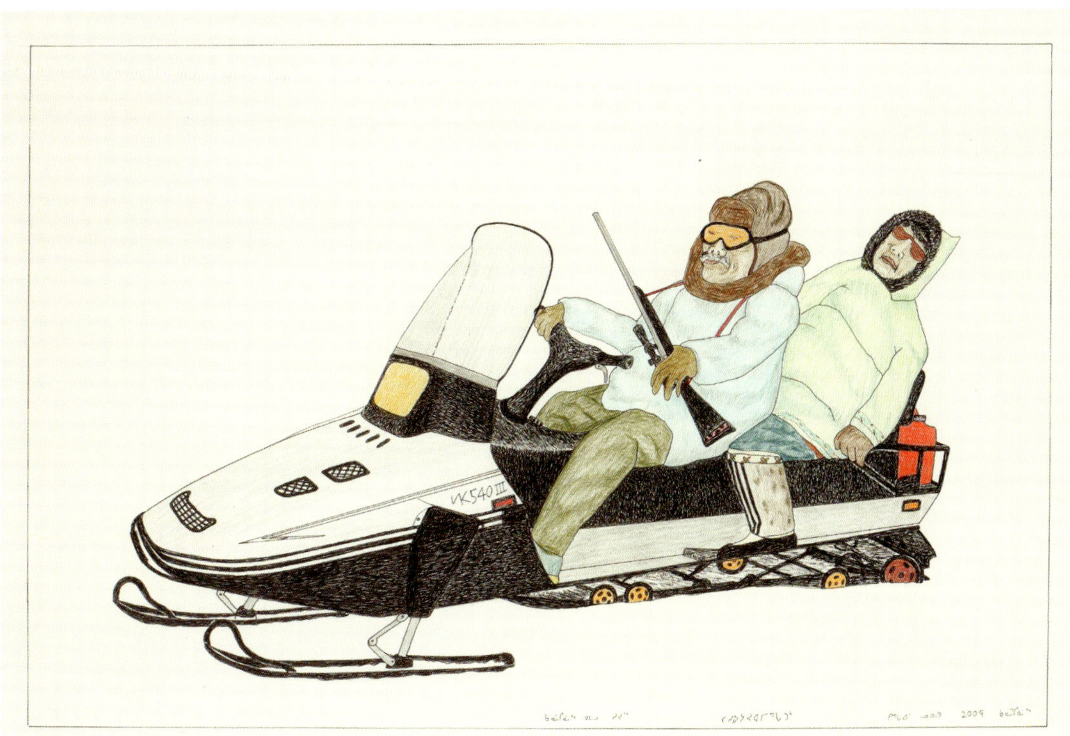

Kananginak Pootoogook, *Man and Woman on Skidoo*, 2009, coloured pencil and ink on paper, 56.0 x 76.0 cm

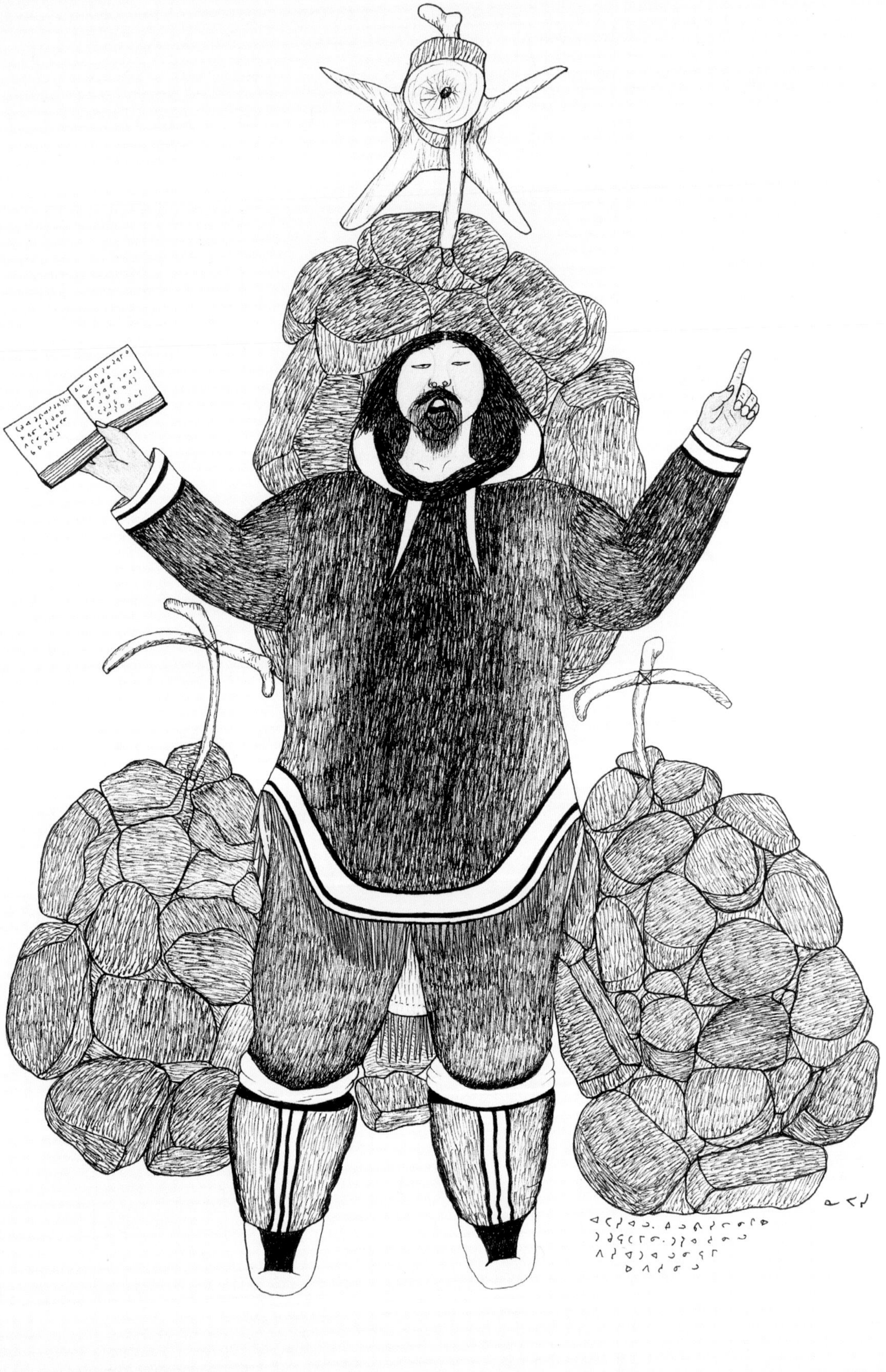

"This book has things to rejoice over. It is said that God recognizes those who have faith in Him."

"This is how much God loved the people of the world. He gave His only son so that all of those that believe in Him will not be lost."

"They buried the one they had put to death and he prayed. He did the right thing and had faith."

"Napachie"

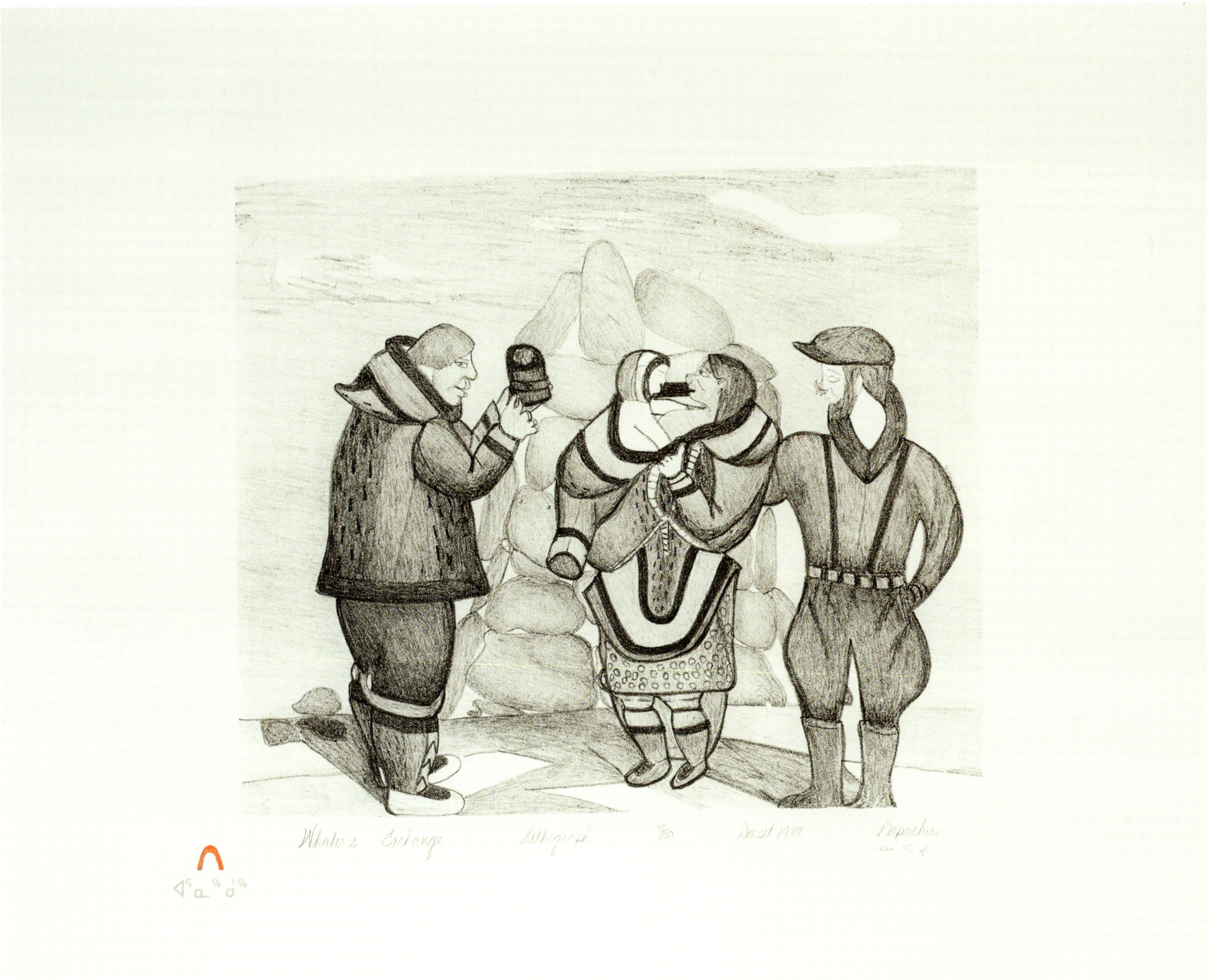

Napachie Pootoogook, *Whaler's Exchange*, 1989,
lithograph, 40.6 x 50.8 cm

Left: **Napachie Pootoogook**,
Shaman/Minister, 1996,
ink and pencil crayon on paper,
66.0 x 51.0 cm

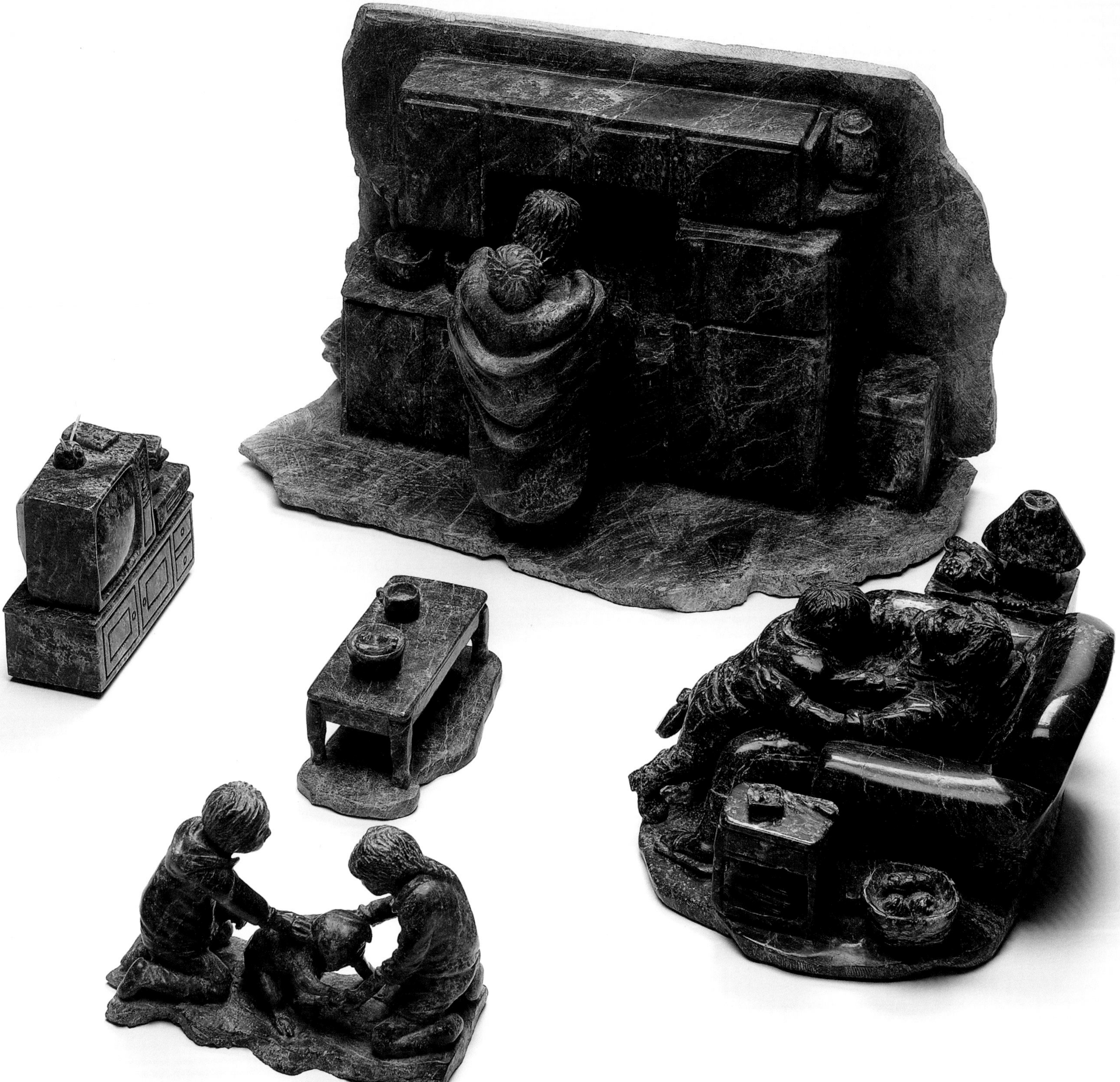

Mark Pitseolak, *Domestic Scene* (5 parts), 2007, stone,
couch/living room: 14.5 x 38.0 x 28.0 cm; kids playing with dog: 15.0 x 22.5 x 10.0 cm;
TV: 17.0 x 18.0 x 8.0 cm; coffee table: 10.0 x 19.0 x 9.5 cm; kitchen: 34.0 x 54.0 x 25.0 cm.
Collection of Samuel and Esther Sarick, Toronto. © Dorset Fine Arts

"I Am an Artist"
Inuit Art Transcends Ethnicity

Ingo Hessel

As individual Inuit artists were developing a new feeling of self-awareness as artists, the Arctic and the Inuit art world continued to evolve. By the late 1960s all but a few Inuit "holdouts" had moved off the land and into one of the fifty villages scattered along Canada's Arctic coast. Federal and/or territorial or provincial government administration, education, welfare, health service and education consolidated their profound control over Inuit society. Fur trapping had dwindled in importance; Inuit now vied for the few, mostly low-paying jobs in their communities. Many had turned to artmaking as a source of income, finding that it, at least, afforded them the flexibility to continue some level of subsistence hunting. Class, social, generational and even political divisions and tensions began to emerge and have accelerated in the decades since:[1] co-op versus private and government enterprise; unilingual elders versus bilingual, educated children and grandchildren; Nunamiut (people of the land) versus Kabloonamiut (people of the white man, people who imitate the white man);[2] the employed versus the unemployed and self-employed; the well-housed versus the overcrowded; Inuit versus (comparatively rich) Qallunaat; federal versus territorial or provincial governments (in particular, the growing insularity of Quebec Inuit[3]); Anglican versus Roman Catholic; and perhaps even successful artists versus more marginal ones. In 1978 Cape Dorset's West Baffin Eskimo Co-operative established its own distribution agency in Toronto, called Dorset Fine Arts, in response to demands from leading artists for a higher share of prices. Elite artists flexed their economic muscles, and the co-operative was forced to comply.[4] The concept of a single Inuit identity has been increasingly difficult to sustain under these circumstances.

At the same time, Inuit began to assert themselves politically: they established the Inuit Tapirisat of Canada (ITC, now Inuit Tapiriit Kanatami or ITK) in 1971; they helped to create the Inuit Circumpolar Council in 1977; they formed Pauktuutit Inuit Women of Canada in 1984; and they founded a host of other local, regional and national political and cultural organizations. Having gained the right to vote as recently as 1962, Inuit elected Peter Ittinuar as the first Inuk federal MP in 1979. By the 1990s, Inuit had begun signing land claims agreements, had successfully negotiated the formation of a brand-new federal territory, Nunavut (1999), and were making their voices heard regarding environmental issues such as climate change.

The 1970s and 1980s saw a rapid expansion in the promotion and exhibition of Inuit art. The large-scale government-sponsored exhibitions *Sculpture/Inuit* and *The Inuit Print* toured internationally in the 1970s. Indian and Northern Affairs Canada established the Inuit Art Section, which organized travelling shows, collected and disseminated information on art and artists and supported marketing and research activities. Commercial galleries specializing in Inuit art sprang up in major cities, and public galleries and museums (notably the National Gallery of Canada, the Winnipeg Art Gallery, the Art Gallery of Ontario and the Canadian Museum of Civilization) expanded their collections and exhibition activities. Inuit artists were showered with honours such as membership in the Royal Canadian Academy of Arts and the Order of Canada, the country's highest civilian honour. The Canadian Eskimo Arts Council, which had been established in 1961 to advise printmakers and officially approve prints for sale, was disbanded in the mid-

"I want [southern people] to truly understand Inuit culture but I don't know how else to explain it to them. The reason I started making drawings... is because in the future our children will not understand or hear of our culture."

Simon Tookoome

artistic vision. Her landscapes and other images, sometimes sparse and at other times oppressively dense, are usually quirky, often disquieting and sometimes downright disturbing (pp. 200–03). Nancy Campbell said it well when she wrote that Shuvinai is "working in the isolation of [her] imagination."[28] And Sandra Dyck noted that Shuvinai's drawings are notable for their "intensity and compelling otherworldliness. By turns whimsical and opaque, they often resist straightforward interpretation."[29] Significantly, Campbell (who has also worked with Annie Pootoogook) and Dyck are both contemporary art curators, not Inuit art specialists; both curators have an interest in the intersection of the two art worlds, and Shuvinai is an exemplar of the "crossover" appeal of some Inuit artists.[30]

Tim Pitsiulak hails from Kimmirut but resides in Cape Dorset. Trained in jewellery making and metalwork, he is one of the graphic artists who have embraced the opportunity to work on a larger scale. It is interesting to note that increases in the scale of Inuit modernist sculpture, first in the mid-1950s and then among avant-garde artists since the 1980s, are being matched to some extent in the art of drawing in the first decade of the 2000s. When Pitsiulak opts to work on a grand scale, he generally chooses imagery to match, be it a pod of whales, a traditional umiak or a piece of modern heavy equipment (pp. 193–95). Like many modern artists, Pitsiulak enjoys visual puns.

The drawings of Itee Pootoogook from Cape Dorset, although they depict Arctic scenery and views of his home community and its residents, are the graphics most removed from any recognizable Inuit art style (pp. 102, 204, 205). More reminiscent of the works of the southern Canadian artist Christopher Pratt than any of Itee's peers, Itee's drawings are painstakingly, one could even say lovingly, rendered in graphite or pencil crayon; they radiate timeless calm and contentment but not always an identifiable locale. As if to make up for this, Itee frequently adds extended inscriptions. Unlike other Inuit graphic artists but like many southern artists, Itee often works from photographs.

Tony Anguhalluq, the adopted son of the elderly artists Luke Anguhadluq and Marion Tuu'luq of Baker Lake, probably does not think of himself as the inheritor of their artistic vision. However, his naive style certainly belies his two-year program in drawing and printmaking, and stylistically his works are about as far removed as possible from the calm, cool landscapes of Itee Pootoogook. Anguhalluq's small, brightly coloured drawings recall Janet Kigusiuq, but more so Shuvinai Ashoona; with their slightly skewed bird's-eye perspective, nervous energy and slight air of claustrophobia, his works are unassuming little gems (pp. 196–97). Anguhalluq seems to look back for reassurance even as he shadows forth an uncertain artistic future.

The evolution of Inuit art is as exemplary as it is unlikely. Who would have guessed that a souvenir art–cum–occupational therapy art–cum–welfare project would bring about a vibrant renaissance in Inuit culture? Who would have predicted that the art from a tiny ethnic minority could become a national treasure? Who would have thought that women, children and the elderly would become valued and successful participants in a six-decade art experiment and that women and artists from the farthest-flung geographic margins could be in the vanguard of the newest achievements? Even today, we are still witnessing this "splendid new art of acculturation."

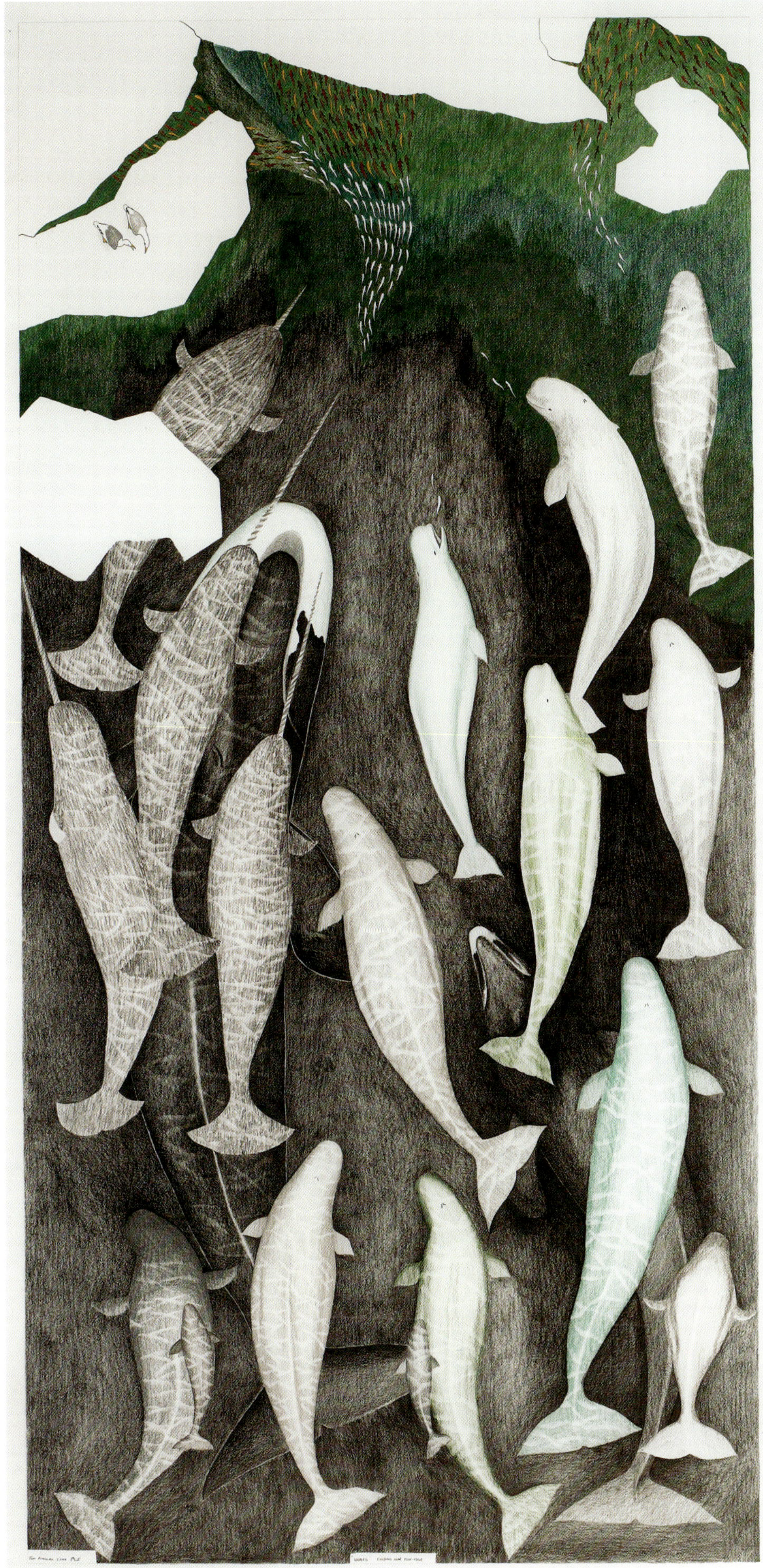

Tim Pitsiulak, *Composition (Whales Feeding)*, 2009, coloured pencil and graphite on paper, 238.8 x 121.9 cm

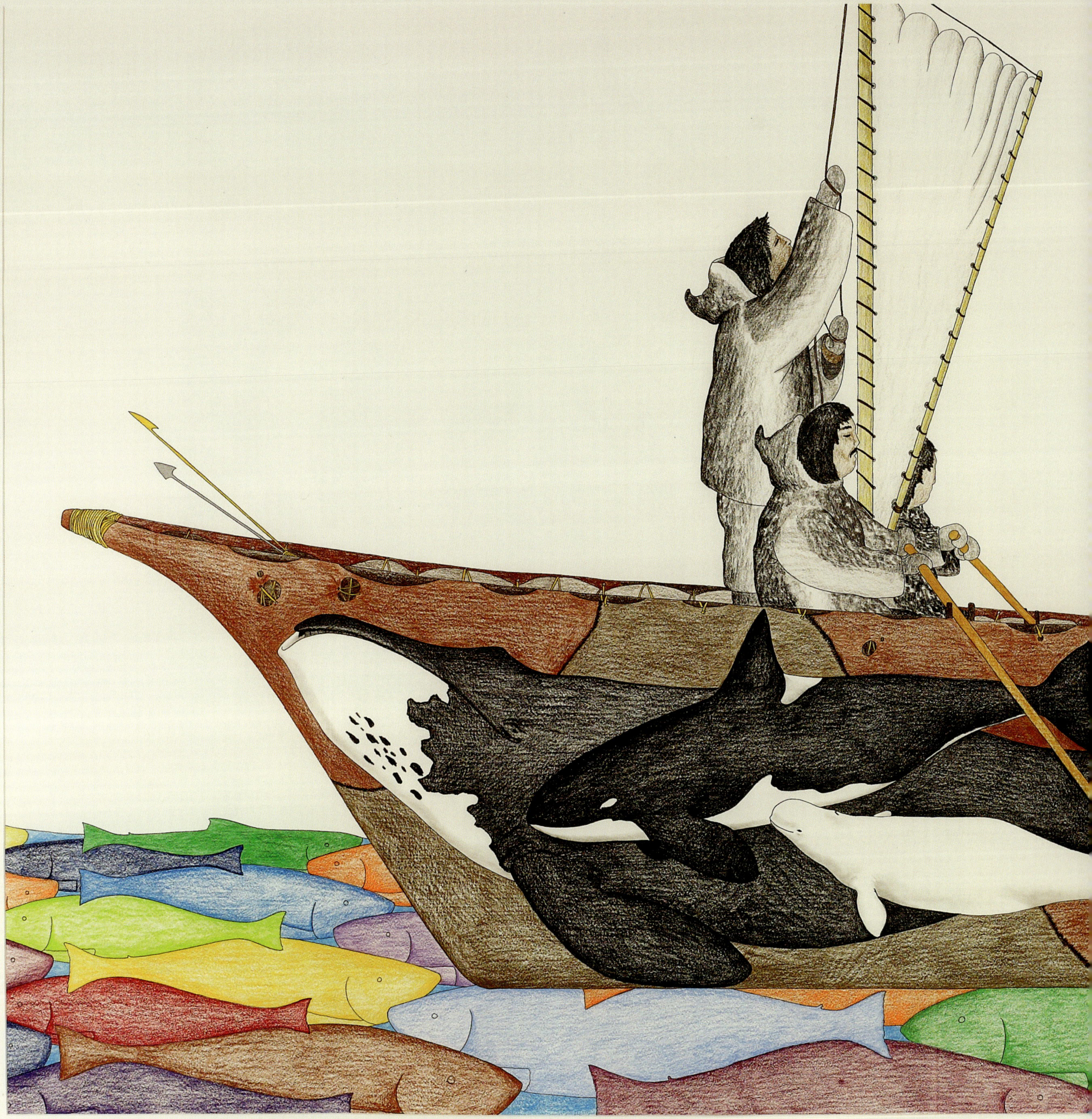

Tim Pitsiulak, *Composition (Whalers)*, 2009,
coloured pencil and graphite on paper, 121.9 x 243.8 cm

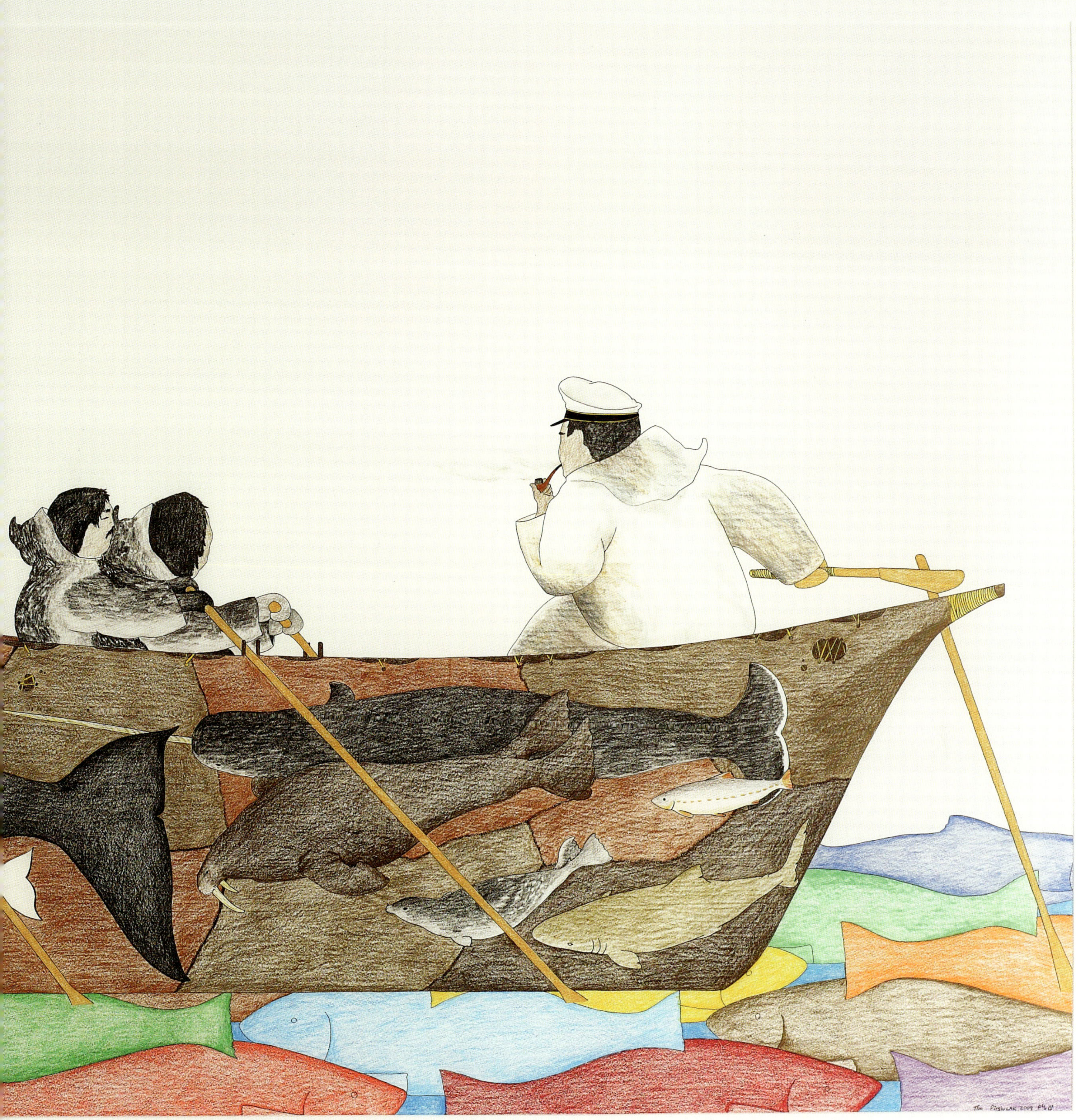

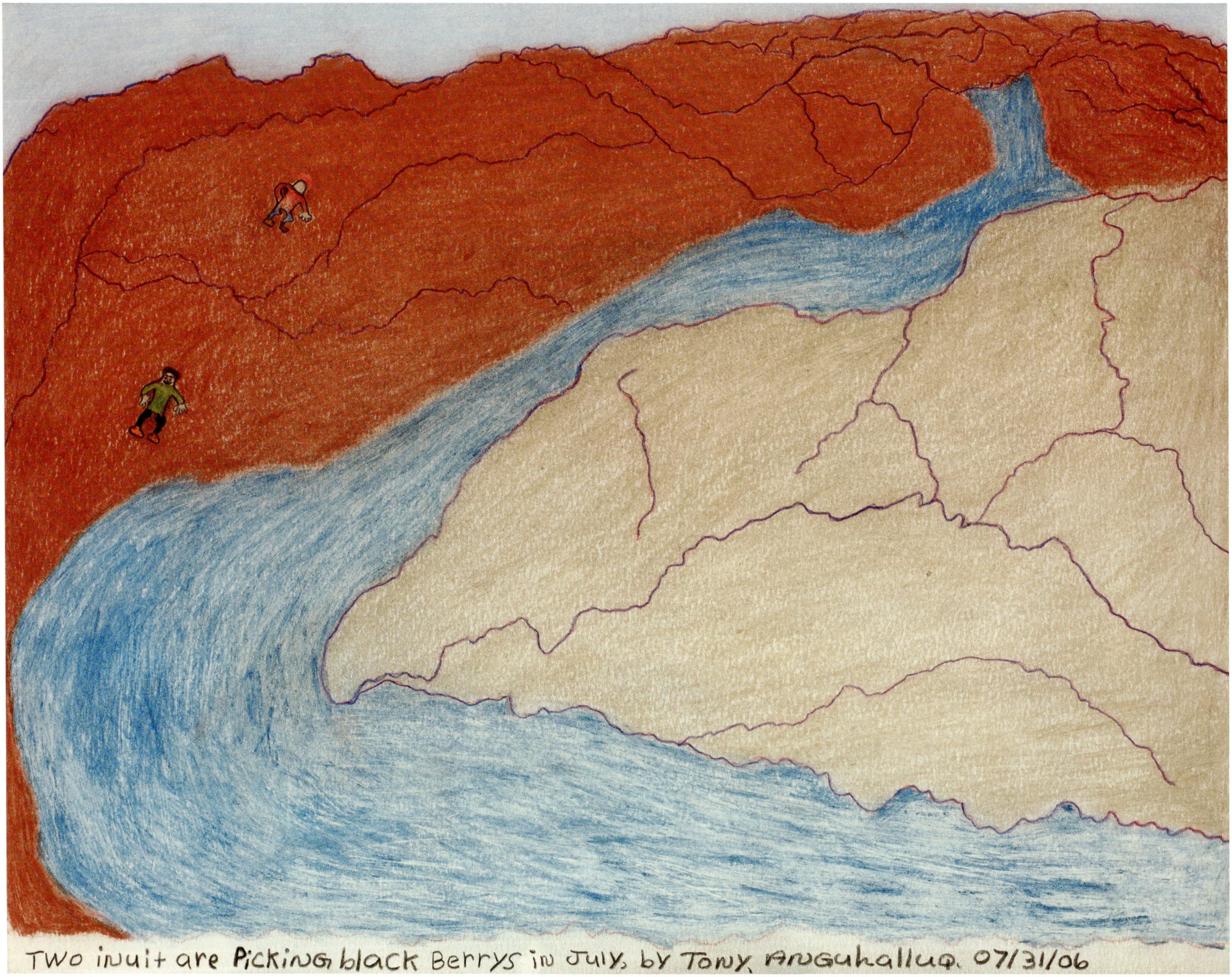

Tony Anguhalluq, *Two Inuit are picking blackberries in July*, 2006,
coloured pencil and wax crayon on paper, 26.7 x 34.9 cm

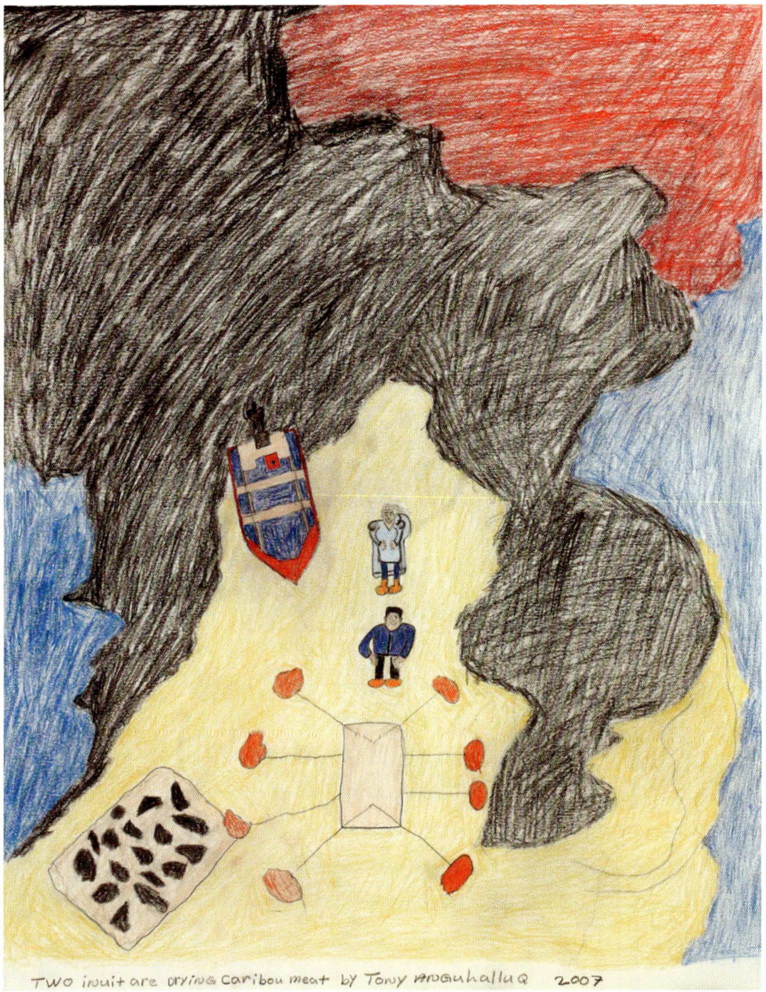

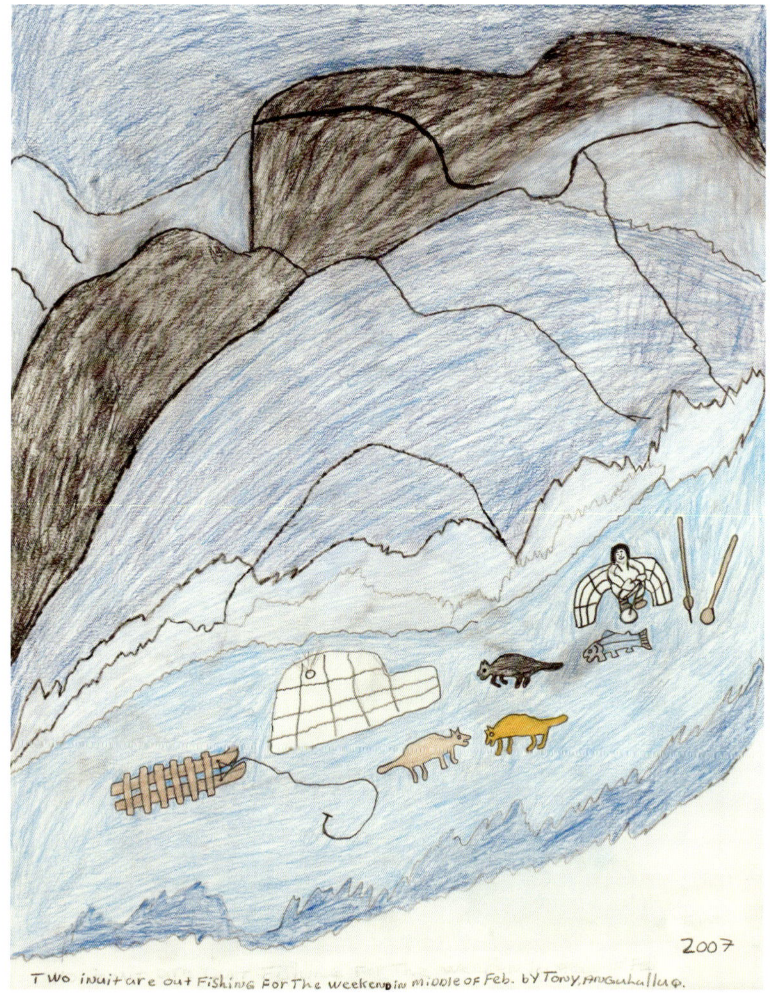

Tony Anguhalluq, *Two Inuit are drying caribou meat*, 2007, coloured pencil and graphite on paper, 61.0 x 48.0 cm

Tony Anguhalluq, *Two Inuit are out fishing for the weekend*, 2007, coloured pencil and wax crayon on paper, 61.0 x 48.0 cm

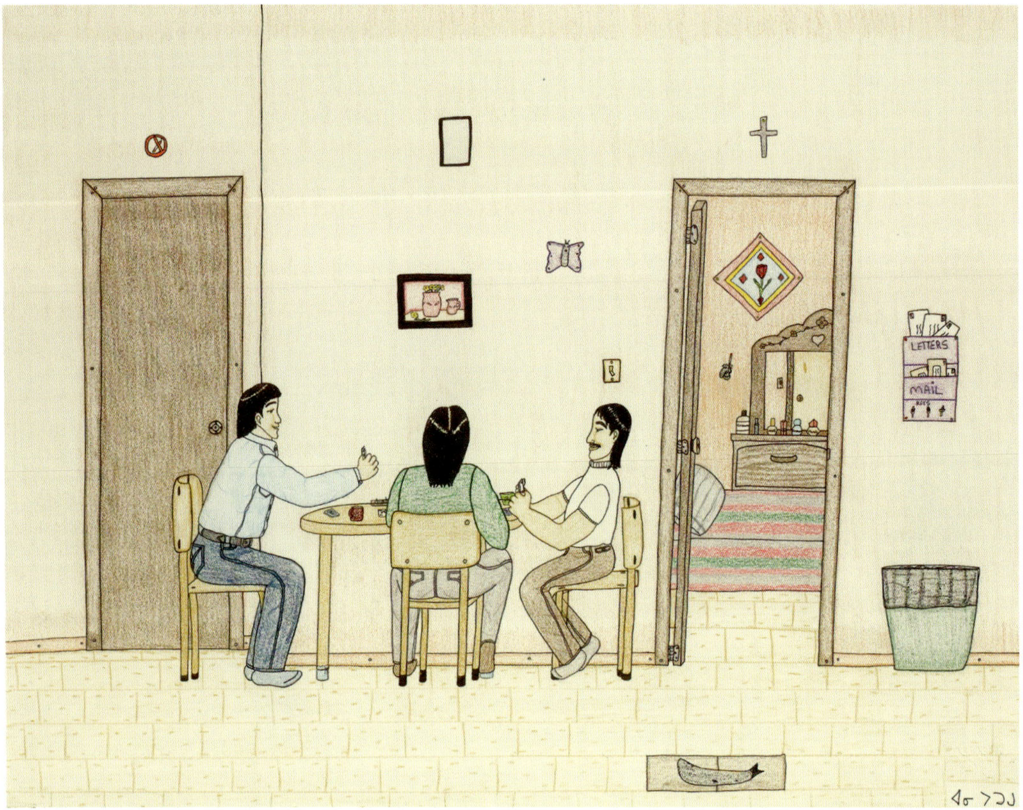

Annie Pootoogook, *Three Men Playing Cards*, 2001–2, coloured pencil and ink on paper, 50.8 x 66.0 cm

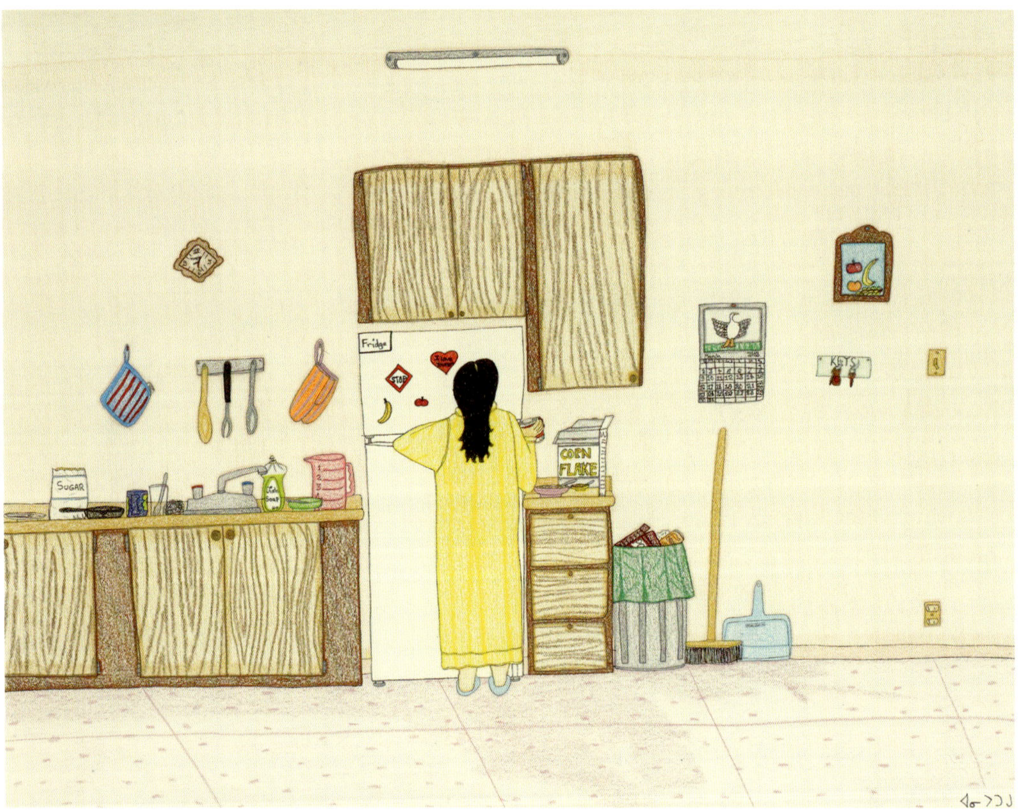

Annie Pootoogook, *In the Kitchen*, 2002–3, coloured pencil and ink on paper, 50.8 x 66.0 cm

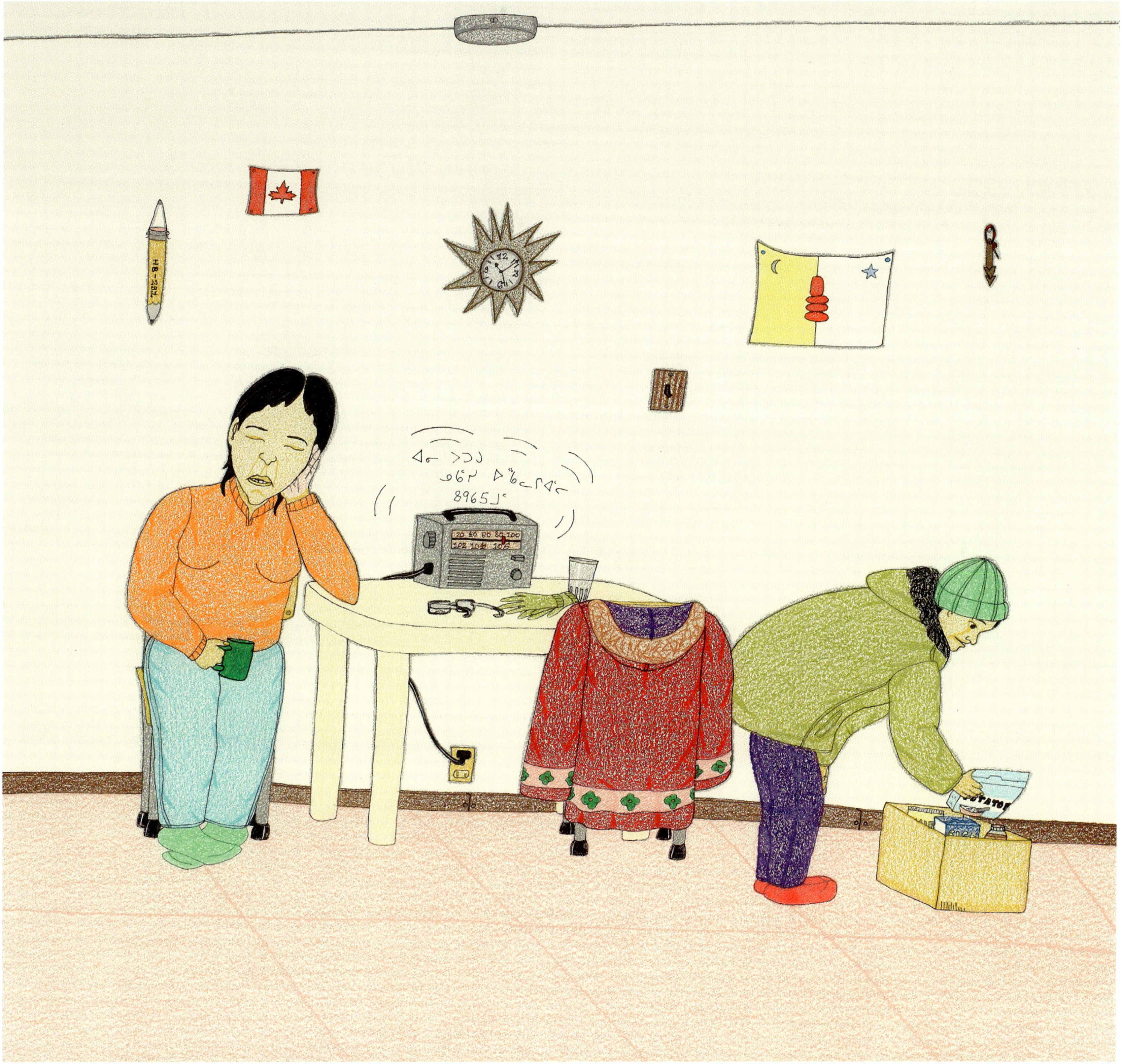

Annie Pootoogook, *Calling Annie*, 2005–6, coloured pencil and ink on paper, 50.8 x 54.6 cm

"Annie Pootoogook, the younger one, must call 8965."

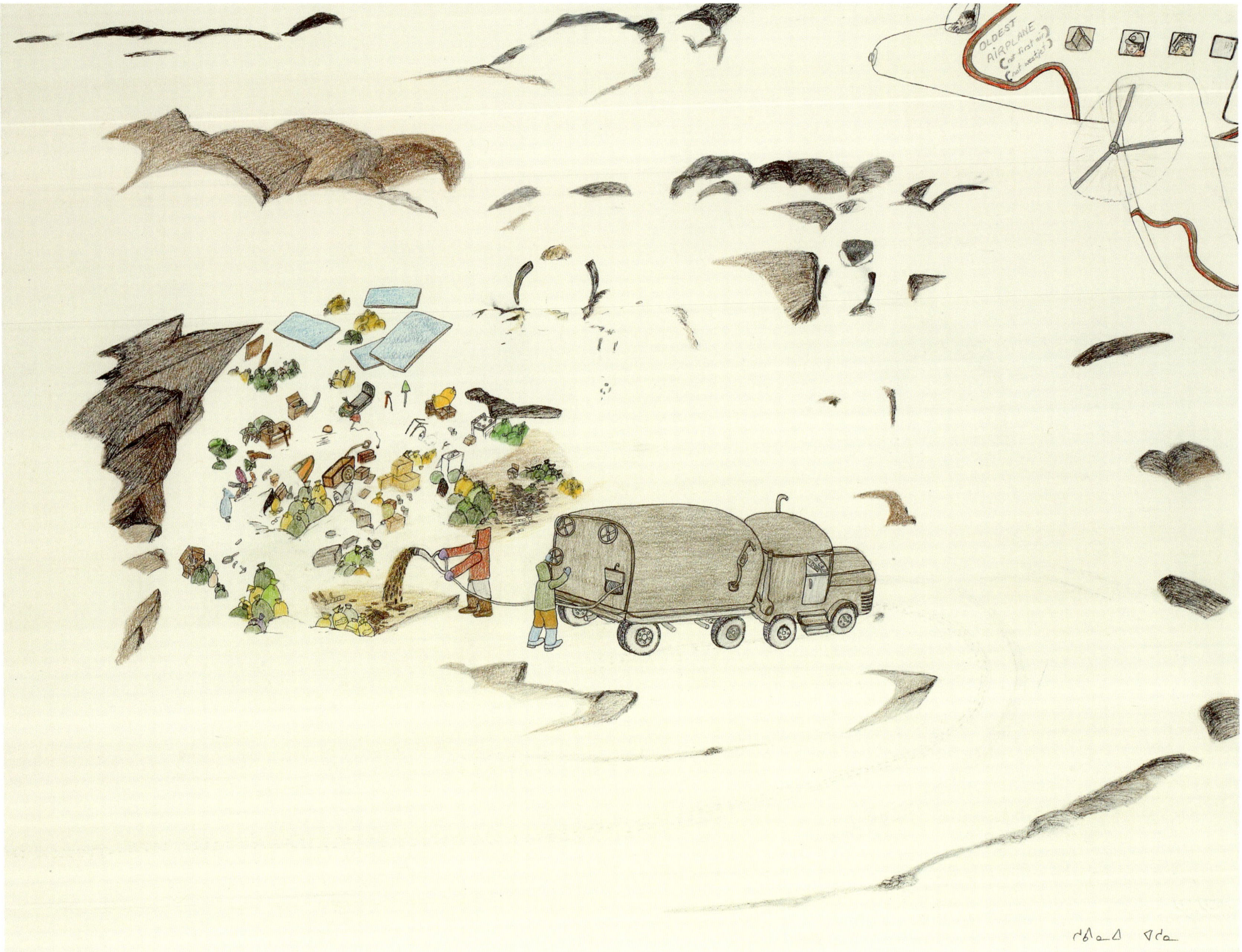

Shuvinai Ashoona, *Composition (Sewage Truck)*, 2007–8, coloured pencil and ink on paper, 50.8 cm x 66.0 cm

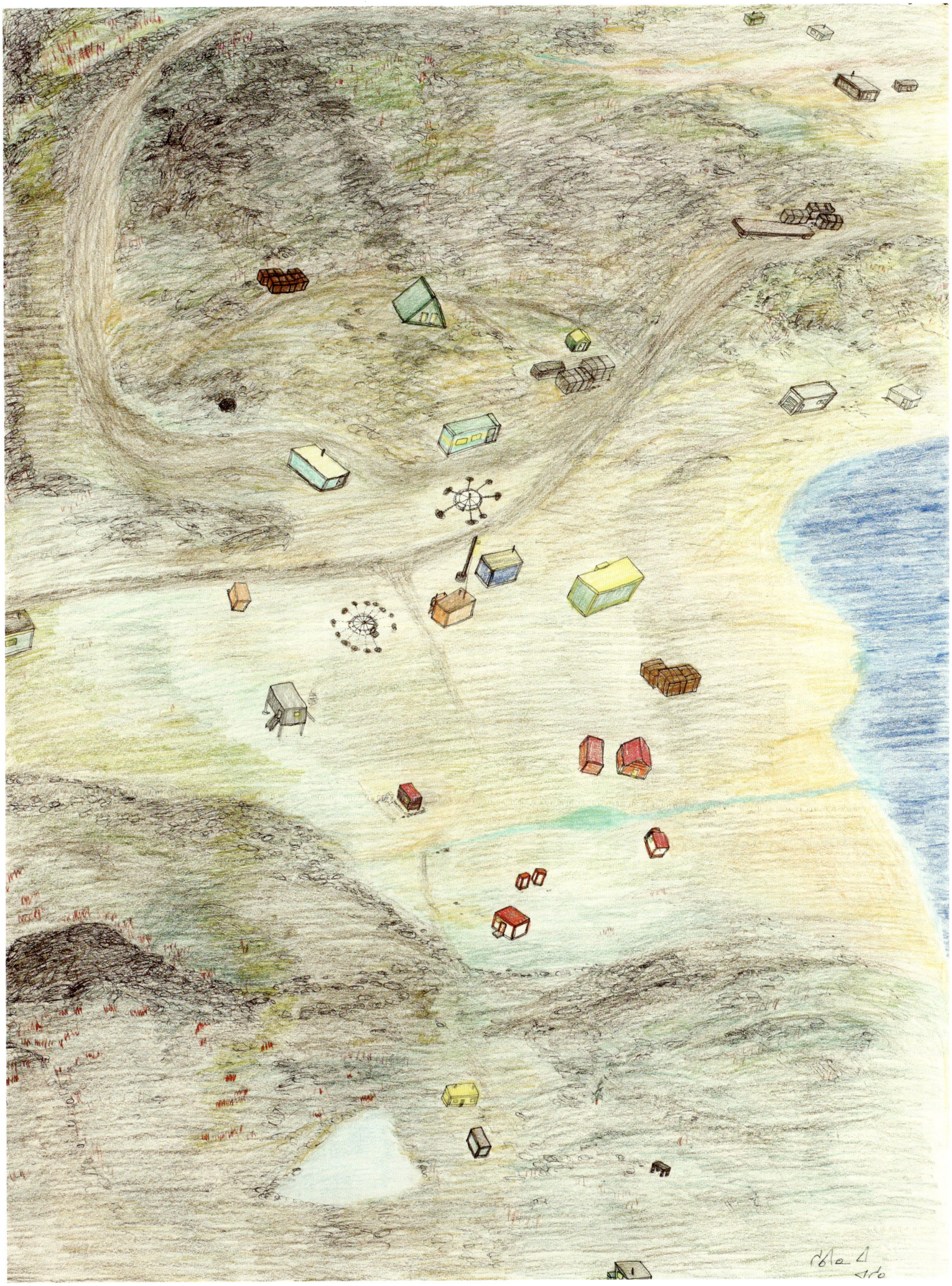

Shuvinai Ashoona, *Cape Dorset from Above*, 2007–8, coloured pencil and ink on paper, 66.0 x 50.8 cm

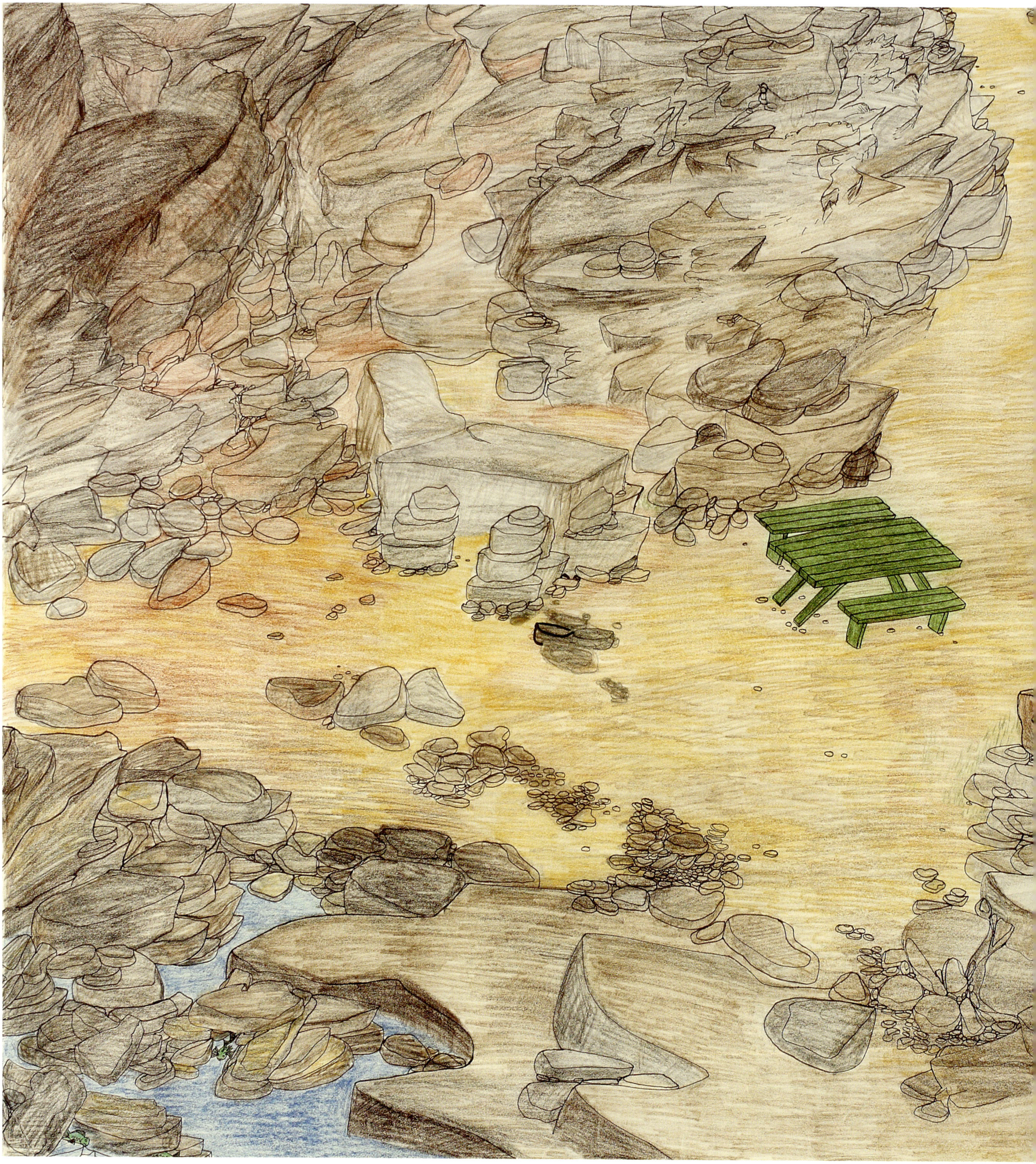

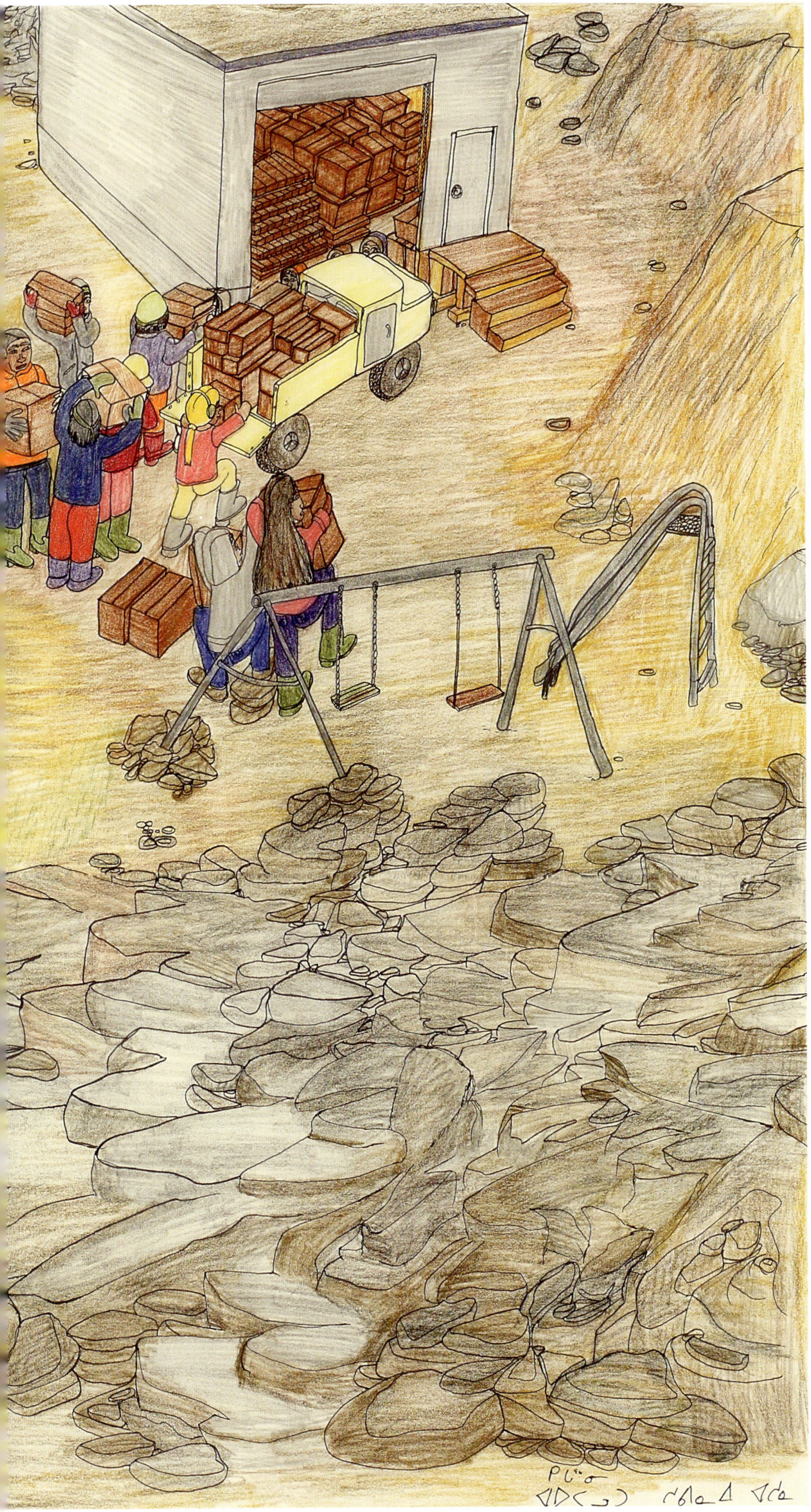

Shuvinai Ashoona, *Composition (Unloading Truck)*, 2009, coloured pencil and ink on paper, 64.5 x 96.0 cm

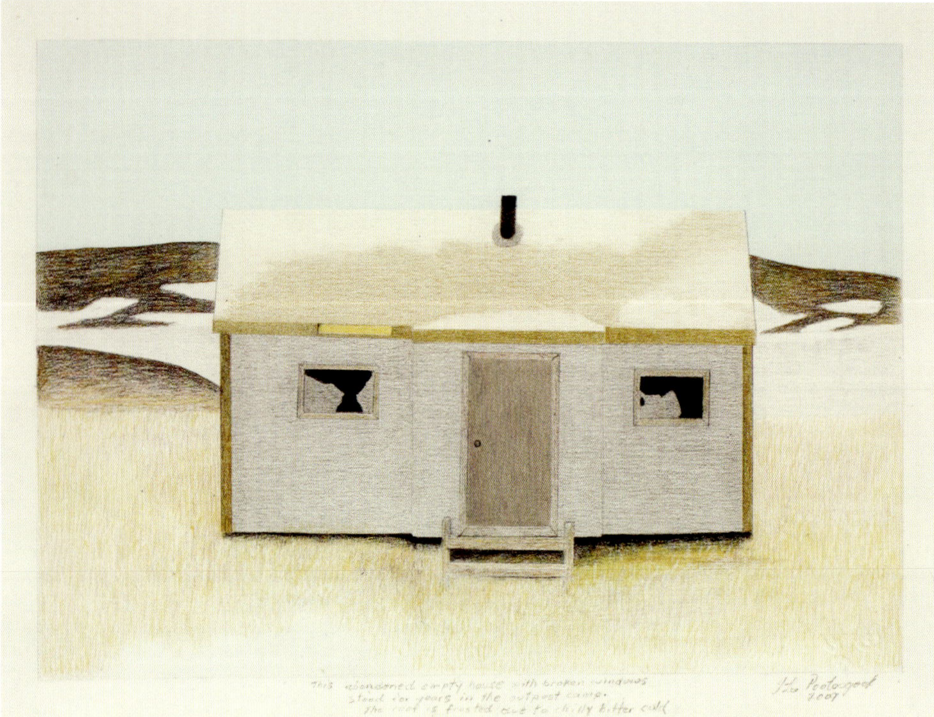

Itee Pootoogook, *Abandoned House*, 2009, coloured pencil and graphite on paper, 27.9 x 38.1 cm

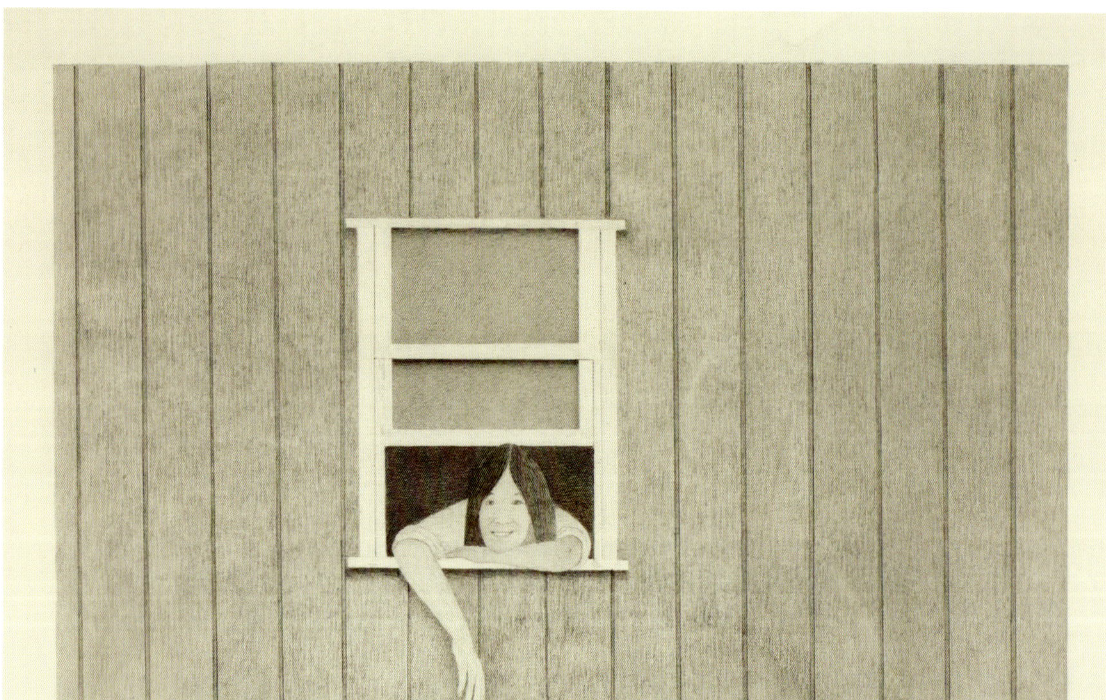

Itee Pootoogook, *Woman in Window*, 2009, graphite on paper, 38.1 x 55.9 cm

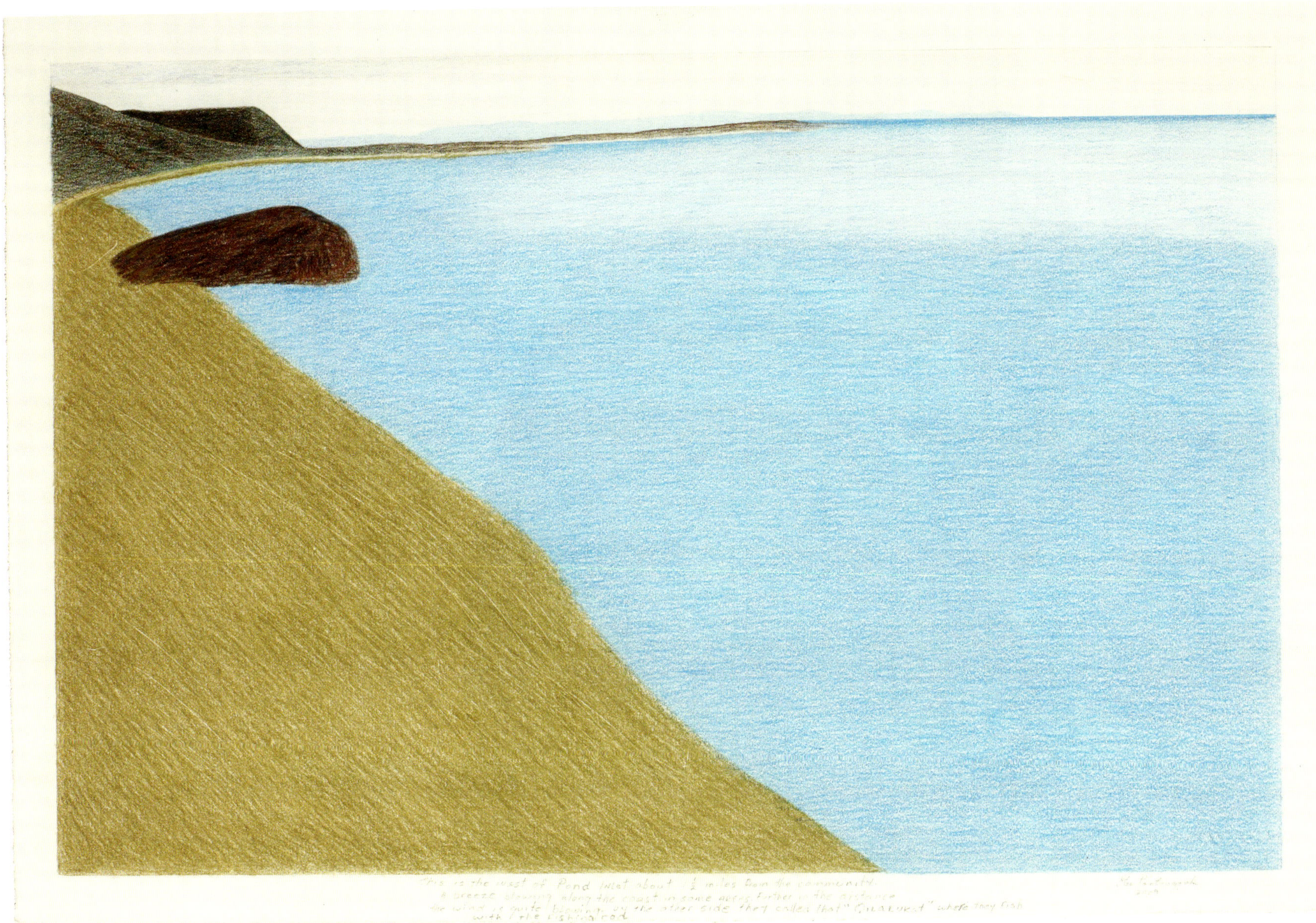

Itee Pootoogook, *Qilalukat*, 2009, coloured pencil and graphite on paper, 38.1 x 55.8 cm

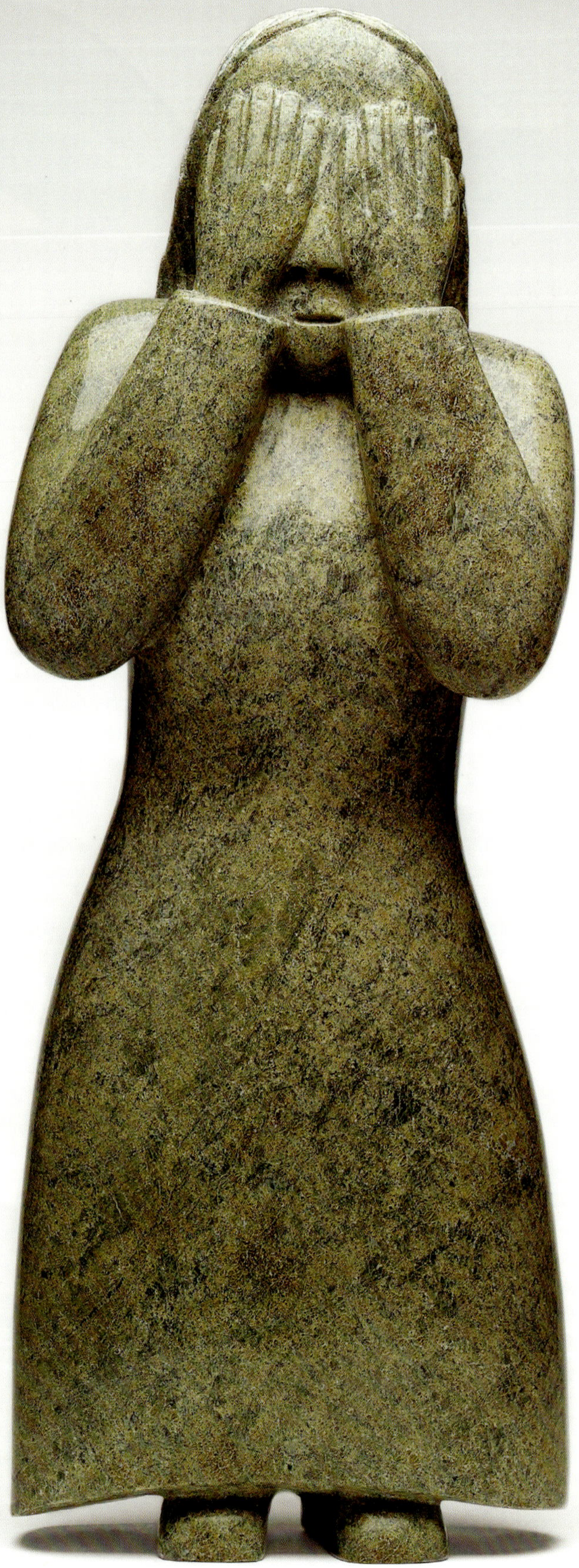

Oviloo Tunnillie, *Untitled (Standing Woman with Hands Cupped over Face)*, stone, 1990s, 55.7 x 21.8 x 11.6 cm

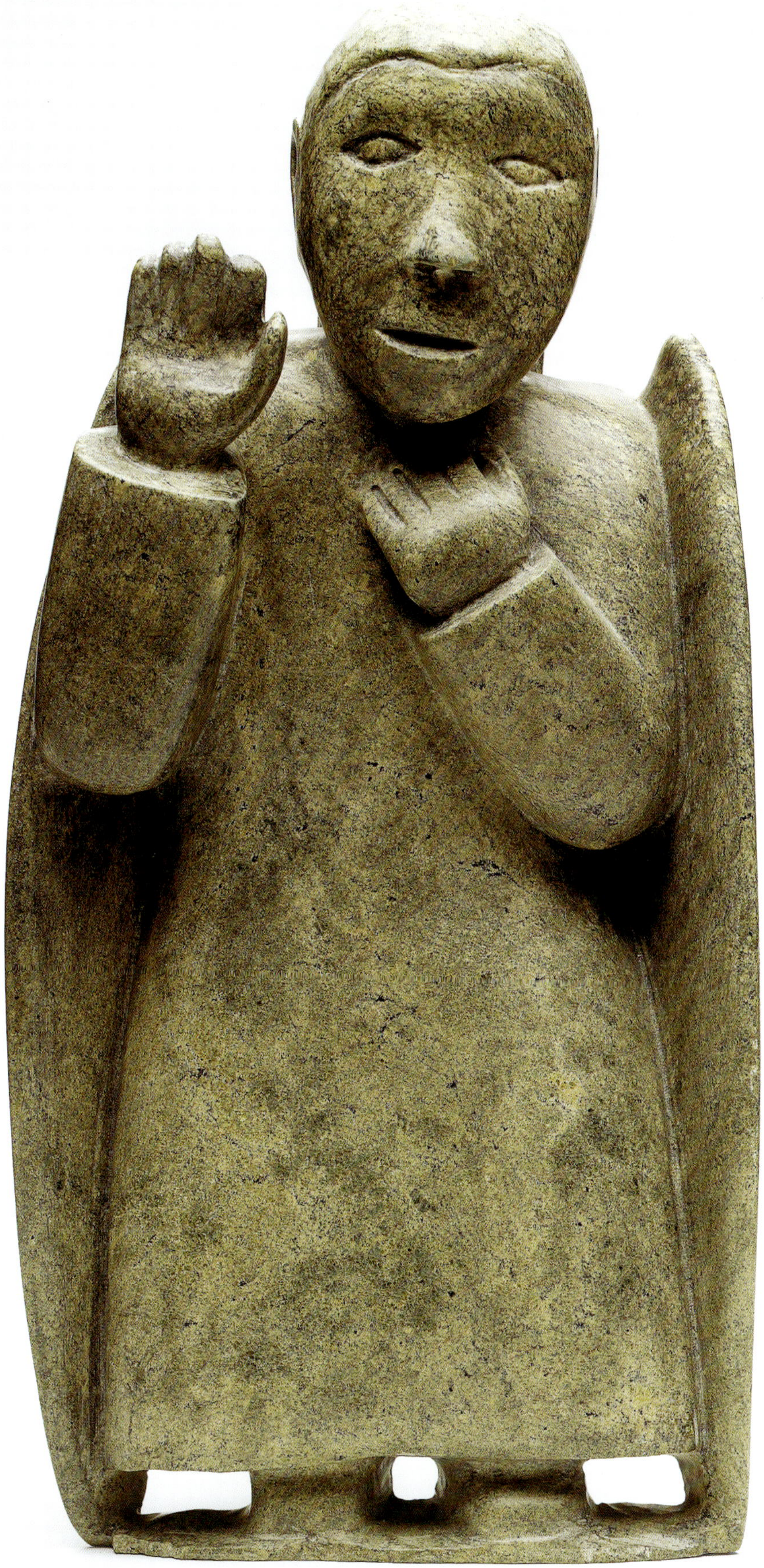

Oviloo Tunnillie, *Angel*, 1997, stone, 46.0 x 23.0 x 14.0 cm

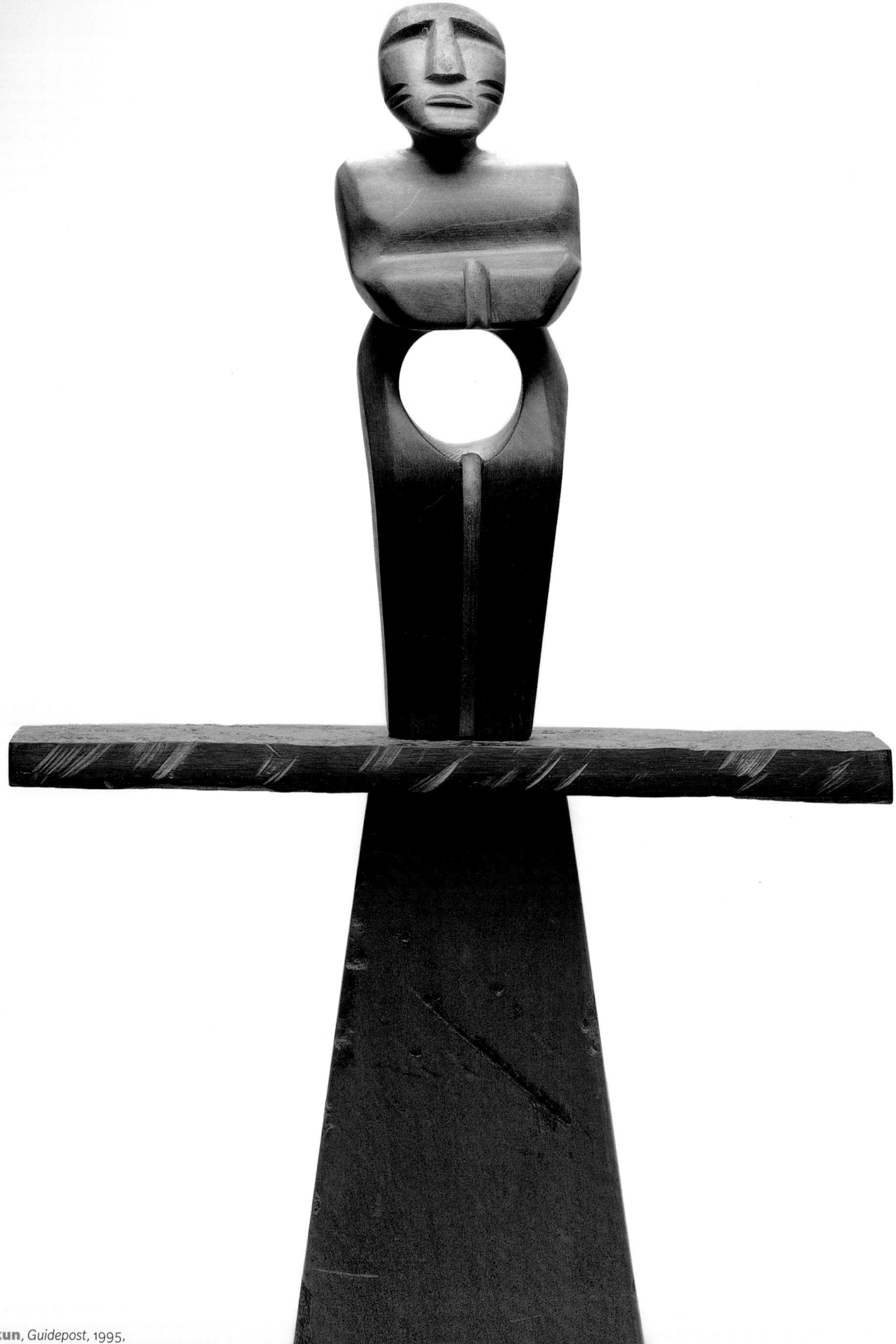

David Ruben Piqtoukun, *Guidepost*, 1995, limestone, Brazilian soapstone, slate, 94.5 x 61.0 x 14.5 cm; base: 41.2 x 25.0 x 14.5 cm

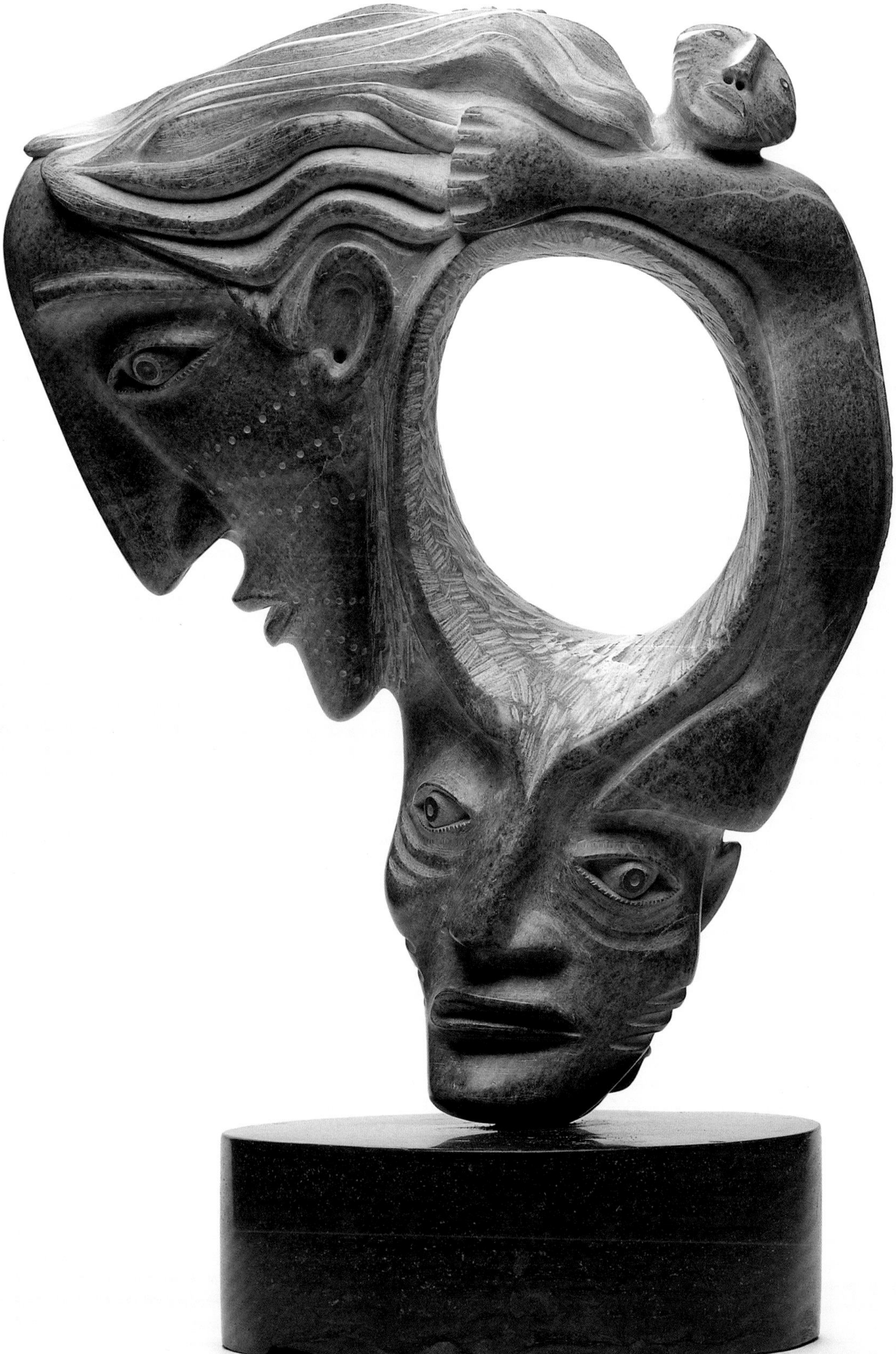

David Ruben Piqtoukun, *Journey to the Great Woman*, 1995,
Brazilian soapstone, Ontario marble, Italian alabaster, African wonderstone,
58.0 x 41.0 x 15.5 cm

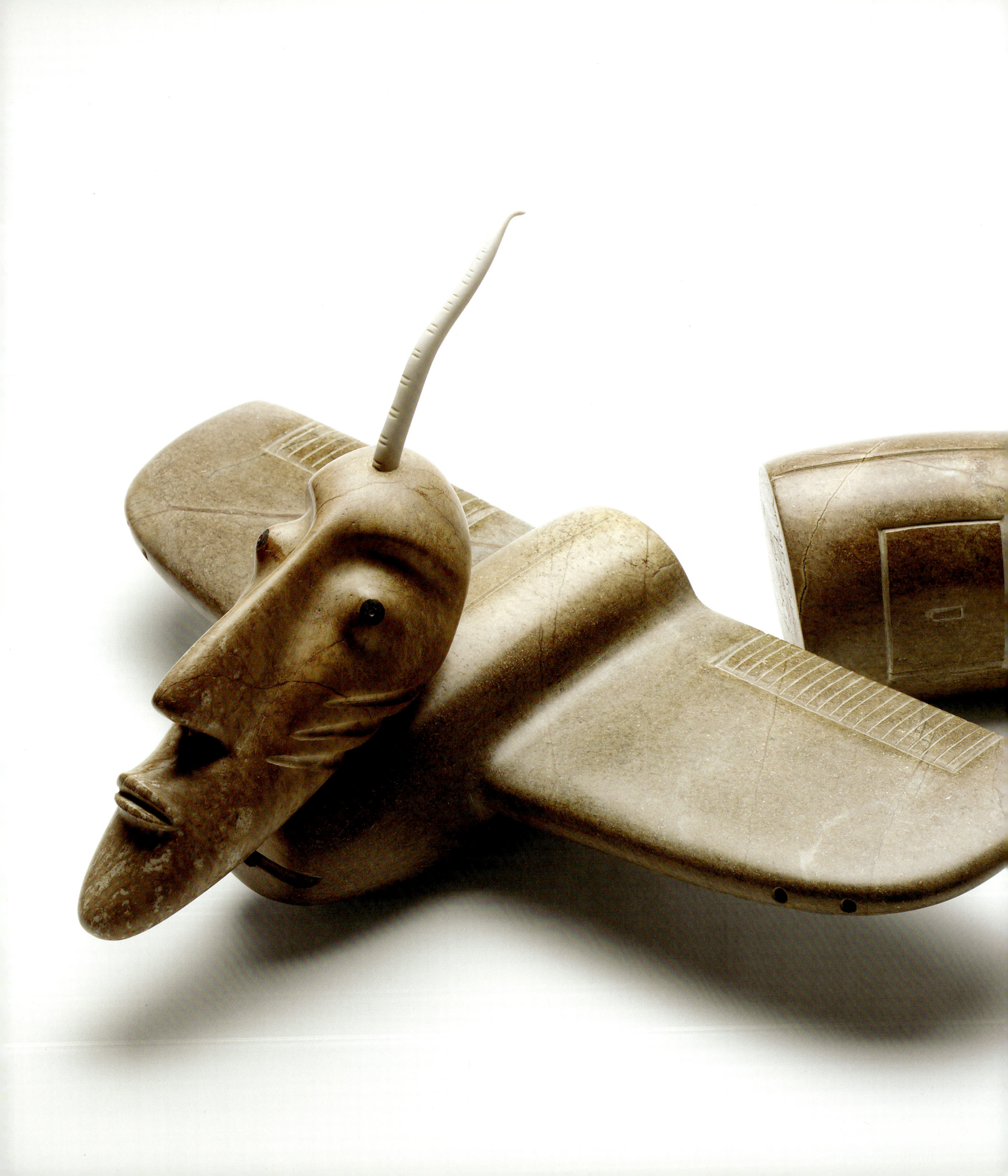

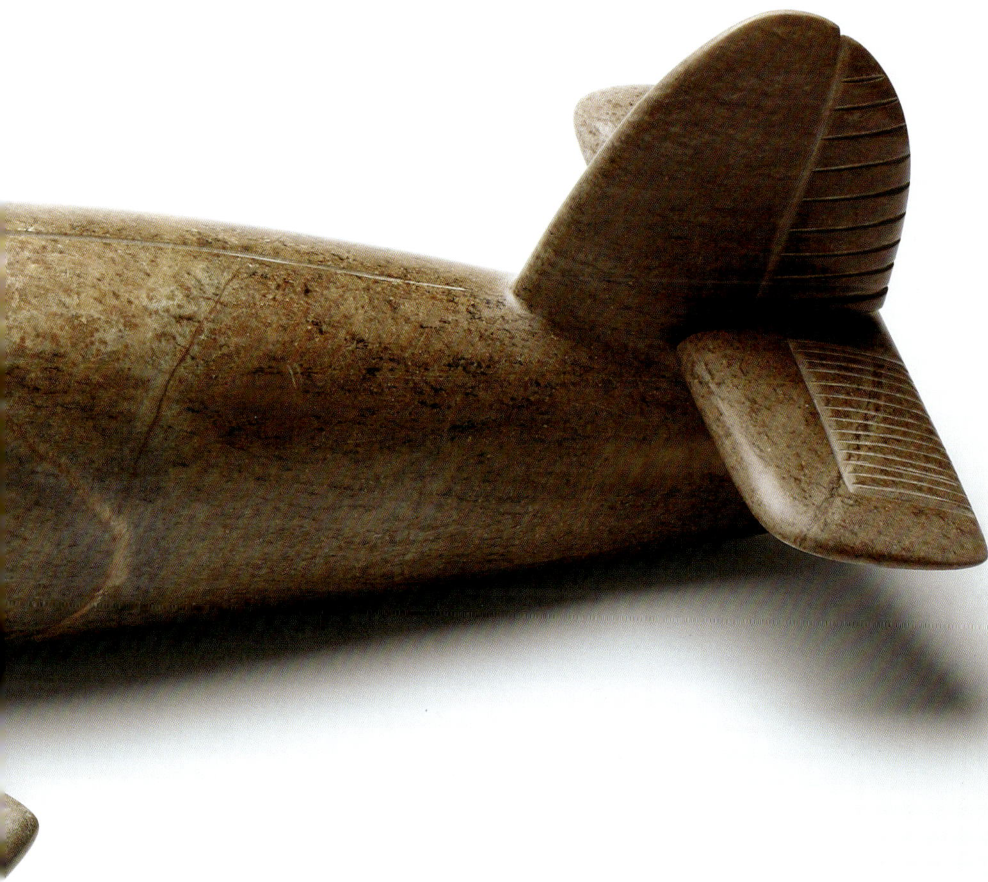

David Ruben Piqtoukun, *Shaman Crash Landing*, 2001, stone, metal, ivory, inlay, 26.5 x 50.5 x 63.0 cm

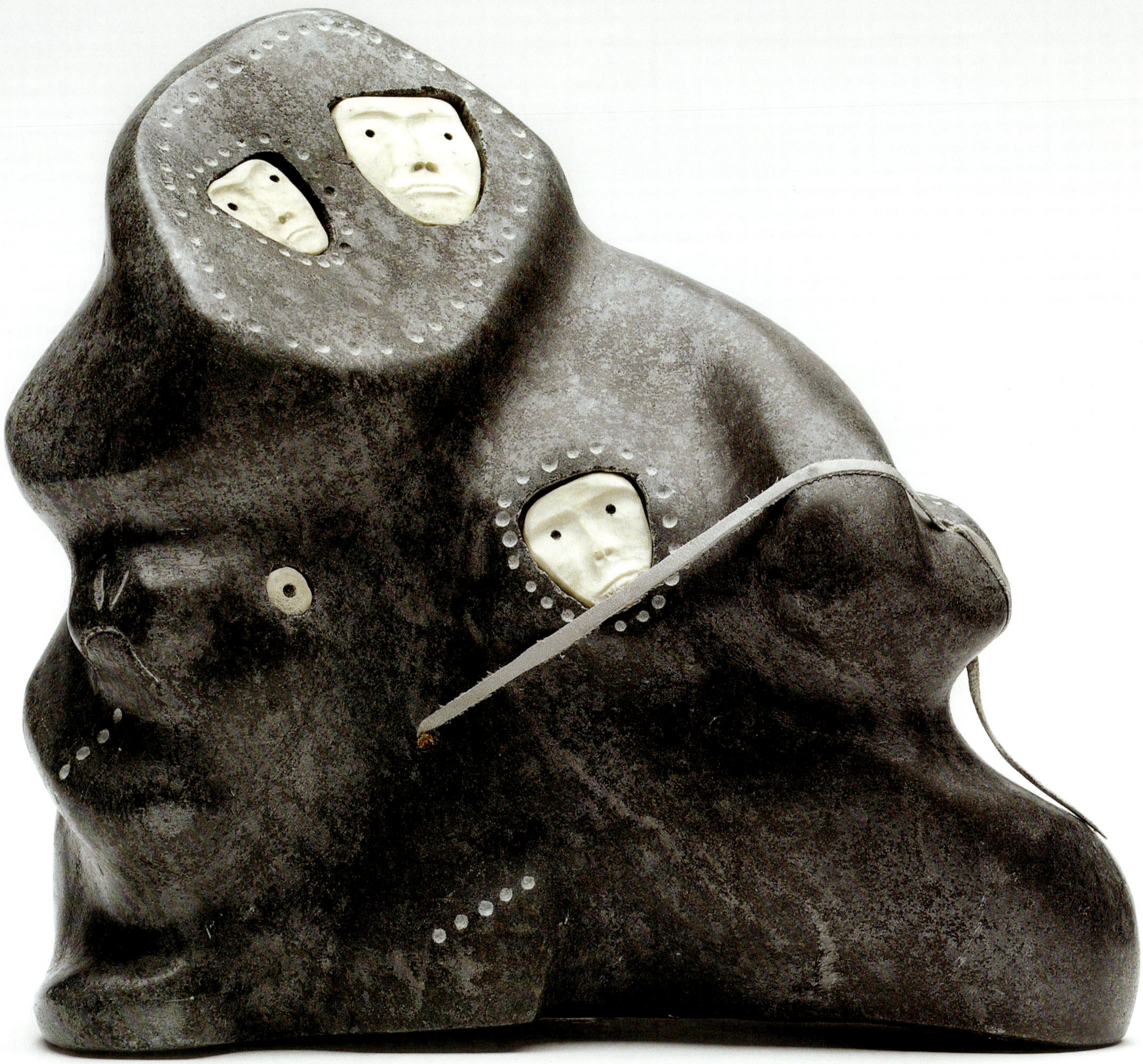

Matiusie Iyaituk, *This woman is happy to see that her son is becoming a good hunter*, 1980, darkened stone, antler, hide, colouring, wood, 21.4 x 24.6 x 22.9 cm

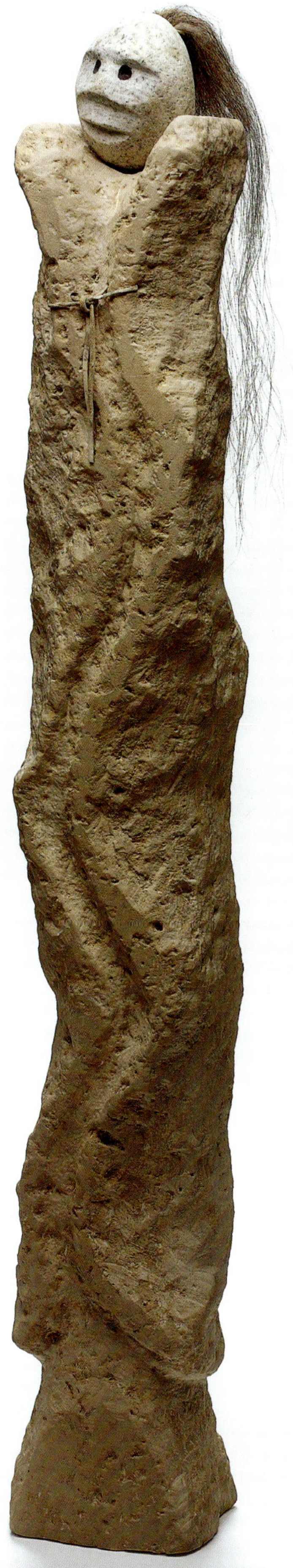

Matiusie Iyaituk, *Sheltered by Caribou Skin*, 2000, stone, hair, 110.0 x 15.0 x 14.0 cm

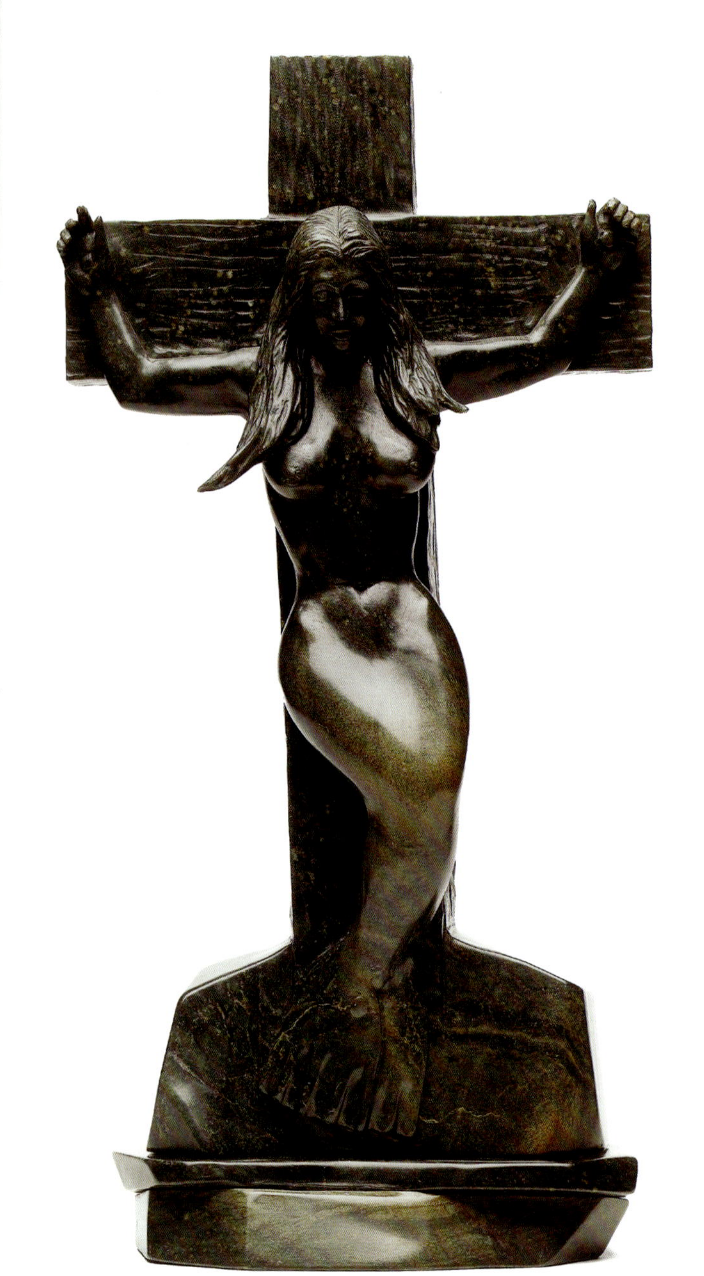

Bill Nasogaluak, *Sedna on Cross*, 2006, stone, metal, 53.8 x 27.0 x 12.0 cm

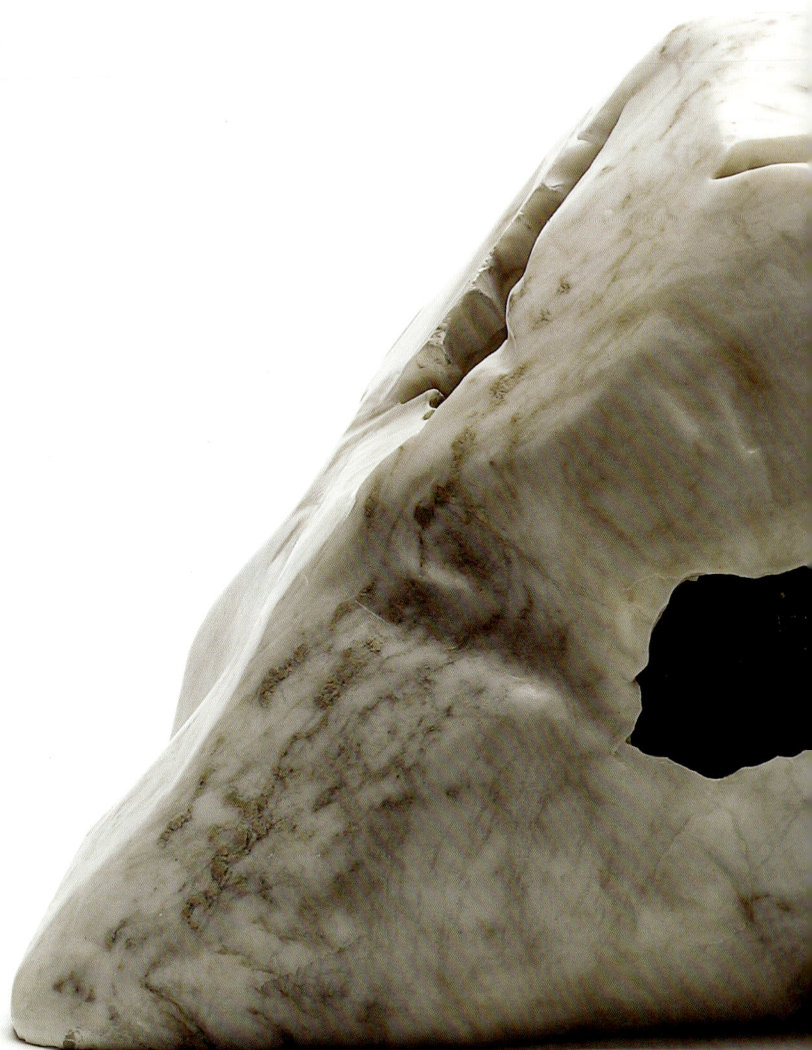

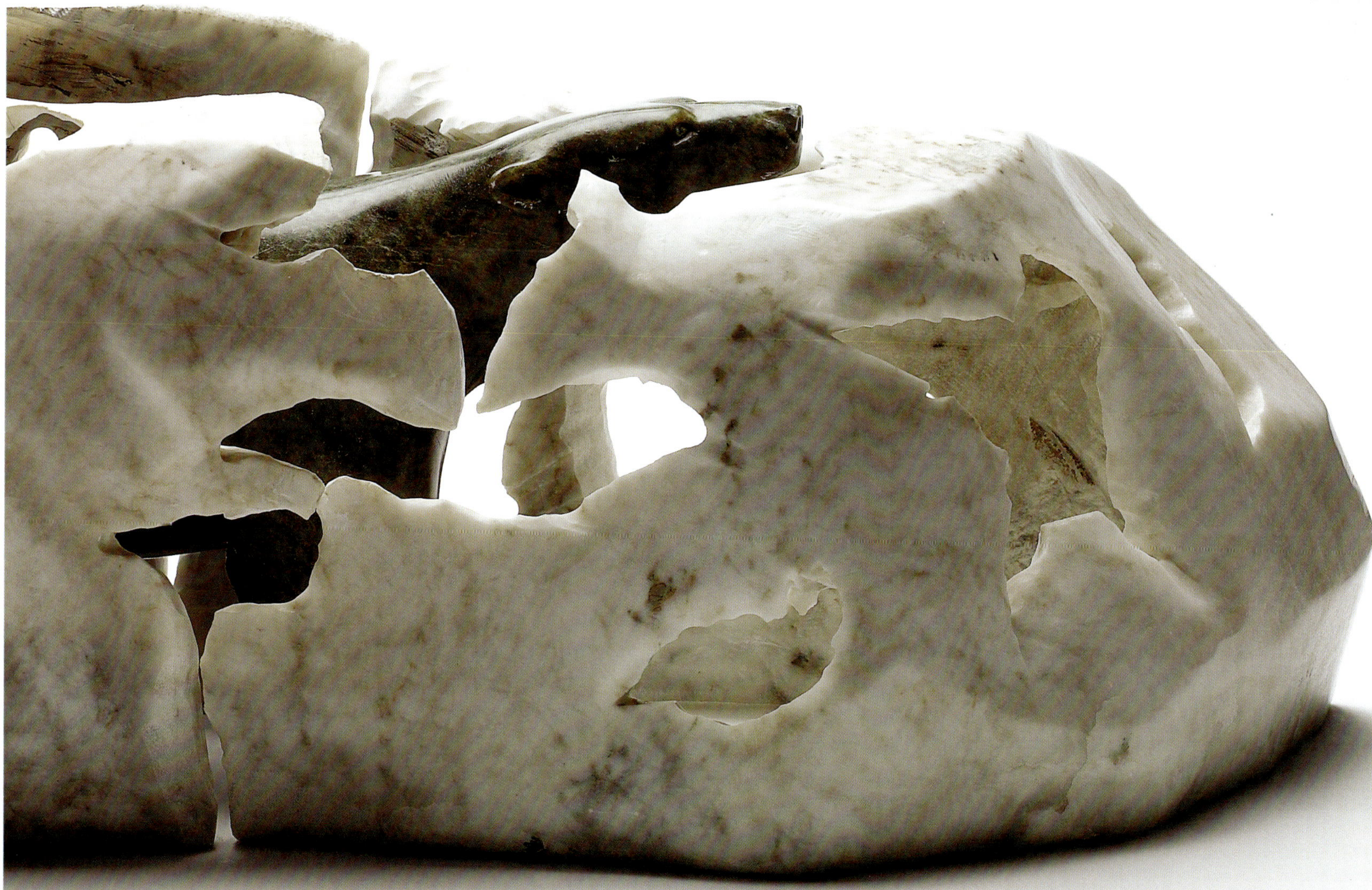

Bill Nasogaluak, *Bear Falling through Rotting Ice*,
2006, stone, 18.5 x 22.0 x 21.8 cm

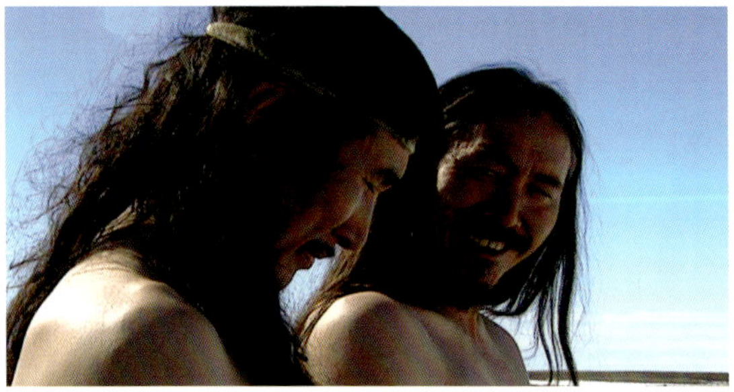

Natar Ungalaaq and Pakak Inukshuk in a still from *Atanarjuat: The Fast Runner*, on location in Igloolik, 1999

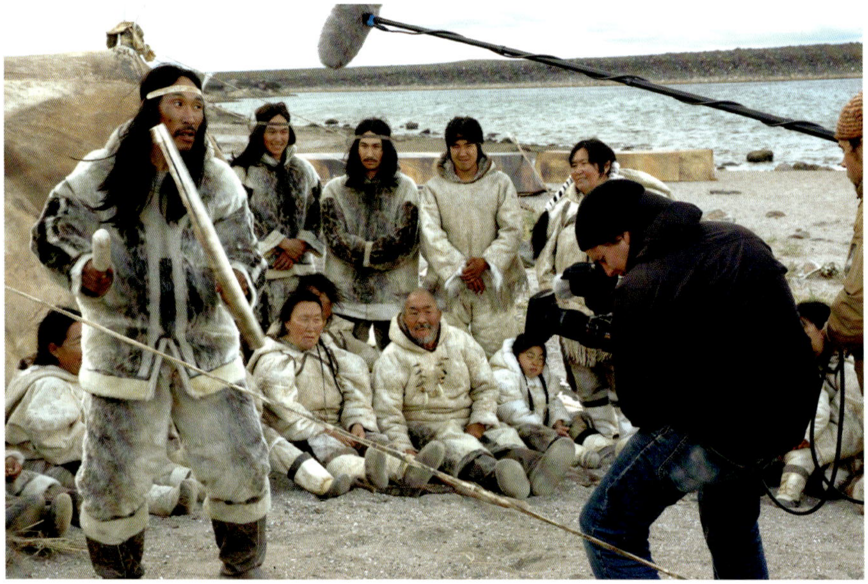

Above: Peter-Henry Arnatsiaq with drum and Félix Lajeunesse filming *Before Tomorrow*, the first feature from Arnait Video Productions, 2006

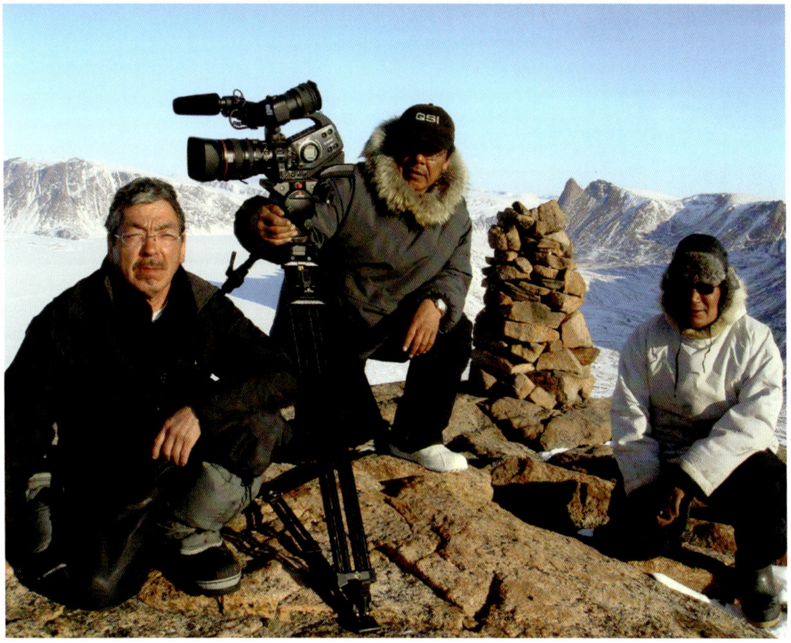

From left to right: Henry Naullaq, David Poisey and Zacharias Kunuk while shooting *Exile* in 2007

I remember a chocolate bar cost maybe ten cents, pop cost twenty-five cents.

I was not thinking of being a movie director. I just wanted to go to a movie. I was fascinated by how you kill two hours entertaining yourself. It's like when we were young, mother telling us stories to put us to asleep. Movies are stories. Filmmaking is in the same tradition as storytelling. And it's a perfect tool we're working with: you don't need paper or pen to express yourself.

I like older stories. When I started out, I'd interview the elders; it's boring when you just have talking heads. You want to see what they're talking about. I was finding that when Inuit try to express themselves in English, it's not on par with the Qallunaat. The only way to be on par is to tell stories in our own language. The camera makes you equal. You watch the story unfold. Later, somebody can sit down and write out the text. Translate it. When it's done the other way around, it doesn't make sense.

Some people say my films are too long, with too much space between the action. There are a lot of things happening in that "space in between." But a lot of non-Inuit moviegoers are not watching. In Hollywood movies, they're constantly being told, "this is coming up next" or "this is happening now." We don't do that. You don't need a lot of talking if you watch.

When I was young I was watching my old man harnessing up the dogs or fixing the sled or tying up the crosspieces. I watched how he was lighting the stove and putting snow in the kettle and how much tea he used. Just constantly watching and learning.

I get very interesting responses to my films from the elders. Now they're telling me to do more, make more films. There are lots of stories. But in this medium, you have to line up the financing, line up the right cast. Lining up the money takes time. The fun part is shooting it. And yeah, there's never enough time.

Interview with David Ruben Piqtoukun

Gerald McMaster

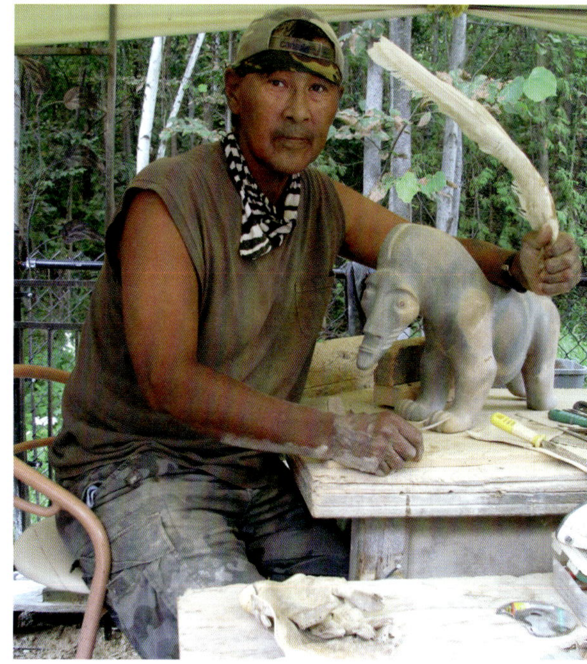

David Ruben Piqtoukun with *The Journey of the Muskox Man*, 2010

David Ruben Piqtoukun was born in Paulatuk, Northwest Territories. He's currently living in Sutton, Ontario, near Lake Simcoe. During this interview in March 2010 I was reminded that I'd first met David when he came through Regina from Vancouver on his way to Toronto. We've remained good friends since then. As he speaks about how he uses his materials, it's evident that his approach is more intellectual than his northern counterparts. He is a product of the new, yet he has managed to resolve the many contradictions that come with being Inuit of mixed ancestry and an Inuk in the modern world. – GM

My name is David Ruben Piqtoukun. Ruben is a Christian name given to my grandfather, Anghik, by the missionaries. I was named Piqtou after a family friend who passed away when I was born. I was expected to follow in his footsteps. This name is well known in the western Arctic: Piqtou translates to "wind" or "like a windstorm brewing."

I didn't use my Inuit name until I started stone carving in 1972, when I was twenty-two. I didn't feel Inuit when I first started carving; I was just a lost soul like everybody else, it seems. I was living in Calgary back then. My brother Abraham came down from Alaska and we hitchhiked through the mountains in March of 1972. When we got to Vancouver, the first thing he wanted to do was find some stone-carving materials. The only stone available at the time was Seattle steatite (soapstone). This material was blasted during asbestos mining; it always fell apart during the carving process like a cheap suitcase.

That's how I was introduced to carving. I watched Abraham as he began to carve. I was fascinated by what he was doing with the stone and decided to try my hand at stone carving also. Initially, I picked up Abraham's stone chips. That's pretty much how I started, feeling the stone first, feeling the silkiness of it. When Abraham introduced me to carving, the stones changed my whole perspective, and I thought, maybe I could make a living out of this. I started off carving little pendants with the stone chips.

I went to the library in Vancouver to look at books on Arctic animals because I'd lost any clear memory of the animals I had grown up with. I etched out owls, bears, seals and caribou, and from there I developed more three-dimensional carvings. I also looked at Inuit carvings in books. At some point, I realized I had to create my own style. I didn't look at art books for many years after that.

I started using my imagination to translate images onto the stone. It's one thing to see the image in your imagination, but to realize the image in stone, that was brutally difficult for me at the beginning. I was introduced to jade carving, which is one of the hardest carving materials on the planet. Jade carving gave me experience with grinding and cutting tools and, most important, the patience to go from start to finish with any given project.

In 1975, I met Dr. Allan Gonor from North Battleford, Saskatchewan. He encouraged me to collect stories from "Eskimo mythology" when I travelled north to Paulatuk and then to create stone carvings inspired by the stories. My work took another leap. I guess that introduction to Dr. Gonor opened many doors into my imagination. Before this introduction, I was only carving Arctic animals and people in daily activities.

I lived in Vancouver for maybe eight years. By then Abraham was getting a name for himself in the art world. When I got an invitation to go to Toronto, I drove my '69 Fleetwood Brougham Cadillac across the country. I'd decided to move to Toronto. This would prove to be a new beginning for my creative endeavours. My brother could take care of the West Coast… I would take this end of the country. Both of us would have lots of elbow room.

In my travels abroad I was introduced to many new materials and often shipped them back home. Initially, I was criticized for using exotic materials and selling my work as Inuit art. But I say, as long as it has an Inuit signature, as long as it's created by an Inuk, it's an Inuit carving. I lived in the South, but I still had the Inuit imagination. The breakthrough occurred when people started to accept who I was and what I was carving. I felt then that I had finally made my presence known. I continue to pursue my own style of work and have enjoyed stone carving on a steady basis.

When I work, I work alone. I am distracted easily by other people; it destroys my carving rhythm. I like to study the materials for long periods of time before I tackle them and also during the carving process. I have a unique dialogue with the subject I am working on. I am always questioning why I am doing this or that with the materials. At some point the stone speaks to me in a silent kind of dialogue, and I learn something new that I did not know when I started the carving. I am always learning something about my "Eskimo past"; words of my youth come back to me, opening doors to keep pursuing my creative endeavours and keeping my imagination sharp. This kind of feedback is vital in my carving and sculpting process. Initially, it really helped to use exotic materials. Not the best materials, but a broad range: jade, marble, granite, feather-rock, alabaster, limestone and all varieties of soapstone and other carvable materials. You need a broad range of tools, too. For harder materials, you have to use tools that are carbide-tipped and tempered for durability. If the material is too hard for cutting with a bowsaw, I pre-cut with diamond-edged cutting saws and then proceed with my hammer and chisels. After that, it's all hand rasping. I use coarse to super-fine sandpaper (1500 grit) before the final polishing of any stone. This effect will give the finished carving a "teardrop" or silky texture. I also highlight certain parts of the stone with the polishing technique and leave a natural raw texture whenever it may be required.

Creating things changes you dramatically. It changes your way of thinking, how you see the world, how you see other people and their art. Right from the start, I used stone bases. People were just shaking their heads, saying if it doesn't balance by itself, the value is not there. So I have to balance them all the way through. After a long period of trial and error, it just becomes natural. You can feel where the centre of gravity is for the best possible balance. You're constantly adjusting things in the process of stone carving and sculpting. Execution for final display is vital.

My earliest recollection of knowing I was an Eskimo, well, it seemed like we were the only people on the planet—we were pretty well isolated. Around our village was a no man's land, but that isolation did not last very long in my youth. I was one of the kids who were "shovelled off" from our families and taken on a plane to a residential school. I was five years old. We were forced to speak English, dress differently and eat foods that we had never tasted before. It took two years before I really accepted that change. But in the end I had no choice.

Before I was taken away, I could speak our language fluently. But that part of my youth is now, sadly, forever dormant. It's like a mysterious vault that I can't open. Little specks of words come out every now and then. Carving is the only thing that allows me to know who I am. I'm still alive because of it.

The first place I was taken is called Aklavik; from there we were all relocated to Inuvik—both are in the Mackenzie Delta of the western Arctic region, Northwest Territories. The exhibition that I did a number of years ago (1996–98) was a recollection of that period. I think of it as my Blue Period. I forced myself to recall various parts of my life journey; I'm talking about going into a dark zone and struggling to get back out.

In the mid-1950s there was very little air travel. In the summertime my people were still nomadic, following migrating animals. You couldn't just call up and say,

"Hey, where are you?" During that period in my life, I was always angry. My hands were always fisted, ready to grapple with anyone. The nuns or supervisors punished me for my frequent outbursts. I spent about twelve years in residential schools. I left the Arctic on August 8, 1968, when I was seventeen.

I wanted to explore the world beyond the Arctic. When I was about twelve years old, I studied the map of North America and drew a line from Inuvik to New York. Mysteriously, the line cuts through Toronto. This mental routing has since become a reality; it's my gateway to the world in search of new ideas and new materials.

Where I come from, if you're darker-skinned, people isolate you. Even within my family, I was the darkest. Most of my brothers and sisters were fair-skinned. On my mother's side, my great-grandfather was a whaler with African and Portuguese ancestry. That's where I also picked up the travelling gene, I guess. He travelled by sea in search of the big whales. I'm exploring the world by air, searching for something even more elusive. What I'm searching for is anybody's guess. I do not rightly know, but maybe the answer is inside a special stone.

There are many factors as to why I do what I do—incorporating materials from abroad, using state-of-the-art tools. At one point, I couldn't afford the sandpaper or the tools, but everything comes in due course. I take after my father, Isoktaq. He would find a piece of a bone or something and see things in it. He always collected and stored materials. He made beautiful ulus out of old saws. [An ulu is a short-handled knife with a curved blade, used by women.] He'd carve a fish from a piece of bone and put the fish handle on the ulu—that made them stand out as far as art was concerned. He carved into his late eighties. Billy Isoktaq Ruben was my father's name. Isok for short. My mother's maiden name was Bertha Thrasher. Her full name was Bertha Badda Qagun Ruben. She was awarded Good Woman of the Year in the Northern Summer Games for many years. Also, she was famous for having so many children. There were seventeen of us.

In 1972, when I went to the travelling exhibition *Masters of the Arctic*, a strange, mythic carving by Osuitok really fascinated me. That work whacked me on the head and awoke the sleeping imagination of my early carving days. Also, Andy Miki, Tiktak and a great many of the other artists in the exhibition were a great influence on me. As far as Andy Miki was concerned, I liked his simplicity. Less is more, whether you're working monumental or on a smaller scale. Having looked through the catalogue and studied the different styles of work and the variety of materials used, I thought to myself, "Maybe one day, I'll be an artist like that, and my work will travel the world in exhibitions." If they can do it, I can make a serious attempt, I thought. That became my dream, my goal, which led to my adventure in the arts.

I guess the person who influenced me the most was my father. When he worked, he got down and dirty. He had a hacksaw and an old snow-goose broom that I still have. Snow-goose wings and other bird's wings were commonly used by my people to keep work areas clean and tidy. I think it's a snow-goose wing that he used to brush away the stone dust. He gave it to me a few years ago on my last trip home, before he passed away. I think he knew he was at the end of his days. I learned from him that if you're feeling weak, rather than pick your nose or scratch your ass, just go and do what you have to do. Keep your focus on what is at hand. Avoid distractions that may redirect your thoughts. Do the job at hand before moving on to the next one!

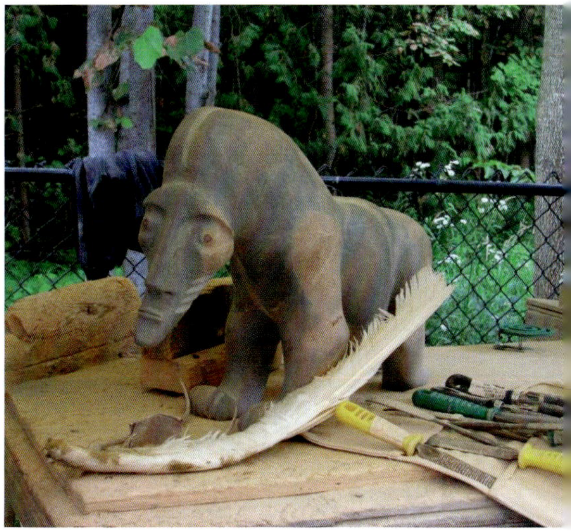

David Ruben Piqtoukun's father, who was also a carver, gave him this snow-goose wing

Many of my carvings come from stories I collected in my early days. Parents, aunts and uncles, people that recall these stories, a lot of my people have passed away. I have to learn how to interpret these stories or reinterpret them to make them work for me. The stories come alive because you can see them now in the carving. Before, it was just oral. Stories that my parents recalled, and their parents recalled, and so on through the generations.

One story can open up the whole imagination. Also, the dream world is very important to me. I'm always searching, I guess. At some point I found my identity through my work. I may not look Inuit, but I sure feel it, and my work shows it.

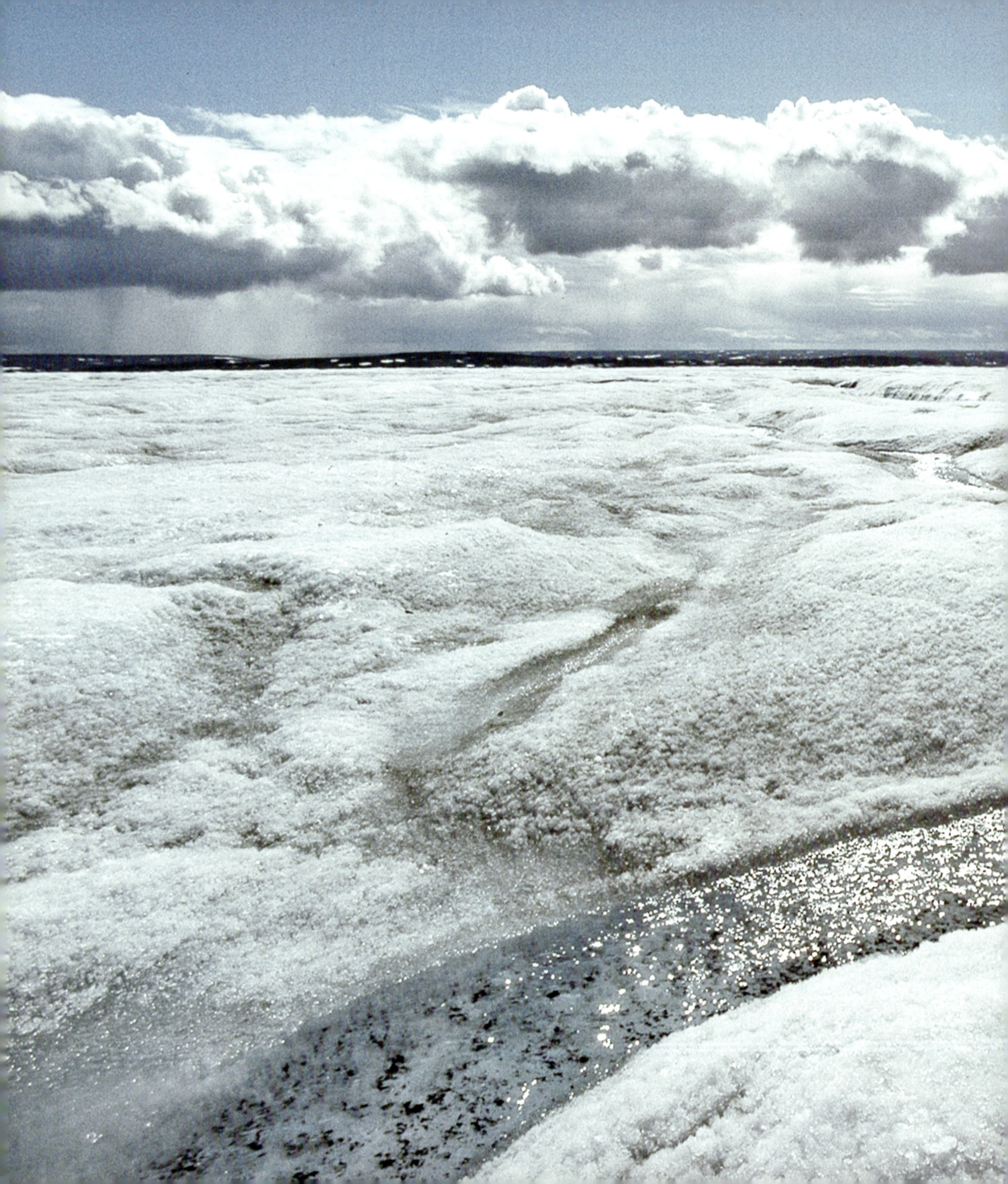

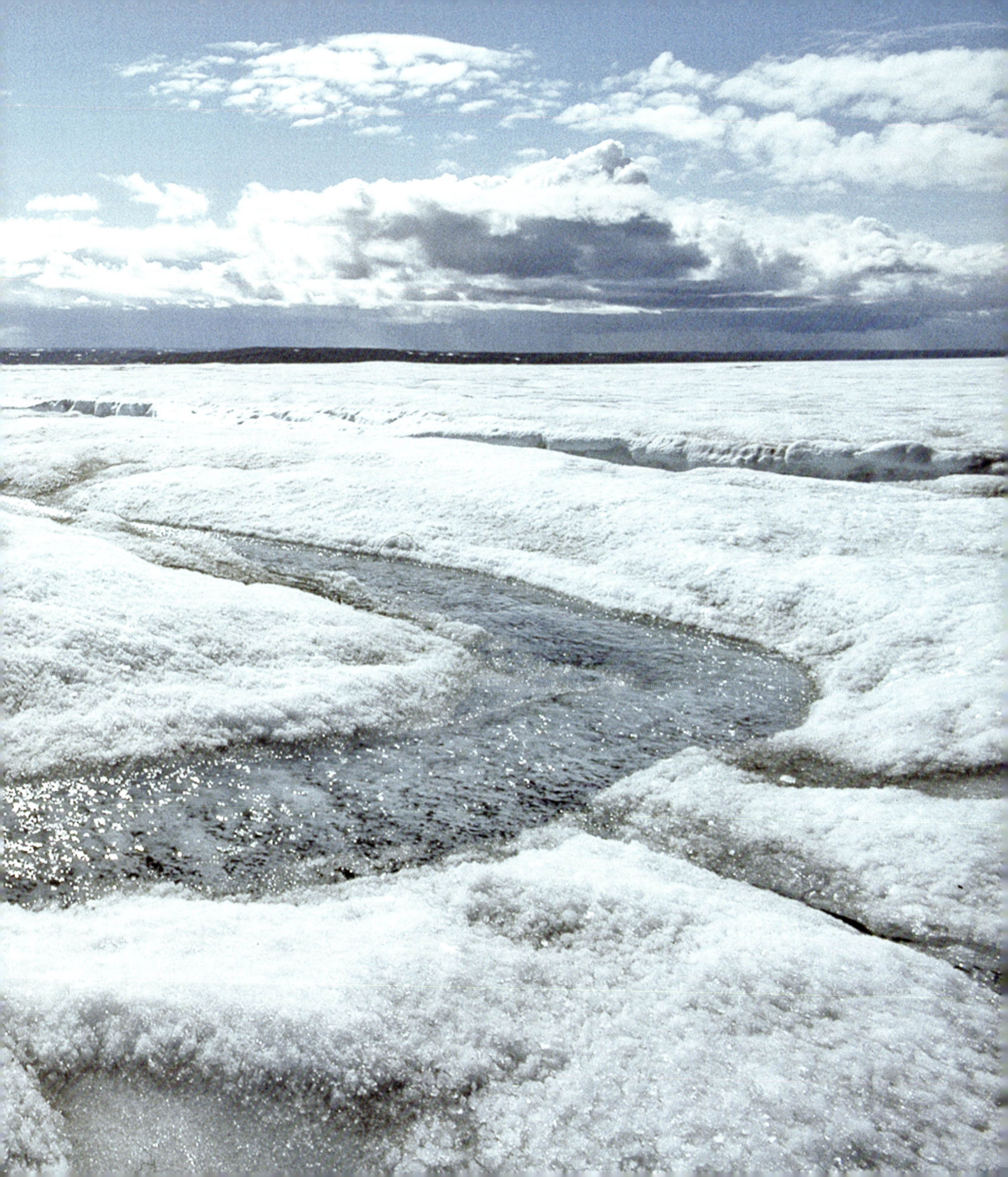

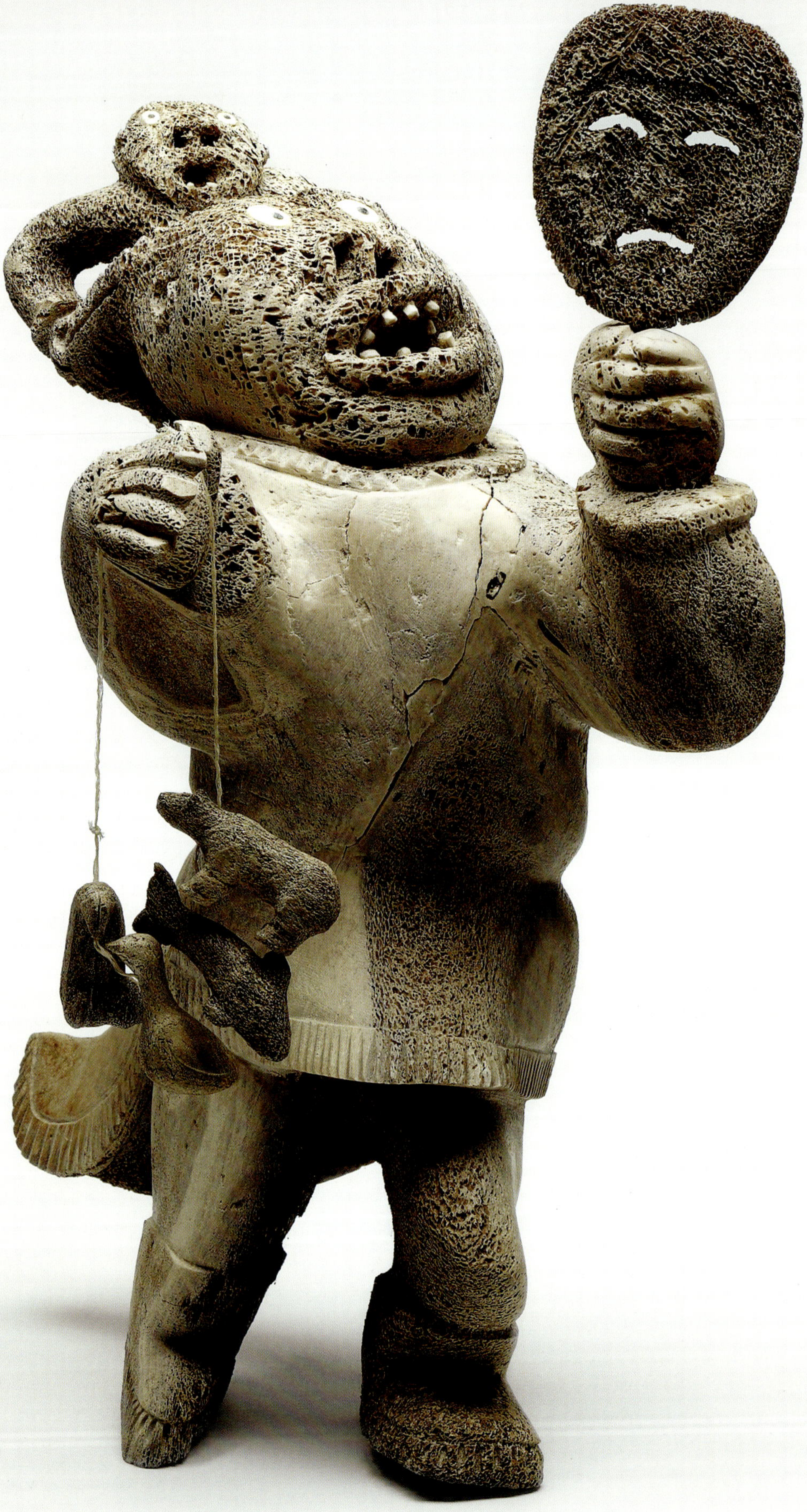

Afterword

John Ralston Saul

My life divides into before and after a meeting in Inuvik early in the spring of 1976. I was there as the young assistant to the chair of Petro-Canada, Maurice Strong. He was already the great father figure of the international environmental movement, and he knew the North well. It was my first trip to the Arctic.

He had organized a conversation with the leaders of the local hunters and trappers associations – probably the Inuvialuit, Dene and Gwich'in. I went into the meeting with my PhD on my brain and my Western certainties that there must be some way I could be helpful to these middle-aged, less educated locals. In other words, I went in with the attitude of a perfect fool – someone enamoured of those Western ideas of progress that have brought us into the world of global warming. Fortunately, Maurice was the boss and so I had to keep my mouth shut.

Ninety minutes later I came out deeply confused. The entire conversation about the Arctic, the environment and development had been reframed by these *locals* into a completely different philosophical approach – one that avoided Manichean false choices, linear logic and pretensions of rationality. Instead they had restructured the whole conversation around a far broader context in which humans were part of the place, not just staring down on it with godly superiority. From an artist's point of view, this was the precise opposite of a beaux-arts approach to imagining reality.

Nobody at school or university had ever mentioned to me that there were other intellectual frameworks that could easily trump that of the West. Put another way, the hunters and trappers were right. And they were postmodern, perhaps because their approach was non-linear and spatial. As for me, along with my doctorate, I was weighed down by the Western linear approach, which suddenly felt particularly heavy and strangely old-fashioned – a bit like nineteenth-century industrial theory.

The arguments about Inuit art and the effects of modernity on that art, as they are explained in this book, deal precisely with this standard Western-imposed conundrum. We see ourselves as the custodians of the idea of progress and therefore of authenticity. It follows that we assume ourselves to be inherently authentic in our own modernizations. We are free to change as we wish. But others are limited – in our linear mindset – to our anthropological rules. If they move off those modernization trails that we have defined as authentic for them, well then, they no longer are.

Interestingly enough, the Canadian people think all of this is nonsense. Over the last half century they have effortlessly abandoned European ideas of what constitutes art and embraced a fascinating combination of Inuit art, Northwest Coast First Nations art, Emily Carr and the Group of Seven, along with near cousins such as Jean-Paul Riopelle and Paul-Émile Borduas. And so millions of Canadians – who know no Inuit or First Nations people, have never been to the North and have probably seen little of the West Coast – somehow feel comfortable in their emotions and imagination seeing themselves through these shapes and colours.

Some of what draws them is not art but tourist-level imitation. Such popularization is common to all art forms everywhere in the world. What actually draws them is the great art that shapes the whole phenomenon of how the world might be seen – the great art that makes the bad art and commercial exploitations possible. From the masterpieces to the plaster copies, these are the images and forms that express the national psyche.

When at home, I sit every day in a room with a large Judas Ullulaq sculpture. A masterpiece. In my office I have a little collection of other Gjoa Haven sculptures. You could argue about where in the evolution of Inuit art the Gjoa Haven school belongs. More to the point, Ullulaq was able to do what those hunters and trappers had done for me in the 1970s. He expressed the context. In the piece I have, he found the relationship between the whale bone he used and the subject of a woman picking lice out of her child's hair – just as Michelangelo found meaning in the marble from which he produced the agony of Mary with her dead son.

What I find exciting is the energy and eagerness with which Inuit artists take on the world as it changes around them. To ask whether they are influenced by the West is to ask the same old Western

Judas Ullulaq, *Shaman with Amulets and Ceremonial Mask*, 1985, whale bone, antler, stone, sinew, 53.5 x 26.5 x 14.3 cm

egocentric question. With the spatial approach, which I believe is still at the core of their new work, Inuit artists are grabbing hold of everything around them and expressing its context. They are using the context, not being used by it. This is true even of utilitarian objects, like the spoons that are coming out of the silver program at Nunavut Arctic College in Iqaluit. The young artists are producing not decorated spoons but sculptures that can be used as spoons.

Not long after the new AGO opened, with its deeply reconceived approach to exhibiting Canadian art, I took the German novelist Bernhard Schlink along to have a look. I explained to him that under the leadership of people like Gerald McMaster, the AGO had reimagined what showing art meant. It wasn't simply that they were presenting Inuit and First Nations art with Western-style art. It was that the way of showing it all was spatial and in a broad context, which belonged to Aboriginal philosophy. So it was not linear, nor even sequential. It was not tied up into neat little schools. Behind the whole approach lay an idea of our relationship to the place of which we were an integral part.

In the old AGO, you got to the Henry Moores via a special ramp, as if rising in isolation to a temple of creative genius. And of course he was a creative genius. On arrival in the gallery you were properly overwhelmed. Now you come up the central stairs and turn right into a series of galleries of indigenous art. The Inuit sculptures set the tone, including a large piece by Judas Ullulaq. It was magical, and I couldn't get Bernhard to move on toward the Moores. We worked our way gradually forward and when we finally reached the Moore gallery his reaction, like mine, was quite simple. Well, of course! Moore now made perfect sense. He was a genius, but in a context of other geniuses who were masters of what most people think of as his highly personal approach. He had in effect been placed in a context – a millennial Inuit context – that made his meaning seem normal.

And that is what this book does. Through great art it draws us into the context of a world – our world – in which we, like these sculptures and images, are one with this place.

Artists' Biographies

Susan Gustavison, with Sarah Chate

Notes:

1. The current nomenclature for Inuit place names has been used throughout the artists' biographies to avoid repetitive clarification and confusion for the contemporary reader. The communities in what is now Nunavut were previously part of the Northwest Territories. Established in 1999, Nunavut is the newest and largest Canadian territory. East of Nunavut, Nunavik (formerly known as Arctic Quebec or Nouveau Québec) extends south to the 55th parallel and comprises the northern third of Quebec's total land mass. Nunavik will be fully independent of Quebec in 2013. Technically it is self-governed by all the people of Nunavik, but Inuit constitute the overwhelming majority in the territory.

2. An artist's place of death, where applicable, is in almost all instances given as the community where the artist resided. It is possible that in some cases the artist actually died in a hospital in a location such as Yellowknife, Edmonton, Montreal or Toronto.

Akeeaktashuk

b. 1898 Inukjuak, Nunavik; d. 1954 Grise Fiord, Nunavut

Among the Inuit, Akeeaktashuk was known as Isakallak or Isa. As early as 1949 Akeeaktashuk was already a prolific, known artist with an identifiable style at a time when the identity of most Inuit artists was still a mystery to anyone outside the Arctic. He even appeared in *Time* magazine in 1954. Akeeaktashuk was a camp leader at Uugarsiuvik, about thirteen kilometres north of Inukjuak. Although he was not an outstanding hunter, most of his subjects are engaged in some aspect of the hunt. His sculptures have an endearing, almost winsome quality; they are full and rounded, much like the artist, whose nickname was "Fatty." Akeeaktashuk was included in the earliest landmark exhibitions of the modern era, including *Eskimo Art* at the National Gallery of Canada in 1951 and the *Eskimo Carvings: Coronation Exhibition* at Gimpel Fils gallery in London, England, in 1953. In 1953 Akeeaktashuk's family was one of seven transferred to Craig Harbour in the Far North, and shortly thereafter to Grise Fiord. The following year he died in a hunting accident, dragged by a walrus into freezing water. (SG)

Latcholassie Akesuk

b. 1919 camp on South Baffin Island, Nunavut; d. 2000 Cape Dorset, Nunavut

Latcholassie Akesuk was the son of Tudlik (1890–1966). Both were well-loved Cape Dorset sculptors active from the earliest years of carving in Cape Dorset. Latcholassie's style – unique among that of his peers in Cape Dorset – is minimalist and abstract but also very expressive. He is known for his almost exclusive preoccupation with birds as a subject, often executed on quite a large scale. His mastery received early recognition with his inclusion in the 1953 *Eskimo Carvings: Coronation Exhibition* at Gimpel Fils in London, England. In addition, six of his sculptures were included in *Sculpture / Inuit: Masterworks of the Canadian Arctic*, an exhibition that toured internationally from 1971 to 1973. In 1999, the artist had a solo exhibition at Spirit Wrestler Gallery, Vancouver. Surprisingly for such a major artist, it was only the third solo exhibition of his career. (SG)

Paulusikotak Alaku

b. 1923 Salluit, Nunavik; d. 1971 Salluit, Nunavik

Paulusikotak Alaku was an artist and community leader; he served on local councils and was a member of the board of directors of the Co-op. Alaku's carvings often incorporate broad, coarse incisions to delineate detail – a technique common to works from the area owing to the hard quality of the local stone. He died in a tragic hunting accident when he was only 48. One of his five children, Susie Angutigirk Kakyok, has become an artist. (SC)

Marc Alikaswa

b. 1928 Arviat, Nunavut; d. 2008 Arviat, Nunavut

Sculptor Marc Alikaswa's carvings display a minimalist aesthetic, emblematic of the Arviat area. Underlying themes of spirituality likely pay homage to the influence of his father, a respected shaman. (SC)

Amidlak

b. 1897 camp near Inukjuak, Nunavik; d. 1961, Inukjuak, Nunavik

This early artist is thought to have been one of the first sculptors to create work for the government's art initiative in the Inukjuak area. The works attributed to Amidlak often have animal subject matter. He was known for using inlays of various stone and bone. (SC)

Davidialuk Alasua Amittu

b. 1910 Nunagirnaraq camp, Nunavik; d. 1976 Puvirnituq, Nunavik

Davidialuk Alasua Amittu's family had various camps in the Puvirnituq area, including a winter camp on a small island in eastern Hudson Bay where he was born. Another camp was at the mouth of the Qugaaluk River, where his cousin Joe Talirunili's family was located. Davidialiuk is believed to have been carving during the 1950s, but no sculptures are known from that time. By the 1960s, however, he was active both in graphics and in sculpture. His prints, about ninety in all, figured prominently in the Puvirnituq print collections from 1962 to 1982. Regardless of the medium, Davidialuk brought all his skills as a master storyteller to his art. A narrative drawn from legends passed down from generation to generation dominates his drawings, prints and sculptures. Davidialuk earned early recognition with his inclusion in the Toronto-Dominion Bank collection and in important exhibitions, such as *Sculpture / Inuit: Masterworks of the Canadian Arctic* of 1971–73 and *The Inuit Print* of 1977–82. The artist was honoured with a solo exhibition, *La Vie et l'oeuvre de Davidialuk Alasuaq*, at the Musée du Québec in 1979. The same year, Davidialuk's personal reminiscences were published in *La Parole changée en pierre*, a multi-year collaboration with Bernard Saladin d'Anglure. (SG)

Augustin Anaittuq

b. 1935 Kasigarsiorvik, Nunavut; d. 1992 Kugaaruk, Nunavut

Augustin Anaittuq, born in 1935, was actively creating from the 1970s until his death in 1992. As is characteristic to the Kitikmeot region, Anaittuq created very detailed intricate carvings from ivory, antler and whale bone. Anaittuq's subject matter is focused on human and animal forms that are fanciful, mystical and sometimes ominous. (SC)

Josephee Angnako

b. 1900 Pangnirtung, Nunavut; d. 1966 Pangnirtung, Nunavut

Josephee was among the first generation of Inuit artists. Although he was carving during this early period, his work has a contemporary aesthetic as he tended to create works that documented his own experiences. (SC)

Luke Anguhadluq

b. 1895 near Chantrey Inlet, Nunavut; d. 1982 Baker Lake, Nunavut

Luke Anguhadluq was a great hunter and camp leader among the Utkuhikhlingmiut. In 1923, the Danish anthropologist Knud Rasmussen wrote of meeting Anguhadluq at Itivnaarjuk camp and noted his quiet but unquestioned leadership. When Anguhadluq and his family moved from the land into the hamlet of Baker Lake in 1961, he continued to live in a tent or an igloo for another six years before finally moving into permanent housing. His earliest graphic work, dating from 1960, has not generally survived. He was most prolific from 1969 onward; from 1970 to 1982, his work was a mainstay of the annual Baker Lake print collections. Although his work has been extensively exhibited in both small and large group exhibitions, the highlights were *Tuu'luq / Anguhadluq* at the Winnipeg Art Gallery in 1976 and *From the Centre: The Drawings of Luke Anguhadluq* at the Art Gallery of Ontario in 1993. His depictions of traditional life on the land have become iconic. Multiple perspectives and selective scale are hallmarks of his spare style. Anguhadluq's third wife was Marion Tuu'luq and his cousin was Jessie Oonark, both famous Baker Lake artists in their own right. At his request, after his death he was taken by dog sled for burial atop his favourite hill. (SG)

Tony Anguhalluq

b. 1970 Baker Lake, Nunavut

Tony Anguhalluq, an adopted son of the late Luke Anguhadluq and Marion Tuu'luq, is a relative newcomer to the art world. His first exposure to creating art was a printmaking workshop offered in Baker Lake from 1995 to 1997. It gave both experienced artists and newcomers alike an opportunity to experiment with a range of printmaking techniques. Since then Anguhalluq has continued drawing, in addition to working in construction. His drawings in pencil crayon are fresh and expansive, covering the entire page with landscape conventions of his own making. Aerial viewpoints combined with other perspectives depict a landscape that dwarfs the human figures. These humans reflect the reality of today's world, equipped as they are with outboard motors, modern fishing gear, snowmobiles and rifles. Anguhalluq usually includes lengthy titles, in English, at the bottom of the image. His work has been championed by Marion Scott Gallery in Vancouver, which included him in a 2006 group exhibition and also in three solo shows, *Tony Anguhalluq: Recent Drawings* and *Tony Anguhalluq: Drawings and Sculptures* in 2007 and *Contours: New Landscape Drawings by Tony Anguhalluq* in 2010. (SG)

Margaret Uyauperq Aniksak

b. 1905 Arviat, Nunavut; d. 1993 Arviat, Nunavut

Margaret Uyauperq Aniksak began carving when she was in her sixties. Aniksak focuses on motherhood and community in her sculpture, themes for which Arviat artists are known. Her body of work deviates from that of the typical Arviat artist, being frequently more detailed and naturalistic. (SC)

Luke Anowtalik

b. 1932 Ennadai Lake, Nunavut; d. 2006 Arviat, Nunavut

Luke Anowtalik's playful nature was visible not only in his infectious smile but also in his whimsical carvings and drawings. Anowtalik's beginnings were difficult. He belonged to the Ihalmiut, an inland group of Inuit, who relied heavily on caribou hunting to provide the necessities of life. But because of weak hunting seasons and poorly thought-out government relocation programs that moved the group to areas around the Kivalliq region, starvation became a major threat to the Ihalmiut people. During this time Anowtalik began carving for income and, in the 1950s, permanently settled in Arviat, Nunavut. Anowtalik's artwork is intertwined with his Ihalmiut heritage as he focuses on humans and caribou and their relationship to each other, often morphing the two. He is best known for his carvings of faces that seem to emerge from the stone and his fanciful characters made out of caribou antler. (SC)

Mathew Aqigaaq

b. 1940 Kazan River Falls, Nunavut; resides in Baker Lake, Nunavut

Mathew Aqigaaq greatly admired the artwork of his brother, David Ikuutaq (1929–1984), and Barnabus Arnasungaaq (b. 1924). As with other Baker Lake carvings, Aqigaaq's sculpture is characterized by bulbous figures in dark stone. Aqigaaq's purpose is not only to depict scenes of daily life but to be evocative of the struggles and joys within the larger Inuit community. Starvation, identity and spiritual connection between humans and animals are themes this artist has tackled in his subtle manner. (SC)

George Arluk

b. 1949 Winnipeg, Manitoba

George Arluk has been a fixture in the Inuit art world for some forty years. He started carving stone in his home community of Rankin Inlet, absorbing the experience of elders John Kavik and John Tiktak. Arluk, a restless individual, has also lived in Arviat, Baker Lake, Churchill and latterly in Winnipeg. His unique style, virtually abstract in nature, is characterized by undulating ripples and sinuous curves along the outer silhouette of the stone. His first exhibition, a solo show at the Winnipeg Art Gallery in 1968, was followed by another in 1969 at the University of Alberta in Edmonton. He has had other solo exhibitions in Toronto, Montreal and Mannheim, Germany. In addition, his work has been included in numerous group exhibitions including *Rankin Inlet / Kangirlliniq* at the Winnipeg Art Gallery in 1981. (SG)

Karoo Ashevak

b. 1940 south of Gjoa Haven, Nunavut; d. 1974 Taloyoak, Nunavut

Karoo Ashevak was a young boy when his family moved to the Taloyoak, or Spence Bay, area in the late 1940s, following his mother's passing. He did not move into the community of Taloyoak itself until 1968. Charlie Ugyuk, an uncle, was an important early carving mentor to Karoo. Karoo won a prize in a sculpture competition organized by the Canadian Eskimo Arts Council to mark the centennial of the Northwest Territories in 1970. In 1972 and 1973, he burst onto the art scene following acclaimed solo exhibitions at The Innuit Gallery of Eskimo Art in Toronto and Lippel Gallery in Montreal, and then *Karoo Ashevak: Spirits* at the American Indian Arts Center in New York. His sculpture was widely praised and sought after in all art circles, not just among those interested in Inuit art. And his evocative style strongly influenced many other artists throughout the Kitikmeot region. He worked extensively in whale bone, creating meticulously finished and wildly imaginative composite sculptures. Karoo tended to work through a subject repeatedly, sometimes as many as six or eight times, before moving on to a new idea. He made about 250 sculptures before he died with his wife, Doris, in a house fire. (SG)

Kenojuak Ashevak

b. 1927 Ikirasak camp, near Cape Dorset, Nunavut

Kenojuak Ashevak is quite simply the most famous and acclaimed Inuit artist of all time. She has had a hugely successful, prolific career marked by numerous commissions and awards, including Companion of the Order of Canada, honorary degrees from Queen's University and the University of Toronto, the Lifetime Achievement Award from the National Aboriginal Achievement Foundation in 1995 and the Governor General's Award in Visual and Media Arts in 2008. Kenojuak received her early art training from artist Harold Pfeiffer at the Parc Savard Hospital in Quebec City where she was treated for tuberculosis from 1952 to 1955. On her return to Cape Dorset, she was encouraged to draw by James Houston when he spotted a sealskin design that she had appliquéd onto a leather bag. This design was the genesis of her well-known 1959 print *Rabbit Eating Seaweed*. Kenojuak is known for her many interpretations of birds, using the shape to investigate line and colour in infinite variety rather than the bird as subject per se. In addition to her thousands of drawings and hundreds of prints, Kenojuak is also an accomplished sculptor. Her son Annago Ashevak was also a very inventive, talented sculptor. In 1986, Kenojuak had a major retrospective exhibition of her work, including a book by Jean Blodgett, at the Art Gallery of Ontario. (SG)

Kiugak Ashoona

b. 1933 Tariugajak camp, South Baffin Island, Nunavut

Kiugak Ashoona has been a prominent Cape Dorset sculptor for more than sixty years. Beginning in 1947 with the sale of his first sculpture – carved from a walrus tusk – to the Baffin Trading Company in Cape Dorset, Kiugak has excelled. Since 1953 his work has been included in more than eighty exhibitions in Canada and abroad. Several of his sculptures were presented to Queen Elizabeth II in Stratford in 1959, and one of his Sedna sculptures was featured on a Canadian stamp in 1980. He received the National Aboriginal Achievement Award in Arts in 1997. In 1999 the depth of his achievement was recognized when he received the annual Canada Council for the Arts Molson Prize, which includes $50,000 prize money. His sculpture, which is primarily concerned with the human figure, is quite flamboyant in composition but always well carved and finished. Other subjects have included fantastic figures, especially in his work of the 1960s. Kiugak is from a family of prominent artists, including his mother, Pitseolak Ashoona, and his siblings – Qaqaq, Koomwartok and Ottochie Ashoona and Napachie Pootoogook. In the current generation of artists, his daughters Shuvinai and Goota are active artists. (SG)

Pitseolak Ashoona

b. 1904 Nottingham Island, Nunavut; d. 1983 Cape Dorset, Nunavut

Pitseolak Ashoona was born on Nottingham Island when her family was en route from Salluit to the Cape Dorset area. Her family settled at Ikirasak, a camp about a day's journey from Cape Dorset (it was also the camp of Peter Pitseolak). She and her husband, Ashoona, followed a very traditional lifestyle, and they moved many times in a year. She bore seventeen children, five of whom became successful artists in their own right. Pitseolak moved into Cape Dorset in the mid-1950s. Although she was initially apprehensive of taking up drawing, seeing the drawings of "the old ways" by her cousin Kiakshuk gave her the confidence to continue. She was one of the early and prolific contributors to the West Baffin Eskimo Co-operative archive of drawings, supplying over 6,400 in all. Daily, she would arrive at the Co-op with a drawing or two to sell, transported in a scarf for protection from the wind. For fourteen years, Pitseolak was well represented in every Cape Dorset print collection. She depicted life as she knew it and with a joyous quality. She was elected to the Royal Canadian Academy of Arts in 1974 and received the Order of Canada in 1977. A 1971 book by Dorothy Eber, *Pitseolak: Pictures out of My Life*, and two 1975 films, *The Way We Live Today* and *Spirits and Monsters*, are tributes to her creativity. (SG)

Qaqaq Ashoona

b. 1928 Cape Dorset area, Nunavut; d. 1996 Cape Dorset area, Nunavut

Qaqaq Ashoona was the oldest son of the famed artist Pitseolak Ashoona. Like his siblings (Kiugak, Koomwartok and Ottochie Ashoona and Napachie Pootoogook), Qaqaq became a prominent artist. He began carving stone at Kangiqsujuaq camp soon after James Houston's arrival in Cape Dorset. He was not particularly prolific in the early years, but over the span of his career, he created an impressive body of work, which has been widely collected in public and private collections alike. His sculptures are often substantial in size. He claimed to be the first artist to use the white marble from the surface deposit to the east of Cape Dorset. With his wife, Mayoreak, Qaqaq was one of the few Inuit to continue to live on the land during summer and winter in a camp east of Cape Dorset called Saturituk. As a result, he continued to use only hand tools to fashion his work. His wife, Mayoreak, was a graphic artist, as is their daughter Siassie Kenneally. Qaqaq died at his outpost camp in November 1996. (SG)

Shuvinai Ashoona

b. 1961 Cape Dorset, Nunavut

Shuvinai Ashoona burst into the consciousness of collectors and dealers when the major exhibition and catalogue *Three Women, Three Generations: Drawings by Pitseolak Ashoona, Napatchie Pootoogook and Shuvinai Ashoona* were unveiled in 1999 at the McMichael Canadian Art Collection. Although she had been drawing for only six years, her style was fully developed. Most typically worked in black and white, and in meticulous and painstaking detail, Shuvinai's landscapes are sometimes rooted in nature. At other times they are drawn from her imagination and can be scary and claustrophobic. Sprinkled here and there are historical images or events, such as the *Nascopie* supply ship; another recurring image is the egg shape. From 2006 Shuvinai Ashoona's drawings have been widely exhibited, especially at Feheley Fine Arts in Toronto and Marion Scott Gallery in Vancouver. Her prints have also been included in the annual Cape Dorset collections. Her work was shown at Art Basel in 2009 paired with that of John Noestheden, a Saskatchewan artist. This pairing was reprised in 2009 in Toronto under the *Nuit Blanche* festival umbrella. Also in 2009, Shuvinai was paired with Shary Boyle in *Noise Ghost* at the Justina M. Barnicke Gallery, University of Toronto. Shuvinai Ashoona has impressive artistic genes: her grandmother was Pitseolak Ashoona, her parents are Kiugak and Sorosiluto Ashoona and her cousins are Annie Pootoogook and Siassie Kenneally. (SG)

Romeo Eekerkik

b. 1923, Padlei, Nunavut; d. 1983, Arviat, Nunavut

It is thought that Romeo Eekerkik was born near Padlei, Nunavut, inland from the west coast of Hudson Bay, and later settled in the community of Arviat, Nunavut. This artist focused on scenes of daily life and family. Eekerkik's unique approach to his work was to combine materials such as string and colouring to represent various parts of his carvings like hair and clothing. (SC)

Ennutsiak

b. 1896 Nunavik region; d. 1967 Iqaluit, Nunavut

A sculptor from a traditional nomadic background, Ennutsiak carved detailed scenes of everyday life. His choice of subject matter ranged from family scenes to hunters on the land to children at play. Ennutsiak's skilled use of stone to create intricate carvings garnered him great respect from fellow artists. (SC)

Luke Iksiktaaryuk

b. 1909 Kazan River area, Nunavut; d. 1977 Baker Lake, Nunavut

Luke Iksiktaaryuk settled in the hamlet of Baker Lake with his family in the late 1950s. He, like so many others of his generation, was driven from the land by starvation during a downturn in the population of the caribou, the foundation of their nomadic lifestyle. He began sculpting in 1960 and gained early recognition when his work was included in *Eskimo Carvers of Keewatin, N.W.T.*, a 1964 exhibition at the Winnipeg Art Gallery. His work is made almost entirely from antler, a restrictive choice as its natural shape offers height and width but very little depth. Iksiktaaryuk, however, made the medium work for him, earning great success as an artist in the process. Many of his sculptures are composite in nature. Without question the drum dance was his favourite subject, one that he conveys with an inherent sense of theatricality. He has been represented in over forty major exhibitions, including *The Inuit Imagination* at the Winnipeg Art Gallery in 1993–94. In addition to his sculpting, Iksiktaaryuk was also a graphic artist; his prints were included in seven Baker Lake print collections between 1970 and 1977. (SG)

Osuitok Ipeelee

b. 1923 Niulijuktalik camp, South Baffin Island, Nunavut; d. 2005 Cape Dorset, Nunavut

Osuitok Ipeelee spent his earliest years in the Amadjuak area and then moved with his family to Tasiujaqjuaq after 1935. It was here that his father, Ohotok (who was a shaman), began teaching him to carve ivory. Peter Pitseolak became his ivory-carving mentor after Ohotok's passing. After his marriage in 1942 to Nipisha, Osuitok moved to Nuvuqjuuaq. Osuitok, further encouraged by Catholic missionaries, sold his first sculpture – a small, fully functional fox trap – made from ivory in the early 1940s. When James Houston first met Osuitok in 1957, he was already widely known among the Inuit for his carving skills. Osuitok had a career that was nothing short of outstanding in every respect. He was included in over one hundred exhibitions in Canada, the U.S. and abroad and has a significant presence in every public collection of Inuit art. He was greatly admired not just by collectors and curators but, more importantly, by his fellow sculptors, who were in awe of his prodigious carving skills. In 1973 he was elected to the Royal Canadian Academy of Arts and in 2004 he received the National Aboriginal Achievement Award in Arts. (SG)

Matiusie Iyaituk

b. 1950 Iyaituite, near Akulivik, Nunavik

For over thirty years Matiusie Iyaituk has had an impressive international artistic career built on diligence, artistic prowess and imagination. His inspiration has come from his brother Nutaraaluk and from the artists Lucy Tasseor Tutsweetok and Henry Moore. Life was harsh in his earliest years, when four older siblings died from starvation and his mother lost her sight. His family settled in Ivujivik in 1955 where Matiusie began high school the following year. He also attended school in Churchill, Great Whale River and Quebec City before he was done. The year 1961 was spent in Clearwater, Manitoba, where he was treated for tuberculosis. Prior to 1979 his sculpture was very detailed and similar in style to that of other artists in Ivujivik. Then, in a seminal moment, his interest shifted to the tactile qualities of the stone itself and the potential of abstract shapes. His work, however, has remained linked to tradition through details like inlaid faces. Throughout his career Matiusie has etched descriptive titles that reference his personal experiences on the underside of his work. Matiusie's earliest exhibition was in 1978, but he really came to prominence in the 1980s, leading him to resign from the Ivujivik police force in 1988 after four years' service. Since 2000, his style has shifted again as he now works more frequently on a larger scale and with mixed media. Matiusie Iyaituk has provided significant leadership to his fellow artists through his nineteen years of service on the board of the Inuit Art Foundation, of which he has been president since 1997. (SG)

John Kavik

b. 1897 near Gjoa Haven, Nunavut; d. 1993 Yellowknife, NWT

John Kavik moved south to Baker Lake around 1957 and then on to Rankin Inlet the following year. In the 1960s, after the local nickel mine closed, Kavik began carving, encouraged by his friend Robert Williamson, an anthropologist who was head of the Arctic Research and Training Centre in Rankin Inlet for ten years. For the next thirty years, Kavik focused almost exclusively on the human figure, endlessly reworking the subject. The expressive power of his sculptures is intimately linked with the roughness of their forms and finish. From 1963 to 1975, Kavik was also deeply involved in the Rankin Inlet ceramics project. His roughly formed figures in clay echo his work in stone. Kavik made his first drawings in 1979, asked to do so by Stanley Zazelenchuk, a Rankin Inlet teacher. He completed only two at the time – finding it far more difficult than sculpting – but did more in 1982 and 1983. By all accounts, Kavik was a small man, quite deaf, and had a lively personality that endeared him to all he met. His work is widely represented in public collections and has been extensively exhibited since 1965. Kavik was the father of Thomas Ugjuk, also a sculptor. (SG)

Kiakshuk

b. 1886 Ungava Peninsula, Nunavik; d. 1966 Cape Dorset, Nunavut

Kiakshuk moved around the turn of the century with his family to southwest Baffin Island, where they established camps along the coast between Cape Dorset and Andrew Gordon Bay. (The quarry site for the distinctive green serpentinite used for Cape Dorset and Kimmirut carving stone was later found here.) Kiakshuk took up carving before he began drawing. He was, however, one of the first Inuk to start making drawings in Cape Dorset, giving others like Pitseolak Ashoona the courage to try this new activity. His prints, a translation of his drawings, appeared in the Cape Dorset collections between 1960 and 1967. His early images were scary, monster-like creatures, but these soon morphed into his distinctive, gnome-like figures. They are engaged in hunting and camp life, and then in village life, perhaps unloading fuel barrels from the sealift. In 1958 Kiakshuk appeared as the storyteller in the National Film Board's *The Living Stone*. There are three large inuksuit at Toronto International Airport originally built by Kiakshuk, though they have now been relocated and rebuilt several times over. Kiakshuk's art has been included in numerous exhibitions including the landmark *Sculpture / Inuit: Masterworks of the Canadian Arctic* and *The Inuit Print*. In 1979 his print *Summer Tent* was reproduced on a Canadian stamp. Kiakshuk was a revered leader among the Inuit in the Cape Dorset area. (SG)

Janet Kigusiuq

b. 1926 Putuqsuqniq camp, near Garry Lake, Nunavut; d. 2005 Baker Lake, Nunavut

Janet Kigusiuq Uqayuittuq was the eldest daughter of Jessie Oonark, a pre-eminent artist who gave her much-needed moral support when she began drawing in the 1970s. Kigusiuq was married to Mark Uqayuittuq, son of Luke Anguhadluq, who was also an artist. Her work was included in the Baker Lake print collections from 1970 to 1988. Her subject matter focused on her early nomadic life, hunting caribou and fishing for Arctic char. She also depicted oral legends and stories handed down from generation to generation. The figures in her earlier drawings, similar in style to those of her sister Victoria Mamnguqsualuk, use the white ground of the paper as a colour and are surrounded by dark outlines in black or solid bands of colour. Some of her most visually stunning work dates from 2002 onward. Kyra Fisher, an arts adviser in the community, introduced Kigusiuq to collage using coloured tissue paper. The new medium allowed her to fully develop her innate sense of colour, depicting the land that she so loved and other iconic images, such as fish drying on a line. She also explored the use of broad, textured colour fields in pencil crayon. Some of these later drawings are worked in layers, as in the collage technique when she establishes an undercoat before overlaying other colours or textures. Several notable solo exhibitions held later in her career include *Janet Kigusiuq: Recent Drawings* at the MacKenzie Art Gallery, Regina, and *Second Nature: Recent Works on Paper by Janet Kigusiuq* at Feheley Fine Arts in 2002. A second exhibition at Feheley's, *Kigusiuq and Her Contemporaries*, was held in 2007. (SG)

Koviak

Not much is known about this early artist. It is thought Koviak may have been born sometime around the beginning of the twentieth century. Koviak lived along the Melville Peninsula, which is near the settlement of Repulse Bay. Playful and intricate carvings attributed to Koviak reveal a creator who was interested in nature and studied wildlife closely. (SC)

Thomassie Kudluk

b. 1910, Ungava Peninsula, Nunavik; d. 1989, Kangirsuk, Nunavik

Born into a traditional nomadic life, Kudluk's family moved into the settlement of Kangirsuk when he was a young man. Kudluk married and had ten children with his wife, who died in 1959. He was a respected elder in his community, known as a storyteller and advocate for his traditional Inuit heritage. Kudluk chose to testify at the James Bay Project hearings in 1974, which affected animal migration paths, thus threatening traditional food sources. Kudluk's artwork reflects his life experiences with both traditional and contemporary subject matter, illuminating how these two worlds collided in his lifetime. He would regularly use shoe polish as a type of paint on his carvings. A natural storyteller, he often inscribed syllabics into the stone to provide a narrative for his work. (SC)

Myra Kukiiyaut

b. 1929 Baker Lake, Nunavut; d. 2006 Baker Lake, Nunavut

Myra Kukiiyaut, born in 1929, experienced the flux of traditional Inuit life meeting settlement life earlier than many of her contemporaries. Her father worked for the RCMP in Baker Lake, yet she spent most of her young life in a traditional nomadic setting, living off the land and learning from elders. Myra married Luke Arngna'naaq, an artist, and they had a daughter and son. Together they continued the traditional way of life. However, in 1957 when their children were still quite young, Luke developed tuberculosis and was sent to a hospital in the South for three years. Unable to sustain the nomadic life on her own, Myra moved with the children to Baker Lake, where she settled permanently. Needing to support her family, she began crafting traditional clothing for sale. In the 1960s, when the Canadian government established an arts and crafts program in Baker Lake, Myra began experimenting with carving, drawing, printmaking and weaving. Clearly a talented artist and craftsperson, Myra has become known for her abstract, lyrical graphics whose inspiration is drawn from traditional stories and her observations of life and nature. (SC)

Victoria Mamnguqsualuk

b. 1930 near Garry Lake, Nunavut

Raised by her grandparents in the Garry Lake area, Victoria Mamnguqsualuk moved with her family to Baker Lake in 1963. She did some carving and sewed wall hangings, and she turned to drawing only in the 1970s. She is best known for her extensive exploration of the Qiviuq legend. Some of these drawings were brought together in the book and exhibition *Keeveeok Awake! Mamnguqsualuk and the Rebirth of Legend at Baker Lake*, organized by the Ring House Gallery, University of Alberta, Edmonton, in 1986. She tends to include several episodes of the legend within a single drawing and sometimes includes syllabic text. Her figures are not unlike those of her sisters Janet Kigusiuq and Nancy Pukingrnak in execution. Her prints were in fourteen Baker Lake collections between 1971 and 1986. In 1982 she did a series of drawings on black paper at the suggestion of Bogus Zdyb, the arts adviser at the time. Her husband, Samson Kayuryuk, was a sculptor, and her mother was Jessie Oonark. Mamnguqsualuk's first exhibition, in 1971, was *Sculpture / Inuit: Masterworks of the Canadian Arctic*, and it has been followed by dozens more. (SG)

Andy Miki

b. 1918 Kazan River area, Nunavut; d. 1983 Arviat, Nunavut

Andy Miki and his wife, Kahootsuak, lived at Ennadai Lake for many years before moving some two hundred kilometres east to the coastal hamlet of Arviat in 1959. Although Miki ended his years in Arviat, he also lived in Rankin Inlet and Whale Cove for a time. He started carving stone animal figures while still living at Ennadai Lake, finding a market for them among the Qallunaat in the Transport Canada camp there. His animals came from his imagination more than they did from nature; they were not meant to be either realistic or even species specific. Although worked in three dimensions, the figures have a strong linear or outline quality to them, as they usually have minimal depth. Miki has a significant exhibition history, including the important *Sculpture / Inuit: Masterworks of the Canadian Arctic* exhibition. He is widely represented in public collections and is a favourite among collectors. (SG)

Mary Kahootsuak Miki

b. 1920 Keewatin (Kivalliq) region; d. Arviat, Nunavut, date unknown

Mary Kahootsuak Miki lived on the land for many years with her husband, artist Andy Miki. Her carvings focus on themes of wildlife and community. Although stylistically minimal, which is typical of artists in the Arviat area, Mary Miki's work conveys emotional depth through the subject matter and precise figuring. Her sculptures have been included in international exhibitions. (SC)

Bill Nasogaluak

b. 1953 Tuktoyaktuk, NWT

A self-taught artist with a passion for art history and the Renaissance masters, Bill Nasogaluak is an accomplished painter and sculptor. Bill considers himself lucky to have been born at a time when the traditional Inuit life was colliding with the modern world of the South. Influences from both Inuit and Western traditions are seen in his work. He portrays the mythology and imagery of Inuit culture while using modern methods and materials, such as power tools and imported stone for his carving and paint for his graphic work. After working for nineteen years as an electronics technician, in 1992 he dedicated himself to his art full-time and taught at Arctic College in the mid-1990s. In recent years, Nasogaluak has also taken on large public commissions. In 1999 he was one of three artists commissioned to create a new Territorial Mace for the Northwest Territories, following the formation of Nunavut. The Government of Canada also commissioned Nasogaluak to create large inukshuk public sculptures for Guatemala City and Monterrey, Mexico, in 2006–7. (SC)

Niviaksiak

b. 1908; d. 1959 Cape Dorset, Nunavut

Niviaksiak, a sculptor and graphic artist, has become a legend in the North owing to the mysterious circumstances of his death. He often focused on animal and hunting scenes in his work, and it is believed that Niviaksiak may have offended the bear spirit, thus contributing to his death. It was while he was out hunting and took aim at a polar bear that he suddenly collapsed. Legend has it that his frightened companions left the scene fearing for their safety and returned shortly after to find their friend dead but untouched, with no bear tracks to be seen. Niviaksiak's sculpture and prints have been featured in exhibitions internationally, and in 1959 his print *Polar Bear and Cub* was figured on a Christmas card for the Museum of Modern Art, New York. Niviaksiak's wife, Kunu, was a graphic artist; his sons, Kiatshuk and Pitseolak Niviaqsi, are accomplished artists as well. (SC)

Maudie Rachel Okittuq

b. 1944 Thom Bay, Nunavut

Maudie Okittuq has been carving stone and whale bone for close to forty years in Taloyoak, formerly known as Spence Bay. It was 1964 when she moved into Spence Bay from Thom Bay, on eastern Boothia Peninsula. She is a steady producer who explores the Sedna theme more than any other, though she might also depict other supernatural creatures. There is a distinctive expressiveness in her work that comes from the mass of her forms and her vigorous carving style. Her output is often hampered by a lack of both quality carving stone and tools. Maudie is a talented seamstress; she usually has a packing doll in some stage of construction. Her husband, James Okittuq, is also a sculptor. Her work was first exhibited in 1974; since then she has had solo exhibitions in Toronto and Germany during the 1980s and has been included in a number of group exhibitions, including *Art and Expression of the Netsilik* at the Winnipeg Art Gallery in 2000. (SG)

Jessie Oonark

b. 1906 Back River area, Nunavut; d. 1985 Baker Lake, Nunavut

Jessie Oonark was an outstanding talent; she gained immediate recognition that has endured to this day. In addition, eight of her children have also had successful artistic careers. Shortly after arriving in Baker Lake from the Back River area, she was given art supplies by Dr. Andrew Macpherson, a biologist working in the area. With the help of the federal government, her drawings were taken to Cape Dorset and translated into prints included in that community's

1960 and 1961 collections. She became a mainstay of the Baker Lake print collections from their outset in 1970. No less accomplished than her drawings and prints are her many wall hangings, sewn in premises too small to roll out the whole work until it was finished and moved elsewhere. As did Pangnark's, her fame increased with the *Oonark / Pangnark* exhibition at the National Museum of Man in Ottawa in 1970. In 1984 she was inducted into the Order of Canada. During Oonark's lifetime her work was shown in some ninety exhibitions and since her passing in countless more. Sadly she died just before her major solo exhibition, with catalogue – *Jessie Oonark: A Retrospective* – organized by the Winnipeg Art Gallery. (SG)

Sheokjuk Oqutaq

b. 1920 Shartoweetok camp, South Baffin Island, Nunavut; d. 1982 Cape Dorset, Nunavut

Sheokjuk Oqutaq was an accomplished sculptor active in the Kimmirut (Lake Harbour) area from the 1940s and in the Cape Dorset area from the 1950s. Earlier he had lived in Salluit with his first wife, Maggie, who died there. Sheokjuk returned to Baffin Island in 1946 with his mother and her husband, Saggiak, settling at Tiku (a camp near Kimmirut). It was probably here that he was first carving ivory miniatures. In 1948 he married Louisa (Maggie's sister) and moved to Itiilliaqjuaq camp before moving into Cape Dorset itself. He was a skilled carpenter as well as a sculptor. Sheokjuk is known for the very carefully rendered details and the quality of his work. His sculptures exude a feeling of calm and serenity. In later years, his loon sculptures became a hallmark with their impossibly fine and sinuous necks. Sheokjuk's sculptures have been widely collected and exhibited in Canada and abroad, beginning with *Eskimo Art* in 1951 at the National Gallery of Canada. (SG)

Anirnik Oshuitoq

b. 1902 aboard the ship Arctic; d. 1983 Cape Dorset

Anirnik Oshuitoq's interesting entrance into the world foretold of the varied life that she would lead. Oshuitoq spent many years following a traditional nomadic life, and at sixteen she gave birth to her daughter Ningeeuga Oshuitoq (1918–1980), who would go on to become a respected artist. Anirnik settled with her family in Cape Dorset in the early 1960s because of Ningeeuga's failing health. It was while in Cape Dorset that both mother and daughter began creating artwork, particularly drawings and prints, and experimenting with various materials. (SC)

John Pangnark

b. 1920 near Windy Lake, Nunavut; d. 1980 Arviat, Nunavut

John Pangnark came from the Windy Lake area to the west of Arviat. Like so many Arviat artists, he moved to the hamlet in the 1950s and began carving in the 1960s. Throughout his career, the human figure was virtually his only subject. His minimalist aesthetic featured the naturally flowing lines of the stone marked with the merest indications of facial features. He first gained wide attention in 1970 when the *Oonark / Pangnark* exhibition was held at the National Museum of Man in Ottawa.

In Osaka, Japan, Pangnark was one of four Inuit who demonstrated stone carving at Expo 70. He stopped carving in 1975. Pangnark's sculptures were more admired by art collectors than by his fellow Inuit in Arviat; in southern Canada and abroad he was dubbed "the Brancusi of the North." (SG)

Parr

b. 1893 Foxe Peninsula, South Baffin Island, Nunavut; d. 1969 Cape Dorset, Nunavut

Parr and his wife, Eleeshushee Parr (also an artist), settled in Cape Dorset in 1961 when he was already sixty-eight years old. Encouraged by Terry Ryan, he took up graphite and colour pencils, felt-tip pens and wax crayons and began recreating a lifetime of memories of life on the land into simple but expressive drawings. His drawings were a subject of some amusement to his peers, but Parr had a dignity and self-confidence that rose above the teasing. Many contemporary artists in particular are drawn to Parr's drawings for their vigour and directness. He did not receive as much recognition and acclaim during his lifetime as he has since by collectors and curators alike. Nevertheless his work has appeared in some eighty exhibitions or more. His prints appeared in Cape Dorset print collections between 1961 and 1974. In 1977 a Canadian stamp reproduced Parr's walrus hunt scene from the print *Hunters of Old*. (SG)

David Ruben Piqtoukun

b. 1950 near Paulatuk, NWT

Between the ages of five and seventeen, David Ruben Piqtoukun was removed from his family and community near Paulatuk and sent to Aklavik, and then Inuvik, where he lived in residential school. He then worked at various jobs, including on the DEW Line at Cape Parry. In 1972 he was introduced to carving by his brother Abraham Apakark Anghik Ruben. Most of his early work was carved from jade. In 1975 he was a participant at the International Stone Sculpture Symposium in Vancouver, and by the end of the decade he was already a leader

Lukta Qiatsuq

b. 1928 Cape Dorset, Nunavut; d. 2004 Cape Dorset, Nunavut

Lukta Qiatsuq's father, Kiakshuk, was a well-respected leader and artist in the Cape Dorset community, encouraging his children to pursue art as well. Qiatsuq became involved with the very first printmaking experiments in Cape Dorset in 1957. He contributed to many Cape Dorset print collections throughout his life. Qiatsuq also extended his talents to carving, and his work, both graphic and sculpture, has been exhibited widely. His passion for artmaking continues in his children, who carry on the family artistic tradition. (SC)

Eli Sallualu Qinuajua

b. 1937 Issuksiuvit camp, Nunavik; d. 2004 Puvirnituq, Nunavik

Issuksiuvit, the camp where Eli Sallualu Qinuajua was born, was located about sixty-five kilometres south of Puvirnituq, on the east coast of Hudson Bay. By the 1960s he was living in Puvirnituq itself. In 1967 he won a local sculpture contest organized by anthropologist Nelson Graburn from the University of California, Berkeley. About twenty-five local artists submitted over fifty sculptures that were *takushurnaituk* (things never seen before) or *adjigiingituk* (different from each other). From that time Qinuajua continued to make sculptures that border on the surreal and the fantastic. In addition to sculpting, he was also a talented radio actor for CBC Northern Circuits. He spent two brief periods in the South for tuberculosis treatment. During the 1970s and 1980s his work was widely exhibited. Qinuajua is well represented in the major public collections of Inuit art. (SG)

Sakiassie Ragee

b. 1924, Baffin Island, Nunavut; d. 2003 Cape Dorset, Nunavut

Sakiassie Ragee spent much of his early years living a nomadic life in the Baffin region, moving between camps and hunting and fishing for survival. He married Eegyvudluk, and together they adopted four children and lived at the Tikerak camp, which was only a few miles from the settlement of Cape Dorset. In the mid-1950s, Sakiassie spent several years in a sanatorium in Manitoba for the treatment of tuberculosis. After returning to the North, Ragee moved with his family into Cape Dorset. Although he had dabbled in artmaking previously, it was during this period that he devoted more time to carving and graphic arts. Ragee's art was inspired by traditional life, but he also drew from his imagination for subject matter. (SC)

Abraham Anghik Ruben

b. 1951 camp southeast of Paulatuk, NWT

Abraham Anghik Ruben spent his early years in the Cape Parry region, north of Paulatuk and east of the Mackenzie River delta. At age eight he was sent to residential school in Inuvik, where, apart from summer vacations, he spent the next eleven years. In 1971 he moved to Alaska and started formal art studies the following year; in 1974 he studied under Ronald Senungetuk, a design professor at the Native Art Center of the University of Alaska Fairbanks. He spent several months in Vancouver in 1975 before establishing a studio in Yellowknife, where he caught the attention of Jack Pollock, a Toronto dealer who held four solo exhibitions of his work between 1977 and 1980. In 1980 Anghik moved back to Vancouver and in 1986 to Salt Spring Island. After a brief period in Chilliwack in the late 1990s, he returned to the Gulf Islands, where he still lives. Anghik's considerable research into his family's and his people's history is often reflected in his subject matter. He most commonly works with Brazilian soapstone, creating sculptures that are often extremely complex and monumental in size. His major exhibitions include *Out of Tradition: Abraham Anghik / David Ruben Piqtoukun* in 1989 and *Abraham Anghik Ruben* in 2001, both organized by the Winnipeg Art Gallery. (SG)

Pauta Saila

b. 1916 Kilapik camp, South Baffin Island, Nunavut; d. 2009 Ottawa, Ontario

Pauta Saila grew up in the Foxe Peninsula area to the west of Cape Dorset, or Nuwata, as it is known to the Inuit. In his youth, he learned to sculpt from his father, Saila, who worked for the Hudson's Bay Company but who sold his ivory carvings to visiting whalers on the side. Pauta moved first to Kimmirut and then, after the death of his first wife, to Iqaluit where he worked on the DEW Line. He married Pitaloosie Saila (also an accomplished artist) in 1960 and moved to Cape Dorset. Although he made about forty prints in all between 1962 and 1981, and then in 2004, Pauta is primarily known as a sculptor. Even more specifically, he is known for his many outstanding sculptures of bears. In 1967 Pauta participated in the International Sculpture Symposium in Toronto. There he made a massive sculpture, *Bear,* which was installed for a time in High Park but has for many years now been installed at the entrance to the McMichael Canadian Art Collection in Kleinburg, Ontario. His career was long and illustrious; both Pauta and Pitaloosie Saila have been elected to the Royal Canadian Academy of Arts. A public collection that did not include some of Pauta Saila's work is hard to imagine. (SG)

Peter Sevoga

b. 1940 Baker Lake area, Nunavut; d. 2007 Baker Lake, Nunavut

The Sevoga family grew up near Baker Lake where both Peter and his half-brother Thomas became artists. At one time Sevoga worked in the mines, but then he became a full-time artist, first a sculptor and then a graphic artist and printmaker as well. His earliest work is similar to that of his brother Thomas, but both soon went on to develop their own styles. Sevoga's sculptures are characterized by a solidity that suggests a mass greater than the actual physical size of the piece. His most common subjects are mother and child or family groupings. They are worked with an economy of detail – the body rests on short, thick legs, the faces are usually framed by the hood of a parka and often one arm is raised. The artist received early recognition for his work: his extensive exhibition history begins in 1964 and includes a solo show at the Raven Gallery in Minneapolis in 1983. He had prints in ten Baker Lake print collections between 1971 and 1988. (SG)

Aqjangajuk Shaa

b. 1937 Satuqitu camp, South Baffin Island, Nunavut

Aqjangajuk Shaa has been carving for over fifty years. He started at age fifteen, when he would sell his sculptures to workers on the *C.D. Howe* ship during the annual sealift visit. By seventeen, he was seriously carving and has continued to the present. He is a grandson of the much-loved artist Kiakshuk and derives his surname from his paternal grandfather, Shaa. His mother, Paunichea, was also an artist. He had one print in the 1961 Cape Dorset collection; otherwise he has remained focused on stone. Aqjangajuk is known for the heroic, exaggerated quality of his imagery whose mannered poses still retain a fine sense of balance. The "dancing walrus" is a particularly favourite subject. He has been in numerous exhibitions, both solo and group, from 1970 to the present in Canada, the U.S. and Germany. In Cape Dorset he is also known for his ability to find and quarry carving stone. In 2003 Aqjangajuk was elected to the Royal Canadian Academy of Arts. (SG)

Nick Sikkuark

b. 1943 near Garry Lake, Nunavut

Nick Sikkuark was orphaned in 1952 when both his parents died during a flu epidemic. Initially he was cared for by his older brother, but then he was raised by Oblate missionaries. In 1956 he was sent to a missionary school in Gjoa Haven, followed by religious schooling in Winnipeg in 1961 and then in Ottawa. In 1965 Sikkuark returned north, having decided not to pursue the priesthood. Around 1967 in Gjoa Haven he began making sculpture from caribou antler and ivory. The following year he moved to Kugaaruk (once known as Pelly Bay), where he still lives. Since 1970 Sikkuark has been a full-time artist, creating his unique sculpture. He is extremely inventive with his subject matter as well as with his use of materials; he makes frequent references to shamanism and often includes a suggestion of landscape in his composite pieces. In 1978 he carved an ivory baton for the opening ceremonies of the Commonwealth Games in Edmonton, and he was also involved in the cultural events of the 1976 Olympics in Montreal. The government of the Northwest Territories published five of his books for school use in 1973. Since 2002, for health reasons, he has turned from sculpture to drawing. Over the years, Sikkuark's work has been highly sought after and exhibited widely, including at *Indigena: Contemporary Native Perspectives in Canadian Art* at the Canadian Museum of Civilization in 1992. Marion Scott Gallery in Vancouver hosted his most recent solo exhibition, *Nick Sikkuark: New Drawings* in 2005. (SG)

Isa Aqiattusuk Smiler

b. 1921 Inukjuak, Nunavik; d. 1986 Inukjauk, Nunavik

This artist, known by his nickname "Isa the Smiler" (Aqiattusuk is his Inuktitut name), lived a varied and interesting life. When he was nine years old, both of his parents died from an illness introduced into the community by a supply ship that came into port near their settlement. He was taken in by Anglican missionaries and soon became confident in English, acting as an assistant by translating and giving Inuktitut lessons. In 1948 he began carving and also dabbled in drawing and painting. Isa is best known for his detailed carvings of Inuit life. Willing to take on any challenge, Isa also wrote his own biography for *Inuktitut* magazine in 1977. (SC)

Nelson Takkiruq

b. 1930, Gjoa Haven, Nunavut; d. 1999 Gjoa Haven, Nunavut

Nelson Takkiruq belonged to an artistic family. His brothers, Charlie Ugyuk (1931–1998) and Judas Ullulaq (1937–1999), and his nephew, Karoo Ashevak (1940–1974), have all been successful carvers. Artists in the Kitikmeot region are known for combining a variety of materials in their carvings, such as whale bone, stone and antler, to create expressive, tactile sculpture. Takkiruq's work often contains mystical and ominous subject matter with what seems to be a sly sense of humour. Takkiruq's nephew, Damien Iquallaq, carries on the family's artistic traditions. (SC)

Quvianatuliak Takpaungai

b. 1942 Cape Dorset, Nunavut

Quvianatuliak Takpaungai, known as Kov, was born into traditional Inuit life and became a well-respected hunter. As Cape Dorset grew into a bustling artistic community, Kov too became interested in trying his hand at carving, creating large stone works. Kov's talent was immediately recognized, and his unique works, ranging from gestural figures to depictions of wildlife, stood out among those of his peers. His work has been exhibited widely, including in the international touring exhibition *Sculpture / Inuit: Masterworks of the Canadian Arctic* from 1971–73. (SC)

Joe Talirunili

b. 1906 Niaqunna camp, Nunavik; d. 1976 Puvirnituq, Nunavik

Niaqunna (or Neahungnuk), where Joe Talirunili was born, is near the mouth of the Qugaaluk River, south of Puvirnituq. It was near here, when he was an infant, that his family had a harrowing experience that later became a favourite, and oft repeated, subject of Talirunili's. They were set adrift for days on an ice floe before managing to build an umiak (a boat made of hides stretched over a wooden frame). They dismantled the wood from their sleds to build the frame and then captured enough seals to cover it with hides before making a precarious journey back to shore. Talirunili probably started carving around 1950, encouraged by James Houston on his early visit to Puvirnituq. He was a particularly prolific artist in drawings, prints and sculptures alike. He worked serially, making many endearing images of owls and many images of single figures of hunters or standing women, the migration boats, hunting scenes and other vignettes of life along the coast of Hudson Bay. Talirunili was one of the first in Puvirnituq to experiment with printmaking, eventually creating over seventy prints. He was an active community member, helping to found the co-operative and serving as a layperson in the Anglican church. In his lifetime his work was widely exhibited but not always appreciated, owing to his inclusion of pieces of string, wood or plastic – materials not approved by purists. Today ownership of his sculpture is hotly contested. One version of his *Migration* sculpture, originally depicted on a Canada postage stamp in 1976, sold for more than $278,000 in 2006, the most yet paid for an Inuit sculpture. (SG)

George Tatanniq

b. 1910 Kazan River area, Nunavut; d. 1991 Baker Lake, Nunavut

George Tatanniq was a stately individual, a proud hunter and a careful, skilled sculptor. He spent half his life in the area of his birthplace, near Sugarloaf Mountain on the Kazan River. After he became ill with tuberculosis he was forced to spend the years 1957 to 1960 in a sanatorium in the South. He began carving in 1963 after his return to Baker Lake and continued until the late 1980s. Tatanniq was never a prolific carver, but the sculptures he did make were always carefully executed, from his thoughtful selection of stone through to the final finishing touches. His sculptures make a quiet but strong statement, much like the man himself. His work has been widely collected and exhibited since 1964, including at the 1971–73 show *Sculpture / Inuit: Masterworks of the Canadian Arctic*. His daughter Irene Niuqtuq is also a sculptor. (SG)

John Tiktak

b. 1916 Kareak camp, Nunavut; d. 1981 Rankin Inlet, Nunavut

Tiktak began life in a camp halfway between Whale Cove and Arviat. In 1958 he settled in Rankin Inlet to work in the newly opened nickel mine. However, within a year he was badly injured in a mining accident and turned to carving instead. As an artist he focused exclusively on the human figure, depicted either as a head or a standing figure. His imagery is simplified, timeless and elegant, giving his figures a monumentality that far exceeds the physical dimensions of the sculpture. Marks of the tools used in the carving process remain evident on the surface of the figures. In 1970 Tiktak was the first Inuit artist to have a solo exhibition at Gallery One One One at the University of Manitoba in Winnipeg. From 1967 to the present, Tiktak has been included in dozens of exhibitions and he continues to be held in great esteem. This small, funny man with a wonderful personality has become a giant. (SG)

Bernadette Iguptark Tongelik

b. 1931 Wager Bay, Nunavut; d. 1980 Repulse Bay, Nunavut

Bernadette Iguptark Tongelik lived off the land with her parents, who were also artists. Tongelik focused on mystical themes and legends in her sculpture and favoured varied materials including stone, bone and ivory. (SC)

Simon Tookoome

b. 1934 near Chantrey Inlet, Nunavut

Simon Tookoome began artmaking in the 1970s, working first in bone, then in stone and finally in graphics. Since moving to Baker Lake in 1968–69, Tookoome has worked in many fields, including construction, mining, fishing, education and printing, and as a cameraman and interviewer for the Inuit Broadcasting Corporation. He has also been a Canadian Ranger. Tookome's accuracy and skills with a dogsled whip, all six metres of it, are legendary. He has demonstrated this skill, as well as traditional games, at many venues, including Expo 86 in Vancouver. In the Baker Lake print shop, he generally printed his own drawings. Tookoome is known for his sculptures and his standing figures, laser-cut from metal – a technique he learned from Saskatchewan artist Joe Fafard. One of Tookoome's drawings was featured on a 1980 stamp, and another was used for a Calgary Winter Olympics poster in 1988. His drawings often represent complex ideas and show different views simultaneously. In 1999 Tookoome received the Norma Fleck Award for Canadian Children's Non-Fiction for his self-illustrated autobiography *The Shaman's Nephew: A Life in the Far North,* co-authored with Sheldon Oberman. He has over one hundred exhibitions to his credit. Tookoome is a half-brother of the late Jessie Oonark. (SG)

Toonoo

b. 1920, outpost camp near Cape Dorset, Nunavut; d. 1969, near Cape Dorset, Nunavut

Toonoo, who married Sheojuke, with whom he had eleven children, was noted as a gifted sculptor when he was a young man. Toonoo and his family followed a traditional nomadic life outside of Cape Dorset. During the 1950s Toonoo travelled into the growing settlement for work to support his large family and connected with other budding artists. His artistic career was short-lived; he died of a gunshot wound in 1969. At the time, Toonoo's death was believed to be an accident; more than two decades later, Toonoo's son-in-law confessed to his murder. The artistic proficiency seen in Toonoo as a young man lives on in his children, Oviloo Tunnillie, Jutai Toonoo and Samonie Toonoo, and his grandchildren. (SC)

Tudlik

b. 1890 Cape Dorset, Nunavut; d. 1966 Cape Dorset, Nunavut

Before focusing on his art, Tudlik was a highly regarded hunter in his community. Failing eyesight and poor health required Tudlik to settle permanently, and he focused on sculpting and printmaking for his income. Inspiration for his artwork came from his traditional Inuit life; he sculpted animals and depicted stories and myths in his printmaking. (SC)

Ruth Annaqtuusi Tulurialik

b. 1934 on a small island, Kazan River area, Nunavut

Ruth Annaqtuusi Tulurialik has created a fascinating body of work during the forty-some years of her career. Annaqtuusi was adopted as an infant by an uncle who raised her in an Anglican mission house in Baker Lake where he worked for the church. Annaqtuusi grew to savour the visits of Inuit who came to Baker Lake to trade, gleaning from them stories of life on the land and other snippets of oral culture. In 1958 she worked at the nursing station, and in the mid-1960s she participated in the sewing project started by Elizabeth Whitton, the Anglican minister's wife. She took up drawing around 1970. From 1971 to 1986, she was included in eleven Baker Lake print collections. She was also part of the *Baker Lake Drawings* exhibition at the Winnipeg Art Gallery in 1972. Her drawings are extremely detailed in subject and technique; it is remarkable that any could be translated into prints. In 1983 Annaqtuusi asked writer David Pelly for help in creating the book *Qikaaluktuk: Images of Inuit Life*, published in 1986. The forty-eight drawings and their stories were culled from seventy that she had been setting aside over a period of time, rather than selling locally. The subjects include historical images like Marble Island as well as legends and other stories from oral culture. The project led to the exhibition *The Vital Vision: Drawings by Ruth Annaqtuusi Tulurialik* at the Art Gallery of Windsor in 1986–87. She and her husband, Hugh (a sculptor), are noted musicians who often perform together. (SG)

Oviloo Tunnillie

b. 1949 Kangia camp, South Baffin Island, Nunavut

Oviloo Tunnillie stands alone among contemporary Inuit for her powerful sculptures: the very personal and poignant nature of their subjects set them apart from other Inuit work. Her childhood was disrupted by three years spent in southern Canadian hospitals at ages five, seven and eight, causing to her lose much of her Inuktitut language and to feel discomfited by the traditional lifestyle that she had known. She began carving in 1965 at Igalaalik, learning from the example of her father, Toonoo, and others in the camp, and took it up in earnest from 1972. It was her work in the 1992 exhibition *Women of the North* at Marion Scott Gallery that really brought Oviloo to the fore. This was followed by the distinctive sculptures in *Isumavut: The Artistic Expression of Nine Cape Dorset Women* at the Canadian Museum of Civilization in 1994. Oviloo is the only Inuit artist to have explored the female nude theme. In other work, she turns upside down the expectation that Inuit art portrays traditional culture for southerners to look at. Often she reverses the gaze by depicting southern cultural images, such as athletes or dancers. She also frequently depicts herself – reflecting on her hospital experiences, her life as an artist and on the social issues of being a woman. Sedna sculptures are her only images related specifically to Inuit culture. Her work has been exhibited widely, both nationally and internationally. Among her solo exhibitions are *Oviloo Tunnillie: In Two Worlds* at the Art Gallery of Ontario in 1997 and *Oviloo Tunnillie: Meditations on Womanhood* at Marion Scott Gallery in 2008. Her brothers Jutai and Samonie Toonoo are also sculptors. (SG)

Lucy Tasseor Tutsweetok

b. 1934 Nunalla, Manitoba

Lucy Tasseor Tutsweetok has been prominent in the art world for four decades now, beginning sculpting at the age of twenty and acquiring her skills from her grandfather. Throughout her career she has focused on maternal and family grouping themes. Her sculptures generally retain the shape of the original piece of stone, with heads, arms and faces emerging from the stone. Sometimes she etches a drawing – an igloo perhaps – into a flat surface between the forms. Her exhibition history is long and prestigious, including *Sculpture / Inuit: Masterworks of the Canadian Arctic* of 1971–73; *In the Shadow of the Sun: Contemporary Indian and Inuit Art in Canada* of 1989–91; and *Indigena: Contemporary Native Perspectives in Canadian Art* in 1992 at the Canadian Museum of Civilization, to name just a few. More recently she has done some drawing, resulting in the 2009 exhibition *Drawings by Lucy Tasseor Tutsweetok and Mary Ayaq Anowtalik* at Feheley Fine Arts. Tasseor has lived in northern Manitoba and in Rankin Inlet, and moved on to Arviat after the closing of the North Rankin Nickel Mine in 1962. (SG)

Judas Ullulaq

b. 1937 Thom Bay area, Nunavut; d. 1999 Gjoa Haven, Nunavut

During his lifetime Judas Ullulaq was the leading artist in the Kitikmeot region, much admired by Inuit and southern collectors alike. He spent his early years into adulthood in the Thom Bay area to the northeast of Taloyoak (or Spence Bay, as it was formerly called) but moved his family to Taloyoak in the 1960s so that his children could attend school. He began sculpting with whale bone in 1961 following the birth of his eldest daughter. After 1973, when the quarry site at Murchison Lake on the mainland was discovered, he used stone as well. His sculptures exude a vibrant energy that mirrors the artist's own puckish sense of humour. They are imaginative, finely detailed and well finished. Some are clearly influenced by the outstanding work of his nephew Karoo Ashevak, created during his brief four-year career (1970–74). In 1982 Ullulaq moved to Gjoa Haven. Ullulaq had two solo exhibitions in 1983, one in Toronto and the other in New York, the latter held in conjunction with the opening of the General Assembly building of the United Nations. His work has been included in countless group exhibitions since 1977 and is an important component of all the public collections of Inuit art. His brothers Joata Suqslak, Stephen Aqqaq, Charlie Ugyuk and Nelson Takkiruq were all sculptors. (SG)

Authors' Biographies

Dorothy Harley Eber is a Canadian writer with a special interest in documentary photography and oral history, based in Montreal. She graduated from the University of Toronto and has worked as a reporter in Canada and England. She first visited the Canadian Arctic in 1968 and has made many return trips to record material for her books, *Encounters on the Passage: Inuit Meet the Explorers* (2008) and *Images of Justice: A Legal History of the Northwest Territories as Traced through the Yellowknife Collection of Inuit Sculpture* (2003), among the more recent. In 1999 she received the Order of Canada for her contribution to preserving the Inuit heritage.

Bernadette Driscoll Engelstad is a writer, researcher and independent curator of Inuit art and cultural history. While at the Winnipeg Art Gallery (1980–85), she organized over thirty exhibitions of contemporary Inuit art, conducted field interviews with artists and collaborated with the Inuit Broadcasting Corporation on art-related programs. As Arctic curator for the exhibition *The Spirit Sings: Artistic Traditions of Canada's First Nations,* she selected historical artifacts from North American, European and (then) Soviet museum collections and contributed to the catalogue. A specialist in the history of Inuit clothing design, she has worked closely with Inuit seamstresses in collaborative research projects. She holds an MA in Canadian Studies from Carleton University, as well as an MA in Anthropology (Program in the History of Art and Anthropology), Johns Hopkins University.

Ingo Hessel is the Curator of the Museum of Inuit Art in Toronto and the Albrecht Adjunct Curator of Inuit Art at the Heard Museum in Phoenix. His publications include *Inuit Art: An Introduction* (1998), widely used as a university text; *Arctic Spirit: Inuit Art from the Albrecht Collection at the Heard Museum* (2006); *Sanattiaqsimajut: Inuit Art from the Carleton University Art Gallery Collection* (2009); *Kananginak Pootoogook: Celebrating Five Decades of Artistic Achievement* (2010); and an essay on Inuit art for *The Visual Arts in Canada: The Twentieth Century* (2010). He curated the exhibition *Arctic Spirit* for the Heard Museum, which toured to ten cities across North America from 2006 to 2009. Since 2008, he has co-taught a course on Inuit art at Carleton University. For fifteen years he was at the federal Department of Indian and Northern Affairs, as Special Projects Officer, and then as Coordinator of the Inuit Art Information Centre; there he oversaw the Inuit artist biography project, produced the video *Keeping Our Stories Alive: The Sculpture of Canada's Inuit* and wrote the booklet *Canadian Inuit Sculpture*. Ingo Hessel is also a sculptor who has exhibited in Canada and Japan.

Heather Igloliorte is an Inuk curator and art historian from the Nunatsiavut Territory of Labrador, currently residing in Ottawa, Ontario. After graduating with a BFA in painting from the Nova Scotia College of Art and Design University in 2003, Igloliorte moved to Ottawa to begin graduate studies at Carleton University, where she earned an MA in Canadian art history and completed a thesis on contemporary Inuit art. She is now is pursuing a PhD in Cultural Mediations at Carleton, specializing in global indigenous art histories with a focus on Inuit art, historic and contemporary. Her most recent curatorial project is the touring exhibition *"We Were So Far Away": The Inuit Experience of Residential Schools* (2009), which features the oral histories of eight Inuit former students of the residential school system.

Alootook Ipellie (1951–2007) was a respected essayist, satirist, poet and cartoonist. Born at his family camp, Nuvuqquq, on Baffin Island, he attended high school in Iqaluit before moving to Ottawa in the early 1970s, though he still spent summers in the Arctic. He chronicled, in his words, "the tribulations and triumphs of his people" in an impressive range of publications including *Inuit Today* (formerly *Inuit Monthly*, where he was also an editor from 1979 to 1983); *north/nord, Inuktitut, Paper Stays Put* (1981); *Indigena: Contemporary Native Perspectives in Canadian Art* (1992); and *The Journals of Knud Rasmussen: A Sense of Memory and High-definition Inuit Storytelling* (2008). A collection of his short stories and drawings, *Arctic Dreams and Nightmares,* was published in 1993.

Zacharias Kunuk is a Canadian Inuk film producer and director. He is the co-founder, with Norman Cohn and Pauloosie Qulitalik, of Igloolik Isuma Productions, an independent Inuit film production company. He produced and directed *Atanarjuat: The Fast Runner* (2001), the first Canadian dramatic feature film in Inuktitut, which won the Camera d'Or award at Cannes, five Genies and the Claude Jutra award. His second film, *The Journals of Knud Rasmussen* (2006), was a co-production with Denmark. He completed his third feature film, *Before Tomorrow*, in 2008. After building a reputation as a sculptor in the 1970s, he turned to video in the 1980s, focusing on recreations of traditional life in such films as *Qaggiq* (*Gathering Place*, 1989), *Saputi* (*Fish Traps*, 1993) and the thirteen-part series *Nunavut* (1993–95). In recent years, he has continued to produce short subject documentaries, such as *Angakkuiit* (*Shaman Stories*, 2003) and *Kiviaq versus Canada* (2006). He was awarded the Order of Canada in 2002.

Christine Lalonde is a curator and art historian who has worked with Inuit art and artists since the mid-1990s and is currently the Associate Curator of Indigenous Art at the National Gallery of Canada. Her many exhibition projects have advanced understanding of Inuit art and represent a balance between theory and practice, between celebrating the artistic accomplishments of Inuit artists and raising awareness of critical issues. Her most notable projects toward this goal include *Artists in the Arctic* (2003), *Inuit Sculpture Now* (2005) and *Uuturautiit: Cape Dorset Celebrates 50 Years of Printmaking* (2009). A regular contributor to *Inuit Art Quarterly* since 1995, Lalonde has also written extensively for journals and anthologies, including *Framing Our Past: Women in Canada in the Twentieth Century* (2001), *On Aboriginal Representation in the Gallery* (2002), *Encyclopedia of the Arctic* (2005) and *Letters from Canada* (2007). Her publications with the National Gallery of Canada include *Beauty in a Common Thing: The Drawings and Prints of L.L. FitzGerald* (2004), *Noah's Ark* (2004), *Itukiagatta! Inuit Sculpture from the TD Bank Financial Group* (2005), *Inuit Sculpture Now* (2005) and the book accompanying the *Uuturautiit* exhibition (2009).

Robert McGhee, PhD, is an archaeologist whose research has addressed the first human habitation of the New World Arctic, the origins of Inuit culture, reactions of prehistoric populations to climate change, and the relations between Aboriginal peoples and early European visitors to Arctic Canada. This work has been reported in over one hundred books and articles, including both academic publications and those designed for a general audience, most recently *The Last Imaginary Place: A Human History of the Arctic World* (2004). He is a fellow of the Royal Society of Canada and the Arctic Institute of North America, former president of the Canadian Archaeological Association and was awarded the Massey Medal by the Royal Canadian Geographical Society.

Gerald McMaster, PhD, is the Fredrik S. Eaton Curator of Canadian Art at the Art Gallery of Ontario. During his tenure as Curator of Contemporary Indian Art at the Canadian Museum of Civilization (1981–2000), he established the first Indian and Inuit gallery at the CMC. In 1992, he curated *Indigena* for the Canadian Museum of Civilization and co-authored the book *Indigena: Contemporary Native Perspectives*. His publications include *Reservation X* (1998), *Native Universe* (2004) and *Remix: New Modernities in a Post-Indian World* (2007). In 1995 he served as Canadian Commissioner and curated Edward Poitras's exhibition at the Venice Biennale. From 2000 to 2004, he was Deputy Assistant Director for Cultural Resources at the National Museum of the American Indian (NMAI), Smithsonian Institution. At NMAI, he curated *First American Art* (2004) and *New Tribe / New York* (2005). He was awarded the Order of Canada (2007) and the National Aboriginal Achievement Award in 2005.

John Ralston Saul is an award-winning essayist and novelist and the president of International PEN. In his latest book, *A Fair Country: Telling Truths about Canada*, Saul argues that Canada is a Metis nation, heavily influenced and shaped by aboriginal ideas. He is perhaps best known for his philosophical trilogy and its conclusion – *Voltaire's Bastards*, *The Doubter's Companion*, *The Unconscious Civilization* (his 1995 Massey Lectures) and *On Equilibrium: Six Qualities of the New Humanism*. His recent essay on globalization, "The Collapse of Globalism and the Reinvention of the World," has been reissued with an updated epilogue to address the current crisis. He has received numerous national and international awards for his work, including the Governor General's Literary Award for Non-Fiction for *The Unconscious Civilization*. His novels and essays have been translated into twenty-two languages. General editor for the Penguin Extraordinary Canadians series, co-chair of the Institute for Canadian Citizenship, founder and honorary chair of French for the Future, and chair of the LaFontaine-Baldwin Symposium, Saul is a Companion in the Order of Canada and a Chevalier in the Ordre des Arts et des Lettres of France. His fourteen honorary degrees range from McGill University to Herzen State Pedagogical University in St. Petersburg, Russia. In 2004 he received the Pablo Neruda Medal of Honor.

List of Works in the Exhibition

Akeeaktashuk
Hunter
before 1954
stone, ivory, inlay
17.5 x 13.0 x 8.0 cm (without harpoon)
Gift of Samuel and Esther Sarick, Toronto, 2001
2001/355
page 69

Akeeaktashuk
Seal Hunter
before 1954
stone, bone, inlay
23.5 x 10.6 x 16.4 cm
Gift of Samuel and Esther Sarick, Toronto, 2001
2001/354
page 69

Latcholassie Akesuk
Bird
c. 1973
stone
41.6 x 43.0 x 16.8 cm
Gift of Samuel and Esther Sarick, 1989
© Dorset Fine Arts
89/553
page 137

Latcholassie Akesuk
Bird
c. 1973
stone
23.6 x 37.3 x 21.5 cm
Gift of Samuel and Esther Sarick, Toronto, 1996
© Dorset Fine Arts
96/1008
page 137

Latcholassie Akesuk
Bird/Man Transformation
c. 1973
stone
56.8 x 18.0 x 12.5 cm
Gift of Samuel and Esther Sarick, Toronto, 1996
© Dorset Fine Arts
96/1010
page 136

Paulusikotak Alaku
Mother and Children
c. 1959
stone
26.9 x 32.0 x 22.4 cm
Gift of Samuel and Esther Sarick, 1990
90/609
page 85

Marc Alikaswa
Mother and Child
1980
stone
40.5 x 20.0 x 19.5 cm
Gift of Samuel and Esther Sarick, Toronto, 1996
96/816
page 87

Amidlak
Figure and Animal Totem
1951–55
stone, ivory, colouring
21.4 x 9.4 x 4.4 cm
Gift of Samuel and Esther Sarick, Toronto, 2001
2001/357
page 65

Davidialuk Alasua Amittu
Two Kajjutajuit on a Sled
c. 1970
porous pointed pen, coloured pencil and graphite on wove paper
59.1 x 66.1 cm
Gift of Samuel and Esther Sarick, Toronto, 2002
2002/10135
page 115

Davidialuk Alasua Amittu
Kajjutajuk and Tunnituaqruk
c. 1972
darkened stone
19.2 x 24.0 x 14.0 cm
Gift of Samuel and Esther Sarick, Toronto, 1996
96/588
page 114

Davidialuk Alasua Amittu
The Hunter Who Encountered the Iqalunappa
1972
stone
24.1 x 41.9 x 8.9 cm
Collection of Samuel and Esther Sarick, Toronto
page 114

Augustin Anaittuq
Muskox
1990
whale bone, antler, bone, stone
50.7 x 62.0 x 36.0 cm
Gift of Samuel and Esther Sarick, Toronto, 1996
96/565
page 97

Josephee Angnako
Whaling Ship
c. 1950
stone, ivory, sinew, thread, pigment
17.5 x 25.7 x 5.8 cm
Gift of Samuel and Esther Sarick, 1990
90/615
page 60

Luke Anguhadluq
Fishing and Hunting Birds
1970
coloured pencil and graphite on paper
56.1 x 76.1 cm
Gift of Samuel and Esther Sarick, Toronto, 2002
2002/10212
page 168

Luke Anguhadluq
Drum Dance
c. 1972
coloured pencil and graphite on paper
58.3 x 79.9 cm
Gift of Samuel and Esther Sarick, Toronto, 2002
2002/10256
page 103

Luke Anguhadluq
Caribou Hunting
1973
coloured pencil and graphite on paper
58.4 x 79.8 cm
Gift of Samuel and Esther Sarick, Toronto, 2002
2002/10218
page 169

Luke Anguhadluq
Muskox and Hunter
c. 1973
coloured pencil and graphite on paper
58.7 x 73.9 cm
Gift of Samuel and Esther Sarick, Toronto, 2002
2002/10225
page 169

Luke Anguhadluq
Hunting Bears
c. 1975
coloured pencil and graphite on paper
58.9 x 79.6 cm
Gift of Samuel and Esther Sarick, Toronto, 2002
2002/10249
page 169

Tony Anguhalluq
Two Inuit are picking blackberries in July
2006
coloured pencil and wax crayon on paper
26.7 x 34.9 cm
Collection of Samuel and Esther Sarick, Toronto
page 196

Tony Anguhalluq
Two Inuit are out fishing for the weekend
2007
coloured pencil and wax crayon on paper
61.0 x 48.0 cm
Collection of Samuel and Esther Sarick, Toronto
page 197

Tony Anguhalluq
Two Inuit are drying caribou meat
2007
coloured pencil and graphite on paper
61.0 x 48.0 cm
Collection of Samuel and Esther Sarick, Toronto
page 197

Margaret Uyauperq Aniksak
Mother and Child
c. 1964
darkened stone
26.5 x 16.5 x 12.8 cm
Gift of Samuel and Esther Sarick, 1988
88/745
page 86

Luke Anowtalik
Mother and Child with Caribou Spirit
before 1992
darkened stone, antler
53.0 x 35.0 x 33.5 cm
Gift of Samuel and Esther Sarick, Toronto, 1996
96/823
page 89

Mathew Aqigaaq
Figures with Bear
1975–76
darkened stone, antler
37.5 x 37.9 x 28.0 cm
Gift of Samuel and Esther Sarick, Toronto, 1996
96/918
page 90

George Arluk
Father and Child
1970–71
stone
32.2 x 19.6 x 8.8 cm
Gift of Samuel and Esther Sarick, 1990
90/387
page 129

George Arluk
Figure
1975
stone
12.2 x 15.4 x 2.8 cm
Gift of Samuel and Esther Sarick, 1989
89/497
page 128

Karoo Ashevak
Bird Spirit
1972
whale bone, antler, ivory
26.6 x 28.3 x 24.3 cm
Gift of Samuel and Esther Sarick, Toronto, 1996
96/747
page 93

Karoo Ashevak
Shaman with Spirit Helper
1972
whale bone, ivory, stone, sinew
47.7 x 23.6 x 16.6 cm
Gift of Samuel and Esther Sarick, Toronto, 1996
96/744
page 118

Karoo Ashevak
Mother and Child with Pulled Tooth
c. 1972
whale bone, antler, stone, ivory, sinew
50.9 x 40.7 x 33.6 cm
Gift of Samuel and Esther Sarick, Toronto, 1996
96/745
page 118

Karoo Ashevak
Spirit Figure
c. 1972
whale bone, antler, ivory, stone
32.7 x 65.5 x 10.5 cm
Gift of Samuel and Esther Sarick, Toronto, 1996
96/746
pages 118–19

Kenojuak Ashevak
Complex of Birds
1960
stonecut on paper
61.1 x 66.1 cm
Gift of Samuel and Esther Sarick, Toronto, 2002
© Dorset Fine Arts
2002/9461
page 174

Kenojuak Ashevak
The Enchanted Owl
1960
stonecut on paper
59.7 x 65.0 cm
Gift of Samuel and Esther Sarick, Toronto, 2002
© Dorset Fine Arts
2002/9460
page 174

Kenojuak Ashevak
Three Birds and Seal
1960–63
graphite on paper
48.5 x 66.5 cm
Gift of Samuel and Esther Sarick, Toronto, 2002
© Dorset Fine Arts
2002/10635
pages 174–75

Kenojuak Ashevak
Five Creatures
1960–65
graphite on paper
46.0 x 60.5 cm
Gift of Samuel and Esther Sarick, Toronto, 2002
© Dorset Fine Arts
2002/10639
page 174

Kiugak Ashoona
Bird and Animal Head Cluster
early 1970s
stone
16.3 x 17.1 x 12.3 cm
Gift of Samuel and Esther Sarick, 1990
© Dorset Fine Arts
90/560
page 140

Kiugak Ashoona
Sea Goddess and Young
before 1986
stone, wood
49.8 x 26.5 x 19.9 cm
Gift of Samuel and Esther Sarick, Toronto, 1996
© Dorset Fine Arts
96/1035
page 141

Pitseolak Ashoona
Tattooed Woman
1960
graphite on paper
41.9 x 53.4 cm
Gift of Samuel and Esther Sarick, Toronto, 2002
© Dorset Fine Arts
2002/10648
page 160

Pitseolak Ashoona
Tattooed Woman
1963
stonecut on paper
75.2 x 62.9 cm
Gift of Samuel and Esther Sarick, Toronto, 2002
© Dorset Fine Arts
2002/9570
page 160

Pitseolak Ashoona
Travelling by Umiak and Kayak
c. 1966–76
coloured pencil and porous pointed pen on paper
50.8 x 66.3 cm
Gift of Samuel and Esther Sarick, Toronto, 2002
© Dorset Fine Arts
2002/10680
page 160

Pitseolak Ashoona
In summer there were always big mosquitoes
1970
porous pointed pen on paper
68.6 x 53.5 cm
Gift of Samuel and Esther Sarick, Toronto, 2002
© Dorset Fine Arts
2002/10664
page 161

Qaqaq Ashoona
Bird/Human Transformation
1986
stone
42.2 x 36.4 x 13.4 cm
Gift of Samuel and Esther Sarick, Toronto, 1996
© Dorset Fine Arts
96/1026
page 90

Shuvinai Ashoona
Cape Dorset from Above
2007–8
coloured pencil and ink on paper
66.0 x 50.8 cm
Collection of Samuel and Esther Sarick, Toronto
© Dorset Fine Arts
page 201

Shuvinai Ashoona
Composition (Sewage Truck)
2007–8
coloured pencil and ink on paper
50.8 cm x 66.0 cm
Collection of Samuel and Esther Sarick, Toronto
© Dorset Fine Arts
page 200

Shuvinai Ashoona
Composition (Unloading Truck)
2009
coloured pencil and ink on paper
64.5 x 96.0 cm
Collection of Samuel and Esther Sarick, Toronto
© Dorset Fine Arts
pages 202–3

Romeo Eekerkik
Family
c. 1972
antler, bone, sinew, string, colouring
20.6 x 31.3 x 18.3 cm
Gift of Samuel and Esther Sarick, Toronto, 1996
96/827
page viii

Ennutsiak
Book Reading Scene
c. 1959
stone, ivory
9.0 x 7.2 x 17.3 cm
Collection of Samuel and Esther Sarick, Toronto
page 83

Luke Iksiktaaryuk
Family
c. 1967
antler
30.2 x 57.6 x 31.2 cm
Gift of Samuel and Esther Sarick, 1990
90/382
page 133

Luke Iksiktaaryuk
The Herd
1972
stonecut and stencil on paper
62.9 x 100.7 cm
Gift of Samuel and Esther Sarick, Toronto, 2002
2002/10549
page 101

Luke Iksiktaaryuk
A Drum Dance
c. 1975
antler, skin, wood, sinew, metal
21.0 x 40.5 x 33.8 cm (assembled)
Gift of Samuel and Esther Sarick, 1990
90/515
pages 132–33

Luke Iksiktaaryuk
Shaman in Flight
c. 1975
antler, hide
46.6 x 46.2 x 20.0 cm
Gift of Samuel and Esther Sarick, Toronto, 1996
96/947
page 133

Osuitok Ipeelee
Woman
c. 1957
stone
32.1 x 11.4 x 6.8 cm
Gift of Samuel and Esther Sarick, Toronto, 1996
© Dorset Fine Arts
96/331
page 67

Osuitok Ipeelee
Bird
1982
stone
30.2 x 26.5 x 7.4 cm
Gift of Samuel and Esther Sarick, Toronto, 1996
© Dorset Fine Arts
96/337
page 138

Osuitok Ipeelee
Bird
1983
stone
27.3 x 16.5 x 7.6 cm
Gift of Samuel and Esther Sarick, Toronto, 1996
© Dorset Fine Arts
96/329
page 138

Osuitok Ipeelee
Caribou Head
before 1988
stone, antler
63.7 x 54.0 x 31.3 cm
Gift of Samuel and Esther Sarick, Toronto, 1996
© Dorset Fine Arts
96/347
page 139

Matiusie Iyaituk
This woman is happy to see that her son is becoming a good hunter
1980
darkened stone, antler, hide, colouring, wood
21.4 x 24.6 x 22.9 cm
Gift of Samuel and Esther Sarick, 1989
89/606
page 214

Matiusie Iyaituk
Sheltered by Caribou Skin
2000
stone, hair
110.0 x 15.0 x 14.0 cm
Collection of Samuel and Esther Sarick, Toronto
page 215

John Kavik
Man Carrying Animal
1970–71
stone
12.6 x 10.5 x 6.8 cm
Gift of Samuel and Esther Sarick, Toronto, 1996
96/679
page 125

John Kavik
Figure and Bird
c. 1972
stone
20.4 x 22.3 x 11.4 cm
Gift of Samuel and Esther Sarick, 1990
90/436
page 124

John Kavik
Mother and Child
c. 1974
stone
14.2 x 13.2 x 7.0 cm
Gift of Samuel and Esther Sarick, Toronto, 1996
96/691
page 125

Kiakshuk
Four Couples
1960
graphite on paper
46.0 x 56.5 cm
Gift of Samuel and Esther Sarick, Toronto, 2002
© Dorset Fine Arts
2002/10690
page 164

Kiakshuk
Kikgavik and the Hunter
1960
graphite on paper
20.4 x 33.2 cm
Gift of Samuel and Esther Sarick, Toronto, 2002
© Dorset Fine Arts
2002/10686
page 165

Kiakshuk
Kikgavik and the Hunter
1960
stonecut on paper
60.1 x 71.3 cm
Gift of Samuel and Esther Sarick, Toronto, 2002
© Dorset Fine Arts
2002/9648
page 165

Kiakshuk
Spirits and Men
1960–65
graphite on paper
46.0 x 53.5 cm
Gift of Samuel and Esther Sarick, Toronto, 2002
© Dorset Fine Arts
2002/10697
page 165

Janet Kigusiuq
Fishing Weir
c. 1970s
wax crayon, coloured pencil and graphite on paper
56.5 x 76.5 cm
Collection of Samuel and Esther Sarick, Toronto
page 172

Janet Kigusiuq
Camp Scene with Mosquitoes
c. 1980s
coloured pencil, wax crayon and graphite on paper
56.5 x 76.5 cm
Collection of Samuel and Esther Sarick, Toronto
page 173

Janet Kigusiuq
Three Large Fish
1984
coloured pencil and graphite on paper
56.5 x 76.3 cm
Gift of Samuel and Esther Sarick, Toronto, 2002
2002/10321
page 101

Janet Kigusiuq
Caribou
c. 1990s
wax crayon and graphite on paper
57.0 x 76.0 cm
Collection of Samuel and Esther Sarick, Toronto
page 172

Koviak
Cribbage Board
1942–45
ivory, stone inlay
16.6 x 87.3 x 11.7 cm
Gift of Samuel and Esther Sarick, Toronto, 1996
96/716
pages 58–59

Thomassie Kudluk
Stacked Up Together
1980
darkened stone
29.8 x 13.8 x 4.4 cm
Gift of Samuel and Esther Sarick, 1988
88/743
page 92

Myra Kukiiyaut
Imaginary Scene
c. 1980s
coloured pencil on paper
57.8 x 76.2 cm
Collection of Samuel and Esther Sarick, Toronto
page 94

Victoria Mamnguqsualuk
Giant Insect
1980s
coloured pencil and graphite on paper
58.5 x 80.0 cm
Gift of Samuel and Esther Sarick, Toronto, 2002
2002/10388
page 176

Victoria Mamnguqsualuk
Imaginary Scene
c. 1980s
wax crayon on paper
56.5 x 76.0 cm
Collection of Samuel and Esther Sarick, Toronto
page 177

Victoria Mamnguqsualuk
Tales of Qiviuq
1980s
coloured pencil and graphite on paper
59.0 x 80.0 cm
Gift of Samuel and Esther Sarick, Toronto, 2002
2002/10379
page 176

Andy Miki
Animal
c. 1967
stone
12.4 x 8.2 x 3.8 cm
Gift of Samuel and Esther Sarick, Toronto, 1996
96/833
page 134

Andy Miki
Animal
c. 1970
darkened stone
10.9 x 22.0 x 15.7 cm
Gift of Samuel and Esther Sarick, Toronto, 1996
96/836
page 135

Andy Miki
Bird
1972–73
darkened stone
14.2 x 3.7 x 8.2 cm
Gift of Samuel and Esther Sarick, Toronto, 2001
2001/282
page 135

Mary Kahootsuak Miki
Mother and Child
before 1979
darkened stone
22.6 x 16.4 x 13.8 cm
Gift of Samuel and Esther Sarick, Toronto, 1996
96/840
page 86

Bill Nasogaluak
Bear Falling through Rotting Ice
2006
stone
18.5 x 22.0 x 21.8 cm
Collection of Samuel and Esther Sarick, Toronto
pages 216–17

Bill Nasogaluak
Sedna on Cross
2006
stone, metal
53.8 x 27.0 x 12.0 cm
Collection of Samuel and Esther Sarick, Toronto
page 216

Niviaksiak
Man Hunting at a Seal Hole in the Ice, from *Niviaksiak Sketchbook*
1950s
ink and graphite on paper
43.0 x 35.5 cm
Gift of Samuel and Esther Sarick, Toronto, 2002
© Dorset Fine Arts
2002/10706
page 72

Niviaksiak
Polar Bear and Cub in Ice, from *Niviaksiak Sketchbook*
1950s
ink and graphite on paper
43.0 x 35.5 cm
Gift of Samuel and Esther Sarick, Toronto, 2002
© Dorset Fine Arts
2002/10706
page 73

Niviaksiak
Man Hunting at a Seal Hole in the Ice
1959
stencil on paper
59.8 x 45.7 cm
Gift of the McLean Foundation, 1960
© Dorset Fine Arts
59/24
page 72

Niviaksiak
Polar Bear and Cub in Ice
1959
stencil on paper
34.1 x 65.8 cm
Gift of the McLean Foundation, 1960
© Dorset Fine Arts
59/23
page 73

Maudie Rachel Okittuq
Sea Goddess
1978
stone
12.8 x 35.6 x 14.9 cm
Gift of Samuel and Esther Sarick, Toronto, 1996
96/754
pages 150–51

Maudie Rachel Okittuq
Woman Giving Birth
c. 1980
stone
19.4 x 12.0 x 11.4 cm
Gift of Samuel and Esther Sarick, Toronto, 1996
96/753
page 151

Jessie Oonark
Female Shaman with Spirit Helpers
c. 1970
coloured pencil and graphite on paper
51.0 x 66.1 cm
Gift of Samuel and Esther Sarick, Toronto, 2002
2002/10433
page 162

Jessie Oonark
Hunters and Bird Spirit
c. 1970
coloured pencil on paper
58.0 x 79.8 cm
Gift of Samuel and Esther Sarick, Toronto, 2002
2002/10434
page 163

Jessie Oonark
Shaman's Flight
c. 1970
coloured pencil, porous pointed pen and graphite on paper
58.0 x 77.4 cm
Gift of Samuel and Esther Sarick, Toronto, 2002
2002/10417
page 162

Jessie Oonark
Capturing Geese
early 1970s
coloured pencil and graphite on paper
56.0 x 76.6 cm
Gift of Samuel and Esther Sarick, Toronto, 2002
2002/10428
pages 100–101

Sheokjuk Oqutaq
Glove Maker
c. 1955
stone, ivory, sinew
15.4 x 10.5 x 14.0 cm
Collection of Samuel and Esther Sarick, Toronto
© Dorset Fine Arts
page 156

Sheokjuk Oqutaq
Woman Standing
c. 1955
ivory, colouring
14.9 x 4.6 x 4.1 cm
Collection of Samuel and Esther Sarick, Toronto
© Dorset Fine Arts
page 157

Anirnik Oshuitoq
Drawing for the print "The Oracle"
1965
graphite and coloured pencil on paper
49.7 x 63.1 cm
Gift of Samuel and Esther Sarick, Toronto, 2002
2002/10710
page 95

John Pangnark
Figure
1968
stone
9.8 x 10.4 x 4.9 cm
Collection of Samuel and Esther Sarick, Toronto
page 121

John Pangnark
Figure
1969
darkened stone
10.5 x 13.9 x 9.2 cm
Gift of Samuel and Esther Sarick, Toronto, 1996
96/861
page 121

John Pangnark
Figure
1970
stone
13.3 x 13.1 x 9.2 cm
Gift of Samuel and Esther Sarick, Toronto, 1996
96/873
page 120

John Pangnark
Figure
1974
stone
21.5 x 22.3 x 18.3 cm
Gift of Samuel and Esther Sarick, 1989
89/552
page 121

Parr
Dog Team, Figures, Walrus and Igloo
c. 1960
graphite on paper
61.0 x 45.8 cm
Gift of Samuel and Esther Sarick, Toronto, 2002
© Dorset Fine Arts
2002/10775
page 167

Parr
Figures and Sea Mammals
c. 1960
graphite on paper
60.7 x 45.7 cm
Gift of Samuel and Esther Sarick, Toronto, 2002
© Dorset Fine Arts
2002/10769
page 167

Parr
Figures with Geese and Animals
1961
graphite on paper
50.4 x 45.8 cm
Gift of Samuel and Esther Sarick, Toronto, 2002
© Dorset Fine Arts
2002/10720
page 166

David Ruben Piqtoukun
Shaman
1989
Brazilian soapstone, antler, ivory, Arizona pipestone, stone inlay
19.9 x 66.6 x 38.2 cm
Gift of Samuel and Esther Sarick, Toronto, 1996
© 2010 David Ruben Piqtoukun
96/563
page 98

David Ruben Piqtoukun
Guidepost
1995
limestone, Brazilian soapstone, slate
94.5 x 61.0 x 14.5 cm; base: 41.2 x 25.0 x 14.5 cm
Gift of Samuel and Esther Sarick, Toronto, 2001
© 2010 David Ruben Piqtoukun
2001/412
page 210

David Ruben Piqtoukun
Journey to the Great Woman
1995
Brazilian soapstone, Ontario marble, Italian alabaster, African wonderstone
58.0 x 41.0 x 15.5 cm
Gift of Samuel and Esther Sarick, Toronto, 2001
© 2010 David Ruben Piqtoukun
2001/409
page 211

David Ruben Piqtoukun
Shaman Crash Landing
2001
stone, metal, ivory, inlay
26.5 x 50.5 x 63.0 cm
Collection of Samuel and Esther Sarick, Toronto
© 2010 David Ruben Piqtoukun
pages 212–13

Tim Pitsiulak
Composition (Whalers)
2009
coloured pencil and graphite on paper
121.9 x 243.8 cm
Collection of Samuel and Esther Sarick, Toronto
© Dorset Fine Arts
pages 194–95

Tim Pitsiulak
Composition (Whales Feeding)
2009
coloured pencil and graphite on paper
238.8 x 121.9 cm
Collection of Samuel and Esther Sarick, Toronto
© Dorset Fine Arts
page 193

Annie Pootoogook
Three Men Playing Cards
2001–2
coloured pencil and ink on paper
50.8 x 66.0 cm
Collection of Samuel and Esther Sarick, Toronto
© Dorset Fine Arts
page 198

Annie Pootoogook
In the Kitchen
2002–3
coloured pencil and ink on paper
50.8 x 66.0 cm
Collection of Samuel and Esther Sarick, Toronto
© Dorset Fine Arts
page 198

Annie Pootoogook
Calling Annie
2005–6
coloured pencil and ink on paper
50.8 x 54.6 cm
Collection of Samuel and Esther Sarick, Toronto
© Dorset Fine Arts
page 199

Itee Pootoogook
Abandoned House
2009
coloured pencil and graphite on paper
27.9 x 38.1 cm
Collection of Samuel and Esther Sarick, Toronto
© Dorset Fine Arts
page 204

Itee Pootoogook
Qilalukat
2009
coloured pencil and graphite on paper
38.1 x 55.8 cm
Collection of Samuel and Esther Sarick, Toronto
© Dorset Fine Arts
page 205

Itee Pootoogook
Waiting for Penny Sale
2009
graphite on paper
55.9 x 76.2 cm
Collection of Samuel and Esther Sarick, Toronto
© Dorset Fine Arts
page 102

Itee Pootoogook
Woman in Window
2009
graphite on paper
38.1 x 55.9 cm
Collection of Samuel and Esther Sarick, Toronto
© Dorset Fine Arts
page 204

Josephie Pootoogook
Grazing Caribou
1957
stonecut and lino block
15.0 x 24.0 cm
Gift of Samuel and Esther Sarick, Toronto, 2002
© Dorset Fine Arts
2002/9735
page 70

Josephie Pootoogook
Grazing Caribou
c. 1957
graphite on paperboard
22.9 x 22.7 cm
Gift of Samuel and Esther Sarick, Toronto, 2002
© Dorset Fine Arts
2002/10783
page 70

Josephie Pootoogook
The Hunter's Signal
1961
stencil on paper (posthumous print)
63.7 x 48.4 cm
Gift of Samuel and Esther Sarick, Toronto, 2002
© Dorset Fine Arts
2002/9738
page 68

Kananginak Pootoogook
Accordion Player
1995
coloured pencil and ink on paper
66.0 x 50.8 cm
Collection of Samuel and Esther Sarick, Toronto
© Dorset Fine Arts
page 182

Kananginak Pootoogook
RCMP and Inuit Family
2007
coloured pencil and ink on paper
57.0 x 76.0 cm
Collection of Samuel and Esther Sarick, Toronto
© Dorset Fine Arts
page 183

Kananginak Pootoogook
Man and Woman on Skidoo
2009
coloured pencil and ink on paper
56.0 x 76.0 cm
Collection of Samuel and Esther Sarick, Toronto
© Dorset Fine Arts
page 183

Napachie Pootoogook
Whaler's Exchange
1989
lithograph (7/50)
40.6 x 50.8 cm
Collection of Samuel and Esther Sarick, Toronto
© Dorset Fine Arts
page 185

Napachie Pootoogook
Shaman/Minister
1996
ink and pencil crayon on paper
66.0 x 51.0 cm
Collection of Samuel and Esther Sarick, Toronto
© Dorset Fine Arts
page 184

Pudlo Pudlat
Scene with Two Airplanes and Church
1976
acrylic, coloured pencil and porous pointed pen on paper
49.1 x 56.2 cm
Gift of Samuel and Esther Sarick, Toronto, 2002
© Dorset Fine Arts
2002/10807
page 170

Pudlo Pudlat
Drawing for the print "Modern Settlement – Traditional Camp"
1978–79
coloured pencil, graphite and porous pointed pen on paper
56.9 x 76.2 cm
Gift of Samuel and Esther Sarick, Toronto, 2002
© Dorset Fine Arts
2002/10813
page 171

Pudlo Pudlat
Drawing for the print "Spirit Embracing Settlement"
1978–79
coloured pencil and porous pointed pen on paper
56.5 x 76.5 cm
Gift of Samuel and Esther Sarick, Toronto, 2002
© Dorset Fine Arts
2002/10812
page 171

Paniluk Qamanirq
Bird Transformation
1971
whale bone
25.4 x 20.2 x 10.1 cm
Gift of Samuel and Esther Sarick, Toronto, 2001
2001/279
page 122

Paniluk Qamanirq
Two Forms on Base
c. 1971
stone, ivory
13.3 x 5.7 x 5.0 cm
Collection of Samuel and Esther Sarick, Toronto
page 123

Paniluk Qamanirq
Animal
c. 1973
stone
5.4 x 20.9 x 3.7 cm
Gift of Samuel and Esther Sarick, Toronto, 1996
96/808
page 122

Nungusuituq Qaqyuraqyuk
Sea Goddess
1988
stone, ivory, plastic
15.1 x 36.0 x 19.1 cm
Gift of Samuel and Esther Sarick, Toronto, 1996
© Dorset Fine Arts
96/376
page 98

Lukta Qiatsuq
Bird Preening
1983
stone
20.9 x 28.2 x 22.5 cm
Gift of Samuel and Esther Sarick, Toronto, 1996
© Dorset Fine Arts
96/378
page 97

Eli Sallualu Qinuajua
Fantastic Figure
1969
stone
54.2 x 47.4 x 14.3 cm
Gift of Samuel and Esther Sarick, 1989
89/657
page 152

Eli Sallualu Qinuajua
Fantastic Figure
c. 1970
stone
19.2 x 28.6 x 13.5 cm
Gift of Samuel and Esther Sarick, Toronto, 1996
96/622
page 152

Eli Sallualu Qinuajua
Fantastic Figure with Man in Mouth
1975
darkened stone
16.3 x 29.6 x 14.7 cm
Gift of Samuel and Esther Sarick, Toronto, 1996
96/621
page 153

Sakiassie Ragee
Sea Goddess Feeding Young
1961
stonecut on paper
31.0 x 41.3 cm
Gift of Samuel and Esther Sarick, Toronto, 2002
© Dorset Fine Arts
2002/9970
page 99

Abraham Anghik Ruben
Sedna
c. 1990
Brazilian soapstone, stone
70.0 x 35.5 x 18.0 cm
Gift of Samuel and Esther Sarick, Toronto, 2001
© 2010 Abraham Anghik Ruben
2001/400
page 206

Abraham Anghik Ruben
Bird Shaman
c. 1990s
Brazilian soapstone, Arizona pipestone
75.0 x 26.0 x 19.0 cm
Gift of Samuel and Esther Sarick, Toronto, 2001
© 2010 Abraham Anghik Ruben
2001/407
page 207

Abraham Anghik Ruben
Journey to the Spirit World
c. 1995
Brazilian soapstone, whale bone
43.5 x 118.0 x 68.5 cm
Gift of Samuel and Esther Sarick, Toronto, 2001
© 2010 Abraham Anghik Ruben
2001/404
page 207

Pauta Saila
Bear
1967
stone
46.0 x 42.0 x 40.0 cm
Collection of Samuel and Esther Sarick, Toronto
© Dorset Fine Arts
page 116

Pauta Saila
Dancing Bear
c. 1973
stone
48.5 x 36.5 x 19.0 cm
Gift of Samuel and Esther Sarick, 1989
© Dorset Fine Arts
89/625
page 117

Pauta Saila
Dancing Bear
1984
stone, ivory
51.2 x 38.8 x 22.8 cm
Gift of Samuel and Esther Sarick, Toronto, 2001
© Dorset Fine Arts
2001/331
page 116

Peter Sevoga
A ptarmigan offers itself to a family
1971
stained stone
28.4 x 29.2 x 11.3 cm
Gift of Samuel and Esther Sarick, Toronto, 1996
96/985
page 155

Peter Sevoga
Family
1972
stained stone
25.2 x 22.7 x 22.5 cm
Gift of Samuel and Esther Sarick, Toronto, 1996
96/982
page 154

Peter Sevoga
Mother and Children
1973
darkened stone
21.2 x 23.7 x 19.3 cm
Gift of Samuel and Esther Sarick, Toronto, 1996
96/978
page 154

Aqjangajuk Shaa
Man with Fish and Seal
before 1974
stone
54.4 x 51.5 x 22.0 cm
Gift of Samuel and Esther Sarick, 1989
89/661
page 142

Aqjangajuk Shaa
Caribou Standing on Hind Legs
1982
stone, antler
64.0 x 37.8 x 36.0 cm
Gift of Samuel and Esther Sarick, 1990
90/594
page 143

Nick Sikkuark
Shaman Performing
1987–88
whale bone, fur, sinew
38.0 x 46.5 x 22.5 cm
Gift of Samuel and Esther Sarick, Toronto, 1996
96/424
page 149

Nick Sikkuark
Spirit Figure Swallowing Animal
1989
whale bone, bone, antler, hide, fur, white pigment, claw
74.2 x 19.4 x 18.9 cm
Gift of Samuel and Esther Sarick, Toronto, 1996
96/422
page 148

Isa Aqiattusuk Smiler
Seated Mother with Child
c. 1953
stone, ivory inlay
14.5 x 15.0 x 9.5 cm
Collection of Samuel and Esther Sarick, Toronto
page 84

Nelson Takkiruq
Mother Delousing Child
1992
whale bone, ivory, stone, horn
58.8 x 35.0 x 25.2 cm
Gift of Samuel and Esther Sarick, Toronto, 1996
96/431
page 91

Quvianatuliak Takpaungai
Female Nude
before 1982
stone
12.3 x 29.2 x 15.3 cm
Gift of Samuel and Esther Sarick, Toronto, 1996
© Dorset Fine Arts
96/401
page 144

Quvianatuliak Takpaungai
Woman Holding Braids
before 1987
stone
29.9 x 45.5 x 14.0 cm
Gift of Samuel and Esther Sarick, Toronto, 1996
© Dorset Fine Arts
96/402
pages 144–45

Joe Talirunili
Building a Large Skin Boat
1970s
pencil and wax crayon on paper
30.1 x 45.0 cm
Gift of Samuel and Esther Sarick, Toronto, 2002
2002/10184.1–.4
pages 112–13

Joe Talirunili
Three Large Figures
1971
porous pointed pen and graphite on paper
35.7 x 27.2 cm
Gift of Samuel and Esther Sarick, Toronto, 2002
2002/10194
page 111

Joe Talirunili
Migration
c. 1974
stone, hide, wood, string
33.7 x 39.5 x 19.5 cm
Gift of Samuel and Esther Sarick, Toronto, 1996
96/640
page 112

George Tatanniq
Fox-Woman
c. 1970
stone
39.1 x 16.3 x 11.0 cm
Gift of Samuel and Esther Sarick, Toronto, 1996
96/989
page 131

George Tatanniq
Muskox
c. 1971
stone, horn
24.5 x 32.5 x 14.0 cm
Gift of Samuel and Esther Sarick, 1989
89/568
page 131

George Tatanniq
Drum Dancer with Helping Spirits
1973
darkened stone, antler, bone
21.7 x 27.1 x 11.6 cm
Gift of Samuel and Esther Sarick, Toronto, 1996
96/992
pages 130–31

John Tiktak
Head
c. 1965
stone
18.0 x 13.2 x 8.0 cm
Collection of Samuel and Esther Sarick, Toronto
page 126

John Tiktak
Mother and Child
c. 1966
stone
20.1 x 17.3 x 6.0 cm
Gift of Samuel and Esther Sarick, Toronto, 1996
96/701
page 126

John Tiktak
Man with Arms Raised
1969
stone
15.0 x 10.2 x 7.9 cm
Gift of Samuel and Esther Sarick, Toronto, 1996
96/703
page 126

John Tiktak
Faces
c. 1971
stone
13.8 x 25.3 x 20.3 cm
Gift of Samuel and Esther Sarick, 1990
90/360
page 127

Bernadette Iguptark Tongelik
Transformed Shaman and Walrus
c. 1973
stone, ivory, sinew, inlay
17.5 x 21.5 x 17.4 cm
Gift of Samuel and Esther Sarick, Toronto, 1996
96/718
page 88

Simon Tookoome
Four Dogs, Four Double-Faced Humans
1980s
coloured pencil on paper
78.5 x 58.0 cm
Gift of Samuel and Esther Sarick, Toronto, 2002
2002/10479
page 180

Simon Tookoome
Wolf and Inuit
1980s
coloured pencil on paper
58.5 x 78.0 cm
Gift of Samuel and Esther Sarick, Toronto, 2002
2002/10480
page 181

Toonoo
Man
before 1959
stone, ivory, hide
15.4 x 8.6 x 8.0 cm
Gift of Samuel and Esther Sarick, Toronto, 1996
© Dorset Fine Arts
96/405
page 67

Tudlik
Bear Standing on Hind Legs
c. 1955
stone, antler
18.6 x 13.5 x 7.8 cm
Collection of Samuel and Esther Sarick, Toronto
© Dorset Fine Arts
page 71

Ruth Annaqtuusi Tulurialik
Camp Scene with Spirits
1980s
wax crayon, coloured pencil and graphite on paper
59.0 x 74.0 cm
Gift of Samuel and Esther Sarick, Toronto, 2002
2002/10497
page 178

Ruth Annaqtuusi Tulurialik
On the Land
1990
coloured pencil, graphite on paper
56.1 x 76.2 cm
Gift of Samuel and Esther Sarick, Toronto, 2002
2002/10494
page 179

Oviloo Tunnillie
Untitled (Standing Woman with Hands Cupped over Face)
1990s
stone
55.7 x 21.8 x 11.6 cm
Gift of Samuel and Esther Sarick, Toronto, 2001
© Dorset Fine Arts
2001/341
page 208

Oviloo Tunnillie
Angel
1997
stone
46.0 x 23.0 x 14.0 cm
Collection of Samuel and Esther Sarick, Toronto
© Dorset Fine Arts
page 209

Lucy Tasseor Tutsweetok
Face Cluster
c. 1969
darkened stone
25.5 x 20.4 x 11.0 cm
Gift of Samuel and Esther Sarick, Toronto, 1996
96/899
page 158

Lucy Tasseor Tutsweetok
Family
c. 1969
darkened stone
16.4 x 17.0 x 4.6 cm
Gift of Samuel and Esther Sarick, 1989
89/608
page 159

Lucy Tasseor Tutsweetok
Mother and Children
c. 1980
darkened stone
15.5 x 9.2 x 8.7 cm
Gift of Samuel and Esther Sarick, Toronto, 1996
96/900
page 158

Judas Ullulaq
Fisherman with Dog
c. 1983
whale bone, bone, horn, stone, sinew
35.5 x 35.6 x 28.0 cm
Gift of Samuel and Esther Sarick, Toronto, 1996
96/438
page 147

Judas Ullulaq
Shaman with Amulets and Ceremonial Mask
1985
whale bone, antler, stone, sinew
53.5 x 26.5 x 14.3 cm
Gift of Samuel and Esther Sarick, Toronto, 2001
2001/351
page 147

Judas Ullulaq
Man Throwing Bolo at Bird
1988
stone, whale bone, antler, wood, sinew, bone
38.1 x 59.0 x 31.4 cm
Gift of Samuel and Esther Sarick, Toronto, 1996
96/441
pages 146–47

Judas Ullulaq
Untitled
c. 1990
whale bone, wood, sinew, hide
22.1 x 19.8 x 18.2 cm (large figure); 10.0 x 13.2 x 7.0 cm (small figure)
Gift of Samuel and Esther Sarick, Toronto, 2001
2001/350
page 96

Unknown Artist
Bear
early 1900s
ivory, colouring
2.9 x 2.1 x 8.1 cm
Gift of Samuel and Esther Sarick, Toronto, 1996
96/785
page 56

Unknown Artist
Sailor
1900–1925
stone, ivory
12.5 x 6.0 x 2.5 cm
Gift of Samuel and Esther Sarick, 1990
90/447
page 57

Unknown Artist, Eastern Arctic
Fox with Leg Trap
1941–42
ivory, colouring
2.5 x 1.1 x 6.4 cm
Gift of Samuel and Esther Sarick, Toronto, 2001
2001/349
page 56

Unknown Artist, Inukjuak
Mother and Child
1948–53
stone, colouring
11.0 x 6.0 x 5.3 cm
Gift of Samuel and Esther Sarick, Toronto, 1996
96/482
page 66

Unknown Artist, Inukjuak
Man with Snow Knife
c. 1954
ivory, colouring
10.5 x 4.5 x 6.0 cm
Collection of Samuel and Esther Sarick, Toronto
page 66

Unknown Artist, Inukjuak
Woman Holding Ulu
c. 1954
Ivory, colouring
11.0 x 4.0 x 3.0 cm
Collection of Samuel and Esther Sarick, Toronto
page 66

Credits for Quotes

Page 2: Oviloo Tunnillie in *Keeping Our Stories Alive: The Sculpture of Canada's Inuit* (Indian and Northern Affairs Canada, 1993); video: 24 minutes.

Page 6: Manasie Akpaliapik in "Carving Is Healing to Me: An Interview with Manasie Akpaliapik" by John Ayre, *Inuit Art Quarterly* 8, no. 4 (Winter 1993): 34–42.

Page 9: Pudlo Pudlat in "Being 'True' to What He Sees" by Sarah Jennings, *Globe and Mail*, July 18, 1990.

Page 31: Jessie Oonark in "Jessie Oonark: A Genuine Natural Artist" by Michael White, *Montreal Gazette*, April 10, 1971.
Johnny Maiko, as quoted by Nelson Graburn in "Inuit Art and the Expression of Eskimo Identity," *American Review of Canadian Studies* 17 (1987): 60.

Page 38: Pudlo Pudlat in "Inuit Artist Draws to Sell" by Nancy Baele, *Ottawa Citizen*, July 7, 1990.

Page 44: Mathew Aqigaaq in *An Inuit Perspective: Baker Lake Sculpture* (Art Gallery of Ontario, 2000).

Page 46: Abraham Anghik Ruben in *Abraham Anghik Ruben* (Winnipeg Art Gallery, 2002), 9.

Page 189: Manasie Akpaliapik in "Sculpting from Polar Roots" by Deidre Kelly, *Globe and Mail*, July 13, 1996.

Page 192: Simon Tookoome in *Arctic Spirit: Inuit Art from the Albrecht Collection at the Heard Museum* by Ingo Hessel (Douglas & McIntyre, 2006), 115.

Back cover: Kenojuak Ashevak in "Art Is My Job and My Love" by Marina Jimenez, *Globe and Mail*, October 20, 2003.
Simon Tookoome in *Arctic Spirit* by Ingo Hessel (Douglas & McIntyre, 2006), 115.
David Ruben Piqtoukun in "Inuit Art Exhibition Marks Turning Point" by Randal McIlroy, *Winnipeg Free Press*, February 4, 1989.

Notes

Part 1: Inuit History, Inuit Art

Inuit Modern: An Introduction by Gerald McMaster

1. George Swinton, *Sculpture of the Eskimo* (Toronto: McClelland & Stewart, 1972), 135.
2. Edmund Carpenter, *Eskimo Realities* (New York: Holt, Rinehart & Winston, 1973), 194.
3. John Houston, personal communication with author.
4. Much to the disappointment of local First Nations of British Columbia who thought a local design should have been used instead of the inukshuk logo; the organizers rightly thought it represented the country, not the region.
5. CBC Sports, "Vancouver 2010 logo unveiled," April 24, 2005, http://www.cbc.ca/sports/story/2005/04/23/2010_vancouver050423.html.
6. Kunuk was awarded the prestigious Camera d'Or at Cannes in 2001 for *Atanarjuat*.
7. Colin Rhodes, *Primitivism and Modern Art* (London: Thames & Hudson, 1994), 8.
8. Ibid., 9.
9. We have come to regard the prevailing discursive frame of ethnography with some skepticism, though today this may be shifting as more and more Aboriginal professionals influence the way museums operate; outside this field I continue to hear the way historic objects are still viewed as "ethnographic" objects, as if to suggest that is the only way to see them, not as "art" or "cultural object."
10. Throughout the twentieth century trading posts were set up in various parts of the North, for example, in 1911 at Lake Harbour (now Kimmirut, Baffin Island) and Chesterfield Inlet; 1916 at Bernard Harbour near Coppermine (now Kugluktuk); 1921 at Pond Inlet; 1923 at King William Island (Gjoa Haven). By 1923 nearly all central Arctic Inuit had access to fur-trading posts. The Hudson's Bay Company was the largest mercantile operation in the North. Canalaska Company established itself in the western Arctic in 1927–38; Reveillon-Frères in northern Keewatin 1924–36; and the Sabellum Company in the eastern Arctic 1911–20.
11. In Lorraine E. Brandson, *Carved from the Land: The Eskimo Museum Collection* (Churchill, MB: Diocese of Churchill–Hudson Bay), 7.
12. George Swinton, *Eskimo Sculpture / Sculpture Esquimaude* (Toronto: McClelland & Stewart, 1965), 25.
13. James Houston, in *Sculpture / Inuit* (Toronto: University of Toronto Press, 1971), 54.
14. Gerald Vizenor, ed., *Survivance: Narratives of Native Presence* (Lincoln: University of Nebraska Press, 2009), 11.
15. Carpenter, *Eskimo Realities*, 200.
16. Swinton, *Eskimo Sculpture / Sculpture Esquimaude*, 18.
17. Carpenter, *Eskimo Realities*, 192.
18. Jean Blodgett, *Karoo Ashevak* (Winnipeg: Winnipeg Art Gallery, 1977).
19. From Isuma Productions, http://www.isuma.tv/isuma-productions.
20. In Marie Bouchard, *An Inuit Perspective: Baker Lake Sculpture* (Baker Lake: Itsarnittakarvik Inuit Heritage Centre; Toronto: Art Gallery of Ontario, 2000), 11.

The Start of Change by Dorothy Harley Eber

1. Except where otherwise indicated, all Inuit quotations are from the author's personal interviews.
2. Ann Meekitjuk Hanson, "Celebrating with George Pitseolak," in *Celebrating Inuit Art*, ed. Maria von Finckenstein (Ottawa: Canadian Museum of Civilization / Key Porter Books, 2006), 14.
3. Peter Pitseolak and Dorothy Harley Eber, *People from Our Side: A Life Story with Photographs and Oral Biography* (Montreal: McGill-Queen's University Press, 1993), 21–26.
4. *Before Tomorrow*, directed by Marie-Hélène Cousineau and Madeline Ivalu (Alliance Atlantis, 2008).
5. Charles Francis Hall, *Life with the Eskimaux*, vol. 11, appendix 8 (London: Sampson Low, Son, & Marston, 1864), 347.
6. Captain George Comer, interview October 21, 1919, transcript, Steffansson Collection, Dartmouth College Library, Hanover, NH.
7. M.J. Ross, *Polar Pioneers: John Ross and James Clark Ross* (Montreal: McGill-Queen's University Press, 1994), 124.
8. Sir John Ross, *Narrative of a Second Voyage in Search of a North-West Passage* (London: A.W. Webster, 1835), 181.
9. Ibid., 591.
10. Dorothy Harley Eber, "New Franklin Stories: The Ship at Imnguyaaluk," in *Encounters on the Passage: Inuit Meet the Explorers* (Toronto: University of Toronto Press, 2008), 84–107.
11. Pitseolak and Eber, *People from Our Side*, 148.

Colonialism Changes Everything by Christine Lalonde

1. Alootook Ipellie, "The Colonization of the Arctic," in *Indigena: Contemporary Native Perspectives in Canadian Art*, ed. Gerald McMaster and Lee-Ann Martin (Hull, QC: Canadian Museum of Civilization; Vancouver: Douglas & McIntyre, 1992), 56.
2. During the first half of the century government administration was largely ad hoc, relying on the RCMP, Hudson's Bay Company managers or even the local missions to dispense services. See Olive Patricia Dickason, *A Concise History of Canada's First Nations* (Toronto: McClelland & Stewart, 1992), 366–67, 380–81, and 395–99; and Marybelle Mitchell, *From Talking Chiefs to a Native Corporate Elite: The Birth of Class and Nationalism among Canadian Inuit* (Montreal: McGill-Queen's University Press, 1996), 107–13.
3. Virginia Watt, ed., "The Beginning: Canadian Guild of Crafts Quebec," in *Canadian Guild of Crafts Quebec: The Permanent Collection; Inuit Arts and Crafts c. 1900–1980* (Montreal: Canadian Guild of Crafts Quebec, 1980), 11–15; James Houston, *Confessions of an Igloo Dweller* (Toronto: McClelland & Stewart, 1995); Christopher Paci, "Commercialization of Inuit Art: 1954–1964," *Études Inuit Studies* 20, no. 1 (1996): 45–62.
4. Increasingly, first-hand accounts are being recorded and published. In addition to Alootook Ipellie referenced above, these include Penny Petrone, ed., *Northern Voices, Inuit Writing in English* (Toronto: University of Toronto Press, 1988); Taamusi Qumaq, "The Autobiography of Taamusi Qumaq: Part 3, 1953–1968," *Tumivut* 8 (Fall 1996); *Inuit Nunamuit: Inland Inuit*, ed. Hattie Mannik (Baker Lake: Qilautimiut, Baker Lake Elders Group, 1998); Nancy Wachowich, in collaboration with Apphia Agalakti Awa, Rhoda Kaukjak Katsak and Sandra Pikujak Katsak, *Saqiyuq: Stories from the Lives of Three Inuit Women* (Montreal: McGill-Queen's University Press, 1999); *The World of Tivi Etok: The Life and Art of an Inuit Elder*, ed. Jobie Weetaluktuk and Robyn Bryant (Inukjuak: Avataq Cultural Institute, 2008).
5. There have been notable exceptions, in particular *Things Made by Inuit*, an exhibition organized by Nunavik co-operatives in 1980, which included recently made traditional objects along with sculpture and prints and toured to ten Nunavik communities. See Marybelle Myers, ed., *Things Made by Inuit* (St. Laurent, QC: Fédération des coopératives du Nouveau-Québec, 1980). Otherwise, exhibitions of clothing and other items have been separate.
6. Paulosie Kasudluak, "Nothing Marvellous," in *Port Harrison / Inoucdjouac* (Winnipeg: Winnipeg Art Gallery, 1976), 21.
7. Geoffrey K. Pullum, *The Great Eskimo Vocabulary Hoax and Other Irrelevant Essays on the Study of Language* (Chicago: University of Chicago Press, 1991).
8. George Swinton, *Sculpture of the Inuit*, 3rd ed. (Toronto: McClelland & Stewart, 1999), 129.
9. Nelson Graburn, ed., "Eskimo Art," in *Ethnic and Tourist Arts: Cultural Expressions from the Fourth World*. (Berkeley: University of California Press, 1976), 52.

10. Osuitok Ipeelee, quoted by Norman Hallendy in *Inuksuit, Silent Messengers of the Arctic* (Vancouver: Douglas & McIntyre, 2000), 85.
11. Marie Bouchard, *An Inuit Perspective: Baker Lake Sculpture* (Baker Lake: Itsarnittakarvik Inuit Heritage Centre; Toronto: Art Gallery of Ontario, 2000), 14–15.
12. Watt, *Canadian Guild of Crafts Quebec*, 11.
13. Darlene Wight, *The First Passionate Collector: The Ian Lindsay Collection of Inuit Art* (Winnipeg: Winnipeg Art Gallery, 1991), 56–58.
14. Mitchell, *From Talking Chiefs to a Native Corporate Elite*, 170–71.
15. Ibid., 149.
16. R.G. Robertson, Deputy Minister, Northern Affairs and National Resources, to Alan Jarvis, Director, National Gallery of Canada, July 20, 1956. 7.4E "Eskimo Handicraft Advisory Committee," National Gallery of Canada fonds, Library and Archives, National Gallery of Canada, Ottawa.
17. Department of Northern Affairs and National Resources, *Eskimo 59 Exhibit Stratford Festival* (Ottawa: Queen's Printer, 1959). Notably, no objects by Labrador Inuit were included.
18. Visual documentation, Stratford Eskimo Exhibition 1959, Ronald Gould fonds, Library and Archives, National Gallery of Canada, Ottawa.
19. *Northern Affairs Bulletin* 6, no. 3 (1959): 32. Abraham Okpik was then starting a distinguished career, first with the Department of Northern Affairs and National Resources; later he went on to become the first Inuk appointed to the Territorial Council of the Northwest Territories in 1965. He led Project Surname (1968–71), which assisted Inuit to choose family names to replace the problematic disc number system of identification. He received the Order of Canada for this work and his involvement in the Thomas Berger Commission. He settled in Iqaluit, continuing to have influence as a politician, consultant and leader, until his death in 1997. His autobiography, *Abraham Okpik: We Call It Survival*, based on interviews with Louis McComber, is the first volume in the publication series *Life Stories of Northern Leaders* (Iqaluit: Nunavut Arctic College, 2005).
20. Department of Northern Affairs and National Resources, *Eskimo 59 Exhibit Stratford Festival* (not paginated). With the exception of the sculptures and prints, all items listed were accompanied by a retail price and order form. The catalogue also included a place for comments to be mailed to the Industrial Division department.
21. Personal interview with Ronald Gould, Ottawa, February 26, 2010. Gould, formerly with the Department of Northern Affairs and National Resources, Industrial Division, from 1955–60, was involved in handicrafts programs and organizing the Stratford show. He recalls that the response to the handicrafts items was negligible. His job was then to promote the prints from Cape Dorset as fine art, rather than craft.
22. Dr. Marion Jackson, "Baker Lake Inuit Drawings: A Study in the Evolution of Artistic Self-Consciousness" (PhD thesis, University of Michigan, 1985).
23. Edmund Carpenter claims that the government appropriated his views and knowledge of older Inuit forms for their promotional "propaganda" to establish this continuity. See *Eskimo Realities* (New York: Holt, Rinehart & Winston, 1973), 193.
24. Ibid., 192.
25. Ibid., 194.
26. As quoted by Nelson Graburn in "Inuit Art and the Expression of Eskimo Identity," *American Review of Canadian Studies* 17 (1987): 60. Graburn notes in this article that there is an aesthetic connection between values appreciated in sculpture and those related to hunting. See also Michele Dupuis, "The Art of Giving: Cooperation, Reciprocity and Household Economic Strategies among Soapstone Carvers in Kimmirut (Lake Harbour), NWT" (MA thesis, McGill University, 1992).
27. Gerald Vizenor, *Fugitive Poses: Native American Indian Scenes of Absence and Presence* (Lincoln: University of Nebraska Press, 1998), 15.
28. John R. Grimes, Douglas Stenton, and Karen Kramer, *Our Land: Contemporary Art from the Arctic* (Iqaluit: Government of Nunavut Department of Culture, Language, Elders & Youth; Salem, MA: Peabody Essex Museum, 2004), 22.

Inuit Art and the Creation of Nunavut
by Bernadette Driscoll Engelstad

1. The homeland of the Inuit and Inuvialuit peoples across Arctic Canada include Nunavut, Nunavik, Nunatsiavut and the Inuvialuit Regional Settlement. With a geographic area stretching over 2 million square kilometres, Nunavut is the largest of Canada's three territories and ten provinces, with a population of 26,745 (2001 census), 85 per cent of whom are Inuit.
2. Leslie Boyd Ryan, *Cape Dorset Prints: A Retrospective; Fifty Years of Printmaking at the Kinngait Studios* (San Francisco: Pomegranate, 2007), 31.
3. Marybelle Mitchell, *From Talking Chiefs to a Native Corporate Elite: The Birth of Class and Nationalism among Canadian Inuit* (Montreal: McGill-Queen's University Press, 1996).
4. Government of Nunavut, http://www.gov.nu.ca/english/pinasuaqtavut/ (accessed March 26, 2010).
5. Knud Rasmussen, *The Intellectual Culture of the Iglulik Eskimos* (Copenhagen: Gyldendal, 1929); Bernadette Driscoll, "Pretending to Be Caribou; The Inuit Parka as an Artistic Tradition," in *The Spirit Sings: Artistic Traditions of Canada's First Nations*, by Julia Harrison (Calgary: Glenbow Alberta Museum, 1988).
6. Personal communication. Manitoba Museum of Man and Nature, Winnipeg, November 1987.
7. Sandra Dyck and Ingo Hessel, *Sanattiaqsimajut: Inuit Art from the Carleton University Art Gallery Collection* (Ottawa: Carleton University Art Gallery, 2009).
8. Maria von Finckenstein, ed., *Celebrating Inuit Art* (Ottawa: Canadian Museum of Civilization, 1999).
9. Personal communication, Qamanittuaq, November 1992. Oonark stated she "lost her mother," apparently referring to her betrothal "at the age of eleven or twelve" when she joined her future husband's family camp. See Jean Blodgett and Marie Bouchard, *Jessie Oonark: A Retrospective* (Winnipeg: Winnipeg Art Gallery, 1985), 10.
10. Personal communication, Qamanittuaq, November 1992.
11. *Port Harrison / Inoucdjouac* (Winnipeg; Winnipeg Art Gallery, 1976), 16.
12. Ibid., 17.
13. Von Finckenstein, *Celebrating Inuit Art*, 59.
14. Artist interview in *Eskimo Point / Arviat* (Winnipeg: Winnipeg Art Gallery, 1982), 29.
15. Following the closing of the nickel mine at Rankin Inlet in 1962, art production was encouraged through the establishment of a ceramic sculpture program.
16. Marybelle Myers, in *Port Harrison / Inoucdjouac*, 15.
17. Terrence Ryan, in Dyck and Hessel, *Sanattiaqsimajut*, 57.
18. Avrom Isaacs, "Foreword," in Boyd Ryan, *Cape Dorset Prints: A Retrospective*, 9.
19. Those honoured as recipients of the Order of Canada include artists Pitseolak Ashoona (1977), Helen Kalvak (1978), Kenojuak Ashevak (1982), Jessie Oonark (1984), Kiugak Ashoona (1999), Zacharias Kunuk (2002) and John Kaunak (2003), as well as James Houston (1972), George Swinton (1979), Andrew Goussaert (1980), Terrence Ryan (1983), Virginia Watt (1985) and Avrom Isaacs (1992).
20. *Inuit Piqutingit (What Belongs to Inuit)* (Isuma Productions, 2009), http://www.isuma.tv/hi/en/isuma-productions/inuit-piqutingit (accessed March 26, 2010).

The Inuit of Our Imagination
by Heather Igloliorte

1. The exception, of course, is Labrador, where Inuit have been in prolonged contact with outsiders for several centuries.
2. Marybelle Mitchell, "Social, Economic, and Political Transformation among Canadian Inuit from 1950 to 1988," in *In the Shadow of the Sun: Perspectives on Contemporary Native Art* (Gatineau: Canadian Museum of Civilization, 1993), 336.
3. Kristen Norget, "The Hunt for Inuit Souls: Religion, Colonization, and the Politics of Memory," in *The Journals of Knud Rasmussen: A Sense of Memory and High-Definition Inuit Storytelling*, ed. Gillian Robinson (Montreal: Isuma Productions, 2008), 222.
4. Richard Diubaldo, *The Government of Canada and the Inuit: 1900–1967* (Ottawa: Research Branch, Corporate Policy, Indian and Northern Affairs Canada, 1985), 163.
5. All schools in the Arctic between 1955 and 1970 (and later in some places) were called Federal Day Schools. These schools had hostels or dormitories built around them, to hold as few as eight to twenty-four students, or as many as over a hundred. Although the government did not use the term residential school to describe this new system of day schools with hostels, the Inuit and northern First Nations children who lived in hostels and dormitories near the schools (which were operated by the Department of Northern Affairs) were considered residential school students by the government. Despite the deceptive name, the experience of residential school children in the North was much the same as in the South, just over a shorter period. For more information on the Inuit experience of residential schools, see David King, *A Brief Report of the Federal Government of Canada's Residential School System for Inuit* (Ottawa: Aboriginal Healing Foundation, 2006).
6. Alootook Ipellie, "The Colonization of the Arctic," in *Indigena: Contemporary Native Perspectives in Canadian Art*, ed. Gerald McMaster and Lee-Ann Martin (Hull, QC: Canadian Museum of Civilization; Vancouver: Douglas & McIntyre, 1992), 53.

7. On the relocations in Nunatsiavut, see Carol Brice-Bennett, *Reconciling with Memories: A Record of the Reunion at Hebron 40 Years after Relocation / Ikkaumajânnik Piusivinnik: Titigattausimajut Katiutusumaningit Hebronimi 40 Jâret Kingungani Nottitausimalidlutik* (Nain: Labrador Inuit Association, 2000). For information on the Nunavik relocations, read Frank J. Tester and Peter Kulchyski, *Tammarniit (Mistakes): Inuit Relocation in the Eastern Arctic 1939–63* (Vancouver: University of British Columbia Press, 1994); and René Dussault and George Erasmus, *The High Arctic Relocation: A Report on the 1953–55 Relocation* (Ottawa: Canadian Government Publishing, 1994) for the Royal Commission on Aboriginal Peoples.
8. Tester and Kulchyski, *Tammarniit (Mistakes)*, 56.
9. Brice-Bennett, *Reconciling with Memories*, 7–9.
10. As Rosemary Kuptana eloquently illustrated in her statement to the Royal Commission on Aboriginal Peoples, the families of the *High Arctic Exiles* agreed to go because of a firmly entrenched cultural belief system that made it impossible for the Inuit to refuse. Because the Qallunaat "could make the difference between success and disaster, sustenance or hunger," Inuit responded to their requests as if they were commands. "In this cultural setting, a challenge to the authority of the Qallunaat or defiance of their requests was almost unthinkable." Rosemary Kuptana, "Ilira, or Why It Was Unthinkable for Inuit to Challenge Qallunaat Authority," reprinted in *Inuit Art Quarterly* 8, no. 3 (Fall 1993): 6. This essay was originally a speech entitled "Providing a Context for Testimony of the High Arctic Exiles: Speaking Notes for a Presentation by Susan Aglukark on Behalf of Rosemary Kuptana, President, Inuit Tapirisat of Canada, to the Royal Commission on Aboriginal Peoples' Special Hearing on the High Arctic Exiles," Ottawa, April 5, 1993.
11. Kuptana, "Ilira, or Why It Was Unthinkable for Inuit to Challenge Qallunaat Authority," 7.
12. Violet Ford, "The Inuit and Issues of Arctic Sovereignty," in *Northern Exposure: Peoples, Powers and Prospects in Canada's North*, ed. Frances Abele, Thomas J. Courchene, F. Leslie Seidle, and France St-Hilaire (Montreal: Institute for Research on Public Policy, 2009), 139.
13. Sheila Watt-Cloutier, "A Principled Path," in Abele et al., *Northern Exposure*, 73.
14. Watt-Cloutier, "A Principled Path," 72.
15. "Land-fast ice" is ice that is frozen to the coastline – fastened to the shore – as opposed to drift ice, which floats according to wind and weather patterns, or pack ice. It is extremely sensitive to climate change. Late ice formation in the winter or early ice breakup in the summer is endangering several species in the Arctic, particularly polar bears and caribou. If the ice stops freezing completely, the Northwest Passage will be extremely vulnerable to international traffic and exploitation.
16. Mary Simon, "Climate Change, Sovereignty and Partnership with the Inuit," in Abele et al., *Northern Exposure*, 524.
17. Frances Abele, Thomas J. Courchene, F. Leslie Seidle, and France St-Hilaire, "Introduction and Overview," in Abele et al., *Northern Exposure*, 4.
18. The Arctic Climate Impact Assessment (ACIA), a peer-reviewed scientific document created by some of the world's leading experts on climate change, outlined the enormity of the impact that the increase of industrial greenhouse gas emissions will have on not only the Arctic but the entire world, if we do not take immediate action to prevent climate change. The summary of this report outlined some of the major threats: animal population, diversity and territories will decrease in the Arctic and around the globe; storms, floods and other inclement weather will have a direct impact on Arctic coastal communities, with devastating outcomes; sea ice will break up, which will lead to increased traffic in the Northwest Passage, threatening sovereignty and further aggravating the fragile ecosystem; sea levels will rise globally; ground thawing will have a negative impact on the infrastructure of the North and disrupt development; food sources will be increasingly threatened; and elevated ultraviolet radiation levels will affect people, plants and animals. Susan Joy Hassol, "Key Findings," *Impacts of a Warming Arctic: Arctic Climate Impact Assessment* (Cambridge: Cambridge University Press, 2004), 10–12, http://www.amap.no/acia/ (accessed March 20, 2010).
19. *Inuit Qaujimajatuqangit* is an Inuktitut phrase that comes from the verb *qaujima*, meaning *to know*; one literal translation could be "that which has long been known by Inuit." It encompasses the oral tradition, environmentally based knowledge, and collective social memory.
20. Laura Westra, *Environmental Justice and the Rights of Indigenous Peoples* (London: Earthscan, 2008), 10–11.
21. Adam K. Johnson, "Country Foods: Are They Threatened?" *Above and Beyond* 21, no. 6 (November/December 2009): 30.
22. Acknowledging the fact that these campaigns often claim that they are not against the Inuit seal hunt but just the commercial hunt, Mary Simon has responded, "Some animal-rights groups, like some governments and legislators in Europe, have been quick to say that their anti-sealing efforts are not aimed at the seal-hunting activities of Inuit, and that seal furs resulting from Inuit hunting should be exempt from such things as import bans. It is hard for Inuit to take any comfort in these promises. These assurances are issued in what appears to be willful ignorance that past anti-sealing activities have destroyed the markets for all seal pelts, whether taken by Inuit or others. They are issued without the prospect of any plausible machinery, methods or communications efforts that would somehow allow Inuit to continue to support themselves and their way of life in the Arctic with a measure of security. No, these assurances are all about salving troubled consciences, not offering respect and reasonable accommodation." Mary Simon, "Inuit Deliver Message on Seal Hunting Practices to European Parliament, Media, and IFAW" (Ottawa: Inuit Tapiriit Kanatami, March 25, 2007), http://www.itk.ca/media-centre/media-releases/inuit-deliver-message-seal-hunting-practices-european-parliament-media-a (accessed February 18, 2010).
23. Steven Loft, "Sovereignty, Subjectivity, and Social Action: The Films of Alanis Obomsawin," in *Transference, Tradition, Technology: Native New Media Exploring Visual and Digital Culture*, ed. Melanie Townsend, Dana Claxton, and Steven Loft (Banff: Walter Phillips Gallery Editions, 2005), 66.
24. Madeleine Dion Stout and Gregory Kipling, *Aboriginal People, Resilience and the Residential School Legacy* (Ottawa: Aboriginal Healing Foundation, 2003), iii–iv.
25. Heather Igloliorte, "Inuit Art: Markers of Cultural Resilience," *Inuit Art Quarterly* 25, nos. 1 & 2 (Spring/Summer 2010): 4–11.
26. See Norman Vorano, "Inuit Art in the Qallunaat World: Modernism, Museums, and the Public Imaginary, 1949–1965" (PhD dissertation, University of Rochester, 2007).
27. In his work *New Age Christ* (2008), Toonoo condemns what he sees as the duplicity of the Church, inscribing on it, "I am the new age Christ and I have been lurking in the shadows for the past several centuries raping and plundering the earth and its inhabitants while I preach peace, financial prosperity in the midst of hunger." This work was a part of the 2008 Cape Dorset prints collection.
28. Jean Blodgett, "After Essay: And What about Inuit Art?" in *On Aboriginal Representation in the Gallery*, ed. Lynda Jessup and Shannon Bagg (Gatineau: Canadian Museum of Civilization, 2002), 210.
29. Gerald McMaster, "New Art / New Contexts," in *Vision, Space, Desire: Global Perspectives and Cultural Hybridity* (Washington: National Museum of the American Indian, Smithsonian Institution, 2006), 19.
30. Sheila Watt-Cloutier was nominated for the Nobel Peace Prize with Al Gore in 2007 for her worldwide contributions to our understanding of climate change and global warming.

Part 2: Inuit Modern
The Samuel and Esther Sarick Collection

Art of the Historic Period – The Spirit of the Thule
by Ingo Hessel

1. Renée Fossett, *In Order to Live Untroubled: Inuit of the Central Arctic* (Winnipeg: University of Manitoba Press, 2001), 33–55.
2. The medical missions founded by Wilfred Grenfell served the Labrador coast and northern Newfoundland for almost a century, from 1893 to 1981. The missions fostered "industrial development," which included the production and marketing of handicrafts.
3. George Lyon, *The Private Journal of Captain G.F. Lyon, of H.M.S. Hecla, during the Recent Voyage of Discovery under Captain Parry* (London: John Murray, 1825), 16.
4. Lyon, *The Private Journal of Captain G.F. Lyon*, 123.
5. Fossett, *In Order to Live Untroubled*, 168.
6. Whalers, and other regular visitors, also sired many children in the Canadian Arctic. For example, research has shown that in the period 1889–1911, nearly half of the forty-six births recorded in the Cape Fullerton area (on northwest Hudson Bay) were sired by Qallunaat. W. Gillies Ross, *Whaling and Eskimos: Hudson Bay 1860–1915* (Ottawa: National Museums of Canada), 122, cited in Marybelle Mitchell, *From Talking Chiefs to a Native Corporate Elite: The Birth of Class and Nationalism among Canadian Inuit* (Montreal: McGill-Queen's University Press, 1996), 80.
7. Dorothy Eber, *When the Whalers Were Up North: Inuit Memories from the Eastern Arctic* (Kingston: McGill-Queen's University Press, 1989).
8. Mitchell describes the increased presence and influence of fur traders, missionaries and police in the early twentieth century as a "community of interest." See chapter 5 of Mitchell, *From Talking Chiefs to a Native Corporate Elite*. By the late 1950s,

according to Mitchell, this triumvirate "had succeeded in delivering the capitalist mode of production to Inuit" (ibid., 117).

9. The federal government's Department of the Interior actually stipulated that the HBC (indeed all applicants for trading post permits) *"must assume full responsibility for the welfare of the natives who trade with them and the destitute natives must be maintained without expense to the Department."* The HBC also assumed other quasi-governmental responsibilities until federal police were in a position to do so. See Mitchell, *From Talking Chiefs to a Native Corporate Elite*, 91.
10. To my knowledge, no one has yet studied the possible influence of whalers' scrimshaw art (both carved and engraved) on Canadian Inuit art of the Historic Period. It is well known that scrimshanding was a favourite pastime of whalers, so I think it would be foolish to discount the influence of their production and their tastes.
11. For an interesting take on the "secular" aspect of Historic Period ivories, see Kenneth Lister, "Looking into the Eye of the Spider: Some Thoughts about Context with Reference to *Tuugaaq: Ivory Sculptures from the Eastern Canadian Arctic*," *Inuit Art Quarterly* 18, no. 3 (Fall 2003): 10–17. George Swinton on the secular: "… fur trapping was initiated and with it the commercialization and secularization of the hunt, and, because the hunt was the central activity of Eskimo existence, the gradual secularization of Eskimo life." George Swinton, "Contemporary Canadian Eskimo Sculpture," in *Sculpture / Inuit* (Toronto: University of Toronto Press, 1971), 39. Swinton directed his readers to Robert G. Williamson, "The Canadian Arctic: Sociocultural Change," *Arch Environ Health* 17 (October 1968): 484–91.
12. Eric Anoee, "The Beginnings of the Carvings in Eskimo Point," in *Eskimo Point / Arviat* (Winnipeg: Winnipeg Art Gallery, 1982), 9.
13. E.W. Hawkes, *The Labrador Eskimo* (Ottawa: Government Printing Bureau, 1916), 100.
14. A. Dudley Copland, *Coplalook: Chief Trader, Hudson's Bay Company* (Winnipeg: Watson & Dwyer, 1985), 124.
15. James Houston reported in 1951 that the HBC had been successfully developing ivory art in Lake Harbour "for many years." (See Virginia Watt, "In Retrospect," *Inuit Art Quarterly* 3, no. 4 [Fall 1988]: 36.)
16. Darlene Wight, *The First Passionate Collector: The Ian Lindsay Collection of Inuit Art* (Winnipeg: Winnipeg Art Gallery, 1991), 49.
17. Charles Martijn described the trading of carvings to outsiders as a "commonplace occupation" for Inuit in the 1930s in "Canadian Eskimo Carving in Historical Perspective," *Anthropos* 59 (1964): 560.
18. See Wight, *The First Passionate Collector*, 47–51; and Virginia Watt, "The Beginning," *Inuit Art Quarterly* 14, no. 3 (Fall 1999): 6–7. The Canadian Handicrafts Guild organized an exhibition of Eskimo arts and crafts in 1930 at the McCord Museum in Montreal that was favourably reviewed in the *New York Times* (read the review in George Swinton, *Sculpture of the Inuit* [Toronto: McClelland & Stewart, 1992], 125).
19. Major David McKeand of the Northwest Territories Administration Office, who, along with Diamond Jenness, was a member of the Canadian Handicrafts Guild Indian and Eskimo Committee in 1939, collected crafts in the Ungava region of Quebec and strongly suggested to both the Guild and the Northwest Territories Council that they undertake handicrafts development initiatives (see Mitchell, *From Talking Chiefs to a Native Corporate Elite*, 168; and Watt, "The Beginning," 7).
20. Dr. Jon Bildfell collected 210 ivories in Pangnirtung in the 1930s and 1940s (see Lister, "Looking into the Eye of the Spider").
21. Lorraine E. Brandson, *Carved from the Land: The Eskimo Museum Collection* (Churchill, MB: Diocese of Churchill–Hudson Bay, 1994).

The World Rediscovers "Eskimos" – A New Art Is Born by Ingo Hessel

1. If this end-date sometimes seems a bit precise and even arbitrary, there is a reason: 1948 was the year of James Houston's first visit to the Arctic, which heralded a rapid series of events and the birth of what we now think of as "modern" Inuit art.
2. Ian Lindsay, in Darlene Wight, *The First Passionate Collector, The Ian Lindsay Collection of Inuit Art* (Winnipeg: Winnipeg Art Gallery, 1991), 21.
3. See Virginia Watt, "In Retrospect," *Inuit Art Quarterly* 2, no. 4 (Fall 1987): 18–20.
4. See Virginia Watt, "In Retrospect," *Inuit Art Quarterly* 3, no. 1 (Spring 1988): 27–29.
5. Virginia Watt, "In Retrospect," *Inuit Art Quarterly* 5, no. 1 (Winter 1990): 39–40.
6. "When we look at the development of handicrafts as adult and child education, we see, perhaps, the only present method of a closer relationship with the Eskimo, which asks the best of him and is the first step into industry, and at the same time directly aids his economy. Handicrafts are done in the camps and in no way disturb his present way of life as a hunter. It does not tend to draw him into the white settlement in large groups, where the scarcity of game would not support him" (James Houston, 1951 letter to the Canadian Handicrafts Guild, in Virginia Watt, "In Retrospect," *Inuit Art Quarterly* 3, no. 4 [Fall 1988]: 39). Houston could not foresee that within one short decade, most Inuit would in fact be living in settlements.
7. The Alaskan Eskimo art expert Dorothy Jean Ray had this assessment of early writings about Canadian Inuit art: "Before 1961 only a few pamphlets had been written about the developments of the then-new Canadian soapstone sculpture, and the ones that I had read were really not an honest appraisal of the art, but rather an idealistic fairy tale treatment." Dorothy Jean Ray, *Artists of the Tundra and the Sea* (Seattle: University of Washington Press, 1980), ix.
8. Norman Vorano, "Creators: Negotiating the Art World for Over 50 Years," *Inuit Art Quarterly* 19, nos. 3 & 4 (Fall/Winter 2004): 11.
9. James Houston, "In Search of Contemporary Eskimo Art," *Canadian Art* 9, no. 3 (Spring 1952): 100.
10. *Canadian Eskimo Art* (Ottawa: Department of Northern Affairs and Natural Resources, 1954), text by James Houston with R.A.J. Phillips.
11. I say "inexplicably" because the booklet remained unchanged even after the advent of Inuit prints in the late 1950s and the publication of another, larger government publication *Innunit: The Art of the Canadian Eskimo* by W.T. Larmour in 1967.
12. However, according to Houston, the carvers of Lake Harbour (who had been relying on ivory imported from Igloolik) were already in 1951 beginning to take advantage of a local serpentine stone deposit. (See Watt, "In Retrospect," *Inuit Art Quarterly* [Fall 1988]: 36.)
13. "A Mesolithic Age Today: Caribou Eskimos Illustrate Its Culture," *Life*, February 27, 1956, 86.
14. *The Epic of Man*, by the editors of *Life* (New York: Time Inc., 1961), 248–55.
15. Farley Mowat, *People of the Deer* (Boston: Little, Brown & Co., 1952).
16. According to Jenness, by 1920 "southerners" had "completely shattered the ancient Eskimo culture over most of the eastern and western Arctic, and were launching an assault on the still primitive central region." Diamond Jenness, *Eskimo Administration:* II, *Canada* (Montreal: Arctic Institute of North America, technical paper no. 16, 1964), 25, quoted in Charles A. Martijn, "Canadian Eskimo Carving in Historical Perspective," *Anthropos* 59 (1964): 558.
17. "Contrary to the perception of the peace-loving nature of the Inuit, hostility with the group appears to have been the norm." Marybelle Mitchell, *From Talking Chiefs to a Native Corporate Elite: The Birth of Class and Nationalism among Canadian Inuit* (Montreal: McGill-Queen's University Press, 1996), 43. She suggests that hostilities were more like feuds than wars. Relations with neighbouring Indian groups were more belligerent (ibid., 44–45).
18. See Nelson Graburn, "Inuit Art and Canadian Nationalism," *Inuit Art Quarterly* 1, no. 3 (Fall 1986): 5–7.
19. Whether or not Inuit had a truly "collective worldview" may never yet be decided. But Mitchell believes that Inuit did not see themselves as constituting a distinct ethnic group, even though they were perceived as such by outsiders. (*From Talking Chiefs to a Native Corporate Elite*, 134)
20. Edmund Carpenter, *Eskimo Realities* (New York: Holt, Rinehart & Winston, 1973), 198.
21. Houston, "In Search of Contemporary Eskimo Art," 104.
22. George Swinton, *Eskimo Sculpture / Sculpture Esquimaude* (Toronto: McClelland & Stewart, 1965), 20.
23. George Swinton, "Eskimo Carving Today," *The Beaver*, Spring 1958, 44.
24. Janet Catherine Berlo, "Autobiographical Impulses and Female Identity in the Drawings of Napachie Pootoogook," *Inuit Art Quarterly* 8, no. 4 (Winter 1993): 6.
25. For an interesting discussion of individuality and autobiography in Inuit art, see Christine Lalonde, "How Can We Understand Inuit Art," *Inuit Art Quarterly* 10, no. 3 (Fall 1995): 6–14. The article focuses on Pitseolak Ashoona of Cape Dorset but has more general application.
26. Swinton, *Eskimo Sculpture / Sculpture Esquimaude*, 13–14.
27. George Swinton, "The Changing Art of the Eskimo," in *Eskimo Sculpture* (Winnipeg: Winnipeg Art Gallery, 1967), 34.
28. Charlotte Townsend-Gault, "Drawing on Inuit," *Inuit Art Quarterly* 4, no. 4 (Fall 1989): 13.
29. Swinton, "Eskimo Carving Today," 40–47.

30. Edmund Carpenter, Frederick Varley, and Robert Flaherty, *Eskimo* (Toronto: University of Toronto Press, 1959), unpaginated; and Carpenter, *Eskimo Realities*, 59.
31. James Houston, "Contemporary Art of the Eskimo," *The Studio*, February 1954, 40–45.
32. Charles A. Martijn, "Canadian Eskimo Carving in Historical Perspective," 583.
33. James Houston, *Sanajaqsaq (Eskimo Handicrafts)* (Montreal/Ottawa: Canadian Handicrafts Guild / Department of Resources and Development, 1951). See Watt, "In Retrospect," *Inuit Art Quarterly* (Spring 1988) for a history of its origin.
34. See Heather Igloliorte, "Sanajatsarq: Reactions, Productions, and the Transformation of Promotional Practice," *Inuit Art Quarterly* 22, no. 4 (Winter 2007): 14–25. Igloliorte analyzes the booklet and its aftermath in some detail and suggests its influence, or lack thereof: "It is possible, then, to imagine that the *real* success of *Sanajatsarq* [*sic*] was, paradoxically, that it failed (17). Martijn ("Canadian Eskimo Carving in Historical Perspective," 564) analyzed it too, and summed it up succinctly by calling the publication "both interesting and peculiar."
35. Department of Northern Affairs, *Eskimo Bulletin: Handicrafts — Senangoat* 1, no. 2 (June 1953).
36. James Houston, *Confessions of an Igloo Dweller* (Toronto: McClelland & Stewart, 1995), 195.
37. The 1952 NFB filmstrip *Eskimo Carvings*, which was shown across the Arctic, probably also exerted some considerable influence.
38. J. Douglas Leechman, "Eskimo Sculpture in Stone," *Canadian Geographical Journal* 49 (September 1954): 96, quoted in Martijn, "Canadian Eskimo Carving in Historical Perspective," 562. Martijn discusses the further implications of this ("Canadian Eskimo Carving in Historical Perspective," 562–63).
39. James Houston, "Eskimo Carvings," *Craft Horizons*, April 1954, 14. He went on to say, "I have shown the work of carvers from Repulse Bay to [Cape] Dorset Eskimos and, although they admired it greatly, they avoided making anything even vaguely resembling it." Interestingly, the contemporaneous Alaskan Eskimo ivory carvers of Nome, or their dealers or customers, did not concern themselves so much with originality (see Ray, *Artists of the Tundra and the Sea*, 120). They valued versatility (Ray, *Artists of the Tundra and the Sea*, 134) and realism (Ray, *Artists of the Tundra and the Sea*, 143–44) more.
40. George Swinton, *Sculpture of the Inuit* (Toronto: McClelland & Stewart, 1992), 110.
41. Ivory is still an important carving medium among Alaskan Eskimos today. According to Dorothy Jean Ray, when Alaskan ivory carvers learned of the success of Canadian Inuit stone sculpture in the 1950s, however, they for a time "glutted the Alaskan market with copies or their own interpretations of this sculpture." She considered the Alaskan stone carvings to be mediocre at best. Ray, *Artists of the Tundra and the Sea*, viii.
42. *Eskimo Art* at the National Gallery of Canada, January 1952; *Eskimo Carvings: Coronation Exhibition* at Gimpel Fils, London, May 1953.
43. See Virginia Watt, "In Retrospect," *Inuit Art Quarterly* 4, no. 2 (Spring 1989): 42–44.
44. Martijn quite rightly describes Houston's efforts as "tenacious." (Charles Martijn, "A Retrospective Glance at Canadian Eskimo Carving," *The Beaver*, Autumn 1967, 14).
45. For an excellent overview of the variety and quality of early modern Inuit sculpture see Darlene Coward Wight, *Early Masters: Inuit Sculpture 1949–1955* (Winnipeg: Winnipeg Art Gallery, 2006).
46. George Swinton, "Eskimo Carving Today," 44–46.
47. James Houston, "Eskimo Carvings," 14.
48. Swinton, *Eskimo Sculpture / Sculpture Esquimaude*, 21.

"We Are Inuit" — Art and Identity
by Ingo Hessel

1. The collapse of the fox fur market in 1948–49 coincided exactly with the beginning of the modernist period of Inuit art (Marybelle Mitchell, *From Talking Chiefs to a Native Corporate Elite: The Birth of Class and Nationalism among Canadian Inuit* [Montreal: McGill-Queen's University Press, 1996], 170).
2. The year 1960 might be considered the tipping point in the modern history of Canadian Inuit. The anthropologist Bernard Saladin d'Anglure wrote that the year 1960 "can be taken as marking the end of a way of life centred on hunting, fishing, and the fur trade, the end of snowhouses for permanent winter occupation, the end of summers spent in traditional hunting camps, and also the end of missionary predominance in schooling and health care" (Saladin d'Anglure, quoted in Mitchell, *From Talking Chiefs to a Native Corporate Elite*, 147).
3. See Alootook Ipellie, "*Nunatsiaqmiut*: People of the Good Land," *Inuit Art Quarterly* 7, no. 2 (Spring 1992), and "*Nunatsiaqmiut*: People of the Good Land, Part Two," *Inuit Art Quarterly* 7, no. 23 (Summer/Fall 1992). For a perceptive early account of the predicament of Inuit, and the role of artmaking in that context, by a southerner, see W.T. Larmour's introduction to the 1964 Winnipeg Art Gallery catalogue *Eskimo Carvers of Keewatin N.W.T.*, 6–15.
4. Federal officials tried to promote arts and crafts as "occupational therapy" in the literal sense of the word in Chesterfield Inlet in 1951 as a response to a polio outbreak in the region. The idea did not pan out. See Virginia Watt, "In Retrospect," *Inuit Art Quarterly* 3, no. 3 (Summer 1988): 23. Occupational therapy projects were attempted in several southern hospitals and sanatoria, with only modest results (see Annalisa R. Staples and Ruth McConnell, *Soapstone and Seed Beads: Arts and Crafts at the Charles Camsell Hospital, A Tuberculosis Sanatorium* (Edmonton: Provincial Museum of Alberta, 1993); and Susan Gustavison, "Inuit Artists and Tuberculosis Patients in Hamilton," *Inuit Art Quarterly* 23, no. 4 [Winter 2008]: 11–16).
5. Thomas McEvilley, *Art and Otherness: Crisis in Cultural Identity* (Kingston, NY: McPherson & Co., 1992), 124. George Swinton had voiced a very similar idea already in 1957: "It is the real miracle that this art arose out of adverse conditions, out of the very destruction of a culture, and not out of the traditional development of old. In a most significant sense this birth of the new art is the *one* way to respond to the challenges which confront the Eskimo's accustomed way of life. The one symbolic way to assert himself, and his ethnic consciousness, in the face of his cultural annihilation, is to produce an art that is all Eskimo art." George Swinton, "Eskimo Carving Today," *The Beaver*, Spring 1958, 47.
6. Nelson H.H. Graburn, ed., *Ethnic and Tourist Arts: Cultural Expressions from the Fourth World* (Berkeley: University of California Press, 1976), 30.
7. Martijn, "Canadian Eskimo Carving in Historical Perspective," *Anthropos* 59 (1964): 577. "From a pseudo-traditional activity, already much influenced by White contact, [Houston] and [Inuit] created a splendid new art of acculturation." To be even more precise, Martijn viewed Inuit art as "one of directed acculturation" (ibid., 583).
8. Dorothy Jean Ray, *Artists of the Tundra and the Sea* (Seattle: University of Washington Press, 1980), 155.
9. Swinton, "Eskimo Carving Today," 46–47.
10. Houston in Virginia Watt, "In Retrospect," *Inuit Art Quarterly* 3, no. 4 (Fall 1988): 36.
11. In Dorothy Eber, "Talking with the Artists," in *In the Shadow of the Sun: Perspectives on Contemporary Native Art* (Gatineau: Canadian Museum of Civilization, 1993), 438.
12. Louis Tapardjuk, in *Report on the Pan-Arctic Co-operative Conference, George River, April 10–25, 1980*, p. 9, quoted in Marybelle Mitchell, "The Eskimo Art Business," *Inuit Art World, IAQ Special Issue* 5, no. 4 (Fall/Winter 1990/91): 29.
13. Houston in Virginia Watt, "In Retrospect," *Inuit Art Quarterly* (Fall 1988): 39.
14. In Richard C. Crandall, *Inuit Art: A History* (Jefferson, NC: McFarland & Co., 2000), 96.
15. See ibid., 147.
16. Graburn, *Ethnic and Tourist Arts*, 2.
17. Marybelle Myers (Mitchell), verbatim notes from a meeting of major organizations involved in the marketing of Inuit art, Montreal 1978, page 67, in Mitchell, *From Talking Chiefs to a Native Corporate Elite*, 329–30. Mitchell: "Since it is the only successful economic activity Inuit have, it is only logical that it would also be the site of power and resistance. Apart from its importance as a major source of income, Inuit have come to value it as a form of collective expression" (*From Talking Chiefs to a Native Corporate Elite*, 329).
18. Peter Millard, "Contemporary Inuit Art — Past and Present," *The American Review of Canadian Studies* 17, no. 1 (Spring 1987): 27. It is perhaps because of this lack of "a clearly established stock of images" that Swinton noted "the Eskimo artists' ability to avoid the uniformity that comes from empty imitation of past traditions" (*Eskimo Sculpture / Sculpture Esquimaude*, 32).
19. Zebedee Nungak, "Inuit Culture: A Deep Well of Artistic Inspiration," in Darlene Coward Wight, ed., *The Harry Winrob Collection of Inuit Sculpture* (Winnipeg: Winnipeg Art Gallery, 2008), 19.
20. Ingo Hessel, *Inuit Art: An Introduction* (Vancouver: Douglas & McIntyre, 1998), 37.
21. Swinton, *Eskimo Sculpture / Sculpture Esquimaude* (Toronto: McClelland & Stewart, 1965), 71–72.
22. Mark Kalluak, "The Importance of Maintaining Language and Culture," in Lorraine E. Brandson, *Carved From the Land: The Eskimo Museum Collection* (Churchill MB: Diocese of Churchill–Hudson Bay, 1994), 6. By "imitation" Kalluak is referring to the Inuktitut concept for art *sananguaq*, which conveys the idea of "model, imitation or likeness" (see Swinton, *Sculpture of the*

Eskimo [Toronto: McClelland & Stewart, 1972], 129). It is *not* "imitation" in the pejorative sense.

23. Ingo Hessel, "Narrative and Anthology in Inuit Art," in Sandra Dyck and Ingo Hessel, *Sanattiaqsimajut: Inuit Art from the Carleton University Art Gallery Collection* (Ottawa: Carleton University Art Gallery, 2009), 34.
24. "William Noah: A View from Baker Lake," in Ingo Hessel, *Arctic Spirit: Inuit Art from the Albrecht Collection at the Heard Museum* (Phoenix: Heard Museum; Vancouver: Douglas & McIntyre, 2006), 230.
25. Janet Berlo, "Autobiographical Impulses and Female Identity in the Drawings of Napachie Pootoogook," *Inuit Art Quarterly* 8, no. 4 (Winter 1993): 9.
26. Edmund Carpenter, Frederick Varley, and Robert Flaherty, *Eskimo* (Toronto: University of Toronto Press, 1959), unpaginated.
27. Carpenter, *Eskimo Realities* (New York: Holt, Rinehart & Winston, 1973), 192.
28. Ibid., 194.
29. Ibid., 193.
30. Ibid., 194–95.
31. Deborah Root, "Inuit Art and the Limits of Authenticity," *Inuit Art Quarterly* 23, no. 2 (Summer 2008): 19.
32. Carpenter, *Eskimo Realities*, 197.
33. In the late 1950s, even George Swinton, who greatly admired Inuit art, was extremely concerned that many Inuit artists were being forced by the Canadian government and marketers to "prostitute" themselves by overproducing and "making carvings pleasing to the white man." See Virginia Watt, "In Retrospect," *Inuit Art Quarterly* 2, no. 2 (Spring 1987): 17–18.
34. The Department of Northern Affairs and Natural Resources developed the "Igloo Tag" in 1959 to combat the flood of fakes and imitations. The Igloo Tag or sticker "certified" the authenticity of the carvings to which it was affixed. One can only guess at the damage that was caused to Inuit art's reputation in Canada and abroad as a result of cheap plaster or "cast stone" knockoffs.
35. For a discussion of "prompted" drawings, see Robert Christopher, "Inuit Drawings: 'Prompted' Art-Making," in *Inuit Art Quarterly* 2, no. 3 (Summer 1987): 3–6.
36. "Johnny Aculiak: 'It seems to me that our culture will die off one day if we do not keep carving'" (artist interview with Henry Kudluk), *Inuit Art Quarterly* 12, no. 4 (Winter 1997): 27.
37. Root, "Inuit Art and the Limits of Authenticity," 21.
38. This is the complete quote: "My own research among Alaska Native artists from a number of different culture groups indicates that tradition is not product, but process. To Native peoples, tradition is an elusive and changing phenomenon subject to a variety of influences. Tradition is the dynamic enactment of value and form by human beings; it *is* process. Further, tradition is not simply of and about the past, it is the present and the future." Susan W. Fair, *Alaska Native Art: Tradition, Innovation, Continuity* (Fairbanks: University of Alaska Press, 2006), 7.
39. Swinton, "The Changing Art of the Eskimo," in *Eskimo Sculpture* (Winnipeg: Winnipeg Art Gallery, 1967), 34.
40. By "folk art" I mean art that expresses cultural identity and values, is not influenced by art movements and academia, is largely made by self-taught artists and is made in small communities. In another real sense, Inuit art is "made by folks for folks," even if much of it has gained acceptance with art "sophisticates."
41. See Hal Oppenheim, "The Inuit Phenomenon in Art-Historical Perspective," in *Inuit Art Quarterly* 1, no. 2 (Summer 1986): 2.
42. Graburn, *Ethnic and Tourist Arts*, 26.
43. Ibid., 45.
44. See the five pages devoted to "The Women's Art" in *Canadian Eskimo Art* (Ottawa: Department of Northern Affairs and Natural Resources, 1954), text by James Houston with R.A.J. Phillips.
45. Art Gallery of Windsor, *Sugluk: Sculpture in Stone 1953–1959* (Windsor: Art Gallery of Windsor, 1992), 12.
46. A. Barry Roberts, *The Inuit Artists of Sugluk, P.Q.* (Montreal: Fédération des coopératives du Nouveau-Québec, 1976), 16.
47. Houston was well aware of the beautiful engravings by Osuitok, Kiugak Ashoona and other Cape Dorset artists on ivory, antler and horn; furthermore, he had purchased many modest works with engraved pictures beginning with his very first buying trips to Arctic Quebec.
48. James Houston, "My Friend, Angotiawak," *Canadian Art* 13, no. 2, 222–24. Furthermore, in his first memoir, *Confessions of an Igloo Dweller* (Toronto: McClelland & Stewart, 1995), Houston described an Inuk sketching a portrait of him on the first day of his first visit to the Arctic in 1948; and later: "The neighbours came in again and I unslung two sketch books, one for me and one for them" (*Confessions of an Igloo Dweller*, 9–11).
49. James Houston, *Eskimo Prints* (Barre, MA: Barre Publishing, 1967), 11.
50. Kenojuak in Jean Blodgett, *Kenojuak* (Toronto: Firefly Books, 1985), 20.
51. Thirteen experimental prints from 1957 and 1958 were exhibited at the Hudson's Bay Company store in Winnipeg in December 1958.
52. For an excellent overview of the history of Cape Dorset printmaking, see Leslie Boyd Ryan, *Cape Dorset Prints: A Retrospective; Fifty Years of Printmaking at the Kinngait Studios* (San Francisco: Pomegranate, 2007).
53. The Department of Northern Affairs shut out the Hudson's Bay Company from marketing Inuit prints in much the same manner as it had tried to effectively shut out the Canadian Guild of Crafts in 1953 by terminating grants to that organization. See Mitchell, *From Talking Chiefs to a Native Corporate Elite*, 174–78, for a discussion of this government strategy.
54. James Houston, "Eskimo Graphic Art," *Canadian Art*, January 1960, 9–11.
55. Christine Lalonde, introduction to *Uuturautiit: Cape Dorset Celebrates 50 Years of Printmaking*, by Christine Lalonde and Leslie Boyd Ryan (Ottawa: National Gallery of Canada, 2009), 18.
56. "James also tried a technique using sealskin with its fur removed, but that did not turn out well." Kananginak Pootoogook, "The Beginning of Printmaking and the Co-op," in Lalonde and Boyd Ryan, *Uuturautiit*, 41. Also, "Sealskin stencils – that, and the old ink from the soot of the lamp – were simply marketing tools. None of that ever happened." Terry Ryan quoted in Patricia Feheley, "Terry Ryan: A Visionary with a Pragmatic Edge," *Inuit Art Quarterly* 24, no. 1 (Spring 2009): 14.
57. Houston also failed to mention his 1958 trip to Japan to study *ukiyo-e* collaborative woodblock printmaking techniques and the influence of the Japanese printmaking style on Houston and, indirectly, on the look of early Inuit images.
58. West Baffin Eskimo Co-operative, *Eskimo Graphic Art 1960*.
59. The CEAC was seen by its many critics as highly paternalistic; it gave critics of "Eskimo Art" further proof that the whole enterprise was inauthentic and was being controlled by southerners for their own purposes. Charles Martijn lamented in 1967 that no anthropologists had been appointed to the CEAC ("A Retrospective Glance at Canadian Eskimo Carving," *The Beaver*, Autumn 1967, 6); needless to say, there were no Inuit on the Committee. For a history of the Canadian Eskimo Arts Council (as it came to be called), see Susan Gustavison, *Arctic Expressions: Inuit Art and the Canadian Eskimo Arts Council 1961–1989* (Kleinburg, ON: McMichael Canadian Art Collection, 1994). Its controversial history is interwoven with the ups and downs of the various Inuit printmaking programs over the decades and reflects the attitudes of outsiders in positions of power vis-à-vis Inuit art and artists over the same period.
60. Some federal bureaucrats were voicing the opinion that Inuit sculpture was being promoted as fine art, whether or not it deserved that status. See Mitchell, *From Talking Chiefs to a Native Corporate Elite*, 175.
61. We know that some carvings were quietly disposed of, particularly in the early years when so many people (including many children) were encouraged to experiment. The former Puvirnituq artist Isah Qopakualuk said: "[S]ome of the works that were produced were not well done. I remember seeing some carvings that had been put aside in a box and I believe those carvings were later dumped in the river when the artists weren't looking." In "People and Places: Qopakualuk Talks about Carvings and Co-ops," *Inuit Art Quarterly* 3, no. 3 (Summer 1988): 13.
62. Leslie Boyd Ryan, "The Dorset Experiment," in Lalonde and Boyd Ryan, *Uuturautiit*, 64.
63. Avrom Isaacs, "Foreword," in Boyd Ryan, *Cape Dorset Prints, A Retrospective*, 10.
64. See Nelson Graburn, "Inuit Art and Canadian Nationalism," *Inuit Art Quarterly* 1, no. 3 (Fall 1986): 5–7, and the ensuing debate with Joan Vastokas of Trent University, also in *Inuit Art Quarterly* 2, no. 1 (Winter 1987), no. 2 (Spring 1988), and no. 3 (Summer 1988). Vastokas argued that the wide acceptance of Inuit art by the general public was because Inuit art forms were "appealing in themselves" and further suggested that the southern public saw in Inuit art an antidote to the largely "formalist and abstractionist" art of the Canadian mainstream in the 1960s and 1970s. I think the truth lies somewhere in between. I would also like to point out a small irony in this debate: many would argue that the dominance of "formalism and abstractionism" of mid-twentieth century art is the direct result of the nationalistic postwar championing of American Abstract Expressionist art by Clement Greenberg and others in the U.S.
65. The premise of John Ralston Saul's 2008 book *A Fair Country: Telling Truths about Canada* (Toronto: Viking Canada, 2008) is

that Aboriginal (First Nations, Metis and Inuit) history, society and culture *are* at the core of Canada's society and identity, even if southern Canadians (and especially southern elites) have mostly denied the fact, or have so far given only lip service to the idea, or are slow in realizing it. If Saul is correct in his assumption, then Inuit art *is* a national cultural icon, regardless of the motives of those who chose to promote it as such. According to Saul, "The fundamental influence on our civilization is revealed in the ease with which we have adopted their art as an expression of ourselves" (ibid., 53).

66. Graburn, *Ethnic and Tourist Arts*, 28–29.
67. The co-ops and CAP competed directly with the HBC, which had enjoyed a virtual monopoly on the marketing of Inuit art until the late 1950s. The HBC held its own, however, as has its successor in the Arctic, the reconstituted North West Company. The wholesale marketing of Inuit art eventually became more fragmented and complex, with the establishment of FCNQ in Quebec, Dorset Fine Arts (for Cape Dorset) and several smaller private players.
68. The role of Inuit co-ops in the history of Inuit art, and Inuit economic and political power and identity, is interesting and complex. See Mitchell, *From Talking Chiefs to a Native Corporate Elite*, for a wide-ranging analysis.
69. "I don't believe that the government is infallible, and the co-ops make it possible for the Eskimos to give us hell." Donald Snowden, chief of the Industrial Division of Northern Affairs, 1963, in Edith Iglauer, *Inuit Journey* (Seattle: University of Washington Press, 1979), cited in Mitchell, *From Talking Chiefs to a Native Corporate Elite*, 181.
70. See Mitchell, *From Talking Chiefs to a Native Corporate Elite*, for a detailed discussion of the Inuit co-operative system and the government's pivotal role. Mitchell makes the case for regarding the Inuit co-op system as capitalist, rather than communal (ibid., 292). She feels that the system eventually had the effect of weakening communal bonds (ibid., 300) and ended up concentrating real power in the hands of southern-based managers and other southerners (ibid., 309–10).
71. For example, George Arluk (pp. 128–29) taught himself to carve at the age of nine, emulating older artists in his hometown of Rankin Inlet.
72. "As it stands now, every Eskimo accepts the development of artistic talent as inevitable. The role of the artist is not the unusual, or deviant, one. No man is faced with the problems of acceptance or rejection by other persons in his own group because of his decision to become an 'artist,' as is so often the case in the non-Eskimo world, but the creative talents of all of the men are brought to flower. The entire culture is much richer for its involvement in artistic activity that pervades the lives of all its people." Ray, *Artists of the Tundra and the Sea*, 155.
73. Examples in the current exhibition include Lucy Tasseor Tutsweetok and Margaret Uyauperq Aniksak from Arviat (where there have been many prominent female sculptors); Paniluk Qamanirq from Arctic Bay (a small community where there have been several); Oviloo Tunnillie from Cape Dorset (where male sculptors predominate, but where several female artists such as Kenojuak Ashevak have produced great sculptural works); and Maudie Okittuq from Taloyoak (where being a female sculptor is the rare exception). Other communities where female sculptors have flourished include Salluit, Repulse Bay and Baker Lake.
74. See Janet Berlo, "The Power of the Pencil: Inuit Women in the Graphic Arts," in *Inuit Art Quarterly* 5, no.1 (Winter 1990): 16–26.
75. "Today it seems that a lot of male carvers are imitating the manner of stone-cut images... But these male carvers are really competing with women when they make with stone what women do on paper. They say they don't but they do, especially when they imitate the patterns and shapes of the bird wings." "Conversation with Joannsie [*sic*] Salomonie," in Bernadette Driscoll, *Uumajut: Animal Imagery in Inuit Art* (Winnipeg: Winnipeg Art Gallery, 1985), 47.
76. Terry Ryan, "Introduction," in Cape Dorset, *Dorset 77: Cape Dorset Annual Graphics Collection 1977* (Toronto: M.F. Feheley Publishers), 6.
77. Swinton, *Eskimo Sculpture / Sculpture Esquimaude*, 12.
78. Berlo, "Autobiographical Impulses and Female Identity in the Drawings of Napachie Pootoogook," 6.
79. Kenojuak Ashevak, Napachie Pootoogook, Pitseolak Ashoona and Anirnik Oshuitoq, to mention a few women; and Pootoogook, Parr, Kiakshuk, Tudlik, and Jamasie Teevee, to name some of the elderly men.
80. *Eskimo Artist: Kenojuak*, directed by John Feeney (National Film Board, 1963).
81. Kenojuak, in Blodgett, *Kenojuak*, 22.
82. Inuit prints (in particular, classic Cape Dorset prints from the 1960s) have been exhibited and published widely. We made a curatorial decision to focus on the drawings, rather than the many fine prints, in the Sarick Collection for this exhibition.

"I Am an Inuit Artist" – The Rise of the Individual Artist by Ingo Hessel

1. In Houston's article "Eskimo Carvings," *Craft Horizons*, April 1954, he identified the carver of each of the eighteen works illustrated.
2. The RCMP conducted a census of Inuit in the 1940s and, for administrative purposes, assigned each person a unique identification number within their eastern or western Arctic region. These numbers were stamped on small round discs similar to dog tags and hence were nicknamed "disc numbers." Syllabics (graphic symbols representing single-syllable sounds) were invented by a Christian missionary for use by the Cree; adapted for Inuktitut in 1876, they were quickly adopted as the written form of Inuktitut in the eastern Arctic (excluding Labrador) and are still used today.
3. Carpenter, *Eskimo Realities* (New York: Holt, Rinehart & Winston, 1973), 201.
4. Dorothy Jean Ray: "Actually, when 'primitive' art is referred to as 'anonymous' art, its anonymous character springs from the appraisal and, it might be said, the ignorance of the group that is discussing it. For the contemporary Eskimo artists, themselves, their art is no more anonymous than that of an artist in another culture who signs his work with letters six inches high, for every Eskimo artist's style is recognizable to everyone else." *Artists of the Tundra and the Sea* (Seattle: University of Washington Press, 1980), 155.
5. Nelson H.H. Graburn, ed., *Ethnic and Tourist Arts: Cultural Expressions from the Fourth World* (Berkeley: University of California Press, 1976), 22.
6. Dorothy Jean Ray's take on the status of Alaskan Eskimo carvers is, I think, widely applicable to the Canadian situation: "Because he is still more oriented to the Eskimo culture where his status is already determined than to the non-Eskimo culture, the carver does not seek further individual recognition from the latter... He grows up in our terms an artist, in his, a carver, the accepted and expected role that he will always play." *Artists of the Tundra and the Sea*, 156.
7. Kenojuak in Jean Blodgett, *Kenojuak* (Toronto: Firefly Books, 1985), 24.
8. Marybelle Mitchell, "The Eskimo Art Business," *Inuit Art World, IAQ Special Issue* 5, no. 4 (Fall/Winter 1990/91): 29–30.
9. *New Yorker*, August 23, 1993.
10. Both George Swinton (*Sculpture of the Eskimo* [Toronto: McClelland & Stewart, 1972]; and *Sculpture of the Inuit* [Toronto: McClelland & Stewart, 1992]) and Nelson Graburn (*Ethnic and Tourist Arts*), among others, have discussed Inuit aesthetics at some length. My view is that "typical" Inuit aesthetic tastes (which favour realism and craftsmanship), although they might be seem to be at variance with late-twentieth-century mainstream Euro-Canadian critical thinking about art and aesthetics, they are actually not very far removed from the artistic tastes of the average southern "person in the street."
11. Marie Routledge, ed., *Inuit Art in the 1970s* (Kingston: Agnes Etherington Art Centre, 1979), 13. She quite rightly suggested that the more highly structured print-shop milieu fostered professionalism and experimentation by its very nature (ibid., 17).
12. Marion Jackson, "Baker Lake Inuit Drawings: A Study in the Evolution of Artistic Self-Consciousness" (PhD thesis, University of Michigan, 1985).
13. Marion Jackson, "Contemporary Inuit Drawings: Reflections of an Art Historian," in *Contemporary Inuit Drawings* (Guelph: Macdonald Stewart Art Centre, 1987), 17.
14. Ibid., 17–18. "[First generation artists] had little consciousness of self-as-artist, self-as-creator, and simply drew the world they knew with no conscious awareness of their own powers to intervene or shape that world... The content and form of their drawings are not only complementary but, in a sense, the same thing. Content and form merge... Younger artists were more self-conscious because they were aware of more choices; they *can* and, in fact, *must* make choices... To achieve a re-integration of information and aesthetic expression similar to the seemingly effortless achievement of the first generation requires a new kind of effort on the part of second generation artists."
15. These six artists, together with Lucy Tasseor Tutsweetok of Arviat, were featured in Norman Zepp's exhibition and catalogue *Pure Vision: The Keewatin Spirit* (Regina: Norman Mackenzie Art Gallery, 1986).
16. "My neighbours sometimes came to tell me that I carved ordinary, pointed objects, and got well paid for them. I would ask them in return whether they could make these carvings that they called ordinary pointed objects. They said no, they couldn't make such carvings." Paniluk Qamanirq, interview in *We Don't Live in Snow Houses Now: Reflections of Arctic Bay* (Ottawa: Canadian Arctic Producers, 1976), 159.

17. Darlene Coward Wight, *Art & Expression of the Netsilik* (Winnipeg: Winnipeg Art Gallery, 2000), 66. Karoo's approach goes well beyond the idea of attaching works to a base or affixing elements such as antlers and tusks, drums and beaters, and so forth.
18. "Our father talked a lot about angakuqs and ghosts when we were small, and I know Ashevak was afraid of them... He was very easy to scare when he was young... I think that he carved what he had been afraid of when he was younger... He laughed at it a lot when he was working on it." Eeteemunga Niviaqsiaq, interview in Coward Wight, *Art & Expression of the Netsilik*, 66.
19. See Marybelle Myers, ed., *Davidialuk 1977* (Montreal: Fédération des coopératives du Nouveau-Québec, 1977); and Bernard Saladin d'Anglure, *La parole changée en pierre: Vie et oeuvre de Davidialuk Alasuaq, artiste inuit du Québec arctique* (Québec: Gouvernement du Québec, Ministère des Affaires culturelles, 1978).
20. In 1958–59 Davidialuk and several other Puvirnituq carvers were actively encouraged to depict oral traditions by the local Catholic missionary Father André Steinmann, O.M.I. (who had established the Sculptors' Society of Povungnituk and in 1961 introduced printmaking to the community). See Eugene Arima, "Foreword," in Zebedee Nungak and Eugene Arima, *Inuit Stories: Povungnituk* (Hull, QC: Canadian Museum of Civilization, 1988), 13. (This is actually bilingual, and a new edition.)
21. Graburn, who has a keen interest in Inuit and cross-cultural aesthetics, enjoined local carvers to make carvings that were *takushurnaituk* ("things never seen before") and *adjigiingituk* ("different from each other"). Four prizes were awarded for originality and technical skill; Davidialuk took the third prize. For more details, see George Swinton, *Eskimo Fantastic Art* (Winnipeg: Gallery One One One, University of Manitoba, 1972); and Diana Trafford, "Takushurnaituk" in *north/nord* 15 (March–April 1968): 52–55 (text reprinted in Swinton, *Eskimo Fantastic Art*).
22. Swinton, *Eskimo Fantastic Art*, 8.
23. Dorothy Eber, ed., *Pitseolak: Pictures Out of My Life* (Montreal: Design Collaborative Books; Toronto: Oxford University Press, 1971).
24. See Marybelle Myers, ed., *Joe Talirunili: A Grace beyond the Reach of Art* (Montreal: Fédération des coopératives du Nouveau-Québec, 1977) for a wonderful account of Talirunili's life and art.
25. For an analysis of Kigusiuq's artistic evolution, see Cynthia Waye, *The Urge to Abstraction: The Graphic Art of Janet Kigusiuq* (Toronto: Museum of Inuit Art, 2008).
26. This is quite different from the approach of Davidialuk, for example, who would create a series of drawings to depict a similar story.
27. Marion E. Jackson, "The Vital Vision: Drawings by Ruth Annaqtuusi Tulurialik," in Marion E. Jackson and David F. Pelly, *The Vital Vision: Drawings by Ruth Annaqtuusi Tulurialik* (Windsor: Art Gallery of Windsor, 1986), unpaginated. Jackson again: "Annaqtuusi's energetic lines, her repetition and juxtaposition of pulsing colors, and the spontaneity with which she constructs her compositions work together to convey a vitality that defies cultural boundaries" (ibid.).
28. Read Kananginak's thoughts on "living at the crossroads" of cultural change in Ingo Hessel, *Kananginak Pootoogook: Celebrating Five Decades of Artistic Achievement* (Toronto: Museum of Inuit Art, 2010).
29. Eber, *Pitseolak*, 80.

"I Am an Artist" – Inuit Art Transcends Ethnicity by Ingo Hessel

1. See Marybelle Mitchell, *From Talking Chiefs to a Native Corporate Elite: The Birth of Class and Nationalism among Canadian Inuit* (Montreal: McGill-Queen's University Press, 1996) for a wide-ranging discussion of these issues.
2. See Mitchell, *From Talking Chiefs to a Native Corporate Elite*, 127–29.
3. See Marybelle Mitchell, "The Eskimo Art Business," *Inuit Art World*, IAQ *Special Issue* 5, no. 4 (Fall/Winter 1990/91): 28–33.
4. Mitchell, "The Eskimo Art Business," 31–32. Mitchell: "This move... is tantamount to imposing a structural separation of art and craft on the co-operative system."
5. Peter Millard, Contemporary Inuit Art – Past and Present," *The American Review of Canadian Studies* 17, no. 1 (Spring 1987): 28.
6. Christine Lalonde, *Inuit Sculpture Now* (Ottawa: National Gallery of Canada, 2005), 4. "Alternating points of cross-over and connection emerge, shift, re-emerge in different patterns with each changing consideration – working conditions, training, aesthetic approach, medium, style, and subject matter. The single thread that forms the starting point and that unites them all remains their Inuit heritage."
7. See Heather Campbell, "Urban Inuit Artists," *Inuit Art Quarterly* 16, no. 2 (Summer 2001): 4–10.
8. Most Inuit (artists and others) who have travelled south have been relieved to return to the relative calm of their home communities. Most Inuit who have chosen to live in the South are younger and bilingual and have worked at Inuit NGOs or in government positions or have married Qallunaat; a good number have eventually returned north.
9. John Ayre, "Carving Is Healing to Me: An Interview with Manasie Akpaliapik," *Inuit Art Quarterly* 8, no. 4 (Winter 1993): 41.
10. Christine Lalonde believes these artists have more of a choice: "The most significant decision these artists make is to choose to make *Inuit* sculpture. Their artistic talents are indisputable: any one could successfully create works without reference to 'Inuitness.'" Christine Lalonde, *Inuit Sculpture Now* (Ottawa: National Gallery of Canada, 2005), 12. In my opinion, contemporary Inuit sculptors have so far been more conservative and more market oriented than, for example, some of their graphic artist peers in Cape Dorset.
11. Matthew Fox, "Cultural Ambassador: Alex Alikashuak," *Inuit Art Quarterly* 16, no. 3 (Fall 2001): 13.
12. In Heather Campbell, "Urban Inuit Artists," 9.
13. "Focus on Bill Nasogaluak, Masterful Apprentice," *Inuit Art Quarterly* 17, no. 1 (Spring 2002): 31 (interview by Michael Olson).
14. Heather Campbell, "Urban Inuit Artists," 10. As Christine Lalonde observed, "Artists are aware that their art will be interpreted, and often provide perspectives on their work themselves through their statements or titles." Lalonde, *Inuit Sculpture Now*, 9.
15. In "An Interview with Abraham Anghik," *Inuit Art Quarterly* 6, no. 2 (Spring 1991): 21.
16. "Focus on Bill Nasogaluak, Masterful Apprentice," 33, 35.
17. Deborah Root, "Inuit Art and the Limits of Authenticity," *Inuit Art Quarterly* 23, no. 2 (Summer 2008): 26.
18. Marybelle Myers, "In the Wake of the Giant," in *Port Harrison/Inoucdjouac* (Winnipeg: Winnipeg Art Gallery, 1976), 15.
19. Lalonde, *Inuit Sculpture Now*, 11.
20. George Swinton, *Eskimo Fantastic Art* (Winnipeg: Gallery One One One, University of Manitoba, 1972); and Diana Trafford, "Takushurnaituk" in *north/nord* 15 (March–April 1968): 52–55 (text reprinted in Swinton, *Eskimo Fantastic Art*).
21. Marybelle Myers, "People Who Know How to Dream," *north/nord*, March/April 1974, 33.
22. Ibid., 35.
23. Darlene Wight's two-person show at the Winnipeg Art Gallery brought the brothers instant credibility and acclaim. See Darlene Wight, *Out of Tradition: Abraham Anghik/David Ruben Piqtoukun* (Winnipeg: Winnipeg Art Gallery, 1989).
24. Wight followed up her 1989 exhibition with two solo exhibitions showcasing the brothers' attempts to deal with tradition, cultural alienation and other issues. See Darlene Wight, *Between Two Worlds: Sculpture by David Ruben Piqtoukun* (Winnipeg: Winnipeg Art Gallery, 1996); and Abraham Anghik and Darlene Coward Wight, *Abraham Anghik Ruben* (Winnipeg: Winnipeg Art Gallery, 2001).
25. See Ingo Hessel, *Arctic Spirit: Inuit Art from the Albrecht Collection at the Heard Museum* (Phoenix: Heard Museum; Vancouver: Douglas & McIntyre, 2006), 145. Robert Kardosh's assessment is similar: "The power and immediacy of Tunnillie's image-making has much to do with the artist's ability to create works that generalize rather than particularize their meaning." Robert Kardosh, "Transcending the Particular: Feminist Vision in the Sculpture of Oviloo Tunnillie," *Inuit Art Quarterly* 24, no. 3 (Fall 2009): 31.
26. She has been featured in several commercial solo shows (accompanied by important catalogues) at the Marion Scott Gallery in Vancouver.
27. Patricia M. Feheley, "Modern Language: The Art of Annie Pootoogook," *Inuit Art Quarterly* 19, no. 2 (Summer 2004), 12.
28. "Noise Ghost: Shuvinai Ashoona and Shary Boyle," *Inuit Art Quarterly* 24, no. 4 (Winter 2009): 15.
29. "Curatorial Notes: Shuvinai Ashoona Drawings," *Inuit Art Quarterly* 24, no. 4 (Winter 2009): 17.
30. The commercial gallery Feheley Fine Arts has worked tirelessly to promote Annie Pootoogook, Shuvinai Ashoona and their contemporaries, successfully steering their careers into the contemporary art world and back again to the mainstream Inuit art scene.

Index

Note: Italicized page references refer to pages on which artwork is depicted; an italicized *i* in a page reference refers to a photograph or other illustration.

This book is set in Dante, a neo-humanist typeface designed by the renowned Giovanni Mardersteig in collaboration with the great punch-cutter Charles Malin. First introduced in 1955, Dante's poise and elegance benefits from a subtle horizontal stress, which makes it extraordinarily easy to read.

The sans serif font used in this book is Slate Pro, designed by Rod McDonald, Canada's most eminent type designer. Slate, released in 2006, is a humanistic sans serif that melds superb functionality and quiet grace.